THE HISTORY OF WALES

GENERAL EDITOR
GLANMOR WILLIAMS

CONQUEST, COEXISTENCE, AND CHANGE
WALES
1063–1415

BY

R. R. DAVIES

Professor of History,
University College of Wales,
Aberystwyth

CLARENDON PRESS · OXFORD
UNIVERSITY OF WALES PRESS
1987

EB

Oxford University Press, Walton Street, Oxford OX2 6DP

Oxford New York Toronto
Delhi Bombay Calcutta Madras Karachi
Petaling Jaya Singapore Hong Kong Tokyo
Nairobi Dar es Salaam Cape Town
Melbourne Auckland

and associated companies in
Beirut Berlin Ibadan Nicosia

Oxford is a trade mark of Oxford University Press

Published in the United States
by Oxford University Press, New York

British Library Cataloguing in Publication Data
Davies, R.R.
Conquest, coexistence and change: Wales
1063–1415—(The History of Wales; v.2)
1. Wales—History—To 1536
I. Title   II. Series
942.902   DA715
ISBN 0–19–821732–3

Set by Hope Services, Abingdon
Printed in Great Britain
at The Alden Press, Oxford

ER CÔF AM FY RHIENI,
HALEN DAEAR CYMRU

PREFACE

It is over three-quarters of a century since the appearance of Sir John Edward Lloyd's *History of Wales from the Earliest Times to the Edwardian Conquest* in 1911. Lloyd's masterpiece laid the foundations of the modern academic study of the history of Wales, notably of medieval Wales. Rarely, if ever, have foundations been so securely laid. His wonderfully controlled narrative, based on an unparalleled mastery of the sources of the period, sustained by his unrivalled knowledge of the early geography, toponymy and genealogy of Wales, and richly garnished with footnotes which laid to rest a host of myths and solved scores of knotty problems with an unerring sureness of touch, set a standard to which subsequent Welsh historians might aspire, but which they had little hope to attain, let alone to surpass. To write in Lloyd's shadow is immediately to be overshadowed.

While I could not hope to escape from Lloyd's shadow—nor indeed had any wish to do so—my aims in the writing of this present volume have understandably been very different from his. In the first place, I have naturally tried to take full advantage of the considerable corpus of published work on, or bearing on, the history of Wales—in edited texts, scholarly monographs, and articles—which has appeared in the last two generations or so. Such work not only constitutes an important addition to our stock of knowledge; it also often represents a substantial, if gradual, shift in the centre of gravity of historical interest. A second aim of this book is, indeed, to reflect and promote that shift of interest. Lloyd's basic intention in the second volume of his *History* was to establish a detailed and firm (sometimes too firm) political narrative of Wales from 1063 to 1282 (or, more correctly, 1277, since he gave the last five crowded years of the period very short shrift). I have taken that achievement largely for granted, even where it has been revised by subsequent research, contenting myself with a fairly rapid chronological survey. Instead I have chosen to focus on those issues which seem to me increasingly to command the historian's attention—such as the nature of native Welsh political society, the making of the March of Wales, the impact of Anglo-Norman colonization, the far-reaching and multi-faceted changes which native and Anglo-Norman societies in Wales underwent in the twelfth and thirteenth centuries, and the identification of those changes in attitude and assumptions which are basic to an understanding of any past society. Likewise, in the period after the Edwardian Conquest of 1277–83, I have tried to provide a framework within which the history of Wales may be discussed as a coherent whole rather than as a collection of discrete and local episodes.

One other general, almost proselytizing, aim has informed my approach: to try to make the history of medieval Wales approachable and interesting not only to scholars and general readers in Wales but to a wider historical audience beyond Wales. With some notable and honourable exceptions, the history of Wales has been regarded by professional historians as a matter for Welsh people only and even among them as a subject not deserving of too serious study. It has been marginalized—as to a greater or lesser extent have the histories of Scotland and Ireland—within British historical syllabuses, at schools and universities alike, even within Wales itself. This act of academic amputation has had two lamentable results. It has deprived historians, especially English historians, of the opportunity to enrich their perceptions and question some of their assumptions from the study of a neighbouring, if often contrasting, society and its development. Equally damaging, it has meant that Welsh history too often has grown in isolation, with the consequent dangers of becoming ingrown and introspective. It is my hope that the present volume, like the series to which it belongs, will spur others, within and without Wales, to take an interest in the history of Wales as part of the histories of western European societies.

I have tried to base the volume throughout on a careful examination of the major printed primary sources for the period which it covers as well as on the not inconsiderable corpus of secondary writing. The format of the series in which the volume appears has imposed on me a self-denying ordinance with regard to footnotes which, I must confess, has often deeply mortified my scholarly flesh. Footnotes have been confined almost exclusively to the identification of quotations in the text. This has meant that the sources and the scholars whose authority underpins every page of this book must remain anonymous, except through the Bibliography. For this omission I crave in particular the indulgence of my fellow-scholars, as I do for the errors of fact and the sins of scholarly omission, commission, and simplification which a general work such as this often entails.

In preparing the book I have incurred the debts which appear all the more desperate since repayment is so delayed and so inadequate. Some of them, indeed, long predate the beginning of this book. I still recall regularly the good fortune which made me a pupil, successively, of May McKisack and Bruce McFarlane. My academic career has brought me friendships which I treasure greatly for personal as well as academic reasons, notably those of Ralph Griffiths, David Morgan, and Colin Richmond. I salute with gratitude and humility the remarkably devoted, hard-working, and companionable band of scholars who have helped to enrich and transform the history of medieval Wales in the generations since the appearance of J. E. Lloyd's *History*. Their number has been small;

their task has been lonely and has rarely attracted the attention and acclaim of more glamorous and popular historical subjects; but their achievement has been considerable and remarkably solid. Without their work this volume would not have been possible. I hope it can be regarded as a tribute, however unworthy, to their achievement, past and present. *Eraill a lafuriasant*, . . . Since this volume originally went to press yet another important contribution has appeared, the valuable study of J. B. Smith, *Llywelyn ap Gruffudd, Tywysog Cymru* (Cardiff, 1986).

Other debts are more recent and particular. My College kindly gave me study leave for a term in the session 1983/4 and relieved me of my administrative duties during that session. The Leverhulme Trust generously made me a grant which enabled me to write the early chapters in the tranquillity of London away from the bustle of Aberystwyth. Michael Thompson and his colleagues at the Institute of Historical Research and my former colleagues and friends in London were kindness itself during those months. Mrs Margaret White coped admirably and promptly with my manuscript amidst all her other tasks. To the General Editor of the series, Professor Glanmor Williams, I am deeply indebted for words of encouragement and kindly exhortation over the years and for the characteristic speed and penetration with which he read the final typescript. His generosity and inspiration are proverbial within Welsh academic circles; I have been privileged to be one of their beneficiaries for over a quarter of a century. The greatest debt of all is to my wife, Carys, and children: others may read or consult this volume; they had to live with its author through the long and often very dark months of its gestation. *Diolch calon.*

R. R. DAVIES

Aberystwyth, 7 May 1986

CONTENTS

MAPS

DIAGRAMS

ABBREVIATIONS

Arch. Camb.	*Archaeologia Cambrensis*
BBCS	*Bulletin of the Board of Celtic Studies*
Brut	*Brut y Tywysogyon or The Chronicle of the Princes. Peniarth Ms. 20 Version*. Translated with introduction and notes by Thomas Jones (Cardiff, 1952)
Brut (RBH)	*Brut y Tywysogyon or The Chronicle of the Princes. Red Book of Hergest Version*. Critical text and translation with introduction and notes by Thomas Jones (Cardiff, 1955)
Cal. Anc. Corr.	*Calendar of Ancient Correspondence concerning Wales*. Edited by J. G. Edwards (Cardiff, 1935)
Cal. Anc. Pets.	*Calendar of Ancient Petitions relating to Wales*. Edited with introduction by William Rees (Cardiff, 1975)
DK	Giraldus Cambrensis, 'Descriptio Kambrie', quoted by book and chapter from *Giraldi Cambrensis Opera*, ed. J. T. Dimock, VI (Rolls Series, 1865)
E.	English
EHR	*English Historical Review*
Episc. Acts	*Episcopal Acts and Cognate Documents relating to Welsh Dioceses 1066–1272*. Edited by J. Conway Davies. 2 vols. Historical Society of the Church in Wales 1946–8
Fr.	French
History G. ap C.	*The History of Gruffydd ap Cynan*. Edited by Arthur Jones (Manchester, 1910)
IK	Giraldus Cambrensis, 'Itinerarium Kambrie', quoted by book and chapter from *Giraldus Cambrensis Opera*, ed. J. F. Dimock, VI (Rolls Series, 1868)
L.	Latin
Litt. Wallie	*Littere Wallie preserved in Liber A in the Public Record Office*. Edited with introduction by J. G. Edwards (Cardiff, 1940)
Llsg. Hendregadredd	*Llawysgrif Hendregadredd*. Copiwyd gan Rhiannon Morris-Jones. Golygwyd gan John Morris-Jones a T. H. Parry-Williams (Caerdydd, 1933)
Mabinogion	*The Mabinogion*. Translated with an introduction by Gwyn Jones and Thomas Jones (1949)

NLWJ	*National Library of Wales Journal*
Trans. Cymm. Soc.	*Transactions of the Honourable Society of Cymmrodorion*
W.	Welsh
WHR	*Welsh History Review*

NOTE ON WELSH PLACE-NAMES

The spelling of Welsh place-names in this volume generally follows the forms suggested in *A Gazetteer of Welsh Place-Names*, ed. Elwyn Davies (Cardiff, 1957) or Melville Richards, *Welsh Administrative and Territorial Units* (Cardiff, 1969). In a book written in English I have naturally used English forms where these are in common use, e.g. Brecon, Cardiff, Carmarthen, river Dee, river Usk, etc. Where the name of a town or a castle derives from an older Welsh district name, I have used the Anglicized form for the former while reserving the Welsh form for the latter, e.g. town or castle of Kidwelly in the commote of Cydweli, Laugharne in Talacharn etc. Likewise when a native Welsh settlement was replaced by an English castle and/or borough, I have referred to the former by its Welsh name (e.g. Aberconwy), to the latter by its English name (e.g. Conway). Complete consistency and uniformity in these matters is neither possible nor, perhaps, desirable. The existence of alternative place-names and of alternative spellings of the same place-names is a reflection of the emergence of that duality of culture and language within Wales which is one of the themes of this volume.

PART I

NATIVE WALES AND THE NORMAN THREAT
1063–1172

CHAPTER I

WALES AND THE WELSH

THE history of medieval Wales is the subject of this book. It behoves us, therefore, at the outset, to ask two fundamental questions: what was Wales? and how meaningful is it to discuss its history as that of a single country and a single people? The answer to the first of these questions is rather less straightforward than might be expected. The sea, of course, provided a natural frontier for Wales to the north, south, and west. Even on its eastern, landward side certain natural boundaries seemed to demarcate clearly the extent of the country in places: the Dee estuary in the north, the Severn valley for a few miles near Buttington, and above all in the south-east the river Wye, which King Athelstan (according to William of Malmesbury) had designated as the boundary between his kingdom and that of the Welsh in the early tenth century. More impressive and far more continuous than these river-boundaries was, of course, Offa's Dyke. This great eighth-century earthwork extended for nearly one hundred and fifty miles along the length of Wales, from just east of the Wye estuary in the south to Basingwerk on the Dee estuary, the last phase of its northern arm running parllel with and being completed by a near-contemporary structure known as Wat's Dyke. Offa's Dyke was much the longest as it was much the most striking man-made boundary in the whole of medieval western Europe. *Clawdd Offa*, as it was known in Welsh, was regarded as the definitive land-boundary of Wales in the medieval Welsh law-texts; in native Welsh usage it has retained that status ever since. To cross *Clawdd Offa* was, and is, to go into England and thereby to become an exile (W. *alltud*).[1]

Offa's Dyke clearly came to play an important part in shaping the perception of the extent and identity of Wales in the medieval period. In a world without maps and border-posts, it served as a reference point, whether literally or metaphorically, to demarcate England from Wales. Furthermore, there was a broad correlation, admittedly closer in some areas than others, between the border as defined by Offa's Dyke and the boundaries of the eastern shires of Wales as they were eventually to be determined by the Act of Union of 1536, and thereby with the borders

---

[1] According to Welsh law, exiles who left their lords 'were not to dwell in this island this side of Offa's Dyke or this side of the sea', *Llyfr Colan*, ed. D. Jenkins (Cardiff, 1963), §634. For other contemporary perceptions of Offa's Dyke, see Walter Map, *De Nugis*, II, xvii (ed. M. R. James *et al.*, pp. 167–9).

of Wales today. It is also true that when contemporaries in the eleventh and twelfth centuries referred to Wales—whether as *Wallia* (the term, in various forms, normally employed by non-Welsh scribes), as *Britannia* (the term preferred by most Welsh writers writing in Latin well into the twelfth century), as *Cymru(y)* (a term already in currency in the vernacular),[2] or as *Kambria* (the name self-consciously adopted by Gerald of Wales in preference to *Wallia*, which he regarded as a pejorative Saxon label)—their geographical image of its extent coincided closely enough to our own usage. Wales, therefore, had emerged as a term and as an identifiable geographical unit before the beginning of our period.

Yet it is important to recognize that, regardless of the clear-cut character of Offa's Dyke, Wales's eastern boundaries were far from being definitively fixed in the late eleventh century. Countries and boundaries are not laid up in heaven. They are shaped by men; and what men shape they may also choose to reshape. The fortunes of war were one obvious reason why the boundaries of Wales might be redrawn. In terms of military power and political control, the border of Wales was not the same in 1086 as it had been in 1060, nor the same again in 1186 as it was in 1086. On the English side, there was no reason why Offa's Dyke should be regarded as a *ne ultra plus* line and no reason why areas well beyond it should not be absorbed into the military and political control of English kingdoms. The Mercian kings had earlier pushed well beyond the Dyke in the north and had even reached as far as the river Clwyd. Their military thrust was accompanied by extensive settlement in the lowlands of the Dee valley and around its estuary. Most of the land east of the Dyke in this district had been absorbed into the Cheshire hundreds of Exestan and Dudestan (later Broxton), while much of the area west of the dyke along and beyond the Dee estuary fell into the ambit of the hundred of Atiscross, extending, albeit rather tentatively, as far as the river Clwyd. It looked in 1086 as if this whole area was henceforth to be fully integrated into the county administration of Cheshire and thereby possibly into the framework of the English kingdom. That suspicion seemed to be further confirmed by the fact that most of this district of north-east Wales lay under firm Anglo-Norman control until the 1140s. Yet by the end of the twelfth century, the Welsh had reversed the process and had done so decisively. They had pushed the border of power eastwards, not only to Wat's Dyke but well beyond it. The whole of the hundreds of Atiscross and Exestan disappeared and were absorbed into the Welsh commotal system, while part of the hundred of Dudestan resurfaces in the records as the Welsh district of Maelor Saesneg (English Maelor).[3] Another border area where

---

[2] For this term see below p. 19.

[3] The first recorded use of the term 'Maelor Saesneg' appears to be in a charter of 1202: A. N. Palmer and E. Owen, *A History of Ancient Tenures of Land in North Wales and the Marches* (2nd edn. Wrexham, 1910), 151.

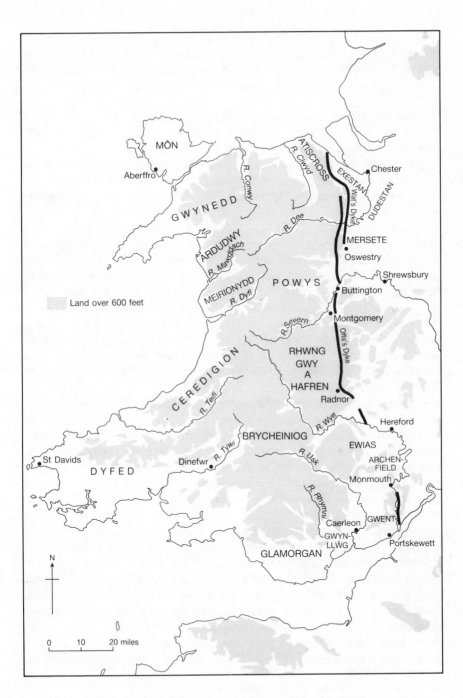

MAP I. Wales and its Borders in the Eleventh Century

the boundary shifted with the swing of the military pendulum lay around present-day Oswestry. In the Domesday survey of 1086 it was regarded as part of Shropshire and assigned to the appropriately named hundred of Mersete (probably meaning 'dwellers on the boundary'); but with the Welsh *revanche* of the mid-twelfth century, part of the area was temporarily absorbed into the lands of the princes of Powys. In the south-east, likewise, the border was far from static: Archenfield had recently been drawn into the orbit of English power and governance; while Harold Godwinson's construction of a hunting lodge at Portskewett (Gwent Iscoed) on the Severn estuary in the 1060s seemed to indicate that the annexation of at least parts of south-east Gwent into the English kingdom was imminent.

A second factor which helps to explain the fluidity of the border was the movement of peoples. The boundaries of peoples and languages and those of political units often do not coincide; but any marked disjunction between the two is a fertile source of conflict and often leads, sooner or later, to the redrawing of frontiers. So it was in Wales in the Middle Ages. To the north of Radnor, itself an important Saxon manor, English colonists had settled well west of the Dyke around Knighton, Knucklas, and Cascob (Maelienydd). It was natural that the boundary should follow them. So it did, for by the time of Domesday Book these areas had been incorporated into the county administration of Shropshire and Herefordshire. Elsewhere the reverse was true: large Welsh settlements survived and sometimes expanded beyond the acknowledged Anglo-Welsh frontier. This was true of the western parts of Shropshire near Oswestry and of the district known as Gorddwr on the eastern bank of the Severn opposite the present-day Welshpool. Most obviously was it true of the districts of Ewias and Archenfield (W. Ergyng) in the south-east. Today these districts are part of Herefordshire and for most purposes they were considered to be such in Domesday Book. Yet even contemporaries acknowledged that their largely Welsh population made their position anomalous. Their customs were separately itemized in Domesday Book; they were, very appropriately, called border districts, *fines*. Their ecclesiastical status confirmed their anomalous position and harked back to the past, for they remained ecclesiastically part of Wales—Archenfield until 1130, Ewias until 1852. It is little wonder that native Welsh poets included them within Wales in their imaginary circuits of the country. Here lay one of the many grey areas of the Welsh border.

Those grey areas grew rather than declined in number as the twelfth and thirteenth centuries progressed. The new Anglo-Norman lords of the Welsh borderlands exploited the fluidity and uncertainty of the frontier to their advantage. They seized on any opportunity to withdraw their frontier estates out of the ambit of English fiscal and judicial administration and to

convert them into virtually autonomous Marcher lordships. Thus, in the
two centuries after Domesday Book, five of the western hundreds of
Shropshire were partially or totally lost to the county and became part of
the March of Wales. Radnor with its surrounding district presents a similar
story: in 1086 it was regarded as part of Herefordshire and still retained
that status in 1250; but gradually and surreptitiously the Mortimer family
withdrew it out of the county and established it as a Marcher lordship.[4]
Such sleights of hand were only possible where borders were fluid and ill-
defined. It is little wonder that contemporaries themselves were far from
clear where the border lay. They indicated their uncertainty by making
entries for the district around Caerleon (Gwent Iscoed) in Domesday Book
under both Herefordshire and Gloucestershire; they pestered the English
exchequer with awkward questions as to whether Glasbury or Montgomery,
for example, were in England or not; they tried to camouflage their own
uncertainties by referring vaguely to 'Herefordshire in Wales' (the normal
designation for the county in exchequer records) and by saying that
Oswestry lay 'in the march between England and Wales'. One sympathizes
with their problems. The truth was that there was no fixed, let alone
predetermined, boundary. The boundary varied from generation to
generation according to the fluctuations of war, colonization, and lordship.

Yet by 1300 the Anglo-Welsh border enjoyed a greater measure of
stability and definition than it had hitherto ever known in its history. The
credit must go in part to Edward I. His conquest of north and west Wales in
1277–83 meant that the borderlands of Wales were no longer a military
frontier. Secondly, the tide of English colonization into the Welsh
borderlands began to ebb at much the same period; there was henceforth
no pressure to adjust the border to accommodate large communities of
English settlers. Thirdly, the process of withdrawing English border
districts into the March of Wales came to an end as the precise extent of
English border counties in terms of fiscal and judicial responsibilities was
more closely defined and as titles to franchises were rigorously scrutinized
by royal commissioners. The days of extending the border by baronial
usurpation and stealth were at an end. Wales, or rather Wales and the
March, had by 1300 acquired a boundary by prescription and by the
stability conferred by peace, though it would not be until the Tudor
legislation of 1536–43 that the Anglo-Welsh border would be definitively
established in the form that it has retained to the present day.

Wales, therefore, was already in the eleventh century a well-recognized
geographical expression; by 1300 its border with England was stable and
would remain unchanged until the sixteenth century. But was Wales more
than a geographical expression? Did it enjoy any measure of unity other

[4] See below p. 276.

than that imposed on it by its peninsular position and its border with England? Wales, it must be conceded at once, does not form a natural geographical unit within itself. In terms of relief, geology, climate, and settlement it is a collection of regions. Most of these regions are isolated from each other, in greater or lesser measure, by natural barriers, be they forbidding mountain ranges, such as isolate Powys from Ceredigion, or Brycheiniog from Glamorgan, or long tidal estuaries and marshy lowlands such as divide Ceredigion from Meirionydd, and Meirionydd in turn from Ardudwy. Furthermore, the mountain massif which dominates so much of upland Wales has concentrated its arable land, and thereby its population, in the coastal plains and a few major river valleys. Wales was a country without a centre, its population living along its peripheries, isolated from each other in pockets, large and small.

Physical geography, therefore, has imposed its own complex pattern of fragmentation on Wales. It was a pattern which made for diversity, not for unity. Within the ambit of this small country there were striking regional variations in wealth and social structure, in settlement patterns and agricultural practice, in commercial and cultural links. So much will become immediately apparent if Wales is divided, however arbitrarily and loosely, into five major regions or 'culture provinces' (in Sir Cyril Fox's famous phrase) in the eleventh and twelfth centuries.

The first of those regions lay in the north-east, extending broadly from the Severn to the Clwyd. Its orientation lay firmly, though not exclusively, eastwards. The rich plains of the eastward-flowing Dee and Severn afforded a tempting and easy route for Saxon penetration, and the extent of that penetration is reflected in an extensive overlay of Saxon place-names along the eastern border (albeit often camouflaged by being subsequently dressed up in Welsh forms, e.g. Preston, W. Prestatyn; Soughton, W. Sychdyn (Tegeingl)). The movement of peoples was by no means a one-way traffic only, for in the twelfth century Welsh settlers in considerable numbers reoccupied the lowlands of the Dee valley and pushed into the district west of Oswestry. In this zone of Wales cultural, commercial, and social links with lowland England were readily forged. They are, perhaps, symbolically manifested in the most famous early medieval monument of the region, the remarkable ninth-century pillar of Eliseg near Llangollen (Nanheudwy). Its affinities are with the round-shaft crosses of Mercia and it is to the east also that other tenth- and eleventh-century monuments of this region—such as those at Whitford (Tegeingl) and Meifod (Caereinion)—look for their inspiration. This lowland zone had long since been vulnerable to the military, political, and economic power of neighbouring England. That relationship did much to shape the personality of the district and the ambivalent and diplomatically calculating attitude of its rulers, the princes of Powys.

Much the same was true of lowland south-east Wales. Here, marshy lowlands and the estuaries of the Wye and Usk acted as a brake on migration from the east, but the routes of former Roman roads and the ease of passage across the Severn estuary made the lowlands of Gwent, Gwynllŵg, and Glamorgan natural targets for raiders and settlers. There is evidence of Saxon and possibly some Scandinavian settlement in these areas, notably in the district around Monmouth, in the middle reaches of the Wye valley and along the coastal lowlands of eastern Glamorgan. The south-east was in many ways the most distinctive region of Wales: rich in good agricultural land, well-populated, its economy and social structure more differentiated and complex than those of the rest of Wales, its settlement pattern more securely established, its links with England close. It also stood rather apart from the rest of Wales politically and Harold's establishment of a hunting lodge at Portskewett in 1065 seemed to announce that parts of the region might soon be annexed to England. Yet later that same year a Welsh princeling destroyed the lodge, thereby serving notice that not even lowland eastern Wales was to be won without an effort.

In between these two eastern border zones lay a third district whose geographical character was utterly different. It was known in Welsh as Rhwng Gwy a Hafren, between Severn and Wye, though it may also be said to extend in the south to the river Usk and indeed across it to the Brecon Beacons. It was a land of eastward-running valleys which here, as elsewhere, could serve as routes for links with England. Early monuments from the region confirm this impression: such as the Saxon church at Presteigne, the intricately carved cross at Llanynys near Builth, and the remarkable early twelfth-century tympanum of the church at Llanbadarn Fawr (Maelienydd), so clearly a distant Welsh outlier of the gifted school of Herefordshire stone-sculptors. Yet in this area of the border, mountains and moor were at their most daunting and uninviting; it was here that the Normans found their progress constantly frustrated. It was at either end of this highland bloc, at Montgomery and Painscastle (Elfael), that Henry III was to erect two of his earliest castles in Wales; it was in this region, near Builth (Buellt) that the last native Welsh prince was killed in 1282. This was a zone which had a strategic significance out of all proportion to its uninviting terrain and thin population.

While the lowland regions of eastern Wales may be said in the eleventh century to be facing eastward, the orientation of the two remaining regions of Wales still lay very considerably westwards. Protected by its own enceinte of mountains and estuaries, north-west Wales was to remain the most vigorously independent and resilient region of Wales. Its natural centre lay at its own extremity, in the rich and old-settled island of Anglesey; it was there at Aberffro that the principal court of its secular rulers lay from sub-Roman times until the final extinction of native Welsh independence. South-west Wales did not form as coherent or resilient a geographical or political unit as did the north-west. It had more obvious routes eastwards, especially along its south-eastern frontiers, and its ancestral political centre lay in the east at Dinefwr (Cantref Mawr) in the rich Tywi valley. Yet for generations much of its orientation lay westwards and its principal shrine was located in the furthest west at St Davids (Pebidiog). In the eleventh century both these western regions of Wales formed part of a western-sea province extending from the Hebrides, Orkney, and Shetlands in the north and comprehending the Isle of Man and the Scandinavian kingdom of Dublin in its ambit. Western and southern Wales suffered recurrent Viking raids, mainly from Dublin, throughout the eleventh and into the early twelfth centuries. North Wales was likewise a target for raids, though the bases for its raiders often lay in the north, in the Hebrides and especially in Man, rather than in the west. Anglesey, itself a Scandinavian name, lay on the crossroads of these Viking attacks from north and west. Its pivotal position was admirably exemplified in 1098: in that year a Scandinavian fleet from Dublin, hired by two Welsh princes to help them withstand the Norman attack on Anglesey, defected to the Normans on being offered a higher reward; but, just as the Normans were celebrating their victory in a rampage of violence and plunder, another Scandinavian fleet under Magnus Barefoot, king of Norway, appeared off the coast of eastern Anglesey and inflicted a crushing defeat on the Normans, in which the earl of Shrewsbury was killed. Magnus returned to the island in 1102 and, according to the native annalist, stripped it of timber to build his castles on the Isle of Man. Scandinavian raids on Wales petered out in the first half of the twelfth century (one of the last recorded raids being that on Llandudoch (St Dogmaels, Cemais) in 1138);[5] but the links with Ireland still remained important. It was to Ireland that Welsh princes recurrently fled for safety from their political rivals,[6] and that disaffected Welsh princelings looked for help to restore their flagging fortunes in Wales (as happened in 1138, 1144, 1157, and 1173). Even as late as 1202 the continuing importance of the western sea orbit in Welsh political strategy was underlined by Llywelyn ab Iorwerth's proposal to marry a daughter of the king of Man. That Llywelyn eventually preferred the hand of Joan, the king of England's illegitimate daughter, may be taken as one indication among many that the pull of the western

---

[5] As late as 1193 Rhodri ab Owain Gwynedd summoned aid from the king of Man to recover, at least temporarily, a share of his patrimony in Anglesey.

[6] Among Welsh princelings who found refuge (often more than once) in Ireland were Gruffudd ap Cynan of Gwynedd (d. 1137), Owain ap Cadwgan of Powys (d. 1116), and Gruffudd ap Rhys of Deheubarth (d. 1137).

sea orbit was by then on the decline, even in north-west Wales.

The links of lowland western Wales with Ireland and the western sea province in the eleventh and twelfth centuries were not confined to politics and plunder. The early literature of Wales shows a lively, if not always well-informed, interest in the Irish world. There is a major Irish dimension to two of the tales of the *Mabinogi* (*Math* and especially *Branwen*); it was on an Irish prototype that Lifris, at the end of the eleventh century, based his *Life of St Cadog* and this biography, like that of St David written by Rhigyfarch at much the same time, is characterized by the lively prominence it gives to the links with Ireland. It was to Ireland that the most distinguished scholar of Wales in the later eleventh century, Sulien, bishop of St Davids (1072–8, 1080–5), travelled to complete his education, while the manuscripts written by his sons, Ieuan and Rhigyfarch, have certain features in common with contemporary Irish practice. It is not surprising that some of the monumental sculpture of south-west and north-west Wales in this period—such as the font at Beaumaris (Anglesey) or the crosses at Penmon (Anglesey) and Nyfer (Nevern, Cemais)—should reveal marked Hiberno-Norse influence. Such contacts may well have entailed some settlement, though now on a very occasional and reduced scale compared with that of earlier centuries. Among the leading figures in Anglesey in the late twelfth century was Cedifor Wyddel (the Irishman), while the mother of Hywel ab Owain Gwynedd (d. 1170), the distinguished poet-prince of the Gwynedd dynasty, was one Pyfog the Irishwoman. Commercial links between western Wales and Ireland, links which indeed extended along the northern and southern coasts to Chester and Bristol respectively, must also have been considerable. The few references that survive—such as those to the harbour of Abermenai (Anglesey) in the biography of Gruffudd ap Cynan or to an Irish ship unloading its cargo at Aberdyfi (Meirionydd) in 1109—can only serve as rare hints of a considerable, if irregular, trade and one in which the distinction between plunder (especially the capture of slaves) and commerce was far from clear.

The westward orientation of the two western regions of Wales until well into the twelfth century served to accentuate the regional differences within the country. These regional differences were in their turn further complicated by sharp local divisions within each of the regions themselves. None of these divisions was more ubiquitous and none more important than that between upland and lowland. It was a contrast which characterized each and every region of Wales as well as the country as a whole. The contemporary poet, Hywel ab Owain Gwynedd, in his exultation in the excellence of Gwynedd, delighted in the contrast between *morfa* (coastal lowland) and *mynydd* (mountain); his was a contrast which was true of every region of Wales.[7] It applied, for example, to the north-east where the broad acres of the Dee plain and of Dyffryn Clwyd were separated from each other by the bleak moorlands of Tegeingl (E. Englefield) and Iâl (E. Yale). It applied equally in the south-east to Gwent and Glamorgan. In medieval times Glamorgan was recognized both as a kingdom and as a region, Gwlad Forgan; but the contrasts within it between upland and lowland, *blaenau* and *bro*, were profound. They shaped the whole social character, or rather characters, of the region and the very different pace at which Norman lordship was imposed within Glamorgan. And what was true of Glamorgan was, in greater or lesser detail, true of every other region of Wales.

Wales, therefore, was a geographically fragmented country, a land of contrasts national, regional, and local. In such a fragmented country it was the locality or district which was often the most meaningful and basic unit of loyalty and obligation. *Gwlad* (pl. *gwladoedd gwledydd*) or *bro* (pl. *broydd, brooedd*) were the loose vernacular terms used to refer to such a district. A *gwlad* might be a kingdom or former kingdom; alternatively or additionally, it might coincide with the local administrative subdivisions of *cantref* (pl. *cantrefi*) or *cwmwd* (pl. *cymydau*) which come to figure prominently in the history of medieval Wales.[8] Yet it was not its political or administrative identity which gave the *gwlad* its cohesion so much as the fact that it was a territorial unit shaped by geography, history, and sentiment, and one which contemporaries recognized and with which they could identify. When a native Welsh poet recounted his imaginary tour of Wales in the early twelfth century, he did so by enumerating more than thirty of its districts.[9] His was no doubt a poetic conceit; but it lays bare one important dimension of contemporary native perceptions of Wales—that of a country which was an amalgam of districts. Even kingdoms themselves often appeared as no more than loose assemblages of such districts: it was as 'the comfort of the districts' (*diddanwch y gwladoedd*) that Bleddyn ap Cynfyn (d. 1075) was memorialized by the native chronicler; likewise, when Madog ap Gruffudd (d. 1236) of northern Powys made a grant of

---

[7] 'Caraf ei morfa a'i mynyddedd . . . Caraf ei brooedd, braint hywredd, A'i diffaith mawrfaith a'i marannedd', (I love its strand and its mountains . . . I love its regions, to which valour entitles, its wide wasteland and its wealth), 'Gorhoffedd Hywel ab Owain', *The Oxford Book of Welsh Verse*, ed. T. Parry (Oxford 1962) p. 26 (original Welsh text); *The Oxford Book of Welsh Verse in English*, ed. Gwyn Jones (Oxford, 1977), p. 22 (trans. by Gwyn Williams).

[8] For *cantref* and *cwmwd* see note at the end of this chapter.

[9] J. Véndryes, 'Le poème du Livre Noir sur Hywel ap Gronw', *Études Celtiques*, iv (1948), 275–300. His list encompassed the whole of Wales. It included kingdoms or former kingdoms (such as Powys, Morgannwg, and Brycheiniog), well-recognized regional subdivisions (such as Dyfed, Ystrad Tywi, and Ceredigon), single *cantrefi* (such as Llŷn, Ardudwy, Rhos, Tegeingl), individual commotes (Edeirnion, Iâl, Nantconwy), and royal centres (Aberffro, Degannwy).

pasture throughout his principality in 1202, he felt obliged to enumerate the districts (L. *provincie*) of which it was composed.[10]

It was the region, large or small, which was often the most obvious focus of communal identity and loyalty for many of its inhabitants. Its boundaries demarcated the horizons of their social contacts and territorial claims, its mother church and its patron saint the focus of their religious affections, its traditions and lore the framework of their collective memories. This attachment to region was all the stronger in a world where political hegemonies and dynastic fortunes were so brittle; in a fluid and uncertain political world the region or *gwlad* represented a welcome element of continuity and stability. No one celebrated this love of region more memorably than Ieuan ap Sulien at the end of the eleventh century: conscious though he was of 'the race of Britons' to which he belonged, it was Ceredigion which he regarded as his homeland (L. *patria*), its sea, mountains, and rivers as the bounds of his world, and its local saint, Padarn, as the focus of his religious affection.[11] Ieuan's love for his region was frequently matched in the vernacular poetry: as in Hywel ab Owain Gwynedd's delight in his 'lovely Gwynedd' (W. *glwys Gwynedd*), or that of Owain Cyfeiliog (d. 1197) in his native Powys or, for a later period, in Sion Cent's memorable exaltation of the excellence of Brycheiniog. Such regional loyalties varied, of course, in their intensity according to time, place, and person. Sometimes they were little more than a harmless and sentimental attachment to the local *pays*; sometimes they expressed themselves more viciously in inter-regional raids and vendettas; sometimes they acted as a brake on ambitious princes and on the development of over-kingdoms: thus Gruffudd ap Cynan's early ambitions were frustrated by 'the men of Llŷn and Eifionydd',[12] while the strong separatist traditions of Meirionydd, Arwystli, Ceri, and Mechain were a constant thorn in the sides of the princes of Gwynedd and Powys. The pull of such regional loyalties declined in the twelfth and thirteenth centuries as the texture of over-kingdoms and princely authority was woven more tightly. Furthermore, patterns of local or regional loyalty were often overridden or at least supplemented at aristocratic level by the personal ties of service and reward to leaders of powerful dynasties and over-kingdoms. But in Wales such regional loyalties died hard and could often be revived in the service of a disinherited local dynasty or even of the cadet branch of a ruling family. Indeed, the emergence of Marcher lordships in Anglo-Norman

[10] *Brut (RBH)*, *s.a.* 1078; *Arch. Camb.*, 3rd ser., xii (1866), 414.

[11] M. Lapidge, 'Welsh Latin Poetry of Sulien's Family', *Studia Celtica*, viii–ix (1973–4), 68–106 at p. 83.

[12] *Historia Gruffud vab Kenan*, ed. D. Simon Evans (Cardiff, 1977), p. 10; *The History of Gruffydd ap Cynan*, ed. A. Jones (Manchester 1910), p. 119. This edition provides an English translation and will henceforth be cited in brackets as *History G. ap C.* in all references to the modern Welsh edition.

Wales was to provide a new context in which such loyalties could be cultivated and perpetuated. It was an inauspicious base on which to build the unity of Wales.

But the greatest stumbling-block of all to such aspirations was the political fragmentation of Wales. Wales in the Middle Ages had never known political unity other than the hegemony temporarily imposed by military might. It was a country of many kings, many dynasties, many kingdoms.[13] What remained to be determined in the eleventh century was the number of kingdoms which would survive. There was no necessary or ineluctable progress towards political consolidation within or between dynasties. Indeed, on the contrary, any move in that direction in one generation was more often than not undone in the next. It is, perhaps, natural with hindsight—especially a hindsight nurtured by the centralist assumptions of English political historiography and reinforced by the nationalist ideology of thirteenth-century native Welsh propaganda—to assume that the will for political unity was always latent in Wales. The evidence suggests otherwise. It assumes multiple kingship as a norm: 'they obstinately and proudly refuse to submit to one ruler' was Gerald of Wales's shrewd comment at the end of the twelfth century.[14] It proclaims that it is morally wrong for a prince to deprive his brother or kinsman of a share of the paternal inheritance in pursuit of a policy of dynastic consolidation. It warns against territorial expansion: 'it is foolish to own more of the world than comes from God' was the stern advice of the twelfth-century poet Cynddelw and his viewpoint was echoed in Elidir Sais's warning to Llywelyn ab Iorwerth to 'beware of raiding beyond boundaries'.[15] The native law-texts likewise assume that Wales is a land of many countries or kingdoms, that the men of one country are not necessarily bound by the rules of an alien country (W. *gorwlad*) and that a king would lead his warband on plundering raids into such neighbouring countries regularly. That is indeed what we find in the annals. The common coin of Welsh politics in the eleventh and twelfth centuries, as in earlier periods, was attack on neighbouring kingdoms, and destruction and pillage of their wealth. To the Welsh such attacks—*cylch gorwlad* as one poet called them—were a normal feature of life; to outside observers they were another expression of 'the universal discord' which was the most

---

[13] See below pp. 58–62.

[14] *DK*, II, ix (*Opera*, vi, 225).

[15] *The Poetry in the Red Book of Hergest*, ii, ed. J. Gwenogvryn Evans (Llanbedrog, 1926), p. 226 (Nid meddwl meddu hefyd/Namyn o Dduw ddim o'r byd), trans. in J. P. Clancy, *The Earliest Welsh Poetry* (1970), pp. 142–4; *The Myvyrian Archaiology of Wales*, ed. O. Jones *et al.* (2nd edn. 1870), 240 (Ystyrych pan dreisych dros ffin). The passage is cited and trans. by D. M. Lloyd in *A Guide to Welsh Literature*, i, ed. A. O. H. Jarman and G. R. Hughes (Swansea, 1976), p. 177.

noteworthy feature of the Welsh.[16] There was little room here for notions of the unity of Wales or for the emergence of a common polity. Political particularism seemed as natural to Wales as did geographical fragmentation and regional loyalties. The three indeed fed upon one another.

Wherever we look at medieval Wales it seems to dissolve into plurality; its history appears to be no more than the sum of its individual parts. Indeed, this impression of fragmentation was to be further accentuated by the character and pace of the Anglo-Norman conquest of Wales: Wales, or rather parts of Wales, now became a country of two peoples as well as of many regions. Yet, in spite of all its divisions, Wales had an identity of its own and so did its people. Outsiders had no doubt about that. In the writs of the first century of Norman rule, the Welsh are invariably greeted as one people and Wales is referred to as one country—an obvious point, maybe, but one which emphasizes that to outsiders the distinctiveness of Wales was as impressive as its fragmentation. Furthermore, during the twelfth century the cultural identity of the Welsh as a distinctive people was brought into much sharper focus, partly because ecclesiastical reformers sought to impose common norms of behaviour on the peoples of Christendom and condemned departures from those norms as unnatural deviations, and partly because shrewd observers (notably Walter Map and Gerald of Wales) began to describe and analyse the customs of the Welsh. 'The Welsh', remarked Bernard, the first Norman bishop of St Davids (1115–48), 'are entirely different in nation, language, laws and habits, judgements and customs'.[17] His comment was hugely amplified by later writers, notably Gerald of Wales, who provided detailed descriptions of the Welsh: of their physical appearance, dress, houses, social customs, morals, marital habits and so forth. A stereotyped image of the medieval Welshman was being shaped by external observers. That image was often simplified, even distorted. It frequently tells us as much about the observer as about the observed; but it also serves to remind us that to outside commentators the Welsh were, indeed, for all their differences, a very distinctive people who shared common characteristics.

This recognition of a common Welsh identity was not a sentiment confined to external observers. The Welsh themselves, in spite of their divisions and differences, were also well aware of it. There is no contradiction here. A strong sense of common unity as a people is not incompatible with a highly particularized local identity. Nor are the institutions of a unitary polity and of centralized governance a pre-requisite for the emergence of a sentiment of national identity. In medieval Wales several other alternative factors contributed to the nurturing of that

[16] *Llsg. Hendregadredd*, p. 69; *Gesta Stephani*, ed. K. R. Potter and R. H. C. Davis (Oxford, 1976), p. 20.
[17] *Episc. Acts*, i, p. 259 (D. 121).

sentiment. One was pride in the frontiers of Wales and conviction of the need to defend them at all costs. The concept of a Wales extending from Portskewett on the Severn estuary to Porth Wygyr in Anglesey and delimited by the gates of Chester in the north and the unidentified Rhyd Taradyr in the south was already a commonplace of Welsh poetry in the twelfth century. When Gwenwynwyn of Powys launched a major campaign in 1198 its declared aim was to restore to the Welsh their ancient 'bounds and limits'.[18] An even more powerful ingredient in the chemistry of national unity was pride in a common descent from the Britons of old. It was as Britons, *Brytaniaid*, that the Welsh normally described themselves until the later twelfth century; 'Britain' was the title they gave to their country. 'I am born of the famous race of Britons', was Ieuan ap Sulien's proud assertion.[19] This same claim was expressed genealogically by tracing the descent of the dynasties of Wales to the heroes of north Britain. A sense of continuity through time from the original and true proprietors of Britain contributed powerfully to the self-identification of the Welsh. It was reinforced by the belief that all Welshmen of noble stock shared common blood and thereby common status. In a society dominated by the terminology and concepts of lineage and status, it was in terms of community of blood and descent that a sense of common identity could be most readily expressed. 'A Welshman born of Welsh parents on either side (*Cymro famtad*)', so proclaimed the Welsh law-texts, 'will be an innate gentleman (*bonheddig cynhwynol*)'.[20] Blood, status, and nationality were intertwined in that definition.

To them was added another potent ingredient in the making of national identity, that of a common mythology, a sense of shared traditions, myths, and sagas. It was a mythology which was jealously cultivated by a professional order of bards and remembrancers; it provided them with a common stock of heroes, onomastic lore, quasi-historical legend, and evocative references. It was a mythology which looked back wistfully and proudly to a glorious past, to victories over giants, to links with Troy and Rome, to memories of a united Britain, to the valour of British heroes, and to the migration of the men of the Old North to Wales. As with all such mythologies, its aim was to provide an interpretation of the past which was consoling for the present and prophetic for the future. It was an immensely powerful element in the creation of national identity, prompting practical action as well as poetic reverie. It was, for example, the prospect of 'repairing and renewing the Brittanic kingdom' which lured young men to flock to Gruffudd ap Rhys's cause in 1116.[21]

---

[18] 'Cronica de Wallia', *sub anno*, 1198, *BBCS* 12 (1946), 5.
[19] *Studia Celtica*, viii–ix (1973–4), 83.
[20] *Llyfr Blegywryd*, ed. S. J. Williams and J. E. Powell (2nd edn. Cardiff, 1961), p. 58.
[21] *Brut (RBH)*, *s.a.* 1116 (p. 87).

Language and a common literary tradition were other important elements in creating an awareness of Welshness. Dialectical differences—such as those which characterized the men of Gwent—were recognized; but they were of small significance compared with the broad linguistic unity of Wales. Welsh was spoken throughout Wales and even beyond its borders in lowland Shropshire and Herefordshire. Archbishop Baldwin on his tours of the country in 1188 required interpreters at its borders, at Usk and at Radnor. An awareness of the Welsh language and pride in its purity were a recurring theme of contemporary court poetry: Cuhelyn Fardd in the early twelfth century was praised for his 'beautiful' and 'refined' Welsh; Cynddelw prided himself on the quality of his Welsh, free from foreign taint and base words; while Gwynfardd Brycheiniog proclaimed that 'good' and 'learned' Welsh alone befitted St David.[22] Equally, those who did not speak Welsh (W. *anghyfiaith*) were immediately designated as aliens (W. *estron*); so it was that the English came to be branded as a 'foreign alien-tongued people' (*estron genedl anghyfiaith*).[23] Language was becoming one of the badges of national identity.

Literary tradition also played its part in forging a sense of common Welsh identity. Welsh poets and story-tellers composed their works self-consciously within a common tradition; they, and particularly so the poets, drew upon a uniform literary language and a common stock of lore and mythology. Furthermore, they moved freely around Wales, both in imagination and in person. They took a delight in making an imaginary tour of Wales (W. *cylch Cymru*); it allowed them to display their knowledge of its various regions. But equally they could tour the country in person, travelling from one princely court to the next. Cynddelw Brydydd Mawr, in his own estimation, as well as that of later literary pundits, the most eminent poet of the later twelfth century, was possibly more eclectic than others in his choice of patrons—including as they did Owain Gwynedd (d. 1170) and Dafydd ab Owain (d. 1203) of Gwynedd, Madog ap Maredudd (d. 1160) and Owain Cyfeiliog (d. 1197) of Powys, and Rhys ap Gruffudd (d. 1197) of Deheubarth—but he was by no means alone in regarding the whole of Wales as his literary stage. When the Lord Rhys of Deheubarth held his famous assembly at Cardigan in 1176 and organized competitions for musicians and poets, it was the men of Gwynedd who carried off the poetry prizes. The native prose tales, notably the *Mabinogi*, likewise assume an audience that can move freely in its imagination across

---

[22] R. G. Gruffydd, 'A Poem in Praise of Cuhelyn Fardd from the Black Book of Carmarthen', *Studia Celtica*, x–xi (1975–6), 198–209 at pp. 203, 206 (Cymraeg hardd, coeth); J. Véndryes, 'Trois poèmes de Cynddelw', *Études Celtiques*, iv (1948), 1–47 at p. 45 (dilediaith, briw-iaith); *Llsg. Hendregadredd*, p. 201 (da Gymraeg, doeth Gymraeg).

[23] For the equation 'estron' and 'anghyfiaith' see, for example, *Historia Gruffudd vab Kenan*, pp. 30–1, (*History G. ap. C.* p. 155); for the phrase 'estron genedl . . . anghyfiaith' see *Llsg. Hendregadredd*, p. 218.

the whole of Wales—from Dyfed and Gwent Iscoed in the south to Talybolion in Anglesey. Poets from Glamorgan are introduced and so are story-tellers travelling from Dyfed to Gwynedd. In prose and poetry alike there is a sense of delight in the geography of Wales, in reciting its place-names and in explaining them, whether through geneaology or through legend. The Wales of the literature is a remarkably intimate and much-loved country. At the level of aristocratic court literature Wales enjoyed a considerable measure of cultural unity.

Wales also knew a goodly measure of legal unity. Law in Wales, it is true, was a customary law, dispensed in a variety of local assemblies and arbitrations and adjusted to the needs and habits of localized societies. It certainly differed considerably in substance, procedure, and enforcement from one region of Wales to another. Yet, in spite of its variations, Welsh law seems to have been informed from an early date (well before the survival of the earliest written texts, from the early thirteenth century) by common legal concepts and basic procedures. Its unity, like that of the native literary tradition, was nourished by the fact that it was taught and transmitted by a class of quasi-professional jurists who were probably responsible for assembling the legal texts as we now have them. Those texts assume that Wales was a legal unit. Their prologues proclaimed that the laws were assembled and revised by Hywel Dda (the Good) as 'prince of the whole of Wales' at an assembly of men 'from every *cantref* in Wales' and that the laws so published were to be current throughout Wales.[24] They doubtless protest too much and are to be interpreted as a deliberate attempt to manufacture an ideology of national unity. In that respect they succeeded. It could be asserted categorically in reply to a royal inquisition in 1278 that Welsh law 'prevailed throughout Wales and the Marches, as far as the power of the Welsh extends'.[25] Welsh law had been converted into a potent symbol of Welsh national identity. It was in the final struggle between Edward I and Llywelyn ap Gruffudd that the full potential of Welsh law was to be exploited;[26] but its role as one of the emblems of Welsh identity had long since been foreshadowed. Already in 1086 the Domesday commissioners noted that three Welshmen in Caerleon (Gwent Iscoed) were living under Welsh law, while in the first extant treaty between an English king and a Welsh prince, that of 1201 between King John and Llywelyn ab Iorwerth, the unitary and distinct character of Welsh law (L. *lex Wallie*) was formally recognized. Whereas Welsh kingdoms and princes might be many, the law of Wales was one. It was, furthermore, a law which proclaimed the distinction between the Welshman (W. *Cymro*) and the alien (W. *alltud*) as basic. Originally, no doubt, that distinction had

---

[24] *Llyfr Iorwerth*, ed. A. R. William (Cardiff, 1960), §1.
[25] *Calendar of Inquisitions Miscellaneous 1219–1307*, p. 333, no. 1109.
[26] See below p. 346.

been a regional one within Wales itself between men of the same region (W. *bro, tud*) and those from other regions (W. *all-fro, all-tud*). But by the time of the surviving law-texts, indeed probably several centuries earlier, the distinction had become a 'national' one: between the Welshman and the man of a foreign county. The line between the two was now drawn explicitly, at the sea, on the one hand, and at Offa's Dyke, on the other. That definition was a cardinal affirmation of the distinctiveness of Wales as a country and of the Welsh as a people.

The Welsh had also adopted for themselves a name, *Cymry*, which highlighted their awareness of themselves as 'compatriots'. They were, it is true, reluctant to abandon their older name of Britons, *Brytaniaid*. It was, after all, a term redolent of memories, of glories, of hope; to surrender it seemed to be to accept that they had indeed come down in the world. So it was that they clung tenaciously to it well into the twelfth century. Yet the growing disjunction between historical mythology and current reality gradually drove them to adopt a new name. That name was in fact already to hand. By the mid-seventh century, at the latest, the Britons of Wales and northern Britain had begun to describe themselves as *Cymry*, people of the same region or *bro*. It was a most serviceable term. It could be applied to land and to people alike (the current distinction between *Cymru* as the land and *Cymry* as its people is a recent orthographic change); from it a word for the Welsh language, *Cymraeg*, had been readily forged. It was a word which had already established itself firmly in the vocabulary of the court poets and during the twelfth century it increasingly ousted the term Britons, *Brytaniaid*, as the common phrase by which Welshmen identified themselves.

The Welsh, therefore, by no means lacked the concept of themselves as a people and of their country as one. 'In that year', records the native annalist under the year 1198, 'Gwenwynwyn' (of Powys) planned to restore to the Welsh (*Cymry*) their ancient liberty and their ancient proprietary rights and their bounds'.[27] Gwenwynwyn and his supporters, who we are told included 'all the princes of Wales' (*holl tywysogion Cymru*), did not realize their hope; but theirs was a vision of a united Wales, of a Wales restored to its former bounds and status. It was a vision to which the poets fully subscribed. Addressing his patron, the Lord Rhys (d. 1197), Gwynfardd Brycheiniog had yearned that he would 'take Wales from end to end', just as in another ode he had cherished the vision of St David 'taking the peoples of Wales to himself'.[28] Poets and politicians alike could dream of a united Wales, of a country politically unified just as it was already in many respects culturally, legally, and linguistically united. For

[27] *Brut (RBH), s.a.* 1198.
[28] *Llsg. Hendregadredd*, pp. 207 ('cymryd Gymru ben baladr'), 198 ('a phobloedd Cymru a gymer ato').

the Welsh, however, such sentiments were by no means incompatible with intense political competition and strong local sentiment. Wales was indeed a single country, but governed by several rulers; the Welsh were one people, but, as so often with families, the segmentary divisions were much more to the fore than the family unity. In the twelfth and thirteenth centuries the paradox of the diversity of Wales on the one hand and its conviction of its own unity on the other came into ever sharper focus. On the capacity of the Welsh to resolve, or to fail to resolve, that paradox would turn very considerably the very survival of Welsh political independence. It was the Normans above all who brought the issue into stark focus, and it is to the challenge that they posed to Wales that we must now turn.

A NOTE ON THE LOCAL DIVISIONS OF WALES

Many of the local divisions of medieval Wales are of great antiquity. Even from such exiguous evidence as survives prior to *c*.1150 a substantial list of such divisions can be compiled. The literary evidence, both the prose tales (notably the *Mabinogi*) and the early court poetry, reveals a ready and often intimate familiarity with these divisions. Furthermore, charter evidence and late surveys show that the boundaries between these divisions were well known, whether they were natural landmarks (watersheds, estuaries, rivers, mountains) or human artefacts (dykes, cairns, standing stones). These regional and local divisions range the gamut from large principalities such as Gwynedd and Powys through intermediate districts such as Ceredigion or Ystrad Tywi to small units such as Ceri or Edeirnion. Some bear names which are essentially geographical descriptions (e.g. Dyffryn Clwyd, i.e. the Vale of Clwyd; Arfon, i.e. land over against Môn (Anglesey)); others carry titles woven from the historical mythology of the Welsh, often referring to the eponymous founder of a royal dynasty or to one of his descendants (e.g. Meirionydd, Eifionydd and Edeirnion were allegedly named after sons or grandsons of Cunedda Wledig, who according to tradition had migrated to north Wales from north Britain in the late fourth century).

These local divisions are known by various names: *provincia* is a common term in Latin charters; *cantref*, *cwmwd*, and *swydd* (largely confined to east central Wales) are among the most familiar vernacular terms. If we look for analogues to these units, both in size and character, we may find them most readily in the early divisions of Anglo-Saxon England, such as the lathe, soke, or rape, or in the early shires of northern England and lowland Scotland. Like these analogues, the Welsh local divisions seem to be units both of lordship, on the one hand, and of community sentiment and organization, on the other. Each district had its lordly or royal centre to which dues were payable and at which services were performed. But each district also often formed a natural geographic and economic unit, its inhabitants often sharing certain common easements (such as grazing rights) as well as responsibilities, and taking pride in their local loyalties and traditions, secular and ecclesiastical. Groups of these districts could be, and indeed often were, historically associated into larger units; thus the *Mabinogi* in common with other early sources, assumes that the region of Dyfed was composed of seven *cantrefi*, Ceredigion of four *cantrefi*, Ystrad Tywi of three *cantrefi*.

It may, therefore, be readily conceded that much of the map of the regional and local divisions of Wales had already taken a firm shape well prior to our period. Yet we must beware of giving a fixity and definitiveness to that map which are not warranted by the evidence. No complete lists of the local divisions of Wales are extant prior to the fifteenth century and by then antiquarians were busy at work on the lists, filling in gaps and trying to impose consistency and uniformity on the administrative map of Wales. Furthermore, it is clear that before and during our period the local divisions of Wales (in common with those of much of northern Europe) were being revised and redivided. Some units disappeared because they were no longer politically or administratively meaningful. Thus the *cantref* of Penychen (Glamorgan), well attested in earlier evidence, disappears from view. The *Mabinogi* comments on another 'lost' *cantref* when it glosses its reference to the *cantref* of Dunoding with the phrase 'which is now called Eifionydd and Ardudwy'. What happened in Dunoding appears in fact to have happened in many other parts of Wales, probably under the impact of a more intensive and regular lordship. Larger regions segmented into smaller districts; in particular, the larger unit of the *cantref* was supplemented and often replaced by the smaller unit of the *cwmwd* (E. commote). In some places (e.g. Arllechwedd, Elfael, Rhufoniog) the *cantref* was divided geographically into two *cymydau*, without however losing its identity; elsewhere (e.g. Ceredigion) the *cantref* organization barely survived, being largely replaced by a collection of small *cymydau*. Furthermore, in the areas that were heavily colonized by the Anglo-Normans, notably lowland Gwent, Glamorgan, Gower, and Pembroke, the Welsh divisions were quickly obliterated or mangled and replaced by knights' fees, lordships, castelries, mesne lordships and manors.

There is, therefore, more uncertainty and fluidity about the local divisions of eleventh- and twelfth-century Wales than the definitiveness of maps, frequently eked out from late medieval evidence and antiquarian speculations, often suggests. Much work remains to be undertaken to assemble contemporary evidence regarding these divisions, thereby consolidating and extending the pioneer work undertaken by such historians as

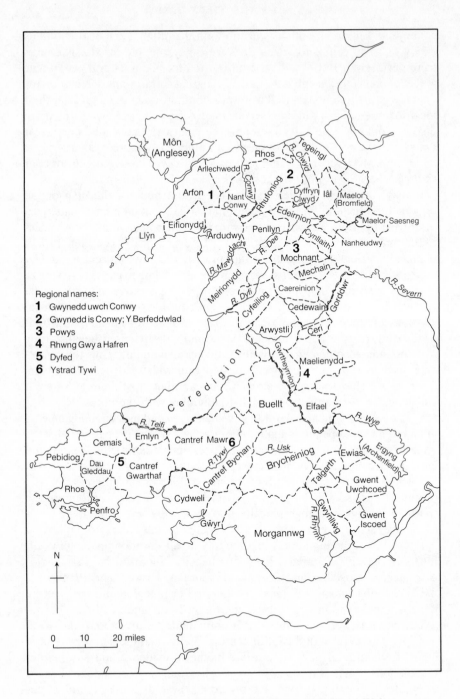

Regional names:
1 Gwynedd uwch Conwy
2 Gwynedd is Conwy; Y Berfeddwlad
3 Powys
4 Rhwng Gwy a Hafren
5 Dyfed
6 Ystrad Tywi

MAP 2. The Regional and Local Divisions of Medieval Wales

Sir John Edward Lloyd, Egerton Phillimore, A. N. Palmer and others, just as local historians such as C. A. Gresham have shown how much can be done to retrace the boundaries of the local vills (W. *trefi*) of medieval Wales. The accompanying map (Map 2) attempts to do no more than to identify the major regional and local divisions of Wales which are well attested before 1200 and which are mentioned in the text. It does not, for reasons of space and clarity, attempt to include all such divisions.

CHAPTER 2

THE STRUGGLE FOR SUPREMACY: WALES 1063–1172

In August 1063 Gruffudd ap Llywelyn was killed by his own men; his head and the figure-head of his ship were dispatched to Harold Godwinson and so, eventually, to Edward the Confessor, as the trophies of a signal victory. From his initial seizure of power in Gwynedd in 1039 and his first major victory over a Mercian army on the Severn in the same year, Gruffudd had been a dominating figure in Wales. During the last eight years of his life (1055–63), he had held the country as a whole under his sway. Contemporary chronicle and folk memory alike agreed in according him an eminence such as few of the Welsh princelings of the eleventh century enjoyed. To the native annalist he was 'the head and shield and defender of the Britons'; to the Anglo-Saxon chronicler, 'king over the whole of Wales'.[1] The defeat and death of such a prince were bound to have far-reaching repercussions.

Within Wales itself his death left a vacuum of authority and power. His hegemony had been founded on military might and personal dependence; it had no institutional base which could outlast his own downfall. The natural fissiparousness of Welsh 'political' life—if such a genteel term may be used for the litany of family and inter-dynastic conflicts, raids, kidnappings, and murders—now reasserted itself. Puppet rulers (such as Bleddyn and Rhiwallon ap Cynfyn, installed by Edward the Confessor in north Wales on his own terms), political exiles (notably Maredudd ab Owain of the dynasty of Deheubarth and Gruffudd ap Cynan of the former dynasty of Gwynedd), and adventurers (such as Trahaearn ap Caradog in north Wales and Caradog ap Gruffudd in south Wales) competed desperately with each other and joined forces in a perplexing kaleidoscope of temporary alliances to further their ambitions. Rarely, even by its own standards, was the Welsh 'political' scene more fluid, its allegiances more brittle and its supremacies more short-lived than in the later eleventh century.

Gruffudd's downfall also had a deep impact on Wales's relations with its neighbours, both to east and west. His reputation was not only that of a prince who had bludgeoned the country into unity but also that of a war-

---

[1] *Brut, s.a.* 1063; *Anglo-Saxon Chronicle*, D, *s.a.* 1063.

leader who had 'hounded the Pagans and the Saxons in many battles'.[2] The Pagans were the Vikings, notably from the Scandinavian colonies in Ireland, who terrorized the coastal lowlands of north and south Wales in the early eleventh century, capturing or killing kings and bishops (Gruffudd himself may have been briefly imprisoned by them in 1042), exacting tributes, ravaging coastal districts and driving the inhabitants to flight (as in parts of south Wales in 1049), and selling their services to any Welsh exile or pretender who was willing to pay for them. During the years of Gruffudd's hegemony, this Scandinavian and Irish menace had been curbed, if only because there were now far fewer political and dynastic divisions within Wales for them to exploit. But once Gruffudd was overthrown Welsh political exiles (such as Gruffudd ap Cynan in 1075 and 1081 and Rhys ap Tewdwr of Deheubarth in 1081 and 1088) once again recruited support from the Irish and from the Scandinavians of Dublin, and the Vikings soon resumed their attacks on the Welsh coastline, ravaging Bangor in 1073 and St Davids in 1073, 1080, and 1091.

But it was in the east rather than in the west that Gruffudd ap Llywelyn's downfall had the most far-reaching repercussions. For centuries English pressure on Wales had been persistent and effective: punitive raids had penetrated deeply into the country (ravaging Gwynedd in 967 and 978, Ceredigion and Dyfed in 992 and 1012); Welsh princelings had been browbeaten into submission and compelled to present themselves at the court of the king of Wessex and to pay him tribute in gold, silver, and oxen; extensive parts of north-east Wales had been brought firmly under direct English political control and a Saxon burh founded at 'Cledemutha' at the estuary of the Clwyd; and in that district and along the central marchland English settlers had pushed beyond Offa's Dyke. There is no indication, it is true, that the Anglo-Saxons meant to press home this advantage: indeed, Offa's Dyke itself, probably constructed in the late eighth century, seems to represent a demarcation of their ambitions in terms of direct rule and settlement, while local agreements (such as the tenth century 'Ordinance of the Dunsaete' from the south-eastern borderlands), suggest an anxiety to work out the politics of co-existence between the two peoples. Yet in the long-term perspective of the relationship, the initiative clearly lay with the English; the Welsh were on the defensive.

The dazzling successes of Gruffudd ap Llywelyn changed all that. Welsh raids now penetrated far into England, notably in the years 1052–6. The city of Hereford and its cathedral were burnt in 1055; its bishop and sheriff were killed in a battle against the Welsh in the next year. English counter-measures proved utterly inadequate: border patrols were overwhelmed, as at Westbury in Gloucestershire in 1053; and the attempts of the new

[2] *Brut, s.a.* 1039.

Norman earl of Hereford, Ralph of the Vexin, to use mounted troops to counter the Welsh proved no more successful. Eventually, the English had no alternative but to seek a peace with the Welsh and concede to them most of the gains they had made. Those gains were indeed remarkable: English settlements in a broad swathe from the Dee estuary in the north to that of the Severn in the south had been devastated; in the north-east Gruffudd now held his court at Rhuddlan, formerly the site of a Mercian burh, and collected renders from the former English manor of Bishopstree (Bistre), near the modern-day Mold; in the south-east Welsh control had been reasserted on the borderlands of Gwent and into disputed frontier zones, such as Archenfield. Nor was the story merely one of military annexation, for it appears to have been accompanied in the north-east and around Oswestry by peasant colonization which eventually regained these districts for Welsh custom and settlement. Gruffudd had not only imposed unity on Wales; he had also apparently extended its bounds and halted the tide of English advance.

His defeat and death in 1063 called this achievement in question. The victor of the devastating campaign of that year was Harold Godwinson. Whether that campaign was primarily undertaken to deal with a Welsh threat that had grown ever more menacing in the last few years, or whether its purpose was also to enhance the standing of the Godwin family and to curb the separatism of the Mercian earldom (which Gruffudd ap Llywelyn had cleverly exploited for his own ends), it was a stunning triumph. It entered into folk memory: more than a century later Gerald of Wales referred to the inscribed stones which had been allegedly raised in Wales as mementoes of Harold's victories and he paid Harold the even greater compliment of suggesting that his victories formed the basis of the achievement of the first three Norman kings in Wales. Militarily Harold's campaigns in 1063 showed that he had learnt lessons which it would take more than two centuries for the Anglo-Normans to master and to implement fully: the use of lightly armed troops to conduct lightning raids into Wales and to engage the Welsh on their own terrain on their own terms, and a co-ordinated pincer movement (Harold himself from Bristol with a fleet and his brother Tostig in command of the land forces) to squeeze the Welsh into submission. Harold's striking successes in 1063 had once more shown how militarily vulnerable Wales was; they had also created a political vacuum which any outsider could exploit to his advantage. Furthermore, Harold had built a fine hunting lodge for himself at Portskewett (Gwent) and had probably annexed part of south-east Wales under his direct lordship, thereby indicating that military victory might be followed by territorial annexation. None of these lessons would be lost on the Norman barons; they were the legatees of Harold's successes.

The Norman kings for their part inherited from their Anglo-Saxon predecessors a claim to overlordship in Wales. There is no reason to believe that the kings of the English before 1066 had contemplated, let alone that they had the ability to undertake, the total conquest and annexation of Wales and the imposition of direct lordship on it. They were well content with the acceptance by the Welsh princes of their client status *vis-à-vis* the kings of Wessex–England. That status could be expressed in a variety of forms and on an ascending scale of dependence: the giving of hostages, visits to the king's court, witnessing his charters as under-kings (L. *sub-reguli*), the payment of tribute, formal oaths of fealty and submission, and open-ended promises of service. Such overlordship had little institutional content or definition; its character varied with the fortunes of military power and political hegemony in both countries, ranging from a nominal claim to suzerainty to a precise and demeaning overlordship. Even in their moments of triumph Welsh princes rarely denied this client status, at least formally: thus, in 1056, in the wake of his military victories, Gruffudd ap Llywelyn 'swore oaths that he would be a loyal and faithful under-king to King Edward';[3] indeed he may have done so in person at a meeting on the Severn. Harold's victory in 1063 enabled that overlordship to be redefined in severe and exacting terms: Gruffudd ap Llywelyn's successors 'gave hostages to the king . . . and swore oaths that they would be loyal to him in all things, ready to serve him everywhere on sea and land, and to render such tribute from that country as had formerly been paid to any other king'.[4] It was this claim to overlordship which the Norman kings inherited, not as a constitutional bequest but as part of the acknowledged political relationships which had prevailed before 1066. Whether they would wish or be able to exploit that inheritance and how they would do so would be their decision. What was beyond doubt was that the inheritance had been greatly enhanced by the nature of Harold's victory in 1063 and by its consequences in Wales.

In the immediate aftermath of Hastings, the Normans were far too preoccupied with the problems of security and control in England and in Normandy itself to give their attention to Wales. It was utterly peripheral to their ambitions and concerns. It was in the late 1060s that it gradually impinged upon their consciousness, partly because the Welsh resumed their attacks upon the border counties but more seriously because the Welsh allied with Saxon dissidents, notably Edric the Wild and Earl Edwin of Mercia, and accompanied them in raids on Hereford and Shrewsbury during 1067–9. William I's response was sharp and purposeful: William fitz Osbern, one of his most trusted confidants and a key figure in imposing

---

[3] *Anglo-Saxon Chronicle*, C, *s.a.* 1056.   [4] *Anglo-Saxon Chronicle*. D, *s.a.* 1063.

Norman control in southern England, was in effect appointed military and civilian governor of Herefordshire (possibly in 1067, though he may not have taken up the post in person until 1069); William the Conqueror himself brought the force of his own terror to bear upon Cheshire at the end of his campaign of 1069–70, built a castle at Chester, and entrusted command and control of the county first to Gerbord and soon after to Hugh of Avranches; by 1071 he had installed another trusted companion, Roger of Montgomery, in a very similar position at Shrewsbury. In each case a new earldom was created; in each case the new earl was granted the royal demesne in the county and control of the county town; in each case most of the rest of the land in the county was henceforth to be held in chief of the earl, not of the king. These were remarkably ample powers and from them in subsequent generations palatine franchises (to use the language of a later age) might be forged. But in the 1070s the Normans were neither living nor planning for the future. The Welsh borderlands posed a dangerous military problem to a much-preoccupied and over-extended conquering force. The obvious solution was to delegate military command there to three talented and proven confidants and to bestow ample feudal, territorial, and civilian powers on them in order to ensure that such command was fully effective. Those powers may also well have included a licence, or indeed a command, to launch campaigns against the Welsh. In any case Norman strategic instinct did not defer to constitutional proprieties. Attack was the best form of defence; and the territorial greed and natural acquisitiveness of the Normans reinforced that truism. Once the border military commands had been created, Norman attacks on Wales were inevitable; only their scale and timing remained to be determined. The attacks fell first on south-east Wales. This was an area which was in many ways ripe for the picking. It was a district from which the most serious Welsh raids on England had been launched in the 1050s and it was, therefore, important to neutralize it militarily. It was here that Harold had sought to establish his base after his success in 1063; the precedent for territorial annexation was therefore to hand. Historically, the area stood apart from the rest of Wales and cultivated a political independence of its own. Geographically, ease of access along the coastal lowlands or across the Severn estuary made it an obvious target for invaders and colonists.

William fitz Osbern, earl of Hereford, was not a man to overlook such opportunities. He was among the most experienced and ruthless of the Conqueror's companions and had already played a key role in the subjugation of England. His stay on the Welsh border was a brief one, for by 1071 he had been lured to fight for even greater fortunes in Flanders. But in two or three hectic years (frequently interrupted by service elsewhere) he had sketched out the strategy for the subjugation of south-east Wales. A line of castles had been built from Wigmore in the north to Chepstow in the south; subsidiary military commands and estates had been granted to leading retainers such as Walter Lacy, Turstin fitz Rolf, Ralph de Limesi, and William of Eu; boroughs were founded at Wigmore and Clifford; and much of the ecclesiastical wealth of the district between Wye and Usk was diverted to fitz Osbern's monasteries in Normandy—Lire and Cormeilles. The detailed work of conquest and settlement was largely delegated to fitz Osbern's followers, such as Ralph de Tosny in Clifford or Turstin fitz Rolf at Caerleon. Progress was initially rapid, if uneven; but the momentum of the advance faltered badly when fitz Osbern's son, Roger of Breteuil, forfeited his estates for treason in 1075 and involved some of his vassals on the Welsh frontier in his downfall. The forfeitures brought the king much more directly into the affairs of southern Wales, and he seems to have chosen a policy of reaching an accommodation with some of the Welsh princes and exacting fealty and tribute from them in preference to a policy of territorial conquest.

The Norman advance in south-east Wales may have faltered after 1075; but there is no reason to believe that it was halted altogether. On the contrary, the Normans took the opportunity to consolidate their position, especially in the valleys of the Monnow and the lower Usk and along the coastal plain from Chepstow to Caerleon. They were to reap their rewards in future generations, for Norman lordship was to be more firmly established here than almost anywhere else in Wales. Indeed, Domesday Book (1086) may lead us to underestimate the scale of Norman penetration in the south-east in these years. The Normans were already fighting in alliance with a group of Welshmen on the river Rhymni as early as 1072 and it is difficult to explain the speed and thoroughness of the Norman conquest of lowland Glamorgan in the next generation without positing considerable preparatory work in the 1070s or at least the 1080s.[5] By then the Normans had certainly opened up another promising line of advance into south Wales, pressing forward up the Wye from fitz Osbern's castle at Clifford and thence across to the upper Usk valley. It was near the Usk, probably not far from a new forward position that the Normans were establishing at Brecon, that Rhys ap Tewdwr, prince of Deheubarth, met his death in 1093 at the hands of 'the Frenchmen who were inhabiting Brycheiniog'.[6] With his death a new phase in the Norman onslaught on south Wales opened.

In the central borderland the cardinal route into Wales obviously lay

[5] The case for a Norman advance into south-east Wales well beyond the limits indicated in Domesday Book is strengthened by the suggestion that coins of William I were being minted at Cardiff from the late 1070s. Four such coins have been tentatively identified by numismatic historians. I wish to thank Mr George Boon for giving me advanced sight of his important work on the Wenallt hoard and associated coins from south-east Wales.

[6] *Brut, s.a.* 1093.

along the Severn valley. It was at Shrewsbury, the target of an attack by
Edric the Wild in 1069, that Roger of Montgomery established himself in
the 1070s and set about to enforce Norman authority in the area. He
rearranged the existing fragmented pattern of Anglo-Saxon estates in
western Shropshire into compact tenurial blocks which could thereby serve
as coherent military units and granted them to personal followers, often
drawn from his dependants and tenants in Normandy—men such as Warin
the Bald (sheriff of Shropshire and husband of the earl's niece), Reynold of
Bailleul (who succeeded both to Warin's office and to his wife), Picot de
Say, and Corbet. These men were the agents of the military consolidation
and expansion of the new earldom—suppressing the earl's Welsh and
English opponents (as Warin the Bald did, according to Orderic Vitalis),
building strong castles such as Reynold of Bailleul's new and appropriately
termed fortress of L'Œuvre (henceforth the *caput* of the lordship of
Oswestry) or Picot's motte at Caus (so called affectionately in memory of
his homeland in the Pays de Caux), and providing military cover and
support for the settlers who established themselves in the lowlands around
Chirbury just to the east of Offa's Dyke. The next stage in the Norman
advance was to reoccupy the areas beyond the Dyke which had once been
in Mercian control and to establish a frontier base from which further
advance might be launched. The site chosen lay between the Severn and
the Dyke and was given the name Montgomery in honour of its founder's
family seat. From Montgomery, Earl Roger's forces moved swiftly up the
valley, building a string of eight mottes from Montgomery to the
appropriately called Moat Lane, near Llandinam, a large motte 40 feet
high with two baileys at its base. From these bases the Normans were able
to impose a loose, if fragile, overlordship over the surrounding Welsh
districts—towards Ceri and Cedewain to the south, Arwystli in the west,
and possibly Edeirnion and Nanheudwy to the north. They were also able
to undertake exploratory sallies even further afield—across the mountains
into Ceredigion and Dyfed (as early as 1073–4) and even north-westwards
into Llŷn. By the time of Earl Roger's death in 1094 the prospects for
steady, if unspectacular, Norman advance in central Wales seemed to be
very promising.

The prospects in north Wales were even better. It was here indeed that
the most striking advances appeared to have been made, partly no doubt
because the lowlands of the lower Dee valley and its estuary had already
long been colonized by Mercian settlers and had been assimilated to the
lordship- and social-patterns of lowland England, but mainly because of
the vigour and ruthless enterprise of two remarkable men, Hugh of
Avranches, earl of Chester (d. 1101) and his cousin, Robert of Rhuddlan
(d. 1088–93). Robert is, indeed, the exemplar of the swashbuckling
Norman warrior: endless in his ambition, pride, and greed, combining the

most ruthless butchery with the most conventional piety, insatiable in his lust for adventure and battle.

The Normans quickly overran the lowland areas immediately to the east of Chester from Basingwerk in the north down to Bangor Is-coed in the south. These districts were once again fully integrated into the county administration of Chester as the hundreds of Atiscross and Exestan; they were measured in hides and assessed for geld after the English fashion; Norman lords were installed in them such as Gilbert Venables at Hope or Robert fitz Hugh at Bettisfield; but the lion's share was reserved for Earl Hugh and his cousin Robert. This area was to remain firmly under the control of the earls of Chester until the 1140s. From this secure base the Norman invaders proceeded swiftly up the coastline—for the forest of Ewloe prevented direct access inland—and by about 1073 they had installed themselves in a new castle built by royal command at Rhuddlan, formerly successively the site of a Saxon *burh* and of Gruffudd ap Llywelyn's *llys* (court). In this secondary area of advance, Norman lordship was less secure: in the language of Domesday Book 'the land of the manor of Rhuddlan and Englefield and the other dependencies (berewicks) belonging thereunto had never been assessed for tax or measured in hides'.[7] Nevertheless, the castle at Rhuddlan was strong enough to withstand a Welsh attack in 1075; a small borough with a church, mint, and fisheries was established there by 1086; and the detailed listing of the vills from the Clwyd to the Dee estuary in Domesday Book suggested that the area would soon be subject to firm Norman lordship, as well as military control. Beyond the Clwyd lay a third area of Norman advance where the character of Norman lordship differed yet again. From Rhuddlan, Robert, with royal consent, advanced along the coast to the river Conwy, building his forward base at Degannwy by about 1078, capturing the local ruler and bludgeoning a reluctant acceptance of his power from the Welsh districts of Rhos and Rhufoniog which he held of the king directly. Nor was this the limit of his ambition, for he had staked a claim to Gwynedd beyond Conwy by proffering to the king a farm of £40 and he and his fellow Normans, with the aid of Welsh confederates, had led plundering raids deep into north-west Wales. Robert himself was killed in a Welsh counter-raid on Degannwy, probably in 1093; but by then the confidence of the Normans in their prospects in north Wales was evident in the appointment of a Norman bishop to the see of Bangor in 1092, in the grant of lands and revenues in Anglesey to the new Norman abbey of St Werburgh's at Chester and above all in the construction of forward castles at Aberlleiniog (a particularly impressive motte in Anglesey), Caernarfon, Bangor, and in Meirionydd.

The Norman advance into Wales by 1093 clearly varied greatly in its

[7] *Domesday Book*, f. 269 b.

geographical range and penetration. It also varied widely in the measure of control that it was able to exercise, ranging from precise and profitable manorial lordship in the lowlands of the south-east to a loose and occasional military hegemony in the north-west. Norman advance in Wales certainly appears hesitant and piecemeal compared with the speed and thoroughness of its achievement in England. In England the Normans built quickly and purposefully on the remarkably firm foundations of authority and institutions bequeathed to them by their Anglo-Saxon predecessors, particularly south of the Humber and the Ribble; in Wales they inherited no more than general claims of overlordship to a politically fragmented and geographically inaccessible country. It would be only through dint of their own efforts that conquest would be achieved and lordship won. Wales, furthermore, did not stand high on the agenda of their priorities; they, and especially the greater barons, were constantly diverted by their military, political, and territorial preoccupations and ambitions in England, Normandy, and even farther afield. Viewed in this light, the achievement of the Normans in Wales was far from inconsiderable. In a generation they had imprinted their authority more successfully and extensively in Wales than any of their Saxon predecessors, recovering areas recently lost to Welsh resurgence, bringing large tracts of north-east, central, and south-east Wales into the ambit of their direct authority, terminating the threat of Welsh raids into the border counties of England, giving a much more precise content to overlordship over much of the rest of the country (including probably south-west Wales), and, through raids and castle-building, establishing the lineaments of a strategy for the final subjection (as it must have seemed) of the country.

Yet hindsight may lead us to over-estimate the impact of the Normans within Wales in these early years. In the native annals, written admittedly in west Wales, they are only mentioned thrice before 1093. In Llanbadarn and St Davids the Vikings appeared a more immediate threat, devastating St Davids in 1073 and killing its bishop in a further raid in 1080 (only a year before William the Conqueror's visit there). Moreover, in the turbulent maelstrom of Welsh dynastic politics—and that turbulence was particularly acute in the years 1069–81—the Normans must intially have appeared as little more than an additional complication. The Welsh were long habituated to pillaging raids from Irish, Vikings, and Saxons and to their ready exploitation of Welsh dynastic conflicts. The Normans at first appeared little different: they also conducted plundering raids into Dyfed, Ceredigion, and Llŷn and were likewise hired by Welsh pretenders to further their dynastic pretensions—by Caradog ap Gruffudd in south-east Wales in 1072 and by Gruffudd ap Cynan in his attempt to wrest control of Gwynedd in 1075. Even when the Normans were imposing direct territorial control, it was initially in areas, such as the Severn valley, north-east

Wales, and the Gwent lowlands, which had already been spasmodically well within the range of Saxon colonization and control.

It was only gradually that the situation in Wales clarified and the true dimension of the Norman threat became more evident. 1081 was an important milestone in that process. In that year William I led an expedition into south Wales. The true nature of his visit is concealed from us (though it was only blind optimism which could have persuaded the Welsh annalist to describe it as a pilgrimage to St Davids). He probably used the occasion to exact fealty and tribute from the newly installed Welsh ruler, Rhys ap Tewdwr.[8] At the very least, it is evident that William had penetrated further into Wales and asserted a greater mastery there than any pre-Conquest king. In the same year the battle of Mynydd Carn (somewhere to the north of St Davids) brought a halt to the political turmoil which had characterized Wales since the fall of Gruffudd ap Llywelyn. Three native princelings (Trahaearn ap Caradog, Caradog ap Gruffudd, and Meilyr ap Rhiwallon) were killed in the battle, bringing the tally of princelings killed or murdered since 1069 to at least eleven. Such blood-letting had at least eliminated many of the contenders in the internecine dynastic strife of the period and allowed the twin victors of the battle to emerge with some prominence and authority in Wales.

The first was Gruffudd ap Cynan, grandson of the ruler of Gwynedd killed in 1039. Gruffudd was born in Ireland of an Irish–Scandinavian mother, and it was from Ireland and with a force of Irish troops that he launched his first attempt to reclaim his grandfather's kingdom in 1075. He has the distinction of being the first and only Welsh prince to be the subject of an extant biography (originally written in Latin in the late twelfth century but subsequently translated into Welsh in its surviving form). This distinction, along with his remarkable achievements after 1100 and his equally remarkable longevity (he survived until 1137), may tempt us to predate his success. During the twenty-five years from 1075 he was still essentially a marauder, pursuing his legitimist claims with the aid of Irish, Danes, Normans, and disaffected groups in Gwynedd, and enjoying periods of success punctuated by even longer spells of defeat, imprisonment (at the hands of the Normans), and exile. The position of the other victor of Mynydd Carn, Rhys ap Tewdwr, was relatively speaking more secure. He had advanced his claim to rule Deheubarth in 1078 on the death of his second cousin (see diagram 2). He survived for fifteen years in spite of several attempts to oust him. He used the temporary discomfiture of Gwynedd, on the one hand, and the agreement he had almost certainly struck with William I in 1081, on the other, to reconstruct the political

---

[8] There is also the intriguing possibility that a mint had already been established at St Davids before the end of William I's reign. This depends on the identification of 'Devitun' on a penny in the Beaworth collection at the British Museum as St Davids.

standing of the kingdom of Deheubarth. His very survival in the turbulent politics of the time may of itself have merited the title 'Rhys the Great' subsequently bestowed on him. But the most eloquent tribute to his standing was the comment, echoed by English and Welsh chronicler alike, that with his death in 1093 royal authority in Wales had collapsed. The total triumph of the Normans seemed imminent.

'And then the French seized all the lands of the Britons' records the Welsh chronicle in 1093.[9] The onslaught may have appeared more sudden and catastrophic in west Wales than elsewhere because of its novelty; but there seems little doubt that there was a marked acceleration of tempo and equally a marked extension of scale in Norman activity in Wales in the 1090s. Striking advances were made in the south-east as the Normans consolidated their hold in Gwent and pushed over the Usk into Gwynllŵg and thence into Glamorgan. In the middle March the groundwork of the Norman settlement of Brycheiniog was being laid and the first tentative steps undertaken in the conquest of the upland districts of Radnor, Builth, Maelienydd, and Elfael. Most dramatically, the Normans surged into south-west Wales, converging on it by land and sea, establishing castles wherever they went, most notably at Cardigan, Pembroke, and Rhydygors (near or at Carmarthen) and ravaging neighbouring districts such as Cydweli, Gŵyr (Gower), and Ystrad Tywi. In the north the Normans overran much of Anglesey in 1098 and compelled the Welsh princes to seek refuge in Ireland.

Several explanations may be suggested for this remarkable surge of activity. The death of Rhys ap Tewdwr in 1093 created a vacuum of authority into which the Normans (as well as Welsh princelings, such as Cadwgan ap Bleddyn of Powys) rushed avidly. It may also have freed William Rufus (if he had not already discharged himself) from any sense of obligation to whatever agreement his father had entered into with Rhys in 1081, an agreement which may well have involved a warranty to Rhys against Norman attack in return for an acknowledgement of his client status and an obligation to pay an annual tribute. In any case Rufus's rôle was probably crucial. He had inherited from his father a major territorial stake in the frontierlands of south-east Wales from Radnor to Chepstow and added to that his mother's lands in Gloucestershire. His foundation of Carlisle in 1092 manifested his interest in border expansion, while his political instincts, sharpened by the revolt of 1088 in which so many of the Marcher barons were involved, doubtless persuaded him to look for an outlet for the aggressive acquisitiveness of the Norman warrior aristocracy. The king's directing hand was certainly in evidence in Wales in the

[9] *Brut, s.a.* 1093.

1090s—commissioning the establishment of a Norman base at Rhydygors on the Tywi estuary; sanctioning the building of castles along the Marches: himself leading two (largely unsuccessful) expeditions into Wales in 1095 and 1097; and, above, all, installing his own associates in key positions in the March—the brothers Hamelin and Wynebald de Ballon at Abergavenny and Caerleon respectively; William fitz Baldwin, his sheriff of Devon, at Rhydygors; and Robert fitz Hamo, a member of his military household, in the lordships of Gwynllŵg and Glamorgan. The detailed work of conquest and settlement would, of course, remain the work of individuals and their retinues, but there is altogether a more co-ordinated look about the Norman thrust into Wales in the 1090s.

The response to it among the Welsh was also more co-ordinated. To talk of 'national resistance' may be misleading:[10] it was Welsh guides and friendlies who led Rufus's forces into Wales in 1097 and the Normans into Anglesey in 1098. Yet there can be no doubt that a new awareness of the dimensions of the Norman threat had dawned on the Welsh. It is witnessed clearly in the poetry of the scholar Rhigyfarch—in his revulsion at the violence of the Normans and in his sense of utter desolation that all the values of his society (law, learning, high renown, the glory of noble descent) were set at naught by them. It is equally clear in the sense of outrage of the native annals at the 'unbearable tyranny, injustice and oppression and violence of the French'.[11] It was this sense of outrage which explains why revolts broke out in almost every part of Wales between 1094 and 1098. There is no reason to believe that these revolts were co-ordinated; but they all drew on a common anxiety to 'throw off the rule of the French' and not to suffer their 'laws and judgements and violence' any longer.[12]

The Welsh inflicted some signal defeats on the Normans in many different parts of Wales in these years, driving them back beyond the river Conwy in the north and capturing all their outposts, except Pembroke, in Dyfed and Ceredigion. But it was from other directions that the really crushing blows were struck against the Normans. In 1098 Earl Hugh of Shrewsbury, who had joined his namesake of Chester on a plundering expedition into north Wales, was killed off Anglesey by Magnus Barefoot, king of Norway. In 1101 Earl Hugh of Chester died, leaving a minor as his heir. In 1102 Earl Robert of Shrewsbury and his brother Arnulf, earl of Pembroke, forfeited all their estates in England and Wales and were exiled after an unsuccessful revolt against Henry I. These three events, and notably the last two, transformed the nature and direction of the Norman

[10] J. E. Lloyd, *A History of Wales from the Earliest Times to the Edwardian Conquest* (3rd edn. 1939), II, p. 400.

[11] *Brut, s.a.* 1094; *Brut (RBH), s.a.* 1098.

[12] *Brut (RBH), s.a.* 1096, 1098 (p. 39).

enterprise in Wales and that for generations. Norman enterprise had relied since the late 1060s on the momentum provided by the three border earldoms and on the driving force of the individual earls. With the forfeiture of the houses of Breteuil (1075) and Montgomery (1102) and the prolonged minority of the heir of the house of Avranches (1101–14), this strategy now finally collapsed. The Norman effort in Wales would have to be reshaped. Its direction geographically would also need to be redefined. It was in north and north-central Wales, above all, that the events of 1098–1102 had their most profound effects. Already before the dramatic happenings of 1101–2, the Normans seem to have sensed that they had overreached themselves in Gwynedd and Powys and that an alternative to their policy of harrying the country and seeking to subjugate it by force was to strike a bargain with the Welsh princelings and to install them as clients. 'Cadwgan ap Bleddyn (of the line of Powys) and Gruffudd ap Cynan (of Gwynedd)', so it is recorded in the native chronicle in 1099, 'returned from Ireland. And, after making peace with the French, they received a portion of the land and the kingdom.'[13] The Normans were beginning to get the measure of the Welsh, of what was the practical limit of their own ambition and how it could best be achieved. The Welsh were also getting the measure of the Normans—learning how to accommodate with them (as the agreement of 1099 showed) but also how to exploit their differences for their own ends. Two could play at the game of 'divide and rule'. The downfall of Earl Robert of Shrewsbury in 1102 was due in good part to the clever duplicity of Iorwerth ap Bleddyn of Powys, who sold his support in turn to Earl Robert and Henry I, calculating that a distant king (especially one who was so generous in his promises) was preferable to a near earl, especially of the cruel and loathed brood of Montgomery. The events of 1101–2 took much of the Norman pressure off Gwynedd and Powys; they thereby allowed the native dynasties to install themselves securely there. Attention now shifted to South Wales.

South Wales certainly witnessed a momentous advance of Norman control and authority during the reign of Henry I. By 1135 virtually no part of the country south of a line from the Dyfi estuary to the valley of the Teme was, in some degree or other, outside the range of Norman authority. The story of this advance is a complex one, for it is composed essentially of tales of local conquest, consolidation, and settlement, pieced together from the fragmentary evidence of chronicles, charters, and ecclesiastical records. Yet the main features of the geography and character of the advance may be briefly indicated. Five major zones seem to stand out. In the south-east the Norman advance, which had been resumed with such gusto in the 1090s, now accelerated further. The

---

[13] *Brut, s.a.* 1099; cf. *Historia Gruffudd vab Kenan*, p. 27. (*History G. ap C.*, p. 149).

Normans' hold on the lowlands of Gwent Uwchcoed and Iscoed was further consolidated; but much more striking was the way in which they now ensconced themselves firmly in lowland Glamorgan and Gower, parcelling them out into manors and knights' fees, colonizing them with settlers from England and even further afield, and appropriating the ecclesiastical wealth of the area for their favoured monasteries in England and France. In the second zone, the middle March, the Norman advance was less impressive: families such as Mortimer, Braose, and Tony certainly made gains in the districts of Maelienydd, Radnor, Builth, and Elfael, but the mountainous terrain deterred alien colonization and inhibited the establishment of firm Norman control. On the southern edge of this zone, however, both the terrain and the story were different: the Normans established themselves firmly in the lowlands of the Llynfi and Usk valleys and even penetrated across the watershed into the upper Tywi valley, establishing a castle at Llanymddyfri (Llandovery, Cantref Bychan) by at least 1116. The third zone may be said to be centred on the lower Tywi valley and specifically on the royal base at Carmarthen. The base (or at least a nearby one at Rhydygors) had been founded in the 1090s and harrying expeditions conducted from it into the neighbouring Welsh commotes. But it was in the first decades of the twelfth century that the temporary military foothold was converted into a permanent civilian base, as the castle was supplemented by a borough and a priory and the outlines of a new administrative unit, the honour of Carmarthen, were delineated. Norman lordship began to radiate from the new base in all directions—northwards into the Tywi valley and Cantref Mawr, eastwards into Cydweli where a castle and borough were likewise founded, and westwards into Cantref Gwarthaf where Robert Courtemain's castle of Abercorram—later to be known as Laugharne (Talacharn)—was an outpost of Norman power.

In western Dyfed, likewise, the reign of Henry I saw momentous advances. The groundwork here had been laid by Arnulf of Montgomery, notably in the region immediately subject to his remote castle of Pembroke; but in 1102 it still remained to be determined whether Norman ambition here, as in Anglesey in the north, had not overreached itself. By 1135 that doubt had been substantially removed. No area in Wales was brought more firmly under Norman rule than the districts on either side of the long and sinuous estuary of the Cleddau rivers. Castles were built and rebuilt, notably at Carew, Manorbier, Wiston, and Haverford; landed estates were created for military adventurers; and the social configuration of the district was transformed and Norman control firmly underpinned by major colonization, notably of Flemings in the district around Haverford. Nowhere in fact, in spite of its isolation, was Anglo-Norman control in Wales in the Middle Ages to be more secure than in an arc of territory from Haverford through Wiston to Tenby. So secure was that control that it

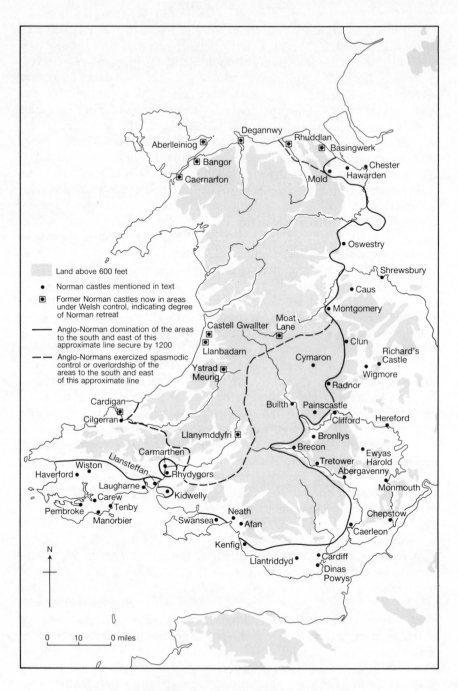

MAP 3. Anglo-Norman Penetration of Wales by c.1200

Map labels:

Land above 600 feet

• Norman castles mentioned in text

◉ Former Norman castles now in areas under Welsh control, indicating degree of Norman retreat

— Anglo-Norman domination of the areas to the south and east of this approximate line secure by 1200

--- Anglo-Normans exercized spasmodic control or overlordship of the areas to the south and east of this approximate line

Aberlleiniog
Degannwy
Rhuddlan
Basingwerk
Bangor
Chester
Caernarfon
Hawarden
Mold
Oswestry
Shrewsbury
Caus
Montgomery
Castell Gwallter
Moat Lane
Clun
Llanbadarn
Cymaron
Richard's Castle
Ystrad Meurig
Wigmore
Radnor
Cardigan
Builth
Painscastle
Cilgerran
Clifford
Hereford
Llanymddyfri
Bronllys
Brecon
Carmarthen
Tretower
Ewyas Harold
Llansteffan
Rhydygors
Abergavenny
Wiston
Haverford
Monmouth
Laugharne
Kidwelly
Carew
Neath
Chepstow
Pembroke
Tenby
Swansea
Afan
Caerleon
Manorbier
Kenfig
Cardiff
Llantriddyd
Dinas Powys

N

0   10   0 miles

seemed not at all inappropriate for it to be organized administratively as an English shire (the county of Pembroke), for its sheriff to account at the royal exchequer, and for royal justices to visit it on eyre. From the safety of this base, Norman enterprise could radiate outwards, gradually imposing its control over eastern Dyfed and bringing the northern districts of Cemais and Emlyn into the ambit of its authority.

The final zone, Ceredigion, is in many ways the most interesting area for the study of Norman penetration in Wales. Here a Norman settlement, which had appeared to be remarkably well-organized, uniform, and centrally controlled, was suddenly overwhelmed by a Welsh onslaught in 1135–6 and its features are thereby fossilized, as it were, at an early and incomplete stage. The Normans had conducted forays, of a prospecting and pillaging kind, into Ceredigion as early as 1073–4. Earl Roger of Shrewsbury and his son, Arnulf, had overrun the country again in 1093–4 as they penetrated into Dyfed and had built a castle on the estuary of the Teifi at Dingeraint, later to be known as Aberteifi (Cardigan); but the castle was no more than a military station and staging post and did not survive the revolt of 1094. It was not until after 1110 that the systematic conquest of Ceredigion was truly begun. Gilbert fitz Richard of Clare was given a licence by Henry I to conquer the country and did so with the help of a group of retainers. He himself built castles at Cardigan (on the former Montgomery site) and just south of Aberystwyth; his followers did likewise in the commotes of the region where, in effect, they were given military commands and powers of lordship; and English settlers were, in the words of the *Brut*, 'brought in to fill the land, which was before that as it were empty'.[14] The settlement of Ceredigion bade fair to be as thorough and as final as that of south-western Dyfed.

Norman lordship in South Wales in 1135 varied greatly in the security of its military control and in the content and profitability of its authority from one area to another. Yet a distinctively Marcher society was beginning to emerge and a temporary military superiority was being supplemented by the institutions of an alien civilian society. In lowland Gwent, Glamorgan, Gower, and Pembroke, along the Usk and Llynfi valleys, even tenatively in the environs of Carmarthen, a pattern of feudal landholding and service was being shaped and the lineaments of a civilian administration, drawing partly on feudal and seignorial practice, but also imitative in some measure of English royal practice, were beginning to emerge. This gradual intensification of Norman lordship was greatly underpinned along the southern coastline from Pembroke to Gwent and even in Ceredigion by extensive alien colonization.[15] It was also accompanied by an ecclesiastical settlement, which perhaps indicates more measurably and clearly than any

[14] *Brut, s.a.* 1116 (p. 42).
[15] The character of this Norman settlement is considered at greater length in Chap. 4.

other feature that Norman control was advancing beyond the primary stage of military forays and hegemony. Much of the ecclesiastical wealth of south Wales had been diverted into the coffers of English and Norman monasteries; the parochial geography, especially of the south-east, was being shaped to conform to the pattern of Norman settlement and lordship; nineteen priories had been founded in south Wales, all, with one exception, dependent on mother houses in England, France, or Normandy and often no more than out-stations for them; and by 1115 Norman candidates had been installed in the sees of Llandaff (1107) and St Davids (1115).[16]

In the background of this advance stalks the figure of Henry I himself. He towers in the history of the subjugation of Wales and of the making of the Welsh March as no other monarch before the reign of Edward I. Of that the contemporary Welsh chronicler was convinced: Henry was, to him, 'the man who had subdued under his authority all the island of Britain' and 'against whom no one could be of avail save God himself'.[17] English chroniclers concurred, even if they expressed the sentiment more prosaically. Wales was not high on Henry's agenda of preoccupations and priorities; but by 1102 he had a far more extensive foothold, and therefore interest, in Wales than either his father or his brother had enjoyed. The fall of the house of Montgomery in 1102 brought him two major blocs of power: Shropshire and the adjoining districts around the castle of Montgomery on the one hand and the areas of Dyfed centred on the castle of Pembroke on the other. He kept both blocs under his direct control. Shropshire was fully assimilated into the county structure of England and placed under a trusted sheriff-justiciar, Richard of Belmeis, subsequently bishop of London; Henry's own confidants (possibly his companions from the Cotentin before 1100) were promoted to key positions along the March—Alan fitz Flaad around Oswestry, the Lestrange family at Knockin and Ruyton, and Baldwin de Bollers in the honour of Montgomery. Pembroke was likewise retained in Henry I's hand: he appointed his own constables there and brought the county firmly under the financial and judicial control of his officers. Another important base for royal authority was Carmarthen. It was not allowed to become the personal fief of the fitz Baldwin family, in spite of the fact that two brothers from that family had been constables there successively. Instead, the castle became the centre of a royal honour and a base for consolidating royal power in Ystrad Tywi and eastern Dyfed.

Henry's influence in Wales was greatly enhanced by the exercise of his powers as feudal overlord of the Norman barons there. Custody was one of those powers: it gave him control of the earldom of Chester for many years

[16] For the ecclesiastical settlement see below, Chap. 7.
[17] *Brut*, s.a. 1116 (p. 42).

after the death of Earl Hugh (1101), and of the lordships of Gwynllŵg and
Glamorgan on the death of Robert fitz Hamo (1107.) Marriage was
another prerogative of the feudal overlord and Henry I used it to good
effect to enrich his own dependants and create his own Marcher baronage.
Fitz Hamo's daughter and heiress was married to Henry's own illegitimate
son, Robert of Gloucester; Sibyl, daughter of Bernard of Neufmarché and
heiress of the vast lordship of Brecon, was given in marriage, by Henry and
during her parents' lifetime, to one of the king's 'new men', Miles of
Gloucester; while another 'new man', Payn fitz John, secured control of
the lordship of Ewyas Lacy on being given the hand of Hugh Lacy's
daughter in marriage.

Henry I exercised his authority above all through his choice and control
of men. His methods in the Welsh March were no exception. He employed
trustworthy clerics, such as Roger of Salisbury, who undertook the
establishment of Norman power in Cydweli; Richard of Belmeis, a former
servant of the Montgomeries, in charge of Shropshire; or the vigorous
Bernard, the queen's chancellor, installed as bishop of St Davids. He used
proven lay servants such as Richard fitz Baldwin, sheriff of Devon, and
Walter, sheriff of Gloucester, who were successively in charge of the royal
base at Carmarthen. He promoted his own favourite aristocratic families in
Wales as elsewhere—the Clares in Ceredigion (Gilbert fitz Richard in
1110) and lower Gwent (Walter fitz Richard, c.1119), and Henry de
Beaumont, earl of Warwick, in Gower in 1106—but equally he favoured
lesser families who could be expected to pursue seriously the task of
imposing Norman control on the Welsh—Richard fitz Pons (ancestor of the
Clifford family) in Cantref Bychan, Maurice de Londres in Cydweli,
Robert fitz Martin in Cemais. Above all, as the reign progressed, Henry I
used the March (as other kings were to do later) as a pool of rewards,
which could be tapped without upsetting the intricate and sensitive pattern
of English feudal estates, to reward his 'new men', the members of the
familia regis. Three of these 'secret and principal advisers', as Gerald of
Wales called them,[18] stand out in particular: Miles of Gloucester, sheriff of
Gloucester and in effect lord presumptive of the vast lordship of Brecon by
marriage from 1121; Brian fitz Count (natural son of Count Alan of
Brittany), who acquired the neighbouring lordship of Abergavenny by
royal gift in 1119 (although its former lord, Hamelin de Ballon, left heirs of
his body); and Payn fitz John, virtual governor of Shropshire and
Herefordshire from the 1120s, who also added Archenfield, Ewyas Lacy,
and possibly Ludlow, to the lands under his control. It is little wonder that
a contemporary observer should remark on the overweening power
exercised by these men along the Welsh border and indeed beyond (for

---

[18] *IK*, I, ii (*Opera* VI, 34).

Payn and Miles also held an eyre in the county of Pembroke). By 1135 almost every single leading Norman baron in southern Wales owed his position to the generosity of Henry I; almost every one of them was a newcomer to the area.

They were beholden to Henry and he never allowed them to forget it. He directed his writs to them; he exercised his powers of feudal control over them; he confirmed their gifts and those of their vassals; he commanded their troops to serve in his Welsh expeditions. His mastery was not of an interventionist kind, nor did it operate necessarily along institutionalized channels; but his ultimate control was not in question. His relations with the native princelings of northern Wales conformed very much to the same pattern. He did not seek to resume the Norman advance into north and central Wales. Instead, he was content with exercising his power as suzerain to the full and exploiting the opportunities which Welsh dynastic politics frequently extended to him. His policies towards the Welsh princelings ranged the whole gamut from cajolery to forfeiture; he showed them to particularly good effect in his dealings with the Powys dynasty and in his clever exploitation of their family squabbles. His ultimate sanction against them was that of the military expedition. He led two such expections into Wales, in 1114 and 1121. The first in particular is remarkable for the thoroughness of its preparation and for the co-ordinated three-pronged strategy of attack: in both respects it anticipates the more successful royal expeditions of the future, notably those of John in 1211–12 and Edward I in 1276–7. The Welsh were certainly impressed, indeed terrified: they assumed that Henry's intention was 'to exterminate all the Britons completely so that the Brittanic name should never more be remembered'.[19] Henry would have been pleased with the impact his preparations had had; but in truth the object of his expeditions seems to have been considerably less dramatic than was imagined. They were punitive expeditions, calculated to show the frailty of the recent Welsh advances (which they certainly did to good effect) and to remind the Welsh princelings of the obligations of their client status. On both occasions, the princes (of both Powys and Gwynedd in 1114, of Powys alone in 1121) quickly made their peace and submissions and the English king's overlordship of them was more clearly defined. In 1114 'the Welsh kings came to him and became his men and swore him oaths of allegiance';[20] in 1121 Maredudd ap Bleddyn and his nephews promised him a tribute of ten thousand cattle as a price of submission. No one indeed could be of avail against such a masterful king.

The sense of despair was most evident in Deheubarth. There the death of Rhys ap Tewdwr in 1093 brought a collapse of Welsh resistance which

---

[19] *Brut (RBH)* s.a. 1114 (p. 79).   [20] *Anglo-Saxon Chronicle*, H, *s.a.* 1114.

appeared virtually total. His heir, Gruffudd, fled to Ireland and Henry I cleverly pandered to and exploited the ambitions and divisions of such local Welsh leaders as survived. Gruffudd, it is true, returned from exile eventually and in 1115–16 led wide-ranging forays in eastern Dyfed, Ystrad Tywi, and Ceredigion. But in very few instances did he capture the inner works of the castles, and the hopelessness of his enterprise is dramatically revealed in the dismissive phrase that the native chronicler chose to describe his followers—'young imbeciles'.[21] Gruffudd himself had to be content with a single commote in Cantref Mawr—such was the sorry plight of the native dynasty of Deheubarth.

The prospects of Powys seemed to be much brighter. Indeed, in some respects the early years of the twelfth century were a propitious period for Powys: it took advantage of royal favour and the vacuum of power left by the decline of Deheubarth to expand westwards—into Ceredigion, Arwystli, Cyfeiliog, and Meirionydd, and it backed its own client princelings to the north in Rhos and Rhufoniog. The opportunity for hegemony was certainly there, but any sustained momentum in that direction was regularly overtaken and shattered by family partitions and repartitions; by bitter and bloody family feuds (at least six members of the Powys dynasty were murdered, blinded or castrated by other members of the dynasty 1100–25); and by crimes of passion, political and otherwise (of which the most daring and disastrous was the abduction of Nest, the wife of Gerald of Windsor, by Owain ap Cadwgan ap Bleddyn in 1109). In such a context, there were few hopes of either consistency of policy or 'state-building'. On the contrary, the greater Powys which seemed to be emerging in the early years of the twelfth century soon began to be dismembered. Ceredigion was detached by Henry I and bestowed on Gilbert fitz Richard, and one by one the former client principalities and commotes were sucked into the orbit of Gwynedd's power—Rhos, Rhufoniog, and Dyffryn Clwyd in the north, Arwystli and Meirionydd in the west. Powys seemed to owe such power as it retained to the grace of royal sufferance on the one hand and to the exhaustion or elimination of family contenders on the other. It seemed ripe for the picking.

By 1135 Gwynedd was the most resilient of the Welsh native principalities. In the early years of the century Gruffudd ap Cynan's position in Gwynedd was still very modest and dependent (as even his biographer conceded) on the generosity of Henry I. Even as late as 1121 he is described, by the admittedly unsympathetic Welsh annals, simply as 'the man who held the island of Anglesey';[22] and the royal expedition of 1114 showed how remarkably vulnerable was his position. Gruffudd's heroism in these years was of an essentially negative kind: he survived. But survival

---

[21] *Brut, s.a.* 1116 (p. 40 'ynfytion ieuainc').   [22] *Brut, s.a.* 1121 (p. 48).

was no mean quality in twelfth-century Wales. It enabled Gruffudd gradually to ensconce himself more firmly in the heartland of Gwynedd: one glimpse of his growing stature was the way the see of Bangor, vacated by Hervé about 1109, was kept vacant for eleven years and eventually filled by David the Scot, 'elected by King Gruffudd and the clergy and people of Wales'.[23] Gruffudd and his sons were also able from the 1120s onwards to exploit the weakness of their neighbours in Chester and Powys—to attract men from neighbouring lordships (especially Rhos and Rhufoniog) to settle in their kingdom, entice smaller local dynasties (such as that of Arwystli) into their orbit, impose a loose hegemony on districts at Gwynedd's frontiers (notably Meirionydd to the south and the *cantrefi* between the rivers Conwy and Clwyd to the east), eliminate rivals ruthlessly (including three of Gruffudd's brothers-in-law in 1125, thereby virtually exterminating the most powerful native dynasty in north-east Wales), and even probe further into Powys itself (Gruffudd's son, Cadwallon, was killed in a foray in Nanheudwy in 1132). Such hegemonies were fragile; but they indicated clearly the directions in which Gwynedd's ambitions would unfold and its security be enhanced. Gruffudd appears also to have had one other instinct which was crucial to the survival of a client prince: that of knowing when and how to bend to the superior power of his overlord. He showed it in 1114 by quickly making his peace with Henry I and by attending his court; he showed it again in 1115 and 1121 by refusing to give succour to other Welsh princelings who had offended the king.

By the time of his death in 1137 Gruffudd ap Cynan had been a leading figure in Wales for over sixty years. That was a truly remarkable achievement. It was pardonable exaggeration for chronicler and biographer to hail him as 'head and king and defender and pacifier of all Wales' and as 'king of the kings of Wales'.[24] The economic revival of the countryside was laid at his door and so was the flowering of ecclesiastical architecture in Gwynedd. Literary antiquarians and historians of a later age promoted his memory by linking the Welsh literary renaissance (especially of court poetry) with his name and patronage, and even ascribed important poetic and musical reforms to Gruffudd himself. Few of these claims have contemporary sanction and those which do are more convincingly explained by coincidence of period; but they are not without a certain appropriateness. The length of Gruffudd's reign and Gwynedd's freedom from Norman and Norse attack from 1100 allowed for a continuity of effort and direction and for the cultivation of the arts of peace. It laid the

---

[23] *Councils and Ecclesiastical Documents relating to Great Britain and Ireland*, ed. A. W. Haddan and W. Stubbs (1869–78) I, 314.

[24] *Brut*, s.a. 1137, *Historia Gruffudd van Kenan*, p. 13 (*History G. ap C.*, p. 125).

foundations for Gwynedd's pre-eminence in native Wales for most of the twelfth century and throughout the thirteenth century.

Gruffudd's achievement is not to be gainsaid; but it needs to be placed in clear perspective. The years of Gruffudd's activity (1075–1137) had witnessed truly momentous advances in Wales by the Normans, kings and barons, vassals and settlers. In the north, the district to the east of the river Clwyd was still under direct Norman control; Powys was a vulnerable and enfeebled client state; even Gwynedd, though now free of Norman castles and incursions, had had to learn to live cautiously under the constraints of a powerful overlordship. In the south, complete Norman control seemed only to be a matter of time, so striking and comprehensive had recent advances been. Taking Wales as a whole, Norman domination in 1135 was in many respects more geographically extensive, more secure, and more confident than it was to be again until 1277. What needs to be explained is why this momentum and control now faltered so badly.

The death of Henry I inaugurated a new era in the history of the Anglo-Norman enterprise in Wales. Revolts broke out in different parts of Wales, especially south Wales—in Gower, Cydweli, Gwent, Brecon, and Ceredigion. The Normans were overwhelmed by a series of dramatic disasters: in April 1136 Richard fitz Gilbert of Clare, lord of Ceredigion, was killed by the Welsh in the Usk valley; at Crug Mawr, just to the north of Cardigan, in the same year, a strong Anglo-Norman and Fleming force was annihilated by the Welsh in a major battle (itself a rare occurrence in Marcher warfare) and memories of the comprehensiveness of that defeat haunted the settler families of west Wales for generations; in July 1137 Payn fitz John, who had lorded it so powerfully along the Anglo-Welsh border of late, was killed while pursuing the Welsh. Some of the local uprisings, such as those in Brecon and Gower, though devastating enough, had little permanent effect; even the capture of castles (such as Caus in the late 1130, Wiston in 1147, Tenby in 1153) did not necessarily entail the restoration of native Welsh control in the surrounding districts. Nevertheless, the map of Norman control in Wales had been substantially redrawn by the end of Stephen's reign.

Three areas of Norman retreat in particular stand out. The most dramatic retreat took place in Deheubarth, where the Normans had made their most striking advances in the previous generation. In three massive raids in 1136–7 the Welsh recovered control of virtually the whole of Ceredigion and captured almost all its castles except Cardigan (in spite of paying for the services of a Danish fleet to help in besieging it in 1135). In Ystrad Tywi, Carmarthen itself was captured in 1137 and though this did not necessarily signal the reintroduction of Welsh rule in the area on a permanent basis, the neighbouring districts of Cantref Mawr and Cantref

Bychan certainly passed out of Norman control. Norman lordship was also seriously called in question in eastern Dyfed and the districts (Emlyn and Cemais) immediately to the south of the river Teifi; even the large alien settlements around Pembroke, Wiston, and Haverford had good reason to feel thoroughly alarmed. The second striking area of Norman retreat appears to be in the Shropshire borderlands: here the capture of Oswestry in 1149 by Madog ap Maredudd was a remarkable manifestation of the way the men of Powys had seized the initiative. The third area of Norman retreat, north-east Wales, is, perhaps, the least surprising. Norman momentum had faltered badly in this district for some time and the Gwynedd dynasty had probably intruded its influence, directly or otherwise, up to the river Clwyd by 1135. The area now at issue was Tegeingl, the district between the Clwyd and the Dee estuary. It was certainly still under the control of the earls of Chester in the 1130s and they had felt confident enough to found the abbey of Basingwerk in 1131; but, by the 1150s, the region was once again under Welsh rule, and when Owain Gwynedd confronted Henry II's forces in 1157 he did so well to the south of Basingwerk.

The Anglo-Norman retreat in Wales was in some measure part of what has been called 'the far-reaching collapse' of Norman power in general during Stephen's reign.[25] Central to that collapse, of course, were the personality and power of the king himself. It is often emphasized that the Norman conquest of Wales was a 'private' baronial enterprise; yet the reign of Stephen makes it immediately evident how crucial strong royal leadership and political stability in England were to that whole enterprise. Stephen quickly lost or gave away the strong, royal, territorial foothold in Wales which he had inherited from Henry I; Carmarthen was captured by the Welsh in 1137 and in the following year Stephen surrendered the county of Pembroke, along with the title of earl, to Gilbert fitz Gilbert of the house of Clare. Royal influence in Wales was further weakened, indeed almost nullified, by the fact that for almost the whole of his reign Stephen had no control over the major border strongholds of Bristol, Gloucester, Hereford, and Chester. A royal expedition to contain the threat of the Welsh and to cow their princes into submission (as in 1114 and 1121) was now out of the question. The best that could be done was to sponsor a small rescue expedition (such as Miles of Gloucester undertook to extricate Richard fitz Gilbert's widow from Cardigan) or a counter-raid by an individual commander (such as that launched by Robert fitz Harold of Ewyas Harold). When the earl of Chester did propose to Stephen in 1146 that he should lead a campaign into Wales, it was construed by the king's advisers as a clever ploy by the earl to ambush Stephen in a trap.

[25] J. Le Patourel, *The Norman Empire* (Oxford, 1976), p. 102.

This abortive proposal of 1146 is but one example of the impact of the tensions and cross-currents of the 'Anarchy' in England on Anglo-Norman fortunes in Wales. At the very least those tensions diverted the attention of the leading Norman barons away from Wales and its concerns. Occasionally, it is true, a Norman magnate might seek to exploit the turmoil of English politics to enhance his standing and power on the Welsh border—most obviously in the case of Miles of Gloucester, who added the earldom of Hereford (1141), the honour of Abergavenny (1141–2), and control of Ewyas Lacy (by his son's marriage in 1137) to the lordship of Brecon, thereby creating a formidable territorial bloc for himself. More usually, however, the leading Norman magnates of Wales—men such as Robert, earl of Gloucester (Glamorgan and Gwynllŵg), Ranulf, earl of Chester (Tegeingl), William fitz Alan (Oswestry), Brian fitz Count (Abergavenny)— found themselves absorbed in political and military conflicts in England. Furthermore, most of them were, sooner or later, supporters of the Empress and committed to pursuing her claims and theirs. It was an eloquent comment on the collapse of royal authority in Norman Wales that Robert of Gloucester issued coins in Matilda's name in Cardiff, while at Swansea Henry of Newburgh went a step further by issuing coins in his own name. The Welsh were now potential allies in the struggles in England rather than an enemy to be defeated: Earl Robert of Gloucester employed a huge force of them in his service in 1139 and 1144, as did Earl Ranulf of Chester at the battle of Lincoln in 1141.

Furthermore, the rivalries amongst the Normans themselves, especially between those who felt themselves to have been 'disinherited' and those who owed their position to recent royal favour, now burst into the open since there was no firm royal authority to keep them in check. Gilbert de Lacy struggled to recover his paternal inheritance in Herefordshire and the March against Miles of Gloucester; he was also a party to the private wars in the Ludlow area which find such an eloquent echo in the Wigmore Abbey chronicle and in the romance *Fouke le Fitz Waryn*. In Wales itself a similar family squabble probably explains why William fitz Gerald (Gerald of Wales's uncle) should join with the Welsh in the attack on Wiston in 1147 and be entrusted by them with the custody of Tenby in 1153. Norman ruthlessness and ambition had turned in on themselves. Their advance in Wales depended on continuing confidence and momentum; when those qualities faltered, retreat followed.

The Welsh saw their opportunity and seized it. Whether their counter-attacks in these years constitute a 'national revival' (in J. E. Lloyd's phrase) in any self-conscious or sustained sense is perhaps open to doubt.[26] But the spontaneous outburst of revolts in different parts of Wales in

[26] J. E. Lloyd, *A History of Wales*, II, chap. XIII.

1136–7 certainly seems to betoken a sense of common grievance against Norman advance and oppression. More striking is the way in which leaders drawn from the dynasties of Gwynedd, Deheubarth, and Maelienydd joined together in a series of recurrent attacks on Ceredigion in 1136–8. But, as so often, such unity was fragile and short-lived; it co-existed with more local loyalties (whether to Norman lord or Welsh prince) and ambitions. So it is that in these years, as usual, an intricate, often inextricable, pattern is woven between attacks on the Anglo-Normans, on the one hand, and the individual, local, and dynastic tensions of Welsh power-politics, on the other.

Gwynedd stood to benefit most by Norman discomfiture. Since the beginning of the century Gwynedd had enjoyed the twin good fortunes of exemption from Norman attacks and the rule of a strong, long-lived prince. Gruffudd ap Cynan's death in 1137 coincided with the eclipse of Norman advance in Wales and thereby enabled his sons, Owain and Cadwaladr, to build on the foundations laid by their father and indeed by themselves during his later years. It was by no means an easy task given the friction within the Gwynedd dynasty itself (leading eventually to Cadwaladr's exile in 1152), nor does the fragmentary evidence allow us to see how Owain Gwynedd, as he was known, extended his control over his principality, its subjects and its resources during a long reign (to 1170). But that he did so seems evident enough from the contemporary references to him as 'Owain the Great' and 'King Owain' and from the remarkble way in which he defended his control over the bishopric of Bangor against pope, king, and archbishop, keeping the see vacant for sixteen years and threatening to send his favoured candidate to Ireland to be consecrated. Likewise, there is little doubt that the governmental and social order, which underlay Gwynedd's power and position in the thirteenth century, was in good measure shaped in his day.

But expansion was just as necessary as consolidation for the political and economic well-being of a native Welsh principality. It was thus that its resources in men, plunder, and power were augmented, the momentum and ambitions of its war-bands sustained, and the bulwarks built to protect its heartland. The directions of Gwynedd's expansion were obvious and paid little regard to the distinction between Welsh and Anglo-Norman neighbours (see map 8). Its earliest thrust was southwards from Meirionydd (itself annexed under Gruffudd ap Cynan). Ceredigion was conquered from the Normans in 1136–7 and, under whatever pretext, was annexed to Gwynedd, ruled as an apanage by members of its dynasty until the early 1150s, and used as a base for foraging expeditions into Dyfed. To the south-east there were no Normans to hand to justify Gwynedd's designs, but that did not deter its ambitions. Iâl was annexed in the late 1140s and protected henceforth by one of the finest Welsh earthwork castles, Tomen y Rhodwydd, and by the 1160s at least three of the outlying commotes of Powys—Edeirnion, Cyfeiliog, and Arwystli—had been brought within the ambit of the pillaging raids and temporary overlordship of the house of Gwynedd. Owain and his sons moved more cautiously in the east, but after the death of Earl Ranulf of Chester in 1153 they ventured with increasing confidence into Tegeingl (the district east of the river Clwyd), control of which was henceforth to be a major target of Gwynedd's ambitions. The capture of Basingwerk in 1166 and of Rhuddlan and Prestatyn in 1167, after a three month siege, realized those ambitions. For the first time for over a century the rule of the prince of Gwynedd extended the whole length of north Wales from Anglesey to the Dee estuary.

It is little wonder that contemporaries were extravagant in their praise of Owain Gwynedd. To the poets he was 'the destroyer of our bondage', the man who had uncovered the glory of former times;[27] even Gerald of Wales, who deplored Owain's marital liaisons, praised him for his great wisdom and moderation. His achievement, it is true, was to prove more insecure than these compliments might suggest; but there can be no doubt that Owain Gwynedd, especially after the death of Madog ap Maredudd of Powys in 1160, was pre-eminent among the native Welsh princes until his death in 1170. It was by his advice that Rhys ap Gruffudd of Deheubarth surrendered to Henry II in 1163 and it was he who assembled and led the remarkable Welsh coalition which dared to withstand Henry II's massed forces in 1165. He was a man with a breadth of vision unusual among the princes of his day: he anticipated the policies of his successors by forming a Franco-Welsh alliance to embarrass Henry II; he may well have signalled his pre-eminence in Wales by adopting the title 'prince of the Welsh' (L. *princeps Wallensium*); he called himself, and was called by others, 'king of Wales' (L. *rex Wallie*). The bardic injunction—'Let princes bear royal tribute to him'—may for once reflect practical power as well as poetic hyperbole.[28]

Gwynedd's power had grown in part at the expense of Powys; but even Powys witnessed an era of expansion in the 1140s and 1150s. After a prolonged period of domestic wrangling, it enjoyed the benefits of unitary rule under a remarkable prince, Madog ap Maredudd, 1132–60. He was, in the words of his court poet, Cynddelw Brydydd Mawr, 'a firm anchor in a deep sea';[29] and a sense of confidence—of the joys of the hunt, the stud, the court, and the retinue—radiates from the poetry addressed to him. That confidence flowed also from his success in taking advantage of the

---

[27] *Llsg. Hendregadredd*, pp. 17–18. This remarkable poem is partly translated in J. P. Clancy, *The Earliest Welsh Poetry*, pp. 119–23; but the quotations in the text are taken from D. M. Lloyd's discussion of it in *A Guide to Welsh Literature*, i, 163–4.

[28] *Llsg. Hendregadredd*, p. 19.

[29] *Llsg. Hendregadredd*, p. 119 ('cadarn angor dyfnfor diffaith'). The translation is by D. M. Lloyd.

discomfiture of the Normans and in extending the bounds of his principality and the range of the activity of his war-bands. His most notable success was in seizing Oswestry in 1149 and three years later his son killed the Norman lord of Montgomery. The poets greeted him as 'the king who owned countries, . . . brilliantly did he strike England as far as the Tern'.[30] They exulted in his victories in Dudleston and Whittington and southwards into Maelienydd. The author of the twelfth-century prose tale, *The Dream of Rhonabwy*, could proudly proclaim that Madog 'held Powys from end to end, from Pulford [just to the south-west of Chester] to . . . the uplands of Arwystli'.[31]

Powys's recovery was remarkable; yet even contemporaries sensed that it was fragile, particularly after the death of Madog ap Maredudd. The expansionist ambitions of Gwynedd threatened its borders and could only be withstood by allying with the Anglo-Normans—whether the earl of Chester, as in 1150, or the king himself, as in 1157—and by taking pensions from them. But the English alliance itself tended to smother Powys's independence and drove its princes back into alliance with Gwynedd, as in 1165. Furthermore, such unity as it had enjoyed under Madog was shattered on his death in 1160. His eldest son was killed shortly afterwards; the principality was divided between five heirs (three sons, one brother, one nephew). Fragmentation led, of course, to weakness; it also led to dynastic quarrels which were soon profitably exploited by the English king and by Powys's other neighbours.

Powys had taken temporary advantage of Norman discomfiture; Deheubarth, the other major Welsh principality, took even greater and, as it proved, more permanent advantage of it. By 1135 Deheubarth and its native dynasty had been all but snuffed out by the great Norman advance in Henry I's reign. It was appropriate, therefore, that it was in Deheubarth that the revolt of 1136–7 and the raids of the following years should be most fierce. By 1155 the native Welsh kingdom had been reconstituted: Cantref Mawr and Cantref Bychan were firmly under Welsh control and Carmarthen castle had been rebuilt, as the *Brut* has it, 'for the strength and splendour of the kingdom';[32] Ceredigion had been gradually wrested out of the control of Gwynedd between 1150 and 1153; and a series of wide-ranging raids to the west and the east—both Tenby and Aberafan (Glamorgan) were attacked in 1153—confirmed that there was potential for further expansion. Furthermore, dynastic disunity, which was the curse of the native Welsh principalities, did not blight Deheubarth's recovery. The four sons, who inherited the dynastic claim from their father,

---

[30] *Llsg. Hendregadredd*, pp. 143–4 ('gwledig gwladoedd berchen').

[31] *Breudwyt Ronabwy*, ed. M. Richards (Cardiff, 1948), p. 1. (*The Mabinogion*, ed. Gwyn Jones and Thomas Jones (1949), p. 137).

[32] *Brut, s.a.* 1150.

Gruffudd ap Rhys, in 1137, forged an unusual unity of purpose in their anxiety to recover their inheritance (relying considerably on Gwynedd's support in the early stages) and by 1155 death and injury had eliminated any future prospect of discord by leaving only one son, Rhys ap Gruffudd, as heir to Deheubarth. What remained to be seen was whether he had the skill to convert the remarkable recovery of the last twenty years into a permanent triumph.

The Welsh recovery of the years 1135–55 is undoubted. It represented the first major and sustained rebuff to Anglo-Norman expansion in Britain since the Conquest. It was more than simply the swing of the military pendulum. It was also almost certainly accompanied in north-east Wales—especially in Tegeingl and Maelor (the areas adjacent to Cheshire) and around Oswestry—by considerable Welsh colonization, which brought these districts back firmly within the ambit of Welsh settlement and customs. The recovery was also important in that it contributed, directly or otherwise, to the definition of the three principalities—Gwynedd, Powys, Deheubarth—which were henceforth to dominate the history of native Wales. But the limits of Anglo-Norman retreat and of Welsh recovery need also to be emphasized. The retreat was by no means universal. The Anglo-Norman conquest of Glamorgan proceeded apace: probably in these very years of retreat elsewhere, castles were founded west of the river Ogwr in Kenfig, Newcastle, and Llangynwyd. In the central March, especially in Builth, Maelienydd, and Elfael, the Anglo-Normans under Philip de Braose, Hugh Mortimer, and Helias de Say were pushing forward ruthlessly and building castles (such as Bryn Amlwg on the borders of Clun or Cymaron in Maelienydd) to demarcate their claims and impose their lordship. Nor was the Welsh recovery as impressive as a cursory list of captured castles and territories might at first suggest. Even their sustained efforts did not give them control of Cardigan, and the apparent ease with which Earl Gilbert of Pembroke recovered temporary control of Carmarthen and the surrounding area in 1145 revealed the precariousness of their successes.

This precariousness was further cruelly exposed by Henry II in 1157–8. In 1157 he led the first royal expedition into Wales since 1121. He certainly met with setbacks: a naval unit sent to attack Gwynedd from the rear in Anglesey (as Edward I was to do later) was overwhelmed, and Henry II himself was taught a timely lesson in the tactics of ambush by a Welsh patrol near Hawarden. Yet the mission was an undoubted success in terms of its purpose—to recover ground lost to the prince of Gwynedd and to reimpose English overlordship on him. Owain was compelled to do homage to the king, to deliver hostages to him, to restore his brother Cadwaladr (who had been in exile in England since 1152), and to surrender Tegeingl, which Henry II proceeded to annex by building castles at

Rhuddlan and Basingwerk. Madog of Powys had accompanied Henry on the punitive expedition and took advantage of Owain's discomfiture to recover the commote of Iâl and destroy Owain's castle there. The lesson which Owain Gwynedd had been so effectively taught in 1157 was repeated for the benefit of Rhys ap Gruffudd in the next year. He likewise was compelled to make his formal submission to the king, give hostages, and see the Anglo-Normans restored to fortresses and lands which they had not held for twenty years—Ceredigion (Earl Roger of Hertford), Cantref Bychan (the Cliffords), Carmarthen (the King). He himself had to be content with Cantref Mawr and some other scattered lands. In two swift campaigns, Henry II appeared to have shown the frailty of the Welsh achievement in both north and south Wales.

Initially, Henry's basic intention in Wales, as elsewhere, seems to have been to restore the status quo of 1135, since he regarded the events of the intervening period as part of an unfortunate and illegitimate interregnum. Military expeditions were a means to that end. There is no reason to believe that he intended to conquer Wales and to impose his direct lordship on it. But restoring the status quo meant reasserting an overlordship which had gone largely by default for a generation; it also meant giving that overlordship a more precise and masterful content. Henry II's policies in Wales in this respect are entirely of a piece with those he followed in England in the same period—destroying adulterine castles, browbeating recalcitrant lords (including two leading Marcher barons, Roger, earl of Hereford, and Hugh Mortimer), recovering alienated royal rights and estates, defining the customs of the church, and instituting an inquiry into feudal obligations. It was in 1163 that he returned to Wales, prompted by a further rebellion by Rhys ap Gruffudd of Deheubarth. The expedition was a complete military success, penetrating into the heart of Rhys's lands and forcing him to accompany Henry in honourable custody to England. But it was the sequel which was alarming, for it showed that Henry II was intent on a definition of his overlordship over the native Welsh princes which was novel in its precision and demeaning in its character. In July 1163 at Woodstock, 'Rhys prince of the southern Welsh, Owain of the northern Welsh and five of the greater men from Wales did homage to the king of the English and to Henry his son'.[33]

Whether the relationship instituted by this ceremony was new or not—and it was a ceremony in which King Malcolm of Scotland was also involved—it was almost certainly seen as an ominous threat by the Welsh, for in the next year, according to the native chronicle, 'all the Welsh united to throw off the rule of the French'.[34] Henry II's response to this challenge to his mastery was to launch an expedition in 1165 which, in the scale and

[33] Ralph of Diss (Diceto), *Opera Historica*, ed. W. Stubbs (Rolls Series, 1876), I, p. 311.
[34] *Brut, s.a.* 1164.

thoroughness of its preparations—forces were commandeered from the continent and Scotland, a fleet was summoned from Dublin, and infantrymen were assembled to cope with the mountainous terrain—seemed to indicate an intention to crush the Welsh, if not to conquer them. That is indeed how the Welsh saw its purpose: 'to carry into bondage and to destroy all the Britons (i.e. Welsh) '.[35] In the face of such an apocalypse, the Welsh of Powys, Gwynedd, Deheubarth, and the middle March stood firm and united, assembling their forces at Corwen in the Dee valley. Henry's ambitions were undone not by the Welsh but by his own ineptitude in choosing a difficult overland route (from Oswestry up the Ceiriog valley and across the Berwyn range) in preference to the seacoast routes he had followed in 1157 and 1163, by the problems of provisioning a large army, and by appalling weather in mountainous terrain. He returned empty-handed, his mission unfulfilled; all he could do was to visit his spleen on Welsh hostages. How far Henry II might have pressed home his attack in 1165 had circumstances been different, it is difficult to know. Like Edward I he was a masterful king whose mastery was not lightly challenged; like Edward I he had the determination and resourcefulness to confront and overcome daunting military problems; unlike Edward I, his preoccupations elsewhere were so many that he could not afford to give Wales other than very brief attention.

The failure of the 1165 expedition allowed the Welsh to resume the initiative. Rhys ap Gruffudd recaptured Cardigan and Cilgerran in the south; Owain Gwynedd, aided by his brother Cadwaladr and by Rhys ap Gruffudd, took Basingwerk and Rhuddlan. Thereby the map of Wales was largely restored to what it had been in 1155. The Anglo-Norman momentum in Wales seemed to be faltering once more: the house of Miles of Gloucester (Brecon and Abergavenny) failed in the male line in 1165; the barons of the south-west despaired of success against the native Welsh and turned instead to Ireland in search of adventure and easy gains; even Welsh allies of the Anglo-Normans in north-east Wales felt so disheartened that they opted for exile in the comparative safety of Lancashire. The king caught the mood of change. When he next returned to Wales in 1171 it was not on a punitive expedition against the Welsh but on his way to demonstrate his mastery over his ambitious Anglo-Norman barons (many of whom were Marcher lords) in Ireland. By then, his policy towards the native Welsh princes and his sympathies for the Anglo-Norman lords in Wales (as in Ireland) had changed radically, no doubt under the pressure of events, experience, and the broader concerns of his 'empire'.

The Welsh princes met him half-way. Owain Gwynedd had died in 1170 and soon a new accord would be struck between Owain's heirs and Henry

---

[35] *Brut (RBH), s.a.* 1165 (p. 145).

which bore ample fruit in the support they gave to the king during the rebellion of 1173. Rhys ap Gruffudd's reconciliation was even more dramatic. He went to meet Henry in the forest of Dean in 1171 and promised him hostages and a large number of oxen as a token of submission. The new accord so begun was sealed in further negotiations which Henry and Rhys held at Pembroke and Laugharne in 1171–2. Rhys acknowledged his client status *vis-à-vis* the king; Henry in return freed Rhys's son, deferred payment of the tribute, confirmed Rhys's territorial gains, and appointed him 'justice on his behalf in all Deheubarth'.[36] It was a remarkable turn-about from the politics of bluster and confrontation of 1165. Henry II had learnt to be content with an acknowledgement of his overlordship and to match his military ambitions in Wales and his support for the Anglo-Norman lords there more realistically to his resources and to the overall needs of his 'empire'. The Welsh princes, and Rhys ap Gruffudd in particular, had relearnt the lesson that under a strong king the acceptance of their client status was the beginning of wisdom; demeaning it might be, but it brought with it a measure of security, especially against the ambitions of the Anglo-Norman barons. Rhys's appointment as justiciar was particularly interesting in this respect: it was an acknowledgement by Rhys that his status in Wales, especially his authority over subordinate Welsh princes, was in some way dependent on the king's grace; it was an acknowledgement by the king that his control over native Wales was best insured by delegating authority in honorary terms to the leading Welsh princes; the title 'justiciar' was an indication that it was in terms of 'justice', 'jurisdiction', and 'law' that overlordship would be increasingly interpreted.

The settlement of 1171–2 marks the end of an era. No English king would again invade Wales for almost forty years. The map of the division of Wales between Anglo-Norman lordship and native Welsh principalities had taken a shape which, in greater or lesser degree, it was to retain until 1277. That map would, of course, be periodically redrawn as military fortunes ebbed and flowed; and, within its crude lines of demarcation, crucial work of consolidation, by Anglo-Normans and Welsh alike, would take place. Nevertheless, a broad equilibrium of power had been established. On the one hand, most of the areas recovered by the Welsh princes since 1135—Carmarthen and Oswestry were the major exceptions— remained in the ambit of Welsh control. On the other, a broad zone in south Wales had fallen under Anglo-Norman rule. Two regions are distinguishable within this zone: in the first (consisting of lowland Pembroke, coastal Gower, the vale of Glamorgan, most of Gwent, and the river valleys of Brecon), Norman control was firm and virtually unassailable; in the second (ranging from Cemais in the west through eastern Dyfed and

---

[36] *Brut*, s.a. 1172.

upland Glamorgan and Brecon to the middle March in the east), such control remained to be confirmed and consolidated.[37] Such, after just over a century, was the achievement of the Anglo-Normans in Wales; such also was the measure of the effectiveness of Welsh resistance.

[37] See map p. 38.

CHAPTER 3

NATIVE WALES 1063–1172:
POWER, CONFLICT, AND HEGEMONY

AT the very time that the princes of Wales were withstanding, with some measure of success, the onslaughts of the Normans, they were also often engaged in bitter conflict with their rivals in Wales. It is to the nature of princely power and conflict in Wales that we turn in this chapter. Power within Wales in the eleventh and twelfth centuries resided in the hands of royal dynasties and a warrior nobility (normally referred to as *uchelwyr* or *gwyrda* in contemporary Welsh sources and *optimates* or *nobiles* in Latin texts), supplemented by such privileges and immunities as had been granted to or arrogated by churchmen. It is the activities of these dynasties and nobility—their rise and fall, their military feats and defeats, their relationships and their quarrels—which constitute the politics of the time. Those politics are essentially the politics of a heroic élite; and it is in terms of the assumptions and values of such an élite—as we can glimpse them not only in the cryptic entries of the native annals but also in the court poetry, prose tales, and law-texts—that we must seek to understand them.

At the apex of Welsh political society stood the kings or princes and the dynasties to which they belonged. There is much that is imprecise about both. 'Kingliness' in medieval Wales, as in Anglo-Saxon England, 'was relative'.[1] The number of power-bases which might qualify as kingdoms still remained, at least in some measure, to be determined; so did the number of kings and even of dynasties. Did, for example, Owain ab Edwin (d. 1105) and his sons, who figure prominently in the history of north Wales in the early twelfth century, or Hywel ab Ithel (d. 1118) of Rhos and Rhufoniog (from an otherwise unknown dynasty) have pretensions or aspirations to princely status? A rather exclusive concentration on the 'winners', on those dynasties which came to dominate native Wales from the mid-twelfth century onwards, may distort our perspective in this respect. The title accorded to or claimed by rulers likewise varied: they might be called *brenin* (L. *rex*) or *arglwydd* (L. *dominus*) or, very occasionally in the early period, *tywysog* (L. *princeps*); but much more often they appear in contemporary sources without title or territorial designation. Thus Hywel ab Ieuaf (d. 1185) appears in the copy of one

---

[1] J. Campbell, E. John and P. Wormald, *The Anglo-Saxons* (Oxford, 1982), p. 53.

charter as 'king of Arwystli' but elsewhere simply as Hywel ab Ieuaf; Madog ap Maredudd (d. 1160) is similarly accorded the title 'rex Powyssentium' in the copy of a charter ascribed to him, but hardly a single one of his successors either assumes, or is given, a title or a territorial designation in chronicle or charters.[2] Dynasties, likewise, cannot be closely defined: the law-texts might declare that only the king's sons, nephews, and cousins were to be regarded as of the royal stock (L. *membra regis*; W. *aelodau y brenin*) for certain purposes, but those who partook of royal descent could not necessarily be expected to subscribe to such an exclusive definition.

Such imprecision is instructive. It reminds us that there was much that was fluid about the titles, structures of authority, and political geography of eleventh-century Wales. Yet the eminence and authority of kingship in Wales were assured and of long standing. In a rigidly hierarchical and stratified society the king's position was amply demarcated in theory by his status—by his honour price, his life-value in the event of homicide (W. *galanas*), the price of his peace and protection, and the privileges extended to his close relatives and officers. Furthermore, in a society based on tradition and custom, the standing of the dynasty was bolstered by the origin-legends, historical mythology, and genealogy which had encrusted around it. Genealogies, in particular, were a potent instrument of dynastic ideology. They upheld the claims of the existing dynasties by grounding their authority in an unbroken descent from the past and by precluding, by implication, the pretensions of intruders.[3]

In these circumstances it was inevitable that lineage was the most important, though not the exclusive, prerequisite in a claim to kingship. The sources of the period are resonant with the phraseology of legitimacy by blood. It is to his patrimony (W. *treftad*) as rightful lord (W. *arglwydd priodor*) that Gruffudd ap Cynan of Gwynedd (d. 1137) lays claim against usurpers (W. *amhriodorion*) and foreigners (W. *arglwyddi dyfod o le arall*); it is likewise as rightful prince (L. *proprietarius princeps*) of south Wales that the Lord Rhys (d. 1197) proclaims himself.[4] The term *priodor* (L. *proprietarius*) itself was significant in this context, since it referred to the basic principle of Welsh law that no title to land was fully established until it had been transmitted in the kin over four generations. The native Welsh annalist echoes the same concern with legitimacy of descent by

---

[2] *Cartulary of Haughmond Abbey*, ed. U. Rees (Cardiff, 1985), pp. 221-2.

[3] The earliest extant Welsh genealogies are to be found in British Library Ms. 3859, most recently published in P. C. Bartum, *Early Welsh Genealogical Tracts* (Cardiff, 1966), pp 9–13. The collection, which contains some thirty brief genealogies, was probably assembled in the mid-tenth century, though the manuscript itself is dated early twelfth century.

[4] *Historia Gruffudd vab Kenan*, p. 7 (*History G. ap. C.*, p. 113); W. Dugdale, *Monasticon Anglicanum* (rev. edn. 1830), v, p. 632.

dwelling on both the lineage (occasionally cognatically as well as agnatically) and affinity of successive princes; while the bards grounded the authority of their princely patrons in the security of an even more distant past, greeting Owain Gwynedd (d. 1170), for example, as of the stock of Rhun ap Maelgwyn Gwynedd (d. 547) ap Cadwallon ab Einion Yrth, or Madog ap Maredudd (d. 1160) of Powys as 'the heir of ancient iron-clad kings'.[5] Nowhere is this cult of descent more explicitly expounded than by the biographer of Gruffudd ap Cynan (d. 1137): for him, Gruffudd's ultimate claim to power lay not in his prowess and victories but in the fact that he was descended 'of royal stock and of exalted lineages', which he then proceeds to expound at great length.[6]

Lineage constituted the claim to kingship; but it did not identify which member of the royal dynasty should succeed. The problem was a particularly acute one in a society where partibility among male heirs up to the fourth degree was the rule in the descent of property rights.[7] Several solutions suggested themselves. One was the designation of an heir during the ruler's lifetime. The Welsh law-texts include eloquent passages on the status of such a designated heir (W. *gwrthrychiad, edling*); but, leaving aside textual ambiguities and the absence of any principle for the choice of such an heir, there is no contemporary evidence that such theorems were closely followed or at least respected in practice. Even if they were followed, there was no reason to expect that the designation of an heir would necessarily settle the issue of succession. Partibility, at least of the royal lands, was itself an alternative solution. It seems to have prevailed in Deheubarth in the 1070s, when two second cousins (Rhydderch ap Caradog and Rhys ab Owain) briefly shared authority (see diagram 2); it also prevailed in Powys on the death of Madog ap Maredudd in 1160 and the murder of his eldest son Llywelyn, in the same year (see diagram 1): Madog's lands and the authority associated with them were divided between five co-heirs—three of Madog's sons, one brother (Iorwerth Goch), and one nephew (Owain Cyfeiliog). The principle of partibility was so deeply ingrained in Welsh society that some element of division was likely to prevail, whether by a formal and agreed division (as seems to have happened in Powys in 1160) or, as frequently in Gwynedd, by the creation of apanages which might always flower into virtually independent kingdoms. That likelihood could only be effectively averted in one of two circumstances: either when death, accidental or contrived, had removed all other major contenders (or at least those of age), or when a powerful and

---

[5] *Llsg. Hendregadredd*, pp. 15, 118 ('hil teyrn yn heyrn henweith'), as translated in J. P. Clancy, *The Earliest Welsh Poetry*, p. 142.

[6] *Historia Gruffudd vab Kenan*, p. 1 ('o frenhinol genedl a llinoedd goruchel'); *History G. ap C.*, p. 103.

[7] See below, p. 126.

overbearing individual was able to impose his own succession to the exclusion of the claims of others. Madog ap Maredudd of Powys was a beneficiary of the first of these routes to unitary rule: by 1132, as diagram 1 shows, death had disposed of his father and of one brother and two cousins in natural circumstances, while two of his uncles, three cousins, and one first cousin once removed had been eliminated by murder or mutilation. Rhys ap Tewdwr (d. 1093) of Deheubarth may serve as an example of how the forcefulness and military skill of an individual member of a dynasty could ensure his succession and exclude other claimants from a share of power with him. Rhys, as diagram 2 shows, was of undoubted royal lineage; but neither his father nor his grandfather nor his great-grandfather figures in the political annals of Wales. Leadership passed to Rhys partly by default. His second cousins, Maredudd, Rhys, and Hywel ab Owain, were all killed between 1072 and 1078 and their sole direct heir, Gruffudd ap Maredudd, was a minor living in exile in Herefordshire. Default, however, only provided the opportunity. It was Rhys's own enterprise and his adept use of allies, native and foreign, which won him the kingdom and it was that enterprise which enabled him to withstand the challenge mounted to his claim by the representative of another segment of the dynasty, his third cousin, Caradog ap Gruffudd ap Rhydderch, in 1081.

Succession, therefore, was determined by military prowess and personal mastery as well as by lineage. Indeed, in the turbulent politics of the eleventh century, the claims of lineage were often overwhelmed by military might. The dynasty of Gwynedd was ousted by such an adventurer, Llywelyn ap Seisyll, in 1018; it only eventually re-established its claim through the heroic efforts of Gruffudd ap Cynan from 1075 onwards. In Powys, likewise, a new dynasty imposed itself in the 1060s and held its grip on power, while soon after, the old native dynasty of Glamorgan was replaced by Iestyn ap Gwrgant and his descendants.

There was clearly a fluidity about the ruling dynasties of Wales in the eleventh century; there was a similar fluidity about the political geography of power itself. The units of political power and dependence overlapped; they expanded, contracted, fragmented, and even disappeared, as military fortunes ebbed and flowed. Four major kingdoms, or perhaps more appropriately kingships, already stood out in the eleventh century: Gwynedd, Powys, Dyfed–Deheubarth and, more uncertainly, Morgannwg. But other 'kingships' certainly survived and preserved a measure of fitful independence—notably Arwystli, Rhos and Rhufoniog, Dyffryn Clwyd, a couple of small 'kingdoms' in the upland district between Severn and Wye, and possibly Brycheiniog and Gwent. The status of these and other districts in Wales still remained to be determined by the swing of the military pendulum. Thus Ceredigion, itself a former kingdom, passed under the control successively of the Normans and of the dynasties of

DIAGRAM 1. Family Violence in a Native Welsh Dynasty, Powys 1075–1197*

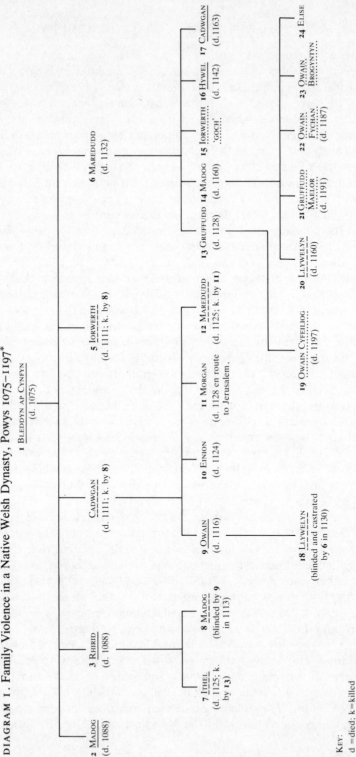

Key:

d = died; k = killed

- - - - killed or maimed by other members of dynasty

——— killed in battle by members of other dynasties or by Normans

.... five co-heirs between whom Powys was divided after 1150

* Note that not all male members of the Powys dynasty are included in the diagram

DIAGRAM 2. Segmental conflict in a Native Welsh Dynasty, Deheubarth 988–1197*

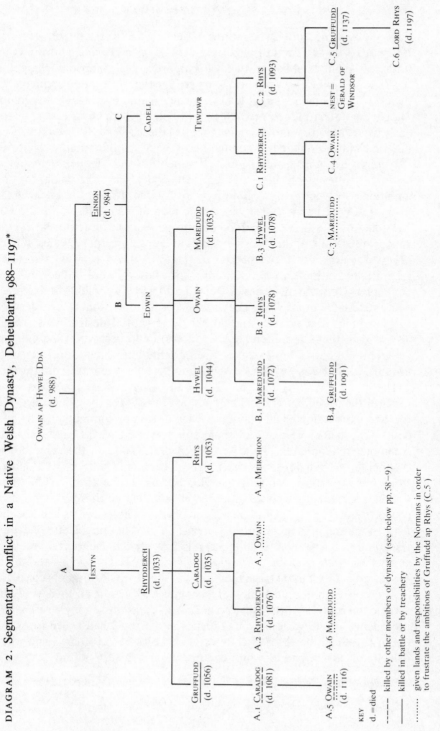

KEY

d. = died

----- killed by other members of dynasty (see below pp.58–9)

——— killed in battle or by treachery

.... given lands and responsibilities by the Normans in order
to frustrate the ambitions of Gruffudd ap Rhys (C.5)

* Note that not all male members of the dynasty are included in this diagram.

Powys, Gwynedd, and Deheubarth, in the first half of the twelfth century. Likewise, it looked for a brief period, 1102–6, as if Hywel ap Goronwy ap Cadwgan might establish, with royal support, a new 'kingdom' composed of Ystrad Tywi, Cydweli, and Gower. Furthermore, the accidents of dynastic arrangements might lead to further fission even within the major 'kingdoms'. Such indeed seemed to be about to happen in Powys in the early twelfth century and did in fact happen there after 1160. Moreover, no king felt himself obliged to confine his activities to the bounds, whatever they might be, of his own kingdom. Competition and conquest were of the essence of successful kingship, and all Wales was fair game for the ambitions of such kings. Bleddyn ap Cynfyn (d. 1075) is normally associated with Powys but it was by the men of Ystrad Tywi that he was slain; his son, Cadwgan, regarded Pembroke as a fair target for his raid in 1096; while at one of the decisive battles of eleventh-century Wales, that of Mynydd Carn north of St Davids (1081), three princes associated territorially with Arwystli, Gwent, and Powys were killed by two contenders from the dynasties of Deheubarth and Gwynedd. The examples could readily be multiplied. They serve as a reminder that it is misleading to bind kings and princes too closely by territorial designations (rarely accorded to them in contemporary sources) or to bestow on the political geography of native Wales a measure of definition which it only began to acquire, with much else, as the twelfth and thirteenth centuries progressed.

The court (W. *llys*) was the seat of the kings's power. 'Arberth', so declares the *Mabinogi* of the 'kingdom' of Dyfed, 'was the chief court (*prif lys*) and from it flowed all honour'.[8] Each district or commote had its own court. The names of many of them still survive, such as Llysfasi in the commote of Llannerch (Dyffryn Clwyd) or Llyswen in the commote of Anhuniog (Ceredigion). As the range of the king's authority extended, some of these courts would be singled out as chief courts: Gruffudd ap Cynan, according to his biographer, 'constructed large churches in his chief courts (*llysoedd pennaf*) for himself and always built his courts and held his feasts honourably'.[9] In a militarily precarious and heroic society, the court was bound to have a prominent military aspect—hence its frequent association with a motte (W. *tomen*, *twyn*), as in Tomen y Faerdref at Llanarmon (Iâl); but its basic function was domestic. It normally consisted of a group of timbered buildings encompassed within an enclosure. Its ceremonial centre was the hall (W. *neuadd*). It was the seating position and precedence of the various court officials in the royal hall which formed a major theme of the legal tractate on 'The Laws of the Court', and when Rhigyfarch in the late eleventh century wished to express the desolation

---

[8] *Pedeir Keinc y Mabinogi*, ed. I. Williams (2nd edn. Cardiff, 1951), p. 51 (*Mabinogion*, pp. 42–3).
[9] *Historia Gruffudd vab Kenan*, p. 30; (*History G. ap C.*, p. 155).

caused by the Normans in his native Ceredigion he did so in the telegraphic phrase, 'tristis est aula', 'the hall is desolate'.[10] The details on the court officers in the native legal texts are doubtless overelaborate and idealized; but they reflect broadly the range of activities centred on the king's court. Some officers (such as the butler, cook, head-brewer, candlemaker, and laundress) attended to the domestic requirements of the king and his entourage; others (court priest, physician) to their spiritual and medical needs; another group catered for the entertainment of the king, whether in the hunt (chief groom, chief huntsman) or of an evening (chief poet, court bard); while a final category performed duties of governance both within the court and in the kingdom (steward, court judge, chamberlain). This entourage, menial and honorific alike, accompanied the king as he toured his lands. He did so in part to satisfy his passion for hunting: it was said of Einion ap Rhys, a princeling of Gwrtheyrnion, that he was addicted to the chase. He did so also because the provision and maintenance of his court still relied considerably on the billeting and renders due to him from his clients and subjects. He did so above all because it was the royal progress alone which ensured that his authority was respected. It is only a bureaucratically governed country which can begin to afford the luxury of a stationary kingship; Wales in the eleventh and twelfth centuries had certainly not begun to approach that stage.

Political control was also exercised in and through the court. It was here that the king dispensed the largess which lubricated relationships and formed ties of indebtedness to sustain his power. One of the qualities which ensured immortality for Bleddyn ap Cynfyn (d. 1075) of Powys was his generosity; his descendant, Gruffudd ap Madog (d. 1191), inherited the same qualities, for he was memorialized as 'the most generous of all the princes of the Britons (i.e. Welsh)'.[11] It was in the court also that the prince entertained his nobility. Entertainment, like largess, was the politically necessary art of companionship and munificence. The king, in the phrase of a contemporary poet, was 'the dispenser of the mead banquet'.[12] Cadwgan ap Bleddyn (d. 1111) of Powys held such a banquet, so the annalist records, at Christmas 'for the leading men of his land'.[13] It was on occasions such as these that the court bards came into their own, drawing deeply on a recondite and archaic vocabulary and on an ample stock of historical mythology, resonant with the names of heroes and places now but half-remembered and less than half-understood. Their odes, like the tales of the story-tellers, provided the ideological confirmation for the status quo, socially and politically. It is not surprising to learn that

---

[10] *Studia Celtica*, VIII–IX (1973–74), 90.   [11] *Brut*, *s.a.* 1078, 1191.

[12] R. G. Gruffydd, 'A Poem in Praise of Cuhelyn Fardd . . . ', *Studia Celtica*, X–XI (1975–6), 204 (meddgwyn gyfran).

[13] *Brut*, *s.a.* 1109 (p. 28, 'i wyrda ei wlad').

Berddig, the court poet of Gruffudd ap Llywelyn (d. 1063), had been granted by his patron three vills in Gwent quit of rent or that Gwrgant ap Rhys, 'the best poet that was', fell by the side of his lord, Morgan ab Owain of Gwynllŵg, in battle in 1158. The bards were the conservative memorialists of an intensely conservative political order.

The king's power derived from his lineage, his war-leadership, and his lordship of men. It also derived from his wealth. The contemporary Welsh noun *cyfoeth* referred significantly to land, to a kingdom, and to wealth. Such wealth was necessary not only for sustenance but also for largess; without both, kingship would wither. The wealth was in part the demesne estates (W. *maerdref*, pl. *maerdrefi*) from which the local court was maintained. Such a demesne estate was that at Dolbenmaen, which served the needs of the court of Eifionydd and which was staffed, as were all such demesne manors in native Wales, by a dependent peasantry holding by the most servile tenure (W. *tir cyfrif*) known to Welsh law and owing heavy labour services and food renders. Such demesne estates, often to be found on the most fertile land, catered for the immediate needs of the court; but they could hardly provide for all the needs of the prince, his entourage, guests, servants, horses, dogs, and so forth. To meet these requirements he drew on tributes, food-rents, services and billeting-obligations from the population, free and unfree, and payable at local royal centres. Little is known in detail about such dues until the thirteenth century; we must clearly beware of projecting backwards the ample details of later surveys or of accepting too readily the mathematically precise formulae of the native law-texts. Yet it is clear that the right of the king to go on circuit around his kingdom, to demand lodging and sustenance for himself and his entourage —often no more than the acceptable and regular face of pillage—and to claim building, carrying, and other services, for his local court was a long-established practice, in Wales as elsewhere. The *Mabinogi* present us with a vignette of Pwyll returning from such a circuit (W. *cylch*) of Dyfed; and some of the earliest surviving charter memoranda from Wales specifically refer to such regular tributes, often under the Latin term *census*. Then again the fossilized remnants of circuit-dues (W. *cylch*, *porthiant*), communal tributes of cows often payable biennially or triennially (W. *commorth*, *treth eidion*; E. *cowgeld*, *horngeld*), and commuted food-renders (W. *gwestfa*) in areas of south-east Wales which were brought under Norman rule at an early date, suggest strongly that a common pattern of obligations and dues to kings or lords prevailed throughout Wales, whatever the regional and local variations in incidence and terminology. Indeed, Domesday Book provides valuable contemporary glimpses of the collection of such dues—of renders of honey, pigs, cows, sheep, and hawks from groups of vills in Gwent and Archenfield and, even more strikingly, of Gruffudd ap Llywelyn's claim to two hundred loaves, a barrel of beer, and a vessel of butter from each of the six ploughs of his men whenever he visited his manor of Bistre (Tegeingl). So did kingship sustain itself and exploit the economic resources of its kingdom.

Royal powers of economic exploitation were clearly considerable even at the beginning of our period; other royal powers are more difficult to trace and to document. Law and justice were spheres in which kingship in medieval Wales had originally but a small foothold. Native law was essentially a customary law, transmitted and expounded by semi-professional jurists, and probably mainly dispensed in communal gatherings and through *ad hoc* arbitrations.[14] Yet kingship was beginning to intrude its claims into both law and justice and thereby to extend its coercive powers over the subject population. Specific legal innovations were attributed to Bleddyn ap Cynfyn (d. 1075) and Rhys ap Gruffudd (d. 1197), and when the Welsh law collections were eventually committed to writing in book-form, the prominence which they accorded to Hywel Dda (d. *c*.950) in causing the native laws to be reformed and promulgated, and to the powers of kings in general, redounded to the benefit of kingship. But it was as the dispenser of justice rather than as the promulgator of laws that the king's authority in particular grew. His initial role was often that of arbitrator: in the earliest extant twelfth-century Welsh poem the local chieftain is eulogized as 'counsellor of judges', 'the acme of reconciliation', 'the upholder of custom'.[15] The status of his court and the coercive powers at his command soon attracted (or compelled) litigants to bring their disputes to him, while the centrality of justice to kingship was acknowledged in the triad in the law-texts which declared that the court judge (W. *ynad llys*) was one of the three pre-requisites of kingship. Already the king was intruding himself into the quarrels of his subjects, claiming, for example (and here the evidence of the law-texts is confirmed by independent testimony from Archenfield from the late eleventh century), that a third of the compensation for settling a feud belonged to him as of right.

Royal powers were doubtless exercised in other directions—in claims to military service from all free men (again mentioned in the Archenfield entry in Domesday Book), in the right to confirm gifts of lands to churches and to free such land from general fiscal or other obligations, in assertions of exclusive royal control over sea, wasteland, and ownerless chattels. Yet there was little that was institutionalized or administrative or bureaucratic about Welsh kingship in the eleventh century. Its powers derived largely from the force of the personality of the individual prince, the power of his retinue, and his ability to extort what he regarded as customary tributes from his subjects and to exploit the bonds and obligations of personal clientship to the full.

[14] See below pp. 132–5.   [15] *Studia Celtica*, x–xi (1975–6), 204.

Above all, royal power in Wales depended on military might. Kings presided over a free, warrior society, which lived, at least in part, by plunder and exulted in war. 'Their minds', comments Gerald of Wales of the native Welsh, 'are always bent on the defence of their country and on plunder; they delight only in horses and arms and their equipment.'[16] His observation is amply echoed in other sources. Einion ap Gwalchmai, an early thirteenth-century poet, writes, with the gusto of a Bertrand de Born, of the delights of the court and of arms—'mead and the feastings of a victorious ruler, a long bright summer, a well-fed horse in April, the play of spears and the waving of banners'.[17] His themes—the exultation in prowess, the delight in the blood and fury of battle, the haunting comparisons with heroes of former days, the plaintive recollections of the dead—are echoed a thousand times in the odes of the period, most poignantly in the remarkable ode, known as *Hirlas Owain* ('Owain's Long Blue Drinking Horn'), which the prince–poet, Owain Cyfeiliog (d. 1197) of Powys, addressed to his companions in arms, alive and dead. Nor are these themes merely the literary conventions of a professional bardic order. The Welsh laws discuss at length the rules on the division of the spoils of war and the occasions on which a king may lead his host in war; military service was regarded as the irreducible obligation of all free men from which, as thirteenth-century charters show, not even princely fiat could grant exemption; while already by the eleventh century a horse with armour was regarded as the appropriate death-duty of a Welsh freeman, an ox that of a villein. So well-recognized were the military talents and training of Welshmen—however indiscriminate their methods and undisciplined their tactics—that, from the twelfth century at least, they were greedily recruited by Anglo-Norman kings and lords to swell their armies. Military training and ambition were widely, almost universally, dispersed throughout free Welsh society. Their endless feuds, conflicts, and wars fed their militarism and were in turn fed by it. Gerald of Wales, with characteristic perceptiveness, described the 'Welsh condition' crisply: 'the young men of this nation move in companies and households, under a chosen leader, and devote themselves to arms and leisure'. 'The whole people', he added, with pardonable exaggeration, 'are dedicated to war.'[18]

Kings had to channel this military energy to their own ends; otherwise it would become a disruptive force and might well destroy them. One major outlet into which it was channelled was the military retinue (W. *teulu*). The *teulu* was more than a royal bodyguard; it was the fighting force which protected the king's authority and title and promoted his cause in the

---

[16] *DK*, I, ix (*Opera*, vi, 182).
[17] *Llsg. Hendregadredd*, p. 39 as translated by D. M. Lloyd in *A Guide to Welsh Literature*, I, 182.
[18] *DK*, I, x, viii (*Opera*, vi, 183, 179).

endlessly competitive world of Welsh dynastic politics. Welsh law showed a due sense of priority when it proclaimed the *teulu* to be one of three indispensable necessities of kingship. How indispensable it was Rhys ab Owain of Deheubarth found to his cost in 1078: when his *teulu* was destroyed in battle he himself was hunted 'like a frightened stag before the hounds through the brakes and the rocks' until he was killed.[19] Another indication of the centrality of the retinue, composed as it was of hand-picked young warriors (*juvenes electi* is Gerald's phrase for them), was that the office of the captain of the retinue (W. *penteulu*, L. *dux familie*, *princeps militie*) was regarded as amongst the very highest in the king's court. It was normally reserved, in practice as in theory, for a close relative of the king: Einion ab Anarawd (d. 1163) acted as captain of the retinue of his uncle Rhys ap Gruffudd of Deheubarth, Iorwerth Goch similarly for his brother Madog ap Maredudd of Powys, and Morgan ap Rhys for his brother Gruffudd ap Rhys (d. 1201) of Deheubarth.

The *teulu* represented one aspect of the king's military resources; the castle increasingly came to be another. The Welsh may already have made some use of the ancient earthworks so common in their land; but it was not until the coming of the Normans that they began to learn the art of castle-building. Initially they were reluctant or slow pupils, often destroying castles (as in Gwynedd in 1096 or Ceredigion in 1136) when they captured them. But, living cheek by jowl with the Normans and even occasionally acting as keepers of their castles (as at Carmarthen in 1116), they soon began to imitate Norman practice. Cadwgan ap Bleddyn had built a castle at Trallwng Llywelyn (near the later Welshpool) by 1111, Uchdryd ab Edwin another at Cymer (Meirionydd) before 1116. By the mid-twelfth century references to native Welsh castles in Gwynedd, Powys, and Deheubarth are common, and Welsh princes, instead of slighting captured Norman castles, now frequently rebuilt them—as happened at Ystrad Meurig (Ceredigion) and at 'Humphrey's castle' appropriately renamed Castell Hywel (Ceredigion). By the 1170s the Lord Rhys could even rebuild the Norman castle at Cardigan in stone and mortar to be a worthy centre for his much-enlarged kingdom, while in north Wales old commotal centres, such as Dolbenmaen (Eifionydd) and Llanbeblig (Arfon), were eclipsed by new castle sites at Cricieth (Eifionydd) and Dolbadarn (Arfon), respectively. The Welsh had indeed learnt their lesson so well that castle-building came to figure in the law-texts as an obligation due from all subjects.

Military power was a means to an end, or rather to several ends. Plunder was one. 'There is no province or realm under heaven', boasts a king of Deheubarth in one of Walter Map's stories, 'from which I could not easily

---

[19] *Brut (RBH), s.a.* 1078.

fetch spoil and return without battle. For who is there who could resist my greatness and that of my household?'[20] Devastation and plunder were common instruments of policy in native Welsh politics, almost seasonal in their occurrence. Vengeance, pure and simple, was sometimes the motive: Gruffudd ap Cynan followed up his victory at Mynydd Carn in 1081 by devastating Arwystli, killing its people, burning its houses, and taking the womenfolk into captivity to avenge himself on its vanquished lord, Trahaearn ap Caradog. The destruction or capture of a rival's resources in men and goods was often a prelude to toppling him. It was thus that Madog and Ithel ap Rhiryd of Powys dealt with their cousin, Owain ap Cadwgan, in 1109—scattering his men in all directions and destroying their crops. Above all, plunder was a major source of income and of largess, as contemporaries freely recognized: it was 'lust for plunder' which persuaded reckless young men to flock to join Gruffudd ap Rhys of Deheubarth on his raids in 1116, and those who forayed into Ceredigion in 1136 returned home 'with a great abundance of captives and spoils and costly raiment and fair armour'.[21] Not only profit came from plunder, but glory also; a prince's success was measured by the plunder he had amassed and distributed. 'And with vast spoil', so it was reported of Gruffudd ap Llywelyn in 1056, 'he returned home eminently worthy'; when his obituary was written seven years later the first compliment in it referred to the 'immense spoils' he had accumulated.[22] Devastation and plunder were also instruments of political pressure and mastery: when Owain Gwynedd devastated Arwystli in 1165 he was punishing its local ruler, Hywel ab Ieuaf, for daring to challenge his overlordship, just as three years later Dafydd ab Owain Gwynedd's devastation of Tegeingl was a prelude to the annexation of the district.

Kings shared their power with the nobility. Between the two, indeed, there were few differences in birth, blood, power, privilege, and life-style. Many whom we, and even contemporaries, might classify as noble freemen regarded themselves as of royal stock. So indeed they were, for they were members of segments, albeit discarded segments, of the royal dynasty. When Gruffudd ap Rhys, heir to the kingship of Deheubarth, launched his revolt in 1116, he was supported by his 'close relations in kindred and acquaintance' from Ceredigion.[23] Others belonged to ancient noble stocks, and the orbit of their power was more local. Such was Rhirid Flaidd, 'the proprietor of Pennant, the chief of noblemen', as he was addressed by the poet Cynddelw;[24] such also were the powerful noblemen of Môn,

    [20] Walter Map, *De Nugis Curialium*, II, xi (ed. M. R. James, C. N. L. Brooke, and R. A. B. Mynors, p. 150).
    [21] *Brut (RBH)*, s.a. 1116 (p. 86 'chwant anrheithiau'), 1136 (p. 144).
    [22] *Brut*, s.a. 1056, 1063.   [23] *Brut (RBH)*, s.a. 1116 (p. 90).
    [24] *Llsg. Hendregadredd*, p. 178 ('priodor Pennant, pennaf uchelwr').

Edeirnion, and Llŷn who figure so prominently in the biography of Gruffudd ap Cynan and who did so much to shape the fortunes, and misfortunes, of his early career. In eminence, wealth and the geographical range of their power there were no doubt vast differences in the standing of these men, differences which were rapidly multiplied by the custom of partibility between male heirs. Between the lesser and the greater nobles there would be woven complex, if frequently temporary, ties of clientship and dependence. They were all, however, united in their sense of the exclusiveness of the nobility of blood and valour they shared. The variety of native Welsh terms by which they were described confirm this outlook, emphasizing their nobility (*boneddigion*), their superiority (*goreugwyr, uchelwyr, arglwyddi*), their leadership (*penaethau, penaduriaid, pendefigion*), their king-like status in the localities (*tywysogion, brehyrion*), and the almost moral qualities of high birth (*gwyrda*).

Such men regarded themselves, in status if not in wealth, as virtually equals of kings. Dues and obligations they certainly owed to princes, but often (as they saw it) of a token and honorary kind. They exulted in their liberty. They were obliged to no one except to their own lineage for their powers over land and men; their standing in a heroic society owed as much to their blood, prowess, and personality as to the favour of princes. Welsh free society was in this respect, as acute observers noted, a much less hierarchical and deferential society than that of contemporary England. One might indeed speak of power being dispersed in a loose federation of lordships rather than in a hierarchy of authority; that is why Wales appeared to men such as Gerald of Wales, habituated to the 'tremendous majesty' of Norman and Angevin kingship, virtually ungoverned and ungovernable, and its people 'bold in speech and ready of response' in the most exalted circles.[25] It was all the more necessary, therefore, for kings to order their relationships carefully with this free nobility. They plied them with entertainment and gifts: it was because they had accepted such a gift (W. *cyfarws*) from Gruffudd ap Cynan that the subsequent treachery of the brothers Tudur and Collwyn appeared the more reprehensible to Gruffudd's biographer. They included them in their civilian and sporting progresses and in their military expeditions. They granted them immunities and privileges on their lands, exempting them from normal obligations and dues. They alienated royal estates or royal rights over lands to them; such, no doubt, is the origin of place-names such as Trewalchmai or Trelywarch (Anglesey); such also was the grant of three vills, with their five plough teams, in Gwent which Gruffudd ap Llywelyn (d. 1063) bestowed on his poet Berddig. Above all, kings associated their nobles with them in their acts, political, judicial, and military. It is not only in the pages of the

[25] *DK*, I, xv (*Opera*, vi, 192).

Mabinogi that the king is depicted sitting regularly with his nobles (*gwyrda*) around him, listening to their advice and indeed being largely bound by it, deferring to their wisdom in dispute-arbitration and high policy matters, and asking them to uphold his grants. Such also is the evidence of contemporary chronicles and charters: thus it was 'through the advice of his nobles' (*gwyrda*) that Owain Gwynedd temporarily settled his quarrel with his brother in 1144, and it was 'by the agreement of his country' (*trwy dyundeb ei wlad*) that the Lord Rhys introduced a change in native law.[26]

Such a powerful and independent free nobility could clearly be a disruptive force. The nobility of south Wales, in particular, had a reputation for ungovernability, harnessing its wealth and status to local particularist sentiment and exploiting to the full the fissures within the ruling dynasty. The events of 1091 in Deheubarth illustrate what a threat the nobility could present to stable rule. In that year Cedifor ap Gollwyn—who traced his descent to a segment of the now displaced native dynasty of Dyfed and who, in the words of the *Brut*, was still 'lord of all Dyfed'—died. Three of his sons instantly proclaimed their refusal to acknowledge Rhys ap Tewdwr as king of Deheubarth; instead, they invited Rhys's second cousin once removed, Gruffudd ap Maredudd, who had been living in exile in Herefordshire, to assume the kingship. It was only with Gruffudd's defeat and death in battle that Rhys's hold on the kingship of Deheubarth was once more assured.

Noble disaffection and fractiousness constituted only part of the reason for the chronic instablity and competitiveness of Welsh political society in the eleventh and twelfth centuries. Gerald of Wales and other contemporary observers might diagnose the moral failing of fickleness as another major source of trouble; but that was to confuse effect with cause. The custom of partibility, albeit confined to the male line, lay at the heart of the matter. Partibility was a deeply ingrained custom within native Welsh society, at all levels. It was a profoundly equitable custom; but it was also one which was inexorably impoverishing and deeply disruptive, particularly at the level of royal dynasties. The powers and wealth of kingship could not be endlessly subdivided; but countering the impact of partibility often created as many problems as it solved. Attempts might be, and were, made to buy off younger sons and cadet branches with office—such as that of the captain of the retinue (W. *penteulu*) or an archdeaconry—but there was no guarantee that such attempts would succeed or that, even if they did so in one generation, they would be respected or regarded as adequate in the next. The more drastic solution of excluding individuals and eventually whole

---

[26] *Brut (RBH)*, s.a. 1144; *Llyfr Blegywryd*, p. 154.

segments of the dynasty from a share of the power and wealth was equally dangerous; it might succeed under a masterful and ruthless prince, but it only served to create a group of *exclus* who regarded their claims as dormant rather than extinct. The problem of partibility was exacerbated by the polygamous habits of many Welsh princes and by an inclusive law of legitimacy: Cadwgan ap Bleddyn (d. 1111) of Powys had sons by at least five different partners, Gruffudd ap Cynan (d. 1137) of Gwynedd by at least four. In Gwynedd after 1170, as in Deheubarth after 1197, some of the bitterness of the family quarrels sprang from the conflict between half-brothers. Thus, immediately on Owain Gwynedd's death in 1170, his eldest surviving son, by a union with an Irishwoman, was killed by his half-brothers, 'Cristin's brood' as the poet contemptuously called them (referring to their mother, Christina, daughter of Gronw ab Owain).[27]

Other factors also contributed to the political volatility of Wales. The militarist ethos of free Welsh society meant that there were always plenty of idle young warriors—'young hotheads', as the *Brut* refers to them dismissively[28]—ever spoiling for a fight and willing to support the escapades of disinherited or love- (or perhaps lust-) lorn princes, to accompany Gruffudd ap Rhys of Deheubarth in his hopeless struggle to recover his inheritance in 1115–16, or to join the dashing, but utterly irresponsible, Owain ap Cadwgan ap Bleddyn of Powys in his escapade to abduct the ravishingly beautiful Nest, daughter of Rhys ap Tewdwr, a lady of easy charm and many lovers, in 1109. If adventure were not a sufficient spur to conflict, the code of honour often was. Vengeance was a solemn family duty on all free Welshmen and one which the passage of time did not extinguish. 'A year after that', reports the native chronicle, 'was the battle of Pwllgwdig in which Trahaearn, king of Gwynedd . . . avenged the blood of Bleddyn ap Cynfyn, his first cousin.'[29]

It is against such a background of a highly competitive and volatile militarist and honour society that the internal conflicts of native Welsh society in this period can best be approached. Aggression was necessary for survival; continued aggression was essential for hegemony. In the absence of an effective central authority, each must dominate or be dominated. The first stage in domination lay within the dynasty; that is why so many of the most savage murders and battles of the period are the products of family quarrels. Even a modicum of family peace could often only be secured by the giving of solemn pledges on relics, the exchange of hostages, and mutual promises not to betray one another. It was thus, for example, that Madog ap Rhiryd and Owain ap Cadwgan of Powys (first cousins) were

---

[27] *Llsg. Hendregadredd*, p. 332 ('o Cristin a'i meibion'). The poem is translated in Clancy, *The Earliest Welsh Poetry*, p. 135.

[28] *Brut (RBH)*, s.a. 1110 (p. 68), 1116 (p. 86 'ynfytion ieuainc').

[29] *Brut*, s.a. 1078.

kept from one another's throats in 1109 and that some temporary accord was struck between Maelgwn ap Rhys of Deheubarth and his brother, Gruffudd, in 1198. Attempts might also be made to defuse family tensions by making grants to younger brothers, nephews, or cousins. Such a magnanimous policy could most readily be pursued when a strong ruler was already firmly ensconced and could, therefore, afford to be generous, and when a period of territorial expansion allowed the creation of apanages without weakening the dynastic base. Thus Owain Gwynedd (d. 1170) was able to keep his younger brother, Cadwaladr (d. 1172), happy by granting him the recently conquered land of Ceredigion. Likewise, Madog ap Maredudd (d. 1160) of Powys created his brother, Iorwerth Goch, his military commander and showered horses, arms, and honour on him. Owain and Madog were, significantly, among the strongest princes of the mid-twelfth century; both were also rulers of expanding kingdoms; and both, equally significantly, ultimately failed to satisfy their brothers. As the contemporary prose tale, *The Dream of Rhonabwy*, remarks of Iorwerth Goch, 'he felt great heaviness and sorrow at seeing the honour and power that were his brother's, whereas he had naught'.[30] For other royal families, living on more restricted resources, the crisis came earlier; more often than not it could only be resolved by a family blood-bath. Between 1111 and 1130 six members of Powys dynasty were so liquidated (see diagram 1). The neighbouring dynasty of the tiny kingdom of Arwystli had an even more gruesome record: in a horrific family vendetta in 1129–30, seven (and possibly eight) first cousins were blinded, castrated, or killed by fellow members of their family and a ninth by a member of the Powys dynasty. It was rare indeed for remorse to be shown, though Morgan ap Cadwgan of Powys felt obliged to go to Jerusalem in 1128 to atone for his murder of his brother, Maredudd, three years earlier. It is little wonder that the English administration in Shropshire felt that it need not bestir itself to subdue Powys, for the Welsh (as it was observed with mordant satisfaction) 'were all killing one another'.[31] Blood-lust and revenge were doubtless factors; but contemporaries were well aware that such feuds were ultimately about land and domination. The *Brut* in its usual telegraphic fashion is admirably concise in its explanations: in 1111 it records that after the eyes of Madog ap Rhiryd of Powys had been gouged out, his uncle and cousin 'divided between them his portion of Powys'; it reports, likewise, that Hywel ab Iorwerth castrated his uncle 'lest he should beget issue who might rule after that over Caerleon'.[32]

The feuds so generated were not only between individuals but often between branches and segments of the dynasty. The conflicts within the

[30] *Breudwyt Ronabwy*, ed. M. Richards (Cardiff, 1948), p. 2. The translation is taken from *The Mabinogion*, trans. G. Jones and T. Jones (1949), p. 137.
[31] *Brut, s.a* 1111 (p. 36).   [32] *Brut, s.a.* 1113 (p 37), 1175 (p. 70).

dynasty of Deheubarth in the years 1072–91 highlight the tensions which were of the essence of the 'political' struggles of the period (see diagram 2). Three major segments of the descendants of Owain ap Hywel Dda (d. 988) were competing for supremacy a century after his death, both within their respective segments and within the dynasty as a whole. Meirchion ap Rhys (A.4) killed his cousin, Rhydderch ap Caradog (A.2), by stealth in 1076 in a struggle for supremacy within his segment; but it was Caradog ap Gruffudd (A. 1) whose bid for hegemony was initially successful. Between 1072 and 1078 he disposed of his third cousins (Maredudd, Rhys, and Hywel ab Owain (B.1–3)), thereby virtually eliminating that segment from the competition. In 1081, however, he himself was killed by Rhys ap Tewdwr (C.2), his third cousin and the representative of yet another segment. The Normans quickly learned how to exploit these fissures within the native dynasties to their own advantage: when Rhys's son, Gruffudd, made his bid for power in 1116, the Normans craftily tried to scotch his ambitions by involving his uncle (C.1) and two first cousins (C.3–4) and two members of another segment of the dynasty (A.3, A.6) in the defence of the Norman settlement in Carmarthen and the Tywi valley.

Family conflicts criss-crossed with inter-dynastic rivalry: the one indeed fed on the other. Rhys ap Tewdwr, as has been shown, had problems enough with his own nobles and his own family;[33] but these were regularly exacerbated by external challenges to his authority, notably from the Powys dynasty. In 1088 he was temporarily expelled by the three sons of Bleddyn ap Cynfyn; later in the same year he returned and killed two of them; but on his own death in 1093 the surviving brother (Cadwgan ap Bleddyn) immediately plundered Dyfed. Whether the conflict was within a dynasty or between dynasties or, as so often, conducted at both levels simultaneously, the tactics employed were the same. Alliances were formed between segments and dynasties; marriages were arranged to pursue dynastic ambitions (thus Rhodri ab Owain Gwynedd (d. 1195) was said to have married the Lord Rhys's daughter 'so that he might gain the support of Rhys against his newphews, whom he had dispossessed of their rightful inheritance');[34] disaffected and underemployed bands of young warriors were enticed with the prospect of plunder; external allies—Irish, Vikings, and Anglo-Normans—were regularly hired (Cadwaladr ap Gruffudd ap Cynan, for example, hiring a force of Scandinavians from Dublin to force his brother to reinstate him in 1144); pillaging raids were conducted to cow an opponent's subjects into submission and to destroy his resources; and eventually the issue would be settled by treachery, ambush, or open battle.

For the loser the result was death, mutilation, or, if he were lucky, exile

---

[33] Cf. above p. 59.   [34] *IK*, II, vii (*Opera*, vi, 126–7).

in Ireland (though some of the exiles, such as Madog ap Rhiryd of Powys, found 'the evil ways and evil manners of the Irish' more than they could stomach).[35] The victor was assured of control, however temporary, within his own family. He might exercise that control generously—appointing his sons, as Gruffudd ap Cynan is said to have done, to be in charge of distant *cantrefi*, or bestowing a district on nephews, as Madog ap Maredudd of Powys did in 1149. But he must never allow his mastery to be challenged nor his gifts to be construed other than as conditional and contingent acts of grace. Firm patriarchal authority within the dynasty was the first-fruit of victory and the precondition of continuing political mastery. But victory, and the honour and prestige it brought, also often allowed the victor to extend his hegemony to neighbouring dynasties and territories (W. *gwladoedd*). The nature of royal power in this period meant that such hegemony was one of military annexation and economic exploitation; it was rarely, if at all, accompanied by any measure of institutional integration or formal annexation. A temporary over-kingdom, a congeries of *gwladoedd*, had been created; no more, no less.

Exploitation and dependence were the hallmarks of hegemony. Tribute, in kind and in cash, would be collected from the annexed district. When Lifris, in his life of St Cadog, pictured Maelgwn dispatching his household troops to exact tribute (L. *census*) from the conquered district of Gwynllŵg, he was depicting a scene that was clearly credible and meaningful in the late eleventh century (when the life was written). Above all, the victor's wealth, as measured in people and animals, in the control of movable wealth rather than of land, had been increased. This is the recurring emphasis in the contemporary sources, nor is it a surprising one in a society where land was relatively abundant but tenants and animals scarce. Gruffudd ap Cynan's growing strength was measured in the way the inhabitants of Rhos and their animals sought his protection, and thereby 'his subjects multiplied';[36] just as his mastery of Meirionydd in 1124 was indicated by the transfer of its men and goods to Llŷn. Similarly, in a later period, Dafydd ab Owain Gwynedd's annexation of Tegeingl was prefaced by the removal of its 'people and all their chattels' with him into Dyffryn Clwyd.[37]

Military victory also brought other returns. The warband of the defeated prince would be amalgamated with the victor's own; the victor's network of clients would be extended; his stock of largess and his means for display had been augmented. Hegemony could be imposed in many ways. Homage (W. *gwrogaeth*) would be demanded: 'surrender your sovereignty to his

[35] *Brut*, s.a. 1110 (p. 35).
[36] *Historia Gruffudd vab Kenan*, pp. 28 ('ac amlhau ei bobl') 36 (*History G. ap C.*, p. 151).
[37] *Brut*, s.a. 1165 (p. 63).

will and do homage to him', as the *Mabinogi* had it.[38] To refuse to do homage was tantamount to rebellion. Hostages would be taken as a guarantee of political compliance, as happened when Owain Cyfeiliog of Powys submitted to the Lord Rhys in 1171. Grants of land would be made strictly conditional on pledges of friendship and alliance, such as the grant of Meirionydd and Cyfeiliog to Uchdryd ab Edwin on condition that he would be 'a true, inseparable friend' to the dynasty of Powys.[39] Dependence would be publicly acknowledged: Hywel ab Ithel recognized that he held Rhos and Rhufoniog through 'the protection and support' of his patrons of the Powys dynasty,[40] just as the ruler of Arwystli acknowledged his dependence on Madog ap Maredudd by allowing Madog to confirm his grants of land.

The strength of such hegemonies varied greatly. If conditions were favourable and if a king's force of personality and reputation were sufficient, he might establish an effective, if often indirect, domination of areas of native Wales well beyond his sphere of immediate political and territorial control. 'When he had a troop of fine men about him', said the poet of Gruffudd ap Cynan, 'kings returned subdued; by fives and fours they came, gentle and obedient'. His biographer echoed the same sentiment: 'other minor kings (*brenhinoedd bychain*) came to his court to seek his protection and to secure his aid and advice'.[41] Even contemporaries, committed as they were to the principle of partibility, were able to recognize the benefits which such unitary rule and hegemony might bring. When Bleddyn ap Cynfyn was commemorated as 'the comfort of the lands', or when the biographer of Gruffudd ap Cynan waxed lyrical about the economic advance and architectural renaissance of his reign, the compliments surely reflect the gratitude of men who had known the horror and devastation of civil war and inter-dynastic strife and yearned to forget years 'wearisome and hateful to everyone'.[42] But peace and prosperity did not last. Hegemonies were short-lived; even in the twelfth century, they were rarely more than loose federations held together by a combination of might, masterfulness, ambition, and fear. They often foundered on the strength of local sentiments and dynastic loyalty or on the return of a claimant or pretender. Even if they could survive these vagaries, they rarely outlasted the life of the man who had founded the hegemony through the force of his own arms and personality.

The politics of eleventh- and twelfth-century Wales were competitive and

---

[38] *Pedeir Keinc y Mabinogi*, p. 42 (*Mabinogion*, p. 35).
[39] *Brut, s.a.* 1116 (p. 46).   [40] *Brut, s.a.* 1118 (p. 46).
[41] *Llsg. Hendregadredd*, p. 2 as translated in A. French, 'Meilyr's Elegy for Gruffudd ap Cynan', *Études Celtiques*, XVI (1979), 263–78 at p. 267. *Historia Gruffudd vab Kenan*, p. 31 (*History G. ap C.*, p. 155).
[42] *Brut (RBH), s.a.* 1078 (p. 30), 1116 (p. 100).

violent to an unusual degree. Politics, it may be argued, are always competitive, but the nature of the competition and the limits of tolerated violence, physical and verbal, differ from period to period and from society to society. The leaders of native Welsh society in our period were hard-drinking, lustful warriors, exulting in prowess, sensitive to a fault of their honour, conditioned by a social code which preached the necessity of vengeance and the shame of dishonour. They were men of violent emotions and those emotions more often than not shaped their actions. Gruffudd ap Cynan (d. 1137) was said by the poet to be 'merciless in his hate . . . he did not love at all'; his son, Owain (d. 1170), was similarly described by Gwalchmai as a man of 'violent passion' and his grandson, Dafydd ab Owain (d. 1203), as a 'harsh man . . . with a hot quick temper'.[43] Such descriptions were not condemnations; they were the attributes expected of rulers in a heroic society. They should not, therefore, be dismissed as mere literary convention. The actions of these men bear out their 'unashamed ferocity' (to borrow a phrase used to describe another heroic society).[44] Sometimes their butchery was so horrific that even contemporaries could not bring themselves to report it.

There were, however, limits even to these men's ferocity. One limit, fortunately, was that of their own power. Their resources were circumscribed. Custom, furthermore, declared that they could only compel military service for a foray outside their country once a year. Their own subjects, who rarely figure in the annals except as a part of a ruler's wealth, sometimes turned on them and on their mercenary bands: thus Gruffudd ap Cynan and his Irish allies were expelled from Arfon by an outraged local population. The teaching and sanctions of the church also acted as an occasional brake on their behaviour. Even these violent men did not lightly incur the wrath of God and his saints by breaching the rules of sanctuary: it was that sanction alone which stood between Gruffudd ap Rhys and the spleen of Gruffudd ap Cynan at Aberdaron in 1115. Nor should one underestimate the role of individual ecclesiastics, such as the influential Simon, archdeacon of Clynnog (Arfon), whose wisdom, leadership, and standing are memorialized on his death in 1152, or Daniel, son of Sulien, archdeacon of Powys (d. 1127), who was specifically commemorated as a man who mediated between Gwynedd and Powys, or his nephew, Sulien ap Rhigyfarch (d. 1146), whose obit praises him as 'a speaker and a pleader for his people and a mediator of various kingdoms . . . and an ornament of secular judgements'.[45] Men such as these brought the teaching and

[43] *Llsg. Hendregadredd*, pp. 2, 15, 262, as translated respectively in *Études Celtiques* XVI (1979), p. 267; *Proceedings of the British Academy*, XXXIV (1948), 183–4; J. P. Clancy, *The Earliest Welsh Poetry*, p. 153.

[44] K. J. Leyser, *Rule and Conflict in an Early Medieval Society. Ottonian Saxony* (1979), p. 1.

[45] *Brut*, s.a. 1146 (p. 54).

example of the Gospel and, no doubt also, reminders of the gruesome fate of Old Testament monarchs, as well as the threat of excommunication, to curb some of the excesses of Welsh royal and noble society.

There was also an alternative, or rather a complementary, image of kingship to set beside that of the warrior leader. The image, based at least in part on the church's teaching, emphasized the qualities of gentle and just rule in peacetime, the ruler's goodness (hence the growing cult of Hywel the Good, *Dda*, from the twelfth century onwards), his mercy and generosity, wise governance, respect for custom, prudence and moderation, and readiness to listen to requests and grant petitions. It is an image memorably reflected in the *Mabinogi* in the characterization of Arawn's governance of the kingdom of Dyfed during his sojourn there as wise, kindly, generous, and just in its judgements. Here again literary convention is echoed by contemporary annals: in the 'mildness and peacefulness' of the rule of Gruffudd ap Cynan, the 'justice and mercy' of Maredudd ap Gruffudd (d. 1155) of Deheubarth, 'the infinite prudence' of Owain Gwynedd (d. 1170)—both of these testimonials given by the *Brut* and Gerald of Wales alike—and the 'wise governance' as well as the sophisticated wit and well-tuned sensibilities of Owain Cyfeiliog (d. 1197) of Powys.[46] Nor are these merely the stilted phrases of annalistic encomia: the *Brut* can condemn harshly those princelings 'who ruled dishonourably' and the condemnation is the harsher in its brevity set beside the compliment paid to Pwyll as ruler of Dyfed as 'successfully beneficent'.[47]

Furthermore, though Welsh political life in the century 1063–1170 appears on the surface as a succession of mindless and meaningless acts of violence and competition, it was conducted within what may be called an ideological and mythical framework to which all Welshmen subscribed. This framework of beliefs, rhetoric, and aspirations had been shaped over many generations. Its primary keepers and transmitters were the court poets, a small coterie of men who underwent a long apprenticeship in the traditional linguistic, literary, and historical lore of Wales. The format, language, and allusions of their poetry were shaped and, and indeed, determined by the corpus of tradition which they were required to master during their apprenticeship—triads, genealogies, foundation-legends, and a mass of literary, quasi-historical, toponymic, and onomastic lore. They themselves were men of noble blood, indeed often of princely stock (such as Hywel ab Owain Gwynedd (d. 1170) or Owain Cyfeiliog (d. 1197) of Powys). Their solemn duty was to compose eulogies and elegies for their patrons and to sing the praises of God and the saints, in short to extol the

---

[46] *Historia Gruffudd vab Kenan*, p. 30 (*History G. ap C., p. 153*); *Brut, s.a.* 1155; *Brut (RBH), s.a.* 1170; *IK*, II, xii (*Opera*, vi, p. 144).

[47] *Brut, s.a.* 1109 (p. 31, 'y llywiasant yn anfolianus ac yn aflwyddianus'), *Pedeir Keinc y Mabinogi*, p. 27. ('llwyddianus garedig'); *Mabinogion*, p. 24.

ruling order in heaven and on earth. Intentionally impenetrable and deliberately archaic though much of their poetry was, the resonance of its personal and toponymic allusions and comparisòns and the recurrent reiteration of its main themes constituted a framework of mythology to which all free noble Welshmen, regardless of dynastic and regional differences and internecine feuds, subscribed.

Central to this mythology was an intense pride in the past or rather in a particular interpretation of it. Two aspects of that past were especially emphasized. One was the unbroken link between the Old North (W. *Yr Hen Ogledd*)—the kingdoms of North Britain of the fifth–seventh centuries—and the contemporary political order in Wales. The genealogies and origin-legends of the major Welsh dynasties were traced back to this Old North homeland. It was from the Old North that Welsh praise poetry throughout the middle ages drew its heroes, its prototypes of virtue, and its poetic exemplars. This northern past—composed of men such as Owain ab Urien and Rhydderch Hael and of battles such as Catraeth and Arderydd—was at once static and living, historical and exemplificatory. It was a mythical, validating past and, thereby, a potent, if gradually diluted, part of the Welsh consciousness. The second point of reference in this native Welsh historical consciousness was a wistful memory of, and pride in, the Roman past of the country. This memory concentrated in particular on the legends which had encrusted around the figure of Magnus Maximus (d. 388), the Macsen Wledig of Welsh lore. Several Welsh dynasties in the medieval period traced their descent, whether directly in the male line or through marriage, from Macsen. He, thereby, served as a convenient bridge from native tradition to Roman glory and thence to Trojan origins; he also served to embody and to explain the transition from the Roman political order to the political dispensation of native Wales.

The Welsh were inordinately proud of their past; for them it was both the fount and mirror for the present. But their pride was balanced by profound sense of loss and shame—the loss of the sovereignty of Britain and shame at the oppressions (W. *gormesoedd*) which the Island of the Mighty had suffered at the hands of alien races. Such a sense of deprivation and failure often led to despair, to a deep conviction of the Britons' sinfulness and a sense of shameful contrition in the face of ineluctable divine retribution. Equally it could and did beget a bitter resentment against those who had, willingly or otherwise, aided and abetted the Saxons to deprive the Britons of the sovereignty of Britain. In this gallery of villains none was more reviled than Gwrtheyrn, or Vortigern, one of the Three Dishonoured Men of the Islands of Britain of Welsh lore. But the Welsh coupled their own sense of failure and betrayal with a bitter enmity towards the Saxons, the heirs of Hengist and Horsa, or the children of Rhonwen as they were called. This deep-rooted historical enmity of the

Saxons was cultivated throughout the Middle Ages. 'Gwalchmai am I called', boasted a twelfth-century poet, 'foe of Saxon . . . enemy of Edwin and the Angles'.[48]

The Welsh could hardly have borne their sense of loss had it not been relieved by a prospect of deliverance. The Welsh—or rather the Britons, as they persisted in calling themselves well into the twelfth century—never surrendered the vision of a single united Britain, centred on the crown of London, once more restored to their control. This vision remained a cardinal axiom of their historical mythology. Thus, according to the native law-texts, the triumphant song which the chief court poet was required to intone as the royal warband returned from a plundering foray was 'The Sovereignty of Britain' (*Unbeniaeth Prydain*). Likewise it was as 'the true proprietor of Britain' that Gruffudd ap Cynan and his son, Owain Gwynedd, were addressed by the poets.[49] Outside observers recognized the force and significance of such pretensions. 'The Welsh', remarked the archbishop of Canterbury in 1199, 'being sprung by unbroken succession from the original stock of Britons, boast of all Britain as theirs by right'.[50]

Such hopes were nurtured in Wales, as in all medieval societies, by the luxuriant elaborations of a corpus of prophecy. Such prophecies were certainly in circulation in Wales well before the advent of the Normans but they were augmented with the passage of each generation. They were associated in particular with the person of Myrddin or Merlin, a poet–prophet whose original connections seem to have been with the sagas of the Old North but whose career and exploits, like those of other North British heroes, were gradually relocated in legend in Wales. Hope was the great theme of the Merlinic prophecies—hope of delivery from, and extermination of, the Saxons and hope of the advent of a messianic deliverer who would once more restore the Britons to their rightful control of the Island of Britain. Several candidates were already front-runners for the role of deliverer: Cynan and Cadwaladr 'the Blessed' (W. *Fendigaid*) certainly, and Owain and Arthur probably (for there is no doubt that Arthur had already been launched on his career as a folk-hero in Wales well before Geoffrey of Monmouth publicized his fame to a much wider audience). These Merlinic prophecies were the staple political ideology of medieval Welshmen. 'They boast', commented Gerald of Wales, 'that in a short time their countrymen shall return to the island and, according to the prophecies of Merlin, the nation of foreigners as well as its name shall be exterminated, and the Britons shall exult again in their old name and privilege in the island'.[51]

---

[48] *Llsg. Hendregadredd*, p. 18, translated in Clancy, *Earliest Welsh Poetry*, p. 121.
[49] *Llsg. Hendregadredd*, pp. 1 ('Prydain briawd'), 18 ('Prydain priodor').
[50] *Episc. Acts*, 1,308 (D. 307).
[51] *DK*, ii, vii (*Opera*, vi, 216), cf. *Speculum Ecclesie* ii, ix (*Opera*, iv, 48–9).

The importance of such prophecies, as indeed of Welsh historical mythology in general, should not be underestimated in any analysis of contemporary political attitudes and behaviour. It was a remarkably resilient mythology. It had already been shaped in its essential features by at least the tenth century, for it informs a remarkable Welsh poem of that period, *Armes Prydain*. It was still vigorous six centuries later when a report on the state of north Wales in Elizabeth's reign recorded how the Welsh gathered in open-air assemblies on hillsides to sing songs, recite their pedigrees, hear tales of the heroism of their ancestors, 'namely of their wars against the kings of this realm and the English nation', and listen to the lives of Taliesin, Myrddin 'and such other, the intended prophets and saints of this country'.[52] The potency of this mythology rarely faded in the intervening centuries. The Welsh were sustained by it in the last dark days of native independence, and one of the first acts of the archbishop of Canterbury after the conquest of 1282–3 was to order that the Welsh be weaned from their ancient prophecies. There is no reason to think that he was successful. The mythology, at once ageless and ever-changing, had become deeply rooted in the Welsh consciousness at all levels of society. It bound a mythical past, a despairing present, and the prospect of future deliverance into one. It was also a powerful instrument in forging a measure of unity in an otherwise politically fragmented and decentralized society, for it presented a vision which could be converted into a programme of action to which all Welshmen might subscribe.

The ideological framework of Welsh political life remained in its essence unchanged during the twelfth century. So did the basic reasons for the vicious competitiveness of Welsh political society—the custom of partibility, the fission and segmentation of native dynasties, the particularism of Wales's political geography, the heroic values and aggressive militarism of its warrior freemen. Yet there is little doubt that the period 1063–1172 witnessed important changes in the character and distribution of political power within natives Wales. These changes need only be hinted at briefly here, for they were to come into sharper focus in the thirteenth century.[53] Most elusive, but no less real for that, is the change in the tone of political behaviour; the language and forms of political conflict became less exultingly brutal. More important, native princes and free noblemen turned increasingly from pillage, plunder, and tribute-taking to more systematic exploitation of the economic resources of their lands and peoples. Here, economic changes and political transformation went hand in hand; the one encouraged the other. The political geography of Wales

---

[52] *A Catalogue of Manuscripts relating to Wales in the British Museum*, ed. E. Owen (Cymmrodorion Record Series, 1900–22), I, 72.

[53] See below pp. 213–5.

and, with it, the status of its leading dynasties gradually assumed firmer definition. Minor kingdoms and dynasties now lived increasingly under the shadow of the three over-kingdoms of Gwynedd, Powys, and Deheubarth and could not hope to compete with them in resources or influence. Conflict would focus on tensions within and between these over-kingdoms. As the map of politics simplified, so the power of native kingship consolidated: there is a growing emphasis, reflected in an exaggerated form in the legal texts, on the status of kingship, its functions of justice and governance, its power of coercion, and its capacity to impose a firmer framework of dependence and unity on its subjects. Such changes—poorly recorded as they are in contemporary evidence and often more easily identified with hindsight—were doubtless accelerated by the Norman onslaught on Wales. If the Welsh kingdoms were to survive they had to learn to match or outwit the Normans militarily and to concentrate and exploit their resources in wealth and in power. After an initial collapse, the Welsh kingdoms did indeed display remarkable powers of resilience and recovery as the twelfth century progressed. What remained to be determined was whether the transformation in the character of political power had been sufficiently far-reaching and rapid to enable native Wales to withstand the even more dangerous challenge which the crown of England would mount against it in the thirteenth century.

CHAPTER 4

THE ANGLO-NORMAN SETTLEMENT OF WALES AND THE MAKING OF MARCHER SOCIETY

BY the end of the twelfth century the Normans had left their imprint deeply on Wales. Their conquest of the country, it is true, was neither as rapid nor as complete as early promise had suggested, and the mid-twelfth century in particular had witnessed a major rebuff to their advance. Yet by the end of the century they had transformed Wales—in terms of political mastery, social configuration, and cultural influence—more profoundly than any other group or movement was to do so until the Industrial Revolution. The story of their advance has been sketched chronologically in an earlier chapter; but its character and the nature of its impact on Wales call for closer attention.

The Norman barons, at whose instigation and under whose direction the conquest of Wales was undertaken, were a small group of men, rarely exceeding twenty in number at any given time. They came not only from Normandy itself but also from other parts of northern France such as Maine (whence came the Ballon brothers to Gwent), Flanders (the home of Turstin of Wigmore), and Brittany (most notably represented by Wethenoc of Monmouth and his nephew and successor, William fitz Baderon). Some of them arrived on the borders of Wales within a few years of the battle of Hastings; others, such as Robert fitz Hamo in Glamorgan, or Alan fitz Flaad (another Breton) in Oswestry, were introduced to the area by William II or Henry I. They had almost without exception risen to eminence, and that often very recently, through service to the royal-ducal family, or to one of its major vassals, and through dint of their own enterprise. Ties of service were often reinforced and overlain by further bonds of kinship and marriage. It was, for example, to his cousin, Robert of Tilleul, later to be known as Robert of Rhuddlan, that Earl Hugh of Chester (d. 1101) entrusted the military command of his borderlands in north Wales; while, in south Wales, William fitz Osbern (d. 1071) similarly placed his brother-in-law, Ralph de Tosny, in charge of the frontier district of Clifford-on-Wye.

The Normans, according to their contemporary historian, Orderic Vitalis, were 'a warlike race . . . moved by fierce ambition to lord it over others'.[1] The barons of the Welsh frontierlands certainly lived up to that reputation. They were violent, ambitious, and acquisitive; they were also, as one of them was described, men of 'extreme arrogance and presumption'.[2] Orderic Vitalis, by no means a hostile critic, has left us memorable portraits of the characteristics of some of them—of 'the pride and greed' of Robert of Rhuddlan, 'who harried the Welsh mercilessly for fifteen years', the savagery and grossness of Hugh of Avranches, earl of Chester, the sadistic cruelty of Earl Robert of Shrewsbury (exiled 1102), and the fiercesome exploits of Warin the Bald, 'a man small in body but great in spirit', against English and Welsh alike in western Shropshire. It is little wonder that *démesure*, the vice of excess so frequently depicted in the feudal *chansons*, was the besetting sin of such men.[3] Arnulf of Montgomery (exiled 1102) certainly succumbed to it. One might have thought that as a younger son he would have been well content with the good fortune which had made him lord of Holderness (Yorks.) and Pembroke, but his success only spurred him to higher ambitions. He dreamt of securing a kingdom in Ireland for himself and married King Muircertach's daughter in order to further his plans there. Their successors in the twelfth century were little different, as we can see in the memorable character sketch of Hugh Mortimer (d. *c.*1150) in the Wigmore abbey chronicle—a swashbuckling, choleric man given over to pleasures and amusements, an evil-tempered and wilful lord, a quarrelsome neighbour, and a lusty warrior, who harried the Welsh of Maelienydd and rebuilt the castle of Cymaron in an attempt to bludgeon them into submission.

The character of the Norman barons in Wales may have changed little during the course of the century from 1070; but the families to which they belonged certainly did, for few of them survived in the direct male line during that period.[4] Sometimes the explanation for the early demise of a family is an unusual one: the first Norman lord of Monmouth, Wethenoc, turned his back on the world to become a monk, while Bernard of Neufmarché's son Mahel, the heir to the great lordship of Brecon, was allegedly disinherited at the insistence of his jealous mother. In most cases, however, the explanation for the failure of a family was either political forfeiture or the absence of a direct male heir of the body. Political forfeiture was a major hazard under the first three Norman kings: it

---

[1] Orderic Vitalis, *Historia Ecclesiastica*, ed. M. Chibnall (Oxford, 1969–80), v, 24.

[2] The phrase is used by Robert of Torigni to characterize Hugh Mortimer (d. 1181) of Wigmore: *Chronicles of the Reigns of Stephen, Henry II and Richard I*, ed. R. Howlett (Rolls Series, 1884–90), IV, 184.

[3] *Historia Ecclesiastica*, IV, p. 139; II, p. 263. The Montgomeries are described as 'gentz trop demesurees' in the romance of *Fouke Le Fitz Waryn*, eds. E. J. Hathaway *et al.* (1975), p. 3.

[4] For a gazetteer of the descent of some of the major Anglo-Norman lordships in Wales, 1086–1400, see Appendix pp. 466–72.

disposed of whole families—notably those of Roger of Breteuil (1075), William of Eu (1096), Robert, earl of Shrewsbury, and his brother, Arnulf of Montgomery (1102)—or of individuals, such as Roger Lacy in 1096. Sometimes a lord's vassals might be involved in his downfall, as happened to some of Roger of Breteuil's vassals in Wales in 1075. Political forfeiture was, however, in general a hazard for the leading Norman families rather than for their vassals, and even for them its capacity to destroy a whole family, rather than an individual member of it, declined as the twelfth century progressed. Not so death without surviving direct male heir of the body; this was the curse of all families, high and low, early and late. In the reign of Henry I alone it disposed of some of the premier Norman families in Wales, such as fitz Hamo of Glamorgan, Ballon of Usk and Abergavenny, Lacy of Ewyas Lacy, and Neufmarché of Brecon.

The impact of such failure was profound. The family's estates were thereby often fragmented among female co-heiresses, as happened to those of the sons of Miles of Gloucester after 1165; the momentum of its policies was halted, as happened to the Montgomery advance in mid-Wales after 1102; and its followers and vassals were required to find a new focus of service. The failure or disinheritance of 'old' families also meant that a 'new' Norman baronage was in process of being created or promoted in the March in each generation, through marriage or royal munificence, or both. Never was the turn-over more dramatic or far-reaching in its impact than in the reign of Henry I. Many of the major Norman lordships in Wales passed through marriage or gift into new hands—Glamorgan and Gwynllŵg (Robert, earl of Gloucester), Brecon (Miles of Gloucester), Abergavenny (Brian fitz Count), Ewyas Lacy (Payn fitz John), Oswestry (Alan fitz Flaad), Chepstow and Usk (Walter fitz Richard of Clare), Ceredigion (Gilbert fitz Richard of the same family). Yet by 1200 all these families, except the Fitzalans (descendants of Alan fitz Flaad) had failed in the direct male line and yet another 'new' Marcher aristrocracy was, as in each generation, in the making.

To refer to a 'Marcher aristocracy' is in fact (as with the word 'Norman') to use a convenient but misleading label. There was no such exclusively, or indeed even predominantly, 'Marcher' aristocracy. The Norman lords in Wales almost without exception held estates also in England, often in Normandy, and not infrequently in 'France', beyond Normandy. Wales might be a challenging and exciting frontier for some of them and royal command might direct them thither; but in the orbit of their territorial interests and concerns it was almost always of secondary, and generally of peripheral, interest. This was obviously true of the premier Norman families, such as the Montgomeries and the Clares; but it was equally true of some of the lesser Marcher barons such as the Fitzmartins (lands in Somerset and Devon as well as Cemais) or Brians (lords of Okehampton

(Devon) as well as of Talacharn (Laugharne)). It was, indeed, often true also of the leading vassals of the Norman lords in Wales: thus the Bloet family held the fee of Raglan of the lords of Usk from the late eleventh to the late fourteenth century but they also had lands in Hampshire, Gloucestershire, Wiltshire, and Somerset, while the Somery family, who held the large mesne-lordship of Dinas Powys (Glamorgan) for a similar period, were also, through marriage, barons of Dudley (Worcs.).

For such men interest in Wales was at best spasmodic. It faltered easily if returns on effort were poor, if quicker or greater gains were to be made elsewhere, or if the distractions and opportunities of Anglo-Norman politics diverted their attention. The families most likely to show a sustained interest in the conquest of Wales were those whose main estates lay in the country itself or on its borders—such as Mortimer of Wigmore, Braose of Radnor and Builth, Say of Clun, Fitzalan of Oswestry, and Lacy of Weobley (until their interests were diverted to Ireland). Thus Roger Mortimer of Wigmore (d. 1214) could refer movingly in one of his benefactions to 'our men who died in the conquest of Maelienydd'.[5] For many other families Wales was a land where young men, and younger sons in particular, might be sent to serve their military apprenticeships, while their elders and betters attended to more pressing and rewarding business in England and Normandy. Thus it was his young son, Hugh, whom Earl Roger of Shrewsbury (d. 1094) sent on a foraging expedition into Ceredigion in 1074; it was Hugh's younger brother, Arnulf, who took up the challenge of establishing Norman rule in the remote outpost at Pembroke; and likewise Richard fitz Pons appears to have dispatched his son, Simon, with a retinue to impose Norman lordship in Cantref Bychan. In much the same fashion, in the later twelfth century, the young Braose and Mortimer heirs were placed in charge of their families' Welsh estates during their fathers' lifetimes and encouraged to take up the struggle against the Welsh.

Wales was not a land of easy opportunities or great rewards; such gains as could be made there could be won and retained only by continuing military effort and constant vigilance. That is why the detailed work of conquest in Wales in the Norman period was mainly undertaken not by the great barons—so easily diverted elsewhere and so often eliminated by forfeiture or failure in the male line—but by their vassals, retainers, and followers. The distinction, it is true, may be misleading, since the vassals of today might be the barons of tomorrow. Thus, the forfeiture of the houses of Breteuil (1075) and Montgomery (1102) allowed their major vassals, such as the Mortimers and Lacies, to step into their shoes, territorially and militarily, in the Welsh borderlands. Yet the distinction has its value in

---

[5] B. G. Charles, 'An Early Charter of the Abbey of Cwmhir', *Trans. Radnorshire Society*, 40 (1970), 68–73 at p. 68.

reminding us that the true Norman *conquistadores* of Wales, the men who battled in the country year in year out, and undertook the gruelling task of converting temporary victory into permanent or semi-permanent conquest, were often the vassals of the great barons. Many of them had but a small territorial foothold, if any at all, in Normandy and in England; they had everything to gain and nothing to lose by pursuing their careers in Wales, for there they would have military adventure in abundance and possibly a territorial fortune as a reward.

Such were Picard, a vassal of Bernard of Neufmarché, lord of Brecon, who established Norman lordship in Ystrad Yw in the Usk valley and built a motte at Tretower, or the de Cardiff family, who constructed a very early ringwork at Llantriddyd in the vale of Glamorgan and saluted their residential intentions by building there the earliest-known medieval domestic hall in south Wales, or Robert fitz Stephen—'a unique example of courage and true endurance', as Gerald of Wales admiringly called him[6]—who, like his father, fought tirelessly but ultimately unsuccessfully to impose Norman authority around Cardigan and eventually went to Ireland in search of easier and greater fortunes. None of them, perhaps, comes into sharper focus from the scanty sources than Gerald of Windsor, maternal grandfather of Gerald of Wales: a younger son of the royal constable of Windsor, he set out for Wales in search of adventure and a fortune; he defended Pembroke castle heroically during the great Welsh revolt of 1096 and harried the estates of the bishopric of St Davids in the next year; he served successively as steward of Arnulf of Montgomery and, after Arnulf's fall in 1102, as royal constable of Pembroke; he sought to ensconce himself more firmly in the area by taking to wife the seductive Nest, daughter of Rhys ap Tewdwr (d. 1093), prince of Deheubarth; he established his home at Carew in the relative safety of the Norman enclave around Pembroke, but his lust for adventure and further gain tempted him to try to win more land and lordship for himself in Emlyn in northern Dyfed. It was there at Cenarth Bychan (probably to be identified with Cilgerran) that he built a castle for himself 'fortified with ditches and walls', and it was there, 'with his wife and sons and his wealth and valuables' around him, that he was ambushed by the Welsh in 1109.[7] He effected his escape through the privy but left his wife to be abducted (perhaps not unwillingly) by the Welsh raiding party. Gerald's career, the considerable fortune he had amassed in wealth and in land, his heroism at Pembroke in 1096, and his undignified escape at Cenarth Bychan in 1109, give us something of the flavour of the lives and adventures of the Norman knights and vassals, the *milites strenui*, who undertook the Norman

---

[6] Giraldus Cambrensis, *Expugnatio Hibernica*, I, xxvi (ed. A. B. Scott and F. X. Martin (Dublin, 1978), p. 87; *Opera*, v, 271).

[7] *Brut, s.a.* 1108 (p. 28).

conquest of Wales, in the service of their lords but also with a keen eye to their own advancement.

The mechanics of Norman penetration in Wales is nowhere explicitly explained in contemporary sources; but its general character seems clear. The original work of conquest was entrusted to a handful of great Norman barons, at the instance and with the permission of the king. ' "Thou wert always asking of me a portion of Wales", Henry I is alleged to have said to Gilbert fitz Richard of Clare, ' "Now I will give thee the land of Cadwgan ap Bleddyn. Go and take possession of it". '[8] The conversation may be imaginary, but it conjures up vividly the atmosphere of prospective gift and licence to conquer which seems to characterize the Norman advance in Wales. That advance owed little to co-ordinated effort (other than an occasional joint harrying expedition, such as that on Anglesey in 1098) or centralized direction (other than the ultimate and occasional control of the king). Rather was it the work of individual barons operating individually. The Norman conquest of Wales was rarely more than the sum of individual baronial enterprises.

A Norman baron would lay claim to a whole Welsh district or kingdom, such as Morgannwg (Robert fitz Hamo), Brycheiniog (Bernard of Neufmarché) or Ceredigion (Gilbert fitz Richard). Such a claim was, initially, often no more than a declaration of intent, calculated as much as anything to warn off other prospective claimants. The Normans acknowledged as much by referring to these districts as *fines*, or frontier zones (the term used in Domesday Book), or by making grants, optimistically, of their 'future acquisitions'.[9] The claim could only be made good by strenuous military efforts by the lord's 'private' army or warband, *comitivae* as they are sometimes called in contemporary sources. The army would be composed of the lord's vassals, relatives, tenants, neighbours, and other adventurers and mercenaries who were attracted to his service by the prospect of booty and reward. Earl Hugh of Chester was said by Orderic Vitalis to 'move around with any army rather than a household',[10] while William fitz Osbern, earl of Hereford, who was noted for his liberality to his knights, had a private army which caused even William the Conqueror some concern. Contemporary sources allow us an occasional glimpse of the bonds of loyalty, adventure, service, kinship, and expectation, which kept these warbands together—Robert of Rhuddlan accompanied on the foreshore at Degannwy by his faithful knight, Osbern of Orgères, who had also witnessed his lord's gifts to the Norman monastery of St Évroul, or

---

[8] *Brut, s.a.* 1110 (p. 34).
[9] 'Cartulary of Brecon Priory', *Arch. Camb.*, IV, xiv (1883), 148; *Episc. Acts*, II, 644 (L. 119).
[10] *Historia Ecclesiastica*, II, 261–3.

Robert fitz Stephen setting out for Ireland in 1169 with a force of 30 knights 'of his own kinsmen and retainers' (including at least three nephews), 60 men-at-arms, and some 300 archers.[11]

The aim of these warbands was brutally clear: to terrorize the country into subjection. They pillaged and plundered ruthlessly in north and south Wales alike: Llŷn was said, doubtless with some exaggeration, to have been completely wasted in a week of relentless harrying, and the earl of Hereford in the mid-twelfth century could still refer casually to the booty which he might take from his enemies in Wales. Animals were driven away in large numbers; men and women were imprisoned and sold into captivity; large tracts of land, especially in north-east Wales, were placed under forest law, especially to satisfy the needs of Hugh of Avranches, earl of Chester, whose hunting, it was said, was a daily devastation of his lands. The terror worked. 'One vile Norman', lamented Rhigyfarch in the last decade of the eleventh century, 'intimidates a hundred natives with his command and terrifies them with his look'.[12] Nor was this merely the hysterical outburst of a lone Welshman. Bishop Urban of Llandaff (1107–33), himself a Norman nominee, spoke bitterly of the impact of 'the incursions of the Normans'; much later, Gerald of Wales, no critic of the Normans, commented on 'the fear and terror' they had instilled into the bishop of St Davids and how he had been 'intimidated by the hostile lances of the newcomers'.[13]

Once the spirit of the people had been broken by such terror, much of the detailed work of conquest was quickly delegated into the hands of camp followers. Many of the grants initially made to them must have been of the nature of military commands, with only the prospect of converting them into territorial lordship through long and exhausting effort. Thus in Glamorgan, the conquest and domination of the large districts of Tal-y-fan and Coety were entrusted to the families of St Quintin and Turberville and they were given an almost entirely free hand in the task, for their duties and obligations to their overlord, the lord of Glamorgan, were nominal. The pattern of delegated conquest is particularly clear in Ceredigion where the Norman settlement was abruptly terminated in 1136–7 and thereby fossilized in the annals. Gilbert fitz Richard of Clare, to whom the district was granted by Henry I in 1110 (as we saw above),[14] certainly played the directing role, leading his army into the district and building or rebuilding castles at Dingeraint (the later Cardigan), near Aberystwyth, and at Ystrad Meurig. But in the rest of the region, conquest and lordship were the work

---

[11] Quoted in A. J. Otway-Ruthven, *A History of Medieval Ireland* (2nd edn. Dublin, 1980), p. 43.

[12] M. Lapidge, 'The Welsh-Latin Poetry of Sulien's Family', *Studia Celtica*, VIII–IX (1973–4), 91.

[13] *Episc. Acts*, II, 617 (L. 33); I, 237 (D. 28) 235 (D. 18).   [14] See above p. 87.

of his vassals, whose names were still attached to the castles they built—Razo's castle, Stephen's castle, Humphrey's castle, Richard de la Mare's castle, and Walter (del Bec)'s castle.

The Normans were certainly outstandingly successful militarily. Even the Welsh chronicler admired their military professionalism, contrasting Norman 'diligence and circumspection' with the impetuous 'imprudence' of the Welsh. In one of the few detailed accounts we have of a military encounter in twelfth-century Wales, he noticed how the Normans first drew the Welsh by the use of archers and then sent in mailed knights to attack them. It was these armed and horsed knights, 'protected by armour and corselets', who above all impressed and terrified the Welsh, accustomed as they were to the ambushes of lightly armed infantry.[15] The Normans were by no means invincible, as was shown at Gelli Carnant (1096) and Crug Mawr (1136); but the suddenness of their appearance, the novelty of their equipment, and the sophistication of their tactics more often than not proved as devastatingly successful against isolated and militarily backward communities in Wales as they were to do later in Ireland.

Victory was converted into conquest and domination by the construction of castles. The building of castles was to contemporaries the visible expression and guarantee of conquest. Earl Hugh of Chester, comments the biographer of Gruffudd ap Cynan, 'made castles and fortified places according to the custom of the French (Normans) and became lord of the land'. The same equation is indicated by the *Brut*, when it records in 1093 how 'the French (i.e. Normans) overran Dyfed and Ceredigion . . . and made castles in them and fortified them. And then the French seized the lands of the Britons.' It was an equation which also worked in reverse. The destruction of the castles represented Norman defeat and Welsh recovery: 'he liberated Gwynedd', so it was said of Gruffudd ap Cynan, 'from its castles'.[16]

The castle was infinitely adaptable. It could be a centre of defence or attack, domination and colonization, or retreat. Norman military organization was focused on the castle. Estates were reorganized to form integrated military command-units or castleries centred on a major castle. It is striking that of the seven castleries specifically mentioned in Domesday Book, five were to be found on the Welsh borderland—at Caerleon, Ewyas Harold, Richard's Castle, Clifford, and Montgomery. The castle was also a springboard from which forays and further attacks were launched. Such, no doubt, was in part the function of fitz Osbern's early castles at Chepstow or Clifford, or the fortress built south of the Severn by the Earl of Shrewsbury and called Montgomery after his family seat in Normandy;

---

[15] *Brut, s.a.* 1116; *Historia Gruffudd vab Kenan*, p. 26 (*History G. ap C.*, p. 147).

[16] *Historia Gruffudd vab Kenan*, pp. 18, 20–21 (*History G. ap C.*, pp. 133, 137–9); *Brut, s.a.* 1093. CF. *s.a.* 1098, 1144.

and such obviously was the role of the string of castles built by the
Normans as they penetrated along the north Wales coast—Rhuddlan by
1073, Degannwy by the late 1070s, Bangor, Caernarfon, and Aberlleiniog
by the 1090s. Such castles, small as they might appear today, dominated
the countryside, overawing the local inhabitants as effectively as Edward
I's fortresses in a later age. Should the tide of Norman advance be halted,
the castles could serve equally well as centres of retreat and defence. They
performed that function admirably. 'The castles', reports the *Brut* in its
account of the great Welsh rising of 1096, 'still remained intact, with their
garrisons in them'.[17] Its comment is frequently re-echoed throughout these
turbulent decades—as in Gruffydd ap Cynan's failure to capture the keep
of Rhuddlan in 1075 or Gruffudd ap Rhys's similar failure before the inner
wards of Llanymddyfri and Swansea in 1116. Nor was the castle's function
exclusively military; it also provided a focus for colonization. Small
boroughs quickly sprouted in its shadow, as at Cardiff, Rhuddlan, or
Brecon; while, in the countryside, a network of castles, often tiny ones,
alone provided the minimum security required to encourage Anglo-
Norman colonization. Such, no doubt, was the purpose of the cluster of
mottes to the north-east of Brecon—at Llandyfaelog, Pytingwyn, Pytinglas
(where the first element is doubtless 'Poitevin') and Alexanderstone—or
the remarkable concentration of 27 castles (many of them tiny 'blockhouse-
mottes', as they have been called) which protected the Anglo-Norman
settlements in an area of some 130 square miles in the vale of Montgomery.

Wales and its borders formed the pre-eminent land of castles in Norman
Britain. There are over 300 pre-1215 castle sites within Wales itself and
the figure would be increased by a further hundred if the adjoining border
districts of England were included. They were particularly heavily
concentrated in the Severn valley and in the lowlands of the south from
Gwent to Pembroke, but the heaviest concentration of all lay along the
central Marcher frontierlands between England and Wales where Norman
advance was slow and hesitant. The number and distribution of castles
within any given district were not necessarily determined mainly by a
coherent military strategy; the extent of alien colonization, the pattern of
subinfeudation, and the anxiety of each Norman knight of any substance to
have a castle of his own were also major considerations.

The castles, almost without exception, displayed the Norman talent for
choosing strategic sites to maximum military and territorial advantage.
Many of them (such as Pembroke, Rhuddlan, or Carmarthen) were built
on tidal inlets and could be supplied or relieved by sea in an emergency.
Some (such as Llansteffan, Hawarden, or Dinas (Blaenllyfni)) took
advantage of an Iron Age fort-site; others (such as Cardiff, Llwchwr

---

[17] *Brut, s.a.* 1096.

(Gower), or Caerleon) were located within the ruins of a Roman fort, though in some instances (as at Brecon or Carmarthen) the Normans deliberately eschewed a Roman site in favour of one nearby of their own choice. The majority were of the well-known motte-and-bailey variety, earthworks defended by timber palisades. Their outstanding virtue was that they could be thrown up quickly by unskilled and, often no doubt, forced labour, as was 'the slender fortress built of stakes and turf' hurriedly constructed by Arnulf of Montgomery at Pembroke in the 1090s.[18] They are perhaps best represented by instances such as Hen Domen, near present-day Montgomery, where careful excavation has revealed the constant process of redesigning and rebuilding over a period of one hundred and fifty years, or by mounds such as Aberlleiniog (Môn) or Castell Gwallter (Ceredigion), abandoned at an early date in the face of Welsh attack. As well as the motte-and-bailey castles, simple banked and ditched enclosures or ringworks were also common, especially in Pembroke and Glamorgan, where they outnumber the mottes.

Some of these early castles had but a short life. A few became redundant militarily as the frontier moved forward. Others, especially in Ceredigion and north Wales, were overwhelmed by Welsh attacks, never to recover. Some were relocated: Caus castle (Salop) seems to have taken the place of an earlier ringwork at Hawcock's mound nearby; Rhydygors was eclipsed within a few years by the new castle at Carmarthen; while two and possibly three different sites were chosen for the castles built between the late eleventh and early thirteenth centuries at the estuaries of the Ystwyth and Rheidol rivers in Ceredigion. Yet other early mottes were abandoned in favour of more comfortable domestic residences, the early Norman ringwork at Llantriddyd (Glamorgan) being so eclipsed around 1200 by the nearby Horseland Moat. The castles most likely to survive were those which continued to fulfil a military or military-cum-governmental function. Such castles were constantly reshaped, partly for military reasons (as fortifications were upgraded, ditches recut, and bridges rebuilt), partly to accommodate changes in military architecture (notably the growing use of stone, especially for building the tower or keep), and partly to satisfy higher demands of domestic comfort for a resident lord and his household. Tretower in the Usk valley is a case in point. Here Picard, one of Bernard of Neufmarché's lieutenants in the conquest of the Welsh district of Brycheiniog, had probably built a motte-and-bailey castle for himself in the late eleventh century to control movement up the Usk and Rhiangoll valleys and to impose his lordship on the surrounding countryside. In the mid-twelfth century the wooden buildings were replaced by a stone shell-keep encompassing a hall, solar, and kitchen. These stone buildings were

---

[18] *IK*, I, xii, (*Opera*, vi, 89).

in turn to be demolished in the next century to make way for a great circular tower which still dominates the site. Tretower castle is a study in miniature of the gradual transformation, architectural and social, of the Norman castle in Wales as it responded to changes in structural design, domestic comfort, and lordly power without surrendering its ultimate military rationale. It is paralleled by two verbal vignettes in Gerald of Wales's memoirs: the one of his grandfather, Gerald of Windsor, desperately defending the motte at Pembroke in the 1090s and, in a calculated act of bravado, throwing his last supplies to the Welsh besiegers, the other a more tranquil and nostalgic picture of Manorbier castle (Pembroke) in Gerald's own boyhood in the 1150s, with its turrets and battlements, fine fish-pond, and outstanding orchards.

Gerald's recollections were happy ones; yet, as so often with childhood memories, they were selective and misleading. Norman control in Wales, especially outside the lowlands, was always insecure. It was constantly frustrated by the natural and political geography of the country. Initially, it is true, this did not appear to be so. The Normans made good use of the decayed Roman road network in the south-east; they penetrated quickly up the river valleys of Wye, Usk, and Severn and along the coast of north Wales; in their raids into Gwynedd and in the intensive colonization of the south Wales coastlands from south-west England, they made highly imaginative and effective use of seapower; their early raids into Builth, Dyfed, Ceredigion, and north-west Wales showed that they were not to be daunted by high mountain passes. Yet penetration proved much easier than control. The problems of supplies, lines of communication, and guerrilla warfare in a mountainous, forested, and marshy country often undid early success. Acute observers soon noted that French warfare (*Gallica militia*), with its emphasis on heavily armoured cavalry, was ill-suited to Welsh conditions; the castle likewise was pre-eminently an instrument for the domination of the lowlands, for few of them were located above the 600-foot contour line.

The political geography of Wales compounded these problems. Wales was a politically fragmented country, each fragment of which had to be individually conquered and controlled. Even the death of a pre-eminent prince, such as Rhys ap Tewdwr of Deheubarth in 1093, did not, in spite of the prognostications of the chroniclers, lead inexorably to the political collapse of Wales. Moreover, the custom of partibility and the consequent segmentation of dynasties meant that there was never any lack of claimants to replace defeated or deceased Welsh princelings. Even a crushing military victory did not necessarily ensure firm Norman control, for in Wales, unlike much of England, the Normans rarely found a firm pattern of political and governmental authority which they could inherit and convert rapidly to their own ends.

For all these reasons Norman control in Wales, in spite of dramatic initial successes and an extensive castle-building programme, was often tentative and precarious. This was obviously true of much of the uplands. It was also true of whole districts, such as Ceredigion and Tegeingl, which were recovered by the Welsh in the 1130s and 1140s after being for more than a generation under the control of the Normans. It was true in a measure even of the lowlands. In 1158 William, earl of Gloucester, his wife, and child were abducted from Cardiff castle itself in a daring ambush; in 1173, a year after Henry II had passed through the area, a local Welsh chieftain (Hywel ab Iorwerth) rampaged through Gwent Iscoed—a district which had been under nominal Norman control for a century—and 'won it all except the castles, and hostages were given to him by the leading men of the land'.[19] It is little wonder that the Neath abbey chronicler should comment despondently that the abbey's estates in Gower were not considered of much value because, whenever a lord of Gower died, the lordship was devastated by the Welsh. Comments and incidents such as these reveal how fragile, even after a century of effort, was Norman control. To depict such tenuous control confidently on a map in terms of large and well-defined lordships is to mislead; it would be more appropriate to represent it as a complex, precarious, and shifting patchwork, ranging from firm control in the environs of castles to barely noticeable overlordship in upland regions.

The Norman conquest of Wales, such as it was, was a joint-stock enterprise conducted by the barons and their vassals under the ultimate control of the king. All three parties—king, barons, and vassals—shared in the lordship which was the fruit and reward of conquest. The role of the king should certainly not be underestimated. He occasionally took a direct military interest in Wales, ordering castles to be built there (as did William I at Rhuddlan and William II at Rhydygors), repairing and provisioning baronial castles under threat (such as Llanymddyfri in the 1150s), and when need arose mounting full-scale expeditions to bolster the Norman position in the country (1095, 1097, 1114, 1121, 1157–8, 1163, 1165). His territorial interest in the country could be very considerable, both through political forfeiture and through the custody of the estate of minors. The Norman barons in Wales were the king's subjects. Most of them were beholden to him for their promotion; all of them held their lands in Wales ultimately of him, either in fee or at farm. Over and above these territorial rights lay his ultimate suzerainty. Wales was part of his dominions: his coinage alone circulated there; his writs were addressed to all his faithful subjects in England and Wales; episcopal estates were held directly of him

[19] *Brut, s.a.* 1173.

and the control of episcopal appointments was likewise his; he confirmed the gifts of his barons there, often in their own lifetimes; and occasionally it was by his licence that they specifically sanctioned their acts. If this ultimate royal authority had rather gone by default in Stephen's reign, Henry II restored it fully and did so masterfully. Never more so than in the early 1170s: in 1171 he reportedly appointed royal constables to take charge of baronial castles in Wales; in 1172 he conferred the honorary title of justiciar of Deheubarth on Rhys ap Gruffudd, confirmed him in his conquests, and thereby in effect took him into royal protection and prohibited Anglo-Norman attacks on him and his lands; and in 1175 he extorted a promise from the leading Marcher lords that, when required, they were obliged to support royal action in Wales. These masterful acts were an abundant reminder of royal overlordship in Wales over native prince and Norman baron alike.

Yet royal interest and direction in Wales remained, until the end of the twelfth century, at best spasmodic. It was at the instance of a handful of Norman barons and under their banners that the conquest of Wales was undertaken; well might their successors in the next century claim to hold their lordships 'by ancient conquest'. It was they who determined the tempo of the conquest; without their commitment the movement faltered. It was they who parcelled Wales into 'honors' and 'lordships', the units of aristocratic feudal power, to correspond to their notions of power and authority—such as 'the honor of Abergavenny' or the 'lordship of the castle of Brecon'.[20] It was they who arrogated some of the powers of overlordship of their Welsh predecessors in the conquered lands and out of them began to shape the immunities known in the next century as 'the liberties of the march'.

But aristocratic power rested on the support of followers and vassals. Their reward, other than glory and plunder, lay pre-eminently in a share of the land and lordship of the baron in whose service they had fought. Subinfeudation, as this process is known to historians, was an act both of military delegation and of necessary largess. Through it, many of the effective powers of lordship in Norman Wales were devolved into the hands of vassals and their descendants. The process began virtually on the morrow of the conquest itself and, in much of the lowland districts of south Wales, it was already well-advanced by 1135. By then, for example, much of the Vale of Glamorgan had been parcelled into knights' fees (as these territorial endowments were called in feudal terminology) and several of the original holders of these fees can be identified as companions of Robert fitz Hamo (d. 1107), the first Norman lord of Glamorgan. The beneficiaries of this delegation of lordship were drawn overwhelmingly from the lord's

---

[20] *Ancient Charters . . . prior to A.D. 1200*, i, ed. J. H. Round (Pipe Roll Society, 1888), p. 43 no. 26; *Episc. Acts*, I, 341, (D. 406).

kinsmen and retainers, often from men who had already served him and been rewarded by him in Normandy and England. The lordship of Brecon may serve as an example. The early Norman lords of Brecon—Bernard of Neufmarché (d. c.1125), Miles of Gloucester (d. 1143) and his sons, and the Braose family—kept for themselves the key castles of Brecon and Hay and direct control of the districts immediately dependent on them. They parcelled much of the rest of the lowlands of the lordship into knights' fees or mesne lordships for their dependants, men with distinctively French names such as Devereux (d'Évreux), le Mans, Waldeboef (possibly Œil de Boeuf); kinsmen, such as Walter Clifford, Miles of Gloucester's nephew, who was granted, or confirmed in, a large estate at Bronllys held by the service of five knights; and tenants drawn from their English estates, such as Ralph Baskerville, who held lands in Bredwardine (Herefs.) as well as in the lordship of Brecon. Norman lordship in Brecon was largely exercised by these men. They, in turn, often created dependent feudal tenures for their followers and so the powers of lordship were further delegated.

Powers delegated are often powers lost, especially in the decentralized and custom-based society of the feudal period. Subinfeudation could easily have led, as in a measure it did in England, to a fracturing of lordship and a dilution of baronial control. Two major reasons help to explain why this did not happen to a marked degree in Norman Wales. In the first place, the feudal lordship or honor in Wales (such as Glamorgan or Brecon) was a compact geographical unit. Within it the lord's ultimate territorial and jurisdictional control was virtually complete, nor was it challenged (as in England) by a co-existing pattern of royal governance and control. The lord of the honor or lordship was thereby able to exercise a tight and continuing control over his vassals and their affairs—summoning them regularly to the court of his honor (such as that held at Cardiff for the lordship, or county, of Glamorgan), acting as their judicial superior, confirming their deeds, reserving certain major criminal cases and judicial profits from their estates for himself, and claiming custody of their lands during a minority. Secondly, the military precariousness of Wales kept alive those very conditions under which feudal tenures were first created and feudal duties defined. In particular, the vassal's obligations of military service in his lord's army and guard-duty at his castle were never in danger of becoming archaic duties in Wales. They were living obligations, all the more incumbent because the major barons themselves were so frequently non-resident. When the castles of Glamorgan were attacked in 1183–4 it was the knights of the honor who were called upon to defend them; those who failed to do so forfeited their lands. The conditions of the frontier helped to maintain the military rationale of lordship and to sustain a remarkable power and depth in lord–vassal relationships in Norman Wales.

The nature of the lordship exercised by the barons and their vassals in Norman Wales varied greatly from place to place. In much of the uplands it was often little more than a loose overlordship over native princelings and kin-groups, reinforced, where possible, by an occasional tribute and the surrender of hostages as a guarantee of good behaviour. Such arrangements were of their very nature brittle. They had to be lubricated by gifts and periodically reinforced by parleys and forays. Such was the character of Norman lordship in much of the middle March—Maelienydd, Radnor, Elfael, Builth—and also in the upland districts of Gwent, Glamorgan, Brecon, and Gower. Even in the thirteenth century the commote of Afan was said to be held by its native lords of the lords of Glamorgan by Welsh tenure 'with royal liberty'; in other words, Norman power there was little more than nominal. And the same was doubtless true of the other upland commotes of Glamorgan—Senghennydd, Meisgyn, and Glynrhondda. In the lordship of Caerleon the local Welsh dynasty kept effective control of most of the uplands until the thirteenth century, alternatively cajoled and threatened by Norman lord and king alike, and occasionally launching devastating raids (as in the early 1170s) on the Norman manors of the lowlands. Elsewhere, as in the lordships of Usk and Chepstow, an attempt was made to integrate the leaders of the native community into a Norman pattern of dependence by creating Welsh knights' fees—held in return for feudal obligations of service but by Welsh inheritance customs. Yet such attempts were at best half-hearted; feudal institutions in Wales were to be confined to the Normanized lowlands.

In these lowlands, the Norman grip was often more secure, its lordship more precise and its profits more ample. Here, as Domesday Book makes clear for south-east Wales, the Normans found a pre-existing pattern of authority on which they could build easily. A dependent peasantry was already organized into groups of vills under local reeves and owed specified renders of honey, swine, cows, and sheep to native Welsh courts (W. *llysoedd*). In such districts a manorial structure of authority could be easily introduced or adopted; a firmer web of territorial, tenurial, and jurisdictional control could be woven around the peasantry and their status and obligations quickly assimilated to those of manorial tenants in England. Thus the lord of Glamorgan soon established manors at Roath and Leckwith to serve the needs of his castle at Cardiff and reserved the demesne lands of the old Welsh centres at Llyswyrny and Llanilltud (Llantwit) for himself. His vassals followed suit: the de Londres family in the mesne-lordship of Ogmore established manorial granges at Ogmore itself and Colwinston and organized the tenantry to work on them. Nor did their economic enterprise end there. They built mills, initially to grind corn for their own halls (as Osbern had done at Gresford (Bromfield) by 1086), but very soon as a major source of seignorial profit. They also began to exploit the pastoral resources of their estates, both for cattle-rearing (as at Brecon) and sheep-rearing (as at Kidwelly and Pembroke). The importance of these early Norman economic enterprises in Wales far exceeded the supplies they provided for the castle and the income which they yielded to the lord. They were the first stage in converting military power into economic lordship.

Norman lordship in Wales was most secure and profitable where it was firmly underpinned by substantial colonization. Alien colonization was no new experience in Wales, for well before the Norman conquest Mercian peasant communities had established extensive colonies in north-east, central, and possibly south-east Wales. But the Anglo-Norman colonization was a much more dramatic and far-reaching movement. It transformed the racial composition and social character of large parts of south and east Wales. It is, unfortunately, a movement which went largely unrecorded at the time. Its character and dimensions have to be deduced from fragmentary references, from place-name evidence, from the retrospective implications of later records, and from analogies with the better-documented colonization in parts of north and west Wales in the days of Edward I.

It is in the boroughs that the impact of Anglo-Norman colonization can be most readily grasped. The story of pre-urban growth and marketing centres in Wales certainly predates the coming of the Normans; but it is with their advent that the history of most Welsh boroughs may be said to begin. Most of them were founded in the shadow of castles and primarily to serve their needs. The burgages of Bernard of Neufmarché's borough of Brecon were said, appropriately enough, to be 'situated in my castle of Honddu', probably in the defended outer enclosure of the castle, later known as Beili Glas (The Green Bailey).[21] Many of these fledgling boroughs were almost contemporary with the earliest days of conquest. Their early burgesses were no doubt foreign settlers: the first recorded burgess of Brecon bore the distinctively English name, Harding. Their early privileges likewise proclaimed the role of Norman inspiration and seignorial initiative in their foundation, for they were often modelled on 'the laws and customs of Breteuil', a Norman castle-borough of which William fitz Osbern had been steward. One of the earliest boroughs to enjoy the customs of Breteuil was Rhuddlan; there the combination of an entry in Domesday Book and recent archaeological excavation provides a welcome insight into the character of these early Norman boroughs in Wales (and one which was later to be overwhelmed by Welsh counter-attack). Norman Rhuddlan was probably built on the site of an earlier Mercian burh; but it owed its security in a hostile environment to the new Norman castle which overlooked it, its own extensive banks and ditches,

[21] 'Cartulary of Brecon Priory', *Arch. Camb.*, IV, xiv (1883), 142.

and the estuarine waters of the Clwyd. In 1086 it was still a tiny settlement of only eighteen burgesses; but it was staking a bright future for itself, for its earthworks enclosed an area of 35 acres. Its optimism seemed to be well-founded, for it was already more than an adjunct to the castle. Its mint (two coins of William Rufus have been discovered there), mills, tolls, fisheries, and interest in the iron industry all proclaimed that the importance and potential of the little borough in extending Anglo-Norman economic control in north-east Wales were out of proportion to its size.

Important as were the boroughs, it was in the countryside of Wales that Anglo-Norman colonization was to have its most profound impact. The story is, of course, but one instance of the great drive for new land to cater for Europe's rapidly growing population in the twelfth and thirteenth centuries. Population growth and land hunger provided the momentum; but in Wales, as in Spain and to a measure on the eastern frontier of Germany, military conquest and seignorial initiative provided the occasion and conditions for the process to get under way. Already in the late eleventh century military overlordship in the vale of Montgomery was underpinned by a policy of settling colonists on waste land and encouraging, indeed possibly ordering, the wealthier of them to build small defensible mottes to protect their newly established farms and hamlets. A similar policy doubtless explains the free tenancies, held by military tenure, which are a common feature of lowland Gwent, Glamorgan, and Gower and whose holders, according to the evidence of later rentals, often bore non-Welsh names. The colonists often settled on virgin lands or on lands which had hitherto not been intensively or permanently cultivated. Such apparently was the case in Ceredigion, where even the native chronicler conceded that the land was 'empty . . . and well-nigh deserted' before Gilbert fitz Richard introduced 'Saxon' colonists in the second decade of the twelfth century.[22] Elsewhere, however, colonization was a much more brutal and drastic process which led to the flight or explusion of the native inhabitants. 'And they', records the *Brut* bluntly of the Flemings, 'occupied the whole cantref of Rhos, near the estuary of the river called Cleddyf, and drove away all the inhabitants from the land'.[23]

Singularly little is known about the mechanics of colonization or the provenance of settlers. Some of them were probably recruited from the lords' English estates by seignorial agents. Many of them arrived in family groups or local bands under the protection of military strongmen, such as Wizo, 'chieftain of the Flemings', or Letard 'Little King' who gave their names, respectively, to the settlements of Wiston (Daugleddau) and Letterston (Pebidiog). The Flemings of Dyfed are in fact the most famous and identifiable group of these colonists. They had been driven from their

---

[22] *Brut, s.a.* 1116 (p. 42).   [23] *Brut, s.a.* 1108.

homeland by overpopulation and by the incursions of the sea. They migrated eastwards to Germany and north-westwards to Britain—to England (notably to Somerset, Lincolnshire, Cleveland, and around Carlisle), Scotland (especially Clydesdale and Moray), and Wales. Their initial settlement in Wales was possibly undertaken as a secondary movement from earlier colonies in England and at the specific invitation of Henry I about 1107–10. Their main settlement was in the *cantrefi* of Rhos and Daugleddau in western Dyfed; but they also established themselves in Ceredigion and at Talacharn and Cydweli, on either side of the Tywi estuary. They were ideal colonists for such frontier districts—aggressive and acquisitive, warriors and peasants by turn, true pioneers in both agriculture and commerce, and deadly enemies of the native Welsh. They retained their racial and linguistic identity until the early thirteenth century and by then they had totally and permanently transformed the character of parts of western Dyfed.

The Flemings may have been the most distinctive group of colonists; but in numbers they were far outmatched by the English. It was they who colonized the river valleys of south-eastern Wales and the coastal lowlands from Gwent to Gower and indeed beyond. Western and midland England were important recruitment areas for such colonists into south-east Wales: many of the settlers of the lowland valleys of Brecon, for example, were drawn from western Herefordshire. Along the southern coastline a large proportion of the immigrants came from south-west England, bringing with them a customary acre based on the pole of nine feet familiar in Devon and Cornwall. They settled initially in the shadow of the Norman castles, but eventually ventured further afield. In Gower, for example, the earliest settlements were probably made around castles such as Pennard and Penmaen, overlooking Oxwich and Port Einon bays, in southern Gower where the 'ancient knights' fees', as they came to be known, were quickly established; only later, and tentatively, did the colonists venture into northern and western Gower.

Most difficult of all is to assess the density and chronology of this alien migration. Place-name evidence can provide valuable hints. Thus the distribution of place-names with the suffix '-ton' is indicative: of the 350 or so recorded in Wales, 155 are to be found in the modern (pre-1974) county of Pembroke, 74 in Glamorgan, 35 in Monmouthshire, and 25 in Flintshire; most of them are not traceable in the records (admittedly scanty) before the twelfth century. Field-name and personal-name evidence is even more significant in providing testimony, however impressionistic, of the density of peasant settlement. An early thirteenth-century deed shows, for example, how thoroughly anglicized were the field-names (such as 'Holegewelle', 'Bromhul', 'Gilbardesmore') to the north-east of Brecon, while the early deeds of Ewenni priory (Glamorgan) reveal the same to be true of the Ogmore district. Above all, it is to the rentals, surveys, and accounts of the late thirteenth and the fourteenth centuries that the historian must turn for a comprehensive and convincing, if still patchy, picture of the impact of alien immigration on the population and on the tenurial patterns of lowland Wales. These different kinds of evidence have, of course, to be used with great care; all of them, in greater or lesser measure, fall short of providing a detailed guide to the chronological stages in the saga of colonization, especially in the early period. Nevertheless, they are unanimous in proclaiming that in lowland Pembroke, Gower, Glamorgan, and Gwent, the lower valleys of the Wye and the Usk, and some other districts along the English border, the Norman conquest of Wales was accompanied and underpinned by extensive peasant colonization, much of it to be dated initially to the late eleventh and twelfth centuries.

Wales by the end of the twelfth century was a country of two peoples, Welsh and Anglo-Norman; the relationship between them was henceforth to be a major theme in its history. The relationship was in part one of deep hatred and mutual fear. The Normans, according to the native chronicler, were guilty of unbearable tyranny, injustice, and oppression; their aim at the very least was to impose their power and laws on the Welsh, at worst to drive out the natives from their land and even 'to exterminate all the Britons'.[24] In the face of such calamities, it is little wonder that the biographer of St Cadog believed that the only way to protect the relics of the saint from the invading Normans was to transfer them, in his imagination, to Benevento in Italy! Rhigyfarch, the scholar–cleric of Llanbadarn (Ceredigion), shared this sense of despair and desolation. It was not only the tyranny of the Normans which offended him; even more devastating were its social consequences: the undermining of native culture and scholarship, the collapse of the social order and values of native Welsh society, the loss of any sense of dignity as a people. It is little wonder that Rhigyfarch modelled himself on Boethius. Nor is it surprising that he should write a life of St David, for it was only in the memory of a distant and heroic past that there seemed to be any antidote to the woes of the present.

This was not merely the hysteria of a conservative, learned élite. The protracted nature of the Norman conquest of Wales and its uneven and spasmodic character meant that resentment was refuelled in each generation from a new stock of memories and atrocities. Thus any accord between Anglo-Normans and Welsh in Brecon and Abergavenny was rudely shattered in 1175 when Seisyll ap Dyfnwal and other Welsh chieftains were killed in cold blood by the Anglo-Normans, so that thereafter, as the native

[24] *Brut. s.a.* 1094, 1098 (p. 21), 1114.

chronicler records, 'none of the Welsh dared place their trust in the French'.[25] Such mistrust was nourished by further incidents, such as that of 1197 when another local Welsh leader, Trahaearn Fychan, was seized on his way to William Braose's court, drawn at the tail of a horse through the streets of Brecon, decapitated, and his headless body ignominiously hung by his feet on the gallows for three days. Tension between Anglo-Normans and Welsh seems to have been particularly acute in three areas: in the middle March districts of Maelienydd and Elfael, where the families of Mortimer and Say were seeking, with only limited success, to impose their authority, killing four sons of the local Welsh ruler, Madog ab Idnerth, in the process between 1142 and 1179; in Gwent Iscoed and Uwchcoed, where the Norman lords of Usk, Caerleon, and Abergavenny were struggling against the recalcitrant Welsh of the upland districts; and in western Glamorgan, where Anglo-Norman attempts to control and colonize the lowlands beyond the river Ogwr were constantly threatened by massive Welsh counter-raids, such as those of 1167 or 1183–4.

Yet brutality and bitterness by no means encompass the whole range of attitudes in the relationship of Welsh and Anglo-Normans. Reasons of mutual advantage and short-term convenience often led them to form temporary alliances with each other, and that from an early date. The Normans became very adept at exploiting the segmentation of Welsh dynasties and the quarrels between them for their own ends. The Welsh likewise quickly learnt the art and benefits of service to the Norman invaders. Bleddyn ap Cydifor was a notable early example: he took charge of the new castle at Laugharne for its Norman lord, Robert Courtemain; stood firmly by his new masters during the Welsh insurrection of 1116; served as their agent and interpreter among the Welsh of eastern Dyfed; and demonstrated his affiliations clearly by donating land to the new Norman priory of Carmarthen.

Bleddyn's example was doubtless followed by scores of others, especially in areas controlled firmly by the Normans. In certain parts of Wales, indeed, compromise and respectful co-existence appear to characterize relationships between Anglo-Normans and Welsh from an early date. This appears to have been the situation in Cemais, where the Norman lords were generally content with a loose and undemanding lordship, easily accommodating itself to the existing native structure of authority. In Brecon, likewise, relationships were cordial in the mid-twelfth century, with local Welsh leaders witnessing the lord's deeds and attending his court. Much no doubt depended on the attitude of individual lords and princes. It was the aggressive policies of the Braose family which seem to have brought the accord to an end in Brecon; whereas two Welsh

[25] *Brut, s.a.* 1175 (p. 71).

princelings, Dafydd ab Owain of Gwynedd (d. 1203) and Hywel ab Iorwerth of Caerleon, were specifically complimented by Gerald of Wales for 'observing a strict neutrality between the Welsh and the English'.[26] Such understanding was doubtless furthered, especially in the higher reaches of society, by marriage. Cadwgan ap Bleddyn of Powys (d. 1111) took the daughter of one of the earliest Norman lords of the northern March, Picot de Say, as his wife; Gerald of Windsor returned the compliment, choosing the daughter of Rhys ap Tewdwr (d. 1093) of Deheubarth as his wife, so that (in the revealing words of Gerald's grandson) 'he might sink his roots and those of his family more deeply in those parts'.[27] The children of such mixed marriages often bore hybrid names: Henri ap Cadwgan ap Bleddyn, Angharad daughter of Gerald of Windsor, Meilir fitz Henry, Maredudd son of Robert fitz Stephen, and so forth. Their very names proclaimed to the world some of the compromises of a frontier society.

Gerald of Wales (c.1146–1223) was the grandchild of such a mixed marriage. It is in his voluminous writings that we see most clearly the ambivalences and nuances which could characterize the attitudes of the Anglo-Normans in Wales towards the native Welsh. Gerald's ultimate loyalty lay clearly to his Anglo-Norman kinsfolk, more particularly to the Geraldines, the common descendants of Gerald of Windsor. He was proud of the part they had played in the conquest of Wales, as later in that of Ireland; and he was quite clear in his own mind that Wales was part of the realms of the king of England. He could on occasion speak with great harshness of the Welsh and castigate them mercilessly for their failings, especially their moral shortcomings. Yet he was proud of his Welsh blood; he flaunted his relationships with his Welsh kinsfolk and used them to promote his career; he genuinely admired the virtues of the Welsh and described them with great insight; he spoke with feeling of Wales as his 'country' (*patria*) and as 'our Wales'.

Gerald's ready sympathy for the Welsh was no doubt sharpened by the constant frustrations of his own career as royal servant and ecclesiastic; it was also heightened by the sensitivities of a widely travelled and infinitely curious man. But Gerald also surely reflected in some measure the attitudes, aspirations, and anxieties of his own family milieu, of the Anglo-Norman knightly circles of the Welsh March, especially of the isolated communities of south-west Wales. Here, for over a century, a distinctive society had been in the making, a society of frontiersmen habituated to war, forced to rely on their own resources, vigorously independent, and deeply distrustful of the brash ways and soft habits of courtiers and outsiders. Common dangers had bred and sustained a close military

[26] *IK*, ii, xii (*Opera*, vi, 145).   [27] *IK*, i, xii (*Opera*, vi, 91).

companionship among them and led them to cultivate and treasure their family links. Above all, living side by side with the Welsh, marrying them and even fighting them had bred in them a respect for the Welsh and generated nuances in their relationships with them which outsiders could only view with suspicion. After all, to outsiders Wales was a land of exclusive racial groups: French (Norman), English, and Welsh. To the men of the March such a confident simplification was a distortion. Wales was now their homeland; they also were Welsh 'by nation if not by descent' (*nacione Kambrensis non cognacione*);[28] many of them, Gerald himself included, were of mixed blood and proud of it. The ingredients of the making of a 'middle nation'—a group caught between, and sitting astride, the normal categorizations of race—were being assembled in parts of Norman Wales. 'Both peoples', remarked Gerald bitterly, 'regard me as a stranger'.[29] His comment tells us much about Gerald's own sensitivities and frustrations; it also heralds the appearance of an Anglo-Norman Marcher society in Wales, distinct from the societies of England and of native Wales alike.

Not only did Welsh and Anglo-Normans learn, in a measure, to live together; they also influenced each other in a variety of ways. Occasions for contact and mutual influence were many. One such occasion, according to Gerald of Wales, was attendance at court. Some such visits were formal 'diplomatic' missions; others were more obviously social. It is Gerald himself who once more provides memorable vignettes of such visits—of Rhys ap Gruffudd of Deheubarth (d. 1197) exchanging pleasantries with Norman barons at a banquet in Hereford, or Owain Cyfeiliog of Powys (d. 1197) delighting Henry II with his ready wit at dinner in Shrewsbury. The courts of Norman barons and Welsh princes in Wales must similarly have been obvious venues for contact and influence. The giving of hostages, so Gerald tells us, was another important route along which Norman influence flowed to the Welsh: Hywel, the son of Rhys ap Gruffudd, spent thirteen years as a hostage at Henry II's court and the nickname given to him on his return to Wales in 1171, 'Sais' (the Englishman), suggests how his exile had shaped his attitude and behaviour. Professional and amateur interpreters, of whom there must have been many in the multilingual frontier districts of twelfth-century Wales, also acted as intermediaries between the two cultures; and so no doubt in their different ways did those who travelled the roads of the country—as builders or merchants, soldiers or pilgrims, scholars or churchmen.

The avenues for mutual influences were many; but it is not easy to characterize the nature and extent of those influences. Gerald of Wales,

[28] *Expugnatio Hibernica*, II, vii (ed. Scott and Martin, p. 151; *Opera*, v, 321).
[29] Quoted in R. Bartlett, *Gerald of Wales 1146–1223* (Oxford, 1982), p. 17.

drawn as he was from a military family, noted two lessons in particular which the Welsh had learnt from the Normans, the use of arms and the management of horses, and to them should certainly be added a third, the construction of castles, even in stone and mortar (such as the one rebuilt at Cardigan by Rhys ap Gruffudd in 1171). The Welsh were a warlike people and particularly adept at learning military lessons; but there is no reason why Anglo-Norman influence, especially in the frontier districts of south Wales, should not also have extended to a whole range of other matters, such as diet, dress, agricultural practices and commercial activities, architectural style and literary inspiration. What it is impossible to determine is how far such influences were mediated through the Anglo-Norman settlers in Wales and how far they are manifestations of the general dominance of French culture in aristocratic, ecclesiastical, and academic circles in twelfth-century Europe, slowly, and often belatedly, percolating to Wales.

Linguistic borrowings pinpoint the problem. Several hundred words were assimilated into medieval Welsh from French or rather from Anglo-Norman. Most of them were almost certainly absorbed as secondary borrowings from middle English; others, especially technical terms, were possibly literary borrowings introduced by translators of French works into Welsh; but it is also likely that others, and some of them among the earliest words borrowed, were assimilated through contact with the Anglo-Normans in Wales itself. This latter category probably includes the handful of French loan-words in middle Welsh which has no parallel loan-forms in English, and the hundred or so loan-words which seem to have been borrowed directly into Welsh rather than as secondary loans from middle English. Most interesting of all from the point of view of cultural diffusion is the nature of the words borrowed, for they reflect the likely areas of Anglo-Norman impact on Welsh society—notably war (words such as *gleif, helmauc*), aristocratic life (*pali, barwn, ffigys*), and commerce (*bwrdais*).

The impact of Anglo-Norman culture on Welsh life is even more strongly marked in literature—not in the formal court poetry, which remained rigidly conservative in language, themes, and allusions, but in the prose tales which are the glory of twelfth-century Welsh literature. The earliest and most famous of those tales—*Culhwch and Olwen* and the so-called *Four Branches of the Mabinogi*—are firmly native in their orientation, themes, and form, their onomastic and mythological lore, and their specific geographical and genealogical references. The contrast between these early tales (which are possibly to be dated in their present form to the late eleventh/early twelfth centuries) and the later ones—notably the so-called 'Three Romances' (*Geraint, Owein, and Peredur*), which may belong to the early thirteenth century—is some measure of the impact of the meeting of Anglo-Norman and Welsh cultures. Linguistically and stylistically these later tales remain within the vernacular Welsh tradition; their heroes are still drawn from a British background; and there is little in them of the indulgent self-analysis so marked in the French romances. But they are also characterized by a much more extensive borrowing of French terminology than the earlier tales. Above all they share with the French romances the common themes of knightly adventure, chivalric love, and *courtoisie*; Arthur's court is central to them; and, in common with French romances, but in sharp contrast with earlier Welsh tales, they lack any precise geographical location or reference. Such common features need not be explained in terms of direct borrowing from the French romances of Chrétien de Troyes. Rather what they demonstrate is that native Wales now partook of some of the themes, topoi, and literary sentiments common throughout the court circles of the Anglo-Norman world. Nothing perhaps indicates this more clearly than the fact that it was probably at Llanbadarn Fawr (Ceredigion), once the centre of native learning, that the *Song of Roland* was first translated into Welsh in the early thirteenth century.

This process of cultural assimilation is to be witnessed in other spheres. In architecture, the churches of Normanized south Wales—from Llandaff, with its splendid Romanesque arch, to St Davids, rebuilt by Bishop Peter de Leia in the late twelfth century—drew heavily in design and decoration on Anglo-French exemplars and doubtless on the services of English architects and masons. Perhaps even more striking was the way in which Celtic motif and Romanesque pattern were integrated in some of the churches of native Wales in the twelfth century—in the south door at Penmon priory (Môn), the chancel arch at Aberffro (Môn) and the shrine at Pennant Melangell (Powys). Even in a conservative Welsh scriptorium, such as that of Llanbadarn Fawr (Ceredigion), the Insular scribal tradition was being eclipsed by the Anglo-Norman script, as indeed was also happening in funerary inscriptions, such as that at Llanfihangel-y-traethau (Ardudwy). Slowly but surely Wales in the twelfth century was being drawn into the orbit of Anglo-French cultural life, both through the agency of Anglo-Norman settlements in south Wales and through its own growing contacts with the international worlds of scholarship, ecclesiastical governance, and monasticism.

The cultural influences did not run in one direction only. The Normans were an infinitely adaptable race, readily assimilating the traditions and institutions of the peoples whom they conquered and harnessing them to their own ends. Such certainly was the case in Wales. They quickly took possession of those parts of the Welsh past which suited their purposes. They might use that past, as in the *Book of Llandaff*, to prop up the claims of a struggling diocese and provide it with the credentials—in saints' lives, charters, papal bulls, and relics—to survive in the rough-and-tumble of the early twelfth century. They might commission biographies of obscure Welsh saints out of curiosity, respect, and self-interest, as was done in the volume (now British Library, Vespasian A. XIV) possibly assembled at Gloucester but probably finally copied at Monmouth priory. They might collect folk-tales and anecdotes about the Welsh and incorporate them in their miscellaneous collections. Walter Map, a Herefordshire man and, therefore in his own words, 'a dweller on the marches of Wales', did just that in his *Courtiers' Trifles (De Nugis Curialium)* in the late twelfth century.[30] Above all, they might be captivated by native Welsh oral tales, embellish them and transform them to make them presentable in their own feudal aristocratic circles.

No one was more captivated than Geoffrey of Monmouth (d. 1155). Geoffrey's father may well have been a first- or second-generation Breton settler in Monmouth, an area rich in opportunities, formal and informal, for contacts between settlers and natives. (In the next generation Gilbert fitz Baderon (d. 1190), lord of Monmouth, had a library of French and Latin books and commissioned two romances from the poet Hue de Rotlande). Geoffrey spent most of his life in England, much of it in Oxford and in ecclesiastical and aristocratic circles. He wrote his *History of the Kings of Britain* (c.1136) and his *Life of Merlin* (c.1150) to please the tastes of men from such cirles and in particular to satisfy their appetite for a combination of history, mythology, prophecy, and romance. Geoffrey was a resourceful author, selecting his material from any source to hand and embellishing it with convincing detail from the ample stock of his own imagination. Welsh historical tradition, literary and oral, was certainly one of his sources. He pillaged Welsh genealogy; he selected some of his characters from the pantheon of Welsh heroes and sometimes, as with Myrddin and Medrawd, mangled their reputation in the process; he drew on native historical traditions about Arthur and his companions; and in his emphasis on the loss and renewal of sovereignty he echoes themes long familiar in Welsh tradition. Geoffrey's *History* shows scant sympathy for the Welsh; but in its plundering of Welsh tradition and in launching Arthur and his companions and their adventures onto the forefront of the European literary stage it showed how rich and fruitful might be the cultural contacts on the frontierlands of Anglo-Norman Wales.

It was one of the towns of that frontierland that principally captivated Geoffrey's imagination. It was Caerleon on Usk, 'famous for its wealth of pleasant things'[31]—the City of the Legions, home of the early martyrs, and seat of Dubricius, Primate of Britain—that Geoffrey chose as the site of Arthur's plenary court for the whole of Europe. His choice was a tribute to

---

[30] Walter Map, *De Nugis Curialium*, ii, xxiii (eds. M. R. James, C. N. L. Brooke, and R. A. B. Mynors, p. 194).

[31] Geoffrey of Monmouth, *History of the Kings of Britain*, ix, xii (ed. L. Thorpe, p. 227).

the captivating power of the Welsh frontierlands on the Norman imagination. The Welsh returned the compliment: by the end of the thirteenth century Geoffrey's *History* had been translated into Welsh several times and Welsh literary tradition was being revised in some of its details to accommodate some of the fabrications of Geoffrey's narrative. So were Welsh and Anglo-Normans learning to adjust to each other and to each other's traditions. Coexistence as well as conquest was one of the themes of these generations.

PART II

THE TRANSFORMATION OF
WELSH SOCIETY
1100–1350

INTRODUCTION

In the two and a half centuries before the Black Death of 1349 Wales underwent economic, social, and ecclesiastical changes arguably more profound and far-reaching than any it experienced prior to the Industrial Revolution and the rise of Methodism. The extent and character of those changes have tended to be underestimated for several reasons. One such reason is that the clatter of battle and conquest has so engaged the attention of the historian, as indeed it did that of contemporary annalists and chroniclers, that it diverts attention from the much less obtrusive and slow-moving changes within society. Another reason lies in the particularity of those changes. All medieval societies were localized; few more so than medieval Wales. Such hints of change as survive are, therefore, of their nature fragmentary and localized. No Domesday Book or foreign trade statistics survive, as in England, to provide the historian with some sort of 'national' foothold for his speculations. Rather is he presented with what appears to be a mosaic of disconnected fragments of evidence.

The nature of that evidence, particularly for native Wales, is another reason for the relative lack of attention that has been paid to the changes of these centuries. The twelfth and thirteenth centuries witnessed a momentous advance in the use of the written word for the ordering and recording of human activities throughout Europe. In particular, in England these centuries saw 'a shift from sacred script to practical literacy'.[1] Wales partook of such a shift only to a very limited degree. Charters and allied documents certainly survive in increasing numbers from the mid-twelfth century and accounts from the mid-thirteenth century, but overwhelmingly from the Normanized districts of south and south-east Wales. From the thirteenth century an increasing, but still minute, corpus of official correspondence and memoranda from *pura Wallia* survives; but virtually all of it emanates from Gwynedd and survives in the archives of the king of England. The remarkable dearth of record evidence for Wales, particularly native Wales, for these centuries is paralysing for the historian; it is also a dearth which calls for an explanation.

The accidents of archive survival provide one obvious explanation. The charters which have survived—such as those copied into the Haughmond Abbey cartulary, or those subsequently included in the royal confirmations

[1] M. T. Clanchy, *From Memory to Written Record. England 1066–1307* (1979), p. 263.

of the foundation deeds of Cistercian abbeys, or those which have survived in post-Conquest family muniments—may well be no more than a tithe of those originally written. There are also clear indications that financial accounts and writs, as well as charters, were being written in Gwynedd in the thirteenth century. Another reason for the dearth of documentation lies in the fact that the arm of English royal government extended to Wales only spasmodically and to a very limited degree. In the triumph of 'practical literacy' and document-mindedness the king's government was, without a doubt, the trend-setter and the pace-maker in medieval England. There is, however, another reason for the dearth of record documentation in medieval Wales. The art of writing in Wales was on the whole reserved for other purposes until the twelfth century, and in most respects until the thirteenth. Charters written in Latin and employing distinctively 'Celtic' formulae were certainly composed at various ecclesiastical centres in Wales both before and after the coming of the Normans; and the marginal entry in the eighth-century Lichfield Gospels shows that an attempt could be made to record a legal dispute in a mixture of Latin and Welsh. But writing was mainly reserved for theological and hagiographical works in Latin. The vernacular literary and legal traditions of Wales were carefully nurtured in professional 'schools'; but they were taught and transmitted orally. No literary manuscript, as opposed to an occasional fragment, in Welsh pre-dates the mid-thirteenth century. The regulation of native Welsh society's affairs was likewise dependent on the spoken word and the collective memory. In these circumstances the documents and records which are the essential grist for the social historian's mill are largely lacking; they were never composed.

Instead the historian must turn to other sources. Three in particular command his attention, and since they will be drawn upon heavily in the following chapters it is essential to mention briefly the problems they pose and the qualifications which need to be borne in mind when basing suggestions and conclusions upon them. The first of these sources is much the most approachable and lively. It consists of contemporary descriptions of, and anecdotes about, Wales and the Welsh. Far and away the most important of these are Gerald of Wales's *Itinerary through Wales* (*c*.1191) and *Description of Wales* (*c*.1194); less valuable but still important is Walter Map's *Courtiers' Trifles* (*c*.1180–93). Both men were born in Wales or, in Walter's case, on its borders; both, especially Gerald, knew Wales and the Welsh well, at least at aristocratic and church levels; both had alert sensitivities, not unduly dulled by academic categories and preoccupations; both were acute observers, particularly Gerald; and both in their different fashions had a wide range of sympathies. Both in different ways presented a rounded and convincing picture of contemporary Wales. Yet the very success of their picture is its own danger. It was a portrait drawn by worldly wise and widely travelled men anxious for literary fame; theirs is as much a work of art, particularly in Gerald's attachment to rhetorical conventions, as of observation. Their image of the Welsh is often as revealing of the values and assumptions of the Anglo-Norman ecclesiastical and aristocratic world as of the society they set out to portray. Their portrait concentrates on those qualities or habits which serve to distinguish the Welsh from their neighbours and to fit them into the contemporary intellectual model of an underdeveloped, primitive, and heroic society. It underrates the wide social and regional differences in Wales, though Gerald himself could be alert enough to some of those differences in his travels around the country. They also, by the very nature of their work, present an essentially static portrait of Welsh society and one which makes little reference to the profound changes at work within that society. Yet, in spite of these reservations, Gerald and Walter cast invaluable shafts of light on the ethos and practices of Welsh society at a crucial stage in its transformation.

Equally valuable, but very different in character, are the texts of Welsh medieval law, *cyfraith Hywel*. None of the manuscripts in which these texts survive is now thought to be earlier than the first half of the thirteenth century. It is not the lateness of the manuscript tradition (a common enough problem with Welsh literary texts) which is the major difficulty, but the still largely unresolved problems of distinguishing between archaic and recent, redundant and current, law within the texts and equally of determining how far legal collections compiled by and for antiquarian-minded jurists reflect the rules and customs which actually governed the ordering of society's affairs and relationships. Welsh medieval law-texts clearly cannot be treated in the same way as the treatises ascribed to Glanville or Bracton, let alone the abundant legal records of thirteenth-century England; they belong to entirely different genres.[2] Yet, if approached with circumspection and a clear awareness of their character, they provide an invaluable point of entry into some of the assumptions about the nature of Welsh society and about the basic concepts and attitudes, if not the precise rules, which governed it.

The final class of sources consists of the financial accounts, court rolls, and great cadastral surveys—notably the *Survey of Denbigh 1334*, the *Record of Caernarfon 1352* (which deals with the counties of Anglesey and Caernarfon), the *Extent of Chirkland 1391–3*, and the unpublished survey of Bromfield and Yale of the same date—which the English kings and lords of Wales caused to be compiled in the post-Conquest period. Their shortcomings are obvious: they are late in date; they seek to construe native society through the categories and assumptions of English formularies

---

[2] See below, pp. 133–4.

and alien clerks; their avowed purpose is to determine fiscal and other liabilities and to record decisions in court cases, not to analyse social institutions or explain social conventions; and, in their anxiety to protect the lord's financial interests, they are often intensely and misleadingly conservative. Yet for the first time they raise the curtain on the character of land tenure and obligations in native Wales and, through the court rolls, on some of the mechanics of relationships within that society. They introduce us to the world of real men and real situations. Thereby, in Maitland's phrase, they help to 'accustom our eyes to the twilight before we go into the night'.[3] It is in the light of these sources, above all, that medieval Welsh society and the changes that were transforming it have to be studied.

[3] F. W. Maitland, *Domesday Book and Beyond* (1960 edn.), p. 415.

CHAPTER 5

NATIVE WALES: THE BONDS OF SOCIETY

'THERE are three grades of men: king, noble (W. *breyr*) and villein (W. *bilain*). So declared the Welsh lawbooks with brisk confidence.[1] The categorization is, of course, grossly over-simplified. It is but one example of the passion of Welsh literary tradition for encapsulating all life and learning in snappy, mnemonic triads. Yet the triad does at least have the virtue of directing attention to the centrality of status in medieval Welsh society. Every man had his status or privilege (W. *braint*); so also did land, office, communities, vills, churches. Even the value of a dog, according to the jurists, was determined by the status of its owner. There is no need, of course, to believe that the detailed provisions and tariffs of the law-texts on status were rigidly or consistently enforced; equally, there is no doubt that a strong sense of the distinctions, privileges, and obligations of status left a deep imprint on early Welsh society and gave it a markedly hierarchical character.

Status was determined by birth and transmitted by descent. Contemporary texts defined the 'innate freeman' (W. *bonheddig cynhwynawl*) as a man of untainted noble Welsh stock on both his father's and his mother's side. Since nobility or freedom (the two words were interchangeable in Wales as in other early medieval European societies) was transmitted by descent, lineage was the key to status. Thus when Ieuan ap Sulien sang his father's praises in the late eleventh century, he could pay him no higher compliment than to emphasize that he was 'of the distinguished stock of noble . . . parents'.[2] A century later, Gerald of Wales observed shrewdly that 'the Welsh valued distinguished birth and noble descent more than anything else in the world. They would rather marry into a noble family than into a rich one'.[3] His statement identified succinctly the centrality of status and lineage among the Welsh. Wealth could not beget status; equally, the loss of wealth or of land did not alter a man's rank, since status was a matter of birth and blood, not of income. On that score the Welsh law-texts and the opinion of native juries in the fourteenth century entirely concurred.

[1] *Llyfr Blegywryd*, ed. S. J. Williams and J. E . Powell (Cardiff, 1942), p. 5.
[2] M. Lapidge, 'The Welsh Latin Poetry of Sulien's Family', *Studia Celtica* VIII–IX (1973–4), 68–106 at p. 85.
[3] *DK*, xvii (*Opera*, vi, 220).

Status was not merely, as in modern society, a matter of perceptions and social esteem. Its value and its obligations could be, and were, precisely estimated. A man's worth in the eyes of the law was relative to his status. His wergild or compensation value (W. *galanas*), his insult- or honour-price (W. *sarhad*) and the standing of his oath were all determined by his status. So also were his dues, services, and obligations—his renders in kind and in money, the various payments to be made on marriage or separation, the virginity fine (W. *amobr*) due for the sexual lapses of his wife or daughters, and his death-duty (W. *ebediw*). At law, likewise, status had practical applications: a man's sureties, it was asserted, had to be of the same rank as himself and it was but natural in a hierarchical society that the value of a man's oath was often proportionate to his status. It is in the law-texts that these status distinctions are most lovingly, and often no doubt artificially, elaborated; but there are echoes of them throughout the documentation of the period—in Lifris's attempt to promote his hero, St Cadog, by asserting that he was superior by birth to St David; in Walter Map's passing references to the insult-payments due to Welshmen according to their respective rank; and, most abundantly, in the way that status distinctions and terminology still underlie the dues and services of native Welsh society in the fourteenth century.

Status distinctions not only determined legal standing and fiscal obligations; they also shaped social behaviour, especially among the free warrior nobility of the eleventh and twelfth centuries. For them honour was the other side of the coin of status. Honourable behaviour was expressed in a code of values and strictly upheld by an etiquette of precedence and propriety. It indicated the appropriate forms of greeting and the order of precedence in hall; it instilled an obligation of largess and hospitality (one of Walter Map's most vivid stories is of how a wife's mindless breach of the code of hospitality triggered a feud between her husband's kin and that of his guest); it defined the range of kin-responsibility; it proclaimed the public mode of behaviour appropriate to a man's status. In such a society to impugn a man's honour was the most heinous offence, for it brought shame (W. *gwaradwydd*) on the man and his kin. That is why the concept of insult (W. *sarhad*) occupies such a central role in the literature and the law-texts of medieval Wales. It was not the physical injury or damage caused by an offence which mattered (for that could be readily emended according to a fixed tariff for each member of a man's body), but the slight on a man's honour and on that of his kinsfolk, on his face-value (W. *gwynebwerth*) as it is dramatically referred to in early texts. Formal public reparation, either in the form of vengeance (W. *dial*) or of compensation and reconciliation, alone could appease the injured party's sense of shame and restore his public standing and that of his kin. It is in the literature of the period, notably in *The Mabinogi*, that the ethos of this honour-centred society is most vividly captured. But that ethos was not merely a literary convention, nor was its potency altogether lost with the decline in the militarism of Welsh free society. When Gerald of Wales dwells on the reckless valour of the Welsh and on their thirst for vengeance, or when Walter Map attributes to the young Welshman the defiant claim that he would 'for honour's sake be caught in a valiant, if foolhardy, attempt at theft and die a hard death', it is echoes of this code of honour which they are recording.[4] Likewise, just as the compensation assigned in a tenth-century settlement was to be 'commensurate with a man's honour and the nobility of his kinfolk' (L. *ad condignum honorem suum et nobilitatem parentele sue*), so some four centuries later the damages awarded in Dyffryn Clwyd for maiming a free Welshman were fixed at £24 'on account of the respect due to him and his kinsfolk' (L. *ob reverenciam sui et parentele sue*).[5] The concepts of status and honour, shame and reparation proved to be remarkably resilient in medieval Wales.

Welsh law recognized various status distinctions; but far and away the most common was that between free and unfree, in the Welsh terminology between *breyr* and *bilain*, or between *uchelwr* and *mab aillt*. The distinction—echoing the Roman law tag so popular in the Middle Ages: 'All men are either free or unfree (*servi*) '—was, of course, inadequate and over-simplified. Yet it was basic. The legal standing of men, their forms of inheritance, their dues and obligations, the status of their vill were all determined by it. It was a distinction deeply embedded in the past of Welsh society and vigorously maintained in the present for reasons of exclusiveness and social conservatism. Freemen regarded themselves as superior: the Welsh term for them *uchelwyr*, appropriately translated by Gerald of Wales as *superiores viri* and by the Latin law-texts as *optimates*, proclaimed that superiority. They regarded themselves as nobles and called themselves such. It was a group of *nobiles* who had appropriated some of the bishop of St Davids lands in Ystrad Tywi in 1222; likewise, it was 'the community of the nobles of Anglesey', or Rhirid ap Carwet 'and sixty other noble free tenants' of Eifionydd and Ardudwy, who forwarded petitions to the king in the fourteenth century.[6]

By the fourteenth century such pretensions to nobility and superiority from men who were now often small peasant proprietors sounded quaint and faintly ridiculous. Two or three centuries earlier such pretensions were less out of place, for the *uchelwyr* of those days were the horse-riding

[4] Walter Map, *De Nugis Curialium*, II, xxv (ed. M. R. James, C. N. L. Brooke, and R. A. B. Mynors, pp. 198–9).
[5] *The Text of the Book of Llan Dâv*, ed. J. Gwenogvryn Evans (Oxford, 1893), p. 233; W. Davies, *The Llandaff Charters* (Aberystwyth, 1979), p. 123; Public Record Office, Court Rolls (SC 2), 215/76 m. 5 (1317).
[6] *Episc. Acts.*, I, 352 D. 454 (1222); *Cal Anc. Pets.*, p. 54, no. 1960; p. 452, no. 13360.

companions of kings and princes. Their militarism was, and remained, one of the distinguishing emblems of their freedom. Domesday Book records that the death-duty payable by the free Welshmen of Archenfield consisted of a war-horse and armour. Military service, often for six weeks as prescribed in the law-texts, remained a common and indeed irreducible feature of free tenure throughout native Wales in the thirteenth and fourteenth centuries. These were not merely the fossils of bygone days: the effigies and seals of fourteenth-century Welshmen and the plaudits of the bards show that military prowess was still regarded as the pre-eminent virtue and one which was widely current at all levels of free society. Such men, it is true, often owed obligations and services to their lord but of an honorary, rather than of a demeaning, kind: to acknowledge his superiority, attend his court, entertain him and his entourage with food and lodging, and repair the buildings of his court. A serviential nobility they might be; but a nobility nevertheless. Furthermore, they owed their territorial and judicial standing to no lord. Their land was theirs by lineage, not by gift; their status was the source of their judicial standing and their kinsfolk were the guarantors that this status would be respected. They might be bound to lords or kings by homage and fealty; but they themselves were lords of men, with under-tenants and villeins beholden to them. It was but natural that a status-group so proud of its privileges should resent any attempt to fudge the distinction between free and unfree. For Rhigyfarch, in the late eleventh century, the collapse of the whole social order seemed imminent when the noble (L. *nobilis*) like the poor man (L. *pauper*) was driven to the plough. Much the same sense of outrage at the subversion of the social hierarchy prompted the community of Gwynedd to protest at Llywelyn ap Gruffudd's alleged disregard for the distinction between free (L. *nobiles*) and unfree (L. *ignobiles*), treating the former as peasants (L. *rustici*), exacting building and carrying services from them, and introducing a third new category between the free and unfree.[7] In Ceredigion much the same charge was levelled against royal officials by Maredudd ab Owain: they compelled free nobles (L. *nobiles*) to judge and to be judged by base-born and common people (L. *ignobiles, subditi patrie*).[8] Welsh society clearly protected its status distinctions jealously.

The unfree, like the free, were a very mixed group in origin, wealth, and the degree of their dependence. Some were the descendants of slaves, others little more than dependent tenants. Some were closely supervised as part of the labour force on the lord's demesnes; on others the powers of seignorial control weighed lightly. But as a status-group they were

---

[7] Llinos B. Smith, 'The *Gravamina* of the Community of Gwynedd against Llywelyn ap Gruffudd', *BBCS* 31 (1984), 158–76 at pp. 173–5.

[8] *Registrum Epistolarum fratris Johannis Peckham*, ed. C. T. Martin (Rolls Series, 1882–5), ii, 453.

encompassed under a common umbrella of disabilities. They were men without a lineage; their status was legally dependent on that of their lord, be he a prince or a free nobleman. They could be sold or left in his will; their right to travel, dispose of their goods, contract marriage, or practise the honourable arts (defined in Welsh law as scholarship, smithcraft, and bardism) was controlled by him. Their land was not theirs; rather did it belong to the lord. Yet it was a measure of their dependence that they were tied to that land, forbidden to leave it without permission, compelled to occupy it when so instructed. In that respect they were a virtual hereditary colonate class. Their dues and obligations, especially on those bond vills such as Aberffro and Llan-faes in Anglesey, which were organized to provide labour and supplies for the prince's demesne and his courts, could be exceptionally heavy, though they were rarely characterized by the weekly labour services so common in England. Thus on the prince's manor of Abergwyngregyn in Arllechwedd, one of the favourite residences of the princes of Gwynedd in the thirteenth century, the bondmen owed renders of barley, wheat, and oats, provision for a groom and his horse, subsistence for one day in each season for 96 members of the prince's entourage, as well as labour and carrying services and other minor dues. Finally, the inferiority of the unfree in a heroic society was underlined in that their duty was not to fight but rather to prepare an encampment, just as their death-duty was appropriately an ox rather than a war-horse. They were the *laboratores*; it was the free men who were the *bellatores*.

In a rigidly and self-consciously hierarchic society, such as that of early medieval Wales, the distinction between free and bond was deliberately sustained by jealousy and privilege and reinforced by seignorial convenience and conservatism. It was at its most meaningful at the beginning of our period. It was then that the gap between free and unfree—in status, wealth, function, and social perception—was at its most acute; it was then that servile tenure, at least on demesne estates, was scarcely to be distinguished from domanial slavery. In the eleventh and twelfth centuries bondmen still seem to have accounted for a considerable proportion, if not the majority, of the population of native Wales. Their ranks were doubtless frequently augmented from the captives who were part of the stock-in-trade of the raids and forays of the period: 'they plundered the land and seized the people and carried them off with them'; 'they carried off with them to Llŷn all the men of Meirionydd and all their chattels' are typical comments from the native chronicler.[9] In a country where land was abundant but men and animals scarce, bondmen, slaves, and their goods were important assets. Wales was still notorious as a source of slaves in the twelfth century and Welsh law continued to draw a distinction between

[9] *Brut, s.a.* 1110 (p. 33), 1124.

native-born and foreign slaves. Whether they are to be classified as slaves (W. *caeth*) or bondmen (W. *taeog, bilain, mab aillt*) there can be little doubt that a dependent servile peasantry formed a major sector of the Welsh population, ruthlessly exploited by a governing warrior nobility and even physically transported by it as part (indeed in some respects the most valuable part) of its movable wealth, in the way that Gruffudd ap Cynan was reported to have moved his bondmen (W. *bileinllu*) into the mountains when his dominion was threatened with invasion. It is only for the border-districts of north-east Wales that there exist any figures to support these suppositions; there, strikingly, some seventeen per cent of the population are classified in Domesday Book as slaves or oxmen (bringing the district into line with other parts of western England where slavery still flourished), while two-thirds of the remainder of the population were villeins (L. *villani*) or bordars. In such a society the distinction between a dependent and largely servile tenantry and a free warrior nobility would be profound and profoundly significant.

Every effort was made to sustain that distinction throughout the Middle Ages. In the fourteenth century free and bond tenants were separately listed; their affairs were frequently administered by different officers; legal distinctions between them—such as separate juries and even on occasion separate courts—were carefully observed; their fiscal and tenurial obligations and services were scrupulously differentiated. Yet, from the twelfth century onwards, the distinction between free and unfree grew increasingly blurred in practice, without ever being extinguished in theory. Their growing convergence is a phenomenon which has as yet been scarcely studied or explained. As Wales gradually turned its back on a pillage economy, the free nobleman became less a warrior, more a landed proprietor. Since partibility, the division of land between male heirs, was the custom which prevailed in Wales, the share of land held by each freeman normally contracted in each generation (assuming a male replacement ratio of 2–3:1). Along that route the descent from wealth to relative poverty, from aristocracy to rural peasantry, was quickly achieved. Much the same process has been documented in detail for the county of Namur, where it has been demonstrated that the small peasant holdings of the twelfth century were the result of the regular repartitioning of the aristocratic estates of the tenth century. In Wales a single contemporary example (which we owe to the curiosity of a contemporary genealogist) illustrates the consequences vividly: the unitary estate of Iorwerth ap Cadwgan (*fl. c.*1220) had been subdivided by 1313 among 27 direct male descendants. Each one of them could claim that he was an *uchelwr*; but with the passage of each generation the disjunction between nobility of status and economic means grew ever wider. At the same time, the renders and obligations of free and unfree came increasingly to approximate to each other, even if they never became identical. Even military service with the host, hitherto the hallmark of free status, was being demanded from the bondmen of Gwynedd. In these circumstances the gap between the small free proprietor, however distinguished his lineage and noble his pretensions, and his bond neighbour, was rapidly closing. Sooner or later the status distinctions would need to be adjusted to accord with that reality.

At much the same period—and much in line with what, in the opinion of many historians, was happening in England—the condition and status of most bondmen improved markedly and the element of seignorial arbitrariness over their lives, chattels, and land was considerably curtailed. The most precarious form of bond tenure (W. *tircyfrif/tregyfrif*) was increasingly confined to the bond vills (W. *maerdrefi*) which were specifically earmarked to maintain the royal courts. It is here that, in the phrase of a later survey, one might find 'pure bondmen'.[10] Yet even the number of such demesne manors worked by bond labour declined dramatically in native Wales in the twelfth and thirteenth centuries. The process was already well afoot in parts of south Wales at an early date: by the thirteenth century bond tenure had virtually disappeared from Ceredigion. Even more far-reaching in its implications was the enfranchisement of bond holdings (of which there is excellent, albeit late, evidence from the estates of the bishop of St Asaph) and, above all, acceptance of the principle that bondmen could hold their lands by the same form of hereditary tenure—known in Welsh as *tir gwelyawg*—hitherto reserved for the lands of freemen. The consequences of this transformation, which had been effected in every part of Wales by at least the fourteenth century, were momentous: the insecurity and seignorial control, hitherto such prominent features of bond tenure, were greatly diminished, if not altogether removed; henceforth, bond and free tenures in most vills were identical in inheritance customs, if not in dues and obligations. This growing approximation of bond and free status was reflected in the hybrid terminology of the surveys: in references to 'free villeins' and in a recognition that there were tenants who were neither 'pure free' not yet 'pure unfree'.[11] In a world of such shifting and uncertain categories, the clear-cut distinctions of the law-texts and estate surveyors looked increasingly academic. Their artificiality became even more apparent as free men came to hold bond land and vice versa, as free and bond persons married, as free and bond men lived and worked together in 'mixed' vills (there were 21 such 'mixed' vills in the lordship of Denbigh out of a total of 81 vills under

---

[10] *Record of Caernarvon*, ed. H. Ellis (Record Commission, 1838), p. 83.
[11] *Record of Caernarvon*, p. 83; *Survey of the Honour of Denbigh 1334*, ed. P. Vinogradoff and F. Morgan (1914), pp. 53, 305, 312; Public Record Office, Duchy of Lancaster Ministers' Accounts (DL 29) 1/2 m. 3 (1305).

lay control), and as it was recognized that a free man might indeed be the sub-tenant of a villein. When that happened—and there is no reason to doubt that the rich evidence of the fourteenth century on such issues reflects developments which had begun much earlier—the status distinctions had indeed forfeited most of their meaning, though social conservatism and seignorial profiteering were to keep them alive until the early sixteenth century. Those distinctions had been devised and elaborated to suit the needs of a warrior nobility and its dependent tenantry; the status divisions of the future would relate more closely to the distribution of wealth and land, patronage and local influence.

Status was one of the bonds of native Welsh society; kinship was another. Contemporary observers, from at least the twelfth century, were struck by the pride of the Welsh in their descent and by their sensitivity to the ties and obligations of kinship. 'Even the common people', commented Gerald of Wales, 'know their family trees by heart and can readily recite from memory the list of their ancestors . . . back to the sixth or seventh generation'.[12] Indeed, even in everyday life the Welsh patronymic form might require a man to trace his ancestry to his great-grandfather as a means of self-identity (Llywelyn ap Hywel Fychan ap Hywel ab Einion Sais, for example). Genealogical collections, originally confined to royal dynasties and saints (for saints likewise had to be of good birth), survive from the late eleventh century; by the later Middle Ages they had expanded into massive treatises claiming to trace the ancestry of all free men of note. The poets were the genealogists *par excellence*; they increasingly loaded, and indeed overloaded, their poetry with genealogical compliments and allusions. The native chroniclers likewise betray a delight in unravelling family relationships: 'Cadwgan ap Bleddyn and Gwladus daughter to Rhiwallon, who was the mother of Nest (wife of Gerald of Windsor), were first cousins; for Bleddyn and Rhiwallon were brothers, sons of Angharad, daughter of King Maredudd', comments the *Brut* in one of its typical genealogical parentheses.[13] The native prose tales show the same scrupulous attention to kin-relationships and the obligations that arise from them: thus in the Welsh version of the Tristan legend, March is at pains to emphasize that since he is more closely related to Arthur than Tristan is (he was a cousin, Tristan only a first cousin once removed), then Arthur was obliged to avenge the insult that March had suffered at Tristan's hand. And so the examples could be multiplied. Welsh society, especially Welsh free society, ordered its vision of the past and arranged its relationships and obligations in the present very considerably in terms of lineage and kinship.

[12] *DK*, i, xvii (*Opera*, vi, 200).   [13] *Brut*, s.a. 1109 (p. 28).

How, then, did the Welsh trace their lineage and what was the circle of effective kin-relationships which they recognized? Kinship ties may be traced downwards through time from an ancestor who is regarded as the founder—whether historical or eponymous—of the lineage. His descendants form, in anthropological terms, a descent-group; their kinship is ultimately based on their claim to be lineally descended from him. Alternatively or additionally, kinship may be traced backwards from the individual, identifying thereby his kindred, his relatives by blood, over a given number of generations. The two methods are complementary, but their point of reference is diametrically different: the descent-group derives its focus from the past and from an ancestor; the kindred from the present and from a living individual. Welsh medieval society used both methods of the computation of kinship in the ordering of its affairs.

The Welsh descent-group (W. *cenedl*, L. *progenies*) was agnatically constituted. It was composed, in other words, of all the men who traced their descent in the male line from a common ancestor—the descent-group of Hwfa ap Cynddelw or Marchweithan, the heirs of Llywarch ap Bleddyn, the *llwyth* (tribe) of Marchudd, to cite a few examples from contemporary record sources. For contemporaries the historicity of the ancestor and the accuracy of the descent traced from him were not vexed issues. The validity of a genealogy in such a society rests on its social acceptability and usefulness, not on its historicity and chronological accuracy. Within a few generations of its founder's lifetime, the descent-group would normally be composed of scores, if not hundreds, of his descendants. It was in terms of the descent-group, as we shall see, that title to land was eventually asserted in native Welsh society; but in other respects the descent-group rarely operated as an organic unit. Welsh medieval society was not a tribal society. The descent-group was too large, too segmented, too diffuse, and too geographically dispersed to act as an effective unit of kin-obligations. That role was fulfilled by the kindred (L. *parentela*). For most purposes, the kindred of a medieval Welshmen consisted of his male relatives who shared their descent in the male line with him from a common great-grandfather. It extended, therefore, laterally as far as his agnatic second cousins male.

In medieval Wales many of the functions which in modern societies fall upon the state or local government were the prerogative and responsibility of the kin-group. The kindred, for example, protected the individual's rights and status and stood surety for his behaviour. Walter Map recounts the story of a young man's kindred—*cognacio* was the term he used—going bail for him when he was unjustly accused of an offence against the king. This aspect of kin-responsbility for crime and public order was exploited to the full by the English in the pacification and governance of Wales. Quoting native law as their authority, they detained kinsmen as warrantors for the good behaviour of their relatives or as a means of compelling escaped suspects to answer for their offences. Other legal responsibilities also fell on kinsmen: thus, according to Welsh law, in a dispute between a debtor and his surety, the former's word should be upheld by the sworn oaths of six relatives, four from his father's kin and two from his mother's kin, and much the same rule applied likewise in cases of contract. Nor were these clauses mere legal casuistry: in Dyffryn Clwyd, in the fifteenth century, a man's defence to a charge of theft collapsed when his brother and another relative 'in the second degree' failed to support him in his compurgation (W. *rhaith*) as specified by Welsh law.[14]

It was in the event of homicide that kin-responsibility came fully and triumphantly into its own. It was the moral duty of the slain man's kinsfolk to avenge his death and to remove the dishonour it had caused them; the slayer's kinsfolk as well as the slayer himself were regarded as a fair target for their wrath and vengeance. That was the force of the plea of the fourteenth-century poet, Iorwerth ap Cyriog, that God the Father would not be moved to avenge the death of His Son on mankind. Homicide triggered a blood-feud. The relatives of the slain man, according to the Domesday report on the customs of Archenfield, assembled and proceeded to plunder the slayer and his kin (as was indeed provided by Welsh law) and to burn their houses. Blood had been replaced by pillage; increasingly both were replaced by money-compensation, referred to (as was feud itself) by the Welsh term *galanas*. The size of the compensation was determined by the status of the man slain. It was collected from the slayer and from his paternal and maternal kinsfolk up to the fifth cousin. Paternal kin were expected to contribute twice as much as maternal kin and the size of the individual kinsman's contribution was proportionate to his degree of relationship to the slayer (the third cousin paying half as much as the second cousin, for example). Similar rules governed the distribution of *galanas* to the slain man's kinsfolk. There is no need to believe that *galanas* was operated with the mathematical precision and actuarial comprehensiveness stipulated by the Welsh law-texts (themselves possibly influenced by Anglo-Saxon practice). Distant kinsmen, especially on the slayer's side, no doubt shirked their responsibility, while force of circumstances and powerful lordship increasingly brought more of the responsibility to bear on the slayer himself. Nevertheless, ample evidence from very different parts of Wales shows that the basic principles of *galanas*—notably the centrality of the kin's responsibility—were still understood and observed, in however attenuated a fashion, until the end of the Middle Ages. When the poet bemoaned his unrequited love and warned his lady to beware of having to pay his *galanas*—'ymgêl, wen, o'm galanas'—for causing his

---

[14] Public Record Office Court Rolls (SC 2), 222/5 m. 15 v.

death through love-sickness, his reference would have been well understood by his audience.[15]

Kinsmen had obligations of a social as well as of a legal kind; and it is these which are the most elusive as they are the most important. They were called upon to appoint a guardian for a minor of their blood; they sorted out family squabbles—or tried to. Their role in marriage arrangements could be very considerable. In the native tale *Culhwch and Olwen*, Olwen had to discuss her marriage with her four great-grandfathers and four great-grandmothers! Native law recognized that a marriage by kin-investiture (W. *o rodd cenedl*) was superior to any other form of union, for it involved the formal transfer of the woman for most (though not all) purposes out of the orbit of the responsibility of her parental kindred into that of her husband. Her close kinsfolk were indeed required to stand warranty for her virginity on being so transferred. Doubtless other aspects of social life and relations—such as festivities, funeral arrangements, credit—were governed, informally and often loosely, by the conventions of kin-consultation and a measure of joint responsibility.

In one crucial area—the inheritance and transmission of land—the centrality of kin-title and the degree of kin-control were beyond doubt. Title to land, or at least to 'hereditary' or 'old land', as it was sometimes called, depended in every part of native Wales on membership of a descent-group, normally, though not invariably, referred to in late medieval surveys by the Welsh terms *gwely* (L. *lectus*, E. bed) or *gafael* (L. *gavella*, E. holding). Thus, to take a single example from the great *Survey of the Honour of Denbigh* of 1334, Gruffudd Fychan ap Gruffudd ap Dafydd was a member of the *gwely* or descent-group of Rhys ab Edrud ap Marchudd (the ancestor-founder of the *gwely*); this entitled him to a share in the *gwely's* lands and appurtenances in Abergele and other vills in the district. Lineage was the key to land. The whole terminology of land title underscored this point: it was by an action of 'kin and descent' (W. *ach ac edryf*) that title to land was claimed; such land was known as the paternal inheritance (W. *treftadaeth*); it was only after a family had occupied the same land by unbroken descent over four generations that it could claim to be the true proprietors (W. *priodorion*, L. *proprietarii*) of that land. It is one of the paradoxes of early medieval society in Wales that it combined intense political instability and volatility with an apparently profound respect for unbroken title and lineal descent to property.

The individual proprietor had no absolute rights in the land. He held it, as it were, on trust as a member of the descent-group. Accordingly, he could not alienate the land, except on a short-term lease; he could not devise it by will; he could in no way defeat or undo the claims of the

[15] *Oxford Book of Welsh Verse*, p. 107 translated in *Dafydd ap Gwilym. Fifty Poems*, ed. H. I. and D. Bell (1942), pp. 221–5.

rightful heirs in the land. Law and custom laid down clearly who those rightful heirs were and on this issue the post-Conquest evidence makes it clear that the provisions of the law-texts were carefully followed in practice. If the proprietor left direct male heirs of his body (sons, grandsons), the land—or rather his right in it and its appurtenances, including meadow, pasture, mills, and even churches—was to be divided equally between them, according to the custom of partibility. If he left no such heirs, his kindred—his male relatives through the male line as far as second cousins—succeeded to his land, again by the custom of partibility. For example, when Maredudd ap Madog ap Llywelyn of Dyffryn Clwyd died without a male heir of his body in 1332 he was succeeded by two second cousins, his closest surviving relatives. Any male relative more distantly agnatically related would not have been a member of the kindred and would thereby be excluded from a claim to the land. It was important for a man to know who were the members of his kindred: they were his co-parceners (W. *cyd-etifeddion*); they were the men who were required to testify on his behalf if his title to land were challenged and to share inheritance-dues and obligations with him; their consent was necessary if he wanted to deforest or assart (i.e., to reclaim from the waste) part of his holding or to alienate any of his land, whether out of piety or out of necessity (that is why monasteries in Wales tried to secure quitclaims from co-parceners when gifts were made to them).

The customs governing the title to and the division and descent of land entrenched the power of lineage and kindred firmly over the most important source of wealth and power in a rural society. Those customs have the appearance of great antiquity; but there is reason to believe that it was only during the twelfth century—a crucial century in the development of Welsh society—that they were fully articulated. It was during this period, or rather earlier, that the lineage system, inheritance practices, and customary laws of much of northern Europe were being defined. Wales followed suit, albeit belatedly. Most of the ancestor-founders from whom the Welsh descent-groups take their names appear to belong to the period c.1150–c1220; and it is significant that, whereas the *gwely* figures but marginally in the earliest law-texts, it dominates the tenurial descriptions in the fourteenth-century surveys. The transformation that was taking place springs, in Wales as in Europe, no doubt from a myriad reasons woven into the very texture of the period. As social conditions became less unstable, as a warrior aristocracy turned increasingly to the exploitation of land, as dues and exactions became more regularized, as the demands of kingship and lordship became more insistent, as jurists began to commit customs to writing and thereby to define them, the fluid and variable practices of earlier days were systematized. This is not to suggest that the inheritance customs and conventions so fully in evidence by the fourteenth century emerged *ex nihilo* in the twelfth century; but that it was in that period that an earlier, more fluid system of kinship conventions acquired, especially with regard to the title and succession to land, the form and definitiveness which it was to retain for the rest of the Middle Ages.

Kinship and lineage were certainly powerful elements in native Welsh society; yet it is easy to overrate the ambit and significance of kinship bonds. The lineage was important for the establishment of title to land and its appurtenances; the kindred, in its various forms (and therein lay part of its weakness), certainly occupied a role in a host of social and legal activities which in England had largely fallen within the ambit of the individual's responsibility and of royal or seignorial jurisdiction. But kinsmen did not live in exclusive territorial groups; their interests constantly overlapped with those of neighbours drawn from different lineages and were compromised by cognatic links (that is, ties through the male or female line) and by the well-recognized obligations towards foster-brothers. The ties and obligations of kinship were, therefore, never exclusive. They were supplemented, and indeed often supplanted, by those of locality and lordship. Already by the thirteenth century the role of the kin was being openly challenged: Dafydd ap Llywelyn, prince of Gwynedd (d. 1246), was reported to have abolished the practice of *galanas* in his principality, while even earlier the men of Ceri had petitioned for the ending of kin-responsibility in cases of homicide. Likewise, when the men of Welsh Gower requested that 'the law of twelve and of inquest' be introduced, they were driving another nail into the coffin of kin-responsibility.

Above all, it was the nuclear family, not the kin-group, which was the operative unit for most purposes in medieval Welsh society, at least within the period of the historical evidence. The individual proprietor shared pasture and meadowland with his co-parceners; he occasionally held some of his arable in common with them. But there is no evidence that they shared the same roof with him or lived as an extended family. Rather it was the nuclear family—husband, wife, children, (occasionally) aged parents, and, in the case of wealthier families, servants—which formed the normal unit of residence, production, and consumption in medieval Wales as elsewhere in north-west Europe.

The family was formed by marriage. The Welsh had a very poor reputation amongst medieval churchmen, such as Archbishop Theobald (d. 1161), Gerald of Wales, and Archbishop Pecham (d. 1292) for their marital practices. They were persistently accused of taking a cavalier attitude towards the bonds of matrimony, choosing partners within the prohibited degrees, keeping mistresses, divorcing their wives, and treating legitimate and illegitimate children as equals. Such accusations reveal more of the standards which churchmen wished to impose on lay society than of the practices of society itself. Welsh society, in common with other customary societies in medieval Europe, regarded marriage as a contract, not as a sacrament. The contract could be terminated with the agreement of both parties and a new contract concluded with another partner. It is, therefore, not surprising that divorce was regarded with equanimity and that Welsh medieval law and marriage-contracts sought to anticipate the problems raised by it. For the same reason, Welsh custom refused to share the church's view, let alone that of English common law, on illegitimacy. Since marriage was a conditional contract, a man might legitimately father children by several partners. Even if his liaisons were extramarital, Welsh law decreed that he could formally adopt the resulting offspring into his lineage, thereby legitimizing them for purposes of inheritance; and this practice, under the name of *cynnwys*, was to survive in parts of Wales until the end of the Middle Ages. Such practices, however, did not mean that the Welsh attitude to marriage was in any way cavalier. On the contrary, it was the solemn duty of the girl's kinsfolk to guard her virginity until she was given in marriage; it would be no small public shame for them, as well as for her, if they were found to have failed in their duty. Math's greeting to his intended bride in the *Mabinogi* was crisply to the point: 'Hail, maiden. Art thou a virgin?'[16] Likewise, within marriage, the highest standard of propriety was demanded from both parties; even to kiss another man was a serious offence which must be amended by the payment of an insult-fine (W. *sarhad*) to the husband.

Within marriage the husband's position was clearly pre-eminent. In an agnatic society, he alone could normally (at least in much of north Wales) hold land, and it was through him that land was transmitted. His wife's legal position was ambivalent, for though for most purposes she was dependent on her husband she still retained formal links with her own family. She had no right to buy or to sell without her husband's permission; she had no status as a surety for, or a witness against, a man. In an agnatic society her prime role was that of a begetter of children: she is sometimes referred to bluntly as *procreatrix* or, as in the *Brut's* description of Maud Braose, as 'the mother of the sons of Gruffudd ap Rhys'.[17] Yet, women's position in Welsh medieval society was not necessarily as inferior or submissive as the legal texts suggest. On the contrary, they often acted on their own initiative—founding churches, as did Gwleder the mother of Hoedlyw at Llanfihangel-y-traethau (Ardudwy), commissioning translations of devotional works into Welsh as did Efa ferch Maredudd in fourteenth-century Ceredigion, and even leading armies into battle, as did the Amazonian Gwenllian, wife of Gruffydd ap Rhys of Deheubarth, in 1136. Through marriage-alliances women played a prominent part in binding

[16] *Pedeir Keinc y Mainogi*, p. 77 (*Mabinogion*, p. 63).
[17] *Brut*, s.a. 1210 (p. 84).

families together, thereby alleviating some of the tensions of a heroic society and of its agnatic kin-groups. The measure of affection and fierce loyalty which such marriages could come to command was occasionally demonstrated vividly in life, as in Owain Gwynedd's refusal to put away his second wife, Cristin, in spite of the blandishments and threats of the church. But it is in literature that the range of affective relationships between men and women in medieval Wales is most vividly displayed—in the centrality of the figure and plight of Branwen in the First Branch of the *Mabinogi*; the utter intoxication of Hywel ab Owain Gwynedd's love for his 'dainty white darling, so gentle her tread . . . so perfect in seemliness'; or the portrait of domestic contentment painted by Iolo Goch in his effusive tribute to Owain Glyn Dŵr's wife, to give a few examples. It is in the literature also that we see that the judicial inferiority of women could easily be lost sight of in the shadow of their personal masterfulness—whether in the shrewish incivilities of the old crone in the *Dream of Rhonabwy* or in the devastating riposte of Rhiannon to her would-be suitor, Pwyll, in the *Mabinogi*: 'Never did man make worse use of his wits than thou has done'.[18]

Kinsfolk were often distant (in every sense); neighbours were close at hand. Accordingly, the bonds of locality were often more immediate and effective than the ties of kinship. The local unit with which the individual identified himself varied with circumstances and social standing. For some, especially for wealthier freemen in pursuit of military glory and political power, the region or *cantref* was the focus of their loyalty: thus the men of Llŷn or Meirionydd or Arwystli appear as identifiable community groups in the sources. But for workaday purposes, the unit of neighbourliness was much smaller, generally the vill (W. *tref*, pl. *trefi*) or a group of vills. Though the *tref* was of ancient origin (it appears in some of the oldest Welsh memoranda) it is in the twelfth century that it comes fully into its own. It was then that it was often assigned fixed geographical boundaries and was increasingly employed by kings and lords for the collection of renders and for the imposition of the powers of governance and justice they were beginning to assume. At much the same time, the parishes of Wales were being demarcated and their boundaries in general followed those of one or more vills (taking in, where appropriate, detached areas).

But though the vill—which might vary in area from a few hundred to several thousand acres—was employed as a unit of royal or seignorial governance and finance, its origins and character were essentially communal. Basically it was a unit of human settlement, a collection of homesteads, either nucleated or, more commonly, dispersed. There were

---

[18] *Oxford Book of Welsh Verse*, p. 28; *Pedeir Keinc y Mabinogi*, p. 14 (*Mabinogion*, p. 13).

some 209 vills on the island of Anglesey,[19] and a hundred or so in the five
commotes of the lordship of Denbigh. It was within the framework of the
vill that the community organized many of those reciprocal obligations of a
practical kind which were essential to sustain and protect life in an
economically underdeveloped and insecure society. The vill frequently had
its own internal organization, though we catch no more than rare glimpses
of it in the seignorial records. It exercised firm control over communal
pastureland, waste and meadow; it appointed its own community shepherd
(the *bugail trefgordd* of the law-texts corresponding to the *clustor ville* of
the records); it determined the seasonal chronology of the communal
agriculture of the vill. Thus, Iorwerth Gethin of Ardudwy was amerced in
1326 'at the suit of the vill of Llanaber because he kept his animals in the
common pasture of the *hendref* (the winter settlement) after the
community of the vill had betaken itself and its animals to the mountains'.[20]
Co-operation was essential for arable agriculture, for rarely had the Welsh
peasant, free or unfree, the means to maintain a plough-team, normally of
eight oxen, from his own resources. Neighbourliness and necessity were
close allies in the vill. The Welsh law-texts from the thirteenth century
devote increased space to a short treatise on co-aration (W. *cyfar*) and lay
down precise rules governing the joint ploughing arrangements between
neighbours, specifying the technical equipment required and the responsibilities and rights of each participant and even giving practical advice—such as
the injunction to the driver (W. *geilwad*) not to overtax the oxen, 'so that
they break their hearts'.[21] The quilleted patchwork nature of open fields
throughout Wales shows the practical significance of these provisions.

Neighbours co-operated in a whole host of other ways. Dues and
obligations in Wales were often communal in character—such as the
biennial subsidy of forty cows which was the sole payment due from the
free Welsh community of Builth. The responsiblity for the distribution and
collection of such renders lay on the community itself, and very
occasionally we catch a glimpse of the process (of three vills meeting at
Llangynhafal church (Dyffryn Clwyd) to allocate a Welsh tribute in 1362,
for example). Such a largely self-governing community readily undertook
other tasks—acting as a corporation to lease land, prosecuting recalcitrant
or defaulting members of the community, even deposing one of its
members from what was portentously called the *collegia communitatis*
when he contracted leprosy. It was a community of sociability as well as of
survival—pooling its resources for the repair of the parish church, as at

---

[19] It is fair to add that Gerald of Wales claims that there were 363 vills in Anglesey: *IK*, II,
vii (*Opera*, vi, 127).
[20] E. A. Lewis, 'The proceedings of the small hundred court of the commote of Ardudwy',
BBCS 4 (1927–9), 153–66 at p. 162.
[21] *Llyfr Iorwerth*, ed. A. R. Wiliam (Cardiff, 1960), p. 97 §150.

Gyffylliog (Dyffryn Clwyd) in 1326; organizing its own poverty-relief, as in Clun in 1326 when the community petitioned for the right to distribute sheaves to neighbours, thereby upholding the reputation of the Welsh for not allowing anyone to go destitute; and doubtless also sponsoring its own entertainment, such as the games of *cnapan* or the open-air assemblies (W. *cymanfaoedd, dadleuoedd*) where genealogies and prophecies were recited, local disputes ironed or fought out, and crythors and harpists, 'rhymers and wasters' (in the phrase of a later statute of 1402, 4 Henry IV c. 27) paraded their talents. There were, of course, tensions, cross-currents and inequalities in abundance within these local communities; yet the neighbourhood remained the necessary framework for economic co-operation and social relations for most men in medieval Wales.

It was within this framework also that the machinery and processes for maintaining 'law and order' operated in Welsh society. Kings, princes, and lords would increasingly intrude their authority into this area, for reasons of power and profit; but law and justice in Wales retained much of the flavour and character of their communal origin until the end of the Middle Ages. It was the authority and status of neighbours, periodically supplemented by seignorial intervention and threat, which were the major guarantees of social peace and order. Thus the native law of suretyship (W. *mechnïaeth* and *gorfodogaeth*) relied on the willingness and ability of neighbours to ensure that obligations would be fulfilled and debts honoured. In a largely pre-literate society, contracts were likewise guaranteed not by written, professionally drafted instruments but by the presence of credible witnesses (W. *amodwyr*, L. *convenciatores*). So well-entrenched was the practice that Edward I conceded in the Statute of Wales (1284) that disputes concerning movable chattels should continue to be determined as heretofore 'by those who saw and heard'. Even at the end of the fourteenth century a seignorial ordinance in north-east Wales still sanctioned the role and testimony of 'witnesses called in Welsh *amodwyr*'.[22] If a man were required to prove or to deny an accusation, it was again to the support of his neighbours (or kinsmen) that he looked in the process of compurgation (W. *rhaith*). Their function as compurgators was to swear to the credibility and good standing of his character in the neighbourhood rather than to the truthfulness of a particular charge. 'He who shall have set a house on fire and been accused thereof defends himself by forty men', according to the customs of the Welshmen of Archenfield as recorded in Domesday Book;[23] the practice clearly persisted, for two centuries later

[22] British Museum Additional Manuscripts 10,013 (Survey of Bromfield and Yale *c.*1393), f. 7v. Cf. The statement made in 1277 that 'pleas of feoffment and pleas of quitclaim are held in Wales without a charter or writing': *The Welsh Assize Roll 1277–84*, ed. J. Conway Davies (Cardiff, 1940), p. 245.
[23] *Domesday Book*, f. 179 a.

the men of Caerwedros (Cards.) were to claim that accusations of homicide, theft, or the harbouring of thieves should be purged by the oaths of six men. In both curial and extracurial cases oath-swearing was crucial. Occasionally, the oaths of as many as two to three hundred men might be involved, as is witnessed by a case from Cardiganshire in the 1430s. It was in effect a character reference supplied by the local community. The testimony of neighbours was equally important in land pleas. The plea was to be heard on the land itself and the whole searchlight of local knowledge was brought to bear on it: local elders (W. *ceidwaid*) swore to the plaintiff's ancestral claim to the land, while it was from among his near neighbours that the witnesses (W. *gwybyddiaid*) to his improper eviction were selected. All in all, the oaths and public witness of neighbours were fundamental to the processes of dispute settlement in native Welsh society.

Judgement itself more often than not likewise rested in the hands of local men, whether it was a medial judgement, indicating the issues to be proved and the method of proof, or a definitive judgement. Courts in early medieval Wales, as elsewhere in much of Europe, were probably occasional and very informal local assemblies. In the settling of disputes and in the formulation of custom, special respect was paid to law-worthy men in the community. The eminence of some of them derived from their seniority in age (W. *henuriaid y wlad*), while others served in respect of the land they held (W. *brawdwyr o fraint tir*). In either case it was their experience, their standing in the local community, and their knowledge of custom which were their prime qualifications. They were the judges; the royal official or representative, if there were such, was no more than the president of the assembly. Judgement often took the form of arbitration; it is only our modern categories which distinguish between the two acts. The purposes of the judgement were to settle the dispute in accordance with custom, but to do so in a way which ensured social harmony wherever possible. In the record of the earliest Welsh dispute extant, the anxiety of the 'good men' was to 'make peace . . . in order that there might not be hatred between the parties'.[24] Their ears were finely tuned to the precariousness of social peace and to the ease with which dispute could escalate to discord and so to violence and feud. Their example was followed across the centuries. Thus it was to the 'judgement of good men who knew the laws of that land' that a dispute at Llandinam (Arwystli)—the only dispute from pre-Conquest native Wales of which we have a full

---

[24] D. Jenkins and Morfydd E. Owen, 'The Welsh Marginalia in the Lichfield Gospels. Part I', *Cambridge Medieval Celtic Studies*, 5 (1983), 37–66 at p. 51. Likewise in the earliest twelfth century poem Cuhelyn Fardd was praised as 'the acme of reconciliation' ('cerennydd nod') and 'the upholder of custom' ('rhychwedis deddf'): R. G. Gruffydd, 'A Poem in praise of Cuhelyn Fardd from the Black Book of Carmarthen', *Studia Celtica*, x–xi (1975–6), 198–209 at p. 204.

record—was referred in the early thirteenth century;[25] it was to the judgement of five law-worthy men that the quarrel between the convent of Enlli (Bardsey) and the secular canons of Aberdaron (Llŷn) was referred in 1252. So deeply ingrained was the habit of local arbitration in Welsh society that Edward I generously conceded in 1284 that in cases concerning land 'the truth may be tried by good and lawful men of the neighbourhood, chosen by consent of the parties'.[26] It was a concession that was eagerly seized upon, for it is clear that most land pleas in native Wales were settled by extracurial arbitration until the end of the Middle Ages. Indeed, so powerful was the belief in community settlements that even cases of homicide were occasionally settled by extracurial arbitration and kin-compensation, in spite of Edward I's stern prohibition on such practices in criminal matters. Medieval Welsh society was to a considerable degree a collection of self-regulating and self-disciplining local communities overlain by a veneer of royal and seignorial authority.

It was also a society governed by customary law. Societies which are politically fragmented and politically fragile, and in which the framework of government is weak, are frequently deeply respectful of law. It is the cement of society, the bulwark against social chaos. 'He who will not give right (or law) has no place in a country', as an ancient Welsh aphorism has it.[27] It is some measure of the respect in which law, or at least law-texts, were held in Wales that some forty collections of Welsh medieval law (six of them in Latin, the remainder in Welsh) survive for the medieval period—far more than for any comparable literary text. None of the manuscripts in which these collections survive is older than the first half of the thirteenth century. They are composed of loose collections of short treatises (or tractates as they are called) on such topics as suretyship, land-suits or the status of women; and it may well be that these tractates were not assembled into a single book in their present form until the twelfth century. In this respect they would be no different from the customary laws of many other parts of Europe, which were likewise first committed to writing in much the same period. Yet it is clear that the Welsh law-texts drew on a very long tradition of legal rules and concepts and on a sophisticated and well-developed legal terminology. The law which they contain is essentially a customary law, a *Volksrecht*. It was not issued by or under the authority of a king, even though the tenth-century king, Hywel Dda (The Good), was claimed to have initiated its codification and even though royal power and royal privilege figure prominently in the surviving

[25] National Library of Wales Wynnstay Collection, no. 34 translated in J. Conway Davies, 'Strata Marcella Documents' *Montgomeryshire Coll.* 51 (1949–50), 164–87 at pp. 182–3. For comment see D. Stephenson, *Thirteenth-Century Welsh Law Courts* (Aberystwyth, 1980), pp. 10–14.

[26] 12 Edward I, c. 14; *The Statutes of Wales*, ed. I. Bowen (1908), p. 26.

[27] *Llyfr Colan*, ed. D. Jenkins (Cardiff, 1963), §553.

texts. Rather was it composed of a selection of the customs for the regulation of society's affairs which long usage had sanctioned and which native Welsh jurists had refined. It is these jurists above all who assembled the law-texts as we have them. Some of them, such as Cynyr ap Cadwgan and his descendants in western Powys, belonged to hereditary families of jurists; others, such as Iorwerth ap Madog (also drawn from a dynasty of jurists), are credited with important innovations in the organization and updating of material in the law-texts. Welsh law, in this respect, was not dissimilar to the native poetic tradition: it was carefully cultivated by a small, traditionally trained and formally sanctioned coterie of quasi-professional learned men. As such the texts they assembled have the status of semi-antiquarian, semi-practical collections of legal lore, probably assembled for reference by jurists and for the training of a future generation of jurists. It was they above all who were responsible for ensuring that, in spite of considerable regional difference in legal usage, the general substantive principles and procedures of Welsh law seem to have prevailed throughout much of native Wales. That is why Wales, in spite of its geographical and political fragmentation, enjoyed a very considerable measure of legal (as indeed of linguistic and literary) uniformity.

The jurists codified and transmitted native law; but, unlike their Irish counterparts, they did not allow that law to become a sacred, unchanging, and obsolete canon. For all its archaism, Welsh law remained a dynamic and flexible customary law, responding (albeit slowly) to social changes and to legal ideas. Thus it developed distinctions between homicides according to the intention of the accused; it classified theft into different categories; its land law grew increasingly sophisticated, especially on questions of short-term leases, guardianship, and seisin; its sections on pleading (W. *cynghawsedd*) and case-law (W. *damweiniau*) became more elaborate; while its law of contract took increasing cognizance of the growing use of credit and exchange in society. It also remained in essence what it had always been, the customary law of a community. Welsh law-texts themselves recognized that an agreement (W. *amod*) or an equitable custom (W. *defod gyfiawn*) was superior to law: that indeed was the hallmark of a custom-based society. The community itself was ultimately the keeper of the law: it was the local suitors (L. *sectatores*) of the court who declared or 'found' the law, especially in north-east Wales; it was local landholders who were required to act as judges (W. *brawdwyr llys*) in south-west Wales; even the role of the Welsh judge–jurist (W. *ynad*), who continued to operate in parts of north Wales until the end of the Middle Ages, was that of a respected wise man, bringing his legal learning to bear on an issue at the request of the parties involved in it. Law-keeping in native Wales remained largely local, arbitrative, oral, and customary in character; its function above all was to enable society itself to maintain a modicum of order and concord, to repair distrust between neighbours and kin-groups and to impose the normative consensus as to proper behaviour within society.

But here, as elsewhere, significant changes seem to have been afoot in the twelfth and thirteenth centuries. Kingship and lordship began to occupy a more prominent and coercive role in the making of law and in the dispensing of justice. 'As to the correction of the laws', said one witness before Edward I's commission of inquiry into Welsh law in 1281, 'the king may reform them to make them better at the instance of the country and by their consent'.[28] Royal legislation as well as community custom was now a source of law. Princely authority intruded itself into law-keeping, staking a claim for itself in matters of crime, insisting on the payment of amercements for offences, claiming that all title to land depended ultimately on seignorial investiture or on a decision by a court, and increasingly favouring the use of the sworn inquest (as is evident from the answers to the 1281 commissioners). It was increasingly—or so the scanty evidence suggests—at courts constituted by and presided over by the prince, his representative, or his officer, that judgements were given. By the thirteenth century a network of such courts, with more or less defined powers and areas of jurisdiction, was beginning to take shape in native Wales. The ties of locality were being woven into the texture of princely authority.[29]

The bonds of status, kinship, and locality were horizontal ties; they bound like with like. They were supplemented and often overridden by the vertical ties of dependence. Clientship and dependence were basic features of early Welsh, as of early Irish, society. It was in the language of personal dependence and submission that social relationships of all kinds were expressed—of wife on husband, child on father, villein or slave on his master, free man on his lord, subject on his king, man on God. Dependence was the most elastic and flexible of concepts: it ranged from formal submission, expressed in symbolic public ceremonies, to the most informal dependence; its constraints and obligations likewise ranged from the exacting and the demeaning to the honorary and nominal.

One form of dependence was that of a people on its king or lord. It was a dependence which was sometimes formally inaugurated and acknowledged by the ceremony of commendation or homage. After his first victory over his enemies in north Wales Gruffudd ap Cynan was encouraged 'to take homage (*gwrogaeth*) from the peoples (*gwerin*) . . . and to go on circuit

---

[28] 'Calendar of Welsh Rolls' in *Calendar of Chancery Rolls Various 1277–1326*, p. 200.
[29] See below pp. 260–1.

around his patrimony'.[30] In much the same fashion just over two centuries later in 1284, when the new English lord of Bromfield and Yale was introduced to his lordship, twenty-nine of the leading men of the district did homage to him individually while the rest of the tenants performed a communal act of homage 'with hands raised and joined unanimously';[31] likewise in Brecon in 1302 a royal commissioner on behalf of the king received the fealty of two thousand Welshmen through an interpreter.

Individuals as well as communities entered formally into a relationship of dependence and that at all levels of society. Welsh law required that the son of every free nobleman should leave 'his father's platter' at the age of fourteen and go to the king to pay his homage. At the level of aristocratic society such an act of dependence was not necessarily regarded as demeaning. It inaugurated an honourable and reciprocal relationship between lord and man: the dependant pledged his loyalty and service to his lord; in return he expected protection (W. *nawdd*), patronage, maintenance, and, normally, some form of gift (W. *cyfarws*) from his lord. In a hierarchic society, where protection and patronage were essential and essentially personal, such a relationship might be regarded as redounding to the honour of both lord and dependant. Furthermore, in a society of hostility and vengeance, formal friendship was a treasured gift. 'The best friendship (*cymdeithas*) that I can show shall be thine, if thou wilt have it', says Pryderi to Manawydan in the Third Branch of *Mabinogi*.[32]

Yet for the majority of the population, ties of dependence were neither voluntary nor honourable. They arose basically out of the inequality in the distribution of wealth and power within Welsh society. Welsh law took it for granted that men would exercise power over other men: they envisaged, for example, a free man becoming the client or dependant of another more powerful man; they assumed that free men would be masters of slaves and serfs (and so indeed they often were); and they stated clearly that 'sons of freemen should exercise lordship (W. *arglwyddiaeth*) over their avowry men (i.e. men who had entered into their protection) just as the king ought to exercise his lordship over his avowry men'.[33] Such also is the pattern suggested by the Domesday entries for south-east Wales: powerful men lording it over whole vills, owning at least a plough-team each, and in charge of their own men. Dependence extended in a graduated scale of dominance and subordination throughout Welsh society. What is much more difficult to guess at is how far the different circles of dependence extended, how far they overlapped, and to what degree the nature of lordship in general changed over time.

[30] *Historia Gruffud vab Kenan*, p. 8 (*History G. ap. C.*, p. 115).
[31] *Calendar of Inquisitions Post Mortem*, II, p. 383, no. 633.
[32] *Pedeir Keinc y Mabinogi*, p. 50 (*Mabinogion*, p. 41).
[33] *Llyfr Iorwerth*, p. 58 §89.

We can but venture a few suggestions. In native Wales the lordship of the prince, the greatest of all lords, seems to have grown apace during the twelfth and thirteenth centuries, especially over his free subjects, placing their renders and services on a more regular basis and claiming an increasing measure of control over their land, including the right of escheat in certain circumstances.[34] The prince's close colleagues and social peers doubtless followed suit. Many of them were close dependants of the prince and held extensive estates in different parts of Wales—men such as Madog ab Einion, who was the lord of vills, mills, and tenants in widely separated parts of north Wales in the mid-thirteenth century, or Ednyfed Fychan, the steward of Llywelyn ab Iorwerth, and his descendants, whose landed interests extended into north-east, north-west, and west Wales. Such men were powerful lords indeed, counting their tenants by the hundreds and their dependants by the score. But the pattern of dependence penetrated much deeper than this into native Welsh society: the records of the fourteenth century show that rich free men often had their own tenants and villeins and, in one of the few glipses that we catch of the inequality of wealth in rural society, the *Survey of Denbigh* (1334) reveals that in the commote of Isaled, thirteen free men had seventy-four under-tenants, whereas the remaining one hundred and thirteen free men had none. Dependence, in some form or another, was deeply entrenched in such a society.

'Therefore as a friend I beseech you, as a lord I command you, as a kinsman I pray you . . .': the plaintive speech attributed by the *Brut* to Iorwerth ap Bleddyn of Powys (d. 1111) signals the clear awareness of contemporaries that the ties of social relationship were multiple.[35] Status, kinship, neighbourhood, dependence: the four ties reviewed in this chapter bound men more or less firmly according to place, time, rank, and circumstance. None of them was an exclusive bond. Kinship and dependence, in particular, were recognized by contemporaries as complementary rather than as alternative bonds. Thus the rape of a woman occasioned 'shame and insult to her, and to her kindred (W. *cenedl*) *and* to her lord (W. *arglwydd*) '.[36] Likewise, the man who wished to deny a charge of dishonour (W. *sarhad*) must satisfy both the kinsfolk, whose right of revenge must be compensated, *and* the lord, to whom a fine (W. *dirwy*) was due. Different social ties, it cannot be too strongly insisted, operated differently at different social planes; they varied in their meaningfulness and force according to the economic circumstances of individuals. The terminology of status, and the distinctions which characterized it, proved remarkably resilient in Wales; so also did the ties

[34] See below pp. 257–60.   [35] *Brut, s.a.* 1110 (p. 32).

[36] *Llyfr Iorwerth*, p. 28 §50.

of kinship, interwoven as they were with concepts of honour, protection, and land-title. But as Wales moved, however uncertainly, from an economy of plunder to one of exploitation, as the 'greatest, strongest and noblest by birth',[37] the *potentes*, regularized their dues and augmented the range of their governance and of their fiscal and judicial powers, as pressure of population and the custom of partibility accentuated the problems of subsistence, and as the economic, social, and tenurial, if not the status, distinctions between free and unfree became increasingly blurred, it was the bonds of neighbourhood and the obligations of lordship which loomed ever larger in the horizon of most Welshmen. What seems beyond doubt—though it can never be precisely documented from the exiguous evidence—is that native Welsh society underwent profound changes in the twelfth and thirteenth centuries. That transformation will come into clearer focus if we consider the economic base of Welsh society in the same period.

[37] *Cal. Anc. Corr.*, p. 70.

CHAPTER 6

THE TRANSFORMATION OF ECONOMIC LIFE

To contemporary observers in the twelfth and thirteenth centuries, Wales's geographical features were readily characterized: it was a mountainous, wooded, and marshy country, remote and inaccessible. Much the best-informed, most widely travelled and most acute of those observers was Gerald of Wales. For him Wales was 'very strongly defended by high mountains, deep valleys, extensive woods, rivers and marshes'.[1] For observers writing at a greater distance—such as William of Newburgh or Matthew Paris—the mental image which Wales evoked was similar: a land of mountain, marsh, and wood. The image of its people could likewise be summarized in a few brisk phrases: they led a pastoral, nomadic existence, living primitively in dispersed settlements; growing few crops; largely restricted to a diet of milk, cheese, butter, honey, and meat; scantily dressed; hardy and eccentric, if not perverse, in their habits and life-style. They were, to put it kindly, a wild people living in a wild country or, to put it more bluntly, an untamed and undisciplined people, who lived like animals in a strange and weird land. Their social, cultural, religious, and economic backwardness was largely to be explained by their physical environment and by the remoteness of their county. Such geographical and social images reveal, as usual, as much about the standpoint and presuppositions of the observer as they do about the people observed. They betray the attitudes of men whose eyes were accustomed to the open plains and nucleated villages, the arable agriculture and social customs of lowland England and northern France. Viewed from such a standpoint, Wales and the Welsh were certainly different.

Its mountains were the primary element in that geographical difference. They shaped the character of the country and of its people, dictating the form and productivity of its agriculture, isolating communities, impeding travel and political integration, and acting as a daunting barrier to would-be conquerors. Almost sixty per cent of the surface area of Wales lies over 500 feet, twenty five per cent over 1,000 feet. In some places, notably in Snowdonia, the mountains, in Gerald's description, 'are very high, with narrow ridges and a great number of very steep peaks all jumbled together in confusion'.[2] More commonly, however, the highland areas consisted of

---

[1] *DK*, I, i (*Opera*, vi, 165).   [2] *IK*, II, v (*Opera*, vi, 123).

rolling acres of moorland and rounded plateaux, intersected by glaciated valleys—as in the Hiraethog uplands in the north-east, Pumlumon in mid-Wales, or the Brecon Beacons in the south-east. In much of this highland area, pastoral grazing alone was possible. The comment of the Domesday commissioners on the two large *cantrefi* of Rhos and Rhufoniog was crisply accurate: 'there is land enough for twenty ploughs only . . . The rest of the land is wood and moor and cannot be ploughed'.[3]

Yet to say that Wales was a mountainous country is to utter only a half-truth. The mountain massif of the interior is girt by large tracts of often fertile lowland, notably in Anglesey and the Llŷn peninsula, along the coastal plain of Ceredigion, in the north-east along the English border, and, above all, along the broad southern-coastal plain from Pembroke to Gwent. Even the massif itself is deeply penetrated in places by broad and fertile river valleys, especially those of Severn, Dee, Clwyd, and Conwy in the north and of Teifi, Tywi, and Usk in the south. Furthermore, Welshmen had adjusted resourcefully to the constraints of their environment. They grew cereals in areas such as Arwystli, Iâl, and upland Brecon, which modern agriculture has long since surrendered to pastoral grazing. They integrated the resources of upland and lowland, which so often in Wales lie cheek by jowl with each other, to best effect. Transhumance was practised from an early date, allowing communities to avail themselves of the pastoral wealth of the uplands in summer and to make maximum use of their limited arable and meadowland resources. The imaginative integration of lowland and upland was practised within individual vills such as Llanaber (Ardudwy), where the restricted terraces of arable of Ismynydd (below the mountain) were supplemented by the isolated farmsteads and extensive pastures of Uwchmynydd (uplands), or in the multiple estates of mixed upland and lowlands vills (such as Meddyfnych in Ystrad Tywi or Dinorben in Rhos), which seem to be such a common and old-established feature of the administrative geography of so many parts of upland Britain. Even on a wider scale the complementary resources of upland and lowland were shrewdly appreciated by contemporaries: Gerald of Wales records the old saying, 'Just as Anglesey can supply all the inhabitants of Wales with corn, so if all the herds were gathered together, Snowdon could afford sufficient pasture for them.'[4] Wales was, indeed, relatively poor in rich arable lowlands; its capacity to produce cereals and thereby to sustain an increasing population was limited. But, for that reason, the serious imbalance between arable and livestock husbandry, which has been seen as one of the critical deficiencies of medieval agriculture in lowland England, was less likely to arise in Wales on a national, regional, or even, most crucially, a local scale. The one major change in the physical environment

[3] *Domesay Book*, I, 269.
[4] *IK*, II, ix (*Opera*, vi, 135). Cf. his comments on Brecon, *ibid*, I, ii (*Opera*, vi, 33).

of the country to which contemporary records drew attention was dramatic, but peripheral in importance. This was the change in sea level and the coastal erosion which affected north and south Wales alike, burying districts such as the old borough of Kenfig and parts of Merthyr Mawr (Glamorgan) under the sand, compelling the parishioners of Pennard and Penmaen (Gower) to relocate their churches, creating the sunken forests of Newgale (Pembroke) which so impressed Gerald of Wales, and overwhelming low-lying land around Beaumaris and Niwbwrch (Anglesey), especially in the early fourteenth century.

Medieval Wales was a thickly wooded country even by contemporary standards. Englishmen approaching Wales on the north-east or south-east were immediately confronted by daunting forests: in the north, the great forest of Ewloe (which was estimated in Domesday as measuring ten leagues by three leagues); in the south, the forests of Strigoil (Chepstow), Tryleg (Treleck), and Wentwood beyond the Wye. Many of the valley bottoms and the adjoining low-lying approaches to them were also densely forested: thus Dinefwr castle in the Tywi valley was said by Gerald to be 'strongly situated in the deep recesses of its thick woods', while the 'impenetrable forests' of nearby Cantref Mawr, Caeo, and Glyncothi proved to be the safest redoubts of the dynasty of Deheubarth.[5] More strikingly, perhaps, much of upland Wales, so notably bare of forests today, other than recently established plantations of alien conifers, was well-covered by scrub and clumps of deciduous woodland. Notable examples were the Great and Little Forest of Brecon, covering over fifty square miles of upland country south of the Usk, or the Upper and Lower Forest of the Epynt range or the extensive forests of Clun. 'When the oaks are felled on the slopes of Snowdon' (*pan dorrir y deri ar ochr Eryri*), ran the Welsh jingle. It is a reminder both of the wooded character of much of upland Wales and of the pre-eminence of the oak, highly regarded for its mast and tanbark as well as for its excellent timber and valued at 120*d*. (half the price of a native slave) according to the law-texts. Wild deer and wolves still roamed in some of these forests.

In many parts of Wales arable agriculture was fitted into the interstices of an otherwise woodland and pastoral economy. The men of Hopedale (Tegeingl) in the early fourteenth century could claim, for example, that 'the greater part of their sustenance is derived from the woods'.[6] Even for settled arable communities woods and woodland pastures were crucially imporant—as sources of fuel, building material for houses, utensils and agricultural implements, and herbage for their stocks, especially in summer to eke out the exiguous resources of their meadowlands. That is why the struggle for the control of, and access to, these resources was so bitter and

[5] *DK*, i, v (*Opera*, vi, 172); *IK*, i, x (*Opera*, vi, 80).
[6] *Cal. Anc. Pets.*, p. 74.

so long drawn out in Wales. From at least the twelfth century, lords, lay and ecclesiastical, native and Anglo-Norman, sought to extend their control over the forests and pasturelands, partly in order to defend their exclusive hunting rights (and Wales was famous for its hawks and peregrine falcons), partly because in an upland region this was one of the shortest routes to seignorial profit and power. Thus, one of the first acts of the new Norman lords of Brecon was to assert their control over the forest uplands and to grant the tithe of hunting and of honey throughout the forest of Brecon to St Peter's abbey, Gloucester. The community fought back with equal determination, asserting repeatedly that free access to and use of woodland and pasture were immemorial communal rights and frequently challenging the profligate gifts of upland grazing to Cistercian houses. The dispute reverberated down the centuries, sometimes erupting into violent confrontations, more frequently smouldering in local resentment and seignorial amercements, occasionally settled (as in Clun in 1292, Maelienydd in 1297, Talgarth in 1299, Gower in 1306), at least temporarily, by local agreements. Such disputes were common throughout medieval Europe. In Wales, however, they had particular urgency, for in a largely upland and wooded country, freedom of access to forest and pasture was the very life-blood of society.

Wales impressed contemporaries not only by its mountains and forest, but also by its weather. 'When it is summer elsewhere, it is winter in Wales', remarked Pierre Langtoft sourly.[7] His sentiments were frequently shared by English visitors to Wales—by Henry II whose expedition of 1165 was almost literally washed away by torrential downpours in the Berwyn mountains, by the English soldiers at Degannwy in 1245 complaining bitterly of the cold and the wet, or by the Black Prince's councillors, who were given a special allowance of winter clothing in order to face the rigours of the Welsh climate. Modern rainfall figures bear out their complaints: much of upland Wales is drenched by 80–90 inches of rain annually, compared with an annual average of 30 inches for most of England. Winters are longer, the growing season is shorter. Only one ray of optimism relieved this climatic gloom: there is some reason to believe that Wales, in common with other parts of northern Europe, witnessd a marked improvement in the weather in the twelfth and thirteenth centuries. Such an improvement may help to explain why cereals were then grown in highland districts, such as Tregaron (Ceredigion), Trawsfynydd (Ardudwy), and upland Brecon. Living in such an unpropitious climate, it is little wonder that medieval Welshmen showed an acute awareness of the seasons. They adjusted their legal calendars to the chronology of their agricultural year: land pleas could only be pursued between 9 November

[7] *The Chronicle of Pierre de Langtoft*, ed. T. Wright (Rolls Series, 1866–8), II, 177.

and 9 February or again, after the ploughing and sowing season was completed, between 9 May and 9 August. A similar sensitivity to the variations of the seasons is reflected in the poetry—in the dread of winter when the earth was encased 'in a mail corslet, cold and hard' and when 'God made hermits of everyone' and in the exultation in the advent of spring and summer with 'its delightful bright weather', the twittering of birds, the finely coloured woodgrove, and the gentleness of the ocean. Summer was indeed, as Dafydd ap Gwilym proclaimed in his celebration of that season, 'the reviver of the world' (*dadeni byd*).[8]

Wales was wet. It was also distant and inaccessible. To say that it was tucked away on the very edge of the world was a common jibe; the rest of the world, added Archbishop Pecham with customary insensitivity, scarcely knew that the Welsh were a people. Distance could be measured in miles as well as in contempt. Wales, according to Gerald, was a fifteen days' journey from Canterbury, though his anxiety to use this claim as a reason for establishing an archbishopric at St Davids doubtless added a few days to the length of his imaginary journey. Nearer the mark was Gerald's other estimate that the journey from Anglesey in the north-west to Portskewett in the south-east across the mountain massif of central Wales would take eight days. Travel was daunting in Wales, particularly to men habituated to the open plains and easy routes of lowland England and northern France. 'The English King', remarked John of Salisbury in 1157, 'has set out to conquer the Welsh amidst their Alps and sub-Alps'.[9] The mountains, especially where they were precipitous, heavily wooded, or boggy, were certainly a major obstacle to travel. But so equally were the rivers, especially the long tidal estuaries of the Conwy and the Clwyd in the north, the Mawddach and the Dyfi in the west, and the notoriously treacherous Nedd estuary in the south, which made the overland approach to Swansea and Gower from the east particularly difficult. Travellers were often at the mercy of quicksands or capricious ferries: Gerald of Wales almost lost his baggage and his invaluable books crossing the Nedd estuary, while the tidal currents of the Dyfi thwarted the ambitions of the love-lorn Dafydd ap Gwilym. Inland routes were often no safer, running as they did through narrow wooded defiles which provided ample opportunities for ambushes: it was at the 'evil pass' of Coed Grwyne near Abergavenny that Richard fitz Gilbert was overwhelmed and killed in 1136. Wales's lack of an adequate network of communications served her both ill and well: it

---

[8] *Dafydd ap Gwilym. Fifty Poems*, trans. and ed. H. I. Bell and D. Bell, pp. 275, 279 (the poem has now been removed from the canon of Dafydd ap Gwilym's work); *Oxford Book of Welsh Verse*, p. 41 (Einion ap Gwalchmai) translated in J. P. Clancy, *The Earliest Welsh Poetry* (1970), pp. 157–8; *Gwaith Dafydd ap Gwilym*, ed. T. Parry (2nd edn. Cardiff, 1963), p. 78.

[9] *The Letters of John of Salisbury*, eds. W. J. Millor, H. E. Butler, and C. N. L. Brooke, I (1955), 52.

helps to explain the country's political fragmentation and the difficulty of sustaining princely control, but it also acted as a major obstacle and deterrent to would-be conquerors.

In fact, medieval Wales was by no means so lacking in roads and tracks as the comments of foreign observers might suggest. Major and well-integrated routes along which the increasingly cumbersome armies of medieval England and their baggage-trains could travel were certainly few; but the much more modest needs of local communities and of their everyday business made more limited demands which might be met. Roman roads still probably retained a measure of vestigial importance, especially in the south-east in the vale of Glamorgan or around Brecon, and even arguably in north Wales where medieval tracks followed the route of the Roman road southward from Segontium (Caernarfon). These, however, were but the crumbling fragments of an old network. More important were the tracks and particularly the upland ridgeways which kept clear of the marshy valleys, such as 'the road which leads from Llancarfan to Llanilltud between the two valleys' or 'the great way (*Y Gefnffordd* as it was known in Welsh) that goes across the mountains of "Torbethel" to Glynywrach'.[10] These well-established routes were supplemented by a host of local tracks and paths, such as the complex network of tracks around Brecon recorded in the early charters of Brecon priory. Rivers and estuaries, of course, presented a major problem. So a piecemeal programme of bridge-building was undertaken—some 'by the alms of good people', others by princes or magnates (such as the bridge which Maredudd ap Rhys proposed to build over the Teifi at Emlyn in 1265, or the one built at Llangollen (Nanheudwy) by Roger Mortimer of Chirk 'for the security of travellers in those parts') or by monasteries (such as the bridge which the abbey of Cwmhir (Maelienydd) was required to build).[11] Five ferries served the passage between Anglesey and the mainland and there were other ferries across the Conwy, Mawddach, Dyfi, and Severn estuaries, as well as boats plying up the major rivers. Along the west and south coasts in particular sea travel was common and that from an early date. It is well to remember that it was across south Wales and from the ports of Pembroke that the Anglo-Norman armies set out to conquer Ireland in the late 1160s and early 1170s and it was along the coast road of south Wales that Henry II and John in turn travelled *en route* to Ireland. Travel, therefore, within and across Wales was not as difficult or as unusual as bland contemporary observations might suggest.

The same was, in a measure, true of travel beyond Wales. Ships plied regularly between north and west Wales and Ireland, carrying goods as

---

[10] *Cartae . . . de Glamorgan*, ed. G. T. Clark. 6 vols. (Cardiff, 1910), II, 441, no. 452; I, 179, no. 174.
[11] *Cal. Anc. Pets.*, p. 101 (no. 3263); *Cal. Anc. Corr.*, p. 141.

well as plunder, slaves, scholars, and political exiles. It is only in these terms that the easy, if often faulty, familiarity with matters Irish in Welsh historical records, literature, and hagiography in the eleventh and twelfth centuries can be explained.[12] This Irish link was quickly appreciated and exploited by the Normans: it was to an Irish bride and an Irish alliance that Arnulf of Montgomery, earl of Pembroke, turned in 1101–2 to try to rescue his family's fortunes. The nature of the link between Ireland and Wales, especially south-west Wales, was transformed with the Anglo-Norman conquest of much of Ireland from the 1170s. Even closer and more regular ties were now forged; but they were the ties of common imperial domination rather than of native contact. When Edward I set about the conquest of native Wales in the 1270s it was to Ireland that he looked, in part, for troops and, above all, for supplies. In south Wales the ease of sea-passage across the Bristol Channel was crucial in fostering a whole host of links—cultural, ecclesiastical, social, and economic—especially with south-west England. Many of these links pre-date the Norman conquest of south Wales; but that conquest and, above all, the settlement and colonization which underpinned it dramatically increased the importance and frequency of these links all along the coast from Chepstow to Pembroke. It is but one manifestation of such links that stones from Wiltshire, Dorset, and Somerset, and lead from the Mendips were used in the building of Llandaff cathedral and other churches in south-east Wales, while St Davids looked for its architectural inspiration towards Glastonbury and for workmen to Bristol and beyond.

Medieval Wales, in common with most parts of rural Europe, was a collection of localized societies, living largely from their own resources, touchily proud of their local customs and identity and deeply distrustful of outsiders. Yet modern perspectives may exaggerate and distort the extent and character of this localism. The frequency and range of travel naturally varied according to social class. The princes of native Wales, their entourages, and officers went on frequent progress around their realms, exacting their food-renders and claiming their billeting rights. Military forays, widely dispersed estates and the demands of the hunt,—'without the solace of hunting, it would be hard and tedious to stay at Frodsham', observed Dafydd ap Gruffudd in 1278[13]—also kept the native nobility frequently on the move. Much the same was true of the Anglo-Norman aristocracy and their followers in Wales; indeed, all the more so, as they were also anxious to retain their social and territorial ties with England and even with Normandy. For ecclesiastics, the twelfth century in Wales, as elsewhere, witnessed a marked increase in the occasion and necessity of travel—whether as scholars *en route* to cathedral schools in England or

[12] Cf. above pp. 10–11.   [13] *Cal. Anc. Corr.*, p. 74.

France, as archdeacons (such as the indefatigable Gerald of Wales) bringing the norms and discipline of an international church to bear on the lives of an errant and dispersed Welsh population, as bishops and their attendants increasingly expected to attend royal and metropolitan councils and synods, to sit as papal judges-delegate, and to take their pleas to Rome, or as monks and, later, friars, attending the chapters-general of their orders.

Most Welsh peasants, it is true, spent their lives within the framework of their localities, relieved only by the seasonal migration of their animals and by visits to local fairs and markets. Yet even their lives were occasionally punctuated by more distant travel. By the fourteenth century, and probably earlier, many of them travelled to England as seasonal labourers for the harvest period, and as such were specifically exempted from the provisions of the Statute of Labourers of 1351. Long before that date, many of them had found an exit from their localities as footsoldiers and archers in the service of Anglo-Norman lords and kings, from the early twelfth century onwards. 5,300 Welshmen accompanied Edward I to Flanders in 1297; 10,500 went with him to Scotland in 1298. If the total population of Wales was of the order of 300,000, these figures for two years alone suggest that foreign travel was not restricted to a tiny minority. For others, pilgrimage provided the pretext to travel further afield, whether to a local shrine, St Davids, Canterbury, or even the Holy Land (four ordinary peasants from Dyffryn Clwyd set out thither in 1360–4). It is impossible, of course, to quantify the scale or to measure the significance of such travel; all that can be done is to bear such impressions in mind when recalling the reputation of Wales as a backward and inaccessible country. Indeed its very backwardness and inaccessbility may, paradoxically, have made Welshmen more widely travelled than most contemporary Englishmen. The Welsh had a reputation among contemporary observers for open-house hospitality to strangers. Such hospitality would hardly have been regarded as a highly esteemed social virtue and obligation in a country where travel was rare. The rhythms of a predominantly pastoral economy made very uneven demands on the time of Welshmen; it freed them for other activities, at least seasonally. Indeed, as population grew beyond the restricted resources of a largely upland country, it was only by periodic and seasonal migration that the needs of such a population could be met.

In any discussion of a largely subsistence society, the size of the population is a crucial issue. Yet in Wales it is an issue which can scarcely be broached. Even the post-Conquest extents of the fourteenth century are of little help for this purpose; they are concerned with the attribution of dues, not with the recording of population; too often they resort to phrases such as, 'and their co-parceners', 'and others', or 'and their tenants and villeins', which are the despair of the demographer. The returns of the subsidy of 1292 are the only source which even begins to provide some foothold, however insecure, for guessing at the size of the population of medieval Wales. This was the only occasion in the medieval period on which a tax was raised for the king from all parts of Wales, from Marcher lordships and Principality alike. Yet only thirteen rolls, covering less than a quarter of the country, relating to the assessment of this tax survive; and even these rolls, as with all medieval tax-records, pose almost as many problems for the would-be demographer as they solve. No satisfactory estimate of the population can be based on such a source; but extrapolating from such returns as survive and utilizing sixteenth-century evidence and analogies, Keith Williams-Jones very tentatively suggested that an estimate of 300,000 for the whole of Wales at the end of the thirteenth century might not be too wide of the mark. It is an estimate which may be compared with the equally very tentative estimates of a population of perhaps one million for Scotland and between four and six million for England at the same date.

This population was far more evenly distributed across the country than it is today. Some districts were naturally richer in taxable wealth and in population density than others. Anglesey, with its high proportion of old settlements and parish churches, was one such district; Cymydmaen, the most westerly commote of Llŷn, and Tegeingl, in the north-east, were, according to the 1292 returns, among the others. Within the newly formed county of Merioneth the main concentrations of wealth and population were to be found in the westerly seaboard commotes on the one hand and in the fertile plains of the Dee valley on the other. But perhaps even more striking is the relatively high density of population in certain upland vills in the county, such as Penaran (Penllyn) and Pennant (Edeirnion). It suggests an increasing pressure of population, driving Welsh communities ever closer to the margins of cultivable land.

That pressure was one of the inevitable consequences of the undoubted increase in the population of Wales in the twelfth and thirteenth centuries. Gerald of Wales with characteristic acuteness had noted the phenomenon, albeit parenthetically, in his *Description of Wales* written in the 1190s. It was an increase which was fed from two sources: from a marked growth of population in native society and from very considerable alien immigration into south and east Wales.[14] The evidence for the increase, though indirect, is cumulatively impressive. New settlements were founded and continued to proclaim their novelty in their names, especially in the Anglicized lowlands—Newton Nottage (Glamorgan), Carew Newton, New House, New Moat (Pembroke). Other settlements—such as Bonvilston in

[14] See above pp. 97–100.

Glamorgan or Flemingston, Herbrandston, or Wiston in Pembroke—assumed the names of their new lords, who thereby provide a *terminus a quo* for their growth, if not for their initial foundation. Much the same process was at work in native Wales. Secondary settlements sprang up to cope with the fast-growing population. The process is particularly vivid (and has been well studied) in Denbigh and on Anglesey, as families were compelled to move out of the richer, sheltered, well-drained soils on the coast to the more exposed and impoverished soils of the upland. Thus in north-east Anglesey the original settlement at Llysdulas—significantly termed in Welsh Hendref (Old Settlement)—became the base from which a burgeoning population gradually spilled over to occupy virtually the whole of the parishes of Llanwenllwyfo and Amlwch, sometimes in vills as far as seven or eight miles from the original base. In Anglesey again, the hamlet of Tresgawen lay some nine miles from its parent vill of Porthaml on the shores of the Menai Straits. Many of these secondary settlements were doubtless established on lands which had hitherto been under temporary cultivation or which had formed part of the summer pastures of earlier days. The establishment of dependent chapelries and the frequent references to the tithes of newly assarted lands (as in Glasbury and Talgarth) are likewise ecclesiastical pointers to the impact of population growth. By the later twelfth century, population pressure was such that native Welsh peasants and Anglo-Norman settlers alike were attracted in considerable numbers to take part in the colonization of Ireland; and the readiness of Welshmen to serve in such large numbers in the armies of English lords and kings was doubtless prompted by the pressures of overpopulation as well as by the natural militarism of the Welsh.

By 1300 Wales was almost certainly more densely populated than it was to be again until at least the sixteenth century. Some of this population was absorbed into the numerous small towns which were founded in Wales in this period; but far the greater part of it would have to be accommodated in the countryside. Land shortage and land hunger were the inevitable result, the more so in a society where partibility among male heirs was the rule of succession. It was, at least in part, in response to this pressure that lineage rights to land (W. *gwely*) in native Wales were more closely defined and that limited arable resources were divided into small open-field strips. The records of the fourteenth century reveal vividly how far the growth of population was outstripping the arable resources of the country. In upland Hay in 1340 two-thirds of the tenant population held less than five acres of arable each, and much the same was true of different parts of lowland Wales—of Bronllys (Brecon) in the fertile Llynfi basin, of the border district of Whitecastle (Monmouth) in the east and of thoroughly Welsh districts, such as Cydweli in the west. Wales had become an overcrowded country.

Such a rapid growth in population naturally had a profound impact on the settlement pattern of the country. Our knowledge of Wales's early settlement pattern is, and is likely to remain, hazy and insecure. There is no Domesday Book to hand to provide us with a gazetteer of settlements in the late eleventh century. Instead, the historian and the historical geographer must rest content with the perilous exercise of piecing together the few shreds of documentary evidence, the beguilingly neat but essentially abstract theorems of the native law-texts, and the interesting but chronologically vague archaeological evidence to form a framework of assumptions about early Welsh society. The emphasis of recent scholarship on this issue has been on the considerable measure of continuity in the social and institutional features of early medieval Wales from Roman and even pre-Roman times, the antiquity of much of the pattern of rural settlement, and the strength of early royal lordship and its capacity to shape and exploit social institutions for its own ends.

Some of the settlements of medieval Wales were undoubtedly old, especially in the coastal lowlands and around royal and ecclesiastical centres, such as Aberffro (Anglesey), Dinorben (Rhos) or Meliden (Tegeingl). Many of the individual settlements were integrated into what have recently been termed multiple estates, corresponding more or less to the Welsh unit of the *maenor* as depicted in the law-texts, and strongly reminiscent of the *scirs* of Northumbria, the *lathes* of Kent, and the sokes of eastern England. Such a multiple estate would consist of several discrete vills with a royal court (W. *llys*) as its focal centre for purposes of collecting food-renders, performing services, and imposing governance. Such a unit was well-suited to the needs of a thinly populated and aristocratically dominated society. The character and extent of such multiple estates have been sensitively reconstructed in different parts of Wales, such as Meddyfnych (Cantref Bychan) and Aberffro (Anglesey). These reconstructions, furthermore, receive considerable support from the glimpses afforded by Domesday Book of groups of seven, thirteen, and fourteen vills, each organized under a reeve in lowland Gwent, and of the royal *llys* at Bistre (Tegeingl) with its five distinct settlements and eight outlying berewicks.

This emphasis on the antiquity of much of the pattern of human settlement and territorial organization in Wales has been hugely illuminating; but it is in danger occasionally of underestimating the elements of change and adaptability, as well as of resilience and continuity, in medieval societies, notably in a period of rapidly changing economic circumstances such as the twelfth and thirteenth centuries. As the population grew, old vills were filled to overflowing and their boundaries carefully defined (as happened in the neighbouring townships of Cemlyn and Caerdegog in northern Anglesey); new vills were formed by segmentation from older, larger vills; secondary settlements were established on pastureland and waste; and districts of hitherto temporary cultivation or summer grazing became the centres of new communities. The settlement pattern of Wales—both of districts under native domination and regions under Norman control—assumed in the twelfth and thirteenth centuries the shape that it was to retain until the end of the Middle Ages and often, indeed, until the advent of industrialism and of mass rural depopulation.

In the process the character of settlement itself may have been changing. Wales is well-known as a country of dispersed settlement. 'They do not live in towns, villages or castles', remarked Gerald of Wales, 'but lead a solitary existence, deep in the woods'.[15] His comment was echoed almost a century later by Archbishop Pecham, who ascribed the moral shortcomings of the Welsh to the fact that 'they do not live together but far from each other', while Leland in the early-sixteenth century likewise commented that in Denbigh 'the people lived *sparsim* not *vicatim*'.[16] That much of upland Wales was a country of dispersed settlement is only to be expected. Indeed, as the population grew rapidly and men were driven to recover land from waste and woodland, they often established isolated homesteads (W. *tyddynnod*) on their newly reclaimed assarts. Thus, in the large vill of Llysdulas (Anglesey), a contrast has been detected between the closely woven pattern of settlement in the original *hendref* (old vill) at Llanwenllwyfo and the much more dispersed character of the secondary settlements towards the Parys mountain. Yet, as this example suggests, nucleated or semi-nucleated settlement was by no means uncommon in native as well as in Anglo-Norman Wales. It particulary characterized the small bond vills of the coastal lowlands, such as the *maerdref* or home farm at Aberffro (Anglesey). These were primarily organized to provide goods, services, food, and labour for their lay or ecclesiastical lords; their affairs were supervised by a seignorial reeve, known unflatteringly as the reeve of the dunghill (W. *maer y biswail*), and the communal and closely regulated character of their obligations and land-inheritance practices (W. *tir cyfrif*) doubtless encouraged nucleation. But nucleation was by no means confined, as is sometimes suggested, to bond vills, especially in a country where the population was increasing rapidly and where the custom of partibility prevailed. The sections in the Welsh law-texts dealing with the damages to be paid when a fire spread to a neighbour's house and on the rules for joint ploughing assume that Welshmen might live close together. It was neither status (free, unfree) nor race (Welsh, Anglo-Norman) which

[15] *DK*, I, xvii (*Opera*, vi, 200).
[16] *Registrum Epistolarum . . . Johannis Peckham*, ed. C. T. Martin (1882–5), III, 776; John Leland, *The Itinerary in Wales*, ed. L. T. Smith (1906), p. 93. Cf. the comment in the Kennington petitions of 1305 'cum ville Walenses sint disperse', *Record of Caernarvon*, ed. H. Ellis (1838), p. 212.

determined the pattern of settlement, but the lie of the land, the constraints of agricultural technology, and the historical development of communities. Small nucleated hamlets or villages with a few outlying farms were characteristic of the lowlands of Anglo-Norman Wales; but equally many of the settlements of the coastal plains and river valleys of native Wales were also at least semi-nucleated. Gerald of Wales's comment, pithy and interesting as it is, should not, therefore, be regarded as a universal truth.

The same may be said of his famous observation on Welsh housing: 'they content themselves with small wattled huts constructed at minimal labour and expense and adequate to last for a year or so'.[17] It may be readily accepted that peasant housing in Wales, as elsewhere in medieval society, was fragile and impermanent and frequently rebuilt and realigned. Yet the texts of the Welsh laws and the researches of modern archaeologists suggest that the truth was much more complex than Gerald's *obiter dictum* suggests. Housing and housing material varied according to area, period, and social status. In many parts of the lowlands, low houses built wholly of timber or of turves and rubble, fitted around a timber frame, and thatched with turf or reeds were probably common: it was to a 'turf-roofed villein's house' (*tŷ taeog do tyweirch*) that the poet rather contemptuously referred.[18] Elsewhere, however, the use of stone both for the house itself and for the enclosure was not unusual. The excavations at Cefn Graeanog (Arfon) suggest that there was a shift from timber to stone-construction in the thirteenth century. Much the same is true of lowland Wales, for in the deserted village of Uchelolau (Glamorgan) there is evidence of the use of dry-stone masonry techniques, with the occasional use of lime plaster; and it is noteworthy that when Dafydd ap Gwilym sang of a dilapidated cottage it was one of stone that he had in mind. Houses also varied according to seasonal usage: Gerald's description would appear to apply more convincingly to the upland summer house (W. *hafoty*), valued in the law-texts at a mere 4*d.* or 8*d*, than the permanent winter dwelling (W. *hendref*, *gaeafty*), valued at 80*d*. Wealthier men might, of course, aspire to greater luxury. They might commission an aisled hall-house divided by partitions, a separate byre, and other buildings, as did the owners of Cefn y Fan (Eifionydd) or Siambr Wen near Dyserth (Tegeingl). Such wealthier houses might even enjoy a moated enclosure, as did Hen Gwrt, Llandeilo Gresynni (Monmouth) or, rather later, Owain Glyn Dŵr's *llys* at Sycharth, so lovingly if extravagantly described in Iolo Goch's poem. The great majority of Welshmen, however, had to be content with houses built crudely to a rectangular plan, often sheltering animals and humans under

---

[17] *DK*, I, xvii (*Opera*, vi, 201).
[18] *Cywyddau Iolo Goch ac Eraill*, ed. H. Lewis, T. Roberts, I. Williams (2nd edn. Cardiff, 1937), p. 198.

the same roof. There was little comfort in such buildings. The author of the native prose tale *The Dream of Rhonabwy* doubtless exaggerated in his memorably revolting description of the uneven floor, the stench of cow-dung, the smoke-filled atmosphere, and the flea-infested blankets of the house where his hero spent one uncomfortable night; but his graphic account probably takes us closer to the living conditions of medieval Welshmen than our modern imaginations could otherwise manage.

Life for most medieval Welshmen was indeed hard. It is little wonder that they were noted for their frugality and hardiness. The contemporary image of the Welshman was that of a scantily dressed, bare-legged, and barefooted character. Even the princes and nobles prided themselves on their hardiness: when Gerald of Wales described one of Lord Rhys's sons he noted that, 'according to the custom of his country and people, he wore only a thin cloak and beneath that a shirt. His legs and feet, regardless of thorn and thistles, were bare.'[19] Their houses were equally bare: in a Welsh house, according to Gerald again, 'there are no tables, no tableclothes, no napkins'.[20] His comment is, as usual, generalized and reflects the domestic expectations of a fastidious man of good Norman family. Standards and habits varied, of course, according to wealth; yet here again it is striking that even the hall of the prince of Gwynedd at Ystumgwern (Ardudwy) was of very modest proportions indeed. The frugality of the Welsh was proverbial and was held up as an example to the Cistercians by their critics. They were—or perhaps had to be—content with one meal a day, consisting mainly of the products of a pastoral society—meat, cheese, butter, and milk, supplemented by fish and wild fruit and washed down with beer and mead. When some of Simon de Montfort's troops took refuge in Wales in 1265 they found that the fare had not changed from Gerald's day; the monotonous diet of meat and milk drove them to return to England in despair. The hospitality of the Welsh was as proverbial as their frugality, while the support they gave to the indigent and poor earned the praise of many observers. The social virtues of the Welsh were those of a proud but poor people; those virtues came under even greater strain as the population increased and as the economy became more complex.

Medieval Wales was pre-eminently a rural society. In such a society wealth lies primarily in land. Later redactions of the Welsh law-texts waxed eloquent on that score: 'Chattels are perishable and land is eternal . . . Therefore land is neither to be given nor exchanged for chattels.'[21] Good cultivable land has always been in short supply in Wales. That shortage grew more acute with the sharp increase in population. It was to counter

[19] *IK*, ii, iv (*Opera*, vi, 119).   [20] *DK*, i, x (*Opera*, vi, 183).
[21] *Ancient Laws and Institutes of Wales*, ed. A. Owen (1841), ii, 381.

such a shortage that every effort was made to reclaim new land, much of it admittedly quickly exhausted and fit only for temporary cultivation. Arable fields were won from waste and pastureland all over Wales: 560 acres were added in two vills alone in Denbigh, 342 acres of 'new land' in two vills in Usk, at least 588 acres in the commote of Carnwyllion (Cydweli). The figures come from the fourteenth-century evidence, but the story had been unfolding for at least two centuries. Upland forests were another natural target for agricultural pioneers: it is some measure both of communal effort and of seignorial vigilance that the Welshmen of Brecon were fined the colossal sum of £400 in 1353 for acquiring land in the forest without licence. Dykes and sea walls were constructed to extend the bounds of coastal settlements, notably in the marshes of Gwynllŵg and Afan (Glamorgan). Individual landlords sometimes played a prominent role in the work of assarting: in Glamorgan, for example, Geoffrey Sturmy 'built his township in the wilderness which no one had previously ploughed', before handing over the fruits of his hard-won labour to Margam abbey.[22] Monks, especially Cistercian monks, were themselves among the most enterprising colonists in Wales: Tintern abbey cleared the appropriately named parish of Newchurch in Gwent and won other lands by drainage in the Caldicot levels; Dore abbey enclosed tracts of arable lands in the Epynt foothills, while the monks of Basingwerk cleared some of the wooded hills of Tegeingl. But pride of place must go to the unrecorded and piecemeal efforts of individual men and communities; theirs was the premier role in the making of the medieval Welsh landscape. The sole record of their achievement is often the suffix 'wood' or 'moor', or the Welsh prefix 'ynys' or 'coed', attached to the lands they cleared by their labour. It is a measure of the economic importance that they themselves attached to their enterprise that the men of the Four Cantrefi, the district between the rivers Dee and Conwy, should insist that the right to assart their own lands and their own woods was one of the principal liberties which they wished the English crown to confirm in the 1250s.

The Welsh landscape was being slowly but fundamentally transformed in the twelfth and thirteenth centuries. In the process, cereal cultivation became a much more prominent feature of the agriculture of the country. Much of upland Wales is, of course, suitable only for stock husbandry and rough grazing. This has encouraged the view, reinforced by theories of social and agricultural evolution, that medieval Wales was a country of pastoral agriculture and even of nomadic societies. In truth, the majority of Welsh people lived in lowland districts below 800 feet and practised mixed agriculture. Even Gerald, anxious as he was to highlight the distinctiveness of the Welsh, noted that their diet of meat and milk was supplemented by

---

[22] *Cartae . . . de Glamorgan*, I, 151, no. 152.

'bread, rolled out large and thin, and baked fresh each day';[23] likewise, it was not the absence of ploughing which struck him but the fact that the Welsh were content with single ploughing and spring-sown crops. The growing importance of arable cultivation is confirmed from every direction. The native law-texts abound with references to joint ploughing (W. *cyfar*), to penalties for trespassing in corn (W. *llwgr yd*), and to the primacy of bread or bread-flour in the food-renders owed to kings. Comparisons with the oxen of the ploughteams, as paradigms of leadership and steadfastness, were commonplaces of Welsh literature; and it was the ploughman (W. *llafurwr*), not the shepherd or hersdman, whom Iolo Goch extolled in his famous ode as the sheet-anchor of Welsh society. Recent archaeological excavation underlines the mixed nature of Welsh agriculture: thus in the farmstead of Cefn Graeanog near Clynnog (Arfon), a large barn for the storage of sown crops stood beside the byre for sheltering stock. Scattered references in the historical evidence confirm the impression—such as the render of two hundred loaves owed to Gruffudd ap Llywelyn (d. 1063) in his manor of Bistre (Tegeingl) or 'the houses and the barns and the crops' deliberately destroyed in a punitive raid by the princelings of Powys in 1109 or 'the great abundance of corn collected into heaps in well-covered granges'[24] in Edeirnion which so impressed a royal commander in the 1270s. Statistically more impressive are the handful of detailed inventories of goods surviving from the 1292–93 tax returns; they show clearly that in the lowland commotes of Llŷn at least three out of every four taxpayers grew some corn.

In most of Wales oats was far and away the most common crop. It was well suited to a land of high relief, acidic soils, and low temperatures; it had the futher advantage of serving both as fodder for animals and food for men. In Penllyn it was, perhaps not surprisingly, the sole crop grown; in the more sheltered lands of Cafflogion (Llŷn) it was five times as popular as wheat; even in favoured districts, such as Aberffro (Anglesey) or parts of the Vale of Glamorgan, twice as much oats as wheat was grown. Barley, rye, and occasionally peas and beans added some variety to the crops. The twin technological foundations of this cereal cultivation were the plough and the mill. Ploughs were constructed locally: 'no one', comments the law-texts, 'ought to undertake the work of a ploughman unless he knows how to make a plough and to nail its irons'.[25] Both the wheeled and the wheel-less plough were known in Wales. They were drawn by teams of oxen, normally four to eight arranged under two yokes; horses, in Wales as elsewhere, were specifically reserved for other agricultural tasks, such as harrowing. As for mills, their importance was well-recognized by Welshmen:

---

[23] *DK*, 1, x (*Opera*, vi, 183–4).
[24] *Brut. s.a.* 1109 (p. 30); *Cal. Anc. Corr.*, p. 172.
[25] *Llyfr Iorwerth*, ed. A. R. Wiliam, p. 99.

the mill, in the picturesque phrase of the law-texts, was considered to be one of 'the three indivisible gems of kindred' (*tri thlws cenedl*).[26] Many mills in Wales remained in kin possession until the later Middle Ages, their ownership being subdivided in ever-smaller portions among the members of the lineage. But in Wales, as elsewhere, the mill also came to figure prominently, and increasingly from the early twelfth century, as a potent and profitable symbol of the lord's authority. The Anglo-Norman kings and lords of Wales were great mill-builders. In Anglesey at least seventeen of over sixty recorded mills belonged to the king in the fourteenth century; in Cydweli the earls and dukes of Lancaster in the same period owned twenty-one mills yielding over £60 to them annually; even in the Great Forest of Brecon, six seignorial mills stood as outposts of the lord's power in the uplands and yielded him 300 *summe* of oats worth £90 annually. The number and distribution of mills are indeed an eloquent comment on the importance of cereals in Wales's economy and on the capacity of lordship to exploit the advance of bread-grains to augment its own profits.

The rapid advance of arable cultivation had a profound impact on the face of the countryside (though by today that impact has been almost completely obliterated by the agricultural changes of subsequent centuries). It was now—under the twin pressures of population growth and the custom of partibility—that much of the best arable land in Wales was laid out in elongated strips in open or subdivided fields. The existence of such open fields in the lowland plains of Anglo-Norman Wales has long been recognized: archaeological and historical evidence indicates pre-Norman examples of ridge-and-furrow husbandry on the Welsh border at Chirbury (near Montgomery) and Tidenham on the Severn estuary, and remnants of open fields survived until recent times at places such as Caldicot (Gwent) and Rhosili (Gower). What is now increasingly recognized, however, is that the quilleted patchwork of long arable strips likewise characterized, or came to characterize, much of the arable land of native Wales. The tractate in the medieval law-texts on joint ploughing (W. *cyfar*) is not readily comprehensible other than in such a context. It is indeed suggestive of the likely chronology of open-field arrangements in native Wales that the tractate is absent from the earlier redactions of the law-texts and only appears prominently in those redactions which are usually associated with Gwynedd in the thirteenth century. The records and land-deeds of the later Middle Ages abound with the terminology and assumptions of open-field cultivation—such as the injunction of 1305 that lands are to be held 'openly' (*aperte*) and not otherwise, or the recurrence of vernacular terms such as *erw* and *cyfar* (acre), *llain* and *dryll* (quillet), or *cae cyd* (joint field) in contemporary deeds. Above all, some highly illuminating reconstructions

[26] *Llyfr Colan*, ed. D. Jenkins, §617.

of late medieval tenurial patterns in widely distributed areas of north Wales—such as Llwydfaen (Arllechwedd), Llysdulas (Anglesey), Pennant (Edeirnion), and Llanynys (Dyffryn Clwyd)—have revealed clearly the prevalence of open-field farming in parts of native Wales. Strips were often less than once acre in size: at Llwydfaen, for example, a holding of seventeen acres lay in seven parcels. The pattern of intermingling might indeed be more complex than in England, for an individual's holding might be scattered, in respect of his membership of a lineage (W. *gwely*), over several vills miles apart in distance and several hundred feet in altitude. In parts of the lowlands of southern Wales large, integrated two- or three-field systems comparable with some of those of midland England might prevail; but frequently the open-field arrangements of Wales had to adapt to a more broken landscape and thereby proliferated into an apparently irregular assemblage of fields, as in Llantrisant (Glamorgan), Bronllys (Brecon), or the rich lowlands of Maelor Gymraeg in north-east Wales.

The balance of agriculture, therefore, may well have been changing dramatically in much of Wales in the twelfth and thirteenth centuries. Yet even in the lowlands the raising of stock remained important, while in the uplands pastoral agriculture of necessity prevailed. Even in the lowland commote of Cafflogion (Llŷn) two-thirds of the taxable wealth of the taxpayers in 1292 derived from their animals; and even if these proportions are distorted by the nature of the returns, they serve as a reminder that this was at best a mixed agricultural subsistence economy. In that economy cattle were without a doubt the most important form of stock and of movable wealth. They were essential as a source of milk, meat, and traction. Their centrality is manifested in many ways—in the fact that the basic Welsh amercement (W. *camlwrw*) was one of three cows, in the large renders of cows that were often the major rent from Welsh upland communities, in the payment of placatory gifts to English kings in cattle and horses (such as the tribute of 300 horses and 4,000 cattle, which the Lord Rhys offered to Henry II, or the fine in three equal parts of money, cattle, and horses, which Senena, the wife of the imprisoned Gruffudd ap Llywelyn, promised to pay in 1241). The late thirteenth-century tax returns reveal the predominance of cattle in peasant households likewise: in Cafflogion (Llŷn) cattle (1045) far outnumbered sheep (711) in number and even more so in value. The sheep had not yet won its supremacy in upland Wales. Sheep were less crucial to a largely subsistence society than were cattle, and most Welsh wool, though adequate enough for domestic cloth production, had much too poor a reputation to be exported. Yet outsiders were already beginning to seize upon the potentialities of Wales's rich pasturelands: from the early twelfth century Anglo-Norman settlers in districts such as Glamorgan, Gower, Cydweli and Pembroke were rearing large flocks of sheep and exporting wool; soon after, the major Cistercian abbeys of south Wales and the borderland, such as Margam, Neath, Tintern, and Dore (but significantly not those of north Wales), became the proud owners of flocks of several thousand sheep each. The advance of cereals in native Wales was thereby paralleled by the advance of sheep in much of Anglo-Norman Wales.

Wales underwent profound social and economic changes in the twelfth and thirteenth centuries. Even contemporaries recognized that a transformation was afoot. 'Thereafter', remarked the author of the life of Gruffudd ap Cynan (originally composed in the second half of the twelfth century but referring to the first quarter of that century), 'all goods in Gwynedd multiplied. The inhabitants began to build churches in every part of it. They planted trees. They established orchards and gardens and enclosed them with hedges and ditches. They also began to eat the fruits of the earth, after the fashion of the Romans'.[27] To the author the economic renaissance which he so vividly described was linked directly to the political mastery secured by Gruffudd. The biographer's instincts were probably right: the sustained political hegemonies of several native rulers (notably Gruffudd ap Cynan (d. 1137) and Owain his son (d. 1170) of Gwynedd, Madog ap Maredudd (d. 1160) of Powys, and Rhys ap Gruffudd (d. 1197) of Deheubarth), the gradual coalescence of larger political units, the growth of princely protection and power, and the sharp decline in the raids of the Vikings and in the plundering forays of Normans were certainly part of the essential backcloth to the economic transformation of Wales from the twelfth century. Equally important, but equally elusive in terms of documentation, was a profound change in the *mentalité* of the ruling classes of the country. In the eleventh century royal dynasties, a warrior aristocracy, and rich ecclesiastical communities held sway over large, if underdeveloped, territories; they treated the dependent peasantry as their property; they commandeered food, goods, lodgings, services, and labour from them; they delighted in the values and habits of a heroic aristocracy— in pillage and booty, precious objects and gift-giving. This, in the terminology of contemporary Europe, was a world of *potentes* and *pauperes*, of warriors and peasants. Inequality and dependence remained features of Welsh society in the twelfth and thirteenth centuries; but the nature of economic exploitation was changing. The emphasis now was on a regular and defined control over a rural peasantry and its land, on rents and mills, on the profits of justice, and on the control of the sale and marketing of surpluses. An economy of plunder was being replaced by an economy of profiteering.

Some of the momentum for this change was generated within native

---

[27] *Historia Gruffud vab Kenan*, p. 30. (*History G. ap. C.*, p. 155).

society itself. The demographic growth of the period and the extensive colonization of new land both opened up new opportunities and imposed new constraints; it was in these very generations that the lineage-system of native Wales as it applied to the descent and division of land seems to have been defined.[28] The Welsh custom of partibility among male heirs (W. *cyfran*) also had profound implications for the distribution and redistribution of landed fortunes. It led to the recurrent haemorrhaging of rural wealth: even Welsh jurists had to concede that 'it may happen that an inheritance of land may descend in small shares among forty or sixty co-heirs'.[29] Estates were thereby assembled and dismantled in a few generations. In these circumstances the relative pattern of fertility and mortality among families was a crucial factor in promoting differentiation between the circumstances of individuals and in the distribution of rural wealth. Princely power and privilege also shaped economic opportunities: individuals who benefited from the munificence of princes (as did Einion ap Maredudd and his son in Dyffryn Clwyd at the hands of the princes of Gwynedd in the thirteenth century) or from the largess of Marcher lords (as did Hywel ap Meurig and his family in mid-Wales from the Mortimers and the Bohuns) found their economic prospects greatly enhanced. Even native Welsh law, conservative as it was in its concepts of property-rights and fiercely protective of lineage title to land ('according to the law of Hywel, called *cyfraith*', so reported one witness to the law commission of 1281, 'no one can sell or quitclaim his inheritance'),[30] began to adjust to a society in which landed wealth circulated more freely. Concepts of custodial rights in land (W. *gwarcheidwadaeth*), of lease and exchange (W. *llog*, *cyfnewid*), and above all of short-term lease by vifgage (W. *prid*) eased some of the rigidities of native custom during the thirteenth century. Powerful men, such as Ednyfed Fychan, the steward of Llywelyn ab Iorwerth, could do even better and effect outright purchases of land.

The momentum for rapid and far-reaching economic change was being generated, therefore, from within native society itself in the twelfth and thirteenth centuries; but this was more than matched by the pressure and pattern for change from without. Among the primary agents of that external pressure were the Anglo-Norman colonists. By the end of the thirteenth century alien settlers had left their imprint deeply on many parts of Wales. In some districts, notably south-western Dyfed and southern Gower, they had almost entirely displaced the native population. Elsewhere they had established themselves firmly in a broad hinterland around the Norman castles, while the Welsh were confined to the foothills and the uplands: such was the contrast between lowland and upland Hay, eastern and western Radnor, the valley of the river Clun and the *multa Walscheria*

---

[28] See above, p. 126.   [29] *Ancient Laws and Institutes of Wales*, II, 433.
[30] *Calendar of Welsh Rolls 1277–94*, p. 195.

of the hills to the west, centres such as Usk, Monmouth, Chepstow, Caerleon, Abergavenny, and Brecon, on the one hand, and the outlying townships of those districts, on the other. After the Edwardian conquest of 1282–3, a further and final wave of English settlers was introduced into northern and western Wales, especially into the fertile lowlands of lordships such as Denbigh and Dyffryn Clwyd. While it is impossible to estimate the number of alien colonists, it can hardly be doubted that, cumulatively over two centuries and in proportion to Wales's existing population, this movement of settlers into the country was highly significant. It was to be one of the last major influxes of population into Wales before the Industrial Revolution. Parts of Wales were now a multi-racial society. Writs were addressed to 'all our faithful subjects, French, English, Welsh' (and occasionally, Fleming) and interpreters were much in demand. Gerald of Wales recounted how Philip of Marcross acted as an interpreter between Henry II and a local Glamorgan man who spoke only English and also recollected how his own brother was addressed in Flemish at Haverfordwest in the late twelfth century.

Many of these new families were colonists in every sense of that word, settling in a foreign country and winning new land for cultivation. Roger de Somery and others had 'colonized lands in the forest of Cibwr' (Glamorgan) and likewise the English peasants who settled in farthest Ceredigion in Henry I's reign came to a land which was, even by the native chronicler's own admission, 'empty . . . and well-nigh deserted'.[31] Their successors in Denbigh almost two centuries later were similarly tempted by the prospect of large tracts of land ripe for cultivation; in two vills alone according to the *Survey* of 1334 English colonists had reclaimed 560 acres from the waste. The colonists, coming from a society dominated by regular and intensive arable cultivation, had a keen eye for good land and easy profits: they quickly seized on land which 'abounded with the best corn'[32] and they built mills as tokens both of their technological superiority and of a new and exploitative seignorial regime. But they also had an equally keen eye for the rich pastoral potential of Wales. Maurice de Londres, according to Gerald of Wales, had large flocks of sheep on his distant Welsh lordship of Cydweli by the mid-twelfth century and so likewise did the earls of Gloucester in Gwynllŵg and Glamorgan. Most enterprising of all were the Flemings. Well-versed as they were from experience in their homeland 'in commerce and the woollen industry', they were soon exploiting the pasturelands of south-west Wales commercially.[33] Gerald remarked, for example, that the Flemings of Talacharn were far richer in sheep than their neighbours, and he gave some indication of the scale of Fleming enterprise

[31] *Cartae de Glamorgan*, I, 140, no. 141; *Brut, s.a.* 1116 (p. 42).
[32] *Episc. Acts*, I, 245 (D. 64).
[33] *IK*, I, xi (*Opera*, vi, 83).

in Wales when he noted in an aside that Roger Bechet of Rhos owed ten stones of wool to his creditors.

The influence of the Anglo-Norman colonists on the character and tempo of economic activity in lowland Wales, especially in the south, must have been profound. Their imprint was, and is, evident on the countryside —in the settlements which bear their names, in the early anglicization of the place- and field-names of much of coastal south Wales, in the introduction of new customary acres (often reminiscent of those of south-west England), in exploiting the mineral, forest, and fishery resources of the newly conquered lands, and, above all, in greatly extending the practice of permanent arable cultivation and market production in lowland Wales. Their impact on the native Welsh, if only by way of imitation, is likely to have been considerable. The settlers, it is true, often kept themselves to themselves. Security dictated that this should be so in early days; and so did differences in language, customs, and dues. The settlers proudly regarded themselves as 'the foreign English' and exploited the privileges of that status to the full; and from at least the thirteenth century the formal separation of native and settler was administratively and legally recognized in the establishment of Welshries and Englishries.[34] Even as late as Elizabeth's day, George Owen could observe of the English and Welsh in his native county of Pembrokeshire that they 'keepe eche from dealinges with the other, as mere strangers' and that the differences between them in 'maners, diett, buildinges and tyllinge of the lande' still remained profound.[35] Yet in spite of good measure of watchful distrust and institutionalized separation between English and Welsh, the settlers were bound to have a profound impact on native society. In many parts of lowland Wales—in the lordships of Chepstow, Abergavenny, Monmouth, Usk, Caerleon, Brecon, and lowland Glamorgan—colonists and natives lived in neighbouring vills, sometimes indeed cheek by jowl with each other in the same vill; rubbed shoulders with each other in the markets and fairs; exchanged land and intermarried. Welshmen periodically participated in the economic life of the Englishry, as did the Welshmen of Cantrefselyf (Brecon) who came down to the English manor of Bronllys to perform their harvest services. In these circumstances it hardly admits of doubt that Anglo-Norman colonization often acted as a major catalyst, however slow-acting, for initiating and accelerating the tempo of economic change in lowland south Wales and, indirectly, in other parts of Wales.

One manifestation of this economic change was the growth of a more

    [34] See below, pp. 283–4.
    [35] George Owen, *The Description of Pembrokeshire*, ed. H. Owen (Cymmrodorion Record Series, 1902–36), I, 39.

complex and differentiated economy and of a more closely interwoven and increasingly monetized network of trade. In general terms, it seems fair to claim that with two notable exceptions—the north-east lowlands up to the river Clwyd, which occasionally formed an economic and political annex of the Cheshire lowlands, and the much more extensive coastlands of the south-east, from the Wye as far as the Ogwr, which probably already had some agricultural and commercial links with the west Midlands and south-west England—Wales in the eleventh century was by contemporary English standards an economically poor, backward, and underdeveloped society. There is singularly little evidence of organized markets or fairs or indeed of the sale of surplus goods on any considerable scale. Rather, wealth and surplus production were transferred from a subject peasantry to a ruling military aristocracy and its retinues, through plunder, tribute, and renders in kind; while much that might in later periods be categorized as trade now took the form of gift-exchange. Wales, like Scotland, had no coinage of its own: the so-called 'Hywel Dda' penny had been minted at Chester, and the coin-hoards discovered in Wales in this period are mainly to be found in coastal areas and consist of English-minted coins. Most trade was probably conducted in barter, and the valuations for goods exchanged or sold were normally expressed in animals or occasionally in silver objects. Some local exchange of goods and some specialization of function there may well have been; but, as so often in such societies, long-distance trade in a few luxury goods—in gold, armour, or precious clothes—was more significant, in value if not in quantity, than local trade. The line between trade and plunder was indistinct, notably along Wales's western seaboard. Slaves remained a major item of 'trade'; more often than not they were sold into captivity to reward foreign allies or buy off Viking marauders. There is singularly little evidence of urban or even proto-urban life in such a society. Small settlements, possibly prompted by trading links with Ireland and across the Bristol Channel, may already have developed in Cardiff, Kenfig (Glamorgan), and Swansea; at Caerwent (Gwent Iscoed) a fine series of Anglo-Saxon and Anglo-Norman pennies suggests continuous occupation of parts of the Roman town from the mid-tenth century onwards; in north-east Wales the Mercian burh at the estuary of the Clwyd on the site of the later Rhuddlan may have formed a focus for the first stirrings of urban life and for links with the emergent town of Chester; elsewhere monastic communities, the only substantial centres of stationary population and regular demand, may well have encouraged the development of urban features in places such as Carmarthen and St Davids. The impression of commercial and urban backwardness may, it is true, be exaggerated by the paucity of written sources; but Gerald of Wales's famous *obiter dicta*, written in the 1190s, seem to confirm that impression. 'The Welsh', he remarked, 'do not live in towns, villages, or castles . . . They pay no attention to commerce, shipping or industry.'[36]

Already at the time when Gerald wrote, his comments were at best bland half-truths, applicable only to parts of Wales. As the thirteenth century progressed, the gap between Gerald's rhetorical assertions and economic realities grew wider. Major changes were afoot in Wales. Money circulated freely if not abundantly in the country. It had probably begun to do so tentatively from the tenth century onwards, as Anglo-Saxon coins, especially from the border mints at Chester, Shrewsbury, and Hereford, began to penetrate Wales; but it accelerated greatly with the establishment of Anglo-Norman mints in the country in the late eleventh–early twelfth centuries—at Rhuddlan, Cardiff, and probably St Davids, before 1087; at Carmarthen (or Rhydygors) and Pembroke before 1135; and possibly elsewhere, as at Abergavenny. As Anglo-Norman lords established themselves in lowland Wales, exploiting the country economically and deliberately fostering trade, and as Welsh troops served for pay in the armies of Anglo-Norman kings and lords, so the circulation of coinage accelerated and so also did the use of money as a medium for sales and a denominator of value. There were doubtless marked regional variations in the speed of this process. The community of west Wales could still plead as late as 1318 that they were 'never accustomed to have money in the Welshry'; they hoped, therefore, that the king would accept their taxes 'in beasts and in corn'.[37] Their plea was probably sincere. It reflects the difficulties caused in a largely pre-monetized rural society by the inroads and fiscal demands of government. Renders in much of fourteenth-century native Wales were still often paid in kind, whether in cattle or in oats. Yet the use of money, both as a unit of account and as a unit of exchange, had certainly been growing rapidly in native as well as in Anglo-Norman Wales. 'Everything', remarked a Welsh jurist, 'was formerly paid in cattle'; now, he implied, it was otherwise.[38] One major incentive to the increased circulation and usage of coins in native society was the growing fiscal demands of princely government. Until the end of the twelfth century, the occasional tributes rendered by Welsh princes to English kings had normally been paid in animals; from the early thirteenth century they were increasingly proffered and paid in cash. Most notably was this true of the vast sum of £20,000 which Llywelyn ap Gruffudd proffered to Henry III in the years 1267–70. The exaction of such sums in so short a time suggests that the prince of Gwynedd had access to considerable liquid assets and that his subjects were rapidly being brought to the knowledge of the use of money by the fiscal demands made upon them. Such a supposition is

---

[36] *DK*, I, xvii, viii (*Opera*, vi, 200, 180).   [37] *Cal. Anc. Corr.*, p. 179.
[38] Quoted in D. A. Binchy, 'Linquistic and Legal Archaisms in the Celtic Law-books', *Celtic Law Papers*, ed. D. Jenkins (*Studies presented to the International Commission for the History of Representative and Parliamentary Institutions*, no. 42, 1973), p. 117.

supported by the contemporary claim that Llywelyn had imposed a tribute of three pence on each head of cattle, under the pretext of raising money to be paid to the king of England. The demands of justice also habituated the inhabitants of native Wales to the use of money; the records preserved in the Red Book of St Asaph (Llyfr Coch Asaph) indicate that, from at least the mid-thirteenth century, fines and amercements were a major source of revenue and were calculated exclusively in cash, at least in north-east Wales.

One measure of the increased use of money in native Wales was the commutation of renders in kind into cash rents. The emergence of a more complex polity and a more stationary court doubtless encouraged such a development; so did the increased opportunities for market-sale and purchase, and the growing demand for ready cash for political and other purposes. The movement first manifested itself in areas close to the market towns of England and Anglo-Norman Wales—in the north-east and in the southern lowlands, in Powys and in Deheubarth. Thus, on the estates of the bishopric of St Davids in south-west Wales, renders of flour and cheese had been commuted into money rents by the early thirteenth century 'for the convenience of the church'.[39] Even in Gwynedd the commutation of renders was well under way before the Edwardian Conquest of 1282–3 and was accelerated by that conquest. The pace of commutation clearly varied from place to place: most of the renders in Anglesey and northern Arfon seem to have been almost totally commuted before 1282; but in Nantconwy, Ardudwy, and Eifionydd the process was still in its early stages and it was still uncompleted in Merionethshire in the fifteenth century. There is also some evidence to suggest that in north Wales at least the pace of commutation was brisker among free tenants than among bondmen.

Much of the momentum for the commutation of renders and for the increased use of money was generated in Wales, as in early medieval Europe, by kings, princes, and lords; but that momentum could not have been sustained had not the tempo of exchange and the circulation of money already quickened within Welsh society itself. Thus it is striking that the level of commutation in Gwynedd was highest in areas which lay closest to native centres of trade such as Llan-faes (Anglesey) or Nefyn (Llŷn). The nature of the transition can be particularly vividly grasped at Nefyn: there, the old bond settlement (W. *maerdref*), inhabited by serfs owing heavy renders and dues for the maintenance of the local court (W. *llys*), was replaced during the thirteenth century by a flourishing borough of fifty householders each of whom owed an individual cash rent and gave no renders in food. Nefyn in north-west native Wales epitomizes the

[39] *The Black Book of St. David's*, ed. J. W. Willis-Bund (Cymmrodorion Record Series, no. 5, 1902), p. 56.

economic transformation which, in greater or lesser degree, characterizes much of Wales in the twelfth and thirteenth centuries. Some measure of rural exchange, informal barter, trading, and specialization of function probably characterized rural society in Wales at an early date. Thus the county of Merioneth, so remote and underdeveloped in many respects, had a considerable number of craftsmen according to the 1292 tax returns— including 29 weavers, 26 cobblers, 17 smiths, and 14 carpenters. But in this direction, as in so many others, it was the twelfth and thirteenth centuries which were to be crucial. A network of markets, coping essentially with local requirements, emerged in lowland Wales; money was circulating more freely and being employed to establish a whole host of new economic relationships; surplus labour and produce were being bought and sold on an increasingly open market. Even the Welsh law-texts, intensely conservative as they are, provide hints of the changing economic climate, in their elaboration of concepts such as loan (W. *benffyc*) and lease (W. *llog*) and in references to the gage-deed (W. *prid*), which in its main features doubtless long pre-dated the Edwardian Conquest and was to be crucial in transforming the market in land in native Wales in the later Middle Ages. Above all, the immediate post-Conquest evidence shows amply that the use of credit and loans, the practice of usury, and the sale of labour for cash were already well-established features of rural society in parts of Wales. Likewise the early *prid* deeds—the earliest to survive to is dated 1289 and refers to the unusually large sum of £60—show that the use of 'good, lawful English money' in land transactions was entrenching itself, particularly in north-east Wales. In much of native north Wales the second half of the thirteenth century appears to have been particularly important in accelerating the tempo of economic change; elsewhere in Wales the change had begun much earlier.

One hub of that change was the town. It is impossible, from present evidence, to identify any community in eleventh-century Wales which might, by the most generous definition, qualify as a town. The best that can be claimed is that there were several proto-urban communities, especially in the coastal lowlands of south and north-east Wales. In the *Mabinogi*, Manawydan and his friends direct their footsteps to England when they decide to find a town where they could earn a living by trade. Yet this is not to suggest that the Welsh were somehow innately averse to urban life. When the Lord Rhys captured Cardigan from his Anglo-Norman enemies in 1165, he seems to have been more than willing to foster the small town there. More significantly, small towns, many of them admittedly minute in size, were emerging in different parts of Wales in the twelfth century and especially the thirteenth. They were often located at or near native bond vills (W. *maerdrefi*): the existence of a nucleated settlement and the demands of a royal court provided a favourable context for urban growth, especially when supplemented by the opportunities offered by coastal trade and fishing. In Gwynedd, Llan-faes (Anglesey) was the most promising of these nascent native towns—a bustling fishing port, the chief point of transit between Anglesey and the mainland, a harbour where already, before the Edwardian Conquest, thirty ships a year on average were calling, and also an important marketing and distribution centre for its hinterland. Nefyn played much the same role for the economy of native Llŷn as Llan-faes did for Anglesey, while other small proto-urban communities were beginning to emerge elsewhere—at Bangor, Caernarfon, Pwllheli (Llŷn), Tywyn (Meirionydd), and Trefriw (Nantconwy). Nor did Gwynedd enjoy a monopoly of native urban development. Much the largest and wealthiest town in native Wales—peopled overwhelmingly, it is true, by English settlers according to the tax return of 1292—was Welshpool in southern Powys. It was probably first granted a charter by its local lord, Gruffudd ap Gwenwynwyn, in the 1240s; but there had been a busy rural market there from the twelfth century. Elsewhere in native Wales, important churches formed a natural focus for the growth of rural markets and settlement. Places such as Llanrwst (Rhos), Machynlleth (Cyfeiliog), Llanidloes (Arwystli), or Llandeilo (Cantref Mawr) would hardly qualify as towns yet; but they were beginning to acquire some of the characteristics from which urban life might possibly develop.

Yet it can hardly be denied that in most of native Wales urban life was still highly tentative and anaemic in the mid-thirteenth century. It was otherwise in much of Anglo-Norman lowland south Wales. There, a vigorous urban renaissance began in the late eleventh century which was already largely complete before 1277 when Edward I began his remarkable programme of town-foundations in west and north Wales. Already by 1075 a small town had been established or enlarged on the west bank of the Wye at Chepstow (or Strigoil, as it was then known); its annual fair already realized £16. By 1086 a Norman borough had been founded or refounded within the remains of an Anglo-Saxon burh at Rhuddlan on the Clwyd estuary. By 1135 many of the major towns of south Wales were already firmly established—Monmouth, Cardiff, Abergavenny, Brecon, Tenby, Kidwelly, Carmarthen, and Pembroke among them. Several were probably located at or near sites which were already important marketing, and often ecclesiastical, centres; but it cannot be gainsaid that the initiative and enterprise of Anglo-Norman lords and settlers were vital in determining the pattern and pace of urban growth. The movement so vigorously begun by the first generations of the Anglo-Norman conquerors of Wales was continued by their successors, though neither the number nor the importance of towns founded in the century after 1150 match those of early days. By 1277 the urban map of most of lowland south Wales was already substantially complete. It was then to be complemented in a dramatic fashion by the clutch of new boroughs which Edward I and his magnates founded in west and north Wales.[40]

The role of seignorial initiative and support in this urban renaissance was crucial. Thus when Hamelin de Ballon bestowed gifts from his newly acquired lands in Gwent on the abbey of St Vincent of Le Mans, in the early twelfth century, he specifically included 'land for making a borough'.[41] In the uncertain conditions which prevailed in Wales, seignorial support and protection were vital to urban survival and prosperity. In early days the infant town was located either within the outer bailey of the castle (as appears initially to have been the case at Brecon) or in the shadow of the castle itself and often joined to it by a single, unified complex of defensive works (as at Monmouth, Tenby, Kidwelly, Chepstow, or later, Montgomery). It was as much a target for Welsh attacks as the castle itself: the history of the borough of Kenfig (Glamorgan) was punctuated regularly by Welsh attacks from the twelfth to the fourteenth centuries. From earliest days the towns of Wales were defended by earthworks, palisades, ditches, and banks, to be replaced later, as the thirteenth and fourteenth centuries progressed, by stone walls and fortified gates (such as the splendid fortified gatehouse which stands astride the Monnow bridge at Monmouth). It is a measure of the insecurity of the plantation towns in Wales that 86 per cent of them (according to Professor Beresford's calculations) were defended by walls, ramparts, or ditches, as compared with 38 per cent in England; it is equally indicative that in Wales alone was military service a normal obligation of burgess status. Seignorial support was not confined to military protection; it extended also to the grant of extensive commercial favours and trade monopolies to the nascent boroughs and even occasionally to investment loans for local merchants.

Military protection and seignorial support were crucial for the fledgling towns; their primary function was indeed to provide for the needs of the castles and their garrisons. Yet, from earliest days, their role was more positive and ambitious: they were intended as centres of Anglo-Norman colonization and exploitation in Wales. Their early population was drawn overwhelmingly from England and northern France. An early twelfth-century writ regarding Kidwelly, for example, refers to 'all the burgesses, French, English and Flemish'; Welshmen are notable by their absence from the list.[42] The alien inspiration of Welsh towns was also reflected in the fact that the customs of the Norman castle-borough of Breteuil, as mediated through the English border town of Hereford, were the exemplar

---

[40] See pp. 371–3 below.

[41] *Regesta Regum Anglo-Normannorum. Henry I 1100–1135*, ed. C. Johnson and H. A. Cronne (Oxford, 1956), no. 800.

[42] *Episc. Acts*, I, 237 (D. 27).

of the liberties of many boroughs of Wales. The long-term success of the boroughs would depend, however, neither on their liberties nor on the military protection of their lord, but on their own capacity to make themselves indispensable to the economic life of the countryside. The entrepreneurial attitude of the Anglo-Norman burgesses in this respect was in evidence from a very early date: already by the time of Domesday Book the well-being of the little borough of Rhuddlan was founded on its market, tolls, and mint, and its links with the iron industry, as well as on the beneficent support of its lord and on the protection of his castle.

Several towns soon outgrew their original ramparts: Cardiff shows evidence of suburban development by the end of the twelfth century, while Abergavenny, Carmarthen, Haverfordwest, and Pembroke quickly spilled over their initial Norman boundaries. Elsewhere, towns displayed their growing confidence by liberating themselves from the apron-strings of castles: thus the burgeoning borough of Brecon quickly transferred itself from the castle bailey on the west side of the river Honddu to a much more extensive site on the eastern bank. The growing confidence of the boroughs was expressed in the thirteenth century in the increasing measure of self-government, especially in judicial and commercial affairs, conceded to them in charters of liberties and in the investment of civic funds in the building of town walls (now often rebuilt in stone) and the endowment and enlargement of town churches. Even the boroughs founded in the wake of the Edwardian Conquest—notably Beaumaris, Ruthin, and Denbigh—grew by leaps and bounds and revealed once more how quickly Welsh society responded to the opportunities presented by urban development. Failures, of course, there were; indeed, there were proportionately more failed towns in Wales and the March than in England. Some nascent boroughs, such as Cefnllys (Maelienydd) or Caus (Shropshire), faltered once the frontier military conditions in which they were born changed; others, such as Radnor or Painscastle (Elfael), remained stunted because their commercial opportunities were too feeble in an upland region; yet others were effectively snuffed out, as were Aberafan (Glamorgan) and Llywel (Brecon), by unfriendly competition from powerful neighbours. Even the towns which survived were tiny: only Cardiff, Carmarthen, and Haverford could boast populations well in excess of a thousand by 1300. Nevertheless, by that date there were some 80 towns (the number depends on one's definition) in lowland Wales, well-located in relation to the distribution of the population. The appearance of these towns is one striking measure of the economic transformation that Wales had undergone in the twelfth and thirteenth centuries.

The primary role of the town—the *raison* of its existence and guarantee of its success—was as a centre of specialization and exchange in what was still a largely rural, subsistence economy. Surviving lists of burgesses reveal that the majority of townsmen in Wales either belonged to the victualling trades (butchers, bakers, brewers, fishmongers) or were craftsmen (traders in leather, metal, or textiles). There was little differentiation of function in the activities of such men; they were producers, craftsmen, wholesale- and retail-traders rolled up into one. The town also served as a centre for the marketing and distribution of surplus produce from its hinterland and as a link for contacts with wider markets beyond the town. Its weekly markets and two or three annual fairs, market cross, and booth-hall (where tolls were paid) became the foci of a network of local trade. The burgesses' control over that trade was, at least in theory, virtually exclusive, since borough charters in Wales normally granted a monopoly of wholesale trade, and even of retail trade, in animals and large goods to local townsmen. 'No alien or foreigner (i.e. no one who was not a burgess or a member of the gild merchant)', declared the borough charter of Brecon in 1308, 'shall henceforth trade within our land (i.e. the whole of the lordship) of Brecon.'[43]

The importance of towns in the economic life of a localized and underdeveloped society, such as that of medieval Wales, was out of all proportion to their minuscule size. They lubricated local trade and accelerated and formalized opportunities for the sale and exchange of produce and, thereby, for the circulation of money. Their burgesses often commanded more liquid assets than other members of the community. They might use them to weave a network of loans and rural credit: it is symbolic that it was to a burgess of Carmarthen that the last of the princelings of Deheubarth, Rhys ap Maredudd, turned when he was short of cash. They used them also to buy land in the vicinity of towns, to rear flocks of sheep (as did John Eccleston of Flint) and herds of cattle for sale on the market, lease mills, demesne land, and escheated tenements, and exploit the mineral wealth of the hinterland (as did the burgesses of Flint in the 1280s). It was thus that the Collier family rose quickly to eminence in the castle-borough of Harlech in the fourteenth century, the Fort family waxed powerful in the Llansteffan area, or the Chester merchant, William of Doncaster, came to dabble in the wool and lead trades of Wales, import wine to Anglesey, and establish himself as a burgess of Beaumaris and mayor of Flint (in 1312). The career of William of Doncaster reveals indeed that the ambitions and horizons of some burgesses were not limited to local trade; they might strive to cut a figure on a wider, regional, inter-town stage; some of them even ventured into long-distance trade.

Wales certainly enjoyed occasional trading contacts with the external world in the eleventh century—notably with Ireland along the western sea coast and with England in the north-east and south-east. But, as with towns

[43] W. Rees, 'The charters of the boroughs of Brecon and Llandovery', *BBCS* 2 (1923–5), 245–61 at p. 248.

so with external trade, the tempo accelerates markedly and the pattern becomes much more regular from the twelfth century onwards. The coming of the Anglo-Normans as soldiers, settlers, burgesses, and merchants was clearly one major impetus for change; the growing population of Wales and the stability and complexity of its economy were others. Already by the late twelfth century two independent and shrewd observers—William of Newburgh and Gerald of Wales—noted that Wales had become economically dependent on England for supplies of iron, cloth, salt, and, even more crucially, of corn, especially in times of famine. Both of them recognized that such economic dependence could easily be exploited as an instrument of political control and submission. The force of that truism was not lost on Edward I: one of his first acts in the war of 1282 was to place an embargo on the sale of corn, wine, salt, iron, and armour to the Welsh. The ties of economic relationships and dependence had, as so often, paved the way for political control.

The major trading contacts between Wales and England were made in a line of border English towns—notably Chester, Oswestry, Shrewsbury, Whitchurch, Ludlow, Leominster, Hereford, and Bristol. Merchants from farthest north and west Wales were certainly visiting these towns by at least the thirteenth century; obstruction to their freedom of passage was to be one cause of tension between the king of England and the prince of Gwynedd. The merchants of the larger and better established boroughs of south Wales were travelling much further afield throughout southern England: merchants from Carmarthen, for example, were taking wool to the Bristol staple by 1218, had reached Winchester by the 1220s, and were soon attending some of the most prominent English fairs, such as those of Lincoln and Boston. English merchants for their part were beginning to venture into Wales and to exploit its resources. Timber, so abundant in Wales, was being exported in the twelfth century to build English abbeys (as at Abingdon) and royal lodges (as at Cheddar); by the fourteenth century the exploitation of the timber trade of south-east Wales was a major source of revenue for several leading English magnate families. Fur, hides, and leather were also natural exports for an upland pastoral country, and its mineral resources—such as the lead of Flint (already mentioned in Domesday) and later, the coal of Cilfái (Gower)—were also exploited by Anglo-Norman lords and entrepreneurs.

Cattle and sheep were, and were to remain, both in bulk and in value, Wales's premier exports. Herds of cattle were driven to England to meet the needs of royal and seignorial larders and increasingly also to satisfy the demands of a growing market in meat, especially in the west Midlands. The wool trade and the cloth industry appear to have been rather sluggish in developing in much of Wales; the inaccessibility of much of the country and the notoriously poor quality of much of the wool were doubtless contributory factors. In this respect, however, as in so many others, regional differences within Wales were crucial. The wool of the border districts of eastern and southern Wales had an outstandingly good reputation and the pastoral resources of these areas were rapidly being exploited for commercial production. The Cistercian abbeys were among the early pioneers: the monks of Margam, Neath, and Tintern owned flocks of 5,245, 4,897, and 3,264 sheep, respectively, by the end of the thirteenth century. But Anglo-Norman lay lords also quickly saw the potential of the district: the Braose family was dispatching merchants to buy Welsh wool by a least 1203 and in the next century great English comital families, such as the Bohun earls of Hereford and the Fitzalan earls of Arundel, built up large flocks on their Marcher estates in Wales. Even the native cloth industry was responding to technological change: at least 25 fulling mills had been built in Wales by 1300 and a further 48 were to be added in the next half-century. Their distribution—overwhelmingly in the north-east, in lowland south Wales, and in the March—reinforces the impression that it was pre-eminently in these districts that commercial attitudes and opportunities were developing most rapidly.

Yet the impact of such changes was being felt even elsewhere. Already by 1212 the monks of the remote abbey of Strata Florida (Ceredigion) were given permission to send wool overseas for three years. The licence is doubly significant. It is a reminder that wool was the commodity *par excellence* which brought parts of Wales, however hesitatingly, into the orbit of international trade. It is also a reminder of the role that powerful corporations, especially Cistercian abbeys and Anglo-Norman lords, played in exploiting the pastoral wealth of upland Wales and in investing capital in large-scale farming and long-distance trade. By the early–mid-thirteenth century, merchants from Flanders and Italy were buying considerable quantities of wool in all parts of Wales; by the next century Welsh wool was being taken in bulk to great warehouses in London prior to export overseas. Most of this profitable foreign trade was in the hands of English and continental merchants; as so often the local merchant community had to be content with the profits of local retail trade. Yet even in this respect some of the larger towns of coastal south Wales—notably Cardiff, Swansea, Carmarthen, Tenby, and Haverford—were coming of age in the thirteenth and fourteenth centuries. They served rich and secure agricultural hinterlands and were not too closely tied, as were inland towns, to the apron-strings of seignorial favour. Their richer merchants were partners not only in a busy coastal trade in Wales and the west of England but also, to some degree, in more wide-ranging activities—sending ships to carry cereals from Ireland, transport wool and leather to England, export hides to Brittany, and import salt from the Isle d'Oléron and wine from Gascony.

Wales in 1350 was a profoundly different country from the Wales of 1050. That is, perhaps, a truism which requires no defence or elaboration. Yet it is a triusm whose dimensions are frequently obscured. Several important reasons suggest themselves by way of explanation—the absence of documentary and statistical evidence to measure the change that took place, the essentially static and conservative view of native Welsh society transmitted by the sources (notably the native law-texts and the fourteenth-century surveys), the seductive simplicity of Gerald of Wales's brilliant characterization of the Wales of his day, the long-established historical tradition of separating the study of native Wales (*pura Wallia*) from that of Anglo-Norman Wales (*marchia Wallie*), and the assumption, implicit if not explicit, that the chronology of political change—in which the final conquest of native Wales 1277–83 is, of course, the major watershed—should also be the framework for the study of social and economic change. This latter change was multifaceted: the population grew rapidly by medieval standards; alien colonization profoundly altered its character in parts of lowland Wales: the bounds of cultivated land were greatly extended; new and subsidiary settlements were founded; the pattern of agricultural exploitation was altered; money came to circulate freely, if not abundantly; towns were founded or grew; and a nexus of marketing links was established at the local, regional, and even, in some measure, international levels. Wales by 1350 was much closer in its economic structures and the pattern of its economic relationships to the Wales of 1650 than to the Wales of 1050. The chronology and pace of transformation naturally varied enormously within Wales; indeed, regional dissimilarities were in a measure accentuated by the transformation. Much of the coastal lowland of south Wales and the river valleys of the south-east were being assimilated, in social configuration, patterns of agricultural and seignorial exploitation, and their marketing and commercial networks, to the practices of lowland England, especially of south-west England. The 1292 tax returns for lowland lordships, such as Monmouth and Abergavenny, reveal a much more complex differentiation in the distribution of taxable wealth, in both countryside and town, than is to be identified in the upland districts of north and south Wales. Important as these regional differences are, it is equally clear that native Welsh society itself was changing rapidly, particularly from the mid-twelfth century onwards. At the very period that political confrontation between native society and English king and baronage was reaching its climax, the circumstances of economic and social change were bringing native and Anglo-Norman Wales into closer, if not close, liaison.

CHAPTER 7

CHURCH AND RELIGION IN
AN AGE OF CHANGE

THE Church in Wales in the eleventh century was fully part of Latin
Christendom as far as religious observance, doctrine, and faith were
concerned. Yet, like many of the churches of western Europe in the early
Middle Ages, it had a strongly regional and distinctive character in its
customs, organization, and institutions. The foundations of much of its
individuality dated back to the period of the conversion and in particular to
'the age of the saints' of the fifth and sixth centuries. That period acquired
in ecclesiastical mythology much of the status and mystique that the era of
'the men of the North' (W. *gwŷr y Gogledd*) occupied in secular
mythology. The individuality of Welsh ecclesiastical practice had been
reinforced and deepened over the centuries by the relative isolation of the
country (especially from the ninth century), by the closeness of its ties with
Ireland rather than with England and the Continent, by the defensive
conservatism of its ecclesiastical personnel, and by the way in which native
ecclesiastical practices and institutions had become entwined with the
fabric and assumptions of Welsh secular society. Changes were certainly
afoot in the church well before the advent of Normans; the example of
Ireland indeed suggests that the native church in Wales would of its own
accord have brought itself, albeit slowly, more closely into line with
ecclesiastical developments in western Europe in the eleventh and twelfth
centuries. The coming of the Normans ensured that the transformation was
effected more briskly, more thoroughly, and often more brutally than
might otherwise have happened. In order to grasp the nature of that
transformation—the most profound and far-reaching change in the Welsh
church between the conversion and the Reformation—a brief sketch of
some of the features of the native church on the eve of the coming of the
Normans must be attempted.

Such a sketch is not easily undertaken. The more research that is
undertaken, the more complex and uncertain does our picture of the pre-
Norman church in Wales become. To talk of it as a 'Celtic' church is to
overestimate its similarities with the early Irish church, whereas the
differences are almost as marked. It is also to overemphasize the
individuality of the Welsh church: many of the features which are often
characterized as distinctively 'Celtic' are in fact common enough in other

parts of the early medieval church. It has also to be remembered that our image of the pre-Norman church in Wales is mediated through the concerns, language, and perceptions of the men of the eleventh and twelfth centuries. Two groups in particular were responsible for creating that image. On the one hand were those anxious to defend the reputation of the native church in face of the Norman assault, and to extol its antiquity. Prominent in this role were the authors of the lives of the Welsh saints written in the late eleventh and early twelfth centuries (notably those of St David by Rhigyfarch of Llanbadarn, c.1085–95, and of St Cadog by Lifris of Llancarfan, as well as those later assembled in the most important volume of Welsh hagiography, British Library Cotton Vespasian A XIV), and those who collected and edited the charters, memoranda, and saints' lives, in the earliest and longest section of the Book of Llandaff, probably compiled in the 1120s. On the other hand were the ecclesiastics who were steeped in the assumptions and categories of the cathedral schools and of the reformed European church of the twelfth century and who judged— and often misunderstood—the native church in Wales in the light of these standards. The most eloquent and most influential of these commentators was Gerald of Wales.

The Welsh church was neither formally nor substantively a unit. Wales was not acknowledged as a separate province of the church; it did not have a unified ecclesiastical structure under a single archbishop; and there were considerable differences in the nature of ecclesiastical organization from one part of the country to another. Bishops already played a prominent part in the Welsh church. There is no indication that in Wales, unlike Ireland, bishops were in any way dependent upon or under the authority of abbots. On the contrary, bishops already exercised a wide range of powers, spiritual, administrative, and jurisdictional. The bishop in Wales was, so it seems, in effect the head of an ecclesisastical community exercising authority over a federation of daughter churches dedicated to, founded by, or donated to the same saint (e.g. Dewi, Teilo, Beuno) and over their lands. His authority grew as the endowment of the mother church and its status outshone those of its competitors and as other mother churches were brought within the ambit of its authority by attraction or annexation. Even so, the churches and ecclesiastical estates subject to one bishop might be intermingled with those subject to another. There was no organized hierarchy of bishops nor an established metropolitan structure within the country, though a bishop might, in respect of either the eminence of his church or that of his own person, come to exercise at least a temporary seniority or primacy over his fellow bishops. That seems to have happened, at least ocasionally, both at St Davids and at Bangor.

Wales, therefore, was already a land of bishops; but the number of bishoprics which would survive still remained to be determined and so did their territorial limits. Bishoprics were still fluid; they were assembled and reassembled at the initiative of individual bishops and their supporters. Thus the bishopric of Llandaff was taking shape in the eleventh century, extending its claims, and assimilating possible earlier bishoprics and ecclesiastical cults, in the east in Welsh Bicknor and Ergyng, in the south in Llancarfan, and in the west in Llandeilo Fawr. Bishops could certainly be powerful and thrustful individuals; some of them were even acquiring territorial designations for their bishoprics. Yet there is little indication that their authority was supported by an infrastructure of ecclesiastical governance. Such power as they exercised co-existed with and did not necessarily override the authority and traditions of regional mother churches and monastic federations. The fluidity of political power and the absence of urban nuclei in Wales further inhibited the development of clearly defined territorial dioceses. Wales's political decentralization seemed to be matched by the inchoate and fluid character of its ecclesiastical governance.

The Welsh church was in origin and essence a monastic church, but 'monastic' in a sense which would barely be recognized within the tradition and practice of Benedictine monasticism in Europe. Each mother church constituted a self-contained ecclesiastical community, consisting of an abbot (who might also, as in St Davids, be a bishop) and a group of canons, sharing a common income but living as secular clerks, often indeed as married clerks and even transmitting their property and ecclesiastical offices to their children. Such *clasau*, as they were known in Welsh, were common throughout Wales. Thus when Bernard, the first Norman bishop of St Davids, came to his see in 1115 he found there a body of *claswyr* or secular canons. *Clasau* of this kind certainly survived in native Wales—at churches such as Tywyn (Meirionydd) and Llandinam (Arwystli)—well into the thirteenth century and dominated the ecclesiastical life of their respective districts.

The church in Wales, as was to be expected in a decentralized and politically fragmented society, was a localized one. Each local district had its own mother church and jealously guarded its own ecclesiastical independence. Thus the mother church, or *clas*, of Llanbadarn Fawr claimed ecclesiastical authority over the whole *cantref* of Penweddig in northern Ceredigion; that of Tywyn initially over the whole *cantref* of Meirionydd, subsequently over the smaller district or commote of Ystumanner; that of Llangollen over the commote of Nanheudwy. These principal churches and their patron saints had been munificently endowed with land and food-rents by kings and princes. They claimed legal immunities and privileges which exempted them from the claims and authority of laymen. They exercised control over satellite chapels within their districts and over other churches dedicated to the same patron as theirs beyond those districts. The saints themselves, on the whole, enjoyed strictly local cults, the major exceptions being Dewi (St David), Teilo, and Beuno. They were the focus of intense regional loyalties, such as that commanded by St Tysilio as chief saint of Powys and patron of the great mother church of Meifod, as is well illustrated by the ode addressed to him by Cynddelw in the twelfth century. The heads of these provincial churches—be they abbots or bishops or bishop-abbots—exercised a range of powers by consent, gift, or usurpation little to be distinguished from those of lay potentates. Indeed, those powers—in terms of concepts of honour, status, and injury-payment—were clearly modelled on the values of lay society.

This assimilation of lay and ecclesiastical values and mores is a striking feature of the native church in Wales. Churches throughout Europe took on the colour of the society in which they operated, and assumed, often unconsciously, many of its values; but rarely had a church so submerged itself into the local social landscape as in Wales. It had adopted many of the values and assumptions of a heroic and violent society. God was a 'ruler' or 'sovereign' (W. *gwledig, mechteyrn*), incomparable as were wordly heroes (*ni'th oes gystedlydd*). Christ likewise was saluted as a 'hero' (W. *arwr*), and his 'prowess' (W. *gwrhydri*) was construed in terms borrowed from the secular world. 'He seized the plunder of Hell into his possession', vaunted one poet; thereby, according to another, 'he had bought reconciliation' between God and man, much as a feud might be terminated by buying off hostility.[1] Saints were similarly depicted as sacred heroes performing wondrous acts of spiritual valour; their protection was as great as that of any lord; their wrath as dreadful and their munificence as generous as that of any prince. Their property and immunities were protected by the same code of privilege (W. *nawdd*), honour (W. *braint*), insult (W. *sarhad*), and punishment (W. *cam*) as that of lay society; and the right of vengeance, so central to the ethos of that society, was likewise jealously upheld in the name of the saint. It is little wonder that Gerald of Wales should observe that Welsh and Irish saints were more vindictive than others; they merely reflected the values of secular society. Piety and vengeance lived cheek by jowl with each other in the lives of ordinary men as well as those of the saints: Walter Map paints a memorable portrait of a Welshman as extreme

---

[1] *Hen Gerddi Crefyddol*, ed. H. Lewis (Cardiff, 1931), pp. 66 ('Dug anrhaith uffern yn ei afflau'), 24 ('Prynesid Mab Duw mad garennydd'). My comments on the religious poetry of the court bards in this chapter are particularly indebted to the following commentaries: D. Myrddin Lloyd, *Rhai Agweddau ar Ddysg y Gogynfeirdd*. Darlith Goffa G. J. Williams (Cardiff, 1977); Catherine McKenna, 'Molawd Seciwlar a Barddoniaeth Grefyddol Beirdd y Tywysogion', *Ysgrifau Beirniadol*, xii (1982) ed. J. E. Caerwyn Williams, pp. 24–39; and J. E. Caerwyn Williams, *Canu Crefyddol y Gogynfeirdd*. Darlith Goffa Henry Lewis (Swansea, 1976).

in his devotion and abstinence as he was savage in his delight in battle and bloodshed.

The Welsh church had also assumed the aristocratic flavour and values of native Welsh free society. Central to that society's ethos was its emphasis on noble descent as the qualification for status and honour. The church had to subscribe to the same criteria. God himself was a well-descended proprietor (W. *priodor*) to the poet Cynddelw; and the saints were provided with genealogies which proclaimed the nobility of their descent and the closeness of their relationship to the royal dynasties. Gildas was given a Pictish king as his father; Dewi was said to be the son of Sanctus, 'king of the people of Ceredigion',[2] and when Cynddelw sang the praises of St Tysilio, he emphasized that the saint was the brother of Cynan Garwyn, the sixth-century ruler of Powys. In the present as in the past, aristocratic birth was a recommendation for high ecclesiastical office: it was as a man 'of the distinguished stock of noble . . . parents' that Rhigyfarch of Llanbadarn presented his father Sulien, bishop of St Davids 1073–8 and 1080–5, while it was from the court of Rhys ap Tewdwr (d. 1093) of Deheubarth that Caradog of Rhos (d. 1124) embarked on his career as a hermit. Men of illustrious birth were reluctant to abandon the values and habits of aristocratic life when they assumed ecclesiastical office. They often hired a *familia* of retainers and travelled around with bands of armed followers. Morfran, abbot of the old *clas* church at Tywyn (Meirionydd) and the subject of an ode of praise by Llywelyn Fardd, also served as steward for one of the princelings of Gwynedd and defended his lord's castle doughtily in 1147, while some forty years later Gerald of Wales was deeply shocked to report that the abbot of the *clas* at Llanbadarn Fawr (Ceredigion) was a layman, who strutted about in armour accompanied by a retinue of warriors. The boundary between the secular and the ecclesiastical seemed to have become hopelessly blurred in the native Welsh church.

That impression seems amply confirmed by closer inspection of some of the customs of Welsh ecclesiastical society. They were customs calculated to give deep offence to anyone conversant with the norms and teaching of the post-Gregorian church. Clerical marriage was common at every level of the Welsh church well into the twelfth century and beyond. Uchtryd, bishop of Llandaff 1140–8, for example, made no attempt to conceal the fact that he had fathered a daughter; appropriately enough he arranged for her to be married into the native Welsh princely family of Gwent, thereby forging further ties between the ecclesiastical and secular dynasties of the district. Clerical marriage begat clerical dynasties; thence it was but a short step to the hereditary transmission of ecclesiastical office. The archdeaconries

[2] *Rhigyfarch's Life of St. David*, ed. J. W. James (Cardiff, 1967), p. 3.

of Bangor and Ceredigion were virtually heritable in the twelfth century; so also were many of the cathedral stalls at St Davids and Llandaff. Great ecclesiastical dynasties—such as those founded, or continued, by Sulien, bishop of St Davids, or Herewald, bishop of Llandaff 1056–1104—monopolized many of the key ecclesiastical posts of their respective dioceses for generations.

Equally offensive to reformed ecclesiastical sensibilities was the proprietary attitude of Welsh laymen towards clerical office and ecclesiastical possessions. They regarded the churches founded by their ancestors and the lands with which they had been endowed as a family investment, upon which they could draw for their own benefit, material and spiritual. Churches were theirs to give to younger sons and relatives: thus, the Lord Rhys (d. 1197) gave one of his sons thirteen mother churches and five vills 'as his hereditary portion' and effected his promotion as archdeacon of Cardigan.[3] At the very least, laymen expected to have rights of presentation (i.e. nomination to ecclesiastical office) to such proprietary churches, and since property rights in Wales were partible among male heirs such a claim quickly came to be divided into small fractions. 'All their churches', remarked Gerald of Wales, 'have almost as many parsons and co-parcenors as there are families of chief men in the parish.'[4] Such portionary churches, as they are known, where the right of presentation was subdivided among co-heirs, were to be found in every part of Wales: there were at least eleven of them in the diocese of St Asaph in 1291, while in the great mother church of Caergybi (Holyhead, Anglesey), in the early fifteenth century, thirty-six men and women exercised their right of patronage as the descendants of two kin-groups. Nor were laymen merely content with exercising rights of presentation; they often appropriated ecclesiastical lands and incomes to their own use and took over the office of abbot, treating it as a marketable and divisible commodity.

All in all, to the critical observer, there was a great deal to cause amazement and prompt condemnation in the organization and practices of the native church in Wales in the eleventh century and indeed for several generations thereafter. At best its idiosyncrasies might be explained in terms of isolation and archaism; at worst they had to be condemned as the deviations of a local church which had ignored the norms and categories of the church universal and surrendered itself entirely to the ethos and practices of a secular, aristocratic, and heroic society. Yet the portrait of the native Welsh church presented by its critics was at best partial, at worst a travesty of the truth. The shortcomings they so self-righteously condemned—such as clerical marriage, hereditary benefices, ecclesiastical dynasties, the proprietary attitudes of patrons towards church offices and

---

[3] 'Cronica de Wallia', BBCS 12 (1946), 15.   [4] DK, II, vi (Opea, vi, 214).

lands, even portionary churches—were common elsewhere in early medieval Europe. It was by the idealized and theoretical standards of reforming churchmen of the twelfth century, rather than by the yardstick of contemporary practice, that the Welsh church most obviously stood condemned. Those standards were frequently flouted by the critics themselves. No critic was more vehement in his condemnation than Gerald of Wales; yet his own uncle, David fitz Gerald, bishop of St Davids 1148–76, was married and was lavish in his use of ecclesiastical lands and patronage to promote his own children and kinsfolk. Even Gerald himself, much to his subsequent regret, arranged for the reversion of the archdeaconry of Brecon to his own nephew. At Llandaff the great ecclesiastical dynasty associated with Bishop Herewald adjusted quickly to the new Norman dispensation and conformed to the norms of ecclesiastical governance acceptable to the Normans, but without surrendering its control over the ecclesiastical patronage and wealth of the diocese. Nor was the native ecclesiastical dispensation necessarily as corrupt and ineffective as its critics wished to depict it. Most obviously was this not true at the great *clas* church at Llanbadarn Fawr in Ceredigion. There Sulien, his sons Rhigyfarch (d. 1099), Daniel (d. 1127), and Ieuan (d. 1137), and his grandsons Sulien (d. 1146), Henry (d. 1163), and Cadifor (d. 1163) exemplified how an ecclesiastical dynasty and a *clas* church could be effective instruments for the transmission of Latin learning, the inculcation of clerical teaching, and bringing the values and teaching of the church to bear on the problems of lay society. By contemporary European standards, the *clas* of Llanbadarn was an anomaly and it was quashed by the Normans after they seized Ceredigion in 1110. Yet here Latin verse and hagiography were composed; St Augustine's treatise on the Trinity and Macrobius's commentary on Cicero's Dream of Scipio were copied; Bede's *De Natura Rerum* was glossed and used for teaching; and a by no means unimpressive classical library was available. One must, of course, beware of generalizing from the history of one remarkable clerical dynasty; but even elsewhere— at Llancarfan (Glamorgan), St Davids or Llandinam (Arwystli)—some of the scholarly traditions of Welsh clerical learning clearly survived. It was at such centres that native annals were composed, charters and legal memoranda copied, saints' lives written and rewritten, and native education imparted by 'special tutors' and 'eminent teachers'. It was the master of such a *clas* school at Llancarfan, Lifris, who penned the biography of St Cadog in the late eleventh century. The image he provided of the saint was one which coincided with his own self-image—that of an educated man, versed in the works of Donatus and Priscian. Contemporaries indeed conceded that native Wales was not without its excellences in the practice of religion. Most notable were its hermits, living either individually, as did Wechelen, the hermit of Llowes in Elfael, consulted by Gerald of

Wales, or in communities, as did the culdees in the religious houses of north Wales, such as Beddgelert (Arfon), Enlli (Bardsey Island), and Ynys Lannog (Priestholm in Anglesey). Welsh law accorded a special status to such men (W. *diofrydogion*), not dissimilar to that of holy men and anchorites in other societies. Their word had an especial force in oath-taking and they frequently acted as mediators in local disputes (as did Meilir the hermit in the difficult negotiations between Margam abbey and the men of upland Morgannwg). Even Gerald of Wales was forced to concede that 'nowhere will you find hermits and anchorites of greater spirituality than in Wales'.[5]

In 1070 the church in Wales was archaic and backwardlooking, isolated (probably more so than in earlier centuries) from England and Europe, and idiosyncratic in many of its customs. Two centuries later it was an integral part of a papally dominated Western Christendom. Its peculiarities had not been entirely eliminated, but they were now little more than the curious fossils of former days. It was the Normans who initiated this process of transformation. For them the subjugation of the Welsh church was at once politically essential and ecclesiastically necessary. Control of the church was a natural corollary of political conquest, exploitation of its wealth but another aspect of the domination and settlement of the country. But, equally, the Normans saw themselves as ecclesiastical reformers, obliged to impose the standards and practices of the recently reformed church of northern Europe on the isolated and deviant native church in Wales. They approached the task, in Wales as in England, with pruposefulness and gusto.

The appointment and control of bishops were obvious ways in which, they sought to impose their authority on the Welsh church. In was in north Wales that the initial Norman advance had been most successful and it was at Bangor that they imposed their first nominee in 1092, Hervé, one of William Rufus's chaplains (though his career there was to be cut short by the Welsh revolt of 1095). Elsewhere, the Normans did not even wait for an episcopal vacancy to demonstrate their intentions: archbishop Anselm of Canterbury temporarily suspended both bishops Herewald of Llandaff and Wilfrid of St Davids and thereby made it clear that they and their sees fell within the ambit of Canterbury's disciplinary powers. The subjugation of the Welsh espiscopate was completed by a few bold strokes: in 1107 Urban, a priest of the diocese of Worcester, was appointed bishop of Llandaff and became the first bishop in Wales who certainly made a profession of canonical obedience to the archbishop of Canterbury; in 1115 Henry I foisted one of his wife's chaplains, Bernard, on the see of St

[5] *DK*, I, xviii (*Opera*, vi, 204).

David, in spite of the vigorous protest of the native *clas*, engineered his 'election' and consecration at Westminster, and ensured that he likewise made a formal submission to the archbishop; in 1120 the new bishop of Bangor, David the Scot, though possibly a Welshman and allegedly chosen with the assent of the local church and of the native prince, was consecrated at Westminster and required to acknowledge his dependence on Canterbury; and so also was Gilbert, who was chosen to occupy the newly created or recreated see of St Asaph in 1143. All the Welsh bishoprics had now acknowledged the supremacy of Canterbury. Nothing proclaimed that supremacy more effectively than the attendance of the three Welsh bishops at a provincial synod at Westminster in 1127.

Ecclesiastical subjugation was underpinned by firm political control. Already in Domesday Book the temporalities of the bishopric of Bangor were specifically excluded from the grant of north Wales at farm to Robert of Rhuddlan; they were to be held directly of the king. The position of bishops in Wales was now to be formally assimilated to that of their colleagues in England: they were tenants-in-chief of the king; they swore fealty and homage to him; they were expected to perform the obligations due from feudal vassals, such as attendance at royal councils. The subjugation of the Welsh episcopate had been achieved with speed and thoroughness; in spite of challenges and setbacks in the twelfth century as the Anglo-Norman advance in Wales faltered, it was a control which was never effectively undermined or overturned.

Control was accompanied by exploitation. The ecclesiastical wealth of the country was not exempt from Norman greed. Some of that wealth, notably many of the estates and endowments of the bishoprics of Llandaff and St Davids, was seized directly into lay hands; it was only under papal and archiepiscopal threat or by solemn compromise—such as that concluded between Urban, bishop of Llandaff, and Robert of Gloucester, as lord of Glamorgan, in 1126—that such spoliation was stopped. More significant was the massive transfer of estates and income to the favoured monastic foundations of the new Norman lords in Normandy or in England. One of the earliest of the Norman *conquistadores* of Wales, William fitz Osbern, set the pattern clearly before 1070 when he granted the whole of the tithes of his lands between the rivers Wye and Usk to the two Norman monasteries of his foundation, Lire and Cormeilles. It was an example soon followed by other Norman lords, especially at the expense of the lands and resources of former Welsh *clasau*. St Peters abbey, Gloucester, grew rich from the former estates and endowments of Llancarfan (Glamorgan) and Llanbadarn Fawr (Ceredigion); St Peters abbey at Shrewsbury benefited from gifts in north-east Wales; the newly founded monastery of Tewkesbury was given a vast endowment of lands, churches, and tithes in the rich Vale of Glamorgan by Robert fitz Hamo and his followers, while the old Welsh sanctuary of Llangynydd (Gower), recently the refuge of the Welsh hermit Caradog, found itself transferred into the ownership of the monks of St Taurin at Evreux. These are but a few examples of the massive disendowment of the churches of Wales, especially south Wales, between 1080 and 1130 to enhance the fortunes of abbeys in Normandy and England. Not until the Reformation was there to be a comparably sudden transfer of ecclesiastical wealth in Wales.

The colonialist flavour of the Norman ecclesiastical settlement of Wales was equally clearly manifested in the nineteen Benedictine and Cluniac priories which were established in the country during the years 1070–1150. They were sited almost without exception in the shadow of the new Norman castles; their very location thereby declared that they were the spiritual arm of a military conquest. They were all initially dependent on a mother abbey either in England or in Normandy—Chepstow, for example, on the Norman abbey of Cormeilles, Monmouth on St Florent of Saumur, Basaleg (Gwent) on Glastonbury. Seven of them—Chepstow, Brecon, Monmouth, Abergavenny, Pembroke, Goldcliff (Gwent), and Ewenni (Glamorgan)—eventually graduated to full conventual status; but they remained essentially alien institutions, tied to the apron-strings of Norman lordship and recruiting exclusively from Anglo-Norman settlers in Wales and from foreign houses. 'Strengthen the locks of your doors and surround your house with a good ditch and an impregnable wall', wrote Gilbert Foliot to the prior of one of these houses in the 1140s.[6] His advice reflects the siege mentality of the Norman ecclesiastical dispensation in Wales; it is matched architecturally by the forbidding cylindrical columns and ponderous rounded arches of Ewenni priory and by the precinct wall that was eventually built around it.

Towards the native church the Normans showed scant respect. Its practices and organization appeared bizarre at best, deplorable at worst; its patrons were a motley crowd of unfamiliar 'saints' sporting outlandish names; its *clas* churches, secularized houses of hereditary canons, seemed to epitomize the very defects which the revived monasticism of Cluny and Bec had set out to reform. The reform of such a church was an obligation, the spoliation of its property fully justified. The fate of the ancient *clas* church of Llandudoch on the Teifi estuary epitomizes the attitude of the new Norman lords. On its site and out of its endowment the Norman lord of Cemais, Robert fitz Martin, founded around 1115 the new priory of St Dogmaels and brought thirteen monks from the house of Tiron to introduce reformed Benedictine monasticism to these distant parts of West Wales. The Welsh saints were treated as cavalierly as the native *clasau*. Some were entirely demoted, to be replaced by patrons drawn from the

[6] *Letters and Charters of Gilbert Foliot*, ed. A. Morey and C. N. L. Brooke (Cambridge, 1967), p. 47.

international calendar: at Glasbury (its Welsh form, Y Clas-ar-Wy, being a clear reminder of its former Welsh ecclesiastical status) St Cynidr was ousted by St Peter, at Caerwent (Gwent) St Tathan by St Stephen, at Cilgerran (Emlyn) St Llawddog by St Lawrence. Elsewhere, the native saints were too firmly established and their cults too profitable for such unceremonious demotion; even so, the merits of a local saint might be supplemented by those of an international colleague. So it was that St John the evangelist came to keep company with St Teulyddog at Carmarthen and St Peter and St Paul to bolster the intercessionary powers of St Trinio at Llandrinio (eastern Powys). Most remarkable was the way in which St David was pushed into second place by St Andrew at the cathedral church of Dewi himself (at least in formal documents, if not in popular usage), just as St Peter naturally took precedence over St Teilo at Llandaff.

The impact of the Normans on the church of south Wales in the period 1070–1140 was profound and enduring; but the transformation which the Welsh church underwent in the twelfth and thirteenth centuries was not solely a by-product of the enterprise, example, and greed of the Normans. It was also part of a more general wave of church reform and reorganization, associated in particular with a revived papacy and a monastic reform movement, and expressing itself in a far greater measure of uniformity in church organization and practice, and in closer international ties, throughout Europe. The impact of this movement on the *ecclesia Wallicana* was profound.

Dioceses were defined and demarcated; diocesan control of the local church was much more amply articulated. Some of the ingredients of territorial dioceses were already being assembled, especially in the south-east, in the tenth and eleventh centuries; but it was in the twelfth century that the diocesan geography of Wales began to assume the definitive shape that it was to retain until the twentieth century. The pioneers of the process were two remarkably forceful and enterprising bishops, Urban of Llandaff, 1107–34, and Bernard of St Davids, 1115–48. It was out of the struggle between these two men that the territorial extent of both their dioceses was forged in the period 1120–34. Urban set his sights high and pursued his claims along two parallel paths, claiming jurisdiction over all churches dedicated to the three patronal saints of Llandaff (Dyfrig, Teilo, and Euddogwy), their disciples, and successors, and also asserting that as bishop of Glamorgan—the title by which he was normally known—his territorial diocese should be commensurate with the ancient kingdom of Morgannwg, extending thereby from the Wye to the Tywi (though in their more immodest moments his supporters claimed that his diocese should range from Moccas in Herefordshire to Ynys Teithi, a lost island in the Irish sea beyond St Davids!). Bernard countered such claims vigorously and, indeed, counter-attacked with great effectiveness by claiming metropolitan authority over the whole of Wales for the see of St Davids. The dispute over diocesan boundaries was conducted with great vigour and resourcefulness, and though Urban seemed to have gained a temporary victory in 1129 it was Bernard who eventually emerged triumphant. Ergyng (Archenfield) was formally incorporated into the diocese of Hereford; Gower, Ystrad Yw, and Ewias into that of St Davids. The bishops of Llandaff had to be content with a consolation prize of a single Teilo church and manor in Gower—Llandeilo Ferwallt (Bishopston). The limits of the northern dioceses do not seem to have involved a similar struggle. Here the key date was 1143, when the old bishopric centred on the *clas* church of St Kentigern was revived as the territorial diocese of Llanelwy or St Asaph. The possibility that north-eastern Wales might be ecclesiastically annexed to the bishopric of Chester–Lichfield was thereby scotched. The creation of the new diocese possibly involved some territorial rearrangement: St Davids may have been required to surrender Powys (though Gerald of Wales made sure that Ceri was not likewise lost), and the see of Bangor, which was now confined west of the river Conwy, was compensated with two major enclaves within the new bishopric of St Asaph—the *cantrefi* of Dyffryn Clwyd in the north and Arwystli in the south. By 1150, therefore, Wales had been divided into four territorial dioceses with clearly defined boundaries.

Such newly delineated dioceses needed traditions to uphold and validate their authority. That is why the early twelfth century was a period of remarkable historical research, myth-making, and hagiography in Wales. The new Norman bishops harnessed the legends and cults of the Welsh in the service of their ambitions and created a past which would sustain those ambitions. The Book of Llandaff, *Liber Landavensis*, is the most remarkable example of this tradition-making exercise. There can be little doubt that the core of the book—represented by Hand A, in which 242 out of the total of 336 columns of the whole volume are written and consisting of the lives of the three founding bishops and patron saints of the see and 158 charters, which purport to range in date from the sixth to the late eleventh century—was part of the empire-building enterprise of Bishop Urban and his *familia* in the 1120s. They were anxious to provide the see of Llandaff (which was probably no older as an episcopal centre of any importance than the early eleventh century) with an unbroken descent from the 'age of the saints', to appropriate the traditions of other monastic centres, such as Llandeilo (Cantref Mawr) and Llandochau (Glamorgan) and possibly Llanilltud (Glamorgan), for Llandaff's greater glory, and to counter the metropolitan pretensions of St Davids, either by asserting (as in the Life of St Euddogwy) Llandaff's own metropolitan status in southern Britain or, alternatively, by protesting that Llandaff had been subject to Canterbury and obedient to the kings of England since the days of St

Augustine and that its customs were in no way different from those of the English. A parallel excercise in historical manipulation was being undertaken at very much the same time at St Davids, partly to consolidate the bishop's authority and partly to promote his claim to be metropolitan of Wales. The Life of St David, originally composed by Rhigyfarch in the late eleventh century, was discreetly, if rather clumsily, revised; Dewi's (David's) position *vis-à-vis* his brother saints Teilo (now patron of Llandaff) and Padarn was deliberately exalted; gifts which according to earlier *vitae* had been made to Teilo and Padarn were now appropriated exclusively for Dewi; and any suggestion that Dewi had been consecrated by Dyfrig, the first bishop of Llandaff according to *Liber Landavensis*, was carefully expunged.

The relics of the saints were also called into service to magnify the status and antiquity of the newly defined bishoprics. In June 1120 Bishop Urban arranged for the bones of St Dyfrig to be translated solemnly from Ynys Enlli (Bardsey Island) and interred in a tomb in the new cathedral church of Llandaff. So, too, were the teeth of Elgar the hermit. Bishop Bernard of St Davids was not to be outdone by such efforts: he initiated several unsuccessful searches for the body of Dewi (St David), possibly arranged for papal confirmation of his status as a saint in 1123, and in the following year secured the body of the recently deceased holy man, Caradog Fynach, for his cathedral, doubtless in the confident hope that in the fullness of time he would be canonized and the cathedral's status thereby enhanced.

The newly constituted territorial dioceses lacked the impressive cathedrals commensurate with their status. Bishop Urban found a tiny church at Llandaff—no larger, he claimed, than 28 feet in length and 15 feet wide, with two aisles and a porch. He soon arranged for a larger one to be built and had it dedicated in 1120. Some of his work still survives in the choir; but Urban's cathedral, no more than begun during his episcopate, was to be replaced by a new church dedicated in 1266 and patterned on the Gothic style of Glastonbury and Wells. At St Davids, Bernard set to work with the same zeal. His cathedral was destroyed by fire in 1182 and was to be replaced by the striking church built by Bishop Peter de Leia, 1176–98; but the dimension of Bernard's work may still be traced and it was clearly, for its time and for his resources, on a grand scale. Similar work was in hand at Bangor and it was in the apsidal-ended cathedral there that Gruffudd ap Cynan was laid to rest in 1137.

The early twelfth century was also a period when the structure of episcopal power and diocesan government began to assume the shape that it was to retain until the Reformation and indeed beyond. The new dioceses were much larger than the areas formerly controlled by mother churches and the range of duties, spiritual and jurisdictional, which fell to the bishop grew apace. A new range of personnel and offices was developed to cope with these responsibilities. The bishop had his own *familia*, consisting of the senior clergy of the diocese, his relatives, household officers, lay administrators of the episcopal estates, and, as the twelfth and thirteenth centuries progressed, university-trained clerks, especially those trained in canon law. The communities of secular canons, sharing a common income, which had served the pre-Norman *clasau*, were replaced at an early date by cathedral chapters, patterned on the Anglo-Norman model with each canon assigned a specific share of the capitular revenue. Bishop Bernard seems to have introduced such a chapter organization at St Davids soon after his election; Llandaff and Bangor quickly followed suit. The organization of the chapter grew more elaborate as time progressed: a dean was appointed to head the chapter, aided by a precentor (first appointed at St Davids in 1224), a treasurer (in St Davids from 1259), a cantor, and, later, a chancellor. By the thirteenth century each chapter had a fixed number of prebends, and detailed ordinances were drawn up to regulate the behaviour, obligations, and income of the canons (such as those issued at St Davids in 1224, 1253, and 1259 or for St Asaph during the episcopate of Llywelyn of Bromfield, 1293–1314).

Even more important in the definition of diocesan control was the fact that the bishop came to head a hierarchy of command and supervision throughout his diocese. There may already have been archdeacons in south-east Wales by the eleventh century; but it was in the years 1120–50, the formative period in the history of the Welsh church, that they first appeared in St Davids and Bangor—four in the former, two in the latter. The archdeacon was 'the eye of the bishop', presiding over the bishop's ordinary courts of ecclesiastical jurisdiction. The key role that he might play in ecclesiastical and, indeed, political affairs in Wales is amply suggested in the fulsome obits in the *Brut* for such men as Simon (d. 1152), archdeacon of Clynnog, and Daniel ap Sulien (d. 1127), archdeacon of Powys. At much the same time groups of parishes were formed into rural deaneries. Their boundaries often followed those of *cantrefi* and commotes; but, as the population grew, some of the earlier deaneries were subdivided into more manageable units—the earlier deanery of Gwent Uwchcoed, for example, being latter divided into those of Abergavenny and Usk, while in the diocese of St Asaph the number of deaneries appears to have doubled, from eight to sixteen. Synods of the clergy, such as that held at Cardiff in 1156, were organized; standards of clerical behaviour were imposed by visitations, such as those conducted by Gerald of Wales in Elfael and Maelienydd; the canons of general, legatine, English, and provincial councils were circulated; above all, the rural chapter and the bishop's consistory courts became the instruments for imposing on lay society the church's norms on matters such as breach of contract, marriage, sexual morality, and testamentary jurisdiction. The bishopric was becoming an effective unit of ecclesiastical organization, command, and jurisdiction.

But for the majority of the people of Wales the most important facet of the ecclesiastical transformation of the period was the definition of parishes, their boundaries, and their claims on the parishioners. Pre-Norman Wales was characterized by a rather loose ecclesiastical organization, with mother churches claiming authority over extensive areas and their dependent chapelries. It is some reflection of this state of affairs that the word *paruchia* seems often to refer in early medieval Welsh documentation to such large regions, even whole bishoprics, rather than to the parish of modern parlance. The creation of defined territorial parishes had probably started before the coming of the Normans; but there is little doubt that it is the twelfth and thirteenth centuries which were crucial in defining the parochial geography of much of Wales in the form which it was to retain, in many cases, until the nineteenth century. Some of the large districts hitherto under the control of mother churches were gradually subdivided into individual parishes: thus the huge district of northern Ceredigion, once dependent on the mother church of Llanbadarn, was divided into seventeen parishes served by twenty churches. Satellite chapels such as those which were said in the 1140s to have been 'lately built in the parish of St. Cadog of Llancarfan'[7] acquired their own endowment and eventually aspired to parochial status. The local parish now became clearly the focus of ecclesiastical obligations and dues: it was to the parish church that tithes and Peter's pence were payable; the rights of that church to exclusive claim over the oblations, customary offerings, and mortuary dues of the parishioners within its jurisdiction were vigorously asserted; the glebe was regarded as a necessary economic endowment for each parish. The parish was now clearly the framework of local ecclesiastical life: 'the whole parish' would be summoned to witness a gift of tithes to the local church, and every layman was expected to know to which parish be belonged or, in the words of one early deed, 'the priest whose parishioner she was'.[8] Indeed the parish was more than an ecclesiastical unit: it might also be employed as the unit for the division and collection of taxes, and the parish church, more often than not the only 'public' building in the locality, was often the venue for communal and secular activities, such as the witnessing of deeds or the division of communal renders.

The delimitation of parishes was a slow process. It proceeded most rapidly in the dioceses of Llandaff and St Davids, more slowly in St Asaph and especially Bangor. In the lowlands of the south—in Gwent, Glamorgan, Gower, Pembroke and around Brecon—the new Anglo-Norman lords created small parishes often co-terminus with the equally new units of manor or knight's fee. Elsewhere, in much of native and upland Wales, the

---

[7] *Episc. Acts*, II, 642 (L. 116).
[8] *Episc. Acts*, II, 661 (L. 175), 639 (L. 105).

parishes were very large—that of Gresford in north-east Wales covered over twenty thousand acres, while the parish of St Elli in Carnwyllion (Cydweli) was virtually co-terminous with the commote of that name. In Wales, as in so many parts of Europe, many parishes were appropriated to monasteries, bishoprics, or cathedral chapters. Thus a large number of the most valuable livings in the Vale of Glamorgan were appropriated to the monasteries of Tewkesbury or Gloucester or to the new foundation at Ewenni; in Brecon the richest churches of the lordship—Brecon itself, Hay, Talgarth, Llangors, and Defynnog, valued in all at over £77 annually in 1290—were bestowed on the new Benedictine priory of Brecon. The result of such appropriation was to improverish greatly the beneficed clergy of Wales, divert much of the ecclesiastical wealth of the country for the maintenance of alien and native monasteries, and augment the revenues of bishoprics and cathedral chapters. Some attempt was made from the later twelfth century to counter, or at least to contain, this movement by the creation of perpetual vicarages, whereby non-resident rectors (such as bishops, cathedral chapters, or monasteries) were required to earmark a specific sum or a proportion of tithes for the maintenance of the vicar and other parish clergy. At least thirty-three such perpetual vicarages had been instituted in the diocese of Llandaff by 1254. Appropriations certainly further improverished an already poor church. The council of Oxford in 1222 conceded that the minimum stipulated income for perpetual vicarages in England (five marks a year) could not be observed in Wales where the clergy 'are content with a smaller stipend';[9] Archbishop Pecham came to much the same conclusion later in the century when he decreed that the satisfactory minimum income for English livings was to be halved for those in Wales. Wales was a country of underendowed parishes and of an often impoverished clergy, beneficed and otherwise.

The most visible expression of the transformation of the local church in Wales in these centuries was the building and rebuilding of its parish churches. Not a single surviving parish church in the country pre-dates the mid-eleventh century or, for the most part, the early twelfth. Just as Raoul Glaber commented how northern France in the early eleventh century came to be covered with a white mantle of new churches, so the author of the biography of Gruffudd ap Cynan (d. 1137) remarked—and his comments were echoed in the *Brut*—how Gwynedd a century later 'came to shine with white-washed churches, like stars in the firmament'.[10] The time-lag between the two comments is significant, but they are united in their awareness of the dawn of a new age in church-building. The churches that were built, or doubtless often rebuilt, were generally small, unimpressive buildings, consisting of a simple square nave and a smaller chancel, and

---

[9] *Episc. Acts*, I, 350 (D. 448).
[10] *Historia Gruffud vab Kenan*, p. 30 (*History G. ap C.*, p. 155).

lacking towers and aisles; their design and stonework were frequently crude. Some of the major *clas* churches of former days were now also rebuilt, often to a cruciform plan—as at Tywyn (the 'glory of Meirionydd' as Llywelyn Fardd called it),[11] Meifod, the premier church of Powys rededicated in 1156, Aberdaron (Llŷn), Llanbadarn Fawr (Ceredigion), or Beddgelert (Arfon). Many small parish churches and satellite chapels were also built for the first time, such as the recently excavated chapel at Uchelolau near Barry (Glamorgan) or the church established by Geoffrey Sturmy at 'Sturmieston' in west Glamorgan in the mid-twelfth century. The small boroughs of Anglo-Norman Wales began to flaunt their increased prosperity and security by founding civic churches, as happened at Carmarthen with the dedication of a new church to St Mary, or by rebuilding them as at Haverfordwest in the 1220s. Members of princely dynasties and Norman barons sometimes provided the capital: Gruffudd ap Cynan 'had built many churches in his time'[12] and among his benefactions was the church at Penmon (Anglesey), where the arch of the south door with its low-relief sculpture and interlace pattern possibly dates from this very period or from that of his son; William, earl of Gloucester (d. 1183), gave some of his considerable fortune towards enlarging the church of St Mary at Cardiff; while the impressive church at Llanaber (Ardudwy), with the carved ornaments of its arcade and south doorway, may well owe its relative splendour to the patronage of the local ruler, Hywel ap Gruffudd ap Cynan (d. 1216). Lesser lay persons also made their contribution—at Llanfihangel-y-traethau (Ardudwy) a remarkable inscribed stone commemorates the munificence of Gwleder, the mother of Hoedlyw, 'who first built this church in the time of king Owain'.[13] Wealthy rectors occasionally used their fortunes to build chapels, as is recorded of Ralph Beneger in an inscription at Pwllcrochan (Pembroke). A few churches enjoyed relics which drew pilgrims from afar and channelled their wealth to the saint's shrine: it is thus, no doubt, that we are to explain the remarkable church of Pennant Melangell (Mochnant) with its sculptured stones, early apse, and shrine, in a remote upland valley. But, perhaps, above all the donations and bequests of ordinary parishioners underlie the church-building which characterized so many parts of Wales in these two centuries.

At much the same time that the church in Wales was being reorganized and rebuilt, its dioceses defined and its parishes delimited, it was also brought firmly under the metropolitan control of Canterbury. The claim of

---

[11] *Hen Gerddi Crefyddol*, p. 85 ('Uchelwawd yw hon i Feirionydd').

[12] *Brut, s.a.* 1137.

[13] V. E. Nash-Williams, *The Early Christian Monuments of Wales* (Cardiff, 1950), pp. 169–70 (no. 281).

Canterbury to exercise such control in Wales was of long standing; but it was one which had almost no practical force prior to the coming of the Normans. Ecclesiastics had certainly travelled to England and occasionally a bishop of Llandaff, such as Herewald in 1056, might have gone to England to be consecrated; but English political and military overlordship of Wales was too insecure and fitful to allow the development of any effective and sustained institutional control of the Welsh church by the see of Canterbury. With the advent of the Normans the situation changed dramatically. Their initial military success provided the impetus to convert theoretical pretensions into practical control. The first two Norman archbishops of Canterbury, Lanfranc (1070–89) and Anselm (1093–1109), pitched their claims in the most expansive terms, asserting that the see of Canterbury was the mother church of the whole of Britain and, in effect, quashing any Welsh pretensions to ecclesiastical autonomy by subsuming Wales within the term 'England'. Furthermore in Wales, unlike Scotland or Ireland, they and their successors gave effect to these pretensions— suspending native bishops, installing Norman nominees in the three Welsh dioceses 1092–1115, exacting oaths of submission and obedience from them, effecting the creation of a new diocese at St Asaph in 1143, and even toying with the idea of placing the two northern Welsh dioceses under the control of York while retaining the two southern dioceses as part of the province of Canterbury. In a matter of a few decades—spanning mainly the reign of Henry I—the church in Wales had been brought firmly under Canterbury's institutional control. As so often, Canterbury went to the trouble of forging the past to uphold its present power and pretensions: in the mid-twelfth century a record was fabricated to show that bishops of St Davids and Llandaff had been consecrated at Canterbury since the early tenth century.

Canterbury was driven to such ruses by the opposition which its metropolitan pretensions encountered within Wales. That opposition, paradoxically, was not spearheaded by the native Welsh princes or by the bishopric (Bangor) which normally remained under their control. It is true that the princes of Gwynedd, especially Owain Gwynedd (d. 1170) in his later years, resisted attempts to make the bishopric a mere pawn of English power, that they threatened on occasion to send their nominees for the bishopric to Ireland to be consecrated, and that, for much of the twelfth and thirteenth centuries, theirs was the decisive voice in the choice of the bishop of Bangor, on occasion of the bishop of St Asaph, and even once (in 1215) of the bishop of St Davids. It is also true that, in the propaganda war which Gerald of Wales conducted on behalf of the metropolitan claims of St Davids from 1198 to 1203, most of the native princes of Wales were eventually persuaded to pledge him their support and to do so in terms of defending the rights of a national church against foreign domination. Yet their support soon withered when Gerald gave up the struggle; and even half a century earlier it was not the metropolitan authority of Canterbury over his see of Bangor, as he called it, which Owain Gwynedd resented so much as the oath of fealty which the bishop was required to swear to the king of England and the political subordination implicit in such an oath.

It was not from the Welsh princes but rather from the churchmen of St Davids—notably its first Norman bishop, Bernard 1115–48, and its most famous son, Gerald of Wales (d. 1223),—that the most vigorous opposition was forthcoming. It doubtless drew on earlier pre-Norman attempts to proclaim and promote the superiority of St Davids, such as are witnessed in the tenth-century poem, *Armes Prydein*, or, even more obviously, in the late eleventh-century life of Dewi by Rhigyfarch. But it was Bishop Bernard, as far as we know, who first pressed his bishopric's claim to metropolitan status over the whole of Wales and, in the 1120s, assembled the arguments to support such a claim. The case rested in part on the distinctiveness of the Welsh as a people and the need, therefore, for them to have an archbishop of their own, in part on the remoteness of the country, and, above all, on a clutch of quasi-historical arguments—notably that St Davids had been a metropolitan see from the first introduction of Christianity to Britain and that Dewi (St David) had been raised to archiepiscopal status either after the miraculous demonstration of his superiority at the synod of Brefi or by promotion at the hands of the patriarch of Jerusalem. The case for St Davids' status would be expanded and elaborated as the twelfth century progressed (notably, of course, by the persistence and verbosity of Gerald of Wales); but in essence the main themes of the case were already firmly identified during the episcopate of Bishop Bernard, to be revived again by the chapter in 1176 and 1179 and to rise to their long coda in the heroic efforts—a combination of melodrama and comedy—of Gerald of Wales's struggle to secure both the see and its metropolitan status in the years 1198–1203.

Historically, St David's claim to archiepiscopal status and metropolitan authority in Wales does not stand up to examination. It was based on arguments about episcopal power, diocesan status, and metropolitan jurisdiction which were largely anachronistic as applied to the pre-Norman Welsh church. Yet they were, in this respect, little different from arguments used throughout Europe, not least by the church of Canterbury itself, in pursuit of power and superiority in an age of fierce ecclesiastical competition and increasing definition. Furthermore, it was by no means a foregone conclusion that St Davids' case would be lost. Bernard enjoyed the support of Henry I and might even have expected that the political turmoil in Wales after 1135 would enhance his prospects. He was shrewd enough to lay his case before the Pope and, as was to be shown in the case of Scotland in the 1190s, the papacy was not altogether unsympathetic to such pleas on behalf of 'national' churches. But it was inevitable that the struggle should increasingly assume political dimensions. Gerald of Wales observed shrewdly that Canterbury's metropolitan jurisdiction was used as the spiritual arm of the English king's political domination, notably by issuing threats of excommunication against the rebellious Welsh; but, equally, the English recognized that to yield metropolitan status to St Davids was a recipe for 'perpetual dissension between the English and the Welsh'.[14] Once the issue was posed in such terms, the chances that St Davids case would succeed were slim indeed.

The struggle was finally abandoned in 1203; but, in spite of Gerald of Wales's torrent of words on the issue, Canterbury in fact had engineered its victory long since. The decision of 1203 merely confirmed it. Welsh bishops had been attending provincial councils at London and Westminster from the 1120s; as suffragans of the see of Canterbury they had attended the consecration of other bishops; they submitted their quarrels to the synod of the bishops of the province of Canterbury (as even the doughty Bernard was forced to do in 1133); they attended English provincial and legatine synods. Canterbury further secured its authority by insisting that Bernard's two successors as bishop of St Davids—David fitz Gerald (1148–76) and Peter de Leia (1176–98)—not only swore an oath of obedience to Canterbury 'our mother church' but also promised not to pursue St Davids' claim for metropolitan status. Canterbury had shown a greater tenacity in asserting its ecclesiastical supremacy over Wales than the kings of England in asserting their political mastery there. The visitation of Archbishop Baldwin in 1188 confirmed Canterbury's success. Though it was undertaken to preach the crusade, the visitation was also an unmistakable demonstration of archiepiscopal power since Baldwin seized the opportunity to celebrate mass at each of the four Welsh cathedrals.

While the grip of Canterbury on Wales was tightening, the native church was also, in common with other churches of western Europe, integrated into the papal governance of Western Christendom. In the eleventh century, Rome was no more than a distant shrine, a pilgrimage centre. Its ultimate authority over the church in Wales was recognized; but that authority barely impinged in a practical fashion on the country. As in so many other spheres, it was the first half of the twelfth century which witnessed the transformation. Formal and regular links with Rome now became the norm: letters were exchanged; cardinals were lobbied; papal sanction became recognized as the most secure insurance for all ecclesiastical title (as in the bull of Calixtus II of 1123 confirming all gifts hitherto made to the see of St Davids); papal legates were dispatched on visits to Welsh sees, the first recorded example being that of Cardinal John of Crema to

---

[14] *Episc. Acts*, I, 308 (D. 307).

Llandaff in 1125; Welsh bishops, or at least those of the two southern sees, became regular visitors to the papal court—Bernard of St Davids travelling to Rheims to attend a papal council in 1119, to Rome in 1123 as royal envoy and proctor of the archbishop of Canterbury, to Rheims again in 1131, and to Meaux in 1147. In institutional terms the acknowledgement of the Pope's authority as universal ordinary—as the ultimate source of all ecclesiastical jurisdiction—was the earliest route by which papal pretensions were given practical and regular effect in Wales, as elsewhere. It was to Rome that Bishops Urban and Bernard referred their long-running dispute about their diocesan boundaries and it was at Siena, in pursuit of a further papal ruling, that Urban died in 1133; it was the papal curia likewise which was the forum for the debate about the metropolitan status of St Davids around 1200 and for the dispute between Llywelyn ap Gruffudd and the bishop of St Asaph in the 1270s. Nor was it merely such *causes célèbres* which came within the purview of papal jurisdiction. Minor cases were likewise referred to Rome and then often dispatched back to the locality to be heard by local ecclesiastics acting as papal judges-delegate, as did David fitz Gerald, bishop of St Davids, in 1175. Such procedures familiarized Welsh ecclesiastics with the machinery and methods of an international jurisdiction and required them to resort to the service of trained canon lawyers and to purchase copies of decretals (as at St Dogmaels abbey).

As the twelfth and thirteenth centuries progressed the plenitude of papal power expressed itself in the Welsh church in other directions. From 1188 taxes were raised from the clergy of western Europe to meet papal demands, normally under the pretext of promoting a crusade. Wales, though it was relatively lightly assessed, was not exempt from such taxes. In 1263, for example, the bishop of St Davids was authorized to collect an annual hundredth of church revenues in Wales for five years in the Pope's name. From the early thirteenth century the papacy assumed a further power which, in the fullness of time, was to augment its control of the Western church hugely, that of nominating (or providing, as it was known) to certain categories of benefices, notably bishoprics and cathedral canonries. The first recorded papal nomination to a Welsh diocese took place in 1219 when Pandulf, the papal legate, provided William, prior of Goldcliff, to the see of Llandaff. The year 1256 witnessed an even more striking manifestation of the growth of papal authority in the Welsh church: the Pope nominated Richard of Carew to the see of St Davids, in spite of royal opposition, and consecrated him bishop in Rome. Lay rulers were also deferring to the Pope's authority and seeking to draw on that authority to bolster their own position. The princes of native Wales were no exception. They might attempt to underwrite their domestic policies by petitioning for the sanction of Papal support, as Llywelyn ab Iorwerth of Gwynedd did in persuading Honorius III to confirm the succession of

Dafydd as his heir in 1222; they might also try to counter the expansionist ambitions of English kings by appeal to the Pope as the international arbiter of Christendom—hence Dafydd ap Llywelyn's bold proposal in 1244 to lay his quarrel with Henry III before papal commissioners; hence also the cordial relations which Llywelyn ap Gruffudd cultivated with Pope Gregory X.

The remarkable advance of papal power in the western church was one expression of, and indeed a major contribution towards, the international integration of Europe in the twelfth and thirteenth centuries. During those two centuries Europe came to enjoy a measure of unity in its academic curriculum and training and in the pattern of its ecclesiastical recruitment, such as it has not known before or since. Wales in its own small way participated in and benefited from this experience: from being an isolated, western-oriented country, where a Latin learning was conservatively sustained by a small coterie of hereditary families in ecclesiastical schools, it gradually became, in so far as its poverty and troubled political fortunes allowed, a province of a European community of learning and ecclesiastical promotion. Welsh students were already attending the schools at Oxford by the 1170s, and though few of them could have had as long and eclectic an academic career as Gerald of Wales (whose studies took him to Gloucester, Paris, Oxford, and Lincoln), their numbers grew slowly throughout the thirteenth century. The impact of such graduates would be most obvious at the higher echelons of the church. Adam, bishop of St Asaph 1175–81, had been a student at Paris and a pupil and friend of the distinguished theologian, Peter Lombard; while, a generation later, Henry of Abergavenny returned to his native diocese as bishop of Llandaff, 1193–1218, after a career as a monk at St Vincent of Le Mans. But perhaps the most striking example of the international outlook and training of the Welsh episcopate was the career of Thomas Wallensis, bishop of St Davids, 1248–55. Born in Wales, he was probably educated at Oxford and Paris, became a regent in the faculty of theology at Paris, and then undertook the direction of the Franciscan school at Oxford. Friend of Grosseteste and Roger Bacon, he accepted the see of St David because, in Matthew Paris's effusive encomium on him, 'he desired to console his wretched fellow-countrymen by his presence, advice and help'.[15] The difference in training and contacts between Bishop Thomas and his distinguished predecessor, Bishop Sulien (1072–8, 1080–5), was one measure of the transformation which the Welsh church had undergone.

How far such a transformation affected the character of the Welsh church beyond its higher echelons is difficult to gauge. Thomas Wallensis had served as archdeacon of Lincoln for the great reforming bishop,

---

[15] Matthew Paris, *Chronica Majora*, ed. H. R. Luard (1872–83), IV, p. 647.

Robert Grosseteste; he doubtless sought to apply in his own diocese some of the methods, broaching on the inquisitorial, which Grosseteste had instituted to improve the spiritual and moral standards of laity and clergy alike. Gerald of Wales, in his own aggressive and somewhat insensitive fashion, had attempted to do the same as archdeacon of Brecon; his *Gemma Ecclesiastica* was written specifically to instruct the clergy of St Davids in the rudiments of theology. Other bishops—such as the Cistercian bishop of Bangor, Cadwgan (1215–36), who wrote several religious homilies, or the Franciscan, Anselm le Gras at St Davids (1231–47), or the two Dominican bishops of St Asaph, Hugh (1235–40) and Anian II (1268–93)—were engaged in the same campaign. So also were the Welshmen who from at least the mid-thirteenth century onwards were busy translating sermon collections, homilies, and manuals of instructions for parish priests into Welsh, notably part of Raymond de Pennafort's *Summa de Poenitentia* under the title *Penityas*. The gap between the exhortations of schools-trained reformers and an often ignorant and poor clergy, enmeshed in the ties and morality of local society, was often wide in Wales, as elsewhere in Europe. Yet on a whole host of issues—such as the marriage of clergy, the prohibited degrees in marriage, inheritance of benefices, portionary churches, divorce—the standards that were now proclaimed were those of an international church. Even the native princes took note of them: Owain Gwynedd (d. 1170) had persistently ignored the advice of Pope and archbishop that he should put away his second wife on grounds of consanguinity; but his grandson, Llywelyn ab Iorwerth, deemed it wise to secure a papal dispensation in 1203 for his proposed marriage to the daughter of the king of Man. The Pope could now insist that the Welsh church follow general ecclesiastical practice even on minor issues, as Alexander III did in requiring the bishops of Wales to promote men to the sub-diaconate only on approved days; provincial councils, such as those of 1175 and 1236, could issue canons to bring Welsh customs into line with the international law of the church; Welsh bishops attended general church councils, such as the Third and Fourth Lateran councils of 1179 and 1215; they even sought papal approval, as did St Davids in 1260, for internal ordinances in their own churches. Even the compilers or copiers of native law-texts felt that the authority of their collections might be enhanced by claiming, in the prologues, that they had been confirmed by the Pope and made at least a nod in the direction of the *lex ecclesiastica* in the substance of their texts. Uniformity with, and conformity to, international standards were increasingly the hallmarks of the Welsh church.

The twelfth and thirteenth centuries saw equally momentous changes in the monastic life of Wales. This was, of course, a period of monastic revival throughout Europe; but in Wales the transformation was even more far-reaching, for here a native monastic tradition was terminated and the country was absorbed into the mainstream patterns of European monastic life. The monastic tradition in Wales went back to the earliest days of Christianity in the country; the vigorous defenders of that tradition in the eleventh century (notably Rhigyfarch of Llanbadarn and Lifris of Llancarfan) proclaimed that its founders 'imitated the monks of Egypt and lived a life like theirs'.[16] Yet, by contemporary European standards, to call these native Welsh houses of married and often hereditary canons 'monasteries' was, to put it kindly, to be guilty of a misnomer. Some such houses survived in an attentuated form even as late as the thirteenth century; but to all intents the long history of native monasticism in Wales was drawing to its close by 1200.

In some places the end came with dramatic suddenness, as the new Norman lords disbanded the *clasau* communities and used their endowments and even their traditions to enrich their own monasteries in Normandy and England. Such was the fate of many of the most famous *clasau* of south-east Wales, such as Llancarfan, Llanilltud, Llandochau (Glamorgan), and Basaleg (Gwent); such also appeared briefly to be the lot of the most flourishing community of all, that of Llanbadarn Fawr (Ceredigion), which was disbanded in 1116–17 to make room for a daughter house of St Peter's Gloucester. Elsewhere, in native Wales, the transition was more gradual; but there also the *clas* was reshaped to conform to the recognized categories of current ecclesiastical institutions. At St Davids and Bangor the *clasau* were converted into cathedral chapters in the early twelfth century, though retention of some common funds for the chapter remained as a vestige of the *clas* origin of these cathedral churches. Elsewhere, as at Llanddewibrefi (Ceredigion) and Caergybi (Holyhead, Anglesey), the *clas* churches were redesignated as collegiate churches; others, such as Llanynys (Dyffryn Clwyd) or Meifod (Mechain), retained their links with the past as portionary churches; yet others, such as Llanbadarn (Ceredigion), were gradually reduced to the status of ordinary parish churches. The days of native religious houses were numbered once the Welsh princes began to transfer their affections to the new orders. Lord Rhys (d. 1197) of Deheubarth announced his sympathies for the new dispensation clearly in the 1180s when he bestowed much of the temporal and spiritual income of one of the most prestigious *clas* churches of Deheubarth, Llandeilo, on the new Premonstratensian abbey of Talyllychau (Talley) founded in the heart of his dominions. Even in north Wales the native religious houses were forcibly reformed to bring them more closely into line with European norms. It was to the Augustinian canons that the task was entrusted. They were particularly well suited to undertake it: they had wide experience in

---

[16] *Rhigyfarch's Life of St. David*, p. 14.

introducing monastic discipline into major churches and they had already shown in Scotland that their rule could be easily grafted onto native Celtic monasticism. The princes of Gwynedd and Powys showed their generosity at an early date to the Augustinian house at Haughmond (Shropshire) and by the early thirteenth century some of the oldest and most distinguished *clasau* of north Wales—notably Aberdaron (Llŷn), Penmon (Anglesey), and Beddgelert (Arfon)—had been transformed into houses of Augustinian canons.

The eclipse of native monasticism was but one facet of the monastic revival in Wales. Throughout Europe, the period from 1050 onwards was characterized by the proliferation of new orders, anxious to rediscover and reassert the original quality, as they saw it, of the monastic vocation. The number of monasteries and monks increased dramatically; and the geography of European monasticism and monastic endowment was radically altered. Wales in its own small way partook of this monastic revival. At first the signs were not encouraging. The Benedictine and Cluniac abbeys and priories which were founded throughout lowland south Wales in the period 1070–1120 were seen for what they were—the ecclesiastical accessories of foreign conquest and colonization.[17] Even the earliest plantations of the reformed orders in Wales were tarred with the same brush: the Tironian abbey of St Dogmaels (*c.*1115) was founded by the new Norman lord of Cemais, the two Savignac houses of Neath (*c.*1130) and Basingwerk (1131) by Richard de Granville and the earl of Chester respectively, the Augustinian canon houses at Llanthony (*c.*1103) and Carmarthen (pre-1127) by Hugh Lacy and Bishop Bernard of St Davids, and the Cistercian houses of Tintern (1131), Whitland (1140), and Margam (1147) by Anglo-Norman lords. Reformed monasticism in Wales seemed to be yet another Anglo-Norman plantation, artificially transported to Wales and dependent on alien recruitment and patronage. Such an impression might indeed be confirmed by the essentially English orientation of houses such as Tintern and Basingwerk, by the flight of the canons of Llanthony to a safer retreat near Gloucester in 1137, by the proposal that Neath abbey be transferred to Somerset to escape out of the range of Welsh raids, or, visually, by the floor tiles of Neath abbey which record graphically the dependence of the house on its Anglo-Norman patrons— the Clare earls and local settler families, such as Berkerolles, Norreys, and Turberville.

Yet the Cistercians in particular established deep roots in Wales, in areas under native as well as Anglo-Norman control. By 1201 thirteen Cistercian houses, including the two Savignac houses of Neath and Basingwerk which were absorbed into the Order in 1147, had been founded in Wales; of these

---

[17] See above, pp. 180–1.

nine were either native Welsh foundations or in areas controlled by native dynasties—Whitland (1140), Strata Florida (1164), Strata Marcella (1170), Cwm-hir (1176, possibly a refoundation), Llantarnam (1179), Llanllŷr (a house for women c.1180), Aberconwy (1186), Cymer (1199), Valle Crucis (1201). The Cistercians had caught the imagination of the Welsh; they had learnt how to tap the strong eremetical and heroic element in the country's religious traditions and to fill the void left by the decline of the *clasau*. Two events in Deheubarth in 1163–4 may be taken as epitomizing the shift in religious outlook that was taking place: in the former year two of Bishop Sulien's grandsons died and with them perished much that was best in the native tradition of clerical dynasties and *clas* learning; in the next year a Cistercian community was established at the original site of the abbey of Strata Florida (Ystrad Fflur) and though its initial patron was a Norman, Robert fitz Stephen, it soon attracted the enthusiastic support and generous munificence of the Lord Rhys. The *clas* at Llanbadarn was eclipsed by the new Cistercian monastery; within ten years it was to be at Strata Florida that the native Welsh annals were kept. In north Wales old and new coexisted for a while: Rhodri ab Owain Gwynedd (d. 1195) gave a third of the vill of Neigwl (Llŷn) to the ancient *clas* at Clynnog Fawr; but his nephew, Maredudd ap Cynan (d. 1212), gave another third of the same vill to the newly founded Cistercian abbey at Cymer. By the early thirteenth century, however, the native dynasties of Gwynedd and northern and southern Powys had all transferred their religious affections to the Cistercians and, to a lesser degree, to the Augustinian canons.

The triumph of Cistercian monasticism in Wales in the period 1131–1201 —only Grace Dieu (1226) and a further house for women at Llanllugan (pre-1236) were established after that date—had consequences out of all proportion to the number of monasteries founded. It gave the whole of Wales a degree of unity in monastic practice and religious benefaction. Tintern and Strata Florida, Margam and Cwm-hir, for all their differences in recruitment and political affiliation, belonged to the same order and adhered to the same rule. Anglo-Norman lord and Welsh prince, feudal vassal and native freeholder alike visited their pious generosity on the Cistercians, sometimes indeed on one and the same house. These benefactions represented a massive transfer of wealth from secular into monastic hands; at a broad estimate, they probably doubled the amount of land under ecclesiastical control in Wales. Thus the abbey of Aberconwy had accummulated an estate of almost 40,000 acres, including one grange of 12,000 acres, within a generation of its foundation in 1186. Much of the land so acquired was, of course, mountain pasture or lowland waste—such as the ten square miles of waste between the rivers Nedd and Tawe and the twenty-eight square miles of undeveloped land between the rivers Afan and Kenfig which formed the huge original endowments of Neath and

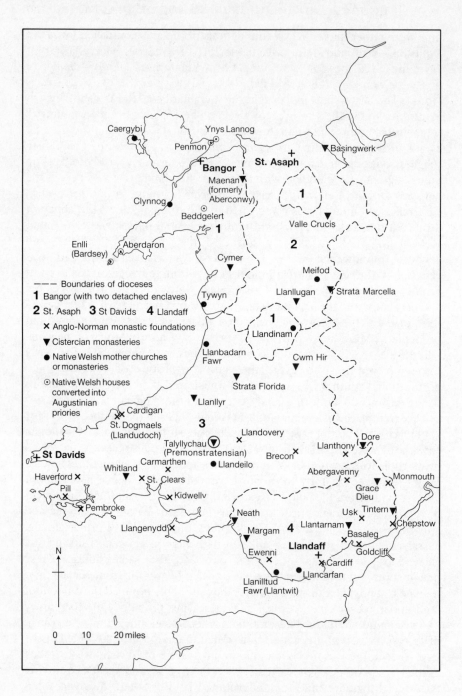

Caergybi

Ynys Lannog

Penmon

Basingwerk

Bangor

St. Asaph

Maenan
(formerly
Aberconwy)

1

Clynnog

Beddgelert

Valle Crucis

1

Enlli
(Bardsey)

Aberdaron

2

Cymer

Meifod

— — — Boundaries of dioceses

1 Bangor (with two detached enclaves)

2 St. Asaph **3** St Davids **4** Llandaff

✕ Anglo-Norman monastic foundations

▼ Cistercian monasteries

● Native Welsh mother churches
or monasteries

⊙ Native Welsh houses
converted into
Augustinian
priories

Tywyn

Llanllugan

Strata Marcella

1

Llandinam

Llanbadarn
Fawr

Cwm Hir

Strata Florida

Llanllyr

Cardigan

3

St. Dogmaels
(Llandudoch)

Llandovery

Dore

Talyllychau
(Premonstratensian)

Brecon

Llanthony

St Davids

Whitland

Carmarthen

Llandeilo

Abergavenny

Monmouth

Haverford

St. Clears

Grace
Dieu

Pill

Kidwelly

Neath

Usk

Tintern

Pembroke

Margam

4

Llantarnam

Chepstow

Llangenydd

Basaleg

Ewenni

Llandaff

Goldcliff

Cardiff

Llancarfan

Llanilltud
Fawr (Llantwit)

N

0   10   20 miles

MAP 4. The Dioceses and Monasteries of Wales *c.*1300

Margam respectively. But the piety, or indigence, of donors and the enterprise and acquisitiveness of Cistercians soon augmented these original gifts: rich lowland manors were secured and depopulated of tenants and secular buildings, as happened dramatically at Llangewydd in the Vale of Glamorgan, where the castle and church were demolished to satisfy the Cistercian lust for solitude; churches were appropriated; and, in spite of earlier prohibitions, Cistercian abbeys were soon enriching themselves with gifts of tenants, rent-rolls, and labour services. Furthermore, the Cistercians were not mere passive beneficiaries; on the contrary, their commitment to the principle of the direct and exclusive exploitation of their own lands made them into enterprising and, indeed, aggressive entrepreneurs. They established granges on their estates—that of Neath abbey at Monknash (Glamorgan), with its embanked enclosure and massive granary over two hundred feet long, is an impressive memorial of their enterprise; they used their own direct labour force of lay brothers to work their land; they exploited the pastoral resources of Wales by rearing large flocks of sheep and by establishing international contacts for the export of their wool.[18]

Important as was the impact of the Cistercians in the distribution and exploitation of rural wealth in Wales, it was their influence as a religious order which was most far-reaching. They brought an entirely new dimension to the religious life of the country. Recruitment was heavy, especially in the twelfth century. Thus, between 1164 and 1224, Whitland founded three daughter houses in Wales and a further two in Ireland, which suggests that a late report that it housed a hundred monks in the late twelfth century was not greatly exaggerated. Furthermore, the Cistercian order opened its recruitment door much more widely than earlier orders, for it encouraged illiterate laymen of poor means to take the monastic vow as lay brothers. As late as 1336 the thirty-eight conventual monks at Margam were still slightly outnumbered by forty lay brothers, and in the early history of the house the proportion would doubtless have been more in the order of two, or even three, lay brothers to each conventual monk. But perhaps the most significant impact of the firm establishment of the Cistercian order in Wales was that it incorporated the country fully into the mainstream of European monasticism. The Cistercians were a self-consciously international and tightly knit religious order: each house was required to follow a uniform rule; each mother house visited its daughter houses annually; each abbot was required to attend the annual chapter-general of the order at Cîteaux. The documents provide an occasional vivid glimpse of the impact of these links: of lay brothers from Strata Florida travelling to Clairvaux in 1195 to be sentenced for their offences against the

---

[18] See above, p. 170.

abbey of Cwm-hir or of the abbeys of Cymer and Valle Crucis raising loans to attend the chapter-general at Cîteaux or to pursue litigation in Rome.

The Cistercians enriched the religious and cultural life of Wales in a host of ways. The abbey churches and the monastic buildings which they built, and frequently totally redesigned and rebuilt, in the twelfth and thirteenth centuries endowed Wales with a corpus of ecclesiastical building in stone such as it had not known previously. It was in its way as impressive and expensive an investment as the castles of Anglo-Norman barons and kings. It drew on the expertise of English masons and, in spite of the initial Cistercian prohibition on decoration and ornament, it brought some of the most recent and innovative departures in stonework and design into the heartland of upland Wales. The spiritual and material confidence and *élan* of the order are still reflected in the grandeur of some of the monastic ruins—in the measured beauty of the dormitory undercroft at Neath, the breathtaking elegance of the polygonal chapter house at Margam, the refinement of the west door at Strata Florida, with its sequence of five bands of roll mouldings, the delicacy of the great west window at Valle Crucis, and that same monastery's rich collection of monumental effigies and slabs which made it into 'the treasure-house of monumental sculpture in north Wales'.[19] Most striking of all, perhaps—though even its outlines are now scarcely to be traced—are the dimensions of the abbey of Cwm-hir in the remote uplands of Maelienydd: its nave at 242 feet was the longest in Wales, while its fourteen bays stood comparison with those of Canterbury.

The Cistercians also contributed handsomely to the literary culture of Wales. There has, it is true, been a tendency to ascribe all Welsh manuscripts indiscriminately to Cistercian *scriptoria* and thereby to overlook the contribution of lay scribes. Thus it has recently been shown that the largest and single most valuable volume of Welsh medieval literature, *The Red Book of Hergest*, which has been variously ascribed to the *scriptoria* of Strata Florida and Neath abbeys, was in fact mainly written in the last quarter of the fourteenth century by a lay scribe from Builth for a lay patron. Yet this is not to gainsay the contribution of the Cistercians in literary matters. Much of their work was doubtless devotional, such as the concordance of St Bernard's Song of Songs compiled by an abbot of Margam, or the translation of the Athanasian creed into Welsh probably undertaken by a monk of Strata Florida. But the abbeys also became important centres for the conservation and transmission of secular learning. The library at Margam included copies of the works of Geoffrey of Monmouth and William of Malmesbury, while the survival of a single early Welsh verse or *englyn* on the flap of a charter there possibly indicates an interest in vernacular literature also. Several

---

[19] C. A. Gresham, *Medieval Stone Carving in North Wales. Sepulchral Slabs and Effigies of the Thirteenth and Fourteenth Centuries* (Cardiff, 1968), p. 254.

Welsh literary manuscripts were probably copied at Cistercian abbeys: they include, for example, a Welsh version of the Charlemagne legend probably compiled at Strata Florida and it was there also, around 1300, that the earliest, most systematic and most comprehensive collection of medieval Welsh court poetry, now known as *Llawysgrif Hendregadredd*, was assembled. Some of the surviving versions of Welsh law may also have been written at and for monastic libraries. The Cistercian houses, from an early date, took upon themselves the role of compiling annals of events in Wales, thereby supplementing and extending the earlier annalistic tradition at St Davids and possibly at Llanbadarn. It was at Strata Florida that the lost Latin chronicle which forms the basis of the Chronicle of the Princes was compiled, in the late thirteenth century, and it was there also that at least one translation of the chronicle into Welsh, *Brut y Tywysogyon*, was effected. But Strata Florida was not alone. Annals and chronicles were also composed at other Cisterican monasteries in Wales and some of them were circulated from one house to another.

This lively literary and historiographical interest in Welsh affairs was matched by the prominence that the Cistercian order had come to occupy in Welsh public life. Cistercian abbeys—notably Aberconwy, Valle Crucis, and Strata Florida—now acted as the mausoleums for native Welsh dynasties and the venues for major Welsh assemblies, such as that held at Strata Florida in 1238 when 'all the princes of Wales swore allegiance and fealty'[20] to Dafydd ap Llywelyn as heir presumptive. It was from the ranks of the Cistercians that the princes of Gwynedd frequently chose their emissaries for their most delicate missions; and they returned the compliment by defending the character of Llywelyn ap Gruffudd vigorously to the Pope in 1274 against the calumnies of the bishop of St Asaph. This most international of monastic orders had become fiercely patriotic in its outlook; it had entrenched itself firmly in the religious, and indeed the non-religious, life of Wales.

Yet, during the later thirteenth century, it had increasingly to share its supremacy with the mendicant friars. In many ways Wales was and remained unpromising ground for the friars; it had neither the large urban centres nor the university schools which were their natural habitat. It is not surprising, therefore, that only three Franciscan houses (Llan-faes (pre-1245), Cardiff (pre-1284), Carmarthen (pre-1284)), five Dominican houses (Cardiff (pre-1242), Haverfordwest (pre-1246), Bangor (pre-1251), Rhuddlan (pre-1258), and Brecon (pre-1269)), and one Carmelite house (Denbigh (pre-1289)) were founded in Wales. Yet their impact was considerable. Already by the end of the thirteenth century they were outstripping the Cistercians in recruitment: there were twenty-three friars

[20] *Brut, s.a.* 1238.

in the Dominican house at Rhuddlan, thirty at Cardiff. They provided the church of thirteenth-century Wales with some of its most vigorous and effective bishops, none more so than the combative Anian of St Asaph (1268–93); they also came to occupy a prominent place in the service of the native princes of Gwynedd. Above all the mendicant ideal—combining practical evangelical work with the monastic life—marked a radical change from the assumptions of the past. By teaching and, above all, by preaching, the friars introduced new standards into the life of parish clergy and laity alike; they undertook the translation of manuals of instruction for use in parochial work; they used the vernacular to communicate the intensity of their religious sentiments and vision—as in Brother Madog ap Gwallter's touching meditation on the nativity of Christ, the earliest such nativity poem in Welsh, or in *Y Cysegrlan Fuchedd* ('The Consecrated Life'), the most important work of piety and devotion produced in medieval Wales and one whose author may have been a Domincan friar. It is, of course, impossible to measure their impact or their success; yet it is, paradoxically, a tribute to the effectiveness of their preaching and to the way in which it impinged on popular concerns that two of the greatest Welsh poets of the fourteenth century, Dafydd ap Gwilym and Iolo Goch, felt impelled to challenge their values and teaching. It was the friars, not the Cistercians, who were moulding the shape of popular devotion and religious practice in later medieval Wales.

The changes in ecclesiastical organization and monastic practice in the twelfth and thirteenth centuries in Wales, as elsewhere, are readily identified; it is much more difficult to penetrate the nature of popular devotion and to characterize the impact of the church on lay society. The medieval church, it has been said, was 'a compulsory society';[21] its beliefs, its rituals, the obligations that arose from membership of it, were woven into the very texture of assumptions and attitudes which provided the framework for medieval man's mentality and cosmology. It was in terms of its calendars and festivals that he organized his weeks and his year; it was by reference to its credo—more often than not mediated through ritual, iconography, and legend—that he ordered, or claimed to order, his personal and social morality and explained the natural world and its relationship to the eternal.

In such a society the church both stood apart from the world and yet stood at its centre. The apartness of the priesthood was expressed legally and institutionally. No monk, hermit, or scholar, according to Welsh law, could act as a surety (W. *mach*). Yet the very fact that such men had estranged themselves, by vow and profession, from the ties and obligations

---

[21] R. W. Southern, *Western Society and the Church in the Middle Ages* (Harmondsworth, 1970), p. 17.

of secular society gave them a special status and power within it. They were holy men, *diofrydogion*; their oath had a special power, especially in serious criminal cases; and their more general role, as prophets, peace-makers, and counsellors, in local society was amply recognized, as is exemplified in the career of Wechelen, the hermit of Llowes (Elfael). The church, as well as its priests, stood apart legally. Each church had its *braint* or honour; he who dared to offend it—be he Welsh prince or English king—brought down upon himself the vengeance of the patron saint of that church. Each church also had its sanctuary (W. *noddfa*), demarcated by fences and ditches and extending, so Gerald of Wales tells us, in the case of larger churches, 'as far as the cattle go to feed in the morning and can return in the evening'.[22] In a violent and vengeful society these areas were havens of peace where political exiles and refugees as well as criminals might flee (as in Meirionydd in 1147); it was rare indeed for a prince, even of the stature of Gruffudd ap Cynan (d. 1137), to dare to incur the wrath of the saint and of heaven by violating such sanctuaries. The church became increasingly assertive of its jurisdictional and fiscal prerogatives and of the immunities of the clerical order as the twelfth and thirteenth centuries progressed. In Wales, as elsewhere, this led to conflict, especially between the prince of Gwynedd and the bishops of Bangor and St Asaph in the 1260s and 1270s.[23]

Yet, in spite of periodic conflict and in spite of its strident insistence on its apartness, the church also set out to shape the norms of behaviour in lay society in a variety of ways. It proclaimed an ethos of love and peace in a society which exulted in valour and vengeance. The Deity himself, in Cynddelw's words, was 'the stronghold of peace'. His saints promoted the same qualities: Tysilio 'hated the love of cruelty'; Cadfan's staff 'restrained a man from murdering his enemy'; Padarn had a particular gift of peacemaking; and love of Dewi helped to contain a man's anger.[24] Nor were these mere poetic or hagiographical compliments, for churchmen sought to contain the violence of society in practical ways. On his death in 1127 Daniel ap Sulien was commemorated as one 'peaceful and beloved by all', and as 'mediator between Gwynedd and Powys', while his nephew, Sulien ap Rhigyfarch, was likewise remembered as 'a peaceful mediator between various peoples'.[25] Such a mediating role continued in the thirteenth century: it was episcopal mediation, for example, which arranged the agreement between Llewelyn ap Gruffudd and his brother in 1269 and underwrote it with ecclesiastical sanction. In the ordering of normal social relations the church and its rituals again played a prominent

[22] *DK.*, I, xviii (*Opera*, vi, 203).   [23] See below, pp. 325–6.
[24] *Hen Gerddi Crefyddol*, pp. 32 ('dinas tangefedd'), 34 ('casau caru creulonedd'), 50 ('a ludd i'r gelyn ladd ei gilydd').
[25] *Brut, s.a.* 1127, *Brut (RBH), s.a.* 1146.

part. In a society which relied so heavily on the pledged oath, the solemnity of the relics on which oaths were sworn and the sanction of divine justice on perjurors were of cardinal importance. According to Welsh law, a contract could be arranged in which God alone was the witness (W. *briduw*); and it was on relics and in the presence of monks and clergymen that solemn oaths (such as that which Maelgwn ap Rhys swore in 1199 to deliver Cardigan to his brother Gruffudd) were sworn, and stolen property reclaimed by the action of *damdwng*. The church itself, according to the law-texts, was to be the venue for taking the oaths of compurgators (W. *rhaith*) and that was to be done 'between the Benedicamus and the giving of the consecrated bread';[26] it was in the church also and in the presence of the priest that solemn accusations of theft were to be made. The church had intruded itself centrally into the peace-keeping and contract-observing mechanisms of medieval Welsh society.

Nor was the church's role merely passive. During the twelfth and thirteenth centuries in particular it employed the machinery of its own courts and the threat of spiritual penalties to impose its own norms on lay society in matters such as marriage, testaments, sexual offences, perjury, and the status of 'illegitimate' children. These were areas of social custom and behaviour where Welsh practice was often at odds with the teaching of the church. The reverberations of the conflict between them are evident in the various texts of Welsh law: in some texts the teaching of Welsh law (W. *cyfraith Hywel*) is pointedly contrasted in defiant fashion with the dictates of canon law (W. *cyfraith eglwys*) on partible succession and the rights of extramarital offspring; in other texts a due measure of deference is shown to ecclesiastical opinion. The conflict itself is, paradoxically, a tribute to the impact of the church on social morality and outlook in Wales.

Some Welsh social customs may have stood condemned in the eyes of reformed churchmen; but few impugned the devotion of Welshmen. Gerald of Wales and Walter Map recognized that they were, by their own light, remarkably devout; even Gilbert Foliot, bishop of Hereford, acknowledged that the Welsh showed unusual respect for holy places and for persons consecrated to God. Popular religious belief and practice did not, it seems, differ in essentials from that common through medieval Europe. It was a religion of ritual and mystery, rather than of structured dogma or frequent preaching. The weekly mass was its focus, but the other sacraments—baptism, confirmation, marriage, and extreme unction—were also public affirmations of the church's control of the key points of transition in the believer's life. 'The Welsh', remarked Gerald, 'more than any other people long to be confirmed by the bishop.'[27] Worship was essentially corporate and communal; the church (and its cemetery), as the

---

[26] *Llyfr Iorwerth*, ed. A. R. William, §60 (p. 35).
[27] *DK*, I, xviii (*Opera*, vi, 203).

only public building in a country of dispersed habitat, served as a centre of sociability as well as of worship. It was there often that bargains were struck, contracts completed, judgements delivered, communal renders divided, ale sold, and games played. Churches, more especially the large mother churches to which processions might be made at high festival, brought an element of visual richness and relative material splendour to a poverty-stricken society: in the artistry of tympanum, font, and rood screen, the vivid colours of wall-paintings and stained glass, and in the richness of ecclesiastical vestments and relics. The atmosphere of opulence and serene security, which pervades the poems of Cynddelw to St Tysilio's church at Meifod and of Llywelyn Fardd to St Cadfan's church at Tywyn, must have been one which struck most contemporary Welsh visitors to these shrines.

Judgement rather than splendour was, however, the keynote of medieval religion. In this respect Wales was certainly no exception. Its religious poetry from the twelfth century onwards is pervaded by a sense of gloom, by a vivid awareness of the presence of the Devil ('the guile of the unseen monster' as the Franciscan poet, Madog ap Gwallter, calls it), a strong sense of the transience of man's life ('no longer than that of a mirror' as one poet vividly puts it), a morbid preoccupation with physical decay, a presentiment of impending doom (W. *arwyddion Dydd Brawd*), and the spectre of Final Judgement.[28] Visions of Heaven and Hell (as reflected in *Breuddwyd Pawl* and *Purdan Padrig*) and legends about the Harrowing of Hell were among the earliest and most popular apocryphal religious tracts to be translated into Welsh. Such an awesome and ever-present prospect of judgement could only be tolerated by invoking the intercessionary powers of saints. Wales had a large pantheon of its own saints, most of whom belonged to the period of the conversion. Their cults were already well-established long before the eleventh century. In most cases those cults were specialized either in function (the staff of St Curig at the church of St Harmon (Gwrtheyrnion), for example, being noted as particularly efficacious for the cure of glandular swellings) or in locality (St Padarn, for example, being especially associated with Ceredigion). The lives of many of these saints, such as Brynach, Cybi, and Illtud, were first composed in writing in the twelfth century and, in the case of Dewi and Beuno, translated into Welsh some two centuries later. With its increasing integration into the religious life of Europe, Wales also came to share more fully in the cult of the major saints of the church. The Normans initiated the process by foisting some of their favoured saints on the churches of

---

[28] *The Myvyrian Archaiology of Wales*, ed. O. Jones *et al*. (Denbigh, 1870), p. 275 ('rhag twyll cawr cêl') as translated by D. M. Lloyd in A. O. H. Jarman and G. R. Hughes (eds.), *A Guide to Welsh Literature*, I, 182; *Llsg. Hendregadredd*, p. 190 ('Nid hyn oes dyn nac oes drych').

south Wales at an early date. But the Welsh were soon to show themselves
eager pupils: they translated the *vitae* of saints old and new (such as
Edmund of Abingdon) into Welsh; they increased their repertoire of
women saints by translating the biographies of St Catherine and St
Margaret; they delighted in the stock of edifying tales provided by the
Legenda Aurea.

The cult of a saint was greatly enhanced if it could be related to a
particular shrine or to physical remains associated with the saint. In this
respect again the Welsh, in common with the Irish and the Scots, had a
reputation for outstanding devotion. They showed remarkable reverence,
so Gerald informs us, for portable bells, pastoral staffs, and other relics of
saints; 'they are more afraid of swearing oaths upon them and then
breaking their word than they are upon the Gospels'.[29] Many of these
relics had a country-wide reputation—such as Dewi's handbell called
'bangu' at Glasgwm (Elfael), the bell of Teilo, the torque of Cynog, which
the Lord Rhys had purloined and hidden in his court at Dinefwr, or
Cyrwen, the staff of Padarn which, in the words of an eleventh-century
vernacular poem, 'much accomplishing, much loved gives protection; its
holy power reaching the limits of three continents'.[30] The most potent
relics, of course, were the bodies of the saints themselves. That is why
Bishop Urban had gone to such trouble to secure the body of Dyfrig for
Llandaff and why Dyfrig's successor, Teilo, had shown remarkable
foresight and consideration by providing three bodies of himself miraculously,
so that the three communities he had served should not battle over and
dismember his remains. Relics attracted pilgrims and so did images, roods,
and shrines. Some pilgrimage centres in Wales were local in their range
and seasonal in their timetable; such was the shrine of St Elyned, just
outside Brecon, which was the focus of processions, dances, and much
religious frenzy on 1 August annually. A few Welsh shrines—such as Ynys
Enlli (Bardsey Island), St Davids, St Winifred's well at Holywell, and
various images of the Virgin—had a national and even international
reputation; while record evidence from the thirteenth century onwards
shows that Welshmen, and not only rich and powerful ones, travelled well
beyond Wales—to Canterbury, Walsingham, Compostella, Rome, and
even Jerusalem—on pilgrimage.

Ritual and sacrament, saints and relics were of the essence of popular
religion in Wales, as elsewhere, in the Middle Ages. How far such
observances were supported by any sustained Biblical teaching and
instruction is a different matter. On the morrow of the Edwardian
Conquest, Archbishop Pecham decreed that each parish priest should
expound a basic programme of instruction to his parishioners four times a

[29] *IK*, I, ii (*Opera*, vi, 27).
[30] Ifor Williams, 'An Old Welsh Verse', *NLWJ* 2 (1941–2), 69–75.

year, concentrating on the Ten Commandments, the Lord's Prayer, the Twelve Articles of the Creed, the Seven Works of Mercy, and the Seven Deadly Sins. Whether such a decree was or indeed could be followed, given the ignorance and near-illiteracy of many parish priests, is very much open to doubt. What is clear, however, is that from the thirteenth century onwards a considerable corpus of basic devotional and didactical religious literature was translated into Welsh, mainly from Latin but occasionally from French. Such texts included translations or summaries of parts of the Bible (notably the popular if mis-named *Y Bibyl Ynghymraec* viz. The Bible in Welsh), apocryphal texts, saints' lives, prayers, and hymns. Most popular of all were manuals of instruction for parish priests, educating them in the basic elements of catechism (notably the tract *Yn y modd hwn* viz. In this fashion, of which twenty-one manuscripts survive) or in methods of listening to confession, and providing them with a convenient and undemanding handbook, or *summa*, of sacred and secular learning, as did Honorius Augustodunensis's *Elucidarium*, which had a great vogue in late medieval Wales. Most of these texts were, or course, utterly derivative, often being translated into Welsh a century or more after they were originally written. Yet they indicate a desire in Wales, as elsewhere, to improve the standard of clerical knowledge, and thereby of lay instruction, especially in the aftermath of the decrees of the Fourth Lateran Council of 1215. Stilted as some of the translations are, they helped to build up a sinewy verncacular vocabulary for the discussion of religious and devotional issues which was to stand the sixteenth-century translators of the Bible into Welsh in very good stead. Above all, perhaps, they show how Wales from the twelfth century onwards was becoming a party to the ecclesiastical culture and popular religious literature of Europe, without altogether surrendering its own traditions.

The changing patterns of religious devotion in this period in Europe were also reflected in Wales. The cult of the Virgin Mary grew rapidly in popularity, particularly under the promotion of her special devotees, the Cistercians and the Franciscans. Wales followed the fashion. When the great mother church of Meifod, the sanctuary of the princes of Powys, was rededicated in 1156 the name of the Virgin Mary was added to those of the native saints, Gwyddfarch and Tysilio. The various apocryphal texts on her life were among the earliest Latin religious works to be rendered into Welsh, and by the fourteenth century, if not earlier, her Office had likewise been translated. Churches and chapels were dedicated to her (143 have been counted in the country as a whole); so were chantries, guilds, and wells. 'Living images' of her were among the most popular objects of lay devotion and from an early date the poets exulted in the paradoxes of her position: 'she is an once mother and father, an undeniable virgin', as one of them noted. Much of her appeal to a society which lived under the spectre of judgement lay in her humanity. She was 'the mother of geniality' (*mam rhadlonedd*) in the memorable phrase of Gwynfardd Brycheiniog in the late twelfth century; her image of a smiling beneficence and serenity had already begun to assert itself.[31]

This same emphasis on compassion and humanity explains the changing perception of Christ himself in these centuries, a change which is as vividly reflected in Welsh poetry as it is in the iconography of Western Europe. Religious devotion came to focus in particular on his birth and his death. Stories about Christ's infancy, particularly those found in the *Pseudo-Mathaei Evangelium*, were translated into Welsh, and the Franciscans in Wales as elsewhere promoted the cult of the nativity. The tone and language of the poem by Madog ap Gwallter, probably a Franciscan friar, on this theme strike an altogether novel and light note, hitherto unheard in Welsh religious poetry: 'the mighty little giant, strong, powerful, frail . . . his chair a little heap of hay'.[32] But it was the crucifixion, rather than the nativity, which was the focus of the most affective Welsh religious poetry of the medieval period. The crucifixion was now seen as a moment of supreme sorrow; it was the ultimate expression, along with the Harrowing of Hell, of the price that Christ was willing to pay to redeem mankind. Even the strict metres and archaic vocabulary of traditional court poetry could not conceal the torrent of emotion of poets, such as Einion ap Gwalchmai and Gruffudd ab yr Ynad Coch, when they chose to write on the theme. When Edward I after the conquest of 1282–3 removed from Wales the fragment of the True Cross (W. *Y Groes Naid*), he took, away not only a valuable national relic (as was Edward's wont) but also the symbol of a much more affective Christo-centric religiosity.

Wales was also at one with Europe in these centuries in searching for a more personal religion concerned with the inwardness of experience as much as with the externals of ritual. One would not normally expect to find such changes reflected in the stylized court poetry of the period; but there is an intensity in the soul-searching of some of the odes, notably those of Einion ap Gwalchmai, which is a far cry from the conventional praise poems to God in earlier generations. The formal insistence on annual auricular confession to a priest, as decreed by the Fourth Lateran Council of 1215, placed a new emphasis on the individual's self-analysis of his behaviour and motives and highlighted the sacrament of penance. This was reflected in Wales in the treatise on how to make a confession penned by Cadwgan, bishop of Bangor, 1215–35, and by the Welsh translation of Raymond de Pennafort's famous manual on the same subject. Laymen

---

[31] *Hen Gerddi Crefyddol*, pp. 24 ('Hi yn fam a thad, hi yn wyryf heb wad'), 52.
[32] *Hen Gerddi Crefyddol*, p. 105 ('Cawr mawr bychan, cryf cadarn gwan, . . . A sopen wair yn lle cadair'). This delightful carol is translated in J. P. Clancy, *The Earliest Welsh Poetry*, pp. 163–6.

increasingly demanded a more satisfying, participatory religion to supplement the apparatus of communal worship. In the late thirteenth century a Ceredigion lady of princely stock, Efa ferch Maredudd, commissioned a translation of the Athanasian Creed with a commentary 'for her spiritual benefit and comfort' and the translator assumed that she could 'read and understand' his work.[33] Efa was the first Welshwoman of whose literarcy we can be fairly confident. Others of her class and district shared her interests: her brother commissioned a translation of the *Transitus Beatae Mariae* (as well as of the Charlemagne epic); while in the mid-fourteenth century the *Book of the Anchorite of Llanddewibrefi* (*Llyfr Ancr Llanddewibrefi*), one of the most valuable and comprehensive anthologies of Welsh religious prose, was compiled at the instance of a leading Welsh squire of Cantref Mawr. Such texts are no doubt but a few remnants of a once substantial corpus of devotional and didactic writings. They illustrate vividly the intense interest among laymen, at least at the higher echelons of native society, in a more personal and book-based religion; they also indicate that Wales had not been untouched by the spirit of mystical piety so characteristic of the later Middle Ages. One of the major texts copied into the *Book of the Anchorite* was *Y Gysegrlan Fuchedd* ('The Consecrated Life'), a mystical work whose final section is concerned to outline 'the ecstasies that spring from divine love and the visions which the Holy Spirit imparts in such ecstasies'.[34] The work, which proved remarkably popular in Welsh, may well have been intended originally for anchorites and men in religious orders; but that it should now be included in a volume commissioned by and for a devout layman was a measure of the change in religious sentiment and aspirations that was afoot in Wales.

The Wales of the *Book of the Anchorite* of 1346 was a very different Wales from that of Bishop Sulien and his sons in the late eleventh century. Nowhere were the changes more striking than in the practice and organization of religion. Continuities, of course, there were in abundance —in the main themes of faith, in the major rituals of the church, in the status of and affection for native saints. But they are less striking than the profound changes which the church had undergone—in organization, the definition of dioceses and parishes, the development of church government, the building and decoration of churches large and small, the introduction of Benedictine and Cistercian monasticism, the financial and judicial control of parishioners, the pattern of popular religiosity, the literature of religious devotion and instruction. None of these changes was unique to

[33] Henry Lewis 'Credo Athanasius Sant' *BBCS* 5 (1929–31), 193–203 at pp. 195–6. Efa was probably the daughter of Maredudd ab Owain (d. 1265) and so a direct descendant of the Lord Rhys. See diagram 3.

[34] Quoted in I. Ll. Foster 'The Book of the Anchorite', *Proceedings of the British Academy*, XXXVI (1950) 197–226 at p. 207.

Wales; they are but local and often pale reflections of the momentous transformation which the western church as a whole underwent in this period. Yet to say as much is to identify once more the greatest change of all that the Welsh church had undergone: it may have retained some of its local practices and idiosyncrasies, but to all intents and purposes it was absorbed fully during these centuries into the observance, practice, and governance of the western church in general.

PART III

THE AGE OF CONSOLIDATION
1172–1277

INTRODUCTION

THE period from 1172 to 1277 witnessed momentous changes in Wales. Some of those changes within society, economic life, and the church have already been outlined. They were equally momentous in the political life of the country. By the late twelfth century the map of political power in Wales had largely assumed the shape it was to retain until the Edwardian Conquest. The age of rapid Anglo-Norman advance had come to an end; it was followed by an age of consolidation. Some districts—notably the Perfeddwlad in the north-east (the district extending eastwards from the river Conwy to the Cheshire plain) and the area around Carmarthen in the south-west—still changed hands in response to the swing of the military pendulum; the skills, fortunes, and preoccupations of individual rulers— English king, Welsh prince, or Marcher lord—could still shape and reshape the map of political power in Wales. Yet a broad equilibrium of power, between native rule and foreign lordship, had been achieved. The acceptance of that equilibrium—and with it an acknowledgement that the conquest of Wales was, and was likely to remain, incomplete—was reflected in the adoption of a new terminology. From the late twelfth century onwards Wales (*Wallia*), or pure Wales (*pura Wallia*) as it was sometimes called, was contrasted with the March of Wales (*marchia Wallie*); likewise, the nobles and magnates of native Wales were contrasted with 'the barons of the March' and the 'English barons holding land in the March'. The duality of terminology reflected the duality of power. The character of this equilibrium, the strains placed upon it, and the changing perceptions of its nature are major themes in the history of Wales in the century or so after 1172.

During the same period the structure of political authority within Wales was being transformed. Particularly was this so within native Wales. There were continuities with the past, of course, in the principles and practice of power, both within and between the ruling dynasties. Yet the changes are even more striking. The political map was simplified, as the greater principalities came to tower in the landscape and as one of them, Gwynedd, came to secure a measure of sustained hegemony; the shaping of institutions of governance, jurisdiction, and exploitation gave native rulers a far greater measure of sustained and systematic control over the resources of their territories, while the temporary federations and brittle military hegemonies of earlier days gave way to a more formal, though often still fragile, pattern of relationships and power between the native principalities. In the March a similar transformation was taking place. Continuing military vulnerability and vigilance meant that Marcher society still retained its militarist flavour; but, in the south-west and, above all, the south-east, the heroic days of conquest and colonization were gradually being succeeded by a period of consolidation. A distinctive Marcher society had emerged and was asserting its own identity; the 'law and custom of the March' were recognized as having a separate existence from those both of England and of Wales; seignorial authority was being consolidated and the lineaments of a pattern of civilian governance—in administration, justice, and finance—were emerging; the growing references to the 'liberty' or 'liberties of the March' manifested an increasing awareness of the distinctive status of Marcher lordships within the lands ruled by the king of England.

The relationship of the king of England with Wales, both native Wales and the March, also changed perceptibly in the same period. The formal language and format of the relationship, it it true, remained the same; they were those of feudal lord and vassal, suzerain and dependant. Yet beneath a façade of continuity, crucial readjustments of attitudes and relationships were taking place. With the loss of Normandy and other lands in France in 1204 and with the formal acceptance of that loss in 1259, England became the centre of the concerns and ambitions of the Angevin kings; their attitude towards Wales, as indeed towards other parts of Britain, was gradually and imperceptibly changed in the process. Furthermore, the thirteenth century witnessed a progressive definition of the relationship between English king and Welsh rulers which, in effect, transformed the character of that relationship: written documents and formal treaties specified the obligations of dependence and the penalties of disobedience; jurisdictional overlordship was increasingly and deliberately exploited as a pretext for intervention, while political or military misfortunes were seized upon as occasions to elaborate the terminology and mechanics of suzerainty and control. The native Welsh rulers, for their part, responded to the challenge not only by exploiting to the full the political discomfitures of English kings but also by developing a theory of the identity of Wales—notably in terms of its customs, its laws, and the status of its rulers—which might act as a bulwark against the pretensions of the English kingdom.

The sharpening of political focus was accompanied by, and expressed in, a sharpening of national identities. Within England an aggressive sense of national pride and identity, and with it a distrust of aliens, grew apace; it was increasingly cultivated and exploited by the monarchy for its own ends. Wales lacked England's political and administrative integration; any measure of political unity that native rulers imposed or achieved was fragile and short-lived. Yet, in spite of this political fragmentation, the sense of a Welsh national identity certainly grew rapidly in the thirteenth century. It was expressed in a pride in the language and laws of Wales, as symbols of its unity, an emphasis on its historic frontiers and the common and exalted descent of its peoples, the self-conscious cultivation of the concept of 'Wales' (*Wallia*) as a political and historical unit, and the cultivation of the prospect of unitary native rule. In the process, the contrast between English and Welsh—both between English settlers in Wales and the native Welsh, as well as between Englishmen and Welshmen generally—was brought into much sharper focus. The plurality of former days (when writs were addressed to French, Flemish, English, and Welsh alike)[1] was being replaced by a sharp and confrontational duality—between English and Welsh.[2] It is increasingly in terms of a conflict between two peoples that the disputes between the English kings and native Welsh princes were fought; even official records conceded as much when they announced, as did the treaty of Montgomery in 1267, that their hope was to terminate 'the war and discord . . . between the English and the Welsh'.[3]

The period from 1172 to 1277 may, therefore, be regarded as an age of consolidation and definition in the history of Wales. It was a period when the powers of native princes, English king, and Marcher lords were all, in different ways, consolidated. It was also a period of definition in the political map of Wales, in the relationship of the English king and native rulers, and in the development of national identity and sentiment. Such are some of the themes which will be considered in the following chapters. It is with the character and transformation of power in native Wales that we begin.

---

[1] One of the last writs in which such a multiple address clause is used is that of William Marshal in 1223: *Monasticon Anglicanum*, ed. W. Dugdale, v, p. 267. It is indicative of changing perceptions that Llywelyn ab Iorwerth in his treaty with the French king in 1212 refers to his enemies as *Angli* and that *Franci* is replaced by *Angli* in one text of the native Latin chronicle, *Annales Cambrie*, in 1216.

[2] One indication of the growth of racial awareness was the licence that Robert Sor felt obliged to secure to marry Gwenllian, sister of Hywel ap Maredudd 'notwithstanding that the said Gwenllian is Welsh', *Patent Rolls 1225–32*, p. 506.

[3] *Litt. Wallie*, p. 1.

CHAPTER 8

NATIVE WALES, 1172–1240

By the 1170s the area of Wales still subject to native rule had assumed the form that it was to retain for the most part until 1277. It covered well over half of the surface area of Wales, though in terms of population and wealth the proportion was very much smaller. The whole of north Wales, from the estuary of the Dee to that of the Dyfi and across to the Severn valley and beyond, lay within the district of native rule; so did much of south-west Wales, from the Dyfi to the Teifi and Tywi. Beyond these districts lay other areas where Anglo-Norman rule was far from secure and where native rulers frequently reasserted their control—notably Maelienydd, Gwrtheyrnion, and Elfael in the middle March, the uplands of Glamorgan and Caerleon, and a great swathe of lordships in the south-west from Cemais to Gower. Not only had the map of Wales acquired a good measure of fixity, so also had the political geography of the native kingdoms. These kingdoms might be partitioned (as was Deheubarth recurrently after 1197, Gwynedd after 1170 and again after 1246, or northern Powys after 1236 and 1269); cadet branches might establish their own sub-kingdoms (such as that of Meirionydd, 1240–56); frontier areas might be annexed (as was Penllyn by Gwynedd in the early thirteenth century). Yet the political geography of native Wales had more fixity than the internal quarrels of its dynasties might suggest and more stability certainly than it had enjoyed in the eleventh and early twelfth centuries. As princes exploited the wealth and resources of their principalities more systematically, as ties of lineage and reward were forged with local nobility, as the nature of princely authority became more territorial and the pattern of governance more sophisticated, so the geographical identity of each kingdom, particularly the greater kingdoms, became more firmly defined.

The pattern of authority within native Wales was also simplified. Some of the lesser dynasties—such as those of Cedewain or Caerleon—could still play a significant role in Welsh politics; others—such as the cadet branches of the Powys and Gwynedd families, established respectively in Mechain and Meirionydd—could prove awkward obstacles to the consolidation of power in the greater principalities; individual local rulers, such as Maredudd ap Rhobert of Cedewain, 'eminent counsellor of Wales', could achieve a distinction out of proportion to their landed wealth and power.[1] Yet, in general, the last century of Welsh independence witnessed a decline in the number and influence of the lesser dynasties. Some, such as the native dynasties of Arwystli and Tegeingl, were reduced to the status of local noble families and their lands and lordships appropriated by the major dynasties; others, such as the native dynasties of the middle March (Elfael, Cedewain, and Maelienydd), of upland Glamorgan, and of Caerleon retained their independent status but moved increasingly in the orbit of the greater kingdoms. It is around the history of these three greater or over-kingdoms—Gwynedd, Powys, and Deheubarth—that the history of native Wales now revolved. Overkingdoms and supremacies there had been in earlier centuries, but they now acquired a measure of definitiveness and stability such as they had not enjoyed hitherto. Law-texts, poetry, and contemporary chronicles now take the threefold division of the country for granted: Gwynedd, Powys, and Deheubarth are the three provinces of Wales; Aberffro, Mathrafal, and Dinefwr their respective 'chief courts'.[2] What remained to be determined was whether or not one of these provinces and its dynasty could secure a permanent hegemony over the other two and, thereby, aspire to the overkingship of native Wales as a whole. In the later twelfth century, the pre-eminence belonged to Deheubarth; its lord may even occasionally have assumed the title of 'prince of Wales'.

(I) THE SUPREMACY AND ECLIPSE OF DEHEUBARTH

Deheubarth was in origin a geographical description rather than a political designation; it referred to the whole of south Wales from Cardigan Bay to the Wye. But, by the twelfth century, it had acquired a much more limited connotation, largely under the impact of Norman advance in south Wales. It now referred to the native kingdom of south-west Wales consisting of such parts of Dyfed, Ceredigion, and Ystrad Tywi as remained under Welsh authority. In the early twelfth century it looked as if the whole of Deheubarth was to be utterly smothered by a concerted Norman advance; indeed, by 1135, the native dynasty was confined to a tenuous foothold in the inaccessible, forested lands of Cantref Mawr. Yet, by 1172, the kingdom of Deheubarth had been reconstituted and for the next generation it dominated the politics of native Wales. This remarkable reversal of fortunes was to be attributed in part to the slowing-down of Norman momentum and to its diversion, after 1170, towards Ireland; in

---

[1] *Brut, s.a.* 1244.
[2] In some of the legal texts only Gwynedd and Deheubarth are referred to: *Latin Texts of the Welsh Laws*, ed. H. D. Emanuel (Cardiff, 1967), pp. 110, 317, 436.

part to the remarkable stamina and tenacity of the native ruler Rhys ap Gruffudd, who refused to treat the crushing royal victories of 1158 and 1163 as the extinction of his claims and aspirations; and, above all, perhaps to the volte-face in the attitude of Henry II towards native Welsh rulers, and his decision in 1171–2 to recognize the status of the revived kingdom of Deheubarth and extend his protection to its ruler.

In 1172 the kingdom of Deheubarth consisted of the whole of Ceredigion (from which the Clares had been finally expelled in 1164), Cantref Mawr (the heartland of the kingdom and refuge of its dynasty in its darkest hour), Cantref Bychan (which had been won from the Clifford family), Emlyn (conquered from the fitz Geralds, who were compensated with land in Devon), and the two small commotes of Ystlwyf and Efelffre to the west of Carmarthen. The kingdom had two centres. The one, Dinefwr, lay in the Tywi valley on the site of an ancient hill fort; it held a particular place in the affections and historical mythology of the Welsh as the principal seat to which 'the dignities of the whole of south Wales . . . belonged'.[3] The other centre, Aberteifi or Cardigan, had altogether different associations. It was one of the earliest of Norman bridgeheads in south-west Wales; its capture by Rhys ap Gruffudd in 1165 was one of the most momentous milestones in the recovery of Deheubarth. He had caused its castle to be rebuilt of stone and mortar and it was there that he held a great eisteddfod in 1176. The surrender of Cardigan, 'the lock and stay of all Wales', as the native annalist eloquently referred to it, in 1200 was to be one of the clearest signs that the days of Deheubarth's glory were coming to an end.[4]

Deheubarth was a rich and fertile kingdom, the tempo of its economic life quickened by contacts with the Anglo-Norman settlements in Pembroke and along Carmarthen Bay. But it was also a vulnerable kingdom: it had few natural boundaries to defend it and the existence of Anglo-Norman lordships and colonies along its borders made for friction and confrontation. To the south-east lay the commotes of Cydweli and Gower. They were traditionally regarded as part of Ystrad Tywi but had been conquered by the Normans at an early date and, in the case of southern Gower, intensively colonized. The princes of Deheubarth longed to recover control of this area, thereby reintegrating Ystrad Tywi and cutting the land route from south-west Wales to the Marcher lordships of the east. They captured Kidwelly in 1190 and besieged Swansea in 1192; in 1215–17 they went even further, destroying Swansea. 'driving all the English away from that land . . . and dividing their lands among Welshmen'.[5] Yet in spite of such temporary successes, the area was never successfully reannexed to Deheubarth. A more immediate danger lay in the enclave of royal and baronial lordships

---

[3] *Cal. Anc. Corr.*, p. 24.
[4] *Brut, s.a.* 1200 (p. 80).
[5] *Brut, s.a.* 1217 (p. 96).

on the Tywi estuary and eastwards—notably Carmarthen, Llansteffan, Talacharn (Laugharne), and St Clears. Here again, castles might be captured in lightning raids (as in 1189) but rarely were they held for any length of time. Carmarthen, in particular, was a thorn in the side of the rulers of Deheubarth. It stood astride the estuary of the Tywi and could be readily relieved by sea (as was well shown in 1233); its borough served as a magnet for the commercial life of its hinterland; above all, as the centre of a royal enclave consisting of three commotes, Elfed, Derllys, and Gwidigada, it served as a base from which royal officials could undermine the authority of the native dynasty. Further west lay an arc of more or less well-established Anglo-Norman lordships from Cemais in the north to Pembroke in the south. The northern lordships—Cemais and Cilgerran—were particularly vulnerable to Welsh raids (Nyfer or Nevern, the *caput* of Cemais, being captured in 1191); even districts such as Wiston, Haverford, and Tenby were not out of the reach of Welsh forays, such as those of 1189 and 1193. But Anglo-Norman lordship in this district was much too firmly entrenched to be permanently dislodged; the best the native rulers could hope for was to compel the inhabitants to pay large sums to buy off the prospect of a Welsh raid. To the east, Deheubarth was protected by the uplands of mid-Wales and by the very uncertain hold that the Normans enjoyed in Brecon and Builth. Yet the rulers of Deheubarth realized that once this eastern bulwark fell, the days of their kingdom would be numbered. Hence their periodic raids into the area (as in 1169, 1196, 1217); hence the establishment of frontier outposts (such as the castle at Rhaeadr built by Rhys ap Gruffudd in 1177 and rebuilt in 1194); hence the assiduous cultivation of alliances and marriage bonds with the native princelings of the district from upland Glamorgan to Maelienydd. To the north, the threat to Deheubarth came not from the Anglo-Normans but from the ambitions of fellow Welsh princes. Rhys ap Gruffudd began the revival of his family's fortunes by expelling the house of Gwynedd from Ceredigion by 1153; he asserted his authority vigorously as far as the river Dyfi, the recognized boundary between north and south Wales; he even made unsuccessful efforts to extend his rule in this frontier area by annexing Cyfeiliog from Powys in 1167 and Meirionydd from a branch of the Gwynedd dynasty (with Henry II's sanction) ten years later.

Such a vulnerable kingdom could not survive, let alone acquire pre-eminence within Wales, without a combination of favourable circumstances—the collapse of the momentum of Anglo-Norman advance, divisions and debility among the other native dynasties, the sufferance and even the support of the English king, and, above all, the quality of leadership of its own ruler. Rhys ap Gruffudd, or the Lord Rhys as he is generally known, towered in the political history of south Wales in the last quarter of the twelfth century. He fully deserved the title he had assumed for himself—

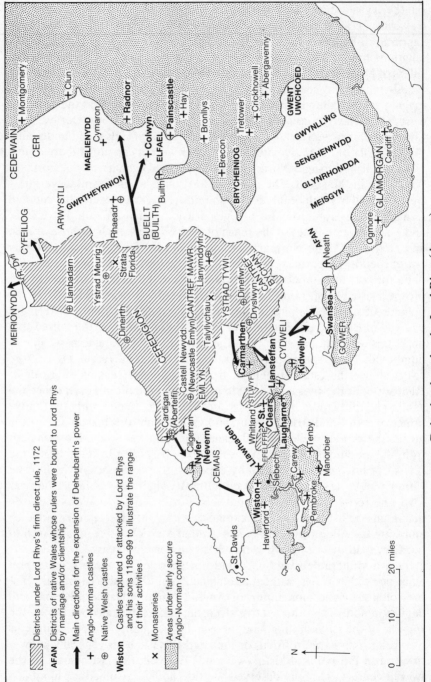

MAP 5. Deheubarth under the Lord Rhys (d. 1197)

Districts under Lord Rhys's firm direct rule, 1172

AFAN Districts of native Wales whose rulers were bound to Lord Rhys by marriage and/or clientship

Main directions for the expansion of Deheubarth's power

+ Anglo-Norman castles

⊕ Native Welsh castles

Wiston Castles captured or attacked by Lord Rhys and his sons 1189–99 to illustrate the range of their activities

× Monasteries

Areas under fairly secure Anglo-Norman control

0   10   20 miles

N

rightful prince of south Wales (*proprietarius princeps Sudwalie*).[6] He reconstructed the pattern of authority within his own kingdom: a major administrative reorganization of his lands appears to have been inaugurated to simplify the dues of his subjects and to effect their collection more regularly and systematically; food-renders were commuted into money-rents, and bond obligations and tenure of earlier days modified or abolished; castles were built or rebuilt (as at Cardigan and Llanymddyfri) and Norman methods of fortification and warfare imitated. As so often in Wales, political reconstruction and cultural renaissance went hand in hand. It is likely that it was under the Lord Rhys's aegis that the texts of Welsh law, as we now have them, were first assembled in book form—not only do those texts refer specifically to one of his legal rulings but their emphasis on Whitland, within the bounds of the greater Deheubarth, as the venue of the assembly at which Hywel Dda was said to have codified the laws, strongly suggests a southern provenance; and the great assembly or eisteddfod of poets and musicians held at Cardigan in 1176 paraded, to the whole of Wales, the cultural pre-eminence of Rhys's court. In religious affairs, likewise, Rhys stole a march on other Welsh princes: his poet, Gwynfardd Brycheiniog, sang the praises of Dewi (St David) as the premier saint of Wales, indeed of the whole of Christendom; it was, as it were, the religious sanction for Deheubarth's pre-eminence and it was at Dewi's shrine that Rhys was to be buried in 1197. But, in religion as in so much else, Rhys had the confidence to come to terms with the new as well as to exult in the old. He was one of the earliest and most enthusiastic patrons of the reformed religious orders in Wales. He was liberal in his gifts to the Cistercian house at Whitland, while Strata Florida was virtually his foundation and became the mausoleum for members of his dynasty (see diagram 3); he founded and munificently endowed the sole house of the Premonstratensian order in Wales at Talyllychau (Talley) in the heartland of his dominions in Cantref Mawr; while Llanllŷr, one of only two Cistercian nunneries in Wales, likewise owed its origin to him. His religious endowments were indeed remarkably catholic, for they also extended to the house of the Hospitallers at Slebech in the Norman lordship of Haverford and the Benedictine priory at Cardigan, (albeit that it was a symbol of Anglo-Norman ecclesiastical colonialism in Wales and a daughter house of Chertsey abbey). The expansive eclecticism of the Lord Rhys's religious patronage seems to reflect the character of the man himself: confident and open-handed, welcoming new challenges and contacts, rather than retreating into a studied isolation.

The same genial self-assurance and easy confidence appear to characterize his hegemony in the lands beyond his dominions. He made no attempt to

[6] The title is given him in a charter to Strata Florida abbey which only survives in a late confirmation.

claim or exercise overlordship in Gwynedd or Powys; but he brought the Welsh princelings of the whole of south Wales within the orbit of his influence and leadership. He did so characteristically, by binding them in marriage to himself rather than bludgeoning them to submit to his authority. The native rulers of Senghennydd, Glynrhondda, Meisgyn, and Afan in upland Glamorgan, Maelienydd, Elfael, and Gwrtheyrnion in the middle March, upland Gwent, and Brycheiniog were all bound to him by ties of kinship and matrimony.[7] His hegemony was truly patriarchal: when he presented these princelings to Henry II at Gloucester in 1175 he did so not only as the king's justiciar in south Wales but also as the head of an extended family. Rhys's methods might have been genial, especially compared with the habits of earlier days; but his purpose was intensely serious. It was only by controlling and, where appropriate, chastising these minor princelings that he could retain the confidence and favour of the king; while his active support of the native rulers not only shored up their tenuous authority and contained the power of the Norman lords of the March, it also acted as a vital bulwark for his own kingdom. What Rhys was, above all, intent upon was the preservation of the status quo so painstakingly achieved in the period 1165–72. Expelling the Anglo-Normans from much of south Wales was no longer a realistic prospect; his sights were set on a much more modest but equally difficult task, that of preventing a renewal of Norman advance and, if possible, of rolling back Norman control at the peripheries of his kingdom. In pursuit of that ambition he used diplomacy as well as force: he hob-nobbed with the Anglo-Normans, aped their manners and customs, wooed them with matrimonial alliances—marrying two of his daughters to leading Norman lords of Cemais, so vital to the defence of his base at Cardigan, and, boldest stroke of all, betrothing his eldest son and designated heir, Gruffudd, to the daughter of the mightiest of the Marcher lords, William Braose, doubtless in the hope thereby of securing the eastern flank of his kingdom.

Above all, Rhys's hegemony depended on the good will of the Crown and on his own good sense in cultivating that goodwill. The *détente* of 1171–2 was the basis of his authority; his prime concern was to maintain it. He did so with remarkable success until 1189, but only by great and continuing effort.[8] The accord with Henry II was recurrently threatened by the ambitions of Marcher lords and by the impetuosity of Welsh princelings. It had to be constantly reviewed and repaired—by timely visits to the king's court, as in 1175, 1177, and 1184; by calculated acts of friendliness, such as the dispatch of Rhys's son to accompany the king to

---

[7] To the list as given in Lloyd, *History of Wales*, II, 545 should be added Trahaearn Fychan of Brycheiniog, who was married to the Lord Rhys's niece.

[8] These developments are considered from the king's angle below, Chap. 11, pp. 290–2.

Normandy, or by support for Henry during the revolt of 1173; by giving tactful permission to levy Welsh troops to meet the king's needs; by parleys and negotiations, such as those held at Worcester in 1184 and Hereford in 1186; by compelling recalcitrant Welsh princelings to render massive tributes as public acts of contrition (as did two of the native rulers of the middle March in 1175, when each proffered the king a thousand head of cattle at Rhys's prompting); and, when a royal expedition seemed imminent, by buying it off with the renewal of fealty and the surrender of hostages, as in 1184. It was Rhys's quality—and in this he was to be followed by Llywelyn ab Iorwerth—that he knew when and how to bend, with good grace and without grovelling.

Rhys's career was indeed a remarkable one. Its very length was a tribute to his stamina and skill: he had occupied the stage of Welsh politics for over fifty years, from his first appearance in his early 'teens, at the capture of Llansteffan castle in 1146, to his death in 1197. But it was his achievement which was astounding: he had reconstituted the kingdom of Deheubarth and made it the premier Welsh kingdom. For once, the poet's compliment was well-deserved: Rhys had restored 'the majesty of the South'.[9] He was truly Rhys the Great, Rhys the Good; 'the unconquered head of all Wales'.[10] Yet the eclipse of his kingdom's pre-eminece so soon after his death suggests that his achievement was flawed. Those flaws indeed had become apparent in the last decade of his life. The first lay in the personal nature of his accord with Henry II, on which all else turned. That accord did not survive Henry's death in 1189. Whether from insensitivity or deliberate choice, Richard I's government chose not to observe the delicate conventions which had governed the relationships of Rhys with the English court since 1172. Royal protection—a protection which had gone so far as to lead to the seizure of the Mortimer estates in Wales and the imprisonment of Mortimer's heir for killing one of Rhys's client princes in 1179—no longer stood between Rhys ap Gruffudd and the ambitions of his Anglo-Norman foes in Wales. Rhys's response was to go on the attack in the hope that his armies could secure by force what Henry II's friendship had hitherto guaranteed him. In a series of spectacular raids and campaigns, from 1189 to 1196, he and his sons waged war on Anglo-Norman lordships throughout the length of south Wales, from Pembroke in the west to Painscastle in the east, culminating in a famous victory at Radnor, on the very borders of England, in 1196. The Lord Rhys had demonstrated that his military might was not to be despised; but once the

---

[9] *Llsg. Hendregadredd*, p. 108, quoted by D. M. Lloyd in *A Guide to Welsh Literature*, I, p. 171.

[10] *Brut*, s.a. 1197 (p. 76). The title 'Resus bonus' is given to him in one of his son's charters; that of 'Resus magnus' in charters issued by his grandson and by later descendants: S. W. Williams, *The Cistercian Abbey of Strata Florida* (1889), Appendix, pp. xiv–xvii.

gloves were off, his own vulnerability might also be revealed. Already in the 1190s the greatest of the Marcher lords, William Braose, had resumed his attacks and by a few bold strokes had demonstrated how exposed Deheubarth was: between 1195 and 1197 Braose recovered the castle of St Clears from the Welsh, reinforced the Crown's position at Carmarthen where he served as royal bailiff, mounted a raid on Cardigan, and showed his contempt for the Welsh by publicly executing one of Rhys's clients and kinsmen, Trahaearn Fychan, in Brecon.

By then the second flaw in Rhys's achievement had also long been evident. Family feuds clouded his last few years: he had imprisoned one of his sons in 1189, while five years later he himself suffered the indignity of being captured and imprisoned by two of his own children. Rhys fathered a huge brood of children—at least eighteen on a modest count—by his wife and by a bevy of mistresses (one of whom was his own niece). Rhys seems to have intended that his kingdom should pass intact to his eldest lawful son, Gruffudd; but Gruffudd had neither the good fortune nor the force of personality to impose his will on his brothers. The feuds which had already erupted in Rhys's last years became rampant once the old patriarch died in 1197; brothers made murderous attacks on each other (thus Hywel Sais was killed in an ambush by the men of his brother, Maelgwn, in 1204); castles were captured and recaptured (the castle of Llanymddyfri appears to have changed hands at least five times between 1200 and 1204); family alliances were made and broken; brothers and nephews were captured and often handed over to the English for imprisonment (as was Gruffudd ap Rhys in 1197); fathers were seized by sons and only released in return for territorial concessions (as happened to Rhys Gryg in 1227). The custom of partibility lay, of course, at the heart of the problem. The native Welsh chronicler recognized that readily enough: he explained Maelgwn ap Rhys's actions in 1197 by observing, almost parenthetically, that he was 'the man who was then without a portion of his patrimony', just as later, in 1213, the cause of a renewed bout of civil war in the Tywi valley was adequately explained by quoting Rhys Gryg's tart retort that 'he would not share with them (i.e. his nephews) a single acre of land'.[11] Some sons were satisfied (or had to be satisfied) with the grant of an ecclesiastical office and appurtenant churches or with the post of captain of the household-guard (W. *penteulu*) for one of their brothers; but most would not rest until they had secured a share of the paternal lands. Even a formal partition was no more than a temporary truce, for no partition would be regarded for long as equitable by all the claimants; and any new death in the family, especially if it were a death without surviving male heirs of the body (as was that of Rhys Ieuanc ap Gruffudd in 1222), precipitated a new crisis and

[11] *Brut, s.a.* 1197 (p. 79), 1213 (p. 87).

DIAGRAM 3. The Male Descendants of Lord Rhys of Deheubarth**

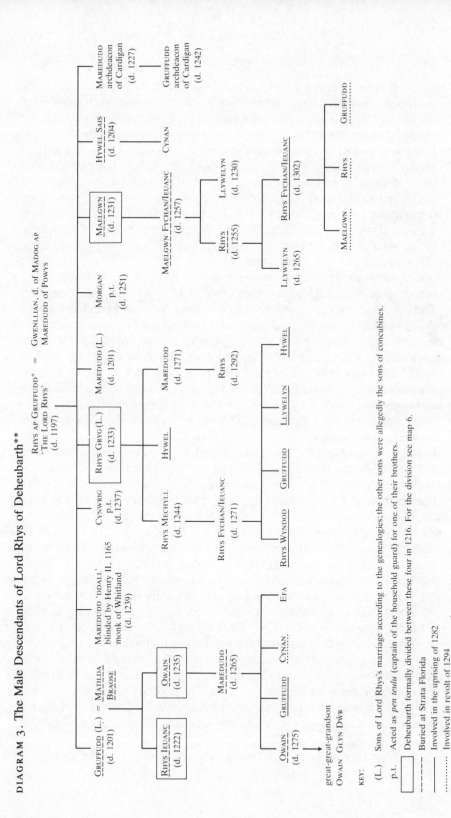

RHYS AP GRUFFUDD* = GWENLLIAN, d. of MADOG AP
'THE LORD RHYS'   MAREDUDD of POWYS
(d. 1197)

GRUFFUDD (L.) = MATILDA
(d. 1201)   BRAOSE

MAREDUDD 'ddall'
blinded by Henry II, 1165
monk of Whitland
(d. 1239)

CYNWRIG
p.t.
(d. 1237)

RHYS GRYG (L.)
(d. 1233)

MAREDUDD (L.)
(d. 1201)

MORGAN
p.t.
(d. 1251)

MAELGWN
(d. 1231)

HYWEL SAIS
(d. 1204)

MAREDUDD
archdeacon
of Cardigan
(d. 1227)

GRUFFUDD
archdeacon
of Cardigan
(d. 1242)

CYNAN

RHYS IEUANC
(d. 1222)

OWAIN
(d. 1235)

GRUFFUDD

RHYS MECHYLL
(d. 1244)

HYWEL

MAREDUDD
(d. 1271)

MAELGWN FYCHAN/IEUANC
(d. 1257)

OWAIN
(d. 1275)

GRUFFUDD

CYNAN

EFA

MAREDUDD
(d. 1265)

RHYS FYCHAN/IEUANC
(d. 1271)

RHYS WYNDOD

GRUFFUDD

LLYWELYN

HYWEL

RHYS
(d. 1292)

RHYS
(d. 1255)

LLYWELYN
(d. 1230)

LLYWELYN
(d. 1265)

RHYS FYCHAN/IEUANC
(d. 1302)

MAELGWN

RHYS

GRUFFUDD

great-great-grandson
OWAIN GLYN DŴR

KEY:

(L.)   Sons of Lord Rhys's marriage according to the genealogies; the other sons were allegedly the sons of concubines.

p.t.   Acted as *pen teulu* (captain of the household guard) for one of their brothers.

☐   Deheubarth formally divided between these four in 1216. For the division see map 6.

―――   Buried at Strata Florida

―――― Involved in the uprising of 1282

········ Involved in revolt of 1294

* For his family ancestry see above, DIAGRAM 2.

** By no means all the descendants recorded in the genealogies are included. All those included above are mentioned in contemporary evidence.

required a new partition or repartition. Furthermore, to add to the confusion, quarrels about partition might develop within each segment of the dynasty as well as between the various segments themselves: such, for example, were the bitter quarrels, which developed periodically in the 1240s and 1250s, between Maredudd ap Rhys Gryg, his brother, Rhys Mechyll, and nephew, Rhys Fychan ap Rhys Mechyll. A compound law of family dissension seemed to be in operation; it reduced the internal history of Deheubarth, from 1197 to 1277, to a recurrent and ever more complicated tangle of domestic squabbles. Only the imposition of a firm settlement by an external authority—whether the prince of Gwynedd (1216–40 and 1258–76) or the king of England (1240–56)—could bring some measure of order and stability.

Deheubarth's dissensions could easily be exploited to the advantage of others. Some of the Marcher lords saw their opportunity and seized it. Thus in the 1220s the young earl of Pembroke, William Marshal, fostered the grievances of one member of Deheubarth's dynasty, Rhys Ieuanc, and won over the support of another, Cynan ap Hywel, by granting him the commotes of Emlyn and Ystlwyf 'in order to hold down the Welsh through him'[12] and associating him with the Marshal raids on Ceredigion in 1223. Likewise, in the early 1240s, William's brother, Gilbert, tried to exploit the weakness of the native rulers of Deheubarth by supporting the pretensions of one member of the dynasty, Maredudd ap Rhys Gryg, and compelling another, Maelgwn Fychan, to take his daughter in marriage and do him homage. The king of England benefited even more handsomely from Deheubarth's discomfiture and divisions. He secured vital footholds in Wales as a result of the family quarrels. The first was won in 1199 when Maelgwn bought King John's support for his cause in return for the grant to him of Cardigan castle and the adjoining commote of Is Hirwern, 'choosing', as the native Latin annals put it devastatingly, 'rather to share with the enemy than with his brother' and bringing down on his head 'the curses of all the clergy and lay folk of Wales'.[13] It was a vital concession, for Cardigan—which was henceforth to be held by the English, with but brief intermissions—was to prove of crucial significance in the growth of royal authority in west Wales. It was another family quarrel which brought a further windfall to the crown, albeit for only a short time, in the same area in 1211, with the cession of the northern commotes of Ceredigion and the building of a royal castle at Aberystwyth. The Crown's intervention in the family quarrels was not, of course, disinterested. It availed itself of every opportunity to extend its authority, not only territorially, but jurisdictionally and feudally as well. It did so with devastating effect in the area around Carmarthen in the 1240s—exacting homage from Maredudd

---

[12] *Cal. Anc. Corr.*, p. 48.
[13] *Annales Cambrie*, ed. J. Williams ab Ithel (Rolls Series, 1860), *s.a.* 1200.

ap Rhys Gryg for all his lands, insisting that family disputes were henceforth to be settled in the king's court, and securing an acknowledgement from the lord of Dinefwr himself that he was justiciable in the royal court at Carmarthen. The days of Deheubarth's independence seemed to be numbered; and the dynasty's quarrels had contributed handsomely to its own decline.

The other native dynasties of Wales likewise exploited Deheubarth's difficulties for their own ends. The first to intervene was Gwenwynwyn of Powys, whose family had long cast covetous eyes on Ceredigion. Barely was the Lord Rhys buried in 1197 than Gwenwynwyn allied with one of the disaffected princelings of Deheubarth in a raid on Aberystwyth, while in 1203 he accompanied him on further raids in the Tywi valley. But it was the star of Gwynedd rather than Powys which was now in the ascendant. In 1208 its prince, Llywelyn ab Iorwerth, overran northern Ceredigion and its rulers became his protégés. After 1212 Llywelyn's power over Deheubarth was to be virtually unchallenged until his death in 1240. He wisely made no attempt to annex it, but its princelings were now clearly, in effect if not in name, his client vassals. He summoned them to Aberdyfi in 1216 and imposed upon them a partition of their lands 'in the presence of the magnates of north and south Wales' and by advice of 'all the learned men of Gwynedd'.[14] (See Map 6, p. 228) It was a measure of his authority that this settlement, further modified in 1222 and 1225, largely survived intact until 1240. The princelings of Deheubarth now fought in his campaigns and attended his court. It was little wonder that when the poets sang the praises of the princelings of Deheubarth, they now felt obliged to nod also in the direction of the prince of Gwynedd.

Deheubarth in the thirteenth century had become a collection of petty principalities, living by grace, or under the thumb, of either the king of England or the prince of Gwynedd. Its rulers strutted proudly on their little stages and the poets and chroniclers flattered their self-esteem by continuing to salute them as 'pillars of Wales', 'tormentors of England', 'defenders of the whole of Deheubarth and counsellors of the whole of Wales'.[15] But in truth they were, in Sir John Edward Lloyd's crushing phrase, no more than 'puny chiefs'.[16] So had been eclipsed the majesty of Deheubarth which had shone so brightly in the days of the Lord Rhys.

(II) POWYS: DEPENDENCE AND SURVIVAL

On the death of the Lord Rhys in 1197 the leadership of native Wales was briefly assumed by Powys. It was not the first occasion on which Powys had

[14] 'Cronica de Wallia', *BBCS* 12, s.a. 1215; *Brut (RBH)*, s.a. 1216 (p. 207).
[15] *Llsg. Hendredgadredd*, pp. 236–8; *Brut*, s.a. 1265.
[16] *History of Wales*, II, 750.

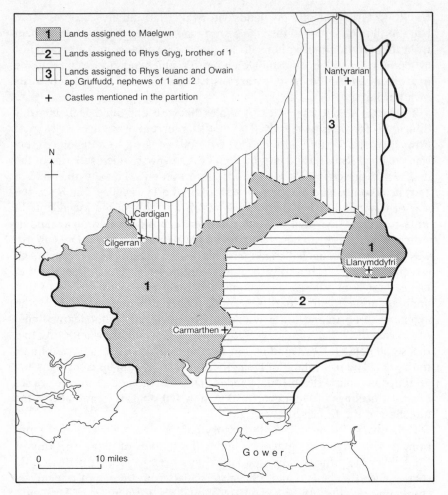

MAP 6. The Partition of Deheubarth, 1216*

* The partition of 1216 is an incident full of significance for an understanding of medieval
Welsh political life. It was undertaken after a protracted period of wrangling among the heirs
of Lord Rhys (d. 1197). The partition was imposed on the claimants at an assembly at
Aberdyfi convoked by Llywelyn ab Iorwerth of Gwynedd, then the dominant figure in native
Wales. It was conducted according to the provisions of Welsh law: the youngest claimant (3)
divided the land, the eldest (1) was given the first choice of the divisions so made. Not all the
lands assigned in the partition (and therefore shaded on the map) were necessarily under
effective Welsh control. Adjustments had to be made to the partition in 1218 to accommodate
Llywelyn's decision to hand over Gower, Cydweli, and Gwidigada (the area immediately
north of Carmarthen) to the English, and in 1222, on the death of Rhys Ieuanc without an heir
of his body. A commission was established in 1225 to make further adjustments to the
partition. The fragmentation of authority and the political debility represented by the
partition of 1216 remained a feature of Deheubarth's history until the extinction of native rule
there. Subsequent partitions after 1240 made the position much more complex.

enjoyed such pre-eminence. There had already been two such periods of glory earlier in the twelfth century—the first from *c.*1099 to 1110, when Powys had exploited the debility of Gwynedd and Deheubarth and the generosity of Henry I to exert its power in north and central Wales and to annex Ceredigion and Meirionydd; the second from 1140 to 1155, when the good fortune of domestic unity under a single ruler (Madog ap Maredudd, d. 1160) and of Anglo-Norman collapse under Stephen allowed Powys to extend its eastern boundaries substantially towards Cheshire and Shropshire. Both these earlier periods of glory were relatively short-lived; both were terminated by domestic squabbles on the one hand and a reassertion of Anglo-Norman power on the other. Powys's bid for hegemony in the late twelfth century proved even more short-lived and its consequent eclipse more dramatic and final. The bid began with extensive raids along the English border in 1196; these were quickly followed in the next year by the annexation of Arwystli in the south-west, the cession of Carreghwfa on the border with England by Richard I's government, and raids into Ceredigion. Flushed by success, Gwenwynwyn, who had finally succeeded his father, Owain Cyfeiliog, as lord of southern Powys in 1197, now assumed the role of national deliverer. 'With the help and support of all the princes of Wales', according to the *Brut*, 'he gathered a mighty host to seek to restore to the Welsh their ancient status and their ancient proprietary rights and boundaries.'[17] He clearly intended to assume the role recently played by the Lord Rhys and in much the same area—in the southern central March, far beyond the frontiers of Powys. It was there, at Painscastle, on 13 August 1198 that his dreams were shattered, when an English army overwhelmed his forces. Gwenwynwyn's prestige as would-be national leader was irretrievably tarnished, though he made several other attempts to show his mettle, leading raids into William Braose's lands, in 1203 and 1208, and exploiting the domestic wrangles of the Deheubarth dynasty for his own ends. He was soon paying the price of failure. Llywelyn ab Iorwerth of Gwynedd had already plotted the destruction of Gwenwynwyn in 1202 and though he was dissuaded from his intention for the time being—satisfying himself with the seizure of some of the lands of one of Gwenwynwyn's allies and kinsmen, Elisse ap Madog of Penllyn—he had served notice that Gwynedd was about to lay claim to the hegemony of native Wales. It was King John who first pulverized the prince of Powys: in October 1208 he summoned him to Shrewsbury, stripped him of his lands, exacted hostages from him, and only restored him to his inheritance on the most demeaning terms—including promises of perpetual service and of jurisdictional submission. Rarely had a native Welsh prince been so publicly and utterly humiliated. Henceforth, Gwenwynwyn was a pawn of

---

[17] *Brut* and *Brut (RBH)*, *s.a.* 1198.

either John (1210–12) or Llywelyn (1212–16); finally in 1216 he was evicted from his lands by Llywelyn and soon after died in exile. So ended Powys's bid for hegemony.

In truth the odds were stacked heavily against Powys. It was admittedly a large kingdom: it extended, in the words of the court poet, Gwalchmai, 'from the summit of Pumlumon to the gates of Chester, from Bangor Iscoed (on Dee) to the forested frontiers of Meirionydd'.[18] It was also a fertile kingdom, famous for the mildness of its contours and for its temperate weather; it was already known as 'the paradise of Wales'. Its long history as a border region had led to the cultivation of a strong sense of its own identity, reinforced by devotion to its patron saint (Tysilio), pride in its links with the Old North and its role in withstanding the Saxon advance, and the well-cultivated ancient privileges which its nobility claimed to enjoy (W. *breiniau gwŷr Powys*). Yet its political prospects in the late twelfth century hardly matched its geographical aspect or historical pride. It was now a fragmented kingdom. On the death of Madog ap Maredudd in 1160 Powys had been dismembered among five of his heirs. Such a patition need not have proved permanent: it could have been reversed either by military force and political skill, or by timely death. But in the case of Powys the division proved to be final and was compounded by further partitions and repartitions in subsequent generations. The major division was that between northern and southern Powys, known also from c.1200 as Powys Fadog and Powys Wenwynwyn. The former consisted mainly of the commotes of Iâl, Maelor Gymraeg, Maelor Saesneg, Nanheudwy, Cynllaith and Mochnant Is Rhaeadr; its lords often used the title lord of Bromfield and their main residence appears to have been the splendid hill-top castle of Dinas Brân (rebuilt in the 1270s). Southern Powys consisted of Mochnant Uwch Rhaeadr, Caereinion, Cyfeiliog, and (by annexation) Arwystli, as well as a clutch of smaller commotes or *swyddi* on either bank of the Severn; its lords titled themselves either 'of Cyfeiliog' or, increasingly, 'of Pool', the site of their new castle on the Severn. There was remarkably little friction between these two divisions of Powys; yet the permanence of the division without a doubt emasculated the kingdom politically. Nor did the process of fragmentation end there: the northern commotes of Penllyn, Edeirnion, and Dinmael became the portion of other branches of the Powys dynasty and fell an easy prey to the ambitions of Gwynedd, while within southern Powys itself the commote of Mechain belonged to a cadet branch of the dynasty, which persistently tried to thwart any attempt at integration into the senior branch or dependence on it. Powys is a classic example of the consequences of partibility, and those consequences threatened to grow more serious with

[18] *Llsg. Hendregadredd*, p. 26.

each succeeding generation: northern Powys was subdivided between five sons in 1236, and yet again between a further four in 1269, while in 1277 southern Powys was to be doled out between the six sons of Gruffudd ap Gwenwynwyn. Powys, to borrow a phrase from the contemporary Powys tale, *The Dream of Rhonabwy*, had indeed become a land of 'little men'.[19]

Even without such weakness, it was the most vulnerable of all the surviving Welsh kingdoms. To the north and west it had long been threatened by any resurgence of Gwynedd's expansionist ambitions, notably in Penllyn, Edeirnion, and Iâl, all at various periods annexed by Gwynedd. In the south-west the key border districts were Arwystli and Cedewain. Both had native dynasties of their own; both dynasties attempted to bolster their independence *vis-à-vis* Powys by forging alliances with either Deheubarth or Gwynedd; and both Gwynedd and Deheubarth for their part were anxious to use these districts as barbicans to defend their southern and northern flanks respectively. It is little wonder, therefore, that in the political tensions of the thirteenth century these two regions occupy a prominent place—Powys seeking to integrate both of them within its boundaries, and Gwynedd being equally determined to take them under its protection, to annex Arwystli (which was already ecclesiastically part of the diocese of Bangor), to convert Cedewain into a client-state (notably during the rule of Maredudd ap Rhobert d. 1244) and eventually to build a castle at Dolforwyn in Cedewain to demonstrate its mastery in the area.

But Powys's most vulnerable borders, of course, lay to the east. Here there was no mountain barrier or sea to inhibit the advance of the English and the Normans; instead, the broad and fertile plains of the Dee and Severn offered a standing invitation to raiders and settlers alike. It was as 'the shepherds of the Severn' that the prince-poet of southern Powys, Owain Cyfeiliog (d. 1197, extolled his troops;[20] and it is to places along the English border—such as Forden, Duddleston, and Caus—that the contemporary eulogies of Powys's princes frequently refer. The Montgomery family in the late eleventh century had shown how easily Powys might be overrun and its lords compelled to pay tribute; and the lesson was repeated on occasion for the benefit of later generations—thus the castle of Chirk on the borders of northern Powys was held by royal troops for prolonged periods from 1165 to 1213, while in 1196 the castle at Pool, the new capital of southern Powys, was itself captured in an English campaign.

Given its geographical vulnerability and also the fractionization of

---

[19] *Breudwyt Ronabwy*, p. 6 (*Mabinogion*, p. 141).
[20] *Oxford Book of Welsh Verse*, p. 31 (bugelydd Hafren) translated in J. P. Clancy, *The Earliest Welsh Poetry*, pp. 124–8. According to *The Dream of Rhonabwy* the lowlands between the rivers Dee and Vyrnwy—Rhychdir Powys as they were known—were worth three of the best commotes elsewhere in Powys.

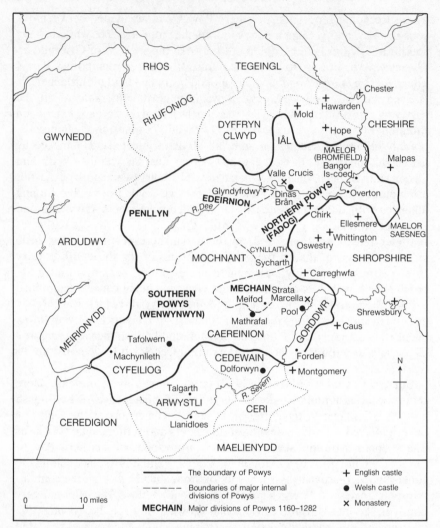

MAP 7. Powys and its Neighbouring Districts in the Thirteenth Century

political and territorial power in the wake of dynastic segmentation, it is
not the eclipse of Powys's hegemony which is remarkable but rather the
survival of Powys as a native principality. After all, in 1277 Powys retained
broadly the same boundaries as it had had at the death of Madog ap
Maredudd in 1160. Part of the explanation for its survival against the odds
lies in the lack of Anglo-Norman drive into Powys, other than an
occasional raid, such as that of the earl of Chester on Maelor in 1177. More
important appears to be the conscious decision of the English Crown,

taken initially as early as the reign of Henry I, that it could achieve its ends in north-east Wales by treating Powys as a pliable, if occasionally recalcitrant, protectorate, rather than by conquering it. It was a policy to which the Crown adhered until the end of the thirteenth century and which, on the whole, paid handsome dividends. But part of the credit for Powys's survival also belongs assuredly to its ruling dynasties, above all to their capacity to trim their sails to every change of wind in the political situation in Wales.

No one learned that lesson more throughly or applied it more successfully than Gruffudd ap Gwenwynwyn (d. 1286) of southern Powys. For more than a generation after his father's death in 1216 he was denied his inheritance by reason of the superior power of Gwynedd and the debility of the English Crown. When he eventually recovered southern Powys in 1241 he abandoned his father's delusions of grandeur. His sights were set on much more modest aims—such as extending the family's foothold beyond the Severn into the area known as Gorddwr (initially acquired from the Corbets as a marriage portion), attempting to bring the cadet house of Mechain into a state of formal dependence and judicial control, laying plans to try to secure mastery in Cedewain and Ceri and, thereby, to protect Powys's southern flank, and drawing up arrangements for a family settlement which would respect both the Welsh custom of partibility and his own anxiety to preserve, as far as possible, the integrity of his estates. These were modest ambitions indeed: but at least they were proportionate to the dynasty's resources and capabilities.

Living as they did on the borders of England, the princes of Powys learned how to reach a *modus vivendi* with their English neighbours and to become acceptable in English border society. Owain Cyfeiliog, prince of southern Powys from 1160 to 1197, had already made the transition. He was a great warrior lord in the tradition of his ancestors and exulted in the joys of war and border-raids; he was also one of the most distinguished poets of his generation, steeped in the traditions and allusions of ancient Welsh verse. But he was also a man who turned easily in the circles of English border society: he was fluent of speech and quick of wit; he exchanged pleasantries—and jibes—with Henry II, over dinner at Shrewsbury; he was noted for his wisdom and justice in the governance of his lands. His kinsmen and descendants followed his example, aping the manners and habits of the English, moving increasingly in English circles, and drawing pensions from the English court. Owain's son, Gwenwynwyn, took a Corbet to wife, and his son in turn married a Lestrange. The dynasty's shift in orientation was reflected in the abandonment of the ancient seat of the Powys princes at Mathrafal and their ecclesiastical centre at Meifod (Madog ap Maredudd (d. 1160) was the last of his line to be buried there) for the new castle on the banks of the Severn at Pool (henceforth

DIAGRAM 4. The Native Dynasty of Powys

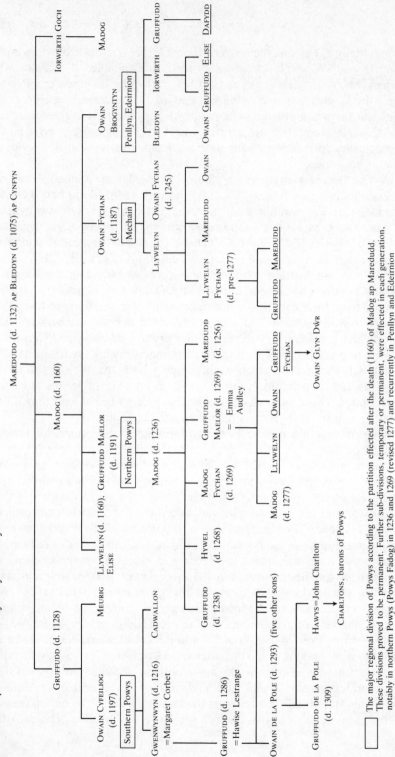

The major regional division of Powys according to the partition effected after the death (1160) of Madog ap Maredudd. These divisions proved to be permanent. Further sub-divisions, temporary or permanent, were effected in each generation, notably in northern Powys (Powys Fadog) in 1236 and 1269 (revised 1277) and recurrently in Penllyn and Ederirnion

—— Involved in the rising of 1282

Welshpool) and the nearby new Cistercian abbey at Strata Marcella (Ystrad Marchell), founded c.1170. A flourishing borough quickly developed at Pool, drawing burgesses from far afield and forging close commercial links with England. The rulers of northern Powys, to a lesser degree, likewise learned to build bridges towards their English neighbours: Gruffudd Maelor (d. 1269) took one of the Audleys of Shropshire as wife; they chose to live at Overton-on-Dee as much as in the hill-top retreat at Dinas Brân; and the family patronized monasteries in Cheshire as well as its own Cistercian foundation at Valle Crucis, founded in 1201. Mastering the arts of co-existence was one of the pre-conditions of survival for the dynasties of Powys in the thirteenth century.

In no instance was that more obviously true than in their relationships with their two most powerful neighbours, the prince of Gwynedd and the king of England. After the débâcle of 1208 neither northern nor southern Powys could hope to survive other than as a satellite of one of those neighbours. Learning to live with that reality, trimming their sails to changes in the balance of power between England and Gwynedd and, if possible, anticipating them, and selling their support to the higher bidder and stronger patron were henceforth the cardinal rules of survival. The dynasty of northern Powys in its own modest fashion flourished under those rules, until the catastrophe of 1282 overwhelmed it. Its ruler, Madog ap Gruffudd (1191–1236), occasionally flirted with King John when the English cause was in the ascendant; but, for the most part, he remained a trusted and well-rewarded ally of the prince of Gwynedd. In the 1240s his sons had no option but to come to terms with the king of England; but they were able to extort concessions from him in return for their support—such as charters to confirm their titles to their paternal lands in their entirety and a further promise that no new laws and customs would be introduced into their petty kingdoms. By 1250 Gruffudd ap Madog (d. 1269) was again conspiring with the prince of Gwynedd and northern Powys was to remain, in effect, a client state of Gwynedd until 1276. Southern Powys did not learn to adjust to its satellite status so easily. That is not surprising; it had been overrun by the prince of Gwynedd in 1216 and was ruled by him or by one of his sons—in spite of periodic plans to reinstate Gwenwynwyn's sons—until 1240. It was not until 1241 that the heir to southern Powys, Gruffudd ap Gwenwynwyn, was restored to his patrimony by royal support. For the remainder of his life he ruled his lands, with the exception of two periods of exile (1257–63 and 1274–7), as a protégé of either the prince of Gwynedd (1263–74) or the king of England (1241–57, 1274–86).

Powys and its princes have received scant sympathy and attention from historians. Powys was, for Sir J. E. Lloyd, 'the weakest of the realms of Wales', 'the temper of its patriotism strictly local and provincial'.[21] It is this

[21] J. E. Lloyd, *History of Wales*, II, 650, 583.

latter charge which in particular has coloured the judgement of historians. Powys stood in the way of the unification of native Wales; its rulers, particularly those of southern Powys, preferred to submit to the king of England rather than subsume their ambitions in the vision of a united Wales ruled by the house of Gwynedd. Such a judgement accords more closely with the sentiments and perspective of modern national aspirations than the realities of thirteenth-century politics and the attitudes of the native dynasties. There was no reason why the princelings of Powys should find the status of being 'Welsh barons' of the prince of Wales more acceptable than that of being tenants-in-chief of the king of England. Indeed, a distant suzerain might be preferable and a less exacting master than a neighbouring prince. Powys's achievement was to have survived and to have adjusted its ambitions to accord more closely with the realities of power. Dependence was the price of survival; the alternative was extinction. Gruffudd ap Gwenwynwyn of southern Powys could congratulate himself, as he lay dying in 1286, that he, his dynasty, and his patrimonial inheritance had survived, while the other two major principalities and dynasties of native Wales had been extinguished (or virtually so).

(III) GWYNEDD: THE SUPREMACY OF LLYWELYN AB IORWERTH

In the first decade of the thirteenth century the leadership of native Wales passed to Gwynedd and there it was to remain until the conquest of 1282–3. Gwynedd was in some ways an unlikely candidate for such a role. Its heartland lay in the remote north-west corner of Wales, far away from the frontiers of tension and conflict; its lines of communication both within itself and with the rest of Wales were difficult; it was probably the most thinly populated and economically the most backward of the native kingdoms. Yet such disadvantages were more than outweighed by other considerations. It was far and away the most easily defensible of the native kingdoms. The lowland approaches to it were protected by a series of treacherous tidal estuaries—those of the Clwyd and Conwy to the east: of the Dyfi, Mawddach, and Traeth Mawr to the south. River defences were, of course, dramatically supplemented by three concentric rings of uplands; the outer perimeter was defended by the semicircle of mountains running from Cader Idris in the south through the Berwyn mountains to the Clwydian range; next came to the inner perimeter of the Migneint range to the south and the moorlands of Hiraethog to the east; finally, of course, lay the inner and most secure citadel of all, Snowdonia. It was an appropriate tribute to the security provided by these mountains that princes of Gwynedd, most notably Llywelyn ab Iorwerth, occasionally assumed the title, lord of Snowdon.

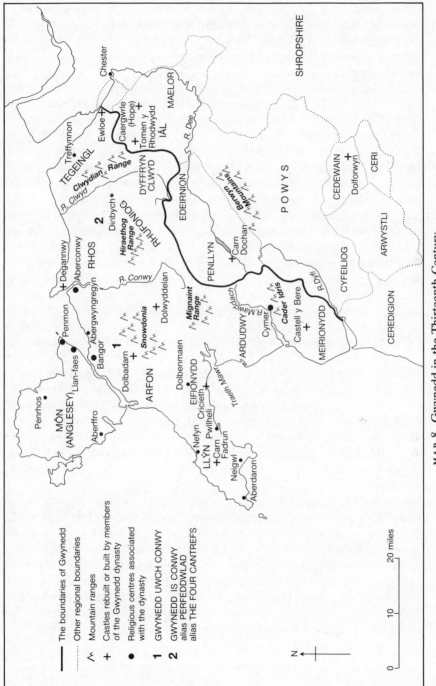

MAP 8. Gwynedd in the Thirteenth Century

The boundaries of Gwynedd
Other regional boundaries
Mountain ranges
Castles rebuilt or built by members of the Gwynedd dynasty
Religious centres associated with the dynasty
1 GWYNEDD UWCH CONWY
2 GWYNEDD IS CONWY alias PERFEDDWLAD alias THE FOUR CANTREFS

SHROPSHIRE

Chester
Ewloe
Caergwrle (Hope)
Tomen y Rhodwydd
IÂL
MAELOR
R. Dee
Treffynnon
TEGEINGL
DYFFRYN CLWYD
Clwydian Range
R. Clwyd
POWYS
Dinbych
RHUFONIOG
EDEIRNION
CEDEWAIN
Dolforwyn
CERI
Degannwy
Aberconwy
RHOS
Hiraethog Range
Berwyn Mountains
Abergwyngregyn
R. Conwy
PENLLYN
Carn Dochan
ARWYSTLI
Penmon
Bangor
Dolbadarn
Dolwyddelan
Mignaint Range
CYFEILIOG
Aberffro
MÔN (ANGLESEY)
Llan-faes
ARFON
Snowdonia
R. Mawddach
Cymer
Cader Idris
Castell y Bere
R. Dyfi
CEREDIGION
Penrhos
Dolbenmaen
EIFIONYDD
ARDUDWY
MEIRIONYDD
Nefyn
Criccieth
Pwllheli
Traeth Mawr
LLŶN
Carn Fadrun
Neigwl
Aberdaron

N

0   10   20 miles

Gwynedd's natural barriers served it remarkably well—only twice between 1100 and 1282 (once from the east under King John in 1211 and once from the south under Nicholas de Molis in 1246) were its inner defences (beyond the Conwy) breached by English armies, and then only briefly. Such a prolonged measure of immunity from Anglo-Norman attacks allowed Gwynedd the luxury to develop as a native principality without having to face the perennial threat of attack, settlement, and subversion which so debilitated Deheubarth and, to a lesser extent, Powys. Furthermore, though Gwynedd was a poor kingdom, it was remarkably self-sufficient economically. Gerald of Wales quotes an ancient proverb to the effect that 'just as Anglesey could supply corn for all the inhabitants of Wales, so could the mountains of Eryri (Snowdonia) provide sufficient pasture for all the herds of Wales, if collected together.'[22] Exaggerated the proverb no doubt was, but it explained some of the resilience and resourcefulness of Gwynedd. It was a kingdom which could sustain setbacks without being utterly overwhelmed. It was also a kingdom with a long tradition of aggressive expansion beyond its boundaries, partly in order to provide a further perimeter of defences for itself and partly because it was only through continuing expansion that the natural acquisitiveness of its military aristocracy could be satisfied. Its most obvious direction of expansion lay to the east, into the district extending from the river Conwy to the Dee estuary and known by a variety of names—Gwynedd Is Conwy, the four Cantrefi (namely, Rhos, Rhufoniog, Dyffryn Clwyd, and Tegeingl), and Perfeddwlad. The capture or loss of this territory was the most accurate barometer of Gwynedd's fortunes. To the south-east its natural line of expansion lay into Penllyn and Edeirnion, to give it control of the Dee valley and the further security of the Berwyn mountains, while to the south the cantrefi of Meirionydd, Cyfeiliog, and Arwystli and the northern commotes of Ceredigion had been frequent targets for plunder or temporary domination at the hands of the men of Gwynedd.

Gwynedd had enjoyed a golden era from 1120 to 1170. Its princes had built their power cautiously but effectively; and by mid-century Gwynedd's pre-eminence in native Wales was assured. Men might even begin to dream of bygone days when Gruffudd ap Llywelyn had used Gwynedd as his base to extend his supremacy over the whole of Wales. But, as so often in the history of the native kingdoms, death and partition put an end to such prospects. On Owain Gwynedd's death in 1170, his lands were divided between his surviving sons; family quarrels inevitably ensued. The kingdom was divided and redivided; politics became a series of shifting and interlocking family feuds; temporary victories were achieved—notably by

[22] *IK*, II, ix (*Opera*, vi, 135).

Dafydd ab Owain in 1173–5—only to be subsequently reversed; external alliances were forged in an attempt to gain the upper hand in the domestic wrangling—Dafydd ab Owain took Henry II's half-sister, Emma, to wife for specifically such a purpose in 1174, while his brother, Rhodri, called in his father-in-law, the king of Man, to restore him to his share of Gwynedd in 1193. For almost thirty years Gwynedd suffered from the chronic malaise endemic to all native Welsh politics in the Middle Ages—the debility which flowed from the custom of partibility.

It was in the 1190s that the situation began to resolve itself. In 1194 Dafydd ab Owain (and possibly his brother Rhodri also) was defeated by two of his nephews in a hard-fought battle at the mouth of the river Conwy. One of the victors of that battle, Llywelyn ab Iorwerth, was to dominate the history of Gwynedd and of Wales for almost half a century. His rise to power was meteoric; in the graphic phrase of one of his court poets, it was like 'the swirl of a great windstorm in a surly February'.[23] His first task was to impose his mastery on his own dynasty and to reintegrate the kingdom of Gwynedd, He did so ruthlessly. His first victim was his uncle, Dafydd: he seized him in 1197 and expelled him from all his lands in Gwynedd, consigning him and his heirs to a life of exile in England and to the status of distressed gentlefolk. Other members of the dynasty were likewise brought firmly under Llywelyn's control: some were peremptorily dispossessed of their lands, as was his cousin, Maredudd ap Cynan, in Llŷn and Eifionydd in 1201; some were allowed to retain their lands so long as they acknowledged their client status, as did Hywel ap Gruffudd ap Cynan; others, sooner or later, resigned themselves to their loss and became members of Llywelyn's entourage, like Gruffudd ap Rhodri and Rhicert ap Cadwaladr. Many of them nursed grievances, but to little avail during Llywelyn's lifetime. Equally vain were the protests of the poets, such as Elidir Sais, at the outrageous flouting of the Welsh rules of inheritance. Llywelyn was intent on mastery, not the observance of custom. Already by 1199 he seems to have arrogated to himself the title of 'prince of the whole of north Wales' (L. *tocius norwallie princeps*).

Others soon recognized that he was now the force to be reckoned with in native Wales. In the first formal written treaty to survive between a Welsh prince and an English king,[24] King John's advisers concluded an agreement with Llywelyn on 11 July 1201, recognizing his title to all the lands which he then held and conceding that, in the event of any dispute, the issues, where appropriate, might be determined by Welsh law. A further major manifestation of John's favour and support was Llywelyn's marriage in 1205 to the king's illegitimate daughter, Joan, and the grant to the young

[23] *Llsg. Hendregadredd*, p. 39. The translation is by D. Myrddin Lloyd.
[24] Relations between the English Crown and Gwynedd in these years are considered more fully in Chap. 11.

DIAGRAM 5. The Dynasty of Gwynedd

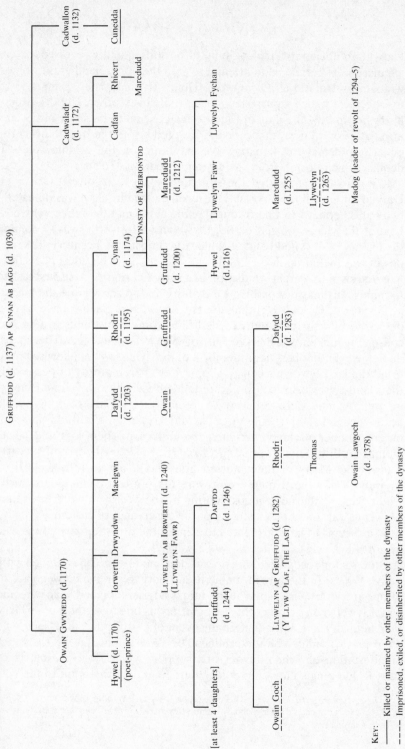

KEY:

—— Killed or maimed by other members of the dynasty

---- Imprisoned, exiled, or disinherited by other members of the dynasty

couple of the manor of Ellesmere in Shropshire (hitherto Dafydd ab Owain's refuge in exile) as a marriage portion. In spite of periodic strains, relations between king and prince remained cordial until 1210: Llywelyn went out of his way to show his loyalty by accompanying John on his expedition to the Scottish border in the summer of 1209. The cordiality of the relationship served both parties well: for John, a quiescent and co-operative Welsh prince was an asset, as he himself pursued his ambitions in France and coped with problems at home (not least the disaffection caused by the proscription of the Braose family, the greatest of Marcher houses, in 1208); for Llywelyn, royal support enhanced his standing and allowed him to extend his mastery beyond Gwynedd into native Wales as a whole. He took the first step in 1202: though dissuaded from the all-out attack on Powys which he had contemplated, he marked out his future intentions by in effect annexing the border *cantref* of Penllyn. But it was in 1208 that Llywelyn revealed the true nature of his pretensions and power beyond the borders of Gwynedd. He took advantage of Gwenwynwyn's arrest by the king to annex southern Powys and, at the same time, he marched into Ceredigion, rebuilt the castle of Aberystwyth, and installed his own candidates as client rulers in the province. His power extended even further afield, for the minor dynasties of the central March (Cedewain, Maelienydd, and Elfael), who had hitherto turned in the orbit of Deheubarth and then briefly of Powys, now looked to him for leadership and patronage. By 1210 his supremacy in native Wales seemed to be beyond question.

The next two years were to prove the most testing of Llywelyn's career. The goodwill of the crown now turned to outright hostility. The results were devastating. In 1210 the earl of Chester advanced his claim to Perfeddwlad and built castles at Treffynnon (Holywell) and Degannwy; in 1211, John, flushed by his successes in Ireland and Scotland and outraged by Llywelyn's insubordination, led two campaigns into north Wales. The second of these was devastatingly successful, penetrating further into Gwynedd than any other royal expedition prior to that of 1282–3 and compelling Llywelyn to agree to the most humiliating terms. The comprehensiveness of the defeat stunned the Welsh into unity (much as had happened in 1165) but their resolve was more than matched by John's anger and by his determination to deliver the *coup de grâce*. In 1212 the king assembled a huge army and seemed intent on nothing less than the conquest of Wales and the destruction of Llywelyn; but at the last moment domestic discord forced him to abandon his campaign. Llywelyn had come as close as could be to disaster in 1211–12. Not only did his nerve and his luck hold; his stature among his fellow-countrymen was also confirmed and even enhanced. In the crisis of 1212, the common Welsh front unanimously chose Llywelyn as its leader. In the next few years he seized every opportunity to exercise that leadership and by 1218 he had secured a position in Wales such as no prince had held since the coming of the Normans.

His first step was to reconquer Perfeddwlad, which he had done by 1213. Two years of truce and negotiations with the king followed, but by 1215 growing domestic discord in England, in which several of the Marcher lords were deeply involved, proved too much of a temptation for Llywelyn and his fellow Welsh princes. While Llywelyn captured Shrewsbury in May, the princelings of Deheubarth caused havoc from Cemais in the west to Swansea in the east. But it was the great campaign of December 1215—made possible by exceptionally mild weather—which was truly remarkable, both in its character and achievement. It was a national campaign under Llywelyn's leadership: the *Brut* records with obvious delight and surprise the names of the eleven princelings who served with him. In a three-week campaign seven castles were captured, of which the greatest prizes were Carmarthen (which had, with a few interruptions, been under royal control for 120 years) and Cardigan (so ignominiously surrendered by Maelgwn ap Rhys in 1199). Almost the only footholds left to the Anglo-Normans west of Swansea were the districts of Pembroke and Haverford. With the return of domestic peace in England and the defeat of the supporters of prince Louis of France at Lincoln in May 1217, the prospects of further territorial gains for Llywelyn and his Welsh allies diminished. But in one final campaign, in the summer of 1217, Llywelyn demonstrated that the whole of Wales, outside the south-east, now lay within the ambit of his military might. Stung into action by the defection of his erstwhile ally, Reginald Braose, he marched down the Wye and threatened Brecon, crossed over the mountains to Swansea (which was surrendered to him and where Reginald Braose made his submission), and then proceeded to the far west to the very outskirts of Haverford (where once again his impending assault was bought off, on abject terms arranged by the bishop of St Davids). It was a remarkable demonstration of military power such as native Wales had not seen since the days of Gruffudd ap Llywelyn. By now Llywelyn deemed it wise to come to terms with the new English government with the papal legate, Guala, acting as intermediary. The terms agreed at Worcester in March 1218 did not, perhaps, represent as complete a triumph for Llywelyn as is sometimes thought. He had to acknowledge his dependence and that of other Welsh princes on the Crown, and his title to several of the key districts conceded to him was a temporary, custodial one. Nevertheless, the concessions that he won were striking: he was given custody of the two key castles of Carmarthen and Cardigan during the king's minority (to the native chronicler this was the most memorable feature of the truce); he was also granted custody of the lands of Gwenwynwyn, and of the key frontier district of Montgomery during the minority of Gwenwynwyn's heirs. His recovery of Perfeddwlad was also in effect acknowledged. There was much that was temporary and contingent about the Worcester agreement, much room for disputes (especially regarding those districts, such as the middle March, where Llywelyn had extended his supremacy, but which were not referred to in the agreement), much that depended on the goodwill and good sense of both parties. Yet there was no denying that for a prince who had come so close to utter disaster in 1211–12 it represented a remarkable recovery of his fortunes.

From 1212 to 1218 Llywelyn had hardly set a foot wrong, militarily or politically. He had exploited the discomfiture of the Crown and the turmoil of English politics, especially as expressed in the division among the Marcher lords, to his own maximum advantage. He had even been invited in October 1216 to participate in the election of a king to succeed John. His success in these years greatly enhanced his pre-eminence in native Wales. His leadership was expressed in a variety of ways: in 1212 the other princes entered into a 'solemn pact' with him, according to the *Brut*; in the same year it was as the spokesman of 'all the princes of Wales' (*universi Vallie principes*) that he concluded a treaty with Philip Augustus of France;[25] no Welsh prince now dared to challenge his mastery and when Gwenwynwyn of Powys was foolish enough to be seduced into an alliance with King John in 1216, Llywelyn tried him in his absence for treachery, summoned the other princes of Wales to him, proceeded to overrun Powys, and forthwith annexed it; he showed a different aspect of his mastery in the same year when he summoned the squabbling princes of Deheubarth to an assembly at Aberdyfi (in Gwynedd), presided over the formal partition of their lands, and ensured that his partition was henceforth observed;[26] it was by his fiat and with his consent that the native princes held lands conquered from the Anglo-Normans—thus it was Llywelyn who entrusted the keeping of Swansea castle to Rhys Gryg of Deheubarth in 1217; finally, his two campaigns of 1215 and 1217 demonstrated that his military interests and mastery encompassed the whole of native Wales and indeed beyond. The English government was driven to acknowledge his pre-eminence: it requested him, in 1218, to persuade 'all the magnates of the whole of Wales' to come to the king to do homage.[27] Llywelyn was now *de facto* prince of native Wales.

It was a position he held for the rest of his life. Admittedly he suffered a considerable set-back at the hands of the English in 1223, losing control of

---

[25] *Brut, s.a.* (p. 8); R. F. Treharne, 'The Franco-Welsh Treaty of Alliance of 1212', *BBCS* 18 (1958–9), 60–75 at p. 74.

[26] See above, p. 228.

[27] *Foedera, Conventiones etc.*, ed. T. Rymer (Rev. edn. 1815–69), I, i, 150; Cf. *Patent Rolls 1216–25*, p. 149.

the key fortresses of Carmarthen, Cardigan, Cilgerran, and Montgomery and forfeiting much of his authority in south-west Wales; he also had to face two further royal expeditions in 1228 and 1231.[28] But neither of these two latter campaigns had much impact on Llywelyn's power. His main aim in the last twenty or so years of his life was to protect and consolidate the gains he had made prior to 1218 and give a measure of permanence to Gwynedd's hegemony within an enlarged native Wales. To this end he bent every effort, military and diplomatic.

His superiority within native Wales from 1218 to 1240 was geographically more extensive and more fully articulated than that enjoyed by any other Welsh prince since the coming of the Normans. He kept southern Powys under his control, or that of his son, until 1240; the lord of northern Powys, Madog ap Gruffudd, was his faithful ally until his death in 1236 and, when one of Madog's sons dared to step out of line in 1238, 'forthwith the Lord Llywelyn took from him all his territory';[29] the princelings of Deheubarth observed the partition he had imposed upon their lands in 1216 and were henceforth his client vassals; he acted as protector and overlord of the Welsh chieftains of central Wales—Cedewain, Ceri, Maelienydd, Gwrtheyrnion, and Elfael; even the native rulers of upland Morgannwg and Gwent acknowedged him as their lord. His authority extended even further, for the magnetism of his power drew men beyond these areas into dependence on him: thus, by 1230, the leaders of Welsh society in upland Brecon were gravitating towards him, and his steward was warning those who tried to prevent them from doing so that they would 'be choosing war and will certainly have war'.[30] Llywelyn made no attempt to forge this augmented native Wales into a single kingdom; but his authority over his dependants was nevertheless extensive and interventionist. He settled their disputes in his court, as he did the succession to Mechain; he adjudicated in their family wrangles, as he did more than once in Deheubarth in the 1220s and 1230s; he took a lively interest in their marital alliances, as in northern Powys in 1222; and in the last resort he could confiscate their lands, as Maredudd ap Madog of northern Powys found to his cost in 1238. Their well-being was subordinated to the overall needs of his policy, even if that meant surrendering lands to the Anglo-Normans: thus, Rhys Gryg of Deheubarth, much to his chagrin, was compelled at Llywelyn's command to surrender the commotes of Cydweli, Carnwyllion, Gwidigada, and Gower to their English lords in 1220 and, in much the same fashion, Llywelyn required the chieftains of upland Glamorgan in 1234 to return lands they had conquered from the English. Individual Welsh lords still led forays on their own initiative; but any major expedition—such as the campaigns of 1220 and 1231—required Llywelyn's sanction and were

---

[28] See below, pp. 298–9.   [29] *Brut, s.a.* 1238 (p. 105).
[30] *Cal. Anc. Corr.*, p. 53; cf. pp. 35–6.

conducted under his command. Llywelyn's mastery of native Wales was beyond challenge. Furthermore, he meant it to outlast his lifetime: in 1238 he summoned all the native Welsh lords to Strata Florida to give allegiance to Dafydd, his son and heir. Gwynedd's 'inherent right' (*hawl greddfawl*)— the phrase is that of the poet, Prydydd y Moch—to the leadership of native Wales was thereby solemnly confirmed.

Llywelyn's overlordship had much in common with that exercised by earlier Welsh princes such as the Lord Rhys. It was founded on military might and leadership, recurrently and triumphantly demonstrated. It was patriarchal, rather than institutional, in its character. Its spirit is perhaps best captured in a letter he wrote to some of the native rulers of mid-Wales early in his career: the tone of the letter is a compound of paternal affection and bluster; it speaks of 'friendship' and 'familiarity' rather than of formal bonds of dependence; but its message is bluntly authoritative: 'I firmly command you, as you love me and my honour, and as you wish to have the freedom to come to me and to depart . . .'.[31] Llywelyn's aim, as that of others who had aspired to overlordship in native Wales, was to create a federation under his presidency rather than to amalgamate the various principalities and regions into a single unit. He had neither the administrative means nor the political resources to create a unitary principality. Conquest and annexation, as in southern Powys in 1216, were only weapons of last resort. No attempt was even made to integrate Powys into a greater Gwynedd; for the most part it was ruled as an apanage by Llywelyn's son; his poets went out of their way to pander to regional sensitivities by emphasising that, through his mother, Llywelyn was descended from the stock of Bleddyn ap Cynfyn, the founder of the ruling dynasty of Powys. In general, Llywelyn operated through the local native dynasties, sorting out their quarrels, installing his preferred candidates, where appropriate, and creating ties of clientship with himself. Yet there can be no doubt that such dependence was growing more exacting, precise, and public. An early indication was the way that Gwenwynwyn of Powys was bound to Llywelyn by a whole host of guarantees—indentures, charters, fealty, homage, and hostages. The ties of fealty became increasingly formal; most of the Welsh princes entered into solemn pacts with Llywelyn in 1212; oaths of fealty were exacted from the leading men of the lands he conquered, as in 1231; and, in at least one instance, a formal feudal relationship was inaugurated, when Morgan Gam of Glamorgan was granted land in Gower in return for knight service. Solemn assemblies were summoned to demonstrate the extent of Llywelyn's mastery—twice in 1216, to arrange the partition of Deheubarth and to plan concerted action against Gwenwynwyn, and in 1226 and 1238 to swear

[31] This letter, which cannot now be traced, is published in *Monasticon Anglicanum*, VI, 496–7.

fealty to Llywelyn's heir. Llywelyn's overlordship was becoming qualitatively different from that of his predecessors: not only was it more comprehensive geographically, it was also more ambitious, more sustained, and more structured.

A conscious attempt appears to have been made to provide a theoretical and ideological basis for his authority. One aspect of the attempt was the elaboration of a historical and legal mythology to explain and justify Gwynedd's hegemony in Wales. Legends were fabricated to show how Maelgwn Gwynedd had demonstrated his claim to be the chief king of Wales with authority over the earls (sic) of Mathrafal, Dinefwr, and Caerleon: dicta were introduced into the legal texts claiming that a special insult payment in gold was due to the prince of Gwynedd and to him alone, and that 'all the kings of Wales' were to accept their lands from him and to pay him a relief and a special recognition due to an overlord (W. mechteyrn dyled). 'His word', the laws majestically pronounced, 'shall be a command to all the kings of Wales, but no other king's word shall be a command to him.'[32] This blatant fabrication of a mythology to justify Gwynedd's hegemony was complemented by the emergence of a new emphasis on the dignity and status of the prince and of his principality. After the first decade of the thirteenth century, the ruler of Gwynedd, alone, is known to have used or been officially accorded the title of prince;[33] indeed, he may even occasionally have arrogated the phrase 'by the grace of God' into his title. Llywelyn referred self-consciously to his principality (noster principatus); he asserted that he had no less liberty than the king of Scotland and, therefore, could receive outlaws from England in his lands with impunity, thereby countering the suggestion, implicit in the act of homage, that he was on a par with any other English baron; he insisted that he should be treated with the respect due to a fellow-ruler and that he ought not to come to any conference outside his own boundaries (and, indeed, that he had written evidence from King John to support such a claim). Llywelyn and his advisers were clearly assembling the propaganda and arguments for his special status as a prince. Those arguments could be taken one stage further, by claiming that Wales, or at least native Wales, was one unit under his authority. In one surviving official document he was accorded the title 'lord of Wales' (dominus Wallie); he himself spoke solemnly and grandly of 'justice and equity according to the status of Wales'; he claimed that the homage of the local rulers of Maelienydd was appurtenant to his principality and that any service due from them should be performed

---

[32] Ancient Laws and Institutes of Wales, ed. A. Owen (1841), ii, 48–50; Latin Texts of the Welsh Laws, pp. 207, 277, 437–8.

[33] Gwenwynwyn used the title 'prince of Powys and lord of Arwystli' in a charter which has been tentatively dated 1200–6: J. Conway Davies, 'Strata Marcella Documents', Montgomery Colls. 51 (1949–50), 164–87 at p. 178.

through him; in 1238 he summoned 'all the princes of Wales' to Strata Florida to swear allegiance to his heir.[34] He stopped short of calling himself prince of Wales, contenting himself (after 1230) with the evocative but local title of 'prince of Aberffro and lord of Snowdon'; but he had assembled all the ingredients—of both the theory and the mechanics of power—for asserting such a claim.

Llywelyn's supremacy in native Wales remained unchallenged until his death; but it was one which relied on his ability to contain the ambitions of the Marcher lords. Gwynedd itself had been largely insulated, except on its extreme eastern frontier with the earldom of Chester, from direct contact with the Anglo-Norman barons; but Llywelyn's dramatic gains in the years 1212–18 brought him, either directly or indirectly through his dependants, into confrontation with the Marcher lords, both in the south-west and the south-east. One area in particular stood out as one where confrontation was likely, indeed inevitable. It comprised a group of commotes and lordships in eastern central Wales from Ceri in the north to Brecon in the south. For almost a century and a half the Normans had been trying to conquer this thinly populated upland district of Wales but with only fitful and mediocre success; in spite of establishing castles in the district—as at Cymaron in Maelienydd, Painscastle in Elfael, and Builth—they had failed to dislodge the native dynasties. For Llywelyn, control of this district was important geographically and politically. Geographically, it formed part of a barbican of defences for his enlarged principality; it was also the district which he must control if he was to keep his lines of communication open with his allies and clients in upland Glamorgan and Gwent. Politically, his authority in native Wales would be measured by his capacity to extend his protection and support to the leaders of local society in this district (as the Lord Rhys had done before him). Much of Llywelyn's effort after 1218 was concentrated in this area—buttressing the position of native rulers in Maelienydd and Elfael and thwarting the Mortimer ambitions in those districts, successfully annexing Builth by a marriage agreement with William Braose in 1229 and razing its castle to the ground, and gradually intruding his authority into Brecon (though he twice failed to take the castle in 1231 and 1233). The English authorities for their part recognized the significance of this district—building two formidable castles at its northern and southern perimeters, at Montgomery and Painscastle respectively, and concentrating much of their efforts in the three campaigns of 1223, 1228, and 1231 in these areas. But until Llywelyn's death they made singularly little headway.

In his politics in the March Llywelyn showed the acumen and judgement which characterized the last years of his long life. He concentrated his

---

[34] National Library of Wales, Wynnstay Collection, no. 7 (Montgomeryshire Collection, no. 30); *Cal. Anc. Corr.*, p. 30; *Brut, s.a.* 1238.

effort on what was realistic. He made no attempt to dislodge the Anglo-Normans from their lordships along the south coast of Wales—even though his punitive raids of 1220 (into Dyfed) and 1231 (which penetrated down the English border to Caerleon, across to Neath and thence to Cardigan, both the latter being captured) were brutal reminders that no area of Wales lay outside his military reach. He was generally well-content to exploit his opportunities in the March as they arose rather than to anticipate them prematurely—making capital out of the dissensions within and the decline of the Braose family, seizing the opportunity presented by the early deaths in 1230–1 of three of the greatest Marcher lords (William Braose, Gilbert Clare, and William Marshal), and exploiting the disaffection of Richard Marshal in 1233–4 to his own ends. Llywelyn recognized that his position in Wales depended ultimately not only on military force but also on being able to come to terms with the Marcher lords. Persuasion and marriage alliances were the instruments used to achieve that end. Llywelyn's greatest success was his alliance with the house of Chester. He had much to fear from that direction, for it was Chester—as had been shown in 1210—which presented the most immediate direct threat to his principality. In 1218 he concluded a peace with Earl Ranulf; two years later he confirmed the friendship by going to meet the earl on his return from crusade; finally in 1222 he sealed the *entente* by marrying one of his daughters to the earl's nephew and heir. It was a policy which paid handsome dividends; henceforth Llywelyn had a powerful friend at court and an amenable neighbour on his eastern borders. Other marriages were likewise arranged to serve his strategic ends, especially in the middle March: one of his daughters was married to Reginald Braose and on his death (1227–8) to Ralph Mortimer, thereby forging a marriage bond with the family which had most to lose by Llywelyn's pretensions in Maelienydd; a second daughter was married successively to John Braose of Gower and Walter Clifford of Bronllys and Clifford (in the Wye valley); a third daughter was wed into the Lacy family, powerful in both the Welsh March and Ireland. The most spectacular marriage coup of all was that which Llywelyn arranged for Dafydd, his son and heir. Taking advantage of the capture of William Braose, lord of Brecon, Builth and Abergavenny in the war of 1228, he wrung a series of concessions from him: the hand of one of William's daughters, Isabel, for Llywelyn's son; the lordship of Builth as her marriage portion; and a promise from her father that he would never again bear arms against the prince of Wales. This series of marriage alliances (all of which appear to have been concluded in the years 1218–33) was forged to serve Llywelyn's territorial and strategic ambitions, to tie two of the potentially most hostile houses of the March (Braose and Mortimer) to him by bonds of matrimony, to make Llywelyn and his dynasty socially acceptable in the circles of the Anglo-Norman court and aristocracy, and in general to consolidate through peace and matrimony what he had initially secured through war and masterfulness. Llywelyn was showing himself to be a clever and adroit statesman was well as a redoubtable warrior.

Yet Llywelyn realized that his domination in Wales depended ultimately also on his domination of his family. It was by asserting the latter in the 1190s that he had been able to aspire to the former after 1200. If his achievement was to outlive him, one precondition was the maintenance of the family unity he had imposed and sustained during his lifetime. He started with one advantage. He had fathered only two surviving sons, one in and the other out of wedlock. But even two sons was one too many. Gruffudd, his son by a pre-marital liaison, was an impetuous youth whom his father had to discipline more than once, expelling him from the lands he had given him in 1221 and imprisoning him for six years from 1228. Nevertheless, Welsh custom and parental duty alike required that Gruffudd be given lands to rule and the means to support his retainers; his father created various apanages for him and seems to have had no intention of disinheriting him totally. But Llywelyn was determined that the principality of north Wales and the overlordship of the rest of native Wales should pass intact to his younger and only legitmate son, Dafydd. He spent a great deal of effort in the last twenty years of his life in pursuit of this ambition. In 1220 the minority government of Henry III acknowledged Dafydd as Llywelyn's heir; in 1222 the Pope confirmed Dafydd's succession and debarred any claim from Gruffudd by condemning the practice whereby illegitimate offspring shared the inheritance with legitimate children; papal support enhanced Dafydd's standing even further in 1226 by declaring his mother, Joan the bastard daughter of King John, to be legitimate, thereby bestowing untainted royal descent on Dafydd; in the same year the leading men of Wales were required to swear an oath of fealty to Dafydd; in 1229, it was the turn of the English government to sanction Llywelyn's arrangements once more by taking Dafydd's homage for all lands and rights which would descend to him on the death of his father and giving him also £40 worth of royal lands; Dafydd's marriage to Isabella Braose in 1229 took the process a step further and associated one of the greatest houses of the March in his succession; finally, in 1238 Llywelyn summoned the magnates of Wales to Strata Florida where they reaffirmed their fealty to Dafydd as his heir. Llywelyn had taken out every insurance policy possible to secure Dafydd's unchallenged succession; he had associated Dafydd in his acts as 'our heir'; above all, he had gone out of his way to secure the assent and support of the Pope and of the English Crown for his arrangements. Such a recurrent search for assurances suggests that Llywelyn remained unconvinced that the arrangements would in fact survive him. His scepticism was well founded. Already in the last years of his life, possibly as a result of a stroke which he suffered in 1237, tension between Dafydd and his brother burst out into the open; once Llywelyn was dead such tension was to be quickly exploited by disenchanted factions within native Wales, by Marcher lords anxious to regain lost lands and above all by the king of England.

In the last years of life Llywelyn indeed seems to have been generally apprehensive about the future; and not without good reason. His augmented principality was no more than a loose federation kept together by the force of his personality and the weakness of his opponents, native and Anglo-Norman. It had been largely assembled as a result of the combination of fortuitous circumstances—the debility of the English Crown, the factiousness of English politics (in the 1230s as well as in the formative years 1212–18), and the discomfiture or mortality of so many Marcher families. Once those circumstances changed, the fragility of Llywelyn's achievement would soon become evident. There were ominous signs in the late 1230s that the circumstances were indeed changing—notably the acquisition of the earldom and county of Chester by the Crown in 1237 and the firm command of the king, in 1238, to the native rulers of Wales and the March that their homage was due to him, not to Llywelyn or to his heir apparent. That is why Llywelyn was involved in negotiations to transform the truce with England into a firm peace, even offering (according to Matthew Paris) to place his lands in the king's protection. Llywelyn had become painfully aware that peace with the Marcher lords and recognition by the English Crown were the preconditions of the survival of his enlarged principality.

Yet hindsight should not be summoned to belittle Llywelyn's achievement. For forty years he had dominated the history of Wales; his success had stemmed the tide of Anglo-Norman advance, notably in the south-west and the middle March; he had forged a measure of unity and purpose in native Wales such as it had not known hitherto. He was a man alive to the dignity of his status and the need to defend his pretensions at a theoretical level as well as pursue them by force. There was a largeness of vision about his policies and methods unusual among Welsh princes—a readiness to appeal to the king and the papacy, to forge an alliance with the king of France, to counter threats of excommunication by an appeal to conscience and to God. He was a man of great passion, personal and political; his wrath could be terrible (as William Braose found to his cost in 1230, when he was publicly executed by Llywelyn for allegedly having an affair with Llywelyn's wife); but he was also a shrewd and wily diplomat and an arch-exploiter of the discomfiture and dissensions of others. His rule appears to have witnessed rapid developments in the internal organization of Gwynedd—in the commutation of renders, the development of princely authority in matters of law, governance, and resources, and the establishment of a serviential aristocracy. He had the confidence, like the Lord Rhys before him, to welcome the new as well as cleave to the old—to patronize the old Welsh *clas* at Penmon and the new Cistercian abbeys at Cymer and Aberconwy, and to found at Llan-faes the first Franciscan house in north Wales. Llywelyn's castles, perhaps, best capture the ambitiousness of his vision and his receptiveness to new ideas—their apsidal towers (at Ewloe, Carndochan, and Castell y Bere) betraying their distinctively native quality but other features, such as the round tower at Dolbardarn or the gatehouse at Cricieth, proclaimining also a willingness to learn from Anglo-Norman exemplars. Castell y Bere, probably built in the 1220s to guard Gwynedd's southern flank, above all, seems to testify to Llywelyn's qualities. Some of its features are distinctively Welsh and there is much that is, by contemporary English standards, crude and outdated about it; but other features—such as the deep undercutting of the ornate foliage capitals, the flanking figures of footsoldiers on the doorway, the human heads on the corbel stops of the roof vaults of one tower—bespeak both inspiration from English style and craftsmen and, above all, an ambition and grandeur matched in no earlier native Welsh castle. Such features reflect some of Llywelyn's own achievement: he had pitched the ambitions and expectations of native Wales at an altogether higher level. For once the plaudits of the bards were not exaggerated when they referred to him as 'the great head of Wales and its orderliness' nor is it surprising that within a few decades the title 'the Great' had been bestowed upon him.[35]

[35] Quoted by D. M. Lloyd in *A Guide to Welsh Literature*, I, 184; *Monasticon Anglicanum*, VI, 200.

CHAPTER 9

THE GOVERNANCE OF NATIVE WALES

THROUGHOUT western Europe the twelfth and thirteenth centuries witnessed rapid and far-reaching changes in the character of secular lordship in general and royal power in particular. Kings retained much of their sacral character and their role as war-leaders still remained pre-eminent; but the increasing emphasis on their powers of governance and justice, and on their capacity to exploit the financial resources of their dominions, gradually transformed the nature and range of their authority. Such changes were reflected, albeit belatedly and often dimly, in the native kingdoms of Wales in the last century or so of Welsh independence. Indeed, if those kingdoms were to survive as independent political units it was essential that their rulers should exploit the resources of their dominions more systematically and concentrate political power much more firmly in their own hands. Such developments occurred very unequally, both in time and in scale, within the native kingdoms: Deheubarth appears to have led the way in the twelfth century, but by the thirteenth century it was in Gwynedd that the most far-reaching changes were taking place, while Powys, weakened by dynastic divisions and territorial fractionization lagged well behind. The evidence for the study of such changes—as with so much that relates to the history of Wales before the late thirteenth century—is meagre and frequently indirect and retrospective; but that important changes in the patterns of authority and governance were afoot hardly admits of doubt.

Central to such changes was the position of the ruler. On his personal ability to control his family, command loyalty, and impose his will depended much of the well-being of his dominions and his subjects. Kingship was an ancient institution in Wales as in the rest of Europe; but there was still much that was vague about its status and authority. The kings or princes of Wales had no formal or consistent titles; often, indeed, they used no title at all; there was no known inauguration ceremony to install them in office; there was little coherent theory on the status and dignity of kingship to which they could appeal. Some attempt now appears to have been made to remedy this deficiency. The native law-texts, first assembled in their present form in the late twelfth or early thirteenth centuries may well have formed part of that campaign. They certainly have a strong royalist flavour: they extol the role of kings in making and reforming law; they dwell on 'the dignity of the king', his special legal status, and the position of the queen and members of the royal household; they give pre-eminence to the 'laws of the court' and emphasize the exalted status of the rulers of Aberffro and Dinefwr in particular. At the same time a measure of definition and hierarchy was introduced into the titles of native rulers. The old designation of king (L. *rex*, W. *brenin*) was abandoned, and after the first decade of the thirteenth century the rulers of Powys and Deheubarth and of other smaller dominions had to content themselves with the title of lord (L. *dominus*). Such demotion only served to highlight further the special status and dignity now accorded to the ruler of Gwynedd within native Wales: he and he alone, was a prince (L. *princeps*), the other rulers were lords, magnates, barons, greater men (L. *domini, magnates, barones, maiores*); his clerks were now much more consistent and self-conscious in the title they accorded him in official instruments; the adoption of the royal plural, common from about 1209, in letters and charters issued in his name, and of phrases such as 'most excellent' and 'most illustrious' in pleas addressed to him likewise betoken a deliberate campaign to emphasize his exalted status; while the assumption of a coronet or *talaith* (first mentioned in 1240) quite possibly forms yet another aspect of the same campaign.[1] When Llywelyn ap Gruffudd finally adopted the title, prince of Wales, in 1258 and won recognition of it from the Crown in 1267, he placed the coping-stone on a sustained effort to elevate the status and dignity of the greatest of the over-kingdoms of native Wales. It was a move intended to consolidate and enhance his status within his own dominions, as well as to reinforce his position *vis-à-vis* the king of England.

The hub of each native kingdom was its court. The three major kingdoms had their own recognized principal seats (Aberffro, Dinefwr, and Mathrafal) and much was made of the historical and sentimental connections of these principal seats. Hence it is that Llywelyn ab Iorwerth exulted in the title 'prince of Aberffro' and Rhys Fychan ap Rhys Mechyll called himself 'lord of Dinefwr'. But the demands of consumption and the chase, as well as the needs of governance, meant that the court was itinerant, rather than stationary. Sometimes it availed itself of ancient commotal centres, such as Nefyn or Pwllheli; often it was satisfied with a makeshift and modest hunting lodge; occasionally it lodged itself at a Cistercian abbey or grange, such as Abereiddon in Meirionydd where Llywelyn ap Gruffudd called frequently; sometimes it took up residence at one of its castles such as Dolbadarn, Dolwyddelan (where Llywelyn ap Gruffudd allegedly kept his treasure), or Cricieth. The domestic buildings

---

[1] A golden coronet belonging to Llywelyn ap Gruffudd was among the insignia carried from Wales to Westminster in 1284.

at some of these centres, notably the more popular ones, such as Aber in Arllechwedd, or Caernarfon, or Denbigh, were fairly substantial; but elsewhere the buildings were very modest, as was Llywelyn's hall at Ystumgwern (Ardudwy), measuring no more than 42 feet by 10 feet, which was later transported to Harlech castle. Much of the business of the court was social and domestic: to cater for the needs of the prince and his retainers, to attend to his delight in the hunt,—Llywelyn ap Gruffudd was said to collect provisions for five hundred men when he came to Penllyn to hunt—and to hold banquets and gatherings especially at Christmas, Easter, and Whitsun. But the court also wore an increasingly governmental and judicial aspect: receiving embassies, settling disputes between competing dependants (such as that between the heirs to Mechain), drawing up treaties, dispatching letters, hearing accounts, and holding formal 'state' trials—such as that of Maredudd ap Rhys Gryg in 1259 on a charge of treachery. The court's domestic servants likewise increasingly assumed responsibilities of a broader kind, in response to the needs of literate governance and a more complex administration. None of the courts of the native Welsh rulers developed the specialization of function which was coming to characterize the *curia regis* in England; but the success of native politics would depend considerably on the degree to which the court adjusted to the new governmental and political tasks that were now imposed upon it.

The court also remained the military centre of the native principalities. The warband (W. *teulu*) was still crucial to the prince's needs and its captain, the *penteulu*, was often chosen from among members of the ruling dynasty and occupied pride of place, after the immediate members of the royal family, in the hirearchy of the court's official personnel. Beyond the *teulu*, the prince could draw on the military resources of Welsh society generally. All free men over the age of fourteen owed him military service, indefinitely within his own dominions and once a year for six weeks outside his lands. The Welsh love of war, their pride in valour, their hardiness, and their fearlessness were proverbial; so was their skill, either with the lance, in north Wales, or the bow, in Gwent. They had already shown that on their own terrain they were more than a match for the Normans; they were not encumbered with heavy armour nor did they rely on long supply lines; they could survive through winter campaigns, as Llywelyn ap Gruffudd's troops showed in 1259–60 and 1262–3, whereas English armies were quickly reduced to despair and starvation by the exigencies of the Welsh diet—Simon de Montfort's troops preferred to brave the wrath of the enemy in 1265 than endure a diet of Welsh bread and milk—and by the inconstancy of the Welsh climate; the lightness of their armour enabled them to move with great speed along mountain ridges—as Llywelyn ab Iorwerth showed to good effect in his rapid march over the Black mountains from Brecon to Gower in 1217—or to retreat with equal promptness out of the range of an English cavalry patrol, as they did at Abergavenny in 1263.

Yet military tactics and resources were changing, and if the Welsh kingdoms were to survive it was imperative that they should make some effort to respond to those changes. Gwynedd certainly seems to have taken up the challenge. There is some evidence of an attempt to extend the obligatory period of service beyond forty days; military service was almost always exempted from grants of immunities made by the princes, for in the words of the law-texts it was 'the principal territorial obligation';[2] fines were imposed on those who refused to perform their military obligation; supplies for the maintenance of armies were more thoroughly exploited, even the mules of the bishop of Bangor's tenants being commandeered for service; above all, English observers and chroniclers noted that Llywelyn ap Gruffudd's armies in the 1260s, though still overwhelmingly composed of footsoldiers, now also included barded, as well as unarmoured, horses—groups of from 80 to 240 barded horses being reported between 1258 and 1263.

In castle warfare, likewise, the native Welsh kingdoms responded to the Anglo-Norman challenge. Castles were being built in native Wales from the early twelfth century onwards; but their numbers increased dramatically after 1180 and their military role was greatly enhanced. There must have been at least thirty castles in more or less active use in native Wales in the mid-thirteenth century. Some of them—such as Llanymddyfri, Cardigan, and Ystrad Meurig in Deheubarth—were originally built by the Norman invaders, but the majority were native Welsh foundations. Some, such as Dolwyddelan in Gwynedd or Dinefwr in Deheubarth, were built on existing sites or, as at Dinas Brân in Powys Fadog, on old hill forts; but others, such as Cricieth and Dolbadarn in Gwynedd and Castellnewydd Emlyn (Newcastle Emlyn) in Deheubarth, were founded on new sites, away from existing commotal centres. In design and construction they were very inferior in comparison with English castles built in Wales in this period, such as Montgomery, Cilgerran, Pembroke, or Whitecastle. Their overall design often appears haphazard; little attempt was made to integrate towers and curtain walls into a sustained defence-system; and the quality of their masonry is frequently poor. Yet in their way these castles—especially the masonry castles of north Wales and the round towers of Dryslwyn and Dinefwr in Deheubarth—represent a not unimpressive response to changes in military strategy and fortification. They were certainly a marked improvement on earlier earth-and-timber castles or on the dry-stone enclosures such as Carn Fadrun in Llŷn. Some of them—notably the Gwynedd castles—represent a conscious effort to

---

[2] *Ancient Laws and Institutes of Wales*, II, p. 402.

respond to contemporary overall military needs, since they involved, as at Dolbadarn and Cricieth, the abandonment of the existing commotal centre; or were located, as at Ewloe in Tegeingl or Castell y Bere in Meirionydd, to guard some of the most vulnerable flanks of the principality or as at Dinas Brân in northern Powys to take advantage of a commanding military site. Even at a technical level they were not without their merits—notably in the quality of their rock-cut ditches, such as those of Dinas Brân and Dolwyddelan—while the readiness of their builder to borrow and to adapt contemporary English ideas in the art of fortification —such as the round tower at Dolbadarn or the gatehouses at Cricieth and Dinas Brân—speaks well for the imagination and receptiveness of the native princes.

The castles of native Wales represented a bold and expensive attempt to provide firmer military foundations for the principalities and rely less on the advantages of geography and terrain or on the exhaustion of the enemy. Some indication of their centrality in the policies of the princes is provided by a new clause introduced into the law-texts specifying that everyone, except the men of the *maerdref*, was required to undertake castle-building duties for the king (prince), while the cost of such building is indicated by the fact that in one year alone (1273–4) the new castle of Dolforwyn in Cedewain consumed £174 of Llywelyn ap Gruffudd's income. Castles not only had to be built; they also needed to be captured from the enemy, if the Welsh were to seize and retain the military initiative. Here again the Welsh showed that they were adept learners. They began to learn the patience that was needed if a strong stone castle was to be taken—laying siege to Rhuddlan for three months in 1167, and even starving Degannwy and Diserth into submission in 1263 after investing them spasmodically for several years. They also learned to use modern engines of war—catapults, slings, hooked ladders and engines— for the purpose, as at Cilgerran in 1176, Painscastle in 1196, or Builth in 1260.

War and defence were costly; they stretched the resources of the native principalities to the limit and indeed beyond. There are no contemporary accounts of the revenues of the native Welsh principalities; we have to make do with fragmentary references and with deductions from post-Conquest accounts and extents. These suggest that the revenue resources of the major principalities were broadly similar. Demesne manors centred on ancient commotal courts—such as Trefilan or Llanfihangel Genau'r-glyn in Ceredigion; Pen-prys and Talgarth in Arwystli in Powys; Aberffro and Pwllheli in Gwynedd—still provided the princes with basic supplies of food, though they were now increasingly (and in much of Deheubarth exclusively) worked by paid labour or by general labour services rather than by the original bond settlements (W. *maerdrefi*) initially attached to them. In the uplands, cattle ranches or vaccaries were established to stock the prince's larder: for example ten such vaccaries, capable of supporting over 550 head of cattle, were located in the hinterland of Dolwyddelan castle. The more general needs of the prince's court and of his treasury were met from the renders and dues that were payable by the free men and the bondmen of his dominions. The post-conquest surveys reveal that though there were wide variations in the terminology, incidence, and collection of these renders from one part of native Wales to another, their general character was broadly similar. They consisted of renders of food—payable in kind or in their commuted monetary equivalent—for the upkeep of the court (W. *gwestfa, twnc, porthiant*), of dues to maintain the household or its officers on their annual circuits (W. *cylch*) and to reward local officials such as the sergeants of the peace, and of a biennial or triennial tribute of cows (W. *commorth*) comparable with cornage in parts of England and cain in Scotland. These various renders formed the single most important and regular source of princely revenue in all the three major principalities of native Wales and in some areas under Norman rule. There were other sources of revenue which were far less regular but which could contribute very significantly to princely revenue. The profits of war could bring in substantial windfalls and much-needed ready cash— whether in pillage and plunder, heavy ransoms paid by individuals (such as the sum of £2,000 which William Braose was alleged to have paid for his release in 1229 or the ransoms exacted from Nicholas fitz Martin and Guy Brian in the late 1250s), protection money paid by communities (such as the thousand marks of silver which the men of Rhos and Pembroke paid to buy off a raid by Llywelyn ab Iorwerth in 1217, with the bishop of St Davids acting as intermediary), or cash to redeem hostages (such as the hundred marks given by the men of Brecon in the same year 'for peace for the town' and to secure the release of the five hostages they had given him). The profits of justice were also from an early date an important, if erratic, source of revenue.

Yet the normal revenue of the princes hardly matched their pretensions. It was under constant threat of erosion from grants to followers and religious houses, the creation of apanges or the permanent subdivisions of kingdoms, and the escalating costs of warfare and defence. The native rulers could only hope to survive financially and match their revenues to their ambitions if they could exploit the resources of their dominions more thoroughly and profitably. Some of them—so at least the exiguous and cryptic evidence suggests—made the effort to do so. The renders and circuit-dues were regularized, simplified, and often (according to the charges brought against Llywelyn ap Gruffudd posthumously) arbitrarily altered and augmented; the complex distinctions between free and unfree renders were simplified or even abandoned; a uniform system of assessment was introduced—thus in Deheubarth, the multiple renders were consolidated into a single sum of 53s. 4d., payable four times a year from each local unit, *gwestfa*, and each *gwestfa* was in turn subdivided into five smaller units (*rhandiroedd*) from each of which 10s. 8d. was payable; and in many parts of native Wales the process of commuting food renders into consolidated cash rents was begun or accelerated. Such reforms, involving major administrative and fiscal reorganization, are difficult to date; but it has been suggested that the Lord Rhys may well have inaugurated such changes in Deheubarth, while in Gwynedd the late twelfth or thirteenth centuries seem to be the most likely period for such innovations. Certain it is that throughout native Wales—in Deheubarth, Gwynedd Uwch and Is Conwy, and northern Powys—the new English lords of Wales inherited a well-established and coherent framework of financial dues and obligations, which stands in marked contrast with the skeletal character of revenue-assessment in several of the Marcher lordships. In that sense the great fourteenth-century surveys, such as the Survey of Denbigh in 1334, or the Record of Caernarfon of 1352, or the Extents of Chirkland, and Bromfield and Yale in 1392–3, are as much a tribute to the quality of financial governance in pre-Conquest Wales as is Domesday Book to that of Anglo-Saxon England.

The princes, notably those of thirteenth-century Gwynedd, appear to have made every effort to maximize their existing sources of revenue. They emphasized their exclusive claims to shipwrecked goods and treasure trove; built mills and exacted suit of mill from their tenants; appointed woodwards (W. *coedwyr*) to increase the profits of their forests; appropriated private woods to their own use; claimed a monopoly of the goods of intestates, including those of the tenants of their free men; seized episcopal temporalities during vacancies in bishoprics; and placed the collection of personal dues such as *amobr* (virginity due) and advowry rents on a more systematic basis and designated local officers to collect them. Above all, their efforts concentrated on two areas in which princely power made rapid advances in the twelfth and thirteenth centuries. The first was land. Here the princes regularized the dues payable on the death of a tenant (W. *ebediw*) and the entry of his successor (W. *gobr-estyn*), extended their control over waste land and escheated tenements, and levied fines for the short-term vifgage of land under Welsh law (W. *prid*). The second area of advance and profitability was justice: the Welsh rulers, notably the prince of Gwynedd, extended the scale of their judicial activities, especially in criminal cases; and the evidence makes it clear that in Llywelyn ap Gruffudd's later years very substantial revenue flowed into his coffers from heavy amercements, the purchase of pardons, fines for favours and goodwill, and so forth.

Not only were existing sources of revenue squeezed to the limit, new ones were also exploited. New boroughs—such as Llan-faes, Pwllheli, and Nefyn in Gwynedd, or Llanidloes, Welshpool, and Machynlleth in southern Powys—were deliberately fostered by native rulers; and market tolls and customs dues began to form a welcome addition to their revenues. In Gwynedd, the first tentative steps were taken on the road to general taxation: it was reported in the 1270s that Llywelyn ap Gruffudd had imposed a heavy tribute of 3*d*. a head on cattle and other animals and had done so at his pleasure. Fragmentary as the evidence is, it leaves little doubt of increased financial pressure and a much more sustained and rigorous exploitation of resources. Written accounts and formal audits begin to appear; and rulers, or at least those of Gwynedd, commanded sufficient liquid assets to lend small sums to indigent Cistercian abbeys. It was only from such increased resources that the native rulers, more particularly the prince of Gwynedd, could meet the expenses that were necessary to match their ambitions: dispatching embassies, building castles, sustaining armies, arranging marriages into leading English families (Llywelyn ab Iorwerth's marriage gift to one of his daughters on her betrothal to the earl of Chester's nephew cost him a thousand marks), and buying peace and recognition from the English Crown. It was a measure of both the magnitude of his expenses and his capacity to meet them that in 1267 Llywelyn ap Gruffudd agreed to pay £16,666 to the king of England and that by 1272 he had actually paid some £10,000. A ruler who could even contemplate such payments had clearly secured a remarkably firm, and probably extortionate, hold on the resources of his principality.

There are indications of a parallel consolidation of princely authority from other directions. In a society in which the primary form of wealth was land, rulers naturally sought to bring it within the ambit of their authority and control. Their prospects were not promising. Title to land in medieval Wales resided firmly in kin-groups and its descent was strictly controlled by customary rules; there was no right of outright sale or alienation of land; even when a ruler donated lands to a religious community, he was obliged to respect the claims of resident proprietors and kin-groups. Outside his own demesne lands and associated vills, the ruler's rights were apparently very limited. Yet the law-texts and such few land-charters as survive suggest strongly that native rulers were making ever larger claims over the lands of their dominions. 'No land', proclaimed the law-texts confidently, 'ought to be without a king'.[3] Such a claim has a propagandist flavour about it; but investiture by a lord or the confirmation of hereditary claims by a ruler (such as Dafydd ap Gruffudd made in a charter to Madog ab Einion ap Maredudd of Dyffryn Clwyd in 1260) were clearly regarded as

---

[3] *Llyfr Colan*, §594.

providing a more secure basis for land title. The prince successfully asserted his right, at least in north Wales, to waste and escheated land and elaborated the occasions on which he could exercise that right—failure to perform the services due from the land, capital offences such as treason (W. *brad*) and ambush (W. *cynllwyn*), failure or inability to pay renders or succession dues, and failure of male heirs beyond the third degree. He claimed and exercised rights of wardship. Disputes relating to land (W. *tir a daear*) were increasingly drawn into the prince's courts; his protection (W. *croes*) was extended to land in dispute; any improper ploughing of another man's lands incurred a fine to the prince; and he alone could exempt land from the general obligations and services due from land. The prince also extended his control over the land market: his permission was necessary for any outright purchase of land (such as Ednyfed Fychan's purchase of Rhos Fyneich in 1230) and, above all every temporary alienation of land by the Welsh practice of *prid* (a vif-gage normally for four years and renewable) required his permission and such licence was only give for a fee. It is only after the Edwardian Conquest that documentary evidence survives in some abundance to illustrate these various aspects of the prince's control of the descent and alienation of land; but it is clear that the mechanics of this control—at least in Gwynedd—had been fully established in the days of the native princes. It represented a great accession of power and authority to the prince.

In the field of law and justice, likewise, princely power appears to have made significant advances. Here again the prospects initially appeared unpromising. Law in medieval Wales was based on custom rather than on princely legislation; it was transmitted and interpreted by professionally trained jurists (W. *ynaid*). Similarly, the dispensing of justice frequently took the form of local arbitration; it relied heavily on communal arrangements and coercion rather than the agencies of princely authority.[4] Yet in both law and justice the authority of the prince came to loom increasingly large. It was certainly recognized that he had the right to amend and augment native law, provided he did so for the common good: thus Rhys ap Gruffudd of Deheubarth was credited with an amendment to the law on formal claims to property (W. *damdwng*), while Dafydd ap Llywelyn of Gwynedd was said to have taken the much more drastic step of abolishing the practice of kin-compensation for acts of homicide (W. *galanas*). Such an arrogation of legislative power clearly enhanced the status of the prince, and that status was further enhanced by the propaganda which ascribed the initial reform and reorganization of native law to the initiative of a king, Hywel Dda. The law-texts also make it clear that the prince was taking an increasingly active role in the enforcement of

[4] See above, pp. 131–5.

law and the dispensing of justice: it was he who enforced the payment of kin-compensation agreements for homicide and claimed a third of such compensation for the service he rendered (W. *traean cymell*); fines for serious offences (W. *dirwy, camlwrw*) could only be remitted by him; it was he who prosecuted in actions of perjury; as increasingly sophisticated distinctions were drawn between various crimes, his role in the maintenance of order became more prominent; it was he who decided whether land disputes were to be determined by inquisition or by the formal proofs prescribed by Welsh law. Above all, courts held in his name and presided over by his officers assumed a much more regular and prominent place in the dispensation of justice in native Wales. The prince's court, in common with royal and seignorial courts throughout medieval Europe, had always had a judicial aspect, and the judge of the court (W. *ynad llys*) was indeed regarded as one of its three indispensable personages. But as the range of the prince's authority extended and business was attracted into his court, the pattern of princely justice became more complex. Litigants from afar—from Mechain and Arwystli—referred their disputes to be settled in the court of the prince of Gwynedd and before his council; abbeys, such as Strata Florida and Aberconwy, received judicial privileges from him; the chief officer of his court occasionally assumed the title of justiciar, thus indicating the prominence attached to his judicial duties; and cases were referred to him for arbitration and judgement. Many of the prince's judicial powers were doubtless exercised in an *ad hoc* fashion and often as acts of grace and command; but it is also clear that by at least the thirteenth century throughout native Wales—in Deheubarth and Powys as well as in Gwynedd—a pattern of commotal courts, regularly held in the ruler's name and presided over by his officials, had been fully established, and that the profits of justice were now an important and elastic source of princely revenue. The authority of the prince had been grafted onto the processes of justice well before the Edwardian Conquest of Wales. In one of the very few official records of a plea to survive from native Wales, a land dispute at Llandinam in Arwystli in the early thirteenth century, the proceedings were presided over by a local ruler, Maredudd ap Robert of Cedewain, acting on behalf of the prince of Gwynedd; and though the judgement lay in the hands of local law-worthy men, the presence of two of the prince's stewards and two local reeves was a further indication of the degree to which the administration of justice was being brought within the framework of princely authority.

As the prince's control of his dominions increased and the pattern of authority and exploitation became more regular and defined, there was obviously need for a more coherent and effective machinery of government. The native Welsh principalities in this respect were following, hesitatingly and belatedly, the same broad pattern of development that characterized kingdoms, principalities, and the greater lay and ecclesiastical estates throughout north-western Europe in the twelfth and thirteenth centuries. Indeed, the native rulers in Wales may well have borrowed or imitated some of the practices—and terminology—of governance now becoming familiar to them in the greater Marcher lordships of Wales, on the estates of their near neighbours, such as the earl of Chester, or in the kingdom of England. The Welsh prince was still pre-eminently a war-leader; his court still provided for his domestic needs and those of his retainers; and there remained much that was patriarchal and familial about his authority, both in his court and in his kingdom at large. But he was now also much more self-consciously a ruler of territories and a fount of governance and justice. Particularly was this true of Gwynedd: there, as the size of the principality and the pretensions of its princes grew rapidly, the character of its governance was also modified to respond to these changes. The first features of bureaucratic government began to emerge in native Wales.

The council was the hub of the prince's government. The duty of the prince to consult with his noble free men (W. *gwyrda*) was a long recognized feature of kingship in Wales as elsewhere in Europe; but, in thirteenth-century Gwynedd, the council assumed a more formal status. It now consisted not only of the lay and ecclesiastical leaders of native society but also of men who were professional or quasi-professional servants of the prince. Its advice would be sought on diplomatic negotiations, great issues of state, major judicial or quasi-judicial matters, in short on those issues which in England would be referred to as the 'great matters of the realm' (L. *magna negotia regni*). 'Because Llywelyn (ap Gruffudd) does not have his council with him', it was claimed in a letter in 1273 'he cannot immediately make a competent reply.'[5] There is no doubt a large measure of deliberate prevarication in such a plea; but there can be little doubt that in Gwynedd, at least, the character of the council and its status changed, as the prince came to rely increasingly on a small body of quasi-professional advisers, lay and ecclesiastical.

The head of the prince's council and his chief lay adviser was the *distain*, whose name was latinized as *senescallus* (steward) or *justiciarius* (justiciar). Such is the title borne by the chief officer not only in Gwynedd, but also in southern and northern Powys, in Deheubarth, and in such of the smaller Welsh principalities (such as Caerleon) of which we have record. The post was initially an honorary domestic office in the prince's court, but by the thirteenth century the *distain* was the prince's chief governmental officer, exercising a wide range of administrative, diplomatic, and judicial duties. He was drawn from one of the premier families of the ruler's dominions: thus Gruffudd ap Gwên and his father, who were stewards to the prince of

---

[5] *Cal. Anc. Corr.*, p. 162.

southern Powys, were drawn from the stock of a powerful family in Cyfeiliog. Such a combination of official status and territorial wealth gave the *distain* a pre-eminent position in his ruler's lands. None more so than Ednyfed Fychan, who was steward of Llywelyn ab Iorwerth and of Llywelyn's son, Dafydd, and who was, with pardonable exaggeration, described by an English annalist on his death in 1246 as 'justiciar of Wales'.[6] Ednyfed was a man who turned comfortably in the company of princes: his own wife was one of the daughters of the Lord Rhys of Deheubarth and his lands lay scattered throughout native Wales—in Perfeddwlad (the original home of the family), Anglesey and Arllechwedd, and, through marriage, Ceredigion and Cantref Mawr.

At least two of Ednyfed's sons—Goronwy (d. 1268) and Tudur (d. 1278)—succeeded him in office as *distain* of Gwynedd. Gwynedd was certainly not unique in this respect, for in southern Powys and Caerleon, also, the post of steward was apparently heritable or nearly so. Indeed heritability was a feature not only of this post but of the lay councillors of the princes in general. So, at least the ample and well-analysed evidence for Gwynedd suggests. There, a group of some six major families seems to have contributed a large proportion of the princes' advisers during the thirteenth century. The dynasty of Ednyfed Fychan himself provides the best example: at least twelve members of the family provided the princes of Gwynedd with officials and counsellors over a period of over sixty years. The rewards of such service were manifold—fees, status, lands, and immunities from fiscal renders and other obligations. Thereby, a ministerial aristocracy was being created and a privileged and largely hereditary status-group, bound to the prince by largess and service, was being installed in his principality. So long as the initial bonds of loyalty and service were maintained, the prince's authority within his dominions was thereby further strengthened.

But as government came to rely increasingly on the written word, the prince also had need of clerks to draft letters, compose charters, draw up accounts, and serve on embassies. He could and did draw on the services of local clergy on an *ad hoc* basis—local archdeacons and priests (such as Master David, archdeacon of St Asaph, who served Llywelyn ab Iorwerth and his son David), members of cathedral chapters (such as Urban, 'my clerk and canon of Llandaff', who witnessed one of the charters of the Welsh ruler of Caerleon), and on the Cistercian monks and Franciscan friars, whose international contacts made them particularly valuable on diplomatic missions. But the princes doubtless also had their own household clerks, doubling up as court chaplains and secretaries (as the Welsh laws had provided, when they had stipulated a fee of 4*d.* for every

---

[6] *Annales Cestrienses*, ed. R. C. Christies (Record Society of Lancashire and Cheshire, 1887), p. 66.

letter patent written by the court priest). Such were Gwrgenau, 'clerk of the lord Rhys (Gryg)', who witnessed a charter of 1222, or Iorwerth and Ieuan, the notaries of Hywel ap Rhys Gryg, in a deed of 1258; and so doubtless were many of the clerks—such as Master Ystrwyth (*Instructus*) and Master Philip ab Ifor—who figure frequently in the service of the princes of Gwynedd. In Gwynedd, indeed, some of these clerks were occasionally given the title of 'chancellor' and 'vice-chancellor'. In Gwynedd, also, as early as the days of Llywelyn ab Iorwerth, the prince had his own secret or privy seal as well as his great seal. Though there is no reason to believe that a chancery as such had emerged in Gwynedd, it is clear that important advances had been made in introducing and regularizing the use of the written word in governance. Similar developments were afoot, at least in Gwynedd, in the organization of princely finances: the keeper of the prince's bed-chamber (W. *gwas ystafell*) evolved naturally into the guardian of the prince's treasure and was occasionally formally termed chamberlain, vice-chamberlain, or treasurer; while, by the later years of Llywelyn ap Gruffudd's principate, formal receipts, regular accounts, and audits were already becoming common.

Important developments, which are equally difficult to document and thereby to define accurately and chronologically, were also taking place in the pattern of local governance. The *cantref* and the commote were already well-established in the early twelfth-century Wales as local divisions of the native kingdoms; but with the advance of the civilian power of the princes a more complex and well-defined, though still far from uniform or neatly hierarchical, framework of local governance seems to emerge. The commote replaced the *cantref* as the effective unit of local governance in most parts of Wales; throughout north Wales the vill (W. *tref*) was confirmed as the unit for the attribution and collection of dues and renders; in Deheubarth, as a result of a major administrative reorganization, each commote was divided neatly and uniformly into smaller units, the *gwestfa*, for fiscal purposes. There were many local anomalies and variations within this pattern of local governance, but in effect the local administrative geography of native Wales as it was to remain—albeit dressed up occasionally in English or Latin terminology—until the Tudor legislation of the 1530s was established. Much the same was true of the pattern of local fiscal obligations. Some of these were still paid in kind; but many were now simplified and systematized, and some were consolidated into commuted money rents. They were collected from groups of co-heirs who were members of the same agnatic descent-group. This was the *gwely* or *gafael*, which figures so prominently in all the fiscal documentation of late medieval Wales.[7] It is in the twelfth and thirteenth centuries that the *gwely*

---

[7] See above pp. 125–7.

begins to figure prominently in the documentation; many of the historical personages whose names are attached to *gwelyau*—such as Ednyfed Fychan, Llywarch ap Brân, or Iarddur ap Cynddelw—likewise flourished in the same period. The poverty of the evidence means that much that relates to the development of the *gwely* remains obscure, in spite of the pioneer researches of the late Professor T. Jones Pierce; but it is at least clear that in the definition of fiscal reponsibilities and the distribution of renders the period 1150–1250 was crucially important. It was then that the pattern of obligations, which emerges clearly in the fourteenth-century surveys and was to survive in many parts of Wales until the sixteenth century, was firmly established. In the same period a local officialdom seems to emerge which is more immediately responsible and responsive to the prince and to his commands. Native rulers had long since had local officials in charge of their local courts and demesne resources; but now that the prince's authority was more broadly based, local officers, with wider judicial and financial responsibilities throughout the commotes, came to occupy a more prominent role. Thus in Perfeddwlad, according to post-Conquest evidence, each commote had its chief administrative officer (W. *rhaglaw*), its sergeant (W. *rhingyll*), its woodward (W. *coedwr*), several sergeants of the peace (W. *ceisiaid*), a local jurist (W. *ynad*), a collector of virginity-dues (W. *amobrwr*), and a keeper of advowry tenants. There is no need to believe that such a schematized and neatly defined pattern always prevailed; there were without a doubt wide variations in practice throughout Wales. It is also clear that, in an essentially decentralized and pre-bureaucratic society, local custom and influence were often more powerful than central direction. But the measure of princely control was certainly on the increase: Llywelyn ab Iorwerth dispatched orders to his bailiffs in Maelienydd and his constable of Builth; Llywelyn ap Gruffudd appointed local bailiffs in the distant districts of his principality, such as Elfael, Gwrtheyrnion, and Brecon, and placed the lands 'beyond Berwyn' under the charge of a steward. There is reason to believe that had the principality of Gwynedd survived, a firmer chain of command and accountability would have been established between the prince's court and the local districts of his principality.

The changes effected in the governance of native Wales in the period from 1150 to 1282 were at best tentative and inchoate. They represent no more than the first hesitant steps in exploiting the resources of the native kingdoms more systematically and placing their governance on firmer administrative and judicial foundations. The pace of change varied from one principality to another, with Gwynedd clearly in the forefront in the thirteenth century. Even in Gwynedd the fluctuations of political fortunes and dynastic conflict recurrently threatened the stability upon which any advance was based. Yet the importance of the changes—frequently obscured by treating the period from the coming of the Normans to the conquest of native Wales in 1282–3 as one entity—is not to be denied. The texture of the native principalities, particularly of Gwynedd, was now woven more tightly; their resources were more firmly under the control of the prince; and the framework of administration, judicial authority, and financial obligation had been established which was to be taken over largely intact by the English conquerors of Wales.

Nevertheless, close examination soon reveals structural weaknesses within the native Welsh kingdoms which would be exposed quickly once pressure was applied to them. They were militarily vulnerable to any sustained or determined English attack, as John showed in 1211, Henry III in 1241, and Edward I in 1276–7. Wales's military strength was essentially of a negative kind: it lay in the capacity of Welsh troops to resist from engaging the English armies on their own terms, relying instead on guerrilla warfare, the exhaustion of the English forces, the weather, and the terrain to wear down their opponents. But once the English Crown was freed from continental preoccupations and had mastered the problems of keeping an army supplied in the field for a long campaign, there was little that Welsh rulers could do to withstand a direct onslaught other than to plead for peace. Even their mountains could not defend them indefinitely, for the English had learned that an economic blockade might drive the Welsh into submission, while Nicholas de Molis's forced march from Ceredigion across upland north Wales to Aberconwy in 1246 showed that English troops could, if pressed, cope with the most daunting Welsh terrain. Development in the art of military fortification placed the Welsh at a further double disadvantage. They had the resources neither in skill nor in money to build the massive and sophisticated stone castles of the thirteenth century: even the most impressive of Gwynedd's stone castles were puny when compared with Caerffili or Montgomery or with other royal and baronial castles in Wales. Equally, such castles proved increasingly beyond the reach of even sustained Welsh sieges. Swansea castle held out successfully against the Welsh for ten weeks in 1192 and Brecon for a month against Llywelyn ab Iorwerth in 1231; most ominously of all, Henry III's twin castles of Degannwy and Diserth withstood intermittent Welsh assaults for seven years before they eventually surrendered in 1263. The military balance of power had turned decisively against the Welsh in the thirteenth century, especially now that the king of England was directly involved in the struggle; only good fortune and political adroitness would postpone the day of reckoning.

The Welsh principalities were also financially fragile. Powys and Deheubarth were fragmented by family divisions, and the economic resources of their rulers were thereby greatly reduced. Thus, on the most generous construction of post-Conquest evidence, the total revenue of southern Powys could hardly have reached £1,000 per annum. For most of the thirteenth century Gwynedd was ruled by a single prince and enjoyed the benefits of expanding frontiers and the windfalls of conquest. Yet, even in its heyday in the 1260s, it is difficult to believe that Llywelyn ap Gruffudd's ordinary annual income much exceeded £5,000–£6,000. In normal years the principality lands in north Wales (the counties of Anglesey, Caernarfon, and Merioneth) yielded c. £2,250 in the early fourteenth century; to this should be added a further £2,500 from Perfeddwlad (Denbigh was valued at £1,100 in 1334, Dyffryn Clwyd at £545 in 1308, Flintshire at £422 in 1301–4).[8] Such a figure might be augmented by casual revenue, tributes, plunder, and taxes, and by the temporary annexation of other territories, notably Powys (in 1216–40, 1257–63, and 1274–7). Yet even such an augmented revenue was inadequate to match the demands that were now being made on Gwynedd—for the payment of armies and embassies, the building and garrisoning of castles, and the payment of huge tributes to the English Crown. The princes might make every effort to maximize their revenues and even to tap new sources of income; but such efforts, apart from the domestic resentment they might generate within Gwynedd itself, could at best produce only marginal results. The native principality of Wales, whose existence was officially recognised by the English Crown in 1267 but which had been in the making for half a century, did not have the resources to match its pretensions and the status it claimed for itself.

Furthermore, the process of state-formation in the Welsh principalities, and in Gwynedd in particular, was recurrently jeopardized by their chronic political instablity. One fundamental aspect and cause of that instability were the absence of a unitary rule of succession. Welsh jurists might proclaim that though the kingdom was divisible, kingship itself was not; they might sustain that belief by emphasizing that each of the three major principalities had only one chief seat; and powerful native princes, such as the Lord Rhys and Llywelyn ab Iorwerth, might designate a single son as heir and make every effort to ensure his succession. Yet the custom of partibility among male heirs and the belief that such a custom was morally

[8] These figures are quoted here to illustrate how much the lands which constituted Gwynedd in the years 1258–77 subsequently yielded to their English lords in the early fourteenth century. It is not, of course, implied that their yield was necessarily similar for Llywelyn ap Gruffudd. The sources for the figures are as follow: (i) Principality lands in north Wales. Average annual gross yield for the years 1304–7 calculated from E. A. Lewis, 'Account of the chamberlain of the principality of North Wales, 1304–5', *BBCS* 1 (1923–5), 256–75, and J. Griffiths, 'Early Accounts Relating to North Wales, temp. Edward I'. *BBCS* 16 (1954–6), 109–33. (ii) Denbigh: *Survey of the Honour of Denbigh, 1334*, Ed. P. Vinogradoff and F. Morgan (1914), 323. (iii) Dyffryn Clwyd: Public Record Office, Chancery Inquisitions Post Mortem (C. 134), 3 no. 5 m. 6. (iv) Flintshire: Average annual gross yield for the years 1301–4 based on A. Jones, *Flintshire Ministers' Accounts 1301–28* (Flintshire Historical Society, 1913).

just, as well as traditionally sanctioned, were too deeply ingrained to allow the triumph of the principle of unitary rule. It was in the name of that custom that Powys was fragmented after 1160 and Deheubarth after 1197; and that Gwynedd was partitioned after 1170 and again, 'by counsel of the wise men of the land', in 1246.[9] Even when a powerful ruler, such as Llywelyn ab Iorwerth or his grandson, Llywelyn ap Gruffudd, succeeded in asserting his mastery within his own family, it was rare for him to proceed to the total disinheritance of his relatives, provided they were willing to acknowledge his supremacy. After all, as the poets reminded him, it was only God who had the right to disinherit men. Yet the principle of partibility was without doubt politically debilitating. It created recurrent family disputes and compounded them in each generation; it inhibited any sustained progress towards political consolidation; above all, it created a focus of dissatisfaction and dissension which could be, and was, recurrently exploited by English kings for their own ends—as by John in 1212 or Henry III in 1241.

Political stability was also threatened by disaffection within the principalities themselves, notably from leading nobles and churchmen. Rulers in Wales, as elsewhere, could only rule by consent; they frequently deferred to the advice of their magnates in making grants of land, reaching major judicial decisions, or undertaking campaigns. Consent had to be won and, once won, it had to be retained both by masterfulness and by concessions: by confirming powerful local men (such as Goronwy ap Heilyn of Rhos) in office; by gifts of land (such as the nine bovates of land in Gafflogion granted to Dafydd ap Gruffudd by Llywelyn ab Iorwerth); by grants of immunities (such as 'the gifts and many freedoms on his land', which Cedifor ap Dinawol secured from the Lord Rhys for his services in improving siege tactics); and by acknowledging the status of leading nobles and their 'liberty and ancient dignity' (as in Dafydd ap Gruffudd's charter to Madog ap Einion ap Maredudd of Dyffryn Clwyd in 1260).[10] Leading ecclesiastics, notably the bishops and Cistercian abbots, were likewise influential in respect of their lands, status, contacts, spiritual weapons, and external links with Canterbury and Rome. Their support had to be delicately cultivated, since—as Llywelyn ap Gruffudd found to his cost—there were ample issues of friction to sour relationships between churchmen and native rulers in Wales, as in other countries.[11]

Such problems of political control were not, of course, peculiar to Wales; but in the native Welsh principalities they were proportionately much more acute. Local loyalties, both within the individual principalities

[9] *Brut*, s.a. 1246.
[10] *Brut*, s.a. 1176 (p. 71 n.); J. Conway Davies, 'A Grant by David ap Gruffudd', *NLWJ* 3 (1943), 29–43.
[11] See below, pp. 325–6.

and between the native principalities of Wales as whole, were still powerful
and asserted themselves quickly in a political crisis. The texture of political
control and dependence within these native principalities was still but
loosely woven. Local noble kindreds claimed and exercised a powerful
lordship over their own lands and men; and, in spite of recent developments,
land and law—those twin pillars of state-formation elsewhere in medieval
Europe—still lay considerably outside the scope of princely power in
native Wales. Furthermore, the individual principalities were too small to
offer an adequate and secure focus of loyalty and sufficient sources of
reward. The political fragmentation of the country and the fissures within
each principality meant that loyalties were unusually brittle, as men tried
to anticipate, and sometimes to promote, changes in political fortunes and
to salvage their lands and their careers, by a deft and timely change of
allegiance. Above all, the Crown of England—provided that it was not
distracted by continental preoccupations or domestic discord—served as an
alternative focus of patronage and protection for Welshmen. It thereby
destabilized Welsh politics—offering refuge to exiles, support to disaffected
members of ruling dynasties, pensions and lands to wavering nobles, and
succour to disenchanted ecclesiastics. Even the close servants and retainers
of the prince of Gwynedd were not immune from its influence: at least nine
members of the dynasty of Ednyfed Fychan, Llywelyn ab Iorwerth's
steward or justiciar, at some stage or other in their careers, accepted posts
or pensions from the king of England and several of them died in his
service. Such brittleness in loyalty was particularly marked in those frontier
districts which would be the first to fall in any English advance—notably
Powys, Perfeddwlad, and Ystrad Tywi.

Internal fissures and external pressure between them meant that the
native Welsh principalities of Gwynedd, Deheubarth, and Powys never
enjoyed the sustained political stability and the conditions of political
growth necessary for their survival as independent or quasi-independent
political units. In those circumstances, the attempt of the princes of
Gwynedd in the thirteenth century to forge a unitary principality of native
Wales was premature. That principality was never more than a loose
federation, held together by fear and power. It lacked, or was not allowed
the opportunity to develop, the institutional, financial, administrative,
military, and above all political unity and infrastructure of authority and
cohesion which would alone give it credibility. It was subject to the same
political weakness as the individual principalities themselves.

The princes of Gwynedd periodically compared their status and
privileges with those of the king of Scotland; but in almost every respect
the comparison was misleading. Scotland had long been an unitary
kingdom and the power of its kings in terms of governance and political
control had grown rapidly in the twelfth and thirteenth centuries, whereas

native Wales only began to take the first hesitant steps on the road to sustained political unity in the thirteenth century. Strong as were local loyalties and regional power-structures in Scotland, they were ultimately subsumed within the notions of a single kingdom and a single political community; but in native Wales the strength of dynastic and regional loyalties and the essentially localized nature of power impeded the native principality of Wales (1258–82) from being more than a loose amalgam under the presidency of the prince of Gwynedd. The Normans came to Scotland by royal invitation, were assimilated into Scottish society, and gave of their experience and talents to bolster the Scottish monarchy; in Wales, on the other hand, the Normans came as conquerors and the consequent tension between them and native Welshmen created a deep chasm of loyalty within a small country. Scotland was a political unit with recognized frontiers; whereas Wales was no more than a geographical unit, in which the boundaries of native power contracted or expanded according to military fortunes. In economic terms, Scotland partook fully of the growth of the twelfth and thirteenth centuries, notably through commerce and the foundation of burghs in eastern and southern Scotland. This enabled its economy to become more diversified, its society more sophisticated, and its kingship more characteristically 'west European' in its resources and power. Important as was the economic and social transformation which it underwent at the same period, native Wales still remained a poor and underdeveloped society. The surpluses produced were small; trade was occasional and fitful; towns were inchoate; money was scarce; and the district was becoming increasingly dependent on the much richer and more economically advanced lowland regions now under Anglo-Norman control. Finally, Scotland and native Wales presented a sharp contrast with each other in their relationships with England. Scotland, it is true, was forced periodically to concede its client status *vis-à-vis* England; but only under duress had it ever acknowledged a formal feudal dependence on the crown of England, while its ruling dynasty regarded the English royal house as virtual equals and was so regarded by it. The princes of native Wales, on the other hand, had never attempted to deny their feudal dependence on the kings of England. The best they could hope to do was to cultivate their own ambitions within the framework of that dependence, whenever their own skills and the circumstances allowed them to do so. In short it is the contrasts between the native principality of Wales under Llywelyn ap Gruffudd (1246–82) and the kingdom of Scotland under Alexander III (1249–86) which are striking, not the similarities; the same is true of their relationship with the kingdom of England. By the same token it is not the collapse of Welsh independence in 1277–83 which is surprising, but rather its survival for so long.

CHAPTER 10

THE MARCH OF WALES, 1172–1277:
THE AGE OF DEFINITION

By the last quarter of the twelfth century the era of rapid Anglo-Norman advance in Wales had drawn to a close. The days of easy pickings and quick returns were now over. The Anglo-Normans had entrenched themselves firmly in the south-east and, in places, along the eastern border of Wales: they had also established a secure foothold for themselves in the far south-west of the country; but they lacked the stamina to extend their lordship permanently or securely into the rest of the country. The lands that were immediately attractive and rewarding to alien colonists had, for the most part, been won; securing and consolidating their control of these districts now took priority over further conquests. For those who were looking for further adventure and easy gains, Ireland offered from the 1170s a much more attractive proposition than did upland Wales: the Norman lords of south Wales took a prominent role in its conquest and immigrants from Wales—English, Flemings, and native Welsh—formed a major proportion of its early settler population. There were yet other reasons why the Anglo-Norman momentum in Wales was faltering by the late twelfth century. After his accord with the Welsh princelings in 1171–2, Henry II positively discouraged further advance at the expense of the native Welsh kingdoms and even severely punished those who threatened that accord. The native Welsh kingdoms had recovered much of their strength and confidence and now presented a formidable obstacle to further Norman expansion; in particular, Deheubarth, under the Lord Rhys (d. 1197), had halted and turned back the tide of Norman advance in the south-west and had extended its protection and support to the beleaguered native dynasties of mid-Wales and upland Gwent and Glamorgan.[1] At much the same time, several major Norman families failed in the direct line and with their passing the Normans, at least temporarily, lost the initiative: Richard fitz Gilbert, earl of Pembroke, or Strigoil, and lord of Lower Gwent, died in 1176 and his estates were in royal custody until 1189; Earl William of Gloucester, lord of Glamorgan and Gwynllŵg, was survived by daughters only on his death in 1183 and for over thirty years his lands were in effect in royal custody; Gower likewise fell to the Crown on the death of the earl of Warwick in 1184; and in north Wales, the one surviving border earldom, that of Chester, was weakened by forfeiture (1174–7) and by a prolonged

---

[1] See above, pp. 218–24.

minority (1181–93) and was otherwise too preoccupied by its Norman and English concerns (especially after the acquisition of the Roumara inheritance in 1198) to concentrate on asserting its claims in north-east Wales.

The Anglo-Norman lords had come to accept by the late twelfth century that the total subjugation of Wales was, at least for the time being, beyond their reach. So had the English government. Wales was to be a partially conquered country. The acknowledgement of this situation was reflected in the increasing use in official documents of a formal terminology to express the duality: on the one hand, that part of Wales which remained under native rule was referred to as 'Wales' (*Wallia*) or 'Wales proper' (*pura Wallia*), while the rest of the country was designated 'the March of Wales' (*marchia Wallie*) and its rulers 'the barons of the March' (*barones de marchia*) or, occasionally, 'earls and barons of England in the March of Wales'. The March was a historical rather than a geographical category. It consisted of a patchwork of lordships, extending from Pembroke in the far west to Oswestry in the north-east, which had been brought, to a greater or lesser degree, under Anglo-Norman control by the end of the twelfth century. It was still a fluid category, since military fortunes and baronial enterprise could add to it here and subtract from it there; but by 1200 it had acquired a broad measure of definition which it was to retain until the final conquest of Wales in 1277–83. A brief review of the March in the late twelfth century will serve to indicate the extent of Anglo-Norman penetration in Wales by that date and to emphasize the very variable quality of Anglo-Norman control.

The March may be divided broadly into four districts. The first zone lay in south-west Wales, extending from the river Teifi to the Gower peninsula. It was a zone which was a mirror image of the March as a whole, for it consisted of an inner core (the lordships of Haverford, Wiston, Pembroke, and southern Gower) where Norman control was firm and securely underpinned by extensive alien settlement, and an outer ring (the lordships of Cemais, Cilgerran, St Clears, Talacharn, and Llansteffan, west of the river Tywi, and those of Cydweli, Carnwyllion, and northern Gower, to the east) where the Anglo-Normans exercised a rather precarious military overlordship and Welsh forays, such as those of 1189–93 and 1217, penetrated easily. The second zone extended from Swansea in the west to Chepstow in the east, northwards along the English border to Hay, and thence across to Brecon. In this zone Norman lordship and an Anglo-Norman society had entrenched themselves firmly along the coastal lowlands, more especially to the east of Ogmore and along the valleys of the Usk and Wye and their main tributaries (especially in the vicinity of Monmouth, Abergavenny, Brecon, and Bronllys). In these districts a resident Anglo-Norman gentry—such as the Pauncefoots of

Crickhowell (Crucywel, Blaenllyfni), the Waldeboefs of Llanhamlach (Brecon), or the Butlers of Marcroes (Glamorgan)—ruled their manors from their castles and moated residences and moved easily in the circles of their English colleagues and often, indeed, owned estates in western England. Outside these restricted and often isolated districts, however, Anglo-Norman lordship was often tentative. Most of the uplands were still ruled by native princely dynasties who owned no more than nominal obligations to their overlords: thus the native ruler of Senghennydd, the commote that extended southwards to within a few miles of Cardiff, owed no service to the Anglo-Norman lord of Glamorgan other than a heriot of a horse and arms at his death. Even in the lowlands outside the boroughs and the seignorial manors, the population remained overwhelmingly Welsh. In lowland Gwent, for example, the tenantry still owed Welsh dues such as *cylch*, inherited their lands by Welsh law, and were organized under their own beadles. It was indicative of continuing native influence in the area that when a Cistercian abbey was founded at Llantarnam near Caerleon in 1179, its mother house should be Strata Florida in the heart of native Wales and its patron and protector was the local Welsh ruler in Gwent, Hywel ab Iorwerth ab Owain. Such a zone, in which Welsh and Anglo-Normans lived cheek by jowl, and often uneasily, with each other, was still militarily vulnerable—not only to major Welsh raids, such as that of Llywelyn ab Iorwerth in 1231, but also to more local forays, such as those of 1173 (in which Caerleon was captured by the Welsh), 1182 (when the sheriff of Hereford was killed while building a castle near Monmouth), or 1183–4 (when Cardiff and Kenfig were burnt and Neath besieged in a Welsh offensive after the death of Earl William of Gloucester in November 1183).

Anglo-Norman power was even more insecure in the third zone, which extended northwards from Brecon to Montgomery. Here the Anglo-Norman lords had made little permanent advance since the late eleventh century. The district was too barren to attract English settlers, and its native rulers—the dynasties of Elfael, Maelienydd, Gwrtheyrnion, Ceri, and Cedewain—successfully appealed to the rulers of Deheubarth and Gwynedd in their attempts to withstand the onslaughts of the Normans. The Norman warlords, it is true, occasionally bludgeoned these native rulers into submission and established castles, such as those of Cymaron and Cefnllys in Maelienydd, or Rhaeadr in Gwrtheyrnion, in an effort to impose their mastery; but until 1277 any such mastery was to prove fragile and short-lived. Much the same was true of the fourth zone extending from Montgomery northwards to Cheshire. Nowhere, indeed, were the collapse of the Norman momentum and the retreat of the Anglo-Norman tide more evident. In the north the earls of Chester, whose ancestors had played such a prominent role in the Norman penetration of north Wales in the late eleventh century, had now virtually turned their backs on Wales. They might still lead an occasional expedition into Wales, such as those of 1177 into Maelor Gymraeg (Bromfield) or of 1210 when castles were built at Holywell and Degannwy; but for the most part they opted for a policy of disengagement, or, from 1218 to 1237, even forged a close alliance with the Welsh. Further south, along the Dee and the Severn, the Anglo-Normans again seemed by the late twelfth century to have opted for a policy of containment rather than of conquest, defending and rebuilding frontier castles, such as Oswestry, Carreghwfa, and Caus, but making no permanent gains at the expense of the native kingdoms of northern and southern Powys. Here, as further south, the March grew not so much by conquests from the Welsh as by withdrawing whole frontier districts, especially the lordships of Caus and Oswestry, out of the purview of English royal administration.

Such then was the March of Wales in the late twelfth century. It was composed of an ill-assorted congeries of lordships, large and small, some of which extended deep into Wales, others of which hardly penetrated beyond Offa's Dyke. It had not grown to an overall plan, nor under any sustained military direction; rather did its shape and extent reflect, on the one hand, the enterprise and preoccupations of individual Anglo-Norman lords and, on the other, the measure of Welsh resistance and the difficulties of the terrain. Its character varied greatly from one district to another, often indeed within one and the same lordship; the social, economic, and seignorial configuration of some of its lowland districts was hardly to be distinguished from that of southern England, but elsewhere the social structure was utterly Welsh and the lord's authority was at best vague and tentative. Thus, to travel the few miles from the lowlands of Radnor into the uplands of Maelienydd, from coastal Newport into the Welsh district of Machen, or from southern to northern Pembroke, was to enter a different world.

In the century after 1170 three major factors determined the development of the March. The first was the resurgence of native Welsh power, at first in Deheubarth under the Lord Rhys and subsequently, and even more menacingly, in Gwynedd. The easy and rapid growth of Anglo-Norman power in Wales was no longer possible in these circumstances. On the contrary, the Welsh now frequently wrenched the initiative from the Anglo-Normans and themselves went on the attack. Welsh raids began to penetrate deep into the March: in 1196, for example, the Lord Rhys's assaults on the March reached to the very frontiers of England itself, while a generation later the great forays of Llywelyn ab Iorwerth in 1231 and 1233 showed that no part of the March was safe from his wrath. This resurgence of native Welsh power in Deheubarth and Gwynedd gave new heart to the native leaders of the upland districts of the March—particularly those of Maelienydd, Elfael, and Gwrtheyrnion in the middle March and of upland Glamorgan and Gwent in the south-east—and thereby frustrated the ambition of the Marcher lords to bring these districts more securely under their authority. In 1236, for example, even the Earl Marshal felt obliged to restore the castle of Machen, only a few miles from Newport, to Morgan ap Hywel 'for fear of the Lord Llywelyn',[2] and in the same year the king himself apologized to Llywelyn for the attacks on Morgans's lands. Even in areas which are designated in historical atlases as being within the March, the power of Marcher lords was retreating in the face of Welsh resurgence. It was only during the period of Gwynedd's discomfiture from 1240 to 1256 that the Marchers were able to wrest back some of the initiative, especially in Glamorgan and the middle March. But even that recovery proved to be short-lived, for with the rise of Llywelyn ap Gruffudd to pre-eminence, the pendulum of power in the March swung once more decisively in favour of the Welsh. Large tracts of eastern and central Wales from the Severn to the Brecon Beacons and extending to the very frontier with England were lost to the March; it is little wonder that the bishop of Hereford should report that 'the whole March is in terror'. By the 1270s the frontier of Llywelyn's ambitions, and thereby of the March, in the south-east lay at Caerffili, less than ten miles from Cardiff. It appeared as if the March, instead of being an expanding frontier, was to be reduced, to borrow an Irish analogy, into an attentuated and embattled Pale.[3]

The power and attitude of the English Crown were the second factor which helped to shape the history of the March in these years. It did so in a variety of ways. Sometimes it acted as a brake on Marcher ambitions; particularly in the period 1172–89 when Henry II, whose suspicions of the motives and loyalty of the Marchers had been aroused by their role in the invasion of Ireland, was anxious to maintain his *détente* with the native Welsh princes under the leadership of the Lord Rhys. The king stepped in on several occasions to admonish and even punish the Marchers for pursuing their assaults against the Welsh in contempt of his prohibition: in 1175 he required the earl of Pembroke to restore Caerleon to its native Welsh ruler, Iorwerth ab Owain; in the same year he cancelled William Braose's appointment as royal lieutenant in south Wales, because of William's alleged involvement in a massacre of Welshmen in Abergavenny; he took even more drastic action against Roger Mortimer in 1179 for killing the Welsh ruler of Maelienydd while he was under the protection of a royal safe-conduct—Mortimer's lands and his castle of Cymaron were confiscated and several of his followers were executed or punished. But on other occasions the Crown in effect encouraged Marcher ambitions in Wales and provided the framework for further Marcher gains. It is no coincidence that the periods of Marcher advance were those when the

[2] *Brut*, s.a. 1236.   [3] *Cal. Anc. Corr.*, pp. 15–16. See map, p. 38.

Crown, tacitly or openly, supported Marcher ambitions (as in the 1190s) or when royal expeditions (especially those of 1211, 1223, 1241, 1245) so diverted and weakened the Welsh principalities that the Marchers could resume their offensive—as did the Marshals in south-west Wales in the 1220s or the Mortimers in the middle March in the 1240s. By the thirteenth century any substantial advance in the March had become dependent, directly or indirectly, on royal support.

The Crown may also be said to have contributed to the growth of the March in another very different sense. During the thirteenth century the March grew not only by the acknowledged manner of conquering lands from the Welsh, but also by subtracting into the March border areas of Herefordshire and Shropshire which had hitherto been subject to English county administration and royal governance and justice. On some occasions the king himself was a party to this process, granting extravagant liberties and immunities to favoured subjects (such as those that were conceded to Roger Mortimer of Wigmore in the 1260s); but more often than not the process was a surreptitious one. Ambitious border lords took advantage of the preoccupations and weakness of the Crown—especially during the period of baronial reform and rebellion 1258–65—to withdraw their frontier estates out of the range of royal governance, justice, and taxation and to claim that they now enjoyed Marcher status. It was by some such process that the lordships of Caus, Clun, Oswestry, and Wigmore were, to a greater or lesser degree, withdrawn into the March during the thirteenth century. And there they were to remain until the Acts of Union of 1536–43.

The men who availed themselves of the opportunity to augment the March at the expense of the kingdom of England were barons, such as William and John Fitzalan of Oswestry and Clun (1175–1240), Thomas Corbet of Caus (1222–74), and Roger Mortimer of Wigmore (1246–82). They bring us to the third and arguably the most important factor in the making of the March, namely the enterprise of individual barons. Seignorial initiative was, as always, the crucial element in the development of the March. Where that initiative faltered or failed altogether, as it did in north-east Wales, the March contracted; where it was maintained, the March was consolidated and even grew. The history of the March is, in this respect, the sum of the history of its major families; around their fortunes and misfortunes, their marriages and minorities, their political successes and failures, turned much of the history of the March. A brief review of three of the premier Marcher families of the period—those of Braose, Marshal and Mortimer—will serve to illustrate this truism.[4]

---

[4] For a genealogical table which traces the descent of some Marcher lordships in the twelfth and thirteenth centuries see p. 278; for a brief gazetteer of the descent of most lordships c.1086–c.1400, see Appendix, pp. 466–72.

The Braose family had been established at Radnor on the Welsh border from the late eleventh century and had been seeking to push the boundary of its power westwards into Builth and Elfael, but with only spasmodic and uncertain success. It was marriage rather than conquest which propelled it into the forefront of the Marcher baronage. On the death of the last of Miles of Gloucester's sons in 1166, William Braose II (d. ?1175) acquired through his wife the great Marcher lordships of Brecon and Abergavenny and became thereby one of the most powerful Marcher lords. He, his son, William III (d. 1211), and grandson, William IV (d. 1210), set about imposing their authority ruthlessly in the district—expelling Welsh noblemen from their lands, massacring and executing others, building castles, annexing lordships, and terrorizing the native population. Nor was that the limit of their ambition: through royal grants (Gower, Kington, Threecastles) and custodies (Monmouth, Glamorgan, Gwynllŵg, the Lacy barony) the family had acquired by 1205 an uncontested dominance of the whole of south-east Wales. Had the Braose ambitions been allowed to grow unchecked, the story of the March and indeed of south Wales in general might have been different. But in 1207 William Braose fell victim to the suspicion and spleen of King John and, with his fall, a vacuum of power and seignorial momentum was created in the central and southern March. The Braose family had recovered most of its patrimonial estates by 1216; but henceforth it was torn by family feuds, and when William Braose V was executed by Llywelyn ab Iorwerth in 1230, his estates were divided between his four daughters, and the main Braose line survived only in Gower.

Unlike the Braose family, the Marshals had no stake in the March until 1189, when the marriage of the dashing William Marshal (d. 1219) to Isabella, daughter and heiress of Earl Richard of Pembroke (d. 1176), brought him two major lordships in Wales—Netherwent (Chepstow and Usk) in the south-east and Pembroke in the south-west. He thereby became at a stroke one of the major barons of the March. He and his sons had other wide territorial interests in England, France, and Ireland; but they devoted a considerable measure of their energy, talents, and fortunes to consolidating and extending their power in the March. The greatest monuments to their efforts are the magnificent castles at Chepstow, Usk, Tenby, Cilgerran, and Pembroke, all of which in their present form are substantially the work of the Marshals. But contemporary records reveal other aspects of the family's enterprise such as recovering Cilgerran from the Welsh in 1204 and again in 1223, expelling Llywelyn ab Iorwerth and his Welsh allies from Carmarthen and Cardigan in 1223, installing a Welsh client ruler in Emlyn and Ystlwyf, raiding into Ceredigion in the 1240s and compelling the local Welsh rulers to submit to them and conclude marriage alliances with them; at the same time they were extending their authority in

DIAGRAM 6. The Descent of Major Marcher Families and their Lordships, 1150–1250 (to illustrate the impact of childlessness and partition between daughters on the Marcher aristocracy)

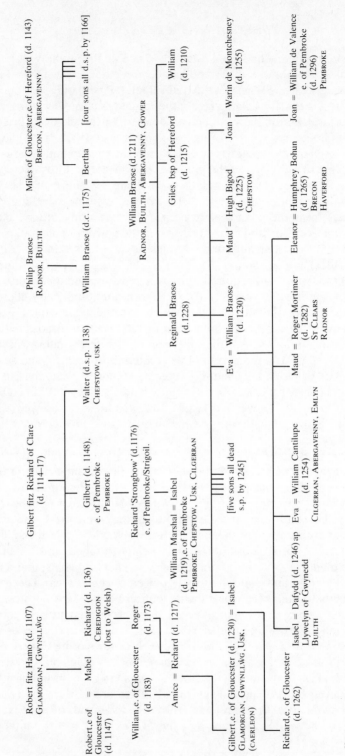

KEY

d. = died

d.s.p. = died without heirs of the body

e. = earl

the south-east, particularly at the expense of the native Welsh dynasty of Machen and Caerleon. The enterprise of the Marshals shows how far the initiative and forcefulness of a single family could shape the history of the March. Indeed, for a time in the 1230s, Gilbert Marshal (d. 1241) was in effect the ruler of most of the southern March: in addition to his own lordships he held Carmarthen and Cardigan of the king's gift and the custody of Glamorgan and the Braose estates in the central March. Yet, as so often, death and childlessness proved the undoing of the family: the five sons of William Marshal failed to produce an heir and when the last of them, Anselm, died in 1245 the Marshal lands were fragmented between five sisters, their husbands, and descendants. Thereby the momentum and coherence which had characterized the policy of the Marshals in the March for over half a century were lost.

One of the few families to escape the mortalities and misfortunes which befell the Braoses and Marshals and other Marcher dynasties was the Mortimer family. Its survival in the direct male line was, by medieval standards, remarkable: already established at Wigmore in the 1070s, it survived there until 1425. Furthermore, unlike so many other leading Marcher families, its major focus of interest lay clearly in the March: its main seat was at Wigmore, its most important estates in Herefordshire and Shropshire, and much of its ambition was directed towards the conquest of the neighbouring districts of Maelienydd and Gwrtheyrnion in Wales. The Mortimers were truly a family of war-hardened *marchiones*: it was as a firm suppressor of the rebellious Welsh that Roger Mortimer (d. 1214) was remembered, and likewise it was as 'a warlike and vigorous man . . . who had tamed the madness of the Welsh' that his son, Ralph (d. 1246), was commemorated by the family chronicler.[5] Periodic success, especially in the years 1195–1212 and 1240–60, attended their campaigns in the March; but they were constantly frustrated by the intractability of the terrain and by the succour given to the local Welsh by the rulers of Gwynedd. In the end their persistence was rewarded: the collapse of Llywelyn ap Gruffudd's principality in 1277 enabled the Mortimers to make good their claim to Maelienydd and Gwrtheyrnion, and two years later royal largess bestowed Ceri and Cedewain on them. It was indicative of the importance of this area of the middle March in the overall balance of power and military strategy in Wales that it was there, in December 1282, that Llywelyn ap Gruffudd was killed, possibly after having been inveigled into the area by the Mortimers. The place of his death has a certain appropriateness, for it was the Mortimers and their like who, through almost two centuries of persistent effort, had paved the way for the conquest of Wales. It is no surprise that when the family eventually attained comital status in 1328, Roger Mortimer should choose the title earl of March.

[5] *Monasticon Anglicanum*, VI, i, 349–50.

The history of the families of Braose, Marshal and Mortimer—and these families may stand as examples of Marcher dynasties generally—shows how far the development of different parts of the March was shaped by the ambitions, preoccupations, and fortunes of individual families. The March did not develop at a single tempo; innumerable balances of power were struck from one part of the March to the other and from one decade, sometimes even from one year, to the next. As such the history of the March is no more than the sum of the histories of its individual lordships. In particular the failure or decline of some of the leading Marcher families in the middle years of the thirteenth century (Braose 1230, earls of Chester 1237, Lacy of Weobley, Ludlow and Ewyas Lacy 1241, Marshal 1245, Fitz Baderon of Monmouth 1256, Clifford of Clifford and Cantrefselyf 1263), the introduction of new families through marriage (Clare 1217, Bohun 1230, Cantilupe 1230, Verdun 1241, Geneville 1241, Bigod 1245, Giffard 1263), and the growing prominence of Crown estates (Montgomery, lands of the earldom of Chester, Builth) were introducing major changes into the complexion of Marcher lordship. Yet, in spite of such diversity and change, certain distinctive common features make the period 1170–1277 one of key importance in the evolution of the March as a whole.

It was a period of military consolidation. The March had been created by war; its future could still be secured only by military vigilance. Warfare had indeed become a way of life for the men of the March: they accepted it not only as the means to pursue their ambitions against the Welsh but also as a way of solving their private quarrels and giving vent to communal tensions. They dated their deeds by reference to Welsh raids or to the siege of a castle; they accepted almost with resignation that their lordships might 'sometimes by fortune of war pass into Welsh hands';[6] as hardened frontiersmen, they had developed conventions for regulating and containing warfare—the display of banners, division of spoils, holding parleys, giving hostages, and arranging local truces and treaties. In such a society, the feudal obligations of castle-guard and service in the lord's army were still of practical and immediate significance: thus it was the leaders of the feudal community of Glamorgan who were required to garrison its castles when they came under Welsh attack in 1183–4, and likewise the army which Walter Marshal raised to raid Ceredigion in 1240 was commanded by the feudal vassals of his county of Pembroke. Those who were tired of war in the March were tired of life: so, for example, Thomas ap Madog transferred the manor of Kinnerley (Oswestry) to James Audley since 'he could not hold it peacefully against the Welsh because of his want of weight and power'.[7]

But the demands of war were changing, partly as military technology and

---

[6] *The Welsh Assize Roll 1277–84*, ed. J. Conway Davies, p. 291.
[7] *Calendar of Inquisitions Miscellaneous 1219–1307*, p. 322, no. 1059.

fortification changed and partly as Welsh resurgence posed a new threat to the March. What was now required, above all, was a strategy for defence rather than attack, to contain the Welsh threat and consolidate the hold of the Marchers on their lordships. So the thirteenth century—and particularly its second half—was a golden age of castle-building in the March. The achievement of the Marcher lords in this respect has been overshadowed by Edward I's later castle-building campaign in north Wales; but in its way the achievement of the Marchers was quite as impressive (if virtually undocumented) and important as that of Edward I. It represented a major investment of money, manpower, and architectural expertise in the defence of the March. Old castles—such as Chepstow, Usk, Whitecastle, Whittington, Caus, Laugharne, and Cilgerran (where in 1223 William Marshal 'began to build an ornate castle of mortar and stones")[8]—were refurbished and virtually rebuilt; and entirely new castles—like Caerffili, Morlais, and Llantrisant in Glamorgan or Cefnllys in Maelienydd—were commissioned. The greater Marcher families—especially the Marshals and the Clares—poured huge resources into the enterprise; but these were proportionately more than matched by the investment made by lesser families, such as the Cliffords of Bronllys, the Picards of Tretower, the Chaworths of Kidwelly, and the Camvilles of Llansteffan. The latest architectural innovations in military fortification were adopted—such as the cylindrical stone keep (an idea probably borrowed from northern France) at Pembroke, Skenfrith, Bronllys, and Tretower; the massive gatehouse as the focal point of the castle's defence, as at Kidwelly and Llansteffan; or the integrated quadrangular defence plan of flanking towers, curtain walls, and inner and outer wards, as at Caerffili (initially begun in 1268). The multiplicity of earthwork and timber castles of the twelfth century had been replaced by much fewer, but more strongly defended, stone castles, which could stand up to a prolonged siege—as Carmarthen did for three months in 1233. The Marchers may have been on the defensive in the thirteenth century but they had at least seen to it that their control of their lordships was firmly underpinned by military strength.

They also set about to consolidate their authority within their lordships. The heady days of rapid expansion at the point of the sword were over; what was now required was to convert a loose and tentative overlordship into a precise and profitable territorial control. Nowhere was the process more dramatic in its impact than in the great lordship of Glamorgan. The lordship had passed through marriage into the hands of the Clare family in 1217 and three members of that family—Earl Gilbert (d. 1230), Earl Richard (d. 1262), and Earl Gilbert 'the Red' (d. 1295)—transformed the nature of seignorial power in the lordship. They browbeat the Welsh rulers

---

[8] *Brut*, s.a. 1223 (p. 100).

of the upland commotes into submission, one by one, and brought their petty kingdoms under comital rule: Hywel ap Maredudd of Glynrhondda and Meisgyn was dispossessed in 1246; the rulers of Afan in effect submitted themselves to the earl's authority in the next year; and the process was completed in 1267, when the ruler of Senghennydd was arrested and imprisoned and a new castle built at Caerffili to proclaim the lord's domination of the area. The earls pursued a similar policy in the neighbouring lordships of Gwynllŵg and Caerleon: they took every opportunity to harass the native Welsh dynasty of the area and eventually, in 1270, they expelled it and brought its lands under their own direct control. Nor were the Welsh rulers the only target of the Clares' campaign: they extended the jurisdictional range of their county court at Cardiff so that its power encompassed the whole lordship; they exercised their powers as feudal lords over their mesne-tenants vigorously and ruthlessly, even confiscating the estates of one of their major vassals, Richard Siward of Llanfleiddan, in 1245; they bullied the major religious houses of their Marcher estates—Margam, Neath, and Llantarnam—to part with their lands so that the earl's territorial control of his lordship could be enhanced. The success of the Clare's policies can be measured in financial terms: Glamorgan was estimated as being worth £1,276 to its lord in 1317; £917 (i.e. 72 per cent) of that sum represented income from lands which had been brought under direct control since 1245. Important as was this striking increase in profitability, more important still was the transformation in lordship which had been effected. The success of the Clares may have been exceptional; but there is no reason to believe that their approach was at all unusual. Other Marcher lords, such as the Braoses, Marshals, and Mortimers, pursued broadly similar policies. They were, thereby, converting a tentative hegemony into a profitable lordship and laying the foundations of Marcher power and revenue for the rest of the Middle Ages.

The thirteenth century was important in another respect in the making of the medieval March, that of elaborating a pattern of governance and justice which was to survive until the sixteenth century. Lordship in the March had partaken for a long time of the character of military command, supplemented by the institutions and conventions of feudal honours. But as the authority of Marcher lords was consolidated and they came to exploit the resources of their lordships more systematically, so a more articulated and ambitious pattern of governance began to emerge. The infrastructure of that governance often remained thoroughly Welsh, based on Welsh units, such as the commote, Welsh officials, such as the *rhingyll* (sergeant), and Welsh dues and obligations; but in its higher echelons it came to be modelled on the practice of English seignorial estates and liberties and also on the pervasive example of English royal government. By the end of the thirteenth century, the greater lordships of the March (such as Glamorgan, Pembroke, Gower, Clun, and Brecon) were administratively and judicially kingdoms in miniature. Their administration was headed by a steward or sheriff, a receiver or treasurer, and a constable; a chancery (though not always so called) issued writs in the lord's name and under his seal, or that of his lordship; and local officials' accounts were audited at the exchequer by the lord's auditors. The lord's authority was imposed on his lordship above all through his courts. Here the lord's authority was untrammelled, for Marcher lords claimed and exercised exclusive jurisdictional rights within their lordships. All writs ran in the lord's name; it was against the lord's peace that offences were committed; and there was no appeal from his courts to the corrective jurisdiction of the king. It is in the thirteenth century, as far as we can see, that the Marcher lordships of Wales acquired a regular pattern of courts to dispense this exclusive jurisdiction in the lord's name and to collect its profits for his coffers. A whole host of courts—local and central, Welsh and English, manorial and burghal, forest and fair—brought the lord's judicial control to bear on his lordship. They drew increasingly on the concepts and practices of English common law and used them to weave the web of seignorial authority more closely around the population of the March. One episode may serve to illustrate this advance of judicial control and, thereby, of seignorial power in general in the March. In 1247 a writ of novel disseisin, issued in the name of Richard, earl of Gloucester, as lord of Glamorgan, initiated a land plea between Margam abbey and the local Welsh ruler of Afan in western Glamorgan; the case was eventually terminated in the county court of Cardiff by a final concord. Here are exemplified the ingredients whereby the judicial authority of the Marcher lords grew so markedly in the thirteenth century—submission to the lord's judicial authority, the acceptance of his court as the forum for judicial decisions, the use of his writ to initiate a plea, and the adoption of the devices of English common law, namely, possessory assizes and final concords.

The March, therefore, in the thirteenth century was rapidly acquiring the lineaments of regular civilian governance and jurisdiction. The character of that governance and its effectiveness varied from one lordship to the next; but regardless of these differences, the March was becoming less of a military frontier, more a collection of lordships where seignorial power enjoyed a measure of authority unsurpassed elsewhere in the king's dominions. The native Welsh of the March were no longer enemies to be conquered, but tenants to be governed and exploited. Hence it is that in the thirteenth century several of the lordships of the March began to be divided for administrative purposes into Welshries and Englishries. It was a division which formalized the distinction between native Welsh and settler English in terms of law, administration, land tenure, inheritance-customs, rents, and dues, and built that distinction into the very framework of Marcher governance.[9] It accepted the duality of Marcher society and made a virtue of that necessity. Paradoxically, the emergence of the Welshries was a tribute to the success of the Marcher lords in bringing their Welsh subjects within the ambit of their effective governance and control; to borrow contemporary Irish terminology, 'the land of war' was being converted into 'the land of peace'. The Marcher lords enhanced their control further within their lordships by forging links of patronage and service with the leaders of local Welsh society. This was by no means an entirely new departure; but it was pursued with renewed vigour in the thirteenth century. The Marshals forged ties of service and obligation with men such as Gwilym ap Gwrwared, the Bohuns with Einion Sais and his powerful kinsmen in Brecon, the Mortimers with Hywel ap Meurig and his sons in the middle March. Such ties yielded handsome dividends, for they began the slow but crucial process of channelling the loyalty of native Welshmen to the Marcher lords through the network of clientship and patronage within native Welsh society itself. Such loyalty was still fragile and could easily succumb to the attractions and threats of a resurgent Welsh principality; but it was some measure of the success of the Marcher lords in tapping the resources of their lordships, in men as well as in revenue, that over half of the foot-soldiers who served Edward I on his first campaign in Wales were themselves Welshmen, most of them from the March and frequently led by Welshmen who had been drawn into Marcher service in earlier generations.

The thirteenth century was, therefore, a crucial period in establishing the authority of the Marcher lords more firmly and effectively within their lordships. It was a process which was quite as important in the eventual domination and control of the country as was the initial military conquest. Just as the Edwardian Conquest of north Wales was followed by a comprehensive settlement to ensure the permanence of that conquest, so the Anglo-Norman conquest of the March was followed by a prolonged process of consolidation. It is only the time-scale of the two settlements which differs—the one being completed within two decades, the other extending over two centuries. Both processes are but two aspects of the Anglo-Norman subjugation of Wales.

By the thirteenth century the distinctiveness of the March within the dominions of the king of England was becoming ever more apparent. It was of Wales and yet it was no part of native Wales (*pura Wallia*); its lords were subjects of the king of England and held their lordships of him (albeit by the loosest and most nominal of feudal ties), yet it was no part of the institutional and legal structure of the kingdom of England. It was a land

---

[9] This division is explored below, pp. 419–25.

which lay between Wales and England, attached to each of them but separate from both. One of the badges of identity and individuality was its law, the law of the March (L. *lex Marchie*). The separate status of that law was announced for the first time in no less august a document than Magna Carta (1215). 'And if a dispute arises', so proclaims clause 56, 'it shall be settled . . . for tenements in England according to the law of England, for tenements in Wales according to the law of Wales, for tenements in the March according to the law of the March'. No attempt was made in Magna Carta, or in any subsequent document, to define the nature of the law of the March—other than in negative terms, as being different from the law of Wales and that of England. In fact there was no single corpus of Marcher law; it was, like the March itself, a loose assemblage, varying from one lordship to another and composed in unequal and changing proportions of native Welsh law, local custom, feudal conventions, and English common law. But however miscellaneous and ill-defined was the law of the March—or more correctly the laws and customs of the March—it had the virtue in a legalistic age of serving to identify the individuality of the March.

To English eyes one of the most astounding manifestations of that individuality was the absence of a single public authority to impose a measure of unity on the actions of the Marchers and to regulate the relations of the Marcher lordships with each other as well as with native Wales. In England, the making of war and the concluding of peace had come to be regarded as the exclusive prerogatives of the king; in the March, each lord claimed the right to wage war and to arrange peace of his own will. Such a claim was not based on a constitutional right or a royal grant; but rather on the conditions of a frontier, where lordship could only be won and retained by war. Such 'private' wars were not only fought against the Welsh but were also used as a means of settling disputes between the Marcher lords themselves, such as the bitter quarrels between the lords of Powys and Caus in the 1250s or between the men of Glamorgan and Brecon in the same period. Each Marcher lordship was, in effect, an almost autonomous unit. Under such conditions it was natural that a body of virtually 'international' conventions should emerge to regulate relationships between Marcher lordships and provide a recognized framework within which conflicts could be defused. Such indeed we find. 'Parliaments' were held, both within and between lordships, to discuss issues of tension (the first surviving written reference to such a parliament being in 1230); days of the March or love days were arranged, where officials and communities met to exchange criminals and stolen cattle; provisions were drawn up for settling boundary disputes; and formal treaties or agreements were concluded between Marcher lordships (such as that between Glamorgan and Brecon in 1245) or between Marcher lords and individual Welsh rulers (such as that between the earl of Chester and Llywelyn ab Iorwerth in 1218 or between Earl Richard of Gloucester, as lord of Glamorgan, and Hywel ap Maredudd in 1245). Such conventions had doubtless developed in the twelfth century and would become increasingly elaborate in the later Middle Ages; but it is in the thirteenth century that they began to be recorded and defended as part of the customs and liberties of the March.

The right to wage war and conclude peace was but the most astonishing of Marcher liberties. It is in the thirteenth century, also, that the other liberties of the March came fully into view and were self-consciously defended by its lords. In terms of civilian governance the most prominent of these liberties was the jurisdictional omnicompetence claimed by Marcher lords. 'He had a regality in the parts of Glamorgan', claimed the earl of Gloucester with considerable self-restraint in 1281, 'and he and his ancestors had always been accustomed to hear all pleas.'[10] It was a claim that was not effectively challenged during the Middle Ages (except in cases relating to advowsons or treason). The corollary of that claim—spelt out as early as 1199 by William Braose, the greatest Marcher lord of his day—was that no royal writ ran in the March, no royal sheriff or other officer had authority there, and no royal justices held their sessions there. It was a corollary reiterated frequently in the thirteenth century, as in John Fitzalan of Oswestry's defiant assertion that in the March he was obliged to do nothing at the king's command nor would he do so. To lawyers, especially to English lawyers attuned to royalist theories that the king was ultimately the source of all jurisdiction and that all liberties derived from him, such claims were breathtaking; they immediately set the March apart. Furthermore, they were supplemented by other liberties which the Marcher lords claimed—such as exclusive territorial lordship within their lands (other than over church estates); the right to treasure trove, wreck, mines, and royal fish; and exemption from royal taxation. Individual items were added to the list of Marcher liberties as occasion required and as challenges were met; but the simple truth was the Marcher lord claimed and exercised within his lordship virtually all the powers which the king exercised within his kingdom. They were, to borrow later phrases, 'lords royal' enjoying a 'royal lordship' with 'royal liberty'; or as an aggrieved Marcher vassal put it in 1247, the Marcher lord was 'virtually king and justiciar' (*quasi rex et justiciarius*) within his lordship.[11] No palatine earl or bishop in England claimed or dared exercise such a comprehensive assemblage of liberties, nor could the greatest franchise-holder in Anglo-Norman Ireland hope to aspire to the measure of immunity from royal administration, jurisdiction, and taxation enjoyed by the Marcher lords of Wales. The March was

---

[10] *Cartae et alia munimenta de Glamorgan*, ed. G. T. Clark, III, 811.
[11] *Cartae et alia munimenta de Glamorgan*, II, 554.

indeed unique in the position it occupied legally and jurisdictionally, administratively and fiscally, within the realms ruled by the king of England.

The assemblage of powers which were now designated 'the liberties of the March' had not been self-consciously assumed at any precise point in time; they had grown as Marcher lordship itself had grown. As the earl of Gloucester, as lord of Glamorgan, put it succinctly, if tartly, in 1281, he claimed his lands and liberties in the March by the conquest of his ancestors and of himself. Yet, as this assertion suggests, it was in the thirteenth century that the liberties of the March began to be defined and defended. The reasons are not far to seek. They lie in part in the development of civilian governance in the March and the need thereby to explain and itemize the powers now exercised by the Marcher lords. But, above all, Marcher liberties were defined in response to a growing royal challenge, particularly from the 1240s. As royal justice grew apace in England and exalted theories of the nature of royal jurisdiction and the dependent and derivative character of all other justice were propounded, so it was inevitable that the powers exercised by the lords of the March should come under scrutiny and challenge. Disputes between Marcher lords were referred to royal judgement; royal commissioners were occasionally dispatched to the March to report on how justice was dispensed; records of Marcher pleas (such as the dispute between the lord of Glamorgan and one of his leading tenants, Richard Siward) might be brought before royal courts for review; and the king asserted briskly and successfully, during the years 1241–7, his control of bishoprics in the March and his right to the custody of episcopal temporalities during vacancies. It may be doubted whether such claims and incidents amounted to a conscious challenge to Marcher privileges; but they were sufficiently menacing and provocative to call forth from the Marcher lords—in the 1240s as later in the 1280s and 1290s—a sustained defence and justification of their powers. That is why the thirteenth century is so important in the making of Marcher liberties.

The period from 1172 to 1277 was, therefore, of cardinal significance for the March of Wales—in the consolidation and definition of the authority of its lords, in laying the foundations of Marcher governance as it was to survive for the rest of the Middle Ages, in proclaiming the individuality of the March in terms of law and jurisdiction, and in the definition of the liberties of its lords. The March, from being a temporary military frontier, had now become, and come to be accepted as, a permanent feature of the landscape of authority and power in the dominions of the king of England. Within those dominions the status of the March was in every way anomalous—archaic in its militarism and feudal ethos, fragmented judicially and governmentally, distinctive in its laws, unique in its hybrid racial and social fabric, and extraordinary in the measure of immunity it enjoyed from the governance and jurisdiction of the king of England. The March had come into being as part of the process of the conquest of Wales; by the end of the thirteenth century it had largely outlived the original *raison* of its creation. It was now an anachronism, a survival from an age of conquest and of untrammelled seignorial enterprise. But anachronisms, once ensconced and bolstered by vested interests, acquire a resilience of their own. So it was with the March of Wales. It survived until the sixteenth century as a monument to the way that a part of Wales had been subjected to Anglo-Norman lordship between the days of William the Conqueror and Edward I.

CHAPTER 11

ROYAL POLICY IN WALES, 1172–1256

THE kings of England in the twelfth and early thirteenth centuries showed no more than a fitful interest in Wales and its affairs. They had taken no sustained part in the Anglo-Norman assault and subjection of the country, and by the later twelfth century their direct territorial stake in it was confined to an enclave around Carmarthen. For the most part their interest in Wales's affairs was essentially negative: in Gerald of Wales's words, 'to keep the country peaceful'[1] and thereby to prevent it from impeding them in the pursuit of more attractive and urgent ambitions elsewhere, in England and on the Continent. Within the overall ambit of those ambitions, Wales occupied a peripheral position. The kings were generally well-content with the acceptance of their claim to the overlordship of the country and that, preferably, at a minimum cost in effort, resources, and money on their part.

Yet, whether they liked it or not, Wales intruded itself onto the agenda of their activities and concerns. It did so whenever the ambitions and success of native Welsh rulers posed a threat to the security of the western frontier of England. So it was that the Crown kept a vigilant eye on that frontier (especially where, as in Powys and the middle March, there was no effective buffer zone between native Wales and lowland England), fortifying and refurbishing border castles, such as Chirk, Carreghwfa, Oswestry, and Caus, and building two impressive fortresses at Montgomery (1223) and Painscastle (1231) to guard the frontier. The Crown may have had no more than a minor territorial foothold in Wales; but the rights of the custody of estates during the minority of heirs and of escheat in the event of political forfeiture gave it a much more prominent role in the affairs of Wales and the March than such a foothold might suggest. Thus Henry II controlled the lordships of Pembroke and Gwent Iscoed (Chepstow and Usk) from 1176 (and possibly earlier) and added Glamorgan and Gwynllŵg to them from 1183; while later, King John, in respect of his custody of Glamorgan and Gower and his confiscation of the vast Braose estates in 1208, was much the most powerful figure in the March. Furthermore, Wales, and particulary that part of it which lay under Anglo-Norman rule, could not be insulated from the more general

---

[1] *Opera*, I, 57.

concerns of royal and baronial politics. The dominions of the Norman and Angevin kings ultimately formed a single arena of territorial ambition and political activity; Wales was part of those dominions. No king of England could safely ignore the activities of his barons there; equally, the tensions of English politics soon spilt over into the March and indeed into native Wales—as the crises of 1215–17, 1233–4, and 1263–5 were to demonstrate clearly enough. Even the claim of the English king to overlordship of the native Welsh kingdoms was not necessarily a recipe for political quiescence. Overlordship was a conveniently elastic relationship; it could mean as little or as much as the respective positions of suzerain and dependant suggested and warranted. It could be intensified as occasion and opportunity arose; its terms could be subtly but profoundly altered by closer definition. When that happened—as it did in Wales as elsewhere in Europe from the late twelfth century—the opportunities and pretexts for intervention grew apace.

Royal interest in Wales grew from the early thirteenth century onwards. It did so in part because the faltering momentum of Marcher advance made it clear that the Crown alone could contain and challenge the resurgence of native Welsh power. It did so also because the loss of his northern French lands allowed and indeed encouraged the king to turn his attention more regularly to Wales. The Welsh rulers for their part found themselves moving inexorably into the orbit of the king of England, drawn to him not merely or mainly by the formal ties of dependence but also by the magnetic quality which the patronage and protection of a powerful neighbour can offer. Relations with the king of England rather than with the Marcher lords came increasingly to dominate Welsh political life. What remained to be determined was whether or not a tolerable *modus vivendi* could be struck between overlordship of the Crown on the one hand and the assertiveness of the native principalities, especially Gwynedd, on the other.

Such a *modus vivendi* had been achieved in 1171–2. In those years Henry II had concluded a *détente* with the rulers of native Wales which was to remain largely intact for the rest of his reign. The Welsh princes, more especially Rhys ap Gruffudd of Deheubarth, were confirmed in the gains they had made since 1165; the Marcher lords were guaranteed against further major attacks by the Welsh; and both parties, in effect, acknowledged the king's own ultimate authority over Wales.[2] In 1175–7 Henry II sought to place that authority on a more formal basis. In a council at Gloucester in May 1175 he met a large delegation of Welsh princes under the leadership of the Lord Rhys and renewed his agreement with

[2] See above, pp. 53–5.

them; at the same council he briskly reminded the Marcher lords, especially the earl of Gloucester and William Braose, that they were required to support any royal action in Wales in the event of a Welsh attack. In 1177 he summoned the princes and magnates of Wales, including on this occasion those of north as of south Wales, to meet him at Geddington and subsequently at Oxford; he exacted oaths of fealty and promises to keep the peace from all of them; and in the case of the two most powerful princes, Dafydd of Gwynedd and the Lord Rhys of Deheubarth, he demanded a more solemn promise of liege homage in return for gifts of land—Ellesmere for the former and Meirionydd for the latter. The councils of 1175–7 represented a conscious attempt to stabilize the situation in Wales as a whole, by assembling Welsh princes and Marcher lords together at a single meeting rather than by striking individual bargains with them, exacting a common oath from them in the royal presence, and spelling out clearly and solemnly to them the character of their obligations. They were masterful demonstrations of royal supremacy.

The councils of 1175 and 1177 and the oaths exacted at them mark an important stage in the intensification and definition of royal overlordship in Wales. Henry II was intent on reconstructing and reasserting his authority in the wake of the revolt of 1173–4; he was also anxious to spell out the obligations of his overlordship in the outlying parts of the British Isles. In 1174 in the Treaty of Falaise he had specified his feudal suzerainty over the king of Scotland in no uncertain terms; in 1175 he defined the nature of his overlordship of native Ireland in the so-called Treaty of Windsor with the king of Connacht. The submissions of the Welsh rulers formed part of the same process. Yet the 'constitutional' significance of these submissions can easily be exaggerated; there was little that was new and less that was permanent about them. A mutual accord and understanding had developed between Henry II and the Welsh rulers since at least 1171–2; the submissions of 1177 did no more than reaffirm that relationship publicly and formally. The need to exact such submissions was in itself a comment on the fragility of the concordat. It was threatened, on the one hand, by the ambitions and actions of the Marcher lords, in particular by episodes such as the murder of the heir of the Welsh dynasty of Caerleon by the men of the earl of Gloucester in 1172, the massacre of Welshmen at Abergavenny by William Braose's agents in 1175, and the slaughter of Cadwallon ap Madog of Maelienydd by the young Roger Mortimer in 1179. It was threatened, on the other hand, by localized Welsh counter-raids, such as the assault on lowland Gwent in 1182 when the sheriff of Herefordshire was killed, or the serious revolt in western Glamorgan in 1183–4. Wales was too politically fragmented for a single unilateral agreement to stand much chance of being universally observed; war and violence were too much of a way life there to be eradicated by oaths and submissions.

Yet in spite of frequent breaches and imminent threats of collapse, the *détente* of 1171–2 survived until Henry II's death in 1189. It survived partly because Henry II had the power and determination to see that it was observed; it survived also because the Lord Rhys had sufficient strength to impose his will on the other native rulers of south Wales and the wisdom to come to terms with the king when the *détente* seemed on the verge of collapse; it survived also because it served the interest of both parties— allowing the Welsh princelings to consolidate their authority, while conceding to the king his overlordship and assuring him that Wales was, relatively, at peace. But an agreement built on personal trust stands little chance of outlasting the life-span of its main architect. The *détente* of 1171–2 quickly collapsed on Henry II's death. The new government of Richard I showed scant respect for the susceptibilities of the Lord Rhys or the etiquette which had governed relationships between the Welsh prince and Henry II. The Lord Rhys, for his part, felt himself discharged from any obligation to observe past pacts; during the remaining eight years of his life he and his sons led a series of raids on Anglo-Norman settlements in south-west and eastern Wales. The Marcher lords likewise resumed their aggressive ambitions; in particular, Roger Mortimer and William Braose once more seized the initiative in the middle March, unrestrained by royal warnings and disapproval. Now that the Crown had, consciously or otherwise, surrendered its neutral and restraining role in the conflict between Marcher lords and native princes, it soon found itself embroiled in Welsh affairs—succouring Welsh dissidents, sanctioning Marcher claims, and countering the resurgence of Welsh power. In 1196 Hubert Walter as justiciar laid siege to the castle of Welshpool and two years later it was Hubert's successor as justiciar, Geoffrey fitz Peter, who led the army which inflicted a crushing defeat on Welsh forces at Painscastle. The policy of *détente* now lay utterly in ruins. The Crown had resumed its earlier, partisan role in the affairs of Wales. Its actions in the 1190s were still essentially permissive and defensive; but sooner or later it would be drawn to take a more positive and aggressive role in Welsh affairs. That quickly became evident in John's reign.

The reign of King John was a formative period in Anglo-Welsh relations, as in so many other directions. Many of his initiatives and policies in Wales, as elsewhere, had eventually to be abandoned, or at least shelved, as political opposition mounted; and by his death in October 1216 the native Welsh had exploited his political difficulties to seize the initiative firmly from him. But during his reign all the major issues of Anglo-Welsh relations for the rest of the thirteenth century had been brought clearly into focus and he himself, in his campaigns of 1211–12, had laid the ground-plans of a military conquest and settlement of the country which it only remained for Edward I to copy and put fully into operation. Our view of the importance of the reign may, it is true, be exaggerated, due to the survival of English chancery rolls from 1199; it is possible, thereby, to study the nature of his policies in Wales in a depth and detail not possible for any previous king. But even when allowance is made for this documentary bias, the significance of John's reign in terms of Anglo-Welsh relations is not to be gainsaid.

John knew Wales and its problems better than any previous Norman or Angevin king of England. He had been lord of Glamorgan since 1189 in respect of his first wife, Isabella of Gloucester, and retained control of the lordship, though not the company of his wife, until 1215. He had used troops from Wales in his bid to oust his brother, Richard, in the early 1190s. Above all, his enforced residence in England after the loss of Normandy in 1204 allowed him to visit the western parts of his kingdom regularly and acquaint himself closely with its affairs. He came to Worcester or Gloucester, Hereford or Shrewsbury, every year from 1204 to 1209; in 1208 he visited the border twice; in 1209 he made two progresses along the border from Gloucester to Shrewsbury; he traversed the length of south Wales on his journey to Ireland and back in 1210; he led two campaigns into north Wales in 1211 and prepared another in 1212; he visited the Monmouth–Hereford district in November 1213 and returned there a year later. No earlier king was personally as intimately informed about the March of Wales and its problems.

His chancery records show that he was equally conversant, if not from direct personal knowledge, with the politics of native Wales. He enticed the native rulers with gifts and pensions; invited them to his court; requested them to attend him on his expeditions and provide troops for his campaigns in France; exploited the domestic squabbles of the Welsh dynasties, notably those of the house of Deheubarth, to his own maximum advantage (his earliest prize being also his greatest, when Maelgwn ap Rhys in December 1199 conceded Cardigan and the neighbouring district to him in return for his support and protection); succoured disaffected and disinherited segments of ruling families; and alternatively cajoled and threatened Welsh princelings and their servants, taking hostages from them one year, flattering them with a marriage alliance the next. In all this John was probably no more than continuing the policies of his predecessors; but his government records do at least reveal how alert and responsive the English government could be to the kaleidoscopic and fast-changing mutations of Welsh political life and how it could keep a sustained and informed interest in Welsh affairs.

In other directions John's policies are more clearly innovative. His reign marked an important stage in the advance of *jus scriptum*, the application of the written word to government, and, thereby, in the closer definition of the obligations of subjects and of the power of the Crown. During his rule the character of his overlordship of native Wales was intensified and its obligations spelt out specifically in written documents. Within a few months of his accession he had confirmed Gwenwynwyn of Powys in all his territories and in what he might win from the king's enemies. Such a confirmation was a political rather than a 'constitutional' move, calculated to win the support and friendship of an influential Welsh prince. Yet the confirmation of a native ruler's title to his patrimony could easily be the thin edge of a wedge, initiating the assertion of a more demanding suzerainty over him. So indeed Gwenwynwyn was to find out to his cost:in an agreement he was forced to conclude with John in 1208 he was required to promise to serve the king in perpetuity 'for himself and his land' (thereby acknowledging his territorial as well as his personal dependence) and be answerable in the king's court at the royal summons.[3] Gwenwynwyn's submission was extorted from him after the king had already broken him militarily; that of Llywelyn ab Iorwerth of Gwynedd, in July 1201, was concluded while his relations with the king were still cordial. Its terms are, therefore, all the more significant, particularly since it is the earliest surviving written agreement between an English monarch and a Welsh ruler. Its tone is indeed friendly; but its definition of the obligations of dependence has an ominous ring to it. Llywelyn was to swear fealty and to do homage to the king as liege lord; more significantly, Llywelyn's greater subjects (L. *maiores*) are also to swear fealty to the king. The king's overlordship is penetrating, as it were, into the political texture of the Welsh principalities; it is to run concurrently with the fealty that Llywelyn's greater subjects owe to the prince himself. Thereby is identified one of the key issues in Anglo-Welsh relations in the thirteenth century: the question of whether or not the fealty and homage of 'the barons' and 'nobles' of native Wales should be reserved to, or at least shared with, the king of England. It was a struggle about power and overlordship dressed up in feudal formulae. The agreement of 1201 also identified the other key issue in Anglo-Welsh relations for the remainder of the pre-Conquest period, that of the jurisdictional content of overlordship. John conceded that cases relating to lands claimed by Llywelyn might be heard by Welsh or by English law, thereby acknowledging for the first time the formal status of Welsh law. But more significant for the future were the provisions that the king might in certain cases send commissioners to hear a case in Llywelyn's land and that other cases might also be referred to the king by Llywelyn. In this single agreement King John and his advisers had indicated clearly how the powers of overlordship might be intensified; they had brought together

---

[3] *Foedera*, I, i, 101.

all the elements from which the final conflict between the English monarchy and the rulers of native Wales would be manufactured.

The ultimate weapon in the armoury of overlordship was that of a military campaign against a recalcitrant vassal. John used it to devastating effect to demonstrate that the native Welsh kingdoms had little chance of withstanding the military might of the English state. John's primary ambition after 1204 was the recovery of his lands in northern France; but, in order to realize it, he had to exploit the resources of his kingdom ruthlessly and ensure that there was no political disaffection within his dominions in Britain which might divert him from his purpose. That involved imposing his authority firmly on Scotland, Ireland, and Wales, as well as on England. In 1209 at Norham he had imposed on the king of Scotland demeaning terms, which were to be confirmed in 1212; in 1210 he led an expedition to Ireland and imposed his will on Anglo-Norman barons and Irish chiefs alike. In 1211 it was the turn of native Wales to experience his wrath and might. Relations between him and his son-in-law, Llywelyn ab Iorwerth of Gwynedd, had been fraught more than once; but on each occasion they had been repaired before a final breach occurred. Not so in 1211: in that year John led two expeditions into Gwynedd, the first royal expeditions into Wales since that of Henry II in 1165. The first, in May, succumbed to the problems of inadequate provisions and the wily retreat of the enemy, which had so often beset royal expeditions into Wales. The second, some two months later, was devastatingly successful. John showed his political skill by detaching almost all native Welsh rulers from Llywelyn; he matched it by his military thoroughness—commandeering supplies from as far afield as Durham, penetrating deep into Gwynedd, sending a patrol to burn Bangor, and 'building many castles in Gwynedd' to consolidate his victory. That victory was complete. Llywelyn's wife was sent to plead for peace 'on whatsoever terms she could'; the whole of Gwynedd east of Conwy was surrendered to the king 'for ever' and so was any claim to the commote of Edeirnion; a huge tribute in cattle and horses was exacted; hostages (including Llywelyn's illegitimate son) demanded; and the king was granted the allegiances of such of Llywelyn's subjects as he wished to have. Llywelyn was also forced to concede that, should he die without a legitimate heir by his wife Joan, all his lands would revert to the king.[4] In south Wales Llywelyn's allies lost the district between the rivers Dyfi and Aeron, and the king's officers proceeded to build a castle at Aberystwyth to control the area. By the end of 1211 John held a much stronger position in Wales than any king of England previously; in addition to the lands he had conquered from the Welsh he also controlled the

---

[4] *Brut (RBH)*, *s.a.* 1211 (pp. 191–3). Our knowledge of the terms imposed by John on Llywelyn in 1211 has been transformed by J. B. Smith, 'Magna Carta and the Charters of the Welsh Princes', *English Historical Review*, 99 (1984), 344–62.

lordships of Glamorgan and Gwynllŵg and the whole of the vast Braose estates, and had installed his garrisons in the castles of southern Powys. His henchmen now held the key positions in Wales—Fawkes de Breauté at Cardiff and Brecon, Engelard de Cigogné in Builth and the other Braose lordships, Gerard d'Athée as 'our bailiff in the parts of Wales', and Robert Vieuxpont in Powys—while royal lieutenants were appointed with authority throughout 'our March of Wales'. 'There was no one', said the Barnwell chronicle, 'who did not obey his nod'.[5] When the Welsh, terrified into unwonted unity by the thoroughness and comprehensiveness of John's supremacy, sought to challenge him, he initiated the preparations for a military expedition such as Wales had never seen. Troops were raised in Scotland, Ireland, and Flanders; the feudal host was summoned out in full strength; and a massive force of more than eight thousand craftsmen and labourers from all parts of England were ordered to be at the ready for building the fortresses which were to convert the military conquest into a permanent settlement. The preparations bear the authentic touch of a later hand, that of Edward I.

John had shown that the English monarchy had assembled the theoretical pretext and the military means to convert overlordship of Wales into direct lordship should it so wish. Whether John wished it in 1212 may be uncertain (though his remarkable preparations and the pitiless vengeance he wreaked on his Welsh hostages are some measure of the seriousness of his purpose). What is beyond doubt is that in mid-August 1212 he suddenly called off the expedition, almost certainly in response to rumours of a plot against his life. John now began to be overwhelmed by the political enmities and suspicions which had accumulated during his reign and these in turn were compounded by the crushing defeat of his allies at Bouvines in July 1214. The grant of Magna Carta in June 1215 provided a temporary respite in the political turmoil; but, within a few months, civil war was resumed in England and was not to be terminated until well after John's death, by the Treaty of Kingston in June 1217. Such a protracted period of political discord provided an ideal opportunity for the Welsh to win back the ground they had lost during John's reign. They did not let the opportunity pass. They displayed an uncharacteristic measure of unity among themselves and stood steadfast against John's blandishments and threats. What is more they learnt how to exploit the atmosphere of distrust and the collapse of political loyalties which John's high-handed actions in the March—notably his proscription of the mighty Braose family, his hounding of Fulk fitz Warin, and his destruction of Robert fitz Richard of Haverford—had generated among the Anglo-Norman families in Wales. It was a measure of John's political ineptitude

---

[5] *Foedera*, I, i, 107; *Rotuli Litterarum Patentium*, I, i (Record Commission, 1835), 88, 109; *Memoriale Fratri Walteri de Coventria*, ed. W. Stubbs (Rolls Series, 1972-3), II, 203.

that he had driven the leaders of native Welsh society and some major Marcher families into each other's arms. By 1213 the Welsh had more than recovered all the lands they had lost to the king; by 1215 they secured concessions in Magna Carta granting them the return of any lands or liberties of which they had been unjustly deprived (clauses 56–7) and restoring to them all hostages (including Llywelyn ab Iorwerth's son, Gruffudd) and security-charters (notably the one conceded by Llywelyn ab Iorwerth in August 1211) extorted from them (clause 58); by 1217 they had made even further gains, winning control of the key royal centres of Cardigan and Carmarthen and demonstrating through their raids that virtually no part of Wales, except the south-east, lay outside the reach of their military arm.[6] Eventually, in March 1218, peace was concluded. Llywelyn ab Iorwerth, as the leader of native Wales, accepted the overlordship of the king and promised to persuade the other magnates of Wales to do likewise; the king's advisers in return conceded most, though not all, of the gains that Llywelyn and his allies had made since 1212. A new *détente* in effect had been struck and the issues which had been sharply, if prematurely, brought into focus in John's reign were allowed to rest. John's political insensitivity and miscalculations had proved his undoing in Wales as elsewhere; he had forced the pace without calculating the costs or the consequences. But his policies had initiated a permanent change in the attitude of the English crown towards native Wales and had identified the issues which were to remain on the agenda of royal policy until 1282–3. His successors recognized as much: when the royal offensive was fully resumed in Wales in 1240 its avowed purpose was to restore the state of affairs which had prevailed in John's reign.

The years 1218–40 may readily be characterized as a period of relative quiescence in the relations between the king of England and the rulers of native Wales. The government of Henry III was too busy reasserting its authority in the country, coping with domestic tensions, and attending to affairs in Brittany and Poitou, to give much attention to Wales, unless and until it was goaded into doing so. Several of the Marcher lords—notably William Marshal and Hugh Mortimer—resented the losses they had suffered at the hands of the Welsh and complained bitterly at Llywelyn's prevarications and evasions; but as a group they were too weak to challenge him and were further enfeebled by recurrent minorities and mortalities in their ranks (the earls of Gloucester and Pembroke and William Braose all died within a few months of each other in 1230–1). Llywelyn for his part was not spoiling for a fight. He was, it is true, willing to seize on any opportunity to reinforce and extend his authority; but his

[6] See above, pp. 241–3.

prime ambition was to preserve the highly favourable settlement he had secured in 1218. He was a shrewd diplomat and knew that the best guarantee of attaining his ambition was to cultivate the goodwill and friendship of the crown, lubricate the channels of diplomacy, curb the ambitions of his client princes (as he did in 1220 by compelling Rhys Gryg to surrender four commotes in south Wales to the king and to their Anglo-Norman claimants), pay tactful social visits to the king's court, protest his loyalty, and secure the king's sanction for the arrangements he made for the succession of Dafydd to the principality of Gwynedd. King and prince had carefully sized up each other and their respective priorities, and had worked out a *modus vivendi*, which survived largely intact until 1240.

Such a *modus vivendi* was bound to come under strain from time to time, if only because Llywelyn felt the need to flex the muscles of his power periodically and to counter any threat, or imagined threat, to his position. Three royal campaigns were launched against Wales in these years (in 1223, 1228, 1231); none of them lasted more than a few weeks, or penetrated more than a few miles into Wales; and not one effected, or was calculated to effect, a major change in the territorial settlement of 1218. Much the most important of these skirmishes was the first. Significantly, the attack on Llywelyn in 1223 was initiated by the earl of Pembroke, not by the Crown; it was only belatedly and very briefly—the royal campaign from Hereford to Montgomery lasted less than three weeks—that the royal forces were engaged. Yet the overall results of the campaign were important and tilted the balance of power in Wales a little away from Llywelyn. He lost control of the south-west and especially of the key castles of Carmarthen and Cardigan, while in the north-east the Crown secured an important foothold at Montgomery. The second campaign of 1228 was a fiasco: its memento was the ruins of a castle, referred to mockingly as Hubert's Folly, which Hubert de Burgh had to abandon when his attempt to annex Ceri to the castle of Montgomery failed. It was Hubert de Burgh's ambitions, and in particular the remarkable assemblage of lands he had accumulated for himself in Wales, which probably lay at the root of the third campaign in 1231. Llywelyn, ever nervous of a potential threat to his hard-won gains, launched a massive foray through the length and breadth of Wales. The royal response was cautious to the point of inaction: a royal army sat at Painscastle for almost two months witnessing, as a contemporary chronicler sourly observed, the erection of one new castle while Llywelyn destroyed ten others. Only once more were royal forces to be engaged in Wales in the 1230s, in 1233–4 in an attempt to scotch the revolt of Earl Richard of Pembroke—a revolt which Llywelyn exploited skilfully for his own purposes—rather than to confront the Welsh.

The royal campaigns in Wales in the 1220s and 1230s had attempted little and achieved less; the initiative lay firmly with Llywelyn. Yet uneventful as these years were, they are not without significance in laying the foundations for increased royal involvement in Wales. The Crown had acquired or reacquired important footholds in Wales from which its authority could grow when the time was opportune: Carmarthen and Cardigan were recovered in 1223 and, though granted to the Marshal earls of Pembroke or Hubert de Burgh, were to be of vital significance in the assertion of royal authority in Deheubarth; the annexation of Montgomery in 1223 and the building of a castle there were to provide a vital bridgehead for royal penetration of north and central Wales, for as it was to be proudly, if extravagantly, claimed in the fourteenth century, 'the greater part of Wales was conquered from the lordship of Montgomery'; the reacquisition of the Three Castles (Whitecastle, Skenfrith, and Grosmont) on Hubert de Burgh's downfall in 1232 provided a base in the south-east; while, perhaps most significant of all, the annexation of the county of Chester in 1237 gave the Crown a direct base from which to confront the power of Gwynedd. Nor was the Crown's military achievement in these years as negative as it appears at first sight. The armies that were led into Wales were large ones by contemporary standards and the role that the household knights played in them—there were perhaps as many as 120 of them in the 1228 force—was a measure of the growing importance of the military hosuehold in the royal armies of the thirteenth century. The two castles that the Crown caused to be built on the frontiers of Wales— Montgomery (which has one of the earliest twin-tower gatehouses in the country) and Painscastle—were important additions to the stock of masonry castles in the country and an indication of the fashion in which the subjugation of the country might eventually be achieved.

Above all, perhaps, the Crown lost no opportunity to assert its overlordship of Wales and to exact from the Welsh princelings public acknowledgement of their dependence. In 1218 not only Llywelyn ab Iorwerth but the other lesser princes of north and south Wales also travelled to Woodstock and Worcester to do homage to the young king, thereby conceding that, however powerful Llywelyn's position might be within native Wales, their loyalty was ultimately due directly to the king himself. The point was reaffirmed even at the nadir of royal fortunes in 1228, when all the princes and magnates of Wales who were present at Montgomery did homage once more to the king. Dependence implied a measure of control and on occasion the king showed what avenues such control might eventually open for him—sorting out disputes among the Welsh princes at Shrewsbury in 1221 and confirming the arrangements that the prince of Gwynedd was making for the succession to his principality. The time was not yet opportune to explore these avenues fully; but the fact that the royal government had already identified the issues and the means whereby it might intensify its overlordship in native Wales became abundantly clear in a series of letters it dispatched from Tewkesbury in March 1238. The letters forbade the rulers of native Wales and those who held of English magnates in the March of Wales from responding to Llywelyn ab Iorwerth's request that they swear homage to Dafydd his son as his prospective heir; their homages, so they were firmly reminded, were owed, either directly or indirectly, to the king, not to the prince of Gwynedd. The supremacy which Llywelyn had in effect exercised since 1218 was being called in question; the English government was preparing for an offensive in Wales. It put that offensive into operation immediately on hearing reports of Llywelyn's death in April 1240.

The years 1240–56 witnessed a remarkable and sustained advance in royal power in Wales, such as the country had not witnessed since the reign of Henry I. The scale of royal achievement in these years has frequently been underestimated—partly because of the extensive retreat in royal power in Wales after 1256 and partly because the thirteenth century is regarded as an unbroken period of resurgence of native Welsh authority under the leadership of Gwynedd. Yet during these years, and particularly during the period 1240–7, the groundwork was laid for the final royal domination of Wales. Henry III now resumed where his father had left off in 1212, and Edward I in turn would do little more than borrow leaves from the book of precedents—in the theory and practice of power—which his father had compiled in Wales in the 1240s and 1250s.

The change in fortunes was evident within a few weeks of the death of Llywelyn ab Iorwerth on 11 April 1240. Dafydd, his son and heir, found his position immediately undermined by power-struggles within Gwynedd itself, focusing on his half-brother, Gruffudd, and by the rapid defection of client Welsh rulers hitherto held on a tight rein by his father. Dafydd's meeting with Henry III at Gloucester on 15 May 1240 was an exercise in humiliation. The former, it is true, was knighted and wore a coronet (*talaith*) as a symbol of his claim to princely status; but the terms of the agreement proclaimed loudly enough that the king had seized the initiative. Dafydd was not accorded the title of prince, but was slightingly referred to as 'the son of Llywelyn sometime prince of North Wales'; he did homage for 'his right to North Wales' (L. *pro jure suo Norwallie*), with the implication that his territorial as well as his personal status was dependent on the king; he quitclaimed to the king and his heirs 'all the homages of the barons of Wales', and acquiesced in a reference to Gruffudd ap Gwenwynwyn and others as 'barons of the lord king'; he agreed that all territorial claims against him should be referred to a joint commission of arbitrators.[7] On all the issues over which Llywelyn had

---

[7] *Litt. Wallie*, pp. 5–6.

prevaricated for more than twenty years, Dafydd had virtually surrendered within a month. Others soon pounced to exploit his weakness, without waiting for the niceties of arbitration. The leading Marcher lords went on the offensive: the Marshal brothers recovered and refortified Cardigan, reduced the local Welsh ruler, Maelgwn Fychan, to submission, and imposed a marriage-settlement on him; Ralph Mortimer resumed his family's campaign to impose its authority on Maelienydd and Gwrtheyrnion; meanwhile the Clare and Bohun families began to wrench back the superiority in upland Glamorgan and Brecon which Llywelyn ab Iorwerth's power had hitherto denied to them. The Crown for its part conducted a highly successful campaign to undermine Gwynedd's superiority over native Wales—enticing some of the local rulers with rewards and promises, threatening some, cajoling others, and posing as upholder of Welsh custom and the defender of the claims of every disinherited and disaffected Welsh dynastic pretender—most notably Gruffudd, Dafydd's half-brother.

So thoroughly had Dafydd's authority as leader drained away from him, and so completely had he been isolated politically in Wales, that it needed only a week-long royal campaign—launched from the new royal base at Chester—in August 1241 to extract the most abject submission from him in two agreements, that of Gwerneigron (29 August 1241) supplemented by even more humiliating terms at London (24 October 1241). The Crown built on the concessions extracted from him at Gloucester in May 1240: Gruffudd and his son, Owain, were released from Dafydd's prison and handed over to the king; Dafydd had to concede that Gruffudd's claim to a share of the principality of Gwynedd would be heard and decided in the royal court, and that, in the event of a partition being made between them, both were to hold their lands directly of the king; all lands seized since the later years of King John were to be restored, thereby forfeiting all the gains made by Llywelyn ab Iorwerth since 1215; Tegeingl or Englefield, the *cantref* of north-east Wales from the Clwyd to the Dee estuary, was surrendered to the king and his heirs 'for ever'; and the prince's claims to Ellesmere and Mold were also abandoned; a forward post for further royal attack was established by the cession to Henry of Degannwy on the Conwy estuary; the surrender of the homages 'of all noble Welshmen' was reiterated; and at much the same time Gwynedd was truncated when the king installed cadets of the native dynasty (the sons of Maredudd ap Cynan) in Meirionydd. Dafydd's humiliation was completed by two menacing supplementary instruments: the one promised that he and his heirs would be faithful for ever to the king and his heirs and that in the event of a breach of this oath of fealty, his land would be forfeited to the king in perpetuity; the other acknowledged that if Dafydd died without a legitimate heir of his body the king would succeed to his principality in perpetuity.

Gwynedd had been comprehensively humiliated; any lands and dignity which its prince salvaged from the débâcle were themselves owed to royal grace and favour. Nor did this represent the whole of the royal achievement in 1240–1. Royal protégés were installed in southern Powys and in Meirionydd; Cardigan and Carmarthen and the lands appurtenant to them were resumed into royal possession; Builth was taken into royal custody; the local rulers of Gwrtheyrnion and Maelienydd submitted themselves to the king; the quarrelsome princelings of Deheubarth did not dare to challenge royal suzerainty; and Dafydd himself could be kept on the straight and narrow by the knowledge that his half-brother, Gruffudd, was in royal custody and that Gruffudd's claim to Gwynedd could be reactivated and supported by the Crown whenever this suited it. Marcher lords and Welsh clients had played an important part in the *bouleversement* of 1240–1; but it was essentially a royal victory and it was the king's authority and power, above all, which had been enhanced throughout Wales.

During the next three years the Crown pursued a vigorous policy throughout the lands it had acquired in Wales—building and fortifying castles, raising troops, instituting inquiries into royal rights, and establishing wide-ranging judicial commissions. Such vigorous policies were seen as 'unrighteous oppression' by the Welsh;[8] and in 1244—as earlier in 1164 and 1212—the experience of alien governance forged a remarkable measure of unity among the native rulers. Under the leadership of Dafydd, who was allegedly outraged by the report of the death of his brother in an attempt to escape from the Tower of London, a revolt swept throughout Wales in 1244–5 recovering much of the land lost in 1240–1 (including Mold) and threatening royal and baronial castles, such as Diserth. The royal response was slow but eventually effective. A large army was dispatched from Chester under the king's command in August 1245; provisions and troops were summoned from Ireland and an impressive royal fortress was built in the forward position of Degannwy; in the summer of 1246 Nicholas de Molis, an experienced household knight and former steward of Gascony and now steward of Carmarthen and Cardigan, led a dramatic expedition through the heart of upland Wales from Carmarthen to Degannwy, showing how a pincer movement might be launched from the newly acquired royal outposts in Wales and also demonstrating, with the help of his Welsh allies, that the Welsh terrain was not the impregnable obstacle which it had so often been proclaimed to be. The Welsh suffered a devastating blow to their morale when Dafydd died on 25 February 1246; but it was the lack of supplies, famine, and the effects of a trade embargo which ultimately proved most debilitating. One by one, during the course

[8] *Brut, s.a.* 1243.

of 1246, the princelings of south and mid-Wales defected to the royal cause in the face of an apparently unassailable royal superiority. By the spring of 1247 the two young heirs to Gwynedd, Owain and Llywelyn ap Gruffudd (the sons of Llywelyn ab Iorwerth's illegitimate son, Gruffudd), saw no alternative but submission.

The Treaty of Woodstock of 30 April 1247 set the seal on the remarkable royal advance in Wales since May 1240. The whole of Perfeddwlad was now quitclaimed to the king of England. Thereby the Crown recovered the position it had held in north Wales for a few brief months in 1211 and Gwynedd's vulnerability was cruelly exposed. Even Gwynedd above Conwy was henceforth specifically to be held by a royal grant (*rex . . . concessit*) and, for the first time in its history, in return for specified military service. The king once more reasserted his exclusive claim to 'the homages and services of all the barons and nobles of Wales', thereby both scotching any claim on Gwynedd's part to the overlordship of native Wales and firmly indicating by the use of the terms 'barons' and 'nobles' that the status of the leaders of Welsh society was being assimilated ever more closely to that of ordinary feudal tenants of the Crown in England. Owain and Llywelyn for their part were brought more firmly within the vice of jurisdictional suzerainty—the instrument *par excellence* for the intensification of feudal overlordship throughout thirteenth-century Europe—by agreeing to appear before the king or his officials at their summons in any territorial disputes. Henry III could claim that he had shown magnanimity in victory: he had not invoked the escheat agreement which he had extracted from Dafydd in 1241 nor had he acted on his legal title to confiscate Gwynedd for a vassal's breach of his sworn fealty (a right which was again specifically spelt out for Owain and Llywelyn's instruction in 1247). Yet in every other respect Henry III's victory in 1246–7 was more thorough and comprehensive —for it extended to every part of native Wales, not merely to Gwynedd— than that achieved by any earlier king of England in Wales.

What, then, had the Crown achieved in Wales in 1240–7 and how had it been achieved? In the first place its territorial stake in the country had been dramatically augmented. In 1237 royal power in Wales was confined to the peripheries—specifically to Montgomery in the north-east and Three Castles in the south-east. By 1247 the king was easily the most powerful territorial figure in Wales and the March: he held the county of Chester and the four *cantrefi* of Rhos, Rhufoniog, Dyffryn Clwyd, and Tegeingl in north Wales; he annexed the lordship of Builth in 1241, in spite of the superior claim to it of Isabella Braose and her husband, Dafydd of Gwynedd; he resumed control of Carmarthen and Cardigan and their appurtenant honors in the same year and secured a foothold further north for himself at Llanbadarn. Furthermore, there was every intention that these territorial annexations should be permanent: in 1247 it was decreed that the king was to retain 'in his hands as always appurtenant to his crown the county of Chester with the castles of Diserth and Degannwy'[9] and Perfeddwlad was henceforth financially and administratively amalgamated to the county of Chester; the process was completed in 1254 when, on the creation of an apanage for the Lord Edward, he was granted all the lands then held by the king in Wales, with the proviso that they 'should never be separated from the Crown but should remain entirely to the kings of England for ever'.[10] So were the Crown's conquests and acquisitions in Wales legally and formally incorporated into its demesne. The Crown's commitment to its newly secured position in Wales was vividly manifested in the massive military investment it made in the country: two impressive stone castles of great strength, built to the latest design, were constructed in the 1240s and 1250s at Diserth (to replace the earlier castle at Rhuddlan) and Degannwy (at a cost of at least £10,000); and major rebuilding was undertaken at other royal castles in Wales—especially Montgomery, Builth, Cardigan, and Carmarthen. Military might was to be underpinned by civilian settlements: burgages were offered to those who wished to settle at Diserth; Degannwy was created into a free borough; town walls were built to protect the well-established community at Cardigan; trade was encouraged; and fairs and markets were established. The Crown, in short, was proceeding to place its acquisitions in Wales on a permanent and profitable footing.

The dramatic advance in the Crown's standing was not confined to its territorial gains. Equally significant was the much closer definition of the character of its suzerainty over the country. Welsh princes had long since accepted that they owed homage to the king of England; but the character and consequences of that homage were now spelt out much more precisely. The Crown insisted, as against the prince of Gwynedd or any aspiring Marcher empire-builder, such as the earl of Pembroke in 1240–1, that it had an exclusive right to the homages of all Welsh rulers and nobles; it began to exact formal written acknowledgements of fealty and homage, reinforced by dire ecclesiastical and secular sanctions, from leading Welshmen throughout Wales; it claimed that homage implied territorial as well as personal dependence—reminding Dafydd that he held his share of Gwynedd 'in chief' (in capite) in 1241 and likewise 'granting' Owain and Llywelyn 'the rest of the whole of North Wales' in 1247 for specified services. Most importantly, the obligations of homage were now specified in writing. The vassal was a dependant: he could be required (as Dafydd was in 1241) to receive and to execute the king's commands and to promise not to receive outlaws from royal or Marcher lands (a right which Llywelyn ab Iorwerth had specifically claimed as his in 1224); he might be asked, as

[9] Calendar of Patent Rolls 1232–47, p. 501.   [10] Foedera, I, i, 297.

the rulers of Gwynedd and Powys Fadog were in 1242, to help the king's foreign expeditions with troops and subsidies; most ominously, in 1247, for the first time in the history of the Welsh principalities, a specific military quota was imposed on Gwynedd, namely, a thousand footmen and twenty-four well-armed horsemen to serve at the prince's cost in Wales and the March, and a smaller contingent at the king's cost in England.[11] With each step the position of the princelings of Wales was being assimilated to that of the king's feudal tenants in England; it was no surprise that the prince of Gwynedd—whose title was, indeed, not acknowledged by the English government—should find his name on a list of the king's tenants-in-chief in 1242 or referred to as one of 'our magnates of Wales'.[12]

Ultimately, the most insidious of the suzerain's claims was that to judicial superiority over his vassal. It could be used—as the king of Scotland found to his cost at the hands of the king of England, and the king of England, as duke of Aquitaine, at the hands of the king of France—to undermine the vassal's authority and as the most convenient and elastic of pretexts to interefere in the affairs of his dominions. The rulers of Gwynedd were now compelled to admit that they were answerable in the king's court in cases relating to the inheritance and division of their own lands—Dafydd, for example, received a safe-conduct to come 'to receive justice in the king's court' in 1241 and four justices were appointed to hear the disputes between Llywelyn ap Gruffudd and his brothers in 1255.[13] The judicial tentacles of the king of England were embracing other native rulers of Wales equally firmly: it was in the king's court that disputes within the dynasties of Powys Fadog and Deheubarth or quarrels between the lords of northern and southern Powys were heard in 1247–8, while at the same time Rhys Fychan of Dinefwr declared his willingness to stand to justice in the king's court at Carmarthen. Judicial superiority, in its own way, could be quite as effective as military force as a method of intensifying the king's authority in Wales. The Welsh rulers were aware that their independence was being drained away from them. Hence their remarkably united front in 1244; hence also David's attempt in that year to persuade the Pope to assume the overlordship of Gwynedd in return for an annual tribute; hence also the dispatch of messengers to Paris, doubtless to seek to renew the Franco-Welsh alliance; hence also his defiant, if rather incongruous, assumption, of the title 'prince of Wales'.[14]

The native rulers were the key targets of the royal offensive in the 1240s;

[11] There had been an earlier attempt to impose an annual service and a military obligation in King John's abortive agreement of October 1212 with two claimants to Gwynedd, Owain ap Dafydd and Gruffudd ap Rhodri.

[12] *Close Rolls 1256–9*, p. 107.

[13] *Cal. Patent Rolls 1232–47*, p. 252; *1247–58*, pp. 362, 432; *Close Rolls 1253–4*, p. 110.

[14] Dafydd's use of this title is recorded in two documents, the one an original letter, the other a later copy: *Cal. Anc. Corr.*, pp. 49–50; British Library Additional MS. 4558, f. 256.

but Henry III was also anxious to extend his mastery over the whole of Wales, the March included. His opportunities to do so were enhanced by the failure of the families of Lacy (1241) and Marshal (1245) in the direct male line, by his continuing custody of some of the Clare and Braose estates in the March, and by his own recently acquired territorial footholds in north and south Wales. The 1240s were certainly a formative period in the assertion or reassertion of ultimate royal control of the March. Between 1241 and 1247 the Crown successfully laid claim to the control of bishoprics and the custody of temporalities and collation to benefices during episcopal vacancies in the March. At much the same period it began to develop a machinery for exercising ultimate judicial supervision over the Marcher lordships—appointing commissioners to settle disputes between Marcher lords (such as that between John of Monmouth and William Cantilupe of Abergavenny in 1248), calling for the record of judgements in Marcher courts to be reviewed by royal justices (as in Glamorgan in 1247 and Blaenllyfni in 1254), and dispatching royal commissioners to hear how justice was dispensed in the seignorial court at Abergavenny. Henry III was making it clear that his judicial authority overrode even Marcher franchise. In much the same fashion, in August 1245, he issued an edict that during a royal campaign in Wales the Marcher lords were expected to support royal policy by waging war on the Welsh, thereby demonstrating once more that the Marcher customs of private war and private truces were subordinate to royal command. Royal initiative was evident in other directions: in the establishment of a far-reaching inquiry into royal rights in the honour of Carmarthen, an insistence on the jurisdictional supremacy of the county courts in south-west Wales, and the appointment of justices with authority to hear pleas 'for all persons of the March and of Wales' and of an officer with the grand title of 'justiciar of the lord king in South Wales'.[15]

By 1247 the Crown had achieved a position of unparalleled pre-eminence throughout Wales; well might Matthew Paris observe that 'Wales was brought to nought at this time'.[16] The king retained this initiative for a further nine years. He exercised it shrewdly—cleverly exploiting fissures within the Welsh princely dynasties, especially that of Gwynedd, where the young Dafydd was asserting his right to a share of the principality with his brothers, Owain and Llywelyn ap Gruffudd; distributing pensions lavishly to native rulers and aristocrats; upholding the claims of disaffected claimants, such as Maredudd ap Rhicert in Llŷn; releasing hostages; remitting fines; taking the homages of Welsh magnates, such as Maredudd ap Gruffudd of Caerleon; and asserting his control over the native rulers of the middle March. Henry III himself showed sensitivity in

[15] Cal. Patent Rolls 1232–47, p. 272; Cal. Anc. Corr., p. 48.
[16] Matthew Paris, Chronica Majora, ed. H. R. Luard (Rolls Series, 1872–83), IV, p. 647.

his dealings with the Welsh on such issues as law, forest rights, military service, and financial dues; he frequently commanded his officials to proceed 'according to the laws and customs of those parts' and 'to bear themselves patiently towards the Welsh'.[17] The need for such commands, however, indicates that his local governors tended to show no such scruples. In Carmarthen and Perfeddwlad, in particular, they rode roughshod over the sensibilities and traditions of the local communities— increasing farms and court perquisites dramatically, imposing English laws and administrative practices, exacting military service, prohibiting the natives from exercising the right to assart their own woods, extending the jurisdiction of English courts, and imposing a poll tax. The conduct of Alan la Zouche as justice of Chester (1251-4)—flaunting the treasure that he had accumulated in Wales and boasting that the whole country was now obedient and subject to English law—and of his successor, Geoffrey Langley, seems to have been particularly high-handed. Nor was the situation improved by the grant of the king's Welsh lands to the Lord Edward: the progress of the royal heir and his entourage through the area in July–August 1256 may well have been the final straw that drove the Welsh to revolt. Miserable Wales, as Matthew Paris was prompted to remark, was leased at farm to the highest bidder.

Yet knowledge of the accumulating tensions of these years and of the great revolt of 1256-7, which swept away so much of the English gains, should not conceal the transformation which had been effected in the Crown's standing in Wales since 1240. It was the Crown, not the Marcher lords, which now set the pace in Wales. All the conditions necessary for the final subjection of the country were in place; what Edward I was to do was to resume in 1276-7 where his father had left off twenty years earlier. His chancery officials recognized as much: when they assembled material relating to Welsh affairs, it was 1240 which they chose as their *terminus a quo* and it was cases from the years 1247–58 which they culled from judicial records to demonstrate how wide-ranging Crown authority had once been. That the royal offensive of 1240–56 was not sustained thereafter was to be explained partly by the problems which now overwhelmed Henry III, partly by the remarkable leadership provided by Llywelyn ap Gruffudd. It is to Llywelyn's career that we now turn.

<hr>

[17] *Close Rolls 1247–57*, p. 541; *1251–3*, pp. 465, 467, 483; *Cal. Patent Rolls 1247–58*, p. 151.

CHAPTER 12

LLYWELYN AP GRUFFUDD:
THE YEARS OF SUPREMACY, 1255–76

NATIVE Wales in general, and Gwynedd in particular, had suffered a massive set-back at the hands of the English Crown during the years 1240–7. Gwynedd has been humiliated militarily and truncated territorially; its pretensions to be the leader and protector of the rest of native Wales had been rudely quashed. Indeed, Gwynedd itself now seemed to be on the verge of disintegration: on the death of Dafydd ap Llywelyn, in February 1246, the principality was, 'by the counsel of the wise men of the land', divided between his two nephews, Owain and Llywelyn ap Gruffudd.[1] Such a partition averted civil war but only at the expense of weakening further an already enfeebled principality. Nor did the partition offer a prospect of permanent peace, for two further brothers, Rhodri and Dafydd ap Gruffudd, lurked in the wings waiting to present their claims to a share of the principality; they were encouraged and manipulated in their ambitions—as were other pretenders[2]—by the king. Native Wales by 1250 appeared to have been reduced to a collection of pliant and fragmented protectorates of the English Crown and the process of the effective subjection, if not the military conquest, of the country seemed now to be set on an inexorable course.

Yet it was not to be so. English control of the areas annexed since 1240 was far from secure; indeed the high-handedness and insensitivity of English officials in these areas were a major cause of the mounting sense of outrage and resentment in Wales which Llywelyn ap Gruffudd was to tap so effectively from 1256 onwards. Not for the first or last time national unity in Wales was forged out of the experience of foreign domination. Furthermore, though Gwynedd had been humiliated in 1240–7, it was still the only native Welsh polity which could hope to act as a focus for Welsh resistance to the English advance. It was to Gwynedd that exiled and disaffected Welsh rulers, such as Hywel ap Maredudd of Meisgyn (in upland Morgannwg), fled for refuge in the 1240s and it was in Gwynedd in 1250–1 that the initial secret moves to forge a new Welsh alliance against the English were planned. Above all, Gwynedd once more produced a

---

[1] *Brut, s.a.* 1246.
[2] In particular Maredudd ap Rhicert was pressing a claim to the rich cantref of Llŷn as one of the great-grandsons of Gruffudd ap Cynan and was being actively supported by the king.

leader who had the vision and the ability to assume the leadership of native Wales.

Llywelyn ap Gruffudd had shown his talents at an early age. Already in the early 1240s, during the lifetime of his uncle Dafydd, he had established himself in Dyffryn Clwyd and had attracted to his company some of the former advisers and officials of his grandfather, Llywelyn Fawr. Llywelyn ap Gruffudd may well have already set himself up as a claimant around whom disaffected elements in Gwynedd might cluster. He was also showing his political acumen—and opportunism—by concluding an agreement with Ralph Mortimer of Wigmore, thereby buying off the opposition of one of the most powerful of the Marcher lords, albeit at a heavy price. By 1244 he had joined the Welsh revolt led by Dafydd, and when Dafydd died in February 1246 Llywelyn quickly laid claim to be one of his successors. The Gwynedd to which he succeeded was in parlous state and he had no option but to share it with his elder brother, Owain, and to conclude a humiliating peace with the king in April 1247. But Llywelyn soon showed his true mettle. In November 1250 he concluded a secret alliance of mutual aid with Gruffudd ap Madog of northern Powys and a year later he and his brother, Owain, forged a similar alliance with Maredudd ap Rhys Gryg and Rhys Fychan of Deheubarth, promising to act together as if they were sworn brothers (L. *fratres conterini*). A new native Welsh confederation was being secretly assembled out of the debris of defeat, and Llywelyn was already its head. But before he could lay claim to the leadership of native Wales, he had to assert his mastery over his own brothers. He did so decisively in mid-summer 1255. Since at least 1253 disputes had erupted between Llywelyn and his brothers over the partition of Gwynedd, with the youngest brother, Dafydd, already casting himself in the role of arch-troublemaker, a role which he consistently played for the rest of his life. The Crown, as ever, saw family dissension in Wales as an opportunity for it to intensify its suzerainty over the country: it appointed justices to hear the disputes between the brothers, thereby proclaiming its ultimate judicial control of Gwynedd; it insisted that each brother should hold his land directly of the king; and it dispatched peremptory orders to Llywelyn to appear before the king. But Llywelyn preferred the arbitrament of battle to the judgement of the royal court and in early June 1255 at Bryn Derwin, on the borders between Arfon and Eifionydd, he decisively defeated his brothers, Owain and Dafydd, in battle. He was now sole master of Gwynedd.

The significance of the victory of Bryn Derwin, as the English government quickly realized, extended far beyond Gwynedd. Native Wales had once more found a leader: the secret alliances of 1250–1 could now be activated; the homages of Welsh magnates, hitherto jealously reserved for the king, were now surreptitiously transferred to Llywelyn;

and it was to him that disaffected Welshmen 'revealed . . . their grievous bondage to the English' and to him that they looked for deliverance.[3] The visit of the Lord Edward and his household to north-east Wales in July–August 1256 may well have been the spark that lit the tinder of Welsh resentment. In November 1256 Llywelyn, accompanied by Maredudd ap Rhys Gryg of Deheubarth, swept through Perfeddwlad, expelled its English rulers and reduced English control to the two isolated fortresses of Diserth and Degannwy. It was the first episode of a remarkable sequence of victories which quickly transformed the situation throughout Wales. Meirionydd was overrun and its native ruler, a royal protégé, forced to flee; northern Ceredigion was restored to native rule and Llywelyn's ally, Maredudd ap Rhys Gryg, was re-established in the Tywi valley; Builth and Gwrtheyrnion were again recovered for the Welsh. The tide continued to run in favour of the Welsh throughout 1257–8: southern Powys was overrun and in due course the ruler of northern Powys defected to the Welsh cause; and Welsh forces ravaged through English-controlled territory in south-west Wales in an arc from Cemais to Gower. English attempts to turn back the tide only served to show its strength and their own weakness: an English counter-attack from Montgomery ended in ignominious retreat; in the south a military expedition in the Tywi valley under Stephen Bauzan in June 1257 was utterly overwhelmed and suffered one of the most devastating defeats inflicted on an English army in Wales in the thirteenth century; while the short campaign which Henry III led into north Wales in August–September 1257 did the king's military reputation no good and achieved little more than some temporary relief for the beleaguered fortresses of Degannwy and Diserth. The king laid plans for a further expedition into Wales in June 1258; but in that very month domestic discontent at his policies and his alien favourites erupted at the parliament at Oxford and put paid to any prospect of a campaign. Instead of a campaign, the English government on 17 June was forced to agree to a truce with Llywelyn which confirmed the status quo in Wales.

1258 was *annus mirabilis* for Llywelyn. He had won his successes, it is true, on the crest of a wave of intense resentment against English rule in Wales. 'Such an union (between north and south Wales) ', remarked Matthew Paris, 'had previously never been seen, since the men of north and south Wales had always been opposed to each other'. Llywelyn cleverly channelled this resentment to his own ends; he acted, so he claimed, 'by the counsel of all the magnates of Wales'; he associated other princelings with him in his raids; he showed magnanimity and sensitivity in his distribution of conquered lands, restoring them to their original dynasties and 'keeping naught for himself', as the *Brut* records proudly,

---

[3] *Brut, s.a.* 1256.

'but fame and honour';[4] while the alliances he concluded in these years—such as that with Maredudd ap Rhys Gryg in April 1258—bear the hallmarks of confederation rather than of supremacy. Yet his ultimate leadership and indeed dominance of native Wales were not in doubt and were to be graphically confirmed in 1258. At an assembly, probably held early that year, 'the magnates of Wales', according to one account, gave an oath of allegiance to Llywelyn ap Gruffudd under pain of excommunication'.[5] This oath or pact was doubtless followd by specific agreements with individual princelings and even by the formal performance of homage to Llywelyn (such as was performed by Maredudd ap Rhys Gryg). Llywelyn was now, to all intents and purposes, prince of native Wales. He adopted—or perhaps, more correctly, was accorded—that title, *princeps Wallie*, in a treaty which was concluded with the Scottish baronial faction led by Walter Comyn at an assembly where almost all the leaders of native Wales were present in March 1258. For a man who three years earlier had been no more than a ruler of part of a truncated Gwynedd it was indeed a notable achievement.

Llywelyn was well content to rest on his laurels in 1258. Indeed he was anxious to do so. He knew full well how fragile was any military superiority in Wales and how transient was any hegemony he might enjoy over the other Welsh principalities. What he now wanted above all was recognition and confirmation of the remarkable gains he had made in 1256–7. Already in 1257 he had made a tentative approach for a peace or, failing that, a truce; he had followed this proposal in 1258 by an offer of 4,500 marks to secure a peace; while, a year later, he raised that sum to £16,500 for a definitive peace and £700 for a seven-year truce. In return he demanded the restoration of the territorial status quo of 1240 and the acknowledgement of his feudal overlordship in native Wales. The English government prevaricated, hoping that the tide might turn in its favour and Llywelyn had to be content with successive renewals of the truce of June 1258. That truce held for over four years; during that period Llywelyn's authority in Wales was further enhanced. In January 1260 he seized Builth from Roger Mortimer and completed his conquest of the lordship by capturing its castle in July of that year and razing it to the ground. Within native Wales his authority was now beyond challenge: he showed it to clear effect in December 1261 when he imposed demeaning terms on Maredudd ap Rhys Gryg of Deheubarth, who had dared to 'withdraw from the prince's unity' and was now readmitted to his 'peace and benevolence'.[6]

---

[4] Matthew Paris, *Chronica Majora*, v, p. 645; *Cal. Anc. Corr.*, p. 50; *Brut, s.a.* 1256.

[5] *Brut (RBH), s.a.* 1258. The account in the Peniarth 20 version of the *Brut* is markedly different: 'all the Welsh made a pact together and they gave an oath to maintain loyalty and agreement together'. That is, it is an oath of mutual aid, not a pledge of dependence.

[6] *Litt. Wallie*, p. 104.

It was in November 1262 that the truce of June 1258 finally collapsed. The resumption of hostilities in that month heralded a major change of direction in Llywelyn's ambitions. Now that northern and southern Powys, Perfeddwlad, and most of Deheubarth were under his direct or indirect control, the key district in his ambitions lay in the middle March. Control of this area, from Severn to Wye, would serve not only as a buffer against any attacks on his augmented principality, but also as a springboard for attempting to extend his own control into Brecon, upper Gwent, and upland Glamorgan. Llywelyn had already seized on every opportunity to intrude his authority into the area—leading raids into Gwrtheyrnion and Builth in 1256–7, capturing the lordship and castle of Builth in 1260, securing the submission of the Welsh claimant to Elfael in the same year, seizing Cedewain on Owain ap Maredudd's death in 1261, and bestowing Ceri on members of the local dynasty. His opportunity to make further advances in the area and to curb the rising power of Roger Mortimer of Wigmore came late in November 1262 when the Welshmen of Maelienydd seized Mortimer's new castle of Cefnllys. The attack seems to have been a spontaneous local uprising, but it was too good an opportunity to be missed. Within a few weeks Llywelyn had overrun the whole of Maelienydd and captured most of Mortimer's Welsh border castles; the 'whole of the Welshry' of Brecon and Blaenllyfni rushed to join him; and his forces pushed through Brecon and down the Usk valley to within a few miles of Abergavenny. 'If they are not stopped', wrote the royal commander of Abergavenny in panic in March 1263, 'they will destroy all the lands of the king as far as the Severn and the Wye; they ask for nothing less than the whole of Gwent.'[7] In 1263 the cup of Llywelyn's success was filled to overflowing: early in August Diserth finally surrendered to the Welsh and was followed by Degannwy in late September; both were razed to the ground and with them were erased the achievements of Henry III in north Wales in the 1240s; while in December, even Gruffudd ap Gwenwynwyn, the bitterest of Llywelyn's Welsh opponents, was compelled to submit hismelf to Llywelyn, doing homage and swearing fealty to him, acknowledging that he and his heirs should hold their lands of him and accepting, in effect, Llywelyn's overlordship in judicial and military matters and his control over his alliances.

Llywelyn's remarkable successes in 1262–3 owed not a little to the growing political disarray in England. During the next two years that disarray grew in intensity as acrimonious political argument escalted into civil war. The March of Wales and some of its lords played a prominent and well-acknowledged part in this political turmoil. Much of the fighting took place in the March or in the contiguous English counties, while the

---

[7] *Cal. Anc. Corr.*, pp. 30, 53.

party of supporters whom the Lord Edward assembled from summer–autumn 1263 drew much of its strength from a group of Marcher barons: notably Roger Clifford, John Fitzalan, John and Hamo Lestrange, and, most prominent of all, Roger Mortimer of Wigmore. Marcher men and Welsh troops were prominent at the two key battles of Lewes and Evesham and there was a grisly appropriateness in the fact that it was to Roger Mortimer's wife at Wigmore that Simon de Montfort's head was sent as a trophy. It is not difficult to explain the prominence of the March and of its barons in the events of these years. Here was an area which lay outside the framework of normal royal governmental and judicial power and one whose lords were inured to war between themselves as well as against the Welsh. It was little wonder that it was a region into which English political disputes were attracted as if by a magnet: it had been so in 1233 (during Richard Marshal's revolt); and would be again in 1297 and 1321–2. The likelihood was all the stronger since several of the leading figures of the English political community were also prominent lords of the March: they exported their quarrels and conflicts thither. Yet the Marcher dimension of the conflict of 1262–5 has frequently been exaggerated: the Marcher barons did not act as a group, since they themselves were torn by conflicts; few of those who are normally classified as 'Marchers' were either predominantly or mainly Marcher in their power and orientation (with the notable exception of Roger Mortimer of Wigmore); and the source of the conflict of these years lay firmly in the tensions of English politics and could only be resolved there. In so far as there was a truly Marcher dimension to the confused political events of these years, it lay in local territorial disputes which cut across and bypassed the alignments of national politics—such as the enmity between Roger Mortimer and Roger Tony over Elfael, the vendetta of John Fitzalan against Bishop Peter of Hereford, the disputes between the Fitzwarins and the Corbets, and the strained relations between Roger Mortimer on the one hand and John Giffard and the earl of Gloucester on the other.

The turbulent politics which impinged so frequently on the March in the years 1262–5 are, therefore, more truly a part of the history of England. Yet the cross-currents of English politics had a marked impact on the political fortunes of Wales, most notably in the way that Llywelyn ap Gruffudd turned the discomfiture of the English to his own ends. In June 1263 he sent his troops to help the Montfortian force which was laying siege to Bridgnorth, thereby signalling clearly his intention to support Simon de Montfort's cause in order to promote his own ambitions. The alliance served both parties well. Twice in 1264 Llywelyn dispatched forces to help capture castles in the Marches for the Montfortians and to compel royalist partisans in the March to capitulate to the Montfortian government (at Montgomery and, later, at Worcester). In return, Montfort plucked out a thorn from Llywelyn's side by requiring the Lord Edward to surrender the county and honour of Chester and taking control of it himself; in January 1265 he went further by conceding that all lands and castles conquered by the Welsh in north Wales should remain theirs. As 1265 progressed and as Montfort's predicament became more desperate, Llywelyn exacted an even heavier price for his collaboration. By an agreement which he negotiated on 19 June 1265 at Pipton-on-Wye—within a few miles of the English border, thereby demonstrating clearly that the middle March was now securely under his control—Llywelyn, surrounded by a bevy of his most powerful vassals, won from Montfort recognition of his title as prince of Wales and his lordship over the magnates within his principality, confirmation of all lands which he and his allies had conquered, and the promise of castles and lands along the border with England, which would greatly enhance the security of Llywelyn's principality—Hawarden, Ellesmere, Whittington, and Painscastle. In return Llywelyn offered to pay £20,000 over ten years for this ample recognition of his status, authority and gains. The terms reveal Llywelyn as a hard bargainer; they also show him as a political realist. Realizing as he did the fragility of Simon de Montfort's position, he insisted that if the king died or defaulted on his obligation to abide by the ordinances for the governance of the kingdom, his own obligations would be cancelled forthwith. It was a wise insurance policy, for just over six weeks later (4 August 1265), Earl Simon was dead.

For over two years Llywelyn had manipulated the Montfortian alliance to his very considerable benefit; Montfort's death could be expected to lead to a sharp reversal in his fortunes. It did not do so. The Lord Edward was not of a mind to resume the initiative again the Welsh, preferring instead to transfer his remaining estates there to his brother; the attempt of the Marcher barons, in the wake of their political victory in England, to recover some of their lands in Wales was an utter failure; meanwhile, the tensions which continued to beset English politics in 1266–7 over the fate of the Disinherited—tensions in which two of the greater Marcher lords, Roger Mortimer and the young earl of Gloucester, were bitterly at odds—nullified the prospects of any co-ordinated action against the Welsh. Exhorted by the papal legate, Cardinal Ottobuono, and exhausted by continuing political dissension in England, the royal government eventually concluded a peace with Llywelyn on 25 September 1267. It was, as was later claimed, doubtless a peace conceded reluctantly by the Crown, but it served the immediate needs of both parties—confirmation and recognition of his gains for Llywelyn, a respite from conflict, and an opportunity for reconstruction, for the Crown.

The Treaty of Montgomery, as that peace is commonly called, set the seal on Llywelyn's success. The title of 'prince of Wales' was confirmed to him and his heirs, and the fealty and homages of 'all the Welsh barons of

Wales' (except the maverick Maredudd ap Rhys of Ystrad Tywi) were reserved to him so that those barons were henceforth to be regarded as his tenants-in-chief. In terms of status and hegemony these were the crucial concessions and were regarded as such by the Welsh chronicler. It was a small concession, indeed, for Llywelyn to acknowledge—what was in any case not in doubt—that he would perform fealty and homage and fulfil the accustomed services to the king of England, promise that he would not receive the king's enemies in his principality, and undertake to restore his brother, Dafydd, to the lands he held before he defected to the king's side in 1263 (or, if he were not satisfied, to an augmented portion of Gwynedd). Even this last clause manifested the strength of Llywelyn's position, for in the event of a dispute the question was to be referred not, as Henry III had insisted in the 1240s and 1250s, to the king's court but to a group of arbitrators who were vassals and servants of Llywelyn; and if Dafydd were still dissatisfied the matter was to be decided by Welsh law and custom (presumably in Llywelyn's court) with one or two English observers present. In short, the feudal and judicial supremacy of the prince of Wales within his newly acknowledged principality was confirmed.

That supremacy was matched by the territorial gains which the Treaty conceded to Llywelyn. His claim, at least in terms of possession (*possessio*) if not of right (*ius*), to Perfeddwlad, Brecon, Gwrtheyrnion, Builth, Ceri, and Cedewain was acknowledged and so was his overlordship of Whittington. In fact his actual territorial control was greater than the treaty seemed to indicate: Hawarden (which Llywelyn had captured and destroyed in 1265) was to be restored to Robert Montalt, but its military significance was nullified by a proviso that no castle was to be built there for thirty years; in Maelienydd, on the other hand, Roger Mortimer was to be allowed to build a castle, but his title to the district was acknowledged to be open to question and in fact Llywelyn retained possession of it; he likewise retained control of the lordship of Elfael (though not of its *caput* of Painscastle) and Moldsdale, though neither is mentioned in the treaty. In return for these ample concessions, Llywelyn agreed to pay to the king a total sum of 25,000 marks in annual instalments of 3,000 marks after an initial payment of 5,000 marks. Such a sum certainly represented a major drain on the prince's finances; but weighed in the balance of the concessions he had won and the security of the acknowledgement of his status and his gains, it was a good, indeed an excellent, bargain.

Llywelyn's achievement in the years 1256–67 was remarkable. 'Since the coming of the Normans no Welsh prince had attained to such a height of authority and landed influence.'[8] He owed his success in part to the feebleness of the English military response: the English found themselves

---

[8] J. E. Lloyd, *History of Wales*, II, 741.

on the defensive against a fast-moving series of hit-and-run pillaging campaigns to which they had no effective reply, while the sole royal expedition that was mounted, that of 1257, though impressive in its planning and in the recruitment and organization of forces, was in the circumstances a cumbersome and clumsy response of doubtful military value and very limited results. Among the Marcher lords themselves, the response to the Welsh assault was characterized, as contemporaries admitted, by apathy and by a lack of co-ordination; their failure was relieved only by the enterprise of a few men, such as Roger Mortimer in 1262–3, or John Grey and Peter de Montfort in the Usk valley in 1265. Welsh tactics, on the other hand, were revealed to best advantage during these years—in guerrilla ambushes (as at Cymerau in 1257), rapid foraging raids (as in south-west Wales in 1258), tactical retreat out of the reach of heavy English cavalry (as in a skirmish near Abergavenny in March 1263), and the deliberate avoidance of pitched battle (against the king in 1257 or the Lord Edward in April 1263). The Welsh also capitalized to the full on the divisions and recriminations in the English ranks: that was obviously so after 1258 (with William Valence accusing the earls of Gloucester and Leicester of being in league with the Welsh) and even more so after 1262; but already, at the commencement of hostilities in November 1256, jealousies and suspicions among the English played into the hands of the Welsh, with reports that some of the Marchers were privately pleased at the embarrassment which Llywelyn's raids had caused to the Lord Edward.

Yet the explanation for Llywelyn's success was not altogether negative. Not a little of it was owed to his capacity to channel resentment and aspiration within Wales to his cause, thereby converting his personal ambition into a 'war of liberation' for all Welshmen.[9] Much of the fighting of these years was local in its aim and leadership; it was bound to be so, given the character of lordship in medieval Wales. Political loyalties were still regional and brittle; alliances between Welsh princelings were as artificial and fragile as ever. Yet there is no mistaking the force of Llywelyn's leadership, on the one hand, and the heightened awareness of a common Welshness, on the other, in these years. Llywelyn kept a tight rein on affairs throughout the whole of native Wales—associating other native rulers with him in his expeditions (as in 1256–7), his major political acts (such as the Scottish treaty of 1258 or the public trial of Maredudd ap Rhys Gryg in 1259), and his peace negotiations (as at Pipton in 1264). He posed as the deliverer of all Welshmen, particularly those who had lived under Anglo-Norman rule: 'and he himself went . . . to Brycheiniog', so records the *Brut* in 1262, 'at the request of the leading men of Brycheiniog to

---

[9] The phrase is used by Dr. R. F. Walker as the title of his final chapter in his important unpublished thesis, 'The Anglo-Welsh Wars, 1216–67' (University of Oxford, D.Phil., 1954).

receive their homage'.[10] Llywelyn rode on the crest of a wave of growing Welsh patriotism and anti-English sentiment. These emotions were expressed in the claim of the men of Perfeddwlad that 'they preferred to be slain in war for their liberty than to suffer themselves to be unrighteously trampled on by foreigners', or in the stridently patriotic tone of one version of the native Latin chronicle, *Annales Cambrie*, for the years 1255–63; they were expressed also in the vernacular poetry of the period, notably in the odes of Dafydd Benfras and Llygad Gŵr—in their delight in the Welsh language, their pride at the discomfiture of the English, and their contempt for the 'foreign, alien-tongued people'.[11] The conflict within Wales and between the Welsh princes and the king of England was increasingly being interpreted as a struggle between two peoples; it was to bring the dissensions between 'the English and the Welsh peoples' to an end that the Treaty of Montgomery was agreed. In this context Llywelyn's adoption of the title 'prince of Wales' had to it more than a 'constitutional' or feudal significance; it also served notice that he was proclaiming his cause as a national struggle of which he was the leader.

Llywelyn ap Gruffudd was undoubted master of native Wales from early 1258 until his death almost twenty-five years later. 'There is no other Welshman who is his peer', claimed the poet without fear of contradiction.[12] The English government shared that opinion, for when reports of Llywelyn's imminent death circulated in the summer of 1262 it took great heart at the prospect and assumed that the political situation in Wales might be immediately reversed. Llywelyn was a born leader of men; some of the charisma of his personality is recaptured in the contemporary observation that Welshmen followed him as if they were glued to him. He was a man of forceful determination and single-mindedness: those qualities alone enabled him to reach and stay at the top in the vicious world of Welsh domestic and dynastic politics. He was also a man of resilience, willing to bide his time and use the bitter experience of defeat to reconstruct the basis of his power, as he showed in the early 1250s and again after 1277. His single-mindedness often broached on the obstinate and called in question the soundness of his political judgement. It is difficult, for example, to explain why he postponed marriage until the 1270s when he was well into his fifties: to do so was not only to endanger his achievements by leaving a power-vacuum at his death, it was also to invite plots over the succession during his lifetime. Again, in his relations with Edward I in the 1270s he seemed incapable of recognizing where legitimate protest ended and intransigence began. He was a man deeply

[10] *Brut*, s.a. 1262.
[11] *Brut*, s.a. 1256; *Llsg. Hendregadredd*, p. 218 ('estron genedl . . . anghyfiaith').
[12] *Llsg. Hendregadredd*, p. 215 ('Nid oes o Gymro ei gymrodedd').

conscious of the dignity of his position and the respect that was owed to it. He was greeted in fulsome terms by his dependants—'most excellent', 'most illustrious', 'your distinguished lordship'—and, in his negotiations with the English king, he himself insisted, even in his darkest hours, on the 'respect that was due to his attributes and status as prince'.[13] Such sensitivity of itself gave a new status to the office of prince and an exalted sense of dignity to his policies. But it also made Llywelyn prickly, suspicious, and high-handed. He resorted easily to the language of bluster and threat; men and institutions were made to pay heavily to buy back his 'benevolence' and to avoid his 'wrath';[14] the bishop of Bangor, admittedly a prejudiced observer, remarked almost hysterically that he could not stir a foot except by the prince's power. Even in the years of his success Llywelyn was a prince haunted by fears of plots and defections, painfully conscious of the fragility of his achievements. He was, one may well believe, a man more feared than loved.

Llywelyn's power in Wales was founded on his domination of his family and of his allies. The fortunes of a single battle in 1255 had given him victory over his brothers; yet he did not use that victory nor any subsequent opportunities to disinherit them completely. He kept his eldest brother, Owain, in prison for over twenty years, it is true, thereby incurring the displeasure of the poets since 'God alone ought to dispossess a man'.[15] Yet Llywelyn himself evidently recognized that Welsh custom required him to share his patrimony with his brothers. That much is clear in his treatment of his two other brothers: Rhodri was kept in confinement but Llywelyn continued to acknowledge his claim to a share of Gwynedd, for he agreed to buy out the claim in 1272; he treated Dafydd, the youngest, ablest, and most treacherous of his brothers, with much greater and arguably misplaced magnanimity, restoring him to a share of the patrimony on more than one occasion in spite of Dafydd's record of defection and treachery. But Llywelyn's scruples with regard to the claims of his brothers were more than balanced by a conviction that his own mastery brooked no challenge. The agreement which he made with Dafydd in 1269 proclaims his position clearly: Dafydd was indeed to be restored to the lands which he had held on his defection in 1263 but in return he was to swear fealty and homage to Llywelyn as his superior and in effect to pledge that he would not henceforth deviate from the path of unity (L. *unitas*). Llywelyn was the arbiter of that unity and the undoubted master of his family.

Llywelyn treated the other rulers of native Wales in much the same

---

[13] *Litt. Wallie*, pp. 334, 29, 24; J. B. Smith, 'Offra Principis Wallie Domino Regi', *BBCS* 21 (1964–6), 362–7 ('habito respectu ad facultates et statum principis'). Cf. his insistence in 1282 on conduct that was becoming to his status ('salva etiam condescentia status sui'): *Registrum epistolarum Johannis Peckham*, II, 465–6.

[14] *Litt. Wallie*, pp. 24–5, 31, 34, 104.

[15] *Llsg. Hendregadredd*, p. 57 ('Ni fedd namyn Duw digyfoethi dyn').

fashion as his brothers—their customary rights and positions were respected, but subject firmly to Llywelyn's control and leadership. Viewed from one angle, his principality was never more than a loose federation of which he was the president. He seemed well content with overlordship and public pledge of fealty such as he secured in 1258; some of the alliances he concluded—notably those with Maredudd ap Rhys Gryg of Ystrad Tywi in April 1258 and with Gruffudd ap Gwenwynwyn in December 1263—present themselves as mutual compacts of friendship (L. *amicitia*), rather than as imposed settlements; he showed, especially in his earlier years, a sensitive respect for the rights of local dynasties, and he intervened in a paternal fashion—as his grandfather had done—to try to compose family quarrels. But where persuasion and agreement failed, Llywelyn did not hesitate to use threat and force to bend local rulers and leaders to his will. He took hostages—often the sons of princelings or the children of local magnates—from would-be allies and defectors; he insisted that groups of warrantors pledge themselves for the loyalty of key figures and for the payment of large sums in which they were bound to him; he released political suspects only on the payment, or pledge of payment, of fines; he imprisoned defectors—Maredudd ap Rhys Gryg in 1259 and Gruffudd ap Gwenwynwyn in 1263—and extorted concessions from them; he demanded the surrender of castles and lands as guarantees of fidelity, requiring Maredudd ap Rhys Gryg to surrender Castellnewydd Emlyn and Dinefwr to him in 1259. It was by such methods—now documented for the first time in the history of Wales—that Llywelyn ap Gruffudd imposed and retained his authority over native Wales in the years 1258–77.

Over and above these strong-arm tactics, he developed more formal mechanisms for exercising his ultimate control in his principality. He demanded personal homage from princelings (such as Maredudd and Hywel ap Rhys Gryg), from the leaders of native Welsh society (such as Einion Sais ap Rhys of Brecon), and even from the sub-vassals of other princelings (such as Hywel Fychan, the 'man' of Owain ap Maredudd of Ceredigion). He required such vassals to acknowledge their military subordination to him, by agreeing (as Maredudd ap Rhys Gryg was compelled to do in December 1261) to come at Llywelyn's command with all their forces and to be ready to harass his enemies in south Wales. He insisted that his vassals should bring their disputes to his court and thereby extended the jurisdictional competence of his court to cover the whole of native Wales (as is shown by cases from Cedewain and Ceredigion that were referred to it). That court was also used as a tribunal in which Llywelyn's vassals might be arraigned for their political misdemeanours, as Maredudd ap Rhys Gryg found to his cost in 1259 and Gruffudd ap Gwenwynwyn in 1274. Finally, Llywelyn made it clear that his territorial control extended ultimately to the whole of native Wales and that he might exercise it in the most masterful fashion. Gruffudd ap Gwenwynwyn of southern Powys was forced to acknowledge in 1263 that he held his lands of Llywelyn and his heirs; while Hywel ap Rhys Gryg conceded in 1258 that he owed the commote of Mabelfyw to Llywelyn's generosity. More ominously, there are plentiful indications of Llywelyn's high-handed intervention in the territorial politics of his enlarged principality—allowing Morgan ap Maredudd to take seisin of the commote of Hirfryn and then expelling him, compelling two of the minor rulers of Ceredigion to exchange lands to Llywelyn's advantage, imposing a territorial partition in northern Powys on the death of Gruffudd Maelor in 1269, scrutinizing and confirming dower arrangements in Ceredigion and northern Powys, annexing Cedewain as an escheat on the grounds of the illegitimacy of the claimants to it.

Llywelyn's masterfulness is not in doubt. Through skill and luck he had assembled a native principality that was more extensive than even that of his grandfather; he had the will and the means to make his authority felt throughout that principality. There was no doubt as to the dependent status of other native rulers: they were his 'vassals', 'barons', 'magnates';[16] he offered them protection against their enemies and guarantees against the consequences of his own wrath. 'Unity' (L. *unitas*) was his ambition: his documents echo to the refrain of the need for 'one peace and one war', 'one war, one counsel and one aid'.[17] It was only through such unity that native Wales could hope to survive. But unity could only be secured by mastery and that in a country where dissension and conflict had been the major motifs of the native political tradition. One of the questions which remained unanswered in 1267 was whether or not native Wales was willing to accept mastery—and an increasingly exacting and interventionist mastery—as the price of unity.

There was no finality about the Treaty of Montgomery of 1267. It closed one episode in the history of Anglo-Welsh relations, but simultaneously opened another. The Treaty was certainly a major triumph for Llywelyn; but one which could not conceal for long the limitations of his success or the doubts about the future. Territorially, Llywelyn had made important gains; but neither in the south-west nor in the south-east had he made much headway against the Marcher lordships. In the south-west, he and his allies had indeed led raids into Dyfed, Cydweli, and Gower, destroying castles and temporarily securing the submission of some of the Welsh tenantry; but any dominance they enjoyed was short-lived and by 1267 the district from Gower to Cemais was still secure under English control. In particular Carmarthen and Cardigan, and the 'honors' or 'counties'

<hr />

[16] *Cal. Anc. Corr.*, pp. 50, 87, 162.   [17] *Litt. Wallie*, pp. 79, 104.

attached to them, lay under royal control and could serve as important bridgeheads of English power and recovery in a vulnerable and volatile part of Wales. In the south-east, Llywelyn's effective power, at least in the lowlands, had rarely reached further than Brecon; the remainder of the district lay under English rule and from it a counter-attack might in time be launched. The newly established principality of Wales fell far short of being co-terminous with the whole of Wales. Even within the bounds—or the putative bounds—of the principality, the Treaty of 1267 was tantalizingly vague or silent about crucial areas; it thereby bequeathed a legacy of uncertainty and dissension for the future. No mention was made of Elfael or the borderlands of Clun and Caus into which Llywelyn had intruded; no definition was offered of who precisely were 'the Welsh barons of Wales' and thereby the status of Welsh rulers in upland Glamorgan and Gwent was left undecided; while the ambiguity of the clauses relating to Brecon and Maelienydd was a standing invitation for future conflict. Over and above these local uncertainties lay much deeper doubts regarding the future of the principality: how secure was it from internal fissure and external attack? How long could it survive the combination of fortuitous circumstances which had allowed it to be assembled in the 1250s and 1260s? It is not the historian's hindsight alone which allows us to pose such questions. They must have haunted anyone who had lived through the traumas of the 1240s, when Llywelyn the Great's principality had been reduced to the status of a small, besieged mountain enclave in a few years, indeed months. Llywelyn ap Gruffudd after 1267 was a man haunted by such fears; recognizing as much goes a good part of the way to explain his behaviour.

Tensions were soon evident in the March, particularly in the middle March and towards the south-east. It was here that Llywelyn had made his most spectacular gains; it was here also that the settlement of 1267 was most patently pock-marked with ambiguities. Llywelyn was intent on retaining the initiative he had won in the area. He demanded hostages and pledges of loyalty from the leading Welshmen of frontier areas, such as Brecon and Elfael; he played the role of protector and patron of the native rulers of upland Gwent and Glamorgan—accepting the allegiance of Maredudd ap Gruffudd of Machen in 1269 and giving his support to the disinherited Welsh dynasty of Senghennydd; he monitored carefully the plans and ambitions of Marcher lords wherever they impinged on his own or his vassals' interests; he consolidated his hold on Cedewain by beginning the construction of a new castle at Dolforwyn in 1273, overlooking the Severn valley and posing a challenge to both the royal frontier post at Montgomery and Gruffudd ap Gwenwynwyn's capital at Pool; at much the same time he showed his determination to defend his gains up to and even beyond the lands formally conceded to him in 1267, by laying the foundations of another castle in the forest of Clun, possibly at the site known as Castell Bryn Amlwg, and one or more castles in the uplands south of the river Usk.

Llywelyn's determination, however, was more than matched by the determination of the Marcher lords to claw back the lands and homages they had lost to him in the 1260s and to reassert their control over their lordships. Three major areas of conflict in particular stand out—Glamorgan, Brecon, and Maelienydd. Gilbert Clare, the young earl of Gloucester, had already gone on the offensive before the peace-settlement of 1267, resuming his father's policies of bringing the Welsh native rulers of upland Glamorgan under his authority. In January 1267 he had arrested Gruffudd ap Rhys of Senghennydd and soon after dispatched him to prison in Kilkenny; by 1268 he had begun to build the castle at Caerffili to demonstrate his control of at least the lower half of the commote of Senghennydd. Llywelyn saw these moves as a direct threat to his authority. Glamorgan, it is true, had not been mentioned in the Treaty of Montgomery; but Llywelyn, by placing the most generous construction on its reference to the homages of all the Welsh barons of Wales, claimed that his overlordship extended to the native rulers of upland Glamorgan and Gwent. Confrontation was inevitable: raids and counter-raids were launched; Caerffili was razed to the ground only to be rebuilt; arbitrators were appointed; royal commissioners sought to defuse the issue. By 1272, however, it was becoming clear that the earl of Gloucester had won the tussle, as he had indeed a parallel struggle in Caerleon. It was an ominous set-back for Llywelyn. It was soon followed by the gradual undermining of his authority in Brecon by the young Humphrey Bohun, the heir to the earldom of Hereford: he and his vassals led raids into the lordship, enticed Llywelyn's vassals there from their allegiance, and gradually won a measure of royal acquiescence for their actions. In Maelienydd, Roger Mortimer likewise set about recovering the authority he had so ignominiously lost to Llywelyn in 1262–3 by rebuilding the castle at Cefnllys and doing so, according to Llywelyn, on a scale quite unwarranted by the terms of the Treaty of 1267. These individual confrontations in the March need not have led to a more general breakdown of Anglo-Welsh relations; each could, with goodwill on both sides, have been settled. Yet their cumulative effect, especially as the years passed, was to create in Llywelyn's mind a suspicion that there was an orchestrated attempt to undermine his hard-won gains, especially in the middle March, and to subvert the terms of the Treaty of 1267 as he interpreted them. What was worse, he could hardly avoid the suspicion that the royal government, regardless of its protestations, increasingly acquiesced in, and possibly supported, the activities of Clare, Bohun, Mortimer, and the other Marcher lords. Already by autumn 1270 Llywelyn was warning that since the Treaty was not being honoured, he might be compelled to ignore it; by February 1274 he was linking his failure to pay the instalments of the tribute due to the king directly with the failure of the Marchers 'to restore to Llywelyn the lands by them unjustly occupied and more unjustly detained'.[18]

Tensions along the borders of Llywelyn's enlarged principality were increasingly matched by tensions within the principality itself. Those tensions, as might be expected, first surfaced in the newly won frontier districts, especially in Maelienydd, Elfael, and Brecon. Here the leaders of the local Welsh communities had begun to come to terms with their English lords and to enter into ties of service and reward with them.[19] Thus the constable of the Mortimer castle of Cefnllys in 1262, when it was captured by the Welsh, was himself a powerful local figure, Hywel ap Meurig. Such men were now required to transfer their allegiance to the prince of Gwynedd. They frequently did so reluctantly and under duress. In November–December 1271 Llywelyn was exacting hostages, sureties, and large fines from some of the leading Welshmen of Brecon and Elfael, as guarantees of their loyalty. Loyalty bought at such a price was hollow indeed. So it was quickly proved in 1276–7 and even earlier: at least two of the commanders who led the Brecon contingent of Edward I's troops into Gwynedd in the summer of 1277 were men from whom Llywelyn ap Gruffudd had exacted solemn pledges of loyalty in 1271.

Llywelyn's principality was never more than a loose federation kept together by fear, success, and the force of his personality. The fissures within it lay just below the surface. In 1270 Llywelyn had bought the homage of Maredudd ap Rhys Gryg of Ystrad Tywi, the only major Welsh princeling whose homage he had been specifically denied in 1267; but the satisfaction that this gave him must have been balanced by the memories of Maredudd's recurrent treachery in the past and by the knowledge that Maredudd (and, after Maredudd's death in 1271, his son Rhys) would flirt with the king's agents at the earliest opportunity. It was from another direction, however, that the first challenge to Llywelyn's authority within his principality came. During the course of 1274 the details of a plot against Llywelyn's life were gradually unfolded. The main conspirators were Llywelyn's brother, Dafydd, and Gruffudd ap Gwenwynwyn of southern Powys. Llywelyn was to be murdered and replaced by Dafydd: Dafydd's daughter was to be married to Gruffudd's eldest son; and Ceri and Cedewain, so crucial to the strategy of Llywelyn's principality, were to be ceded to Powys. The sources for the plot, it is true, all emanate from Gwynedd; but, given the outstanding records of both conspirators for defection and treachery, there is no reason to doubt the essential truth of the story. Equally, there is no reason to be surprised at the plot: Llywelyn's

---

[18] *Cal. Anc. Corr.*, p. 93.   [19] Cf. above, p. 284.

increasingly high-handed behaviour in the 1270s must have alarmed Dafydd and Gruffudd, while the construction of the new castle at Dolforwyn in 1273 must have fuelled Gruffudd's growing sense of political suffocation. The original judgement against Gruffudd on 17 April 1274—before the full details of the plot had come to light—required him to surrender some of his western lands to Llywelyn; restored the rest of southern Powys to him, but with the proviso that all his estates would be forfeit in perpetuity in the event of further treachery; demanded his son, Owain, as a hostage and transferred to Llywelyn the homages of twenty-five of the leading men of Powys. The judgement could have left Gruffudd in no doubt that, if he put another foot wrong, he and his dynasty would be destroyed and his lands forfeited. It is little wonder that, when further and more incriminating details of the plot were leaked in November 1274, Dafydd and Gruffudd fled to England rather than face Llywelyn's wrath.

The backing that the two refugees now received from the king of England contributed substantially to the deterioration of Anglo-Welsh relations after 1274; but the conspiracy itself is also significant. It laid bare the atmosphere of fear and mistrust within the principality. It revealed Llywelyn's power at its most menacing. Immediately on hearing of Gruffudd's flight, so the *Brut* records, Llywelyn 'overran all the territory of Gruffudd without opposition and set his own officers over it all'.[20] It was a demonstration of masterfulness which must have sent shudders of fear down the backs of Llywelyn's other client princelings. The speed with which Welsh resistance to Edward I crumbled in the outer perimeters of Llywelyn's principality in the winter of 1276–7 is perhaps as much a comment on native disaffection as it is on the purposefulness of the initial English onslaughts. One of the first to capitulate—on 26 December 1276—was Llywelyn ap Gruffudd ap Madog of northern Powys; and one of the promises made to him was that, in the event of Edward I being reconciled with the prince of Wales, Llywelyn ap Gruffudd ap Madog's homage would be retained by the king and not granted again to the prince of Wales. A principality where the bonds of loyalty could be so quickly dissolved and where fear of future recrimination loomed so large in vassals' minds could hardly be said to be in a sound state of political health.

Nor was the disaffection limited to the satellite districts which had been encompassed within Llywelyn's principality. It was not altogether absent from Gwynedd itself. Tension had always been a feature of Gwynedd's political life, as ousted segments of the princely dynasty sought to recover their position, as younger sons acted as a focus for political dissidents, and as trimmers, especially in Gwynedd Is-Conwy, took out insurance policies against the possibility of a resurgence of English power. To these tensions

---

[20] *Brut (RBH)*, s.a. 1274.

were now added the strains of the financial pressure of sustaining and defending a greatly enlarged principality. Llywelyn's masterfulness also brought its own strains within Gwynedd: in 1269 Rhys ab Ednyfed—one of the sons of Ednyfed Fychan, Llywelyn the Great's justiciar—had to provide sureties for his future good behaviour towards Llywelyn, while the speed with which several other members of the family tried to defect to Edward I in 1276–7 suggests that disaffection, as well as a calculated estimate of Llywelyn's chances, may have lain at the root of their action.

Llywelyn could break or contain the opposition of individuals; he could not so easily dispose of the opposition of the Church and its leaders. Tension between lay and ecclesiastical authorities was a recurring feature of all medieval societies. It grew in intensity during the twelfth and thirteenth centuries, as the theoretical pretensions and practical control of the church over secular life increased and its claims to immunity for its own personnel and property were defined. Conflict was all the more likely in Wales as attempts were made to bring Welsh practices, especially concerning the status and privileges of clerics and their property, more into line with international norms. Welsh law and custom accorded an unusually wide and, by canon law standards, unacceptable degree of authority to secular rulers over such matters as testaments, the goods of deceased bishops, sanctuary, criminous clerks, the goods of intestates, and fiscal rights over ecclesiastical lands and tenants. In these circumstances periodic conflict was inevitable, all the more so since the bishops of Bangor and St Asaph found their loyalties further entangled by their relationships with the archbishop of Canterbury as their metropolitan, with the king of England as their ultimate feudal lord, and occasionally (as in the 1240s and 1250s) with disaffected members of the ruling dynasty in Gwynedd. Yet such periodic conflicts were normally eventually terminated either by arbitration (as in Bangor in 1261) or by the verdict of a jury and a subsequent confirmation of ecclesiastical liberties (as in St Asaph in 1269).

In 1274, however, Llywelyn ap Gruffudd was caught up in a quarrel with the bishop of St Asaph which proved to be more bitter and politically damaging than earlier disputes. Both parties contributed handsomely to the quarrel. There can be no doubt that Llywelyn was aggressively pressing his claim to a share of the profits of justice from the bishop's tenants and dependants; the evidence assembled by the bishop, selective as it no doubt is, is convincing enough on this issue. It is but another example of the hard-fisted and high-handed character of Llywelyn's governance throughout his principality in these years. But equally there is no doubt that the fiery personality and indomitable spirit of Anian, bishop of St Asaph 1268–93, were major factors in the quarrel. As a Dominican friar, he was alert to the wider and canonical context of church–state relations; as a clever and tireless disputant he knew how to whip up local feeling through diocesan synods and how to lay his case before the Pope, the king, and the archbishop of Cantberbury. So a quarrel over a fairly minor issue was broadened out into a much more serious dispute about ecclesiastical liberties in general and used to Llywelyn's maximum embarrassment as his political problems multiplied. The Cistercian houses in Wales leapt to Llywelyn's defence; but their support was more than counterbalanced by the way that Anian cleverly manipulated English support for his own ends. Edward I mischievously confirmed the ancient liberties of the see of St Asaph in November 1275 and January 1276; Anian attended the royal council of November 1276 at which Llywelyn was declared a rebel; a month later, he presented his most comprehensive list of grievances against Llywelyn. Early in 1277 Llywelyn tried to buy off the bishop's opposition by conceding many of the issues at stake in a charter of liberties. But to no avail: the bishop of St Asaph had betaken himself into royal custody and was soon followed there by the bishop of Bangor. By then the writing was no doubt on the wall. Even so, Llywelyn had shown a quality which any political leader can well afford to do without—the ability to make enemies on different fronts at the same time.

The conflicts with the Marcher lords and the strains within the principality of Wales were no more than the tensions to be expected in any body politic. They could have been contained had they not been compounded by, and fed upon, deteriorating relationships with the Crown of England. In the years immediately after the Treaty of Montgomery, relations between Llywelyn and the Crown were apparently marked by punctilious correctness and even cordiality. Llywelyn paid the instalments of his tribute under the Treaty of Montgomery promptly until 1270 and, though he then began to fall into arrears, he had by January 1272 (the date of his last payment) handed over half of the total sum owed. The king, for his part, showed his goodwill by conceding the homage of Maredudd ap Rhys to Llywelyn in August 1270, while in the disputes which arose in the March, the Crown and, after Henry III's death in November 1272, the regents acting on behalf of the absent Edward I proceeded circumspectly, seeking to observe the terms of the Treaty and settle differences through parleys and commissions. Nor was there any reason to believe that Edward I's accession would herald a change of attitude: Edward had disposed of all his lands in Wales; he was referred to as 'the friend of the prince' (Llywelyn) and had apparently promoted the latter's interests in Wales; as late as May 1275 he could protest vigorously that he did 'not want Llywelyn to have any cause for complaining about the settlement' and wished 'peace to be observed'.[21] There is no reason to believe that the English Crown and the prince of Wales, or Edward I and Llywelyn as individuals, were necessarily set on a collision course from the early 1270s.

[21] *Cal. Anc. Corr.*, pp. 11, 210, 57–8.

Yet collision did occur. Its root cause lay in the tensions in the March, discussed above. Llywelyn became convinced that he was in effect being denied or defrauded of the gains he had won in 1267 and that the Crown was turning a blind eye to, or even conniving at, the process. Failure to abide by the terms of the Treaty of 1267 and the inability or unwillingness of the Crown to enforce them were for Llywelyn the basic reasons for the breakdown in relations; the other reasons were secondary. The first of those other reasons—the withholding of fealty and homage—became for the Crown, however, the *casus belli*. Llywelyn failed to obey the summons to swear fealty to Edward I in January 1273; he was guilty of a flagrant breach of etiquette by absenting himself from Edward's coronation in August 1274; most seriously, he failed to respond to five summonses, between December 1274 and April 1276, to do homage to Edward as his lord. For Llywelyn the withholding of homage was a negotiating ploy: he never denied his obligation to swear fealty and do homage, but he claimed that he should not do so until his grievances had been redressed and he was confirmed in this attitude by the opinion of an assembly 'of all the barons of Wales'.[22] Edward I saw matters entirely differently: fealty and homage were legal obligations due from a vassal to his lord; to withhold them, whatever other disputes there might be, was a formal act of defiance which turned a vassal into a rebel. Edward I was a king unusually prickly about his regality; Llywelyn was but the first of many who was to discover that truth. 'In order to receive his homage and fealty', wrote Edward I to the Pope in August 1276, 'we had so demeaned our royal dignity (*regiam dignitatem*) as to go to the confines of his land.'[23] He was referring to his journey to Chester in August 1275 when Llywelyn failed to turn up to perform homage. Edward was beside himself with anger at the insult to his dignity: his last three summonses to Llywelyn called upon him to come to Westminster and Winchester and made no promise of a safe-conduct.

By that date two other issues had driven Llywelyn and Edward further apart. The first was the refuge afforded to the two conspirators of 1274 in England and the raids they conducted thence into Wales. To Llywelyn's deeply suspicious mind this was convincing evidence that the Crown was not only ignoring the terms of the Treaty of 1267 but was also fostering those who were plotting his overthrow. Such suspicions were amply confirmed in the winter of 1275-6 when his bride-to-be, Eleanor de Montfort, was captured *en route* to Wales and was held in royal custody along with her brother. The marriage, though probably originally contracted some ten years earlier, was seen by Edward I as a deliberately provocative act, aimed at rekindling the embers of Montfortian opposition within and without England. For Llywelyn the arrest of Eleanor was an illegal act, which confirmed him in his view that he himself would be

---

[22] *Brut (RBH), s.a.* 1275.   [23] *Treaty Rolls 1234-1325*, p. 54.

detained if he dared to venture to England to perform homage. The truth was that after Llywelyn's failure to appear at Chester in August 1275 the attitudes of both parties hardened, Llywelyn's intransigence and suspicions being matched by Edward's outraged sense of slighted dignity. Short of a climb-down by one of the two parties, conflict was inevitable. On 12 November 1276, after further fruitless negotiations, Llywelyn was condemned as a rebel and disturber of the peace. It was war.

Historians have not viewed kindly Llywelyn's policies after 1267, and particularly after 1272. They have charged him with over-ambitiousness, with putting together a principality that was well beyond his military and political power to sustain, with high-handedness which lost friends and won enemies, and with imposing intolerable political and financial strains on native Wales. More specifically they have charged him with gross political misjudgement in the 1270s: he forfeited the gains he had made and the recognition he had won by his intransigence in refusing to perform fealty and homage. 'In five years', runs one of the most restrained but damning judgements, 'he had just fumbled his way to disaster.'[24] The charges are difficult to gainsay, especially with the benefit of hindsight. Yet such judgements do less than justice, perhaps, to Llywelyn's ambitions and the changing character of Anglo-Welsh relations in the thirteenth century. Paradoxically, the very success of Llywelyn and the fact that he was now prince of Wales made the prospect of serious confrontation more likely and more serious. There was now no buffer between him, on the one hand, and the Marcher lords and English king, on the other; he could not conduct his policy by proxy; any attack on any part of his principality was an attack on him. The defence of native Wales now lay formally and legally on his shoulders. The poets did right to salute him as 'the man who was for Wales', 'the governor of the Welsh host', 'the true king of Wales'; defender of Deheubarth and Powys and upholder of Glamorgan, as well as lion of Gwynedd.[25] That is how he saw himself.

Such poetic compliments arguably take us closer to the nature of Llywelyn's ultimate ambitions in these years than does the diplomatic correspondence. He had fought hard to build his principality and to impose his suzerainty on native Wales; he had gone to the trouble in 1274 to win from the Pope the concession that neither he nor his subjects would be cited to appear in England in ecclesiastical disputes: he had paid—and was still paying—heavily for the recognition of his title as prince of Wales and for the feudal overlordship of native Wales. Such recognition not only

[24] J. G. Edwards, *Litt. Wallie*, p. lxi.

[25] *Llsg. Hendregadredd*, pp. 66 ('gŵr oedd tros Gymru'); 68 ('llywiawdwr llu Cymru'), 219 ('gwir frenin Cymru'): Cf. also the poem by Dafydd Benfras in *The Poetry in the Red Book of Hergest*, ed. J. Gwenogvryn Evans (Llanbedrog, 1911), pp. 144–5 and the quatrains published in T. Roberts, 'Englynion Marwnad i Lywelyn ap Gruffudd', *BBCS* 26 (1974–6), 10–12.

flattered his ego, 'magnifying his person and honouring him in his descendants', as the Treaty of Montgomery put it; it was politically the only hope of retaining a semblance of true political independence for native Wales. The alternative was an eventual return to the conditions of the 1240s—the effective pulverization of native Wales politically, as the grip of feudal control was tightened around each of the puny principalities and as the English Crown promoted the further fragmentation, and thereby emasculation, of those principalities, in the name of defending the Welsh custom of partibility. The political alternatives had come into ever sharper focus as the thirteenth century progressed. Llywelyn deserves the credit of having recognized that what was at stake after 1267 was not his *amour propre* but the survival of the ambition which he and his predecessors had struggled so hard to attain and which, so he believed, had been confirmed by the Treaty of Montgomery.

He felt duped. The Treaty had not given him the territorial security which he sought for his enlarged principality; instead, the Marcher lords nibbled away at his authority all along its frontiers. More seriously, the title of prince of Wales had not accorded him the measure of political independence commensurate with his ambitions. Llywelyn had an exalted view of his title as 'prince' and of the 'liberties' it conferred on him.[26] As he put it forcefully in a letter to the king in July 1273: 'the rights of our principality are entirely separate from the rights of your kingdom, although we hold our principality under your royal power'.[27] Even in the desperate negotiations in 1277 he could insist on the 'respect that was due to his attributes and status as prince'.[28] The reality was quite otherwise: he was treated as a 'man' of the king of England, on a par with the earl of Gloucester and other vassals;[29] he could be summoned to appear in the king's court if he wanted redress; he could be sent a command not to build a castle or establish a market without royal permission; his vassals conspiring against his life were accorded asylum in England. This was no way to treat a prince; more seriously it opened endless opportunities for royal intervention in his principality and for undermining his authority there. To Edward, Llywelyn was no more than 'one of the greater among the other magnates of our kingdom' and was bound not only to do homage and fealty but also 'to do and receive right in the court of the kings of England'.[30] Edward's intentions were clearly revealed in a grant he made at Flint on 23 August 1277, while his first campaign against Llywelyn was in

[26] *Diplomatic Documents 1101–1272*, ed. P. Chaplais (1964), p. 279. The contents of this letter suggest that it belongs to the negotiations of 1276–7 rather than to 1267.

[27] *Cal. Anc. Corr.*, p. 86.   [28] Above p. 318 n. 13.

[29] F. M. Powicke, *King Henry III and the Lord Edward. The Community of the Realm in the Thirteenth Century* (Oxford, 1947; 1 vol. edn. 1966), p. 581 n. 1.

[30] *Treaty Rolls 1234–1325*, no. 134, p. 54 ('qui est unus de maioribus inter magnates alios regni nostri'); *Cal. Anc. Corr.*, p. 252.

progress. Edward, it is true, posed as the upholder of Welsh law and customs and promised to restore Llywelyn's brothers, Dafydd and Owain, to a share of their paternal inheritance. But there could be no mistaking the sinister undertones of the document: Anglesey might be retained entire by the king; even parts of Snowdon might for reasons of security be reserved for him; the 'land of Wales (*terra Wallie*) was to be regarded as forfeit to him; the two brothers would only secure recompense by royal grace and on strictly feudal terms; and—to make clear that the political incorporation of the native principality was the king's intention—Dafydd and Owain and their heirs were to 'come to our parliaments in England, as our other earls and barons (come) '.[31] Perhaps, after all, Llywelyn had read Edward I's intentions better than historians have done. The struggle was not one about feudal etiquette but about power and the survival of a measure of political independence for native Wales. Edward I's imperious, even imperial, concept of the nature of overlordship could not be squared with Llywelyn's concept of a native principality of Wales. Collision was well nigh inevitable. And so was victory for the one, defeat for the other.

[31] *Litt. Wallie*, p. 104. It is worth adding that some contemporaries believed that under the terms of the Treaty of 1277 Llywelyn was obliged to come to parliament once or twice a year and that his failure to do so in 1278 immediately aroused Edward I's suspicions.

PART IV

CONQUEST AND SETTLEMENT
1277–1317

CHAPTER 13

CONQUEST

EDWARD I's first campaign against Llywelyn ap Gruffudd lasted in its entirety just under one year. Llywelyn was proclaimed a rebel on 12 November 1276; he submitted to the king's terms on 9 November 1277. The campaign was carefully planned, well co-ordinated and, above all, well paced, so that it reached its climax effortlessly. The Marcher lords were the first off the mark; their forays and incursions, which had done so much to undermine the Treaty of 1267, were now officially encouraged. The young earl of Hereford recovered most of Brecon, Ralph Tony Elfael, Peter Corbet the western half of the lordship of Caus, while in Glamorgan the earl of Gloucester's officer refused the Welsh a truce and imposed a trade embargo against them. But the campaign was not to be left to uncoordinated Marcher enterprise; that was not Edward I's style. Three military commands were created based on Chester, Montgomery, and Carmarthen. The task of the commanders was to win control over the outer bulwarks of Llywelyn's principality, driving him back into his patrimony in Gwynedd. So successfully did they undertake their work that all that was left to Edward I, when he appeared at Chester in July 1277, was to deliver the *coup de grâce*. Royal forces from Chester soon persuaded two of the princelings of northern Powys to submit, while in May 1277 the native garrison at Dinas Brân burnt the castle rather than see it fall into English hands. The successes achieved from Montgomery and Oswestry were even more striking. Dolforwyn, Llywelyn's recently built castle overlooking the Severn, capitulated on 8 April 1277 after an eight-day siege. Builth was taken; by May a new castle was under construction there. Gradually, English rule was re-imposed on the whole crucial area of the middle March from Cedewain in the north to Brecon in the south. Patrick Chaworth, the local commander at Carmarthen, proved equally successful in Deheubarth: one by one the castles of the Tywi valley fell to him; during April and May the leading princelings of Deheubarth submitted to him, stumbling over one another in their anxiety to turn surrender to the English into a means of furthering their ambitions at the expense of other members of their own family; Ceredigion was overrun with surprising ease and speed; by 25 July Edmund of Lancaster, the king's brother and now commander of his forces in south Wales, had reached Llanbadarn and began to erect a new castle at Aberystwyth.

By that date Edward I had arrived with his army at Chester, confident in the knowledge that Llywelyn had been isolated, that the whole of his principality other than Gwynedd had already been overrun, and that his allies had either defected or been forced to surrender. Edward's own task was thereby much more limited and well-defined. Nevertheless, he proceeded with great care and deliberateness. His army moved by slow stages along the coastal route into north Wales, clearing large swathes of woodland as it went to avoid the danger of ambush and to facilitate the movement of supplies, and establishing firm bases at Flint (now making its first appearance in history) and Rhuddlan to cover its rear, before proceeding to Degannwy on the Conwy estuary by 29 August. There Edward awaited the results of a major military initiative he had undertaken in sending a large force of troops by sea to Anglesey to harass Llywelyn in the rear of his principality and to harvest the crops so essential to him if he were to withstand a prolonged siege in his mountain fortress. The impact of that initiative on Llywelyn, both economically and psychologically, was devastating, coming as it did at the end of nine months of accumulated disasters. He soon entered into negotiations and by early November he had made his submission.

In terms of military strategy Edward I's first Welsh campaign heralded no major departures from earlier royal expeditions against north Wales. It followed much the same route as the expedition of John in 1211 and those of Henry III in 1241 and 1245; it penetrated less far than the former and less speedily than the latter. Like Henry III before him, Edward relied heavily on his own household knights and sergeants as an advance force which could undertake some of the essential reconnoitring work, as the nucleus of the cavalry strength of his main army, and as a permanent headquarters staff. More innovative was his recruitment of large forces of footsoldiers, which were to become such a notable feature of Edward's later campaigns. By August 1277 he had some 15,600 such troops in his pay, more than half of whom had been recruited within Wales itself. The problems of managing such large forces were already proving daunting, and within one month many of the footsoldiers had been sent home. Even so, Edward had shown that he had the will and the means to raise and to deploy military forces on a scale unprecedented in the history of warfare in medieval Britain. Indeed, the real significance of the 1277 campaign lies in demonstrating the speed and thoroughness with which the resources of the English kingdom could be mobilized for war. Crossbowmen were recruited from Gascony; heavy war-horses were imported from France; carts, wagons, ships, and boats were commandeered and brought to Chester; provisions were assembled in abundance, so that the problems of victualling, which had reduced the English army to such penury in 1245, were readily overcome; armies of woodcutters, carpenters, diggers, and

masons were forcibly recruited—some 1,800 axemen were employed
cutting a road through the woods between Flint and Rhuddlan in August
1277, while another 530 men were at work on the new fortifications at
Flint; and a ready flow of cash was more than amply provided by the credit
afforded by Edward I's Italian bankers, notably the Riccardi of Lucca. It
was a remarkable display of the capacity of the nascent nation-state to
mobilize its resources for a co-ordinated and centralized war-effort. Faced
with such a display, the best that Llywelyn could do was to resort to the
tactics of withdrawal and the occasional guerrilla ambush; deserted by his
allies, even such tactics could do no more than postpone the hour of
reckoning. It had become a conflict of David and Goliath.

The Treaty of Aberconwy represented a comprehensive humiliation for
Llywelyn, all the greater than the Peace of Woodstock thirty years earlier,
since his ambitions in the mean time had soared to such dizzy heights. He
submitted himself to the will and mercy of the king and offered a massive
fine of £50,000 for his 'disobedience'. He was made to eat humble pie in
ample measure: he travelled forthwith to Rhuddlan to swear fealty and,
before the year was out, he journeyed to London—not to the frontiers of
Wales as he had once demanded—to do homage to the king in the most
public manner at the Christmas court. He was required to hand over ten
hostages from the leading men of Gwynedd and to free and reinstate his
political enemies. He was still addressed, incongruously and almost
mockingly, as prince of Wales. It was now an empty title, a cruel memento
of former days of glory.[1] The king reserved to himself the homages of all
but five of the princelings of Wales—four members of the Powys dynasty
holding small estates in the upper Dee valley and Rhys Fychan ap Rhys ap
Maelgwn, a landless exile from Deheubarth. Llywelyn was allowed to
retain the homages of these five as a sop to his dignity, but for his life only;
thereafter their homages were to revert to the Crown. Llywelyn was
further embarrassed and impoverished by being compelled to take
cognizance of his brothers' claims to a share of their patrimony. From the
outset of the war Edward I, like earlier English kings, had cast himself in
the role of not only an offended feudal lord but also the upholder of the
Welsh custom of partibility. The right of Owain Goch, Llywelyn's eldest
brother and his prisoner for over twenty years, to his share of Gwynedd
was recognized; he soon came to terms with Llywelyn and was settled in
the *cantref* of Llŷn. Another brother, Rhodri, succeeded in persuading
Llywelyn in the king's presence in September 1278 to honour his
commitment to buy out Rhodri's claim to his share in the principality in

---

[1] The Oseney annals in a French summary of the terms of the peace suggest that no one
was to bear the title of prince after Llywelyn's death: *Annales Monastici*, ed. H. R. Luard
(Rolls Series, 1564–9), IV, 273–4. Several English chroniclers reveal detailed knowledge of
the terms of the Treaty, which suggests that official summaries of it were circulated.

return for a gift of 1,000 marks. It was Dafydd, the youngest brother, who had posed much the most serious threat to Llywelyn; and it was he who was now treated most generously. Llywelyn was allowed to hold Dafydd's hereditary share in Gwynedd uwch Conwy for life while the king recompensed Dafydd by a grant of the two *cantrefi* of Rhufoniog and Dyffryn Clwyd and the lordship of Hope. Territorially, Llywelyn's humiliation was completed by the surrender to the king of the whole of the Four Cantrefi (i.e. the district between the Conwy and the Dee estuary) and any other lands which the king had conquered from him. The territorial status quo as it had prevailed in 1247 was virtually restored: that was the measure of Edward's victory.

In the circumstances which faced him in the autumn of 1277 the terms conceded at Aberconwy were, perhaps, the best that Llywelyn could hope to secure. Edward I had indeed shown a measure of calculated magnanimity in victory—pardoning the fine of £50,000 and the annual rent of 1,000 marks for Anglesey, leaving Llywelyn his title of prince of Wales, conceding to him the homages of five minor rulers, and providing for Dafydd out of his own conquests. Yet the ambiguities and security clauses in the Treaty made it clear enough that there was ample room for continuing royal supervision and intervention. The position with regard to Anglesey was ominous: it was dealt with separately from the rest of Gwynedd in the various peace instruments and at one stage Edward had toyed with the idea of keeping it for himself. It was now granted to Llywelyn and to the legitimate heirs of his body; in the event of his dying without such heirs—and the actuarial possibilities were high, given that he was an unmarried man probably approaching, if he had not already reached, his fiftieth year—it was to revert to the king.[2] The status of Dafydd's potential share in the lands of Gwynedd (including Anglesey) was equally ominous: Llywelyn was indeed allowed to hold that share, but for his life only, with a clear hint that on Llywelyn's death, with or without heirs, the issue of whether or not Dafydd should then be allotted his share of the inheritance in Gwynedd itself could be re-opened, especially as the king's grant of land to Dafydd was to lapse on the death of either Dafydd or Llywelyn. Llywelyn was required to pay 500 marks annually to the king in discharge of his outstanding debts under the Treaty of Montgomery; these instalments were to serve as recurrent reminders to him of the royal munificence, for they were to be treated as token payments for Anglesey and for Dafydd's rightful claim to Gwynedd. Most ominous of all, Llywelyn's submission was to be reiterated annually. Each year twenty

[2] The uncertainty was further compounded by the exclusion, in the grant of Anglesey to the heirs of Llywelyn's body, of the portion that should belong to Dafydd. The various instruments of the peace to be found in *Litt. Wallie*, pp. 116–22 need to be supplemented by the letters in 'Calendar of Welsh Rolls', *Calendar of Chancery Rolls Various 1277–1326*, pp. 157–60.

men from each *cantref* in the prince's possession were to swear, in the presence of the king's agents, that they would observe, and cause the prince to observe, the terms of the Treaty and withdraw from his fealty and homage if he failed to do so. Llywelyn was on parole for his good behaviour, with his own subjects as the warrantors of his fealty.[3]

The Treaty of Aberconwy was concerned only with Edward I's relations with Llywelyn ap Gruffudd; it thereby conceals the extent of the royal advance in Wales in 1276–7. In north-east Wales the king not only kept the two *cantrefi* of Rhos and Tegeingl in his own hands, he also retained the lands of the young sons of Madog ap Gruffudd Maelor of northern Powys under his effective control. Southern Powys, now restored to Gruffudd ap Gwenwynwyn, was a pliant English protectorate and the arrangements that Gruffudd made for the division and descent of his estates were enrolled in the royal chancery. Royal power was equally prominent in the middle March, which had been so crucial a district in the Anglo-Welsh balance of power throughout the thirteenth century: the key districts of Ceri and Cedewain, in spite of a token nod in the direction of the claims of the native dynasty of the area, were retained in royal control until they were granted to the royal favourite, Roger Mortimer, in 1279; while Builth was restored to its status of the 1240s as a royal lordship guarding the routes down the Wye valley. But it was in Deheubarth that the map of royal power in Wales was most dramatically redrawn. The speed with which the various descendants of the Lord Rhys rushed to come to terms with the king in the spring and summer of 1277 did not save most of them—Rhys ap Maredudd was the notable exception—from extensive territorial expropriation. In Ystrad Tywi, Rhys Wyndod surrendered the fortress of Dinefwr, the traditional centre of the kingdom of Deheubarth; it was henceforth a base for English authority in the area. Royal bailiffs were also placed in charge of Rhys's two former castles of Llanymddyfri and Carreg Cennen, while his prolonged attempts to recover the commotes of Perfedd and Hirfryn from the royal protégé, John Giffard, were recurrently frustrated by contrived judicial delays. Most remarkable of all were the royal acquisitions in Ceredigion: there, through surrender and confiscation, royal control was imposed on the whole district from the Dyfi to the Aeron.[4] Edward I had ensured for himself a measure of direct dominion in native Wales such as no earlier king had enjoyed.

---

[3] There are recurrent references, both in the chronicles and in Llywelyn's charges in 1282, that Edward wrung further secret concessions from Llywelyn, either at Westminster in December 1277 or at Worcester in October 1278, regarding the succession to Gwynedd or the right to receive men there against the king's will.

[4] The descendants of Maredudd ab Owain surrendered Mefenydd and Anhuniog on 2 May 1277, while the northern commotes of Genau'r Glyn, Perfedd, and Creuddyn were forfeited when Rhys Fychan ap Rhys ap Maelgwn defected to Llywelyn in August 1277 and the forfeiture was confirmed in the Treaty of Aberconwy.

Edward I's success in 1277 was comprehensive. It involved much more than bringing a recalcitrant vassal to heel; it represented a major redistribution of power in favour of the English, and in particular of the king, throughout Wales. Edward was now intent on ensuring that this redistribution of authority should prove permanent, not merely dependent on the fortunes of war or of a single campaign. In the next few years he gave affairs in Wales a measure of sustained and detailed attention—including a personal visit to Rhuddlan in September 1278—such as it had hitherto never received from an English king. Much of that attention was personal: his leading officers there were briefed by him 'by word of mouth'; and issues were referred to him for his personal consideration and decision, if they involved important policy matters or created significant precedents or turned on the interpretation of the peace terms of 1277.[5] It was some indication of the importance that Edward I now attached to the affairs of Wales that from November 1277 copies of all official correspondence relating to Wales were entered on separate Welsh Rolls.

Edwards's first task was to ensure the military security of the new dispensation he had created in Wales. In that task the stone castle occupied the premier place. Henry III had already demonstrated the cardinal role of the stone castle in containing the Welsh and in serving as an instrument of military domination and, thereby, of civilian control. More recently, that lesson had been reinforced by Marcher experience, notably in Gilbert Clare's magnificent new fortress of Caerffili. Edward I, for his part, had had ample occasion on his recent crusade to observe the latest developments in the art of military fortification—as at Aigues Mortes, whence he set sail in 1270, or at St Georges-d'Espéranche in Savoy on his return journey in 1273. He now set about to apply the lessons he had learnt to his newly conquered lands in Wales. During 1277 work was begun on four major new castles—Flint, Rhuddlan, Aberystwyth and Builth; royal initiative and resources were also involved in at least three other new, or newly constructed, castles, those at Ruthin, Caergwrle (Hope), and Hawarden. Edward's castle-building in Wales was informed from the outset by certain distinctive characteristics—intelligence in the choice of site, the remarkable speed at which each castle was built, thoroughness and even ruthlessness in the deployment of resources and manpower, and enterprise and innovation in the application of the latest principles of military architecture. Edward showed his independence of judgement by choosing new sites for three out of four of his new major castles (Builth being the exception) and by abandoning the sites at Degannwy and Diserth on which his father had expended such energy and money. At Rhuddlan he reverted to an earlier Norman site; but it was the measure of the ambition and determination of

---

[5] *Cal. Welsh Rolls*, pp. 160, 167, 182-3; *Welsh Assize Roll 1277-84*, pp. 237, 340.

the man that, in order to make the site fully accessible to supplies and relief by sea, he undertook the construction of a new deep-water canal, some two–three miles long: a remarkable feat of civil engineering. The canal and the four major new castles had been substantially completed by 1280 at a total cost of some £25–£30,000; that is, considerably more than the total recorded cost of the 1276–7 war. Such speed of execution was only made possible by the remarkable deployment of the resources of the English kingdom: the dimensions of Edward I's achievement in this respect are perhaps best indicated by recalling that already in August 1277—while the campaign against Llywelyn was still in progress—more than 2,300 diggers alone had been assembled at Flint, some of whom had been force-marched there from as far away as Lincoln.

Nor were Edward's military efforts confined to the four major new castles he commissioned. He kept some of the key native castles under his control even when the surrounding district was restored to native rulers—notably Dinas Brân in northern Powys, Dinefwr, Carreg Cennen, and Llanymddyfri in Deheubarth. Considerable sums were forthwith spent on their repair, so that by 1282 the king had an arc of new or newly repaired castles from Flint and Rhuddlan in the north-east to Aberystwyth and Cardigan in the south-west. He also initiated a campaign to clear and widen routes through the Welsh forests to ensure ease of passage for troops and supplies. The Marcher lords and native rulers were ordered to undertake such clearance work on their lands, and if they failed to do so, the king's justiciar in west Wales was to do the work for them at their expense. The command demonstrates vividly the masterfulness of Edward: no 'constitutional' scruples, on the part of Marcher lord or native ruler, were to be allowed to stand in the way of his determination to bring Wales firmly under his military control.

He showed the same purposefulness in consolidating his territorial and administrative position in the country. The campaign of 1276–7 had given Edward I a larger and more widely distributed territorial stake in Wales than that of any previous English king. He now set about to increase it. The feudal right of custody brought him the temporary control of certain important Marcher lordships during these crucial years—Cilgerran, Abergavenny, Oswestry, Clun, Mold, and Hope—but it was in native Wales that Edward made his important permanent acquisitions. In November 1279 he assumed control of the castles of Carmarthen and Cardigan and their appurtenant 'counties' from his brother Edmund who had held them since 1265; they were now to resume their role as centres from which royal military, administrative, and judicial authority radiated throughout south-west Wales. They were joined in that role by Dinefwr in the Tywi valley which Edward had confiscated in 1277; he reinforced his position there in June 1280 by forcibly annexing the commote of

Maenordeilo from Rhys ap Maredudd and in the same month he installed his confidant, Thomas Bek, as bishop of St Davids. Edward was also determined to extend his power in northern Powys, taking over the custody of Maelor Gymraeg and seeking to gain the reversion of dower lands in Maelor Saesneg. Royal bailiffs—sometimes chosen from loyal Welshmen, at other times from among well-tried royal servants—were initially appointed to govern and administer these royal lands in Wales; but here again Edward showed that he had recognized the need for a more permanent and coherent administrative organization. In January 1280 all the royal estates in west Wales were brought under a single civilian and military command, known as the justiciarship of west Wales; and the post was entrusted to Bogo Knovill, a former sheriff of Shropshire. In north Wales, after various experiments with the appointment of local Welshmen, the two *cantrefi* of Rhos and Tegeingl were placed clearly under the administrative, judicial, and financial control of the justice and chamberlain of Chester in June 1281. The lineaments of a permanent and centralized administration for the royal lands in Wales were beginning to emerge.

It was, in jurisdictional matters, however, that what turned out to be the most far-reaching developments were inaugurated. Short of the imposition of direct lordship, jurisdictional control was the most effective way of bringing royal suzerainty to bear on vassal rulers and their lands throughout the thirteenth century. So it now proved to be in Wales. Commissions were issued to deal with the claims of the successive widows of the rulers of northern Powys, to consider the pleas of the princelings of Deheubarth, and to sort out disputes between Welsh abbeys and local rulers: thereby the status of the king's court as the fount of justice for the native dynasties of Wales—a role which had fallen into abeyance since 1258—was restored. In west Wales the courts of the royal bailiffs of Carmarthen, Dinefwr, Cardigan, and Llanbadarn extended their jurisdictional authority aggressively over the surrounding countryside; even Thomas Bek, faithful royal servant and newly appointed bishop of St Davids, was stung to protest at the jurisdictional high-handedness of the new justice of west Wales. But it was Edward I himself who launched much the most significant jurisdictional initiative. On 10 January 1278—within less than two months of the Treaty of Aberconwy—he appointed seven justices 'to hear and determine all suits and pleas both of lands and of trespasses . . . in the marches and in Wales and to do justice therein according to the laws and customs of those parts'.[6] Later in the year the number of justices was reduced to four, with Walter Hopton, a Shropshire man and an experienced royal judge, serving as president.[7] Similar commissions were

---

[6] *Cal. Welsh Rolls*, p. 163.
[7] The three other members of the commission were Welshmen: Hywel ap Meurig, a long-standing servant of the Bohuns and Mortimers in the March and now royal bailiff at Builth;

issued for west Wales and for the lands of the bishop of St Davids. These commissions, more particularly the Hopton commission, announced clearly that the king intended to extend his judicial authority throughout Wales. The Hopton commission, it is true, held its sessions at royal centres in Wales (21 out of 38 of them at Montgomery); the original summonses referred to lands which could be regarded, by the most generous construction, as coming within direct royal authority; there was no direct reference in the terms of the commission to jurisdiction over Gwynedd or over the Marcher lordships of the south and east as such. Yet there was no doubting that, potentially at least, the new commissions marked an important extension of royal jurisdiction. They referred to 'the Marches and Wales' *tout court*; they specifically commanded the princelings of Deheubarth and Dafydd ap Gruffudd in north-east Wales to be attendant; in the reissued commission in June 1278, some even of the major Marcher lords were required to see that their men appeared; and the proceedings of the Hopton commission reveal that litigants from all parts of native Wales and the March alike (even the south-east March) brought their cases before it. The king who paraded his wish to be 'debtor of justice . . . to every man of his power' seemed determined to discharge that debt throughout Wales.[8]

No one could have been more alarmed than Llywelyn ap Gruffudd. In the original commission of January 1278 he was ordered to appear before the justices 'to propound the suits of himself and his men and to do and receive justice'.[9] The peremptoriness of the command, the way he was treated as an ordinary litigant before an English court, and the summons to appear at Montgomery or Oswestry, all served to bring home to him during 1278 that his defeat in 1277 entailed not only major losses of land and authority in Wales but also a crippling blow to his dignity. Relations between king and prince, it is true, appeared at first proper and even cordial in the wake of the Treaty in November 1277. Edward I, as was his wont, showed considerable magnanimity once his mastery was acknowledged. He agreed to release Llywelyn's bride in January 1278; he handed back Llywelyn's hostages in September 1278 and presided at a settlement of Gwynedd's family disputes at Rhuddlan in the same month; he and his queen were present when Llywelyn and Eleanor de Montfort were eventually married in Worcester cathedral on 13 October 1278 and, indeed, he met the costs of the wedding feast and the transport of the bridal party to Wales; gifts were exchanged and a general atmosphere of geniality seemed to prevail. Edward promised that he would 'be

Rhys ap Gruffudd, formerly a servant of Llywelyn but now also on the royal payroll; and Gronw ap Heilyn, a confidant of Llywelyn and one of his negotiators in 1277 but now also serving as the king's bailiff in the cantref of Rhos.

[8] *Cal. Welsh Rolls*, p. 173.   [9] *Cal. Welsh Rolls*, p. 163.

benevolent and a friend to Llywelyn in all things'.[10] Llywelyn, for his part, went out of his way to display his good intentions: he paid his outstanding debts to Edward with scrupulous punctuality, and even delighted the king by the speed with which he accepted the new judicial procedures. 'With good will he seeks and receives justice and judgement', said Edward I of him in self-congratulatory terms.[11]

Yet such mutual amicability could hardly be expected to last, once Llywelyn had overcome the trauma of defeat and addressed himself to the restraints on his power and independence. The catalogue of Edward I's paternalistic interventions in Llywelyn's affairs must have stuck in the prince's gullet—reviewing the lands that Llywelyn was to assign in dower to his wife, giving his licence for grants of land which Llywelyn made within his own principality, ordering Llywelyn not to harass one of his political enemies, unctuously urging Llywelyn to act 'courteously and modestly' towards ecclesiastical liberties and threatening to send his justices to review complaints if he failed to do so, warning Llywelyn that if he defaulted on his financial obligation to his brother, Rhodri, royal officers would be sent into the principality of Wales to distrain on his lands and chattels, underlining the precariousness of Llywelyn's title to Anglesey by giving royal letters of protection to men going thither and instituting royal inquiries there, and baring his judical teeth by encouraging an aggrieved litigant to come to the king for redress 'if Llywelyn does not do him justice'.[12] Such admonitions would have irked any self-respecting magnate in England; to a man so hypersensitive to the dignity of his own princely status and so mindful of his own recent independence as Llywelyn ap Gruffudd, they must have galling in the extreme.

Llywelyn's sense of being deliberately belittled was compounded by his feeling of insecurity within his principality. Loyalties were brittle after 1277; tempers were short; suspicions ran deep, as men tried hard to keep their options open. The air was full of recriminations against men, such as Iorwerth Foel of Anglesey or Madog ab Einion of Dyffryn Clwyd, who had come to terms with the king in 1277 with unseemly speed. Llywelyn as ever tried to ensure loyalty by issuing threats: in December 1281 Rhys ap Gruffudd ab Ednyfed bound himself to the prince in £100 'on account of the disobedience we showed to the prince at Aberffro'.[13] Men's loyalties, especially in districts such as Perfeddwlad, were put under intolerable strains, as they tried to square their former support for Llywelyn with service to their new masters. Thus Ithel ap Bleddyn, Llywelyn's former keeper of his castle of Ewloe, was allowed to continue in the prince's service but only on condition of observing his overriding fealty to the Crown. Tensions with ecclesiastics continued: Anian, bishop of Bangor,

---

[10] *Ibid.*, p. 174.
[11] *Calendar of Close Rolls 1272-9*, p. 493.
[12] *Cal. Anc. Corr.*, p. 60.
[13] *Litt. Wallie*, p. 31.

took his complaints to the English king. Even former allies, such as the abbey of Aberconwy, wavered in their loyalty. The political atmosphere was undoubtedly fraught: one late manifestation of it was the plot against Llywelyn's life in the belfry at Bangor by his own men at the height of the war of 1282.

Yet in these difficult years Llywelyn showed remarkable resilience. He did not accept the defeat of 1277 as final. Rather did he secretly initiate plans to reassemble the strands of loyalty in different parts of Wales. Already in May 1278 five members of the dynasty of Deheubarth paid him a visit in his court at Dolwyddelan.[14] But it was in Powys that Llywelyn made his most determined attempts to pave the way for a come-back. In May 1278 the abbot of Aberconwy and the dean of Arllechwedd drew up a copy of the submission which Gruffudd ap Gwenwynwyn and his son had made to Llywelyn in 1274 and insisted that the submission was still valid. This would provide ecclesiastical and legal sanction for Llywelyn to move against Gruffudd when the time was ripe. In August of the same year he struck a significant secret deal with Gruffudd's steward or justiciar, Gruffudd ap Gwên of Cyfeiliog, whereby the latter agreed to defect to Llywelyn with all his resources when required to do so. Cyfeiliog lay next to Llywelyn's lands in Meirionydd. In another move to strengthen his position in this important frontier district Llywelyn took a lease of all Cymer's abbey's lands there for twelve years. He was also casting his eyes further afield. On 9 October 1281 he concluded a remarkable agreement at Radnor with Roger Mortimer of Wigmore, formerly one of his most bitter enemies. Both men pledged to support each other in peace and in war against all men except the king of England, his brother, and heirs. Llywelyn further flattered Roger by quitclaiming certain lands in Gwrtheyrnion to him. Most of these secret deals and agreements were probably directed against Gruffudd ap Gwenwynwyn. Be that as it may, they show that Llywelyn had not passively accepted his defeat. He was slowly and patiently laying the foundations for a recovery, much as he had done in the 1250s. He was still at work when the events of 1282 overwhelmed him.

Yet, however much he schemed, Llywelyn must have realized that his prospects and fears ultimately depended on the attitude of the king. The royal stake in Wales was now too extensive, and Edward I's own personal interest in and commitment to its affairs too great, for him to overlook any challenge to his authority or that of his allies there, however indirect it might be. Tension between king and prince certainly grew between 1277 and 1282. There were ample local incidents to fuel such tension—disputes about border areas and jurisdiction, high-handed actions by royal officials in frontier districts of Llywelyn's principality, the execution of two of

---

[14] It is possible that the deed, which survives only in a copy in *Litt. Wallie*, p. 43, is wrongly dated and belongs to the early 1270s rather than to 1278.

Llywelyn's men at Oswestry, and the distraint of Llywelyn's goods by the justice of Chester in retaliation for what Llywelyn regarded as his undoubted claim to the right of wreck. Annoying and indeed humiliating as some of these incidents were, none was an issue from which renewed conflict was likely to erupt. The dispute over Arwystli, however, became such an issue, for it eventually laid bare the unbridgeable chasm between the expectations and ambitions of Llywelyn, on the one hand, and the intentions of Edward I, on the other.

Arwystli was an upland *cantref* in central Wales. Until the late twelfth century it was ruled by its own dynasty but was always in danger of succumbing to the superior strength of its powerful neighbours, Gwynedd and Powys. Its rather anomalous position in the political geography of Wales—not dissimilar to that of Cedewain and Ceri—was reinforced by the fact that ecclesiastically it was an outlier of the diocese of Bangor rather than part of the bishopric of St Asaph. During the thirteenth century Arwystli was alternatively under the control of Gwynedd and Powys. Llywelyn ap Gruffudd had confirmed Gruffudd ap Gwenwynwyn's claim to it in 1263; but had deprived him of it in 1274, and was in possession of it himself on the outbreak of war in 1277. In February 1278 Llywelyn laid his claim to Arwystli against Gruffudd ap Gwenwynwyn before the Hopton commission. Strategically, Arwystli was certainly important for Llywelyn in the years after 1277: it would extend his rule into mid-Wales, and give his truncated principality a southern flank from which he could penetrate into the crucially important lordships of the middle March. As the dispute unfolded, however, issues of first principle were raised which overshadowed such strategic considerations.

When he first presented his plea, Llywelyn doubtless expected it to be quickly dispatched and that in the presence of the king himself. Instead, it meandered slowly and tortuously through four years of litigation and was still unresolved when the revolt of March 1282 broke out. It was heard—or aspects of it were considered—before the king himself, by the king and his magnates in parliament, and before the Hopton commission; it was recurrently adjourned on technicalities, such as the lack of proper credentials for attorneys or (as late as November 1281) the absence of the appropriate writ; it prompted two important inquiries into legal usage and practice in Wales, the Grey–Hamilton inquisition of October 1278 and the much more thorough investigation of early 1281; it triggered a search of royal judicial records for precedents from Henry III's reign; and it generated a vast amount of correspondence.

The issues in the Arwystli dispute were from an early stage confused, probably deliberately so. It is important to identify, however briefly, what those issues were, because from them and the mutual misunderstanding they occasioned developed the growing distrust between king and prince.

To Llywelyn the dispute and the procedures to settle it were straightforward; the application of those procedures would be a test of the king's adherence to the Treaty of Aberconwy. Two clauses in the Treaty dealt with future disputes about land in which the prince was involved. The first promised that the king would show full justice to Llywelyn 'according to the laws and customs of those parts in which the land lie'; the second provided that disputes should be settled 'according to the laws of the March for cases arising in the March and according to the laws of Wales for disputes arising in Wales'.[15] Arwystli, so Llywelyn not surprisingly claimed, was in Wales; therefore, the dispute ought to be heard according to Welsh law, by Welsh procedure, and accordingly—a point often overlooked by historical commentators—on the land itself, as Welsh law required. This remained the essence of Llywelyn's case throughout the dispute. It was a case which was difficult to gainsay. Gruffudd ap Gwenwynwyn, admittedly, tried to undermine it by claiming that, as a baron of the March and therefore a tenant-in-chief, any case against him (Gruffudd) ought to be heard in the king's court by common law. Yet that same argument when advanced by Gruffudd in a case against Roger Mortimer concerning the neighbouring district of Cedewain was dismissed by the justices, who decreed that the issue should be determined by Welsh law since it related to Welsh land.

Gruffudd ap Gwenwynwyn's counter-arguments would have counted for little had not Edward I himself in effect become a party to the dispute. Edward did not deny, though equally he did not concede, Llywelyn's claim that the dispute should be heard by Welsh law. What he did instead was to shift the argument away from the question of law to be used to the question of the nature of his own jurisdiction and of Llywelyn's position as litigant. He made the point in a rather short-tempered letter he wrote to Llywelyn as early as July 1278: 'disputes', he told Llywelyn peremptorily, 'ought to be heard and determined . . . at certain days and places that he (the king) shall cause to be prefixed for the parties. Therefore Llywelyn shall come before the king's justices in those parts at days and places that they shall make known to him to do and receive what justice shall dictate . . .'.[16] He repeated the point almost two years later when he informed Llywelyn that 'the magnates of Wales had of their own free will recognized that disputes which arose ought to be determined by the king's majesty by the king's writs before him or his justices'.[17] Edward I had turned the Arwystli dispute into a demonstration of his own mastery and masterfulness. Llywelyn was to be treated as an ordinary litigant—required to secure writs, expected to observe the due procedures of the king's court,

---

[15] *Litt. Wallie*, pp. 119–20.
[16] *Cal. Welsh Rolls*, p. 175. The first part of the first sentence was a quotation from the Treaty of Aberconwy; the second half was Edward I's gloss.
[17] *Welsh Assize Roll 1277–84*, p. 59.

summoned by royal justices at their convenience and to their sessions. Any concession to Welsh law would be made within the framework of the recognition of the king's jurisdictional supremacy; and since the king was the master of the judicial ceremonies, he would decide at what pace the game would be played. It must also have appeared to Llywelyn that the king would eventually decide who would be the winner, on a technicality or otherwise.

As the dispute dragged on, the issues broadened out. Llywelyn's appeal to Welsh law was no longer a technical issue; it was converted into a platform on which the identity of the Welsh as a people (L *nacio*), with a right to their own laws and customs, was to be defended. The propaganda of a national struggle was being born out of the Arwystli dispute. Edward I, for his part, set out to counter the case. His law commission of January–February 1281 was concerned in part to establish that Welsh law was by no means as universal in its application within Wales as Llywelyn claimed and that there were ample precedents for disputes from Wales being initiated by writ, heard before royal justices and terminated by jury. More ominously, he began to call in question the status of Welsh law itself, declaring that he could only allow it to stand if it were not derogatory to his Crown and to the rights of his kingdom and proclaiming that he would only uphold such Welsh laws as were 'just and reasonable'.[18] What had started as a dispute about land was developing into a full-blown political struggle, with the status and validity of Welsh law at its centre.

The Arwystli dispute was neither as simple as Llywelyn suggested nor as complex as Edward I made it out to be. Llywelyn was disingenuous in his assertion that the legal situation in native Wales was as clear-cut as he claimed: Welsh law was patchy in its application, regional in its practices, and changing rapidly in the thirteenth century, partly under princely direction. He was equally disingenuous in his claim, reiterated by many of his allies, that Edward I had 'granted to all Welshmen their Welsh law';[19] Edward I is not known to have made such a grant nor would such a 'national' grant have been meaningful in the political conditions of 1277. Edward I, for his part, made a mockery of justice by turning the law into an instrument of his own power (as he did likewise in his dealings with English magnates and Scottish kings), by his deliberate refusal to consider evidence which might prove awkward (whether the Grey–Hamilton inquiry of 1278 into Welsh law, or some of the evidence submitted to the 1281 inquiry), by his failure to apply precedents created by his own justices (as in the case concerning Roger Mortimer's claim in Cedewain), and by his highly selective reading of history and legal precedents for his own ends in support of the cause of his client, Gruffudd ap Gwenwynwyn. In any

---

[18] *Welsh Assize Roll*, p. 59.
[19] *Welsh Assize Roll*, pp. 258, 266, 269; *Register . . . Johannis Peckham*, II, p. 446.

review of the evidence concerning the Arwystli dispute it is difficult to
dissent from the view that Edward I was guilty of 'double dealing', just as
historians in other contexts have charged him with 'moral shabbiness' and
'wilful abuse of his power'.[20] Even if we refrain from such moral
judgements, Edward's prevarications and legal chicanery in this case can
hardly be construed other than as a sustained display of gross political
insensitivity or as a calculated act of political humiliation. Edward was
exhibiting one of the most unattractive and consistent features of his
character as king—the gratuitous belittling of his opponents and greater
subjects. Llywelyn, as he himself said, was being 'altogether put in
despair', his sense of being disgraced far outweighing any value that
attached to the land in question.[21] Desperate men are dangerous men.

Llywelyn's despair, however, would not of itself have sparked a national
revolt; such a revolt would only be possible if Llywelyn's personal
grievances could be aligned with a more general sense of resentment and
outrage throughout native Wales. It quickly became apparent in 1282 that
such pent-up anger had indeed been welling up within Wales. Native
princelings found royal policy and behaviour as offensive as did Llywelyn
himself: Rhys Wyndod of Ystrad Tywi was galled by the way that his claim
to the commotes of Hirfryn and Perfedd was being balked and royal favour
shown to his adversary, John Giffard; the sons of Maredudd ab Owain in
Ceredigion complained bitterly of the way they were maltreated and their
jurisdiction over their own men undermined; Dafydd ap Gruffudd, prickly
and ambitious as ever, resented every royal intrusion on his lands and
liberties. Most significant of all, and best-documented, was the growing
disenchantment of Llywelyn ap Gruffudd Maelor, one of the rulers of
northern Powys. He was one of the first to defect to Edward I in 1276; his
disillusion was, therefore, all the more bitter. He found himself harassed
by summonses and citations, bullied by the constable of Oswestry, and
forced to defend his title to his property against every vexatious litigant; he
became deeply suspicious of royal interference in his own family's
territorial settlement, openly doubted the impartiality of the king's judicial
commission, and became a doughty defender of Welsh law and the
customary rights of his men. The royal partisan of 1276 was being
converted into the rebel of 1282: Llywelyn ap Gruffudd Maelor's attack on
Oswestry was one of the opening salvos in the revolt of that year.

That revolt, however, fed on a more general communal resentment of
English rule within Wales as well as on the bruised pride of particular
princelings. Such resentment was particularly virulent in districts such as

[20] J. Conway Davies in Welsh Assize Roll, p. 81; G. W. S. Barrow, Robert Bruce (2nd edn.
Edinburgh, 1976), p. 72; K. B. McFarlane, The Nobility of Later Medieval England (Oxford,
1973), p. 266.
[21] Cal. Anc. Corr., p. 91.

north Ceredigion and north-east Wales, which had been brought under English rule in 1277. Alien officials rode roughshod over cherished Welsh customs, such as the practice of allowing kinsmen to redeem the lives of condemned criminals; ancient rights of forest and pasture were disregarded; English burgesses in Wales, in the infant boroughs of Flint, Rhuddlan, and Aberystweyth, grossly abused their commercial privileges; the status-distinctions and privileges so beloved of Welshmen were ignored; promises of compensation for land seized to build castles were broken; and the clause in the Treaty of 1277 which promised that the men of the Four Cantrefi would continue to enjoy their liberties and customs had been flagrantly flouted. Resentment in particular focused on two issues. The first was the behaviour of royal officials in Wales. Local Welshmen, such as Goronwy ap Heilyn and Gruffudd ab Iorwerth, who sought to co-operate with and to serve the new English administration and could have made that administration acceptable to the native community, were increasingly thrust aside. Instead high-handed and tyrannical officials, such as Reginald de Grey in Perfeddwlad, Roger Lestrange in Oswestry, Roger Clifford in Moldsdale, and Bogo de Knovill in Llanbadarn, widened their authority and did so insensitively. The charges against them were doubtless exaggerated; yet Edward was repeating the mistake of his father in the 1240s—that of allowing alien governors too free a hand to bully native society into submission. The second issue which united native opposition throughout Wales was the defence of their laws and their hostility to the imposition of English laws and procedures. The defence of their laws and customs was a banner under which all Welshmen could unite. As the Dunstable annalist put it, Llywelyn and his brother Dafydd made accord 'that they would stand together for their laws'.[22] The war of 1277 had been fought in pursuit of the personal quarrel of the native prince of Wales with Edward I; the war of 1282 was truly a war of national liberation under the leadership of Llywelyn ap Gruffudd.

The Welsh burst into rebellion in late March 1282. Dafydd ap Gruffudd swooped down on Hawarden castle on the night of March 21; the next day a huge raid, under the leadership of Llywelyn ap Gruffudd Maelor, ravaged Oswestry, and in the next few days the princelings of Deheubarth captured the castles of Aberystwyth, Llanymddyfri, and Carreg Cennen. The outburst was clearly well-planned and co-ordinated. Llywelyn ap Gruffudd himself claimed that he was not cognizant of the original plot; its timing and the role that his brother had played in the initial moves, both in north and south Wales, might indeed well have displeased him. Yet he had little option but to join the revolt and to assume its leadership; indeed he

[22] *Annales Monastici*, III, 291.

had probably every inclination to do so. The revolt was without a doubt 'a widespread popular rising of the Welsh'.[23] Neither south-east nor south-west Wales, it is true, participated and they were to contribute handsomely to Edward I's forces. It is also true that Edward I found ready support from Gruffudd ap Gwenwynwyn of Powys and Rhys ap Maredudd of Ystrad Tywi, and that men, such as Hywel ap Gruffudd ab Ednyfed and his brother, Rhys, or Gruffudd ap Tudur, whose families had long been associated with the dynasty of Gwynedd, were now sufficiently disillusioned with Llywelyn or his prospects to join the king's forces at the earliest opportunity. But it is not the exceptions or the defections which are impressive, but rather the remarkably broad-based support—regionally, dynastically, and socially—that the revolt elicited.[24] Like all such movements, it fed on a whole host of tangled motives; but in its essence it appears to have been a massive act of protest against English rule. It leaders may have expected that the English dispensation in Wales might be swept away as effectively and quickly as in 1256–8, that Edward I would be worn down by guerrilla warfare, and that a measure of native recovery might be effected as so often in the past history of Wales. If so, they had mistaken their man.

Edward I's response was one of outrage and determination. Llywelyn was not now, as in 1277, simply a contumacious vassal; he was a faithless betrayer of his sworn word and, what was worse, the leader of a faithless people. The king announced his intention 'to repress the rebellion and malice of the Welsh' and before the year was out he had proclaimed that he would be content with nothing less than the final solution of the Welsh problem: 'to put an end finally to the matter that he has now commenced of putting down the malice of the Welsh'.[25] Words were matched by action. Edward could not prepare his campaign with the same leisurely deliberation as in 1276–7; he had to act quickly if he was to prevent the revolt from engulfing the whole of Wales. Within four days of the outbreak of the revolt he had created three military commands to organize the initial response to the challenge and had entrusted them to three of his close confidants, Reginald Grey in Chester, Roger Mortimer in mid-Wales, and Robert Tibetot in the west. Yet speed was not allowed to dilute the thoroughness of the preparations for the major onslaught. The county levies, mainly from the western counties, and the hired retinues were supplemented by a force of 1,500 highly effective, if expensive, Gascon crossbowmen; more than 40 ships were commandeered from the Cinque Ports to carry supplies and prepare for the assault on Anglesey; provisions were ordered to be purveyed in Ponthieu, Gascony, Ireland, and every

[23] J. G. Edwards in *Litt. Wallie*, pp. lxvi–lxvii.
[24] For support from the princely dynasties of Deheubarth and Powys see genealogical tables above pp. 225, 234.
[25] *Cal. Welsh Rolls*, pp. 213, 275.

part of England and dispatched to two huge depots at Whitchurch and Chester, to be placed under the charge of a royal paymaster; already by 31 May a muster of 1,010 diggers and 345 carpenters was to be assembled at Chester 'for the king's works in Wales'.[26] No expense was spared: the Riccardi were as usual a convenient source of ready cash and when money ran short Edward had no scruples in seizing funds collected for the crusade in the Temple and various cathedrals; clergy and townsmen were encouraged to make voluntary loans; parliament in January 1283 imposed a tax of a thirtieth on movables; and the money was channelled through the wardrobe (i.e. the royal household office), and a special wardrobe account was kept for the campaign. Indeed, there was need for such an account, for the campaign costs were to total some £150,000, about seven times the cost of the 1277 campaign.

Edwards's second Welsh campaign bore many of the hallmarks of the first. It was, by medieval standards, a remarkably well-coordinated campaign. Local commanders had, of necessity, to be given some free hand; but their correspondence reveals their clear awareness of the general strategy underlying the campaign and their deference to central command. The king himself directed the course and tempo of the offensive; he was not afraid to remove commanders, such as the earl of Gloucester, who showed themselves militarily wanting; he relied heavily, as in 1277, on tried knights of his own household: men such as Robert Tibetot, Otto Granson, Bogo de Knovill, Grimbald Pauncefoot, and Roger Lestrange. He proceeded with the same cautious deliberateness which had characterized his actions in 1277—forbidding his commanders (as Roger Lestrange reported) from putting their troops in undue peril; carefully repairing castles, such as Hope, as the campaign proceeded, so that his rear was covered; moving slowly down the Clwyd valley and up that of the Conwy to make sure that Perfeddwlad was securely in his grasp before he embarked on the assault on Snowdonia; and making all the preparations, including the issue of warm clothing for the troops, for a sustained winter campaign in Wales—a prospect which no earlier king had dared contemplate.

The general aims of Edward I's strategy in 1282 were very similar to those of 1277 and, with the exception of some notable set-backs, they were well executed. His first task was to reduce native Wales outside of Gwynedd to submission. It was certainly a more daunting task than in 1277, for this time there was fierce resistance and few rapid defections. The flames of revolt had to be extinguished in each area in turn; and English forces might be overwhelmed by disastrous guerrilla ambushes, as happened to the earl of Gloucester's patrol in the Tywi valley on 16 June. Yet in spite of such occasional successes, it was difficult for scattered and

[26] *Cal. Welsh Rolls*, pp. 247–8.

localized Welsh forces to mount sustained resistance to the advancing English forces. By the end of the summer the fighting had been extinguished in Ystrad Tywi and Ceredigion, and though the picture was less clear in the middle March, local commanders, such as John Giffard, Roger Mortimer, Roger Lestrange, and Roger Springhose, were more than holding their own. In the north Edward's first task was the complete subjection of Perfeddwlad. It was a task which took him the better part of three months; but the thoroughness of his progress—crowned by the fall of Dafydd ap Gruffudd's castles at Ruthin and Denbigh in September–October —meant that Edward could contemplate the final stage of his campaign, the assault on Snowdonia, confident in the knowledge that his lines of communication with his base at Chester were secure. Edward had already opened a second front in late August by sending a large force under Luke Tany, former steward of Gascony, to subdue Anglesey (as in 1277) and to make the preparations for an assault thence on the mainland to link up with Edward's forces as they moved westwards. Llywelyn was caught in a classic military trap: English troops were ready to advance on him from south, south-east, and east, and from Anglesey; his supplies were running desperately short.

Under similar circumstances in autumn 1277 he had capitulated. It was at this stage that Archbishop Pecham of Canterbury chose to launch a diplomatic initiative in an attempt to bring the bloodshed to an end and prevent further acts of sacrilege (such as the recent burning of St Asaph cathedral). His credentials for the task were far from promising: in earlier negotiations with the Welsh he had shown himself tactless, irascible, and insensitive, all too ready to issue *ex cathedra* statements on the morals of the Welsh and on the shortcomings of their laws, to act as a defender of the superiority of royal custom and his own authority over the Welsh dioceses, and to respond to royal requests to excommunicate the Welsh. Yet his initiative in October–November 1282 was imaginative and brave, and undertaken in the face of Edward I's hostility. Well-intentioned as it was, it only served to show that there was no hope for compromise. Edward I was intent on nothing less than the total conquest of the whole of north Wales and the disinheritance of the house of Gwynedd; the most that he was willing to offer to Llywelyn was land to the value of a thousand pounds in England and the prospect of a hereditary earldom, if he begat male heirs by a new wife (Eleanor de Montfort had died in childbirth on 19 June), and to Dafydd honourable provision so that he would go on crusade, returning only with the king's permission; no specific promises were made that the libeties, customs, and laws of the inhabitants of Gwynedd and Perfeddwlad would be protected; they would have to be content with vague promises of the royal clemency and mercy, and even vaguer references to their well-being and honour. Such terms—and it is rare for secret conditions, as on

this occasion, to be much more humiliating than the public proposals—
were clearly unacceptable.

They elicited from the Welsh not only a comprehensive dossier of their
individual grivances against royal justices and bailiffs, but also an eloquent
and highly dignified defence of their revolt as a struggle to maintain their
national identity as a people. Llywelyn could appeal, as in earlier days, to
his obligation to his conscience and to his status as a prince; but he and his
apologists now cast their case in much broader terms. They drew on a
historical mythology which emphasized the prince's rights as the descendant
of Kamber, son of Brutus; they declared that in any submission they must
stand by their 'laws and rights' (*juribus nostris et legibus nobis . . .
reservatis*); they claimed that their struggle was not merely that of the
prince or people of Gwynedd but of the people of Wales as a whole and
that such was the oppression of the English that 'the people preferred to
die rather than to live'; and they asserted that even if the prince himself
submitted, his subjects would refuse to do homage 'to any stranger of
whose language, manners and laws they were entirely ignorant'.[27] Such
declarations savour of the rhetoric of propaganda; but they also surely
make it clear that Llywelyn, his advisers, and his allies had come to view
and to present their struggle as one to defend the national identity of the
Welsh people—*nostra nacio* was a phrase that came easily to their
pens—and to preserve a measure of political independence for native
Wales. Edward I, for his part, cast the struggle equally uncompromisingly
in terms of a conflict of two peoples. Not only did Llywelyn and Dafydd
belong to a 'family of traitors', the Welsh themselves were a perfidious
people—'full of treason', as the chronicler Pierre Langtoft put it—whose
history was one prolonged record of deception and of treacherous attacks
on the English.[28] It is not only historical hindsight which has come to
record the revolt of 1282 as 'the last serious struggle for Welsh
independence'; so it appeared to many contemporaries.[29]

It was not a struggle which the Welsh could hope to win. They were
given a temporary fillip to their morale during the negotiations with
Archbishop Pecham by the disaster which overcame Luke Tany and his
forces as he, prematurely and possibly in a treacherous attempt to take
advantage of the peace discussions, sought to effect a crossing from
Anglesey to the mainland across a pontoon bridge of specially constructed
boats. One disaster, however, could not change the course of the war;
instead, it hardened Edward's determination to make preparations for a
prolonged campaign and to summon extra troops and supplies. Llywelyn

---

[27] *Registrum . . . Johannis de Peckham*, II, 437–40, 469–71.
[28] *Cal. Welsh Rolls*, p. 281; *Chronicle of Pierre de Langtoft*. ed. T. Wright (Rolls Series, 1866–8), II, 220.
[29] F. M. Powicke, *The Thirteenth Century* (Oxford, 1953), p. 421.

had little option but to try to open a new front. There was much to attract him to the middle March: it was an area where the death of Roger Mortimer on 26 October had created a vacuum of lordship and where the local communities, under leaders such as Rhys ap Gruffudd of Builth, needed to be bolstered in their resistance to the English forces; it was also an area where Llywelyn and his grandfather had assiduously woven ties of loyalty and service which might now stand the prince in good stead. There is also more than a possibility that Llywelyn was lured into the district by a treacherous invitation from Roger Mortimer's sons, an invitation made all the more plausible by the accord which he had struck with their father just a year earlier. Over and above such considerations was the need for Llywelyn to try to seize some measure of the military initiative from Edward while the king was still recovering from news of the disaster to Luke Tany's force and, above all, to break free from the royal stranglehold which was threatening to suffocate his principality.

Militarily, the decision to open a new front in the Wye valley had much to commend it; but for Llywelyn and his cause it proved fatal. On 11 December 1282 he was killed within a few miles of Builth, probably in or after a major skirmish with a larger Marcher force led by the Mortimer brothers, John Giffard and Roger Lestrange. It was Roger Lestrange who dispatched the news in a communiqué to the king: 'Know, sir, . . . that Llywelyn ap Gruffudd is dead, his army broken, and all the flower of his men killed'. The Welsh chronicler was equally telegraphic in its brevity: 'And then all Wales was cast to the ground'.[30] The poets, so often worthily conventional and wooden in their elegies, felt the loss to be so cosmic in its significance that their poetry scaled heights rarely paralleled before or since in Welsh literature. 'Is it the end of the world', mused one of them despairingly. 'Do you not see the whole world is a danger'? asked another.[31] The tone of almost suicidal despair that characterized their elegies betokened their awareness that there was an awesome finality about the events of December 1282 for Wales as for Llywelyn.

Llywelyn's brother, it is true, carried on the struggle, henceforth known as 'Dafydd's war'. Edward I did not allow Llywelyn's death to change the tempo of his advance; he still moved with cautious deliberateness, not crossing the Conwy until January 1283. But his progress was inexorable: the princelings of Deheubarth began to surrender; Dolwyddelan was taken on 18 January; the Anglesey troops crossed the Menai straits and soon overran the major centres of Snowdonia; Edward now felt confident

---

[30] *Cal. Anc. Corr.*, pp. 83–4; *Brenhinedd y Saesson*, ed. T. Jones (Cardiff, 1971), *s.a.* 1282 (p. 259).
[31] T. Roberts, 'Englynion Marwnad i Llywelyn ab Gruffudd', *BBCS* 26 (1974–6), p. 11 ('Oes derfyn byd'); *Oxford Book of Welsh Verse*, p. 45 ('Poni welwch chi'r byd wedi r'bydiaw').

enough to move his headquarters from Rhuddlan to Aberconwy on 13 March; on 25 April the garrison of Dafydd's last major outpost, Castell y Bere, surrendered. Dafydd kept up the pretence of power for a few more weeks, confirming territorial arrangements in Ceredigion (long since under royal control) and dispatching a messenger to summon the men of the middle March to his aid; but in June Dafydd himself was captured by 'men of his own tongue' and dispatched to face a gruesome death. During July local assemblies were held throughout north Wales at which the leaders of each *cantref* in turn bound themselves in the sum of £2,000 for the maintenance of peace under threat of excommunication by the local bishop. The conquest of Wales was at last complete.

CHAPTER 14

SETTLEMENT

EDWARD I meant to savour his great victory in Wales in 1282–3 to the full. The Welsh had been a thorn in his side since his youth. Even now in his hour of triumph he recalled with pain some of the humiliating defeats he had suffered at their hands. One of his acts in 1284 was to commission tombstones to be transported from Bristol to Carmarthen to mark the graves of two of his commanders who had been killed in a notorious Welsh ambush at Cymerau in 1257; later, in 1290, he arranged for special masses to be celebrated for their souls. But in general the mood was one of exultation in recent victory rather than recollection of past defeats. In late July 1284 Edward, lover of tournaments and avid devotee of Arthurian mythology that he was, invited English and foreign knights alike to a lavish 'round table' and other festivities at Nefyn—one of the most important courts (W. *llysoedd*) of the former house of Gwynedd—to celebrate his victory. Later that autumn a large troupe of Welsh minstrels was summoned to Overton to entertain the king before he set out, accompanied by some of his most trusted advisers, on a great triumphal progress around Wales.

Edward took a particular delight in appropriating the residences of the Gwynedd dynasty, thereby making clear to all the definitiveness and finality of his conquest. In August 1284 he set up his court in two of Llywelyn's favourite residences, Abergwyngregyn and Caernarfon; he refurbished Llywelyn's hall at Aberconwy and converted it into a privy palace for his son as prospective prince of Wales; he dismantled another of Llywelyn's timber-framed halls at Ystumgwern and had it transported to the inner ward of his new castle at Harlech; and he showed that sentiment could have no place in the victor's heart by ordering the transfer of the abbey of Aberconwy—the favoured Cistercian house of the Gwynedd dynasty and the resting-place of the Llywelyn the Great—seven miles up the Conwy valley to Maenan to make room for his new castle and borough of Conway. With equal deliberateness he removed all the insignia of majesty from Gwynedd: Llywelyn's golden coronet, so it is recorded by an English chronicler, was solemnly presented to the shrine of St Edward at Westminster; the jewel or crown of King Arthur was an even more prized treasure; the matrices of the seals of Llywelyn, of his wife, and his brother Dafydd were melted down to make a chalice to be donated, appropriately enough, to Edward's new monastic foundation of Vale Royal: the most precious religious relic in Gwynedd, the fragment of the True Cross known as *Y Groes Naid*, was paraded through London in May 1285 in a solemn procession on foot led by the king, the queen, the archbishop of Canterbury and fourteen bishops, and the magnates of the realm. Edward was thereby appropriating the historical and religious regalia of the house of Gwynedd and placarding to the world the extinction of its dynasty and the annexation of the principality to his Crown. He was to mete out exactly the same treatment to the kingdom of Scotland in 1296.

Edward the Conqueror—as he was appropriately entitled, at least in retrospect—had little difficulty in justifying his conquest or spelling out its consequences. It was, he commented, a conquest justified by right as well as by power. In his own flowery metaphors, he had 'cut away the rotten portion and extinguished the poison'.[1] In feudal terms the justification presented no awkwardness: the lands conquered in Wales had previously been held of the king by feudal right; they had now escheated into the direct possession of the Crown (*in proprietatis nostre dominium*) through the rebellion of Llywelyn and his allies. Edward's apologists later took the argument a step further and thereby crossed the threshold from the defensible to the absurd: the conquest effected the reannexation to the Crown of lands and liberties which had indeed belonged to the Crown before they had come into the hands of the princes of Wales! What was not in doubt was that native Wales was now, with some exceptions, 'conquered land';[2] the native principality of Wales, formally recognized in 1267, had been extinguished; any reference to it was studiously avoided; henceforth, native Wales would be referred to as 'the land of Wales' (just as the 'realm of Scotland' was demoted to 'the land of Scotland' in 1305) or as 'the king's land of Snowdon and his other lands in Wales'. Likewise the status of the tenants of those lands was that of a conquered people: they had submitted themselves completely (L. *de alto in basso*) to the king's will; therefore, they could not appeal to their laws, customs, and liberties as a bulwark against his policies; references to their petitions were curtailed in the Statute of Wales and allusions to their consent, included in the original draft, were deleted. Edward was not to be denied the completeness of his conquest nor the free hand that it gave him; any concession that he made to his Welsh subjects would be of his grace.

Edward set about making the arrangements for the governance of his newly acquired lands with characteristic thoroughness and dispatch. He

[1] *Cal. Close Rolls 1279–88*, p. 350.
[2] 'The land of Wales is conquered land . . . By that conquest the whole land, both in demesne and in services, was annexed to the Crown of England', *Monasticon Anglicanum*, IV, 660 (royal attorney in 1370). For an earlier expression of a similar claim see *Rotuli Parliamentorum*, I, 93–4.

spent almost the whole of 1284 there, personally attending in detail to all matters, giving precise oral instructions to his officials and castle-builders, briefing the men appointed to prepare the surveys of the conquered lands, and reviewing the judicial and administrative dispensation for those lands with legal and other experts. By the time he left Chepstow on 17 December 1284, not to return to Wales again until 1291, the main configurations of the new order were firmly established. It was, it is true, in many respects a very partial settlement: it applied only to the king's own lands in Wales; no attempt was made to bring the Marcher lordships, even those new lordships created by Edward I during the year 1279–83, within its ambit; it did not extend to the royal lordships of Montgomery and Builth; many of its legal and administrative aspects referred only to 'the land of Snowdon' and the new county of Flint; it reinforced the governmental fragmentation of Wales by accepting, in effect, the division of the country into native-ruled enclaves, Marcher lordships, and royal lands. None of this can be gainsaid. Yet on a broader and longer perspective it is the scale of Edward I's achievements in these years which is astounding. In two short campaigns he had utterly transformed the map of political and territorial power in Wales; he had inaugurated a major and co-ordinated policy of castle-building to ensure the permanence of his conquest; and in a few bold strokes he had laid the institutional and legal foundations of the dispensation under which much of Wales was to be governed for well over two centuries. The year 1283—'after our peace proclaimed in Wales in our eleventh year', as the formula in royal writs ran—marked as definitive a break in the history of native Wales as did 1066 in the history of England; it did so legally, for throughout north Wales hereafter it was effectively the limit of legal memory in actions relating to land. It was little wonder that the king who had inaugurated this new era should be regarded admiringly by later generations as 'the good King Edward the Conqueror', 'the wise and noble King Edward the First'.[3]

Edward set out, remarked the chronicler, 'to pacify and to organize that land'.[4] His first task was to ensure that his victory was militarily secure; it was an urgent task given the remarkable record of the Welsh for recovering quickly from military disaster. Large numbers of hostages were taken and dispatched to various castles in England. Garrisons were stationed at strategic places—forty men each at Harlech, Cricieth, and Conway, thirty at Bere and Caernarfon—and the king on his frequent to-ing and fro-ing through north Wales during 1284 was accompanied by a considerable detachment of bannerets, knights, and mounted crossbowmen. Orders

[3] Cal. Anc. Corr., p. 234; Rotuli Parliamentorum, III, 476.
[4] The Chronicle of Walter Guisborough, ed. H. Rothwell (Camden Society, vol. 89, 1957), p. 222.

were dispatched for clearing passes, and two trusted royal servants, Bogo de Knovill and Roger Lestrange, were commanded to supervise the work and to do so 'nothwithstanding any liberty'.[5] But it was in the great stone castle that Edward I placed his faith, above all, as the prime instrument 'to contain and thwart the attacks of the Welsh'.[6] Flint and Rhuddlan, built in the wake of the 1277 invasion, had shown their sterling worth in withstanding the Welsh attacks of 1282 and serving as bases from which counter-attacks could be launched. So Edward had no hesitation in inaugurating a massive programme of castle-building as his immediate and main policy for ensuring that his conquest of Wales was indeed final. The work was set in motion at once: Hope was being repaired in June 1282; Ruthin, Denbigh, and Holt were under construction by his barons by the autumn; repairs began at the native castle of Dolwyddelan on 18 January 1283, the very day it was captured; and between March and June 1283 work had begun on the three great new castles of Conway, Harlech, and Caernarfon.

This second phase of Edwardian castle-building in Wales was, organizationally and architecturally, even more breath-taking than the first in its achievement. Resources were commandeered from every part of Edward's realm: lead from the Isle of Man; iron and steel from Newcastle-under-Lyme; rope from Lincolnshire; timber from Liverpool. Manpower was assembled with a speed and on a scale which were truly remarkable: already in 1283 and 1284 as many as 4,000 workmen—diggers, carpenters, masons, carters, and quarrymen—drawn from almost every county of England were working at Harlech, Caernarfon, and Conway alone. The best master-craftsmen that Edward I could find were hired to supervise and co-ordinate the king's works in Wales. Pride of place must go to Master James of St Georges, the master-mind behind Edward's Welsh castles for almost thirty years. When he joined Edward's staff in 1278, he had already major building-experience in Savoy to his credit—notably at the comital palace at St Georges-d'Espéranche and the castle of Yverdon. He was a military architect of genius and also an administrator of great skill; Edward showed his appreciation of his qualities by giving him unusually handsome rewards, creating him constable of Harlech in 1290, and inviting him to join the royal party to Gascony and Scotland. It is Master James who 'must be credited with the basic design of all the great Edwardian castles in Wales'.[7] But he was by no means the only man who travelled from the Continent to offer his expertise in Edward's service in Wales: Stephen the Painter from Savoy, Master Bertram the military engineer from Gascony, Master Manasser (in charge of the diggers at Caernarfon and eventually a

[5] *Cal. Welsh Rolls*, p. 274.
[6] *Chronica . . . Willelmi Rishanger*, ed. H. T. Riley (Rolls Series, 1865), pp. 91, 105, 148.
[7] H. M. Colvin in H. M. Colvin *et al.*, *The History of the King's Works* (1963–), I, 204.

burgess there, but originally of Vaucouleurs in Champagne) are among others. Leading English craftsmen were also pressed into service—men such as Master Nicholas Durnford, who had worked at St Augustine's Bristol, Burton-on-Trent, and Repton Priory before he succeeded Master James of St Georges at Beaumaris, or Master Walter of Hereford, who laboured for Edward I at Vale Royal as well as at Caernarfon.

These men worked at break-neck speed. Conway was virtually completed in four and a half years; most of the major building was finished at Caernarfon by 1287 and at Harlech by 1289. No expense was spared: between 1283 and 1291 at least £23,000 was spent on the castles of north Wales; by 1301 Edward had expended some £80,000 on his eight major new castles in Wales and, if to this were added the repairs and renovations of other royal castles and former native Welsh castles (including those of south Wales) and contributions towards non-royal castles, the total sum cannot have fallen much short of £90,000. It represented a massive investment and was no mean drain on the resources of the English kingdom (and on the lordship of Ireland whose treasure funded much of the building expenditure of the 1280s). Each castle presented its own problems of construction and had to take account of the lie of the land; each castle thereby has its own distinctive character. Yet the Edwardian castles in Wales—from Builth and Flint begun in May–July 1277 to Beaumaris begun in the wake of the Welsh revolt of 1294 and substantially completed in its main features in two seasons of frenzied activity in 1295–6—were more than the sum of the individual parts. They formed part of a coherent strategy for the subjugation of native Wales, the site of each castle being selected in relation not only to local considerations but also to the overall plan for the military settlement of the country. There is, accordingly, a remarkable unity about the castles. Built under common supervision, constructed in a few years, and commissioned as part of a single overall plan, they are truly one of the most remarkable examples of 'a medieval state enterprise'.[8] They are also a testimony to the ruthless energy of Edward I, a ruthlessness which removed a Cistercian abbey (at Aberconwy) and utterly destroyed the most flourishing urban centre in north Wales (at Llan-faes) to provide secure sites for his new fortresses.

Architecturally, it is in these Welsh fortresses that 'the medieval castle reached the limits of its capacity as a military device'.[9] Here—and particularly at Harlech and Beaumaris—the idea of the keepless castle, whose strength lay in its twin set of curtain walls and in massively imposing gatehouses, was taken to its logical conclusion. Some of the detailed constructional and architectural features of the castles—such as the use of

[8] J. G. Edwards, 'Edward I's Castle-Building in Wales', *Proceedings of the British Academy*, 32 (1946), 16.
[9] H. M. Colvin in *The History of the King's Works*. I, 228.

helicoidal or inclined scaffold paths, the appearance of full-centred semicircular arches, and distinctive characteristics of garderobe and window construction—can be paralleled only in Savoy, and once more underline the formative role of Master James of St Georges and his fellow-workers in their construction. It can be said of each and all of them that they combine 'a marvellous sense of power with great beauty of line and form',[10] whether in the dramatic, cliff-top splendour of Harlech, the wonderful integration of castle and town-walls at Conway, the imperial expansiveness of Caernarfon, or the faultess symmetry of Beaumaris. Militarily and psychologically they achieved their purpose: they broke the spirit of the Welsh. Furthermore, Edward's example and success were imitated throughout Wales—in the construction of castles in the new Marcher lordships of the north-east (Denbigh, Ruthin, Holt, and Chirk) and the major refurbishment of many of the older Marcher castles of south Wales (such as Chepstow, Brecon, Usk, Kidwelly, Laugharne, and Llansteffan). Wales by 1300 lay more firmly and securely than ever under military rule or, as a poet later put it, under the control of 'the tower of the bold conqueror'.[11]

Edward's castles were primarily instruments of military domination. But they were more: they were to be the seats of civilian governance, the headquarters of a new administrative, financial, and judicial dispensation. They inaugurated a new regime as well as secured a conquest. They also proclaimed proudly, almost extravagantly, the quasi-imperial character of Edward's vision of his conquest of Wales. This was most obviously demonstrated at Caernarfon. There, Edward, drawing on the legendary links of the area with imperial Rome in Welsh lore and on the alleged discovery of the body of the Emperor Constantine (or his father Magnus Maximus) there in 1283 and its reinterment at the king's command, caused to be constructed a remarkable castle whose polygonal towers and bands of differently coloured stone were almost certainly a deliberate imitation of the Theodosian wall of Constantinople. The imperial analogies were underscored by mounting an eagle on each of the triple turrets that crowned one of the principal towers of the castle and by placing a carved statue of the king over its main gate. Caernarfon was to be the administrative capital of the new province of north Wales; the calculated grandness of its building was a comment on the way that Edward perceived the task which faced him in Wales.

One aspect of that task had already commanded Edward's attention. As the conquest of 1282–3 unfolded, he had to decide the fate of members of the native Welsh dynasties who had opposed him and the fortune of their

[10] A. J. Taylor, *Harlech Castle. Castell Harlech* (Official Handbook, Cardiff, 1980), p. 3.
[11] *Cywyddau Iolo Goch ac Eraill* (2nd edn. 1937), p. 310 ('twr dewr goncwerwr').

lands. Edward was not disposed to show mercy; nor did he. The dynasty of Gwynedd was in effect exterminated: Llywelyn's sole child was consigned to the nunnery of Sempringham; Dafydd's daughters were likewise forced to take the veil and his two sons were incarcerated for life; Owain seems to have died before or during the conquest; and the fourth brother, Rhodri, had already opted for the secure obscurity of the life of a Cheshire gentleman. Edward's venom against the house of Gwynedd was understandable: but his spleen was directed no less against those of northern Powys and Deheubarth. The five surviving heirs of the dynasty of northern Powys (including the two young sons of Madog Fychan) were summarily dispossessed, whether they had openly supported the rebellion or not. The minor princelings of Deheubarth surrendered in time to save their skins, but not their lands. They spent their remaining years either as English prisoners (as did Rhys Wyndod and his brothers of Ystrad Tywi), or as royal pensioners and soldiers, serving with the king's army in Flanders in 1297 (as did three of the former lords of Ceredigion) and receiving the honour of a burial in Windsor at the king's expense (the fate of Rhys Fychan in 1302). The descendants of the dynasties of the middle March fared no better; they survived the conquest, but only to be reduced to the status of impoverished country squires or harassed out of their lands by the new Marcher lords. Only two major branches of Welsh dynasties emerged unscathed from the débâcle of 1282. In south Wales Rhys ap Maredudd of Dryslwyn, who 'alone of the nobles and magnates of West Wales adhered to the king at the time of the late disturbance',[12] waxed rich at the expense of his disinherited relatives and assembled a considerable estate, consisting of almost the whole of Cantref Mawr and two commotes in Ceredigion. In mid-Wales Gruffudd ap Gwenwynwyn of southern Powys, who had suffered so much for his opposition to the house of Gwynedd, was fully restored to his lands, though he must have been disappointed not to be more amply rewarded for his long-suffering loyalty to the king. For the rest Edward I showed very selective and limited mercy: some of the smaller barons of Edeirnion and Dinmael—men of proud lineage but little weight—were restored to their lands; one of the princelings of Ceredigion, Llywelyn ab Owain, was allowed to salvage a small estate for himself, and so was one member of the dynasty of northern Powys—but specifically during the king's pleasure and at his will. These were indeed small crumbs of comfort compared with the massive programme of disinheritance which Edward had engineered. For the native dynasties of Wales the disinheritance of 1282–3 (soon completed by that of Rhys ap Maredudd in 1287) was as traumatic as were the events of 1066–70 for the Anglo-Saxon aristocracy.

The king himself was the greatest beneficiary of this disinheritance. He

---

[12] *Cal. Welsh Rolls*, p. 236.

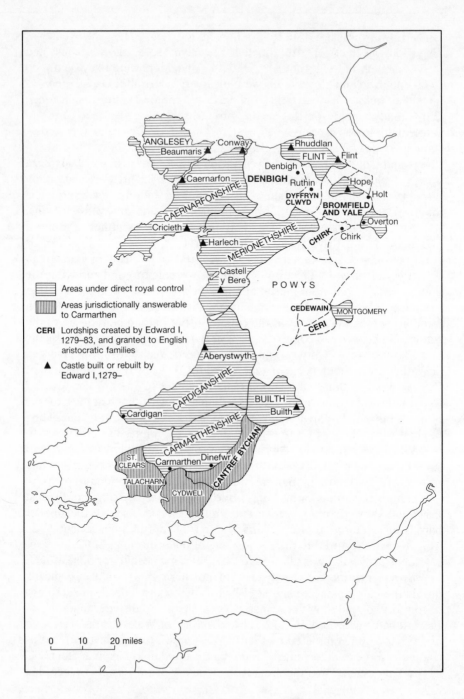

MAP 9. The Edwardian Settlement of Wales, 1277–95

Legend:

Areas under direct royal control

Areas jurisdictionally answerable to Carmarthen

CERI Lordships created by Edward I, 1279–83, and granted to English aristocratic families

▲ Castle built or rebuilt by Edward I, 1279–

Map labels:

ANGLESEY
Beaumaris
Conway
Rhuddlan
Flint
FLINT
Denbigh
Caernarfon
DENBIGH
Ruthin
Hope
Holt
CAERNARFONSHIRE
DYFFRYN CLWYD
BROMFIELD AND YALE
Overton
Cricieth
Harlech
MERIONETHSHIRE
CHIRK
Chirk
Castell y Bere
POWYS
CEDEWAIN
MONTGOMERY
CERI
Aberystwyth
CARDIGANSHIRE
BUILTH
Cardigan
Builth
CARMARTHENSHIRE
CANTREF BYCHAN
ST. CLEARS
Carmarthen
Dinefwr
TALACHARN
CYDWELI

0   10   20 miles

reserved for himself the whole of Gwynedd uwch Conwy and the newly forfeited lands in Ceredigion. He also kept any other districts which he considered to be strategically important for his control of Wales: Hope and its associated lordships in the north-east, the township of Faenol and the marshland of the river Clwyd to protect his castle of Rhuddlan, the commote of Creuddyn to control the Conwy estuary, and the castle of Dinefwr and its associated lands (which he compelled Rhys ap Maredudd to quitclaim to him in October 1283) in order to buttress royal authority in the Tywi valley. These lands, added to those which Edward had inherited or secured in Wales in the years 1277–9, made the Crown far and away the single most powerful landowner in Wales.

For the rest Edward I used the massive territorial disinheritance of 1282–3 as an occasion for a display of royal munificence to his magnates. He had already shown the way by his grant of Ceri and Cedewain to his close confidant, Roger Mortimer of Wigmore, in 1279. Once the campaign of 1282 was in progress he resumed the policy; and from the outset he meant it to be a permanent one, for in Pecham's negotiations with Llywelyn in early November the king made it clear that the grants made to the magnates were not open for discussion. Between June and October 1282 he carved four large lordships for his followers out of forfeited lands in northern Powys and Perfeddwlad: the lordship of Chirk for Roger Mortimer junior (the second son of Roger Mortimer of Wigmore), Bromfield and Yale for John Warenne, earl of Surrey, Denbigh for Henry Lacy, earl of Lincoln, and Dyffryn Clwyd for Reginald Grey, justice of Chester. In south Wales the major beneficiary of the king's munificence was John Giffard of Brimpsfield (Gloucs.), who secured in 1282–3 the whole of Cantref Bychan, the area lying south of the river Tywi. Others, such as Roger Lestrange, placed their bids for a share in the royal carve-up of north-east Wales, but without success. The significance of these grants was far-reaching. They were handsome gifts indeed: Denbigh, and Bromfield and Yale were, or were soon to be, worth £1,000 each p.a., Chirk and Dyffryn Clwyd some £400–500 p.a. They associated leading members of the English aristocracy in the pacification and settlement of Wales. They were simultaneously acts of royal largess and of the delegation of military and governmental command. They created in north Wales a new Marcher aristocracy which held its land on clearly specified feudal terms (unlike the old Marcher lordships) and by the king's gift, as Edward I was not slow to remind the recipients.

The next step was to determine the pattern of government which was to prevail in these newly conquered lands, particularly in those which were retained under direct royal control. No attempt was made to deal with the royal lands in Wales as a single unit: some of those lands had come under royal control over a long period of time and had developed their own institutions of governance piecemeal; elsewhere, most obviously in Gwynedd, both the opportunity and the need presented themselves to devise an administrative structure *de novo*. The two lordships of Builth and Montgomery were isolated from other royal estates in Wales and were in effect administered as self-contained units, barely to be distinguished from other Marcher lordships. In south-west Wales a pattern of royal governance had developed from at least 1240 around the twin centres of Cardigan and Carmarthen, both organized as 'honors' or miniature counties; a third bailiwick was added at Llanbadarn in 1277; and in 1280 these units were brought together under the rule of a new (or rather revived) officer, the justiciar of west Wales. Yet the streamlining of royal administration in south-west Wales was a slow process: it was impeded by the fact that most of the land north of the Tywi and in south Ceredigion remained under native rule until the revolt of Rhys ap Maredudd in 1287, and also by the extraordinarily wide powers which Robert Tibetot exercised as justiciar of the area 1281–98. In north Wales, on the other hand, Edward and his ministers were given *carte blanche*. There they introduced at a stroke a fully fledged governmental structure drawing on the fullness of English experience. The basic guidelines were laid down in a statute issued at Rhuddlan on 19 March 1284. Henceforth, this statute was to be regarded by future generations in Wales as the one 'whereby they should be managed and governed'.[13] Edward I's governmental dispensation, like his castles, had been built to last.

By the Statute of 1284 the royal lands in north Wales were divided into two major blocs. Those in north-east Wales—the three discrete units of Tegeingl, Hopedale, and Maelor Saesneg—were amalgamated into the single new county of Flint, and that county in turn was placed uner the control of the justiciar of Chester (as had often happened to royal lands in north-east Wales since the 1240s). The remaining royal lands in north-west Wales, consisting of Gwynedd uwch Conwy, were treated as a single governmental unit and ultimately acquired to the title of 'the principality of north Wales'. This district was not assimilated into the governmental structure of medieval England; it was too remote from Westminster and too alien in its social structure for that. Instead, it was treated, in effect, as a separate province into which many of the features, practices, and procedures of contemporary English governance were introduced. A justiciar, the king's governor-general in the province, was appointed to head the administration and was given the most wide-ranging military, governmental, and judicial powers. He was aided in financial matters by a chamberlain, who was in charge of the provincial exchequer at Caernarfon

---

[13] *Register of Edward the Black Prince*, III, 91–2.

and also headed the province's secretariat. A broadly similar pattern of provincial administration prevailed on the royal estates in south-west Wales, with Carmarthen acting as provincial capital.[14] Such a provincial administration was not without its parallels in England, most obviously and relevantly in the county palatine of Chester; but its closest affiliations were with those 'delegated, dependent governments' which ruled the 'overseas territories' of the English crown in the thirteenth century, notably Aquitaine, Ponthieu, the Channel Islands, and Ireland.[15] The royal estates in north and south Wales were now among the outlying provinces of what had become increasingly during the thirteenth century a Westminster-based English monarchy.

Beneath the provincial level, Edward introduced the shire as the key unit of financial and judicial organization in his Welsh lands. Flint, as has already been mentioned, was created as a county out of the disparate royal estates in north-east Wales; in south Wales the existing inchoate shires of Cardigan and Carmarthen became the centres around which larger units eventually grew; while in north-west Wales Edward eventually decided to divide the conquered land into three shires—Anglesey, Caernarfon, and Merioneth. With the shire arrived other features of English county administration: the post of sheriff as the linchpin of shire governance (in north Wales, much less obviously so in the south) and a very handsome fee of £40 attached to it 'by reason of the newness of the office in the parts of Wales';[16] the monthly county court; the twice-annual sheriff's tourns as the assembly for the preliminary investigation and declaration of criminal offences; and the office of coroner—normally two per shire in spite of the Statute's provision that there should be one in each commote. At the local level Edward I's administrative settlement was much less innovative. Here the existing Welsh unit of the commote, albeit now parading in acceptably English garb as the hundred, remained the basic unit for the dispensing of justice and the collection of dues; here local customs, boundaries, offices, and fees remained largely unchanged; at this level, above all, Edwardian governance had to accommodate itself, in terms of appointments and institutions, to the existing native Welsh social pattern.

The Edwardian administrative settlement of Wales, particularly of north Wales, is remarkable for its thoroughness, overall coherence, and single-mindedness of purpose. It was created as the civilian arm of a military occupation and for the first generation or so it retained its military character. The first justiciar of north Wales, Otto of Granson, was appointed 'to keep that land';[17] much of his attention and that of the

---

[14] The first chamberlain in south-west Wales was not appointed until 1299.

[15] J. Le Patourel, 'The Plantagenet Dominions', *History*, 50 (1965), 302–3.

[16] *Cal. Welsh Rolls*, p. 283.

[17] *Cal. Close Rolls 1279–88*, p. 273; cf. A. J. Taylor, *The King's Works*, I, 373 n. 6.

sheriffs and the constables of castles in these early years was devoted to the pacification of the countryside, supervising the building of castles, and anticipating and coping with military emergencies. It was not a bureaucratic structure but hand-picked men, wielding immense power and not too punctilious in the way they wielded it, who ensured that the Edwardian conquest was a governmental as well as a military success—men such as John Havering, successively deputy-justiciar and justiciar of north Wales, 1284–7 and 1295–1301, or the powerful and ruthless Robert Tibetot, close confidant of Edward I, a soldier and diplomat of experience, and sole unquestioned governor of south Wales 1281–98, or busy and efficient clerks, such as Richard Abingdon, the first chamberlain of north Wales who laid the financial foundations of the new province before graduating to become eventually one of the paymasters of Edward's campaigns in Scotland and a baron of the exchequer, or the royal clerk, Walter Pederton, who served Edward I in countless ways in south Wales for twenty years after 1288 and accumulated a canonry and six rectories in the diocese of St Davids as his reward. Such men were the makers of the Edwardian settlement.

That settlement had a distinctively colonial flavour, particularly in north Wales. It imported the institutions and the norms of English administration for the governance of the royal lands in Wales. It assumed that governmental practice in Wales ought increasingly to approximate to that followed in England. It allowed a large measure of initiative and discretion to the provincial governors, especially in the early years. But there was no doubting ultimate metropolitan control and direction: it was to the exchequer at Westminster that the chamberlains of Caernarfon and Carmarthen submitted their accounts; it was from the king and through his chancery that the justiciar received his instructions; it was to the king in council that petitions were addressed. The personnel of the new governmental dispensation in Wales was also 'colonial' in its recruitment. In its higher echelons—from the level of constable and sheriff upwards—it was almost exclusively non-Welsh in its appointments. It drew heavily on men who had already served, or were to do so in future, in other parts of Edward's empire: John Havering graduated from Wales to Gascony and back again; Adam Wettenhall, the first controller of the Caernarfon exchequer, had previously been receiver of the royal revenues in Ireland; and Ralph Broughton, who was royal paymaster in west Wales from 1277, had served his apprenticeship as deputy-warden of the Channel Islands. It was through the experience and service of such men that the royal lands in Wales were, in Edward's own words, being 'united and annexed . . . to the crown of the realm as a member of the body of that realm'.

Edward I was anxious that these lands should yield him a fixed and regular income as soon as possible. In June 1283, as the military conquest was drawing to a close, he issued oral instructions for extents of north-west Wales to be prepared, detailing the obligations due from the tenants and the revenues owed annually to the king. By March 1284 those extents had been completed. They displayed the characteristic arrogance of the conqueror: they made no attempt to comprehend the categories and customs of native Wales; instead they strait-jacketed them within the formulae of the English manorial extent. But the speed with which the extents were compiled was an eloquent tribute to the brisk efficiency of the new dispensation and to the king's determination to start exploiting the resources of his conquered lands at once. During the 1280s and much of the 1290s, it is true, Wales was a drain on royal resources, as huge subventions were dispatched to finance the cost of castle-building there; but already by 1300 the new province had begun to yield a handsome profit for the king's exchequer. Rents were being rigorously collected; judicial profits were mounting steadily (those from the three counties of north-west Wales averaging close on £600 annually by the first decade of the fourteenth century); while in 1291–2 and 1300 royal taxes were levied from the king's estates in Wales. Llywelyn ap Gruffudd's rule had been increasingly oppressive in its last years; but it was more than matched by the ruthless, exploitative efficiency of the new English dispensation in Wales.

It is, however, in legal and judicial affairs that the Edwardian settlement of Wales appears at its most majestic and masterful. The late thirteenth century was a great age of royal legislation throughout Europe, and no king exulted in the role of law-maker more than Edward I. He had already inaugurated a far-reaching series of administrative inquiries and reforms in England and had launched a programme of statutes which was to earn for him the title of 'the English Justinian'. The conquest of Wales provided him with a new opportunity to display his legislative talents in the most ample manner. During the years immediately before the conquest of 1282–3 Edward's attitude towards Welsh law had gradually become more clearly defined, largely in response to the attempts of Llywelyn ap Gruffudd and his allies to use native law as a bulwark against English jurisdictional pretensions. Edward was by no means outright in his hostility to Welsh law; he had not dismissed it, as he had the Irish laws in 1277, as being 'detestable to God and . . . not to be deemed laws'.[18] But he had made it clear that provincial customs such as Welsh law were subject to his scrutiny, that they must in no way derogate from the rights of his crown and kingdom, and that he would uphold only those which were 'just and reasonable' and consonant with 'God and justice'.[19] These were ominous warnings, all the more so since Archbishop Pecham, who had acquired a copy of the Welsh law-texts, had launched vitriolic attacks on certain

---

[18] *Foedera*, I, ii, 540.
[19] *Welsh Assize Roll*, pp. 59–60; *Cal. Anc. Corr.*, p. 60.

aspects of native Welsh legal practice. The way had, therefore, already been prepared for a formal scrutiny of Welsh legal practice once the conquest was complete. In the Statute of Wales or Rhuddlan (as it is alternatively known) issued on 19 March 1284, Edward announced the results of his deliberations.

Welsh law was by no means totally ousted by the Statute. It specifically conceded—in response to popular request, so it was claimed—that existing native procedures should still prevail in disputes concerning lands and pleas about movables: specifically, the appointment of mutually agreed arbitrators for the former and reliance on proof by witnesses or wager of law for the latter. These were wise concessions to the needs and practices of a largely pre-documentary society. Even in certain actions initiated by writ in the English fashion, it was conceded that the penalty for non-appearance should be the Welsh amercement of three cows. But it was with respect to the descent of land that Edward made his most momentous concession, when he confirmed the Welsh custom of dividing inheritances between male heirs. The landed customs and civil procedures of native Welsh society thereby emerged from this legislative review almost intact. In other directions, however, Edward and his advisers had no hesitation in proscribing Welsh law and practice where they contravened, in their opinion, the canons of natural justice and Christian morality as mediated through contemporary English practice. It was on these grounds that he expressly precluded bastards from inheriting land or sharing land with legitimate heirs. For the same reasons he insisted that English criminal law was henceforth to prevail in all major felonies—theft, larceny, arson, murder, homicide, and robbery. Welsh juristic theory still regarded many such offences as essentially personal actions between private parties and, what is more, as actions which could be emended by the payment of an agreed or stipulated compensation. Such notions were totally alien to English common law as it had developed from the mid-twelfth century onwards: major crimes were felonies; they involved a breach of the king's peace and therefore could not be privately settled; they were to be punished by death or mutilation and, therefore, could not be emended by a money compensation. These views were now imposed on native Wales, whether by statute as in the north or by the justiciar's fiat as in the south. Compensation-settlements for homicide, it is true, survived unofficially in parts of Wales; and as late as the fifteenth century the poet, Dafydd ab Edmwnd, could contrast the barbaric severity of 'the law of London' with the equity of 'the law of Hywel' in cases of homicide.[20] But from 1284 it was 'the law of London' which officially prevailed in Wales in criminal matters.

[20] *Oxford Book of Welsh Verse*, p. 139.

Edward's legal settlement in 1284 was concerned not only to scrutinize native law and procedure but also to extend the benefits of English common law to Wales. So it was that many of the characteristic institutions and procedures of English law were now transferred *en bloc* to Wales. The administration of justice was remodelled on English lines: supreme judicial authority was vested in the justiciar's court or sessions, which exercised many of the functions of the central royal courts and the assize courts of England; county and hundred courts were established; the offices of sheriff and coroner were introduced; and many of the basic procedures of English criminal law—indictment, appeal, hue and cry, and outlawry—now became the norm in Wales. In civil matters the Statute of 1284 made available in Wales many of the standard writs of English common law—such as those of dower, debt, contract, and novel disseisin (recent dispossession of land)—and laid down the forms of action to be followed in cases commenced by such writs. In some instances simplified and amended versions of existing writs and forms of action were issued (such as that which allowed judgements by default in actions of debt in Wales, whereas such judgement was not available in England), so that the Statute of Wales represents some of the latest thinking on current legal issues. Finally, on two substantive issues of land law Edward introduced English customs which ran contrary to long-established Welsh practice: he allowed a widow to enjoy a third of her late husband's lands as dower (whereas dower in much of native Wales had hitherto been confined to movable goods), and permitted females to succeed to land where the male line failed.

Edward's legal settlement in Wales was by any standards a magisterial achievement. The Statute of 1284 was, in Maitland's words, 'the most comprehensive code that any English legislator issued during the middle ages'.[21] Its comprehensiveness, it is true, can be overstated: though known as the Statute 'of Wales', the Statute of 1284 in fact only extended to the king's lands in north Wales, and as an introduction to contemporary English law it was certainly selective. Yet such reservations hardly serve to qualify Edward's achievement. Even in geographical terms his legal settlement cast its shadow well beyond the royal lands. It provided the pattern for the legal governance of the new 'private' lordships in north-east Wales; indeed, in the lordship of Bromfield and Yale a revised seignorial version of the Statue of 1284 was eventually to be issued. The Statute of 1284 represented, by the standards of the time, a considered and balanced response to the difficult questions posed by the relationship of the common law of the king's realm to the legal traditions of a recently conquered province. Edward and his lawyers were convinced of the superiority of English common law and the benefits it could bring; but,

[21] F. Pollock and F. W. Maitland, *The History of English Law before the time of Edward I*, (2nd edn. 1968), I, 220–1.

with the exception of criminal matters, they did not impose it on Wales. Nor did they, on the other hand, as in Ireland, exclude the natives from the benefits and privileges of English law extended to a settler population: that would have been a sure recipe for racial tension. Instead, they created the royal lands of Wales into largely self-contained judicial provinces (almost entirely independent of normal judicial control from Westminster) and introduced the processes and instruments of English common law on a largely permissive rather than obligatory basis. Such a process of gradual legal assimilation was already well under way in several of the Marcher lordships of south Wales by the early thirteenth century; it was now extended by royal fiat to the newly acquired districts of native Wales. Wales was to be won to the common law by stages: we catch a glimpse of one of those stages in 1302, when a volume containing some English statutes, a register of English writs, and Chief Justice Hengham's breviate was dispatched to Carmarthen for use by the justice and chamberlain.

Beyond the ranks of the native princely dynasties, the Edwardian conquest of Wales was not followed by a sustained campaign of disinheritance. On the contrary, Edward I was acutely aware, in spite of some of the virulent anti-Welsh propaganda issued from his chancery, of the need to win over the support of the leaders of the native Welsh community and to reward those who had supported him in the recent war. Some Welshmen were immediately granted key posts, the most obvious case being Gruffudd ap Tudur, who was appointed constable of Dolwyddelan for life in August 1284; others were granted annuities, lands, or local offices; yet others, such as the barons of Edeirnion, had their jurisdictional liberties confirmed; while a few were enrolled as members of the king's military household. In more general terms, Edward magnanimously granted that those who came into his peace should retain their lives and lands. There was to be no massive campaign of expropriation. Yet it was inevitable that a comprehensive military victory such as that of 1282–3 should be followed by some measure of territorial reordering. Many Welshmen had died in revolt against the English regime (L. *contra pacem*) and their lands had escheated; on the English side, the demands of largess and security alike dictated that some attempt should be made to establish English settlements in the recently conquered districts of Wales.

As far as the Welsh countryside was concerned, such a policy had no more than a limited success. Most of the districts conquered by Edward's enterprise in Wales were too inaccessible and too unattractive to tempt English colonists to settle there in any numbers. It was in the new seignorial lordships of north-east Wales—Bromfield and Yale, Dyffryn Clwyd, and Denbigh—that the most sustained and effective attempts to introduce such a policy were made. Large estates were created for some of the lord's closest dependants: thus, in Bromfield and Yale, John de Breous secured an estate of almost 2,000 acres to be held by knight service; Sir Robert Crevequer abandoned his family lands in Kent in return for handsome grants in Flintshire and Dyffryn Clwyd; the families of Hanmer and Puleston moved into Maelor Saesneg; while in Denbigh all the major officials of the earl of Lincoln—his steward, marshal, and chamberlain—and some of his household servants (including two of his cooks) were granted a considerable territorial stake in his new lordship. It is in Denbigh also that we can witness the most remarkable, though by no means the only, attempt to create a new rural enclave of English peasant settlers. In the two commotes of Ceinmeirch and Isaled at least 10,000 acres were transferred—either through forfeiture or compulsory exchange—from native Welshmen to new English settlers, more particularly in vills near the new castle-borough of Denbigh and in the fertile lowlands of the Vale of Clwyd. A similar process, though possibly not on such a scale and certainly not so well-documented, was inaugurated in the lordships of Dyffryn Clwyd and Bromfield and Yale. The settlers were a motley group: adventurers in search of a fortune, craftsmen and soldiers, who had come to Wales originally to work on or to guard the new castles, and land-hungry peasants (one of whom bore the revealing nickname 'Lackland', *Saunz Terre*). Many of them came from the border counties; many others from the English estates of the new lords of Wales—as is amply indicated in the pages of the great *Survey of Denbigh* in 1334 by the catalogue of Yorkshire and Lancashire placenames and surnames, such as Pontefract, Clitheroe, Blackburn, Runcorn, Ramsbottom, and Birkenshaw. It was a colonization movement which was effected with considerable speed and under firm seignorial control. The native Welsh proprietors who were expelled from their lands to make room for the colonists were often, though by no means invariably, compensated with land elsewhere in the lordship; but the lands so given to them frequently lay in remote and infertile upland districts. What might be construed mathematically as fair exchange must often have been regarded by native Welshmen as virtual internal exile and brazen dispossession. It was to leave a bequest of bitterness which soured relationships between natives and settlers in north-east Wales throughout the fourteenth century.

Beyond the river Conwy, rural colonization by Englishmen was out of the question. There, as indeed elsewhere, the town was the prime instrument for establishing an English civilian presence in the new province. These new towns were self-evidently part and parcel of the Edwardian military settlement. They were built as adjuncts of the castles, their walls integrated with those of the castle itself, as at Caernarfon, Denbigh, and Conway. The constable of the castle was the mayor of the newly born borough, while the premier obligation on the burgesses was to defend the ramparts of the town and to provide the castle garrison with supplies. But the role of the towns was more ample than that of sustaining the English military regime in Wales. Edward and his advisers doubtless saw the new boroughs as important civilizing and anglicizing agents in native Welsh society; indeed, Archbishop Pecham had openly expressed the view that it was only by being herded into towns—as the Burgundians had been herded by the Romans—that the Welsh could be brought to the knowledge of civilized manners and living. More realistically and more immediately, the towns were to play a key role in the economic subjugation, or at least control, of the newly conquered province, for the boroughs were given a monopoly of wholesale trade over large areas of their hinterland.

The new towns established by Edward I and his barons in north Wales represented the last major phase of the urban foundations of the kings and lords of England in the Middle Ages. It was a phase inaugurated by Edward I immediately in the wake of his first victory over the Welsh in 1277 with the establishment of entirely new boroughs at Flint and Aberystwyth and the relocation and effective re-establishment of the borough of Rhuddlan. After the second victory of 1282–3, Caernarfon, Conway, and Harlech were added to the list, and the existing Welsh settlements at Cricieth and Bere were brought into the English burghal fold. Finally, in 1295 the new town of Beaumaris was founded by Edward I in the shadow of his new castle in Anglesey. This movement of town-foundation was neither confined to north Wales nor to the king. In south-west Wales two anaemic boroughs were founded at the old Welsh royal centres of Dryslwyn (1287) and Dinefwr (1298), the latter significantly bearing the title Newtown; while in north Wales major new boroughs were established by seignorial fiat at Holt, Denbigh, Ruthin, and (later) Overton. It was a policy which was pursued ruthlessly: the establishment of Beaumaris involved the suppression of Llan-faes, much the most populous and prosperous borough in native Wales, and the transfer of its inhabitants to a site some twelve miles away, henceforth to be known as Newborough; the homesteads of Welsh tenants were likewise compulsorily appropriated at Overton (Maelor Saesneg), Ruthin, Holt, and Dryslwyn to make room for the neatly patterned streets of the new towns. The sheriffs of the border counties of England were commanded to recruit burgesses for the new plantations and offer remission of rents for three years or more in order to entice them; generous grants of land and rights of common were also made to the burgesses to ensure that they were self-sufficient in food: those of Caernarfon, for example, being endowed with almost 1,500 acres.

These 'plantation boroughs' formed an important aspect of the Edwardian settlement of Wales. Some of them, it is true, had no more than an anaemic existence (such as Cricieth) or even failed altogether (such as

Bere); but others—notably Beaumaris, Conway, Ruthin, and Denbigh—prospered and quickly overspilled the limits of their original embankments and walls. The towns quickly transformed the economic life and pattern of marketing of native Wales. They were granted a commercial stranglehold over the surrounding countryside: thus the three commotes bordering on Beaumaris were commanded to trade there and not elsewhere; likewise, all districts within eight miles of Caernarfon were covered by the burgesses' monopoly; while a general ordinance proclaimed that no Welshman was to trade outside the mercatorial towns. The burgesses used their extensive privileges, their access to liquid capital in a largely pre-monetized society, and the favour of local administrators to secure control of key sectors of the rural economy, such as mills and fisheries, and buy escheated lands. They also exploited to the full their favoured status as colonies of loyal English settlers in a hostile Welsh countryside, 'the English burgesses of the English boroughs of Wales' as they called themselves. They played the card of racial exclusiveness to their own advantage, proclaiming unctuously that their towns had been established 'for the habitation of Englishmen', and excluding 'mere Welshmen' from their privileges and from the right to trade on the grounds that they were 'foreigners' in the borough. Nowhere was the spirit of conquest and of racial superiority so vigorously and selfishly kept alive as in the Edwardian boroughs. It was little wonder that they were the most consistent target of Welsh resentment throughout the fourteenth century.[22]

While Edward I was busily laying the foundations of the new English dispensation in native Wales, his archbishop of Canterbury was simultaneously attending to the affairs of the church there. The work of the two men was indeed complementary and overlapped: Archbishop Pecham's visitation of Wales in June–August 1284 coincided with Edward's period of most intense activity in Gwynedd. Pecham had shown a genuine concern for the spiritual welfare of the Welsh since his elevation to the see of Canterbury (1279), even if some of his attempts to act on that concern had been ham-fisted. His first task, now that the conquest was complete, was to aid in the pacification of the country. Much of the detailed work was deputed to the able and loyal Anian, bishop of Bangor: it was he who in June 1283 arranged for the formal surrender of the various districts of north-west Wales and who was well rewarded for his pains by grants of land, wardships, and regalian rights. But the archbishop himself shouldered some of the more delicate tasks: it was he who, in spite of his better judgement, made the arrangements for the transfer of the Cistercian abbey of Aberconwy eight miles up river to Maenan to make room for the king's

---

[22] See below, pp. 433–4.

new castle and borough of Conway; and he also effected a reconciliation between Edward and Anian, the disgraced bishop of St Asaph, who had been exiled from his see and fined 500 marks for his independent stand during the war of 1282–3. But Pecham was not merely the king's ecclesiastical poodle; he was a doughty and outspoken defender of the liberties of the church and of proper standards of Christian behaviour at all times. He showed that to good effect in Wales. He quickly won from the king a commission to inquire into damage suffered by Welsh churches; over a hundred claims were submitted and already by November 1284 more than £1,730 had been distributed in compensation payments, ranging from a few shillings to £250. It was a remarkable act of reconciliation and constructive generosity. Pecham also stood up vigorously for the liberties of the Welsh church: he reminded Edward I pointedly that those liberties represented the privileges which ancient British kings had extended to churchmen and as such were a model to which he should aspire. The archbishop did not mince his words in condemning high-handed and arrogant royal officials—'carnally wise but spiritually foolish'—who now rode roughshod over those liberties.

Pecham was one of the leading ecclesiastical reformers of his day; the constitutions issued at the Lambeth provincial council in 1281 stand as one of the many monuments of his reforming zeal. The Welsh church was now to receive the benefit of his attention. In June 1284 he embarked on a visitation of the whole of Wales, giving particular attention to the two recently conquered northern dioceses. It was the first such visitation that an archbishop of Canterbury had conducted in Wales. It provided Pecham with an occasion to assert and display his metropolitan authority over the whole country, much as Edward I's progress later in the year did, in military and political terms. Only at St Davids did he meet with opposition and then from an ambitious former royal servant, not from a Welshman. Thomas Bek was bold enough to revive St Davids' metropolitan claims in Pecham's presence, only to be quickly browbeaten into submission by the archbishop. It was in the field of reform, however, that the visitation was most notable. Pecham found, as he expected, much to dismay him in the ecclesiastical, moral, and spiritual life of the native Welsh. Welsh laymen were incorrigibly idle and attached to reprehensible customs, such as sending their children out to be fostered. Pecham saw little hope for them other than to jolt them out of their indolence by denying them the sacrament, herding them into towns to be civilized, and dispatching their children to England to be educated. The state of the clergy caused him even more alarm; nowhere was there a more illiterate, incontinent, and secularized clergy. Detailed injunctions were issued for the two northern dioceses: friars (Pecham himself was a Franciscan) were to be dispatched to help with parochial work; portionary churches were gradually to be

amalgamated to form single benefices; perpetual vicarages were to be
established; proper clerical education was to be provided; and the
corporate life of the cathedral churches was to be reorganized. It was a
programme intended to bring ecclesiastical standards and practices in
native Wales into line with those of England. While its primary aim was
ecclesiastical reform, the programme also had strong moral and political
overtones. Hard work was to cure the Welsh of their natural laziness and of
the political unreliability which often came in its wake; education would
gradually wean them from their social idiosyncrasies; and the clergy were
to be charged with the duty of political re-education, by persuading the
Welsh to abandon their Trojan fantasies and their messianic hopes of
recovering mastery of the whole of Britain.

Pecham's injunctions were stronger on condemnation and exhortation
than on practical, enforceable advice. But at least his active interest
ensured that the military victors did not ride entirely roughshod over the
interest of the Welsh church in the generation after the Conquest. Racial
aspects there certainly were to the religious settlement: the native monks
of Talyllychau (Talley) were expelled in 1284 to make room for 'others of
the English tongue who were able and willing to observe the religious
life'.[23] Welsh benefices were also brazenly exploited for royal and
aristocratic advantage: seven of the sixteen canons of St Davids by 1291
were men employed in royal service, and royal servants were appointed to
some of the richer Welsh livings (such as Hugh Leominster, chamberlain of
north Wales, who was nominated rector of Caernarfon). Most significant
of all, the Welsh church and its resources were brought much more firmly
under royal and papal fiscal control: the valuation of the two northern
Welsh dioceses for papal taxation in 1291 showed an increase of over 400
per cent over that of 1254; then in 1294 for the first time the Welsh clergy
were required to contribute to a clerical tax raised by the king, and in 1297
a proctor from each of the Welsh dioceses was summoned to attend the
convocation assembled to consider Edward I's extraordinary request for a
third of clerical temporalities. Yet, in spite of this closer fiscal integration
into the province of Canterbury and the English kingdom, Edward I made
no attempt to plant his own men in the Welsh episcopate (except in the
case of Thomas Bek who had been appointed to St Davids in 1280). The
turbulent Anian of St Asaph (1268–93) was succeeded by one of his own
canons Llywelyn ab Ynyr (1293–1314) and he by another canon, Dafydd
ap Bleddyn (1314–45). Likewise at Bangor the long-lived Anian
(1267–1305) was succeeded by two local men, Gruffudd ab Iorwerth
(1307–9) and Anian Sais (1309–28). At St Davids the royal clerk, Thomas
Bek (1280–93), was followed by a man of good Pembroke stock, David

---

[23] H. M. Colvin, *The White Canons in England* (Oxford, 1951), pp. 237–8.

Martin (1296–1328), while the see of Llandaff left vacant on the death of William de Braose (1266–87) was eventually filled by a notable local theologian, John of Monmouth (1297–1323). The Welsh sees, therefore, were filled without exception by local men of high calibre. Furthermore, the momentum of reform inaugurated by Archbishop Pecham's whirlwind visitation of 1284 was not lost: the bishops of all four Welsh dioceses issued constitutions for their clergy (often based on Pecham's injunctions) and drew up regulations on the organization of their cathedral chapters between 1287 and 1296; the cathedral church at St Asaph, largely destroyed in the war of 1282–3, was rebuilt; in the same period a major rebuilding programme was undertaken at the bishop's palace at Llandaff; and, most enterprisingly of all, Bishop Bek of St Davids founded two collegiate churches, at Abergwili (originally Llangadog, 1283) and Llanddewibrefi (1287), to cater for the needs of deserving clerics, and two hospitals in 1287 at Llawhaden and St Davids. The age of the Edwardian settlement was, therefore, also an era of reconstruction and reform in the Welsh church.

The Edwardian settlement of Wales was restricted to those parts of the country which lay under the king's direct authority. Edward I made no attempt to extend his legal and administrative settlement to the Marcher lordships, even to those lordships created by his own munificence in the years 1277–83. The liberties of the March were already firmly entrenched; they accorded to the lordships a virtual immunity from the administrative, judicial, and fiscal control of the Crown, at least in the ordinary course of events. It was only during a minority or as a result of political forfeiture that royal control extended into the March and it was only in exceptional circumstances that the royal claim to ultimate judicial supervision in the March was exercised. Edward I showed no inclination to challenge this status quo. Indeed, he specifically decreed that disputes between Marcher lordships should be settled by 'the custom of those parts';[24] only in the last resort should such disputes be referred to royal justices.

Edward I was no enemy of Marcher liberties; but equally he was not a king who would brook any challenge to his ultimate authority anywhere within his dominions. He had made his standpoint clear as early as the first statute of Westminster, 1275: 'in the Marches of Wales, or in any other place where the king's writ does not run, the king who is sovereign lord will do right . . . to all such as will complain'. Royal authority could, and would, override Marcher franchise. That authority was greatly enhanced by the final conquest of Gwynedd. That conquest was a royal achievement and one in which the Marcher lords had played a subordinate part, and that

[24] *Welsh Assize Roll*, p. 309.

strictly within the needs of overall royal strategy and under royal command. Their claim to be conquerors and defenders of Wales was thereby palpably diminished. Militarily and territorially the king now towered in the affairs of Wales as never before; the new lordships of the March were his creation and their holders were his favourites; and his triumphal progress through Wales in 1284 took in the whole country, March and royal lands alike. A king who enjoyed such dominance and who took such an exalted view of his regality would not hesitate to display his mastery in the March.

He had already given an occasional hint of his approach. As early as 1278 he had appointed a judicial commission whose powers in theory embraced the March of Wales and he had summoned Marcher jurors to appear before his justices. In 1281 he had fired an early shot across the earl of Gloucester's bows as lord of Glamorgan by requiring him to reply to a case brought against him by the lord of Gower; in 1285 he revived one of his father's methods of exercising judicial superiority in the March by dispatching royal commissioners to review the record of a case heard in the county court at Cardiff; and in the same year he bared the teeth of his masterfulness even more menancingly when he reminded William Valence, lord of Pembroke, that 'since all lands in the kingdom were held of the king in chief, the king was entitled to send justices to hear pleas wherever he wished'.[25]

It was in the 1290s, however, that Edward I displayed the fullness of his mastery in the March. He did so in several directions. Between 1290 and 1293 he asserted the Crown's claim to be the sole guardian of temporalities and collator to benefices during an episcopal vacancy in the March. It was a claim which flew in the face of well-documented precedent, especially in the diocese of Llandaff, and met fierce opposition from the earl of Gloucester. But Edward I was not to be deterred by Marcher custom; he appealed instead to the superior and inscrutable authority of 'the dignity of the Crown', and one by one the Marcher lords were browbeaten into submission. Even more ominously, the king began to extend his direct fiscal and military power to the March: in 1291–2 a royal tax of a fifteenth was for the first time raised in the March and the lords must have treated with scepticism the king's promise that no precedent for further royal taxes was thereby created; in 1297–8 he dispatched his own commissioners directly into the March to raise troops for his armies, instead of following the normal custom of sending requests for troops to the Marcher lords themselves.

Above all, Edward I overlooked no occasion on which he could humiliate the Marcher lords and display his own ultimate mastery. His

[25] J. R. S. Phillips, *Aymer de Valence, Earl of Pembroke 1307–24* (Oxford, 1972), p. 251.

earliest victims were also the greatest. In 1291-2 he summoned the earls of Gloucester and Hereford, as lords of Glamorgan and Brecon respectively, to appear successively before royally appointed judges, then before the king's great council at Abergavenny, and finally in parliament at Westminster to answer charges of flouting a royal injunction prohibiting them from waging 'private' war on each other in the March. The case ended dramatically: the Marcher estates of both earls were confiscated for life and they themselves were sentenced to imprisonment at the king's will. The earls were, in fact, quickly released on payment of large fines and their estates were restored after five months in royal custody. The *cause célèbre* was the culmination of a long history of sour relationships and suspicions between Edward I and the two earls; but it was also clearly interpreted by contemporaries as a direct challenge to Marcher liberties. That is certainly how the Marcher lords summoned to Llan-ddew (Brecon) saw it: they affirmed as a body that the King's actions and demands were unprecedented and contrary to Marcher usage; one of them forbade a group of jurors summoned from his lordship to take the oath. Edward I, however, was not to be deterred. Instead, he appealed to his 'crown and dignity', to his role as 'debtor of justice to all' and guardian of 'the common utility', and ultimately to his prerogative right to act 'in many cases above the laws and customs used in his realm'.[26]

The confrontation with the earls of Gloucester and Hereford might be dismissed as a personal vendetta were it not that there is other ample evidence of Edward I's determination to display and assert his mastery in the March in the 1290s. The liberties of Wigmore and Oswestry were briefly confiscated; records of the judicial decisions of Marcher courts were ordered to be scrutinized by royal justice; Marcher lords were firmly warned that their claims of immunity would not deter royal officers from entering their lordships to collect debts due from them to the king; the disaffection of Marcher communities was deliberately fostered by the king in Maelienydd, Talgarth, and Gower in order to compel their lords to grant charters of liberties to their tenants; Theobald Verdon, the lord of Ewyas Lacy, was imprisoned, and his lands and liberties forfeited for the contempt he showed to the king's officers; and in 1295 the largest of Marcher lordships, Glamorgan, was peremptorily seized into royal hands. There is no reason to believe that Edward I had deliberately launched a co-ordinated and pre-meditated assault on the Marcher lords and their liberties; but, equally, there can be little doubt that each and every action was calculated to show to the Marcher barons, individually and as a group, that ultimately the king's mastery and authority were beyond challenge, even in the March. As he put it crisply and bluntly in a letter to his uncle,

---

[26] *Cal. Welsh Rolls*, pp. 336, 343-4.

the earl of Pembroke, Marcher lands were 'within the king's realm' and therefore 'in his obedience'.[27] Once that truism was fully understood and acknowledged, Edward I was well content to permit and even to confirm Marcher liberties. Edward's settlement of Wales in the 1280s may have stopped short of the March; but his actions in the 1290s made it abundantly clear that the whole of Wales, the March included, now lay, in the words of a contemporary lawyer, 'within the power of the king of England'.[28]

The conquest of Wales left a deep legacy of despair and bitterness among Welshmen. Many of them, it is true, adjusted rapidly to the new alien dispensation and learnt quickly how to work with it. Edward I showed no vindictiveness in victory, except in the case of the native princely dynasties; there was to be no mass campaign of victimization or expropriation. Yet the trauma of that victory naturally left deep scars on the Welsh consciousness. The remarkable hiatus in the Welsh court poetry tradition in the generation or so after the Conquest, though it may have been exaggerated, is eloquent in this respect. The elimination of many of the native princely dynasties created a vacuum in the hierarchy of power and patronage to which the professional bardic order in Wales was habituated; it was only gradually that a new pattern of patronage and new literary forms emerged. As the completeness of their defeat dawned on them, some Welshmen turned more than ever to the prophecies of Merlin as a source of consolation and hope; others looked forward wistfully to the day (in the words of one drunkard in Dyffryn Clwyd) when 'the English would hear such threats that they would never dare return to Wales'.[29]

Yet it was not at this messianic and apocalyptic level that the experience of conquest bred resentment most readily among Welshmen but rather at the more prosaic level of day-to-day novelties and irritations. The petitions of the period help to identify their grievances.[30] Territorial resettlement in the environs of the new castle-boroughs begat great resentment and so also did the privileges of the newly settled burgesses and the commercial monopolies they sought to impose. The zeal of financial officials in collecting and augmenting rents, imposing new obligations, and ignoring communal claims to rights of forest and pasture provoked a large sheaf of complaints. Judicial innovations were another major target of community grievance: suit of court at hundreds and tourns proved irksome, while non-attendance was punished by fines and occasionally by confiscation of lands;

---

[27] *Cal. Anc. Pets.*, p. 105, no. 3397.

[28] *Year Book 12 Edward II 1319* (Selden Society, 1964), p. 130.

[29] *The Court Rolls of the Lordship of Dyffryn Clwyd*, ed. R. A. Roberts (Cymmrodorion Record Series, 2 (1893), pp. 2–3.

[30] Some of these themes are considered more fully below pp. 431–5; they are mentioned here where there is contemporary evidence that they were a source of grievance in the period 1284–1317.

even the justiciar himself admitted that 'the land was much troubled and irritated' by some of these practices;[31] while the brusque denial of Welsh practices (such as the use of compurgation in accusations of robbery and homicide) and the arbitrary imposition of English practices bred deep resentment. Above all, in a deeply traditional society, the disregard for the laws, usages, franchises, social distinctions, and practices of native society and the high-handedness and insensitivity of many of the local English governors in Wales—such as Reginald Grey, justice of Chester and north-east Wales (1281–99), Robert Tibetot, justiciar and virtual sole ruler of west Wales (1281–98) and his deputy, Geoffrey Clement (1284–94), Roger Puleston sheriff of Anglesey (1284–95), or Robert Bures, the queen's bailiff in Maelor Saesneg—created an accumulation of grievances which in the tinder-dry political atmosphere in Wales could easily lead to conflagration. Many of these grievances were exaggerated; others were doubtless contrived. But Welshmen now enjoyed the prerogative of conquered peoples, that of ascribing all their social ills to alien rule and rulers. It was a prerogative which they exercised to the full. Edward I's fault in this respect, as in so many other directions, was that of lack of imagination. His rule was not particularly oppressive; but he had not learnt from his earlier experience that, in the governance of a subject people, restraining the zeal and greed of his officials, taking the leaders of native society into his confidence, and working with the grain of local custom were quite as important as a military occupation and a legal and administrative settlement.

The first post-Conquest revolt that Edward I had to face came from an altogether unexpected quarter. It drew more on the resentment of one man than the grievances of a whole community. On 8 June 1287 Rhys ap Maredudd of Ystrad Tywi broke into revolt. He was an embittered and deeply disappointed man. He and his father had paid dearly for their resistance to the pretensions of the house of Gwynedd for more than a generation, and in the wars of 1277 and 1282 Rhys had been virtually unflinching in his loyalty to the king. Edward was indeed not slow to reward such loyalty. Rhys was given the forfeited lands of his kinsman, Rhys Wyndod; he thereby brought almost the whole of Cantref Mawr under his authority and augmented it with a grant of two commotes in Ceredigion. He could now proudly title himself 'lord of Ystrad Tywi', and he sought to ingratiate himself further with the English establishment in Wales by marrying the sister of John Hastings, lord of Abergavenny. But he had already been taught some sharp and unpleasant lessons about the nature of royal power in post-Conquest Wales: in October 1283 he was required to quitclaim the castle of Dinefwr, the ancestral capital of the

---

[31] *Cal. Anc. Corr.*, pp. 140–1.

kingdom of Deheubarth, to Edward I and in the same month he was publicly humiliated by Edward I in full council for taking seisin of lands in Wales (which the king had already granted to him) without waiting for formal investiture by a royal official, 'contrary to the custom of our realm'. In addition to these deeply hurtful blows to his dignity, Rhys was further disappointed by his failure to establish claims to land south of the Tywi against the royal protégé, John Giffard. Worse was to follow. He found himself increasingly harassed by Robert Tibetot, the justiciar of west Wales, and by the constable of the royal castle of Dinefwr: he was summoned, as the English chronicler puts it, 'to follow the county and hundred courts'; he and his men were 'compelled to plead by English law';[32] the judicial immunities granted to him by Edward I were ignored; he was the victim of financial extortion and administrative harassment; he found his authority over his tenants and followers diluted by the competing demands of royal governance and patronage. In short, his princely pretensions were no longer compatible with the ambitions and assumptions of the new royal dispensation. Edward I dealt with Rhys's complaints with a good measure of forebearance; but he could not begin to understand Rhys's deep sense of disillusion and disappointment. Revolt was inevitable.

That revolt was short-lived. It was confined to south-west Wales and even in that area Rhys was by no means able to command the support of his own men. The royal response was swift and crushing. Within a few weeks huge armies totalling about 24,000 men were assembled, well over half of them being recruited within Wales and the March; the Marcher lords co-operated closely and effectively with the local royal commanders and raised some 12,500 troops on their own account. Early in September Rhys's stronghold at Dryslwyn was captured. Rhys, it is true, raised the flag of revolt again in November, but by January 1288 his revolt had been finally crushed and all his castles taken. He himself remained at large for four years; but he was eventually betrayed in April 1292, taken to York and executed. So in effect was extinguished the ancient royal dynasty of Deheubarth; only a junior branch now survived in penury in southern Ceredigion. The six commotes of Cantref Mawr were formed into a single stewardship, and eventually, in 1290, they were assimilated into the financial and judicial structure of the county of Carmarthen. A new borough was established at the old Welsh commotal centre at Dryslwyn and English burgesses were invited to settle there on favourable terms. The revolt of 1287 had provided the occasion for completing the Edwardian conquest and settlement of Wales.

Rhys ap Maredudd's revolt could be dismissed as a small local difficulty caused by a disaffected and superannuated Welsh princeling. The English

---

[32] *Annales Monastici*, III, 338; IV, 310; J. B. Smith, 'The Origins of the Revolt of Rhys ap Maredudd', *BBCS* 21 (1964–6), 151–63 at p. 163.

government and its agents in Wales learned no lessons from it. Instead, the early 1290s witnessed a growing intensification of royal lordship in the country and the increasing alienation of the native community from its new rulers. Taxation contributed hugely to that alienation, all the more so in that it was a grievance shared by all. In January 1291 Edward issued a request for a fifteenth of their movables from the 'whole commonalty' of Wales to help him to pay his outstanding debts. It was an unprecedented demand and heralded Edward's determination to bring the whole of Wales—March and royal lands alike—within the ambit of his fiscal power. The response to the request was slow: individual negotiations had to be held with each community and it was not until the winter of 1292–3 that the assessments were finally made. The tax was undoubtedly heavy, particularly in a society where ready coin was in short supply and payment often only possible by selling off valuable stock. The tax probably yielded £9,000–£10,000 over Wales as a whole; but it is the assessment of individual districts which communicates how burdensome the tax must have been. The thinly populated county of Merioneth, for example, was assessed at £566, more than a third of the sum (£1,604), as it has been pointed out, which was to be levied from the much richer county of Essex ten years later. The tax caused widespread disaffection, inflaming the other grievances which were already festering within the native community. At this stage Edward I reduced the garrisons of some of his key castles—there were only 19 men in the garrison at Harlech, and even when burgesses and other reinforcements were added the force was only augmented to 37—and summoned some of his leading officials, including Robert Tibetot, the justiciar of south Wales, to help him in his Gascon campaign. He also issued writs for raising large contingents of infantry in Wales. It was the captain of one of these contingents, Geoffrey Clement, deputy-justiciar of south Wales, who was the first victim of the new revolt and it was on the day that the Welsh levies were to assemble at Shrewsbury for the start of the journey to Gascony (30 September) that the great revolt of 1294–5 erupted.

    This revolt was remarkably widely based and was altogether a much more serious affair than the rebellion of 1287. It affected almost the whole of the country—the royal lands in the north and south, 'old' Marcher lordships, such as Glamorgan and Brecon, and 'new' ones, such as Denbigh and Dyffryn Clwyd, alike. The leadership of the revolt varied from one area to another: in the north the leader was Madog ap Llywelyn, an embittered member of a cadet segment of the Gwynedd royal family whose forebears had been rulers of Meirionydd; in the south-east another disinherited local princeling, Morgan ap Maredudd of the dynasty of Machen and Caerleon, took the lead; other local leaders drawn from ancient dynasties also emerged in Brecon and Cardiganshire. The targets of the rebels varied from place to place: the revolt in Glamorgan, in particular, was specifically directed against the vigorous policies of Earl Gilbert 'the Red' of Gloucester; the men of the lordship described their rebellion as a 'war against the Earl'[33] and transferred their homages to the king of England. Yet, in spite of these differences, the revolt drew on a common groundswell of deep resentment against alien rule, Marcher and royal alike, in Wales. As such it was a classic anti-colonial revolt. It vented its fury in the massacre of English royal officials (such as Roger Puleston, the sheriff of Anglesey or Geoffrey Clement, the deputy-justiciar of south Wales), the destruction of records and memoranda, and attacks on and capture of castles (among those taken were Caernarfon, Denbigh, Ruthin, Hawarden, and Morlais (Glamorgan)). Wales had found a new unity in a common experience of conquest. It was yet another measure of the 'national' dimension of the revolt that its leader, Madog ap Llywelyn, assumed the title 'prince of Wales'.

The revolt took Edward I completely by surprise; but his response was as speedy and as devastatingly thorough as it had been on earlier occasions. Wales was in effect created into a single military unit, overriding any distinctions between Marcher and royal lands; as on previous campaigns a three-pronged military campaign was prepared to squeeze the Welsh into submission—with Chester in the north, Montgomery in mid-Wales, and Brecon and Carmarthen in the south, acting as the bases. By the end of the year unprecedentedly large detachments of infantry—totalling at least 35,000, of whom 16,000 were assembled to meet the king at Chester—had been raised and were ready to crush the rebellion; supplies were moved quickly and effectively by sea, ships being commandeered from as far afield as Bayonne; and the besieged castles of Cricieth, Harlech, and Aberystwyth were relieved. Winter weather and successful Welsh guerilla tactics kept Edward cooped up in Conway from January to March 1295 (apart from a risky foray as far as Nefyn); but with the advent of spring the revolt collapsed quickly. The earl of Hereford won striking victories in the south-east: Reginald Grey penetrated through the heart of north Wales to Ardudwy; most importantly, the earl of Warwick inflicted a crushing defeat on Madog ap Llywelyn at Maes Moydog (west of Welshpool) on 5 March. Early in April Edward I set out from Conway on what was more a victory march than a military campaign, receiving submissions, taking hostages, and issuing commands as he went. Within three months he was back at Conway after his rapid circuit of the country; by 17 July he left Wales to resume the business from which he had been so rudely interrupted ten months earlier.

The revolt of 1294–5 showed that the Welsh had neither the stamina nor

---

[33] *Cal. Anc. Pets.* p. 217, no. 6839.

the resources to sustain a rebellion. It was the first major revolt in Wales after the Edwardian Conquest; it was also to be the last for over a century. Edward I once more demonstrated his military and political mastery of Wales as a whole: not only had he crushed the Welsh rebels, he had also used the revolt as a pretext for taking at least three Marcher lordships (Glamorgan, Bromfield and Yale, Mold) into his temporary custody; and he had again availed himself of the opportunity to humiliate his old adversary, the earl of Gloucester, by receiving the rebels in Glamorgan into the royal peace 'against the earl's wishes'[34] and by extending his favour as well as his pardon to their leader, Morgan ap Maredudd. The devastating military capacity of the English state had once more been impressively demonstrated, while the interspersing of cavalry forces, crossbowmen, and archers at the battle of Maes Moydog and the massive use of large forces of infantry foreshadowed tactics to be used in Scotland some three years later. Yet the revolt of 1294–5 was undoubtedly deeply embarrassing to Edward I: he suffered the indignity of being pinned down for three months by the Welsh in distinctly uncomfortable conditions at Conway; he was detained for a full eight months in Wales at a particularly awkward moment in his reign; and the cost of the campaign (£55,000), the building of Beaumaris castle, and extensive repairs at Caernarfon (at least £16,000 by 1300) contributed to the financial crisis which overwhelmed him in the late 1290s. Above all, the revolt was deeply hurtful to the pride of a king who was not used to set-backs and who thought that the problem of Wales had already been settled.

Edward's immediate response was to institute punitive and security measures to ensure that the settlement was not challenged again. Almost 200 hostages were taken from the royal lands in north and south Wales and dispatched to various castles throughout England; similar precautions were taken by several Marcher lords. Heavy fines and recognizances were imposed on local communities as an insurance against future revolts: thus the men of Rhos and Rhufoniog in Denbigh bound themselves in £3,000 to the earl of Lincoln for their future behaviour; those of Glamorgan paid large fines to recover their laws and ancient franchises; while in Oswestry and Bromfield and Yale, the Marcher lords used the rebellion as a pretext to extend their powers over forest and waste. The tendency to rule Wales through absentee governors was reversed: the widely experienced John Havering, formerly steward of Gascony, took over from Otto of Granson as justiciar of north Wales with the specific instruction that he was to 'supply the place of the king there',[35] and later he was to take control of all royal lands in Wales. Above all, Edward I decided that his earlier policy of building massive stone castles as symbols of the irreversibility of his

---

[34] *Annales Monastici*, IV, 526.
[35] *Cal. Patent Rolls 1292–1301*, p. 146.

conquest must be reinforced. By April 1295 the foundations of the new castle at Beaumaris were being laid. During the next two seasons work on the new castle proceeded at frantic speed, even by Edward I's exacting standards. Simultaneously, extensive repair and rebuilding work was in progress at Caernarfon, which had been badly damaged during the revolt, and at Harlech. It was a measure of the importance that Edward I attached to this work that castle-building and repairs in Wales were only one of two major categories of work which were exempted from a general prohibition on all royal building operations in January 1296. English lords in Wales were also compelled to follow the royal suit: a new castle was built by the Clares at Llantrisant, while at Denbigh the earl of Lincoln rebuilt his castle on a much more ambitious scale—with higher and thicker curtain walls and a massive gatehouse.

The revolt of 1294–5 had jolted the English rulers out of their smug self-confidence; but it left even deeper scars on the relations of English and Welsh. In English eyes the utter faithlessness of the Welsh had once more been demonstrated. They could never again be trusted: 'as you well know', wrote two royal officers in Wales in February 1296, 'Welshmen are Welshmen, and you need to understand them properly'.[36] Racial hatred now rarely dwelt far below the surface: the burgesses of Aberystwyth claimed that they were afraid to go among the Welsh 'because of the great enmity that was between them since the war of Maelgwn' (the local leader of the revolt in Cardiganshire), while a royal command had to be issued to free an ecclesiastic arrested simply 'because he is a Welshman'.[37] Furthermore, practical measures were introduced which institutionalized this atmosphere of racial distrust. At Denbigh the process of territorial resettlement to establish a self-contained Englishry around the castle was pursued with renewed vigour and the burgesses were granted a new charter which specifically restricted the descent of their properties to their English heirs and assigns. Much the same spirit of apartheid pervades ordinances which Edward I issued almost certainly in the wake of the revolt: no Welshman was to carry arms in the English boroughs of north Wales or reside in them or trade outside them; Welshmen were only allowed to assemble with the permission of the king and in the presence of his chief ministers of the area. For the settler population in Wales, notably in the isolated boroughs and Englishries of the north and west, the revolt of 1294–5 was a traumatic experience; it put paid to any prospect of easy assimilation or accommodation with the indigenous population. The 'war of Madog' was henceforth not only a point of reference in their memories

---

[36] The original letter is published in J. G. Edwards in 'Edward I's Castle Building in Wales', *Proc. of the British Academy*, 32 (1946), 80–1 and in translation in *History of the King's Works*, i, p. 398–9.

[37] *Cal. Anc. Pets.*, p. 398, no. 11883; *Cal. Close Rolls*, 1288–96, p. 406.

and in their deeds; more importantly it also coloured their attitude to the Welsh. The worst of their settler prejudices and fears had been confirmed.

It was easier for those who lived at a distance to forgive. Edward I was soon building bridges towards the Welsh community. Morgan ap Maredudd, the leader of the revolt in Glamorgan, was soon acting as a royal agent in Wales, while the son of Madog ap Llywelyn was taken into the royal household and eventually rose to be a king's esquire. Edward I showed equal sensitivity in other directions: he appointed commissioners to investigate cases of administrative oppression in north Wales in 1295 and in west Wales in 1297; he arranged for the liberties of the Welshmen of Hopedale to be confirmed; and he posed as the defender of oppressed Marcher tenants against their lords. In December 1296 he assured a delegation of four representatives from north Wales that he held 'no suspicion towards them' but rather regarded them as 'faithful and devoted subjects'.[38] Both parties were anxious to repair the breach: Edward had problems enough on his hands in Scotland and France and wished to draw on the military and financial resources of Wales to help him solve those problems (summoning large contingents of Welsh troops to serve in Flanders and in Scotland in 1297–8 and requesting a tax of £2,400 from the royal lands in Wales in 1300); the Welsh for their part needed a focus of service and reward to fill the vacuum created by the extinction of their native dynasties.

Edward I went a good part of the way to meet this latter need in February 1301 when he granted the royal lands in Wales to his eldest surviving son, Edward 'of Caernarfon', and probably invested him with the title and insignia of prince of Wales at the same time. The prime purpose of the grant was to provide the royal heir with a suitable title and an appropriate apanage; but it was an act which also gave Welshmen a focus of worship and service of their own. It was one of the few roles which the future Edward II was to fill with any measure of success. Though he was to be kept on tight leading-strings by his father until 1307, he gradually built up in his principality of Wales ties of service, reward, loyalty, and even affection which were to serve him well throughout his troubled reign. Native Welshmen were enlisted as knights, esquires, and minstrels in his household; leaders of the native Welsh community—such as Gruffudd Llwyd, Rhys ap Gruffudd, Hywel ap Gruffudd, and Goronwy ap Tudur—were taken into the king's confidence, employed to raise troops for him, and used as channels of communication with native society; Welshmen began to be appointed for the first time since the Conquest to key posts in the royal administration in Wales—notably as sheriffs of Merioneth (1300), Caernarfon (1302), and Anglesey (1305); and the young

[38] *Cal. Patent Rolls 1292–1301*, p. 223; *Cal. Close Rolls 1296–1302*, p. 75.

Edward gave a sympathetic hearing, if rarely a satisfactory answer, to the grievances of native society. The tensions of the post-Conquest years were gradually being reduced as a pattern of trust and dependence was being woven between English lordship and native community.

Yet grievances there remained in abundance: the long list of individual and common petitions, submitted by the men of north Wales to Edward as prince at Kennington in 1305, and again by the communities of north and west Wales at Lincoln in 1316, make that obvious enough. Nor had the passage of years dimmed the expectation in many quarters of the return of native political independence. Wales was still politically volatile. Indeed in 1315–17 the country seemed once more to be on the brink of revolt. It was, in common with the rest of northern Europe, in the grip of a serious famine, with 'a great dearth of victuals' being reported from every part of the country. More menacingly, the success of Edward Bruce and his Scottish troops in Ireland in the summer of 1315 raised the spectre that the Scots would next launch an attack from Ireland into Wales. The notion of a pan-Celtic alliance against the English seemed a distinct possibility; propagandists were exploiting to the full the theme of the common kinship of the peoples of Wales, Ireland, and Scotland and an equally common resentment of English rule. Nor were these merely the bad dreams of English settlers, for Scottish ships were already active on the west coast of Wales, capturing a Haverford vessel in Cardigan bay and launching a raid on Holyhead in September 1315. If external threat could be combined with internal disaffection, the elements for a new conflagration could have been readily assembled. The English government took urgent precautionary measures: castles were munitioned and the coasts defended against the prospect of 'tumults'; a commission was instituted into accusations of oppression by royal officials; the Welsh were encouraged to send some of their kinsmen into virtually honourable custody in the royal household, 'without', however, 'stirring the Welsh'; discreet negotiations were conducted with the leaders of native society, 'men of position who can be a help or a hindrance', and they were invited to meet the king at Clipston; the grievances of the Welsh were sympathetically examined and at the Lincoln parliament in February 1316 many of their petitions were granted 'for their greater tranquillity and convenience' by a king who made much of the fact that he had been 'born in the land of Wales'.[39] It was a clever exercise in defusing a political crisis. That crisis recurred in the winter 1316–17: Scottish fortunes temporarily revived in Ireland; secret negotiations proceeded between Robert Bruce and Gruffudd Llwyd, the most powerful figure in native Welsh society; and Gruffudd Llwyd himself (on whom Edward II and his father had relied heavily) was briefly imprisoned. Yet

---

[39] *Cal. Close Rolls 1313–18*, pp. 186, 406; *Cal. Anc. Corr.*, pp. 253–4; *Foedera*, II, i, 283.

ultimately the crisis passed; the ties of loyalty and service, which had been woven since 1301, held and indeed made the Principality lands in Wales one of the most reliable bulwarks of royal authority for the remainder of the reign.

Revolt had been avoided in north Wales. Not so in Glamorgan. There, a brief but furious rebellion flared for some six weeks in January–March 1316. It was led by a powerful Welsh nobleman, Llywelyn Bren, the son of the native Welsh ruler of Senghennydd who had been dispossessed by the earl of Gloucester in 1266. The revolt drew on a strong sense of oppression and disenchantment throughout the Welsh community of upland Glamorgan, particularly after the death of the young earl of Gloucester (the lord of Glamorgan) at Bannockburn in June 1314. The royal custodians who took over the lordship had shown insensitivity in ignoring the delicate social relationships upon which 'good lordship' ultimately depended, in the March as in the Principality: higher yields had been demanded from the lordship at a time of great hardship; local officers had been peremptorily removed; promises of patronage made by the earl were rudely broken; and the dignity and respect which men such as Llywelyn Bren expected as the price for their co-operation were withheld. The revolt was confined to Glamorgan, though it encompassed the whole of that large lordship. Yet its significance was more than local. The wide measure of support it elicited from all sections of Welsh society in Glamorgan was a comment on the breadth of resentment within the lordship; the attacks on castles, boroughs, and mills throughout the lordship identified the obvious targets of that resentment. It was a resentment which drew not only on recent insensitivities and on the bruised susceptibilities of individual noblemen such as Llywelyn Bren, but also on a much deeper conviction of dispossession and on the mythology which it bred. As late as 1365 a leading Welshman in Glamorgan could recall bitterly how his ancestors had lost their inheritance to Robert fitz Hamo some two and a half centuries earlier. The memories of a conquered people are long indeed.

The revolts and threats of revolt which troubled Wales from 1294–1317 were reminders to the English government and English settlers in Wales that peace could not be taken for granted in Wales. Their response could take more than one form. One reaction was to raise the racial barriers further. It was such a view which informed the command to the custodian of Glamorgan in 1316 to remove the Welsh from the plains to the mountains and to inhabit the plains with Englishmen for the greater safety of the lordship. An alternative approach was to win the confidence of the Welsh community and to forge ties of dependence and patronage which might ensure that native society at least accepted alien lordship. It was on the capacity of lordship and community to reach some such sort of a *modus vivendi* that the quiescence of post-Conquest Wales would depend.

PART V

POST-CONQUEST WALES
1317–1415

CHAPTER 15

FOREIGN LORDSHIP
AND NATIVE COMMUNITY

AT no stage in its history could it be more appropriately said of Wales that it was merely a geographical expression than in the fourteenth century. The whole of Wales, it is true, had now been conquered; but conquest had not been followed by the integration of the country within itself institutionally or by its assimilation into the body politic of England. On the contrary, the essentially piecemeal and protracted character of that conquest had only served to entrench and indeed to deepen the particularism so characteristic of medieval Wales. Almost two-thirds of Wales was fragmented into forty or so Marcher lordships, old and new, large and small. Regardless of their age, size, or ownership all these lordships by the fourteenth century were virtually self-contained and self-governing units in administrative, jurisdictional, and financial terms. They enjoyed a measure of independence of the Crown and of each other such as no other seignorial liberty within the dominions of the king of England enjoyed. Their lords exulted in a phraseology which emphasized the regality of their position: they were 'lords royal' enjoying a 'royal lordship', 'with royal liberty', and exercising a 'royal jurisdiction'.[1] During the fourteenth century they defended the status and privileges of their lordships vigorously and successfully against all challenges—whether from the king of England (notably Edward II in the years 1319–21), the prince of Wales (especially in the years 1343–54), or the sheriffs and communities of the English border shires (in the 1330s and again in the 1370s). They thereby entrenched their position as virtual petty kings of petty kingdoms, at least in governmental terms. The remainder of Wales lay under the direct control of the king or of his eldest son, and was divided into shires on the English model. But even within this district—known as the Principality—there was further fragmentation: the two shires of south Wales (Carmarthen and Cardigan) formed one administrative province; the three shires of north Wales (Anglesey, Merioneth, and Caernarfon) another; while the composite county of Flintshire was attached administratively to the palatinate of Chester.

Fragmentation, *morcellement*, was therefore the keynote of Wales's

[1] For these phrases see R. R. Davies, *Lordship and Society in the March of Wales 1284–1400* (Oxford, 1978), p. 217.

institutional and administrative life in the later Middle Ages. The country lacked the semblance and institutions of governmental unity. The extent of that fragmentation stands out starkly if Wales is compared with another province of the king of England's dominions, Ireland. Ireland, like Wales, had only been partially shired; about half of Ireland likewise was composed of large liberties. But there the similarity ends, for the liberties of medieval Ireland were under ultimate royal control and subject to the powers and processes of royal jurisdiction. Furthermore, Ireland, or rather English Ireland, enjoyed a considerable measure of governmental unity—a single common law, that of England; a single justiciar and a unitary royal administration; a single parliament which could act as a forum and focus for the Anglo-Irish political nation; and a single taxation levied from shires and liberties alike. Not so Wales. There was no legal uniformity in the country: English and Welsh law co-existed, in different proportions, throughout the country and each lordship prided itself on the individuality of its own amalgam of laws and customs. There was no common supervisory jurisdictional authority within the country; the king's writ did not run in the March of Wales and there was no royal jurisdiction in error there or in the Principality. There was no Welsh parliament; on the only two occasions (1322 and 1327) when Welsh representatives were summoned to parliament at Westminster, the invitation extended only to the Principality lands. Nor was there general taxation in Wales: with the single exception of the subsidy of 1292, each individual lord (including the king) raised such extraordinary revenue from his lordship as he wished, for his own purposes and under his own pretexts.

Wales, therefore, was a patchwork of lordships, royal and seignorial. Such fragmentation created its own problems. The power of the lord extended no further than the boundary of his lordship; the inhabitants of contiguous lordships were regarded, and indeed designated, as 'aliens' who lay beyond the reach of his protection and punishment. Under such circumstances abuses flourished readily: men fled from one lordship to another to seek sanctuary; others removed their goods and animals to nearby lordships, thereby placing them beyond the reach of their own lord's power of distraint. It is little wonder that late medieval Wales became a byword, especially among Tudor propagandists, for disorder and the disastrous consequences of the absence of a uniform and centralized judicial authority. Indeed, the absence of such an authority prompted the lords of medieval Wales themselves to evolve mechanisms for dealing with the judicial and governmental fragmentation of the country. Letters of protection or 'letters of the march' were issued to officially sanctioned travellers to protect them on their travels between lordships; 'lovedays' or 'days of the march' were held on the boundaries between lordships to settle inter-lordship disputes; and formal written agreements (L. *composiciones*;

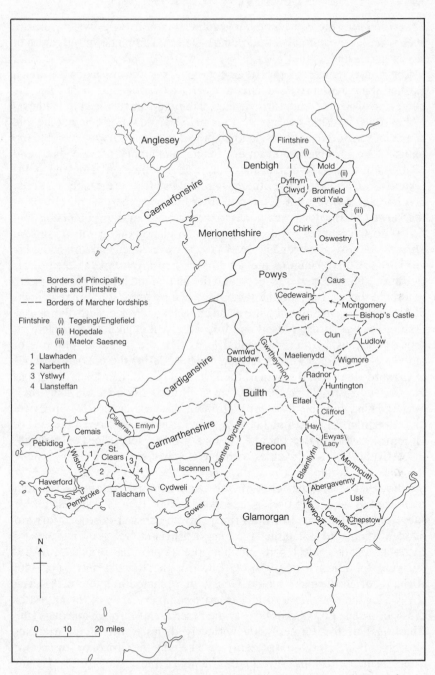

Anglesey

Flintshire
(i)

Denbigh Mold
(ii)

Caernarfonshire Dyffryn
Clwyd Bromfield
and Yale

(iii)

Merionethshire Chirk

Oswestry

Powys Caus

Cedewain Montgomery
Bishop's Castle

Ceri

Clun
Ludlow

Cwmwd Maelienydd Wigmore
Deuddwr

Cardiganshire Radnor

Builth Huntington

Elfael
Clifford

Cligerran Emlyn Hay
Cemais Ewyas
Lacy

Pebidiog Carmarthenshire Monmouth

Wiston St.
Clears 3 Blaenllyfni

1 4 Brecon Abergavenny

2 Iscennen Usk

Haverford Cydweli

Pembroke Talacharn Newport
Caerleon Chepstow

Gower

Glamorgan

| | Borders of Principality |
| shires and Flintshire |
| Borders of Marcher lordships |

Flintshire (i) Tegeingl/Englefield
(ii) Hopedale
(iii) Maelor Saesneg

1 Llawhaden
2 Narberth
3 Ystlwyf
4 Llansteffan

N

0 10 20 miles

MAP 10. The Major Administrative and Lordship Divisions of Wales
in the Fourteenth Century

W. *cydfodau*) were concluded between neighbouring lordships to sort out such issues as the mutual extradition of suspected criminals or the return of stolen goods and cattle.[2]

The consequences of the fragmentation of authority extended much further than administrative and judicial awkwardnesses; it shaped the character of loyalty and patronage, worship and service in late medieval Wales. Each lordship was an integral unit. The lord was ultimately the sole source of territorial and jurisdictional power within it; he was, thereby, the natural focus of loyalty and service for its inhabitants, as individuals and communities, Anglo-Norman and Welsh. The contrast with England in this respect is highly instructive: there, baronial estates were widely scattered and interspersed with the estates of other lords. Furthermore, in England the power of the lord was continuously diluted by the competing and supervisory powers of royal governance and justice and by the alternative attractions of royal patronage. In Wales, however, the local lord could lay virtually exclusive claim to the governance and loyalty of the men of his lordship. Thus the men of Brecon and the men of the lord of Brecon were, at least in theory, one and the same; they had no obvious alternative focus of loyalty and worship. 'Political' allegiances in Wales were thereby as multiple as was lordship itself and it is largely, though not exclusively, in terms of loyalty to their individual lords that the 'political' postures of individual Welshmen were determined. Thus, during the political turmoils of Edward II's reign, the men of the Principality and their leaders (such as Sir Gruffudd Llwyd and Sir Rhys ap Gruffudd) stood steadfast by their lord, the king; but equally other Welshmen, such as Master Rhys ap Hywel or Iorwerth ap Llywarch of Lleweni, stood firm by their lords, the earl of Hereford, as lord of Brecon, and Thomas of Lancaster, as lord of Denbigh, respectively. Political loyalties within Wales had become fractured along the lines of lordship.

Who, then, were the lords of fourteenth-century Wales and how did their careers and ambitions shape the lives of their Welsh tenants or subjects? For the shires of the Principality the answer is straightforward enough: their lord was either the king of England (1283–1301; 1307–43; 1377–99) or his eldest son and heir presumptive as prince of Wales (Edward 'of Caernarfon' 1301–7; Edward 'the Black Prince' 1343–76; Richard 'of Bordeaux' 1376–7; Henry 'of Monmouth' 1399–1413). The answer for the Marcher lordships is more complex.[3] One of the largest of those lordships, Powys, was held by the descendants through marriage (the Charltons) of the former native princely dynasty; two other Marcher lordships (Builth and Montgomery) were held by the Crown or leased out; three further lordships were in the hands of the bishops of St Davids

---

[2] Cf. above pp. 285–6.
[3] For a summary of the descent of the major Marcher lordships 1284–1400 see Appendix.

(Pebidiog and Llawhaden) and Hereford (Bishop's Castle). The remaining lordships were held without exception by leading English families of comital or baronial status. Some of those families (such as Corbet, Clare, Fitzalan, and Mortimer) had held a major stake in Wales for generations; others (such as Lacy, Valence, and Warenne) had only very recently made their entrée into Wales, either through marriage or royal generosity.

During the course of the fourteenth century the composition and character of the English aristocracy in Wales underwent significant changes. Many families were extinguished, occasionally through penury (as happened to the Fitzreginald family of Blaenllyfni) or political forfeiture (as was the lot of the Mortimers of Chirk in 1322), much more frequently through the failure of the direct male line (extinguishing thereby some of the most distinguished families, such as Bigod (1306), Lacy (1311), Clare (1314), Warenne (1347), and Bohun (1373)). New families from the ranks of the English aristocracy took their place, most notably Beauchamp (1309), Despenser (1317), and Stafford (1347). More, however, was involved than simply the replacement of one group of baronial families by another, for in the process territorial power in Wales was concentrated in fewer hands. Whereas twenty-five major English aristocratic families held lordships in Wales in 1300, that number had been reduced to fifteen by 1370. Two families in particular were the major beneficiaries of this process and came thereby to tower in the March in wealth and in power—the Fitzalan earls of Arundel, who controlled an extensive bloc of four major lordships in north-eastern Wales, and the Mortimer earls of March, who by the end of the century had accumulated as many as sixteen lordships in Wales. They were the Marcher barons *par excellence*.

Yet of very few of these families could it be said that their primary interest lay in the March or that they were members of a self-conscious Marcher aristocracy. Some of the smaller families—notably the Camvilles of Llansteffan, the Brians of Talacharn (Laugharne), and the Greys of Dyffryn Clwyd—admittedly paid regular visits to their Welsh estates; and by the end of the century the Mortimers had good reason to do so, since they drew more than two-thirds of their income (£2,410 out of a net revenue of £3,400) from their Welsh and border estates. Yet even the Mortimers chose to live in Wigmore or, later, in Ludlow rather than in Wales itself. Most of their fellow Marcher lords visited their Welsh estates only very occasionally—to hunt or make a grand and profiteering progress on their first entry into their lands (as Roger Mortimer, earl of March, himself did for forty days in 1393). They were overwhelmingly absentee lords. Their estates in Wales were only a means for them to pursue their ambitions elsewhere. Absentee lordship created a vacuum of power which was often filled by the emergence of an alternative local leadership—be it resident nominated officers (such as the justiciar and his associates in the

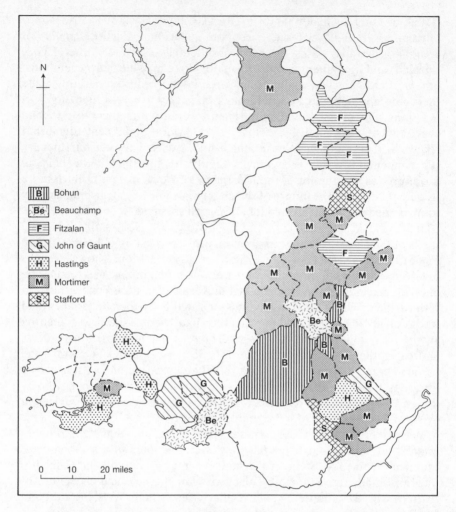

N

Bohun
Beauchamp
Fitzalan
John of Gaunt
Hastings
Mortimer
Stafford

0   10   20 miles

MAP 11. Lordships in Wales held by Major English Aristocratic families c.1370

Principality shires or the steward and constable in the Marcher lordships)
or, increasingly, local men, Welsh and English. Absenteeism and the wide
dispersal of the estates of the English aristocracy also meant that no
specifically Marcher of Anglo-Welsh aristocratic group-identity emerged.
The contrast with English lordship in Ireland is again illuminating in this
respect. Many of the English lords of Ireland, it is true, were primarily
English landowners whose residence and interests lay in England; but in
Ireland there was also a major group of lords whose main territorial
fortunes and normal residence lay in the country itself and who thereby

developed their own identity and particular demands as an Anglo-Irish community, especially in the fourteenth century. Such a development could not, and did not, take place in Wales.

Absentees the English lords of Wales might be, yet their personalities and careers, their demands and policies did much to shape the fortunes of their lordships and the lives of their tenants, even at a great distance. The demands and impact of lordship varied from one generation to the next and from one district to another, for lordship, like kingship, was ultimately personal. An affable and considerate lord could win the loyalty and even the affection of the local community and its leaders. Earl Humphrey (d.) 1298) of Hereford did so in Brecon, and so did the dashing young Roger Mortimer (d. 1398), earl of March, in Denbigh a century later. Edward II may have cut a poor figure as king of England but he forged strong ties of loyalty with the men of north and west Wales.[4] They stood staunchly by him in the crisis of 1321–2 and were in the forefront of the movement to restore him in 1327 and subsequently to overthrow Roger Mortimer. Other lords, however, earned the lasting hatred of their Welsh communities: the rapaciousness of the younger Despenser (d. 1326) and the lawless greed of Roger Mortimer of Chirk (d. 1326) and of his namesake and nephew of Wigmore (d. 1330) alienated the men of their lordships, while the covetous miserliness of Earl Humphrey of Hereford (d. 1361) became part of the folk-memory of the people of his lordship of Brecon. In death as in life the fortunes and misfortunes of their lord impinged on the men of his lordship. The men of Brecon certainly had good reason to know that. When their lord, Earl Humphrey of Hereford, was killed at the battle of Boroughbridge, in 1322, the sins of his political failure were visited heavily on his distant Welsh lordship: royal forces rampaged through Brecon; the lordship was stripped of its timber; the leaders of the local Welsh community were imprisoned; and the tenantry paid for their loyalty to their lord in a fine of 3,000 sheep.

Over and above the impact of the personality and policies of the individual lord on his lordship lay the fact that each Marcher lordship was ultimately part of a structure of governance and control whose base lay in England. The lord's council was the highest decision-making and appeal body for the lordship; the lord's chief steward and other central officers visited his lordship regularly 'to supervise its affairs, to examine the conduct of the officials', and in general to attend to its 'well-being, governance and rule';[5] the accounts of the local officials were closely scrutinized by the lord's auditors; while a regular flow of letters, commands, petitions, bills, and visits further helped to maintain a close liaison between the lord's central administration and the affairs of his

[4] See above, pp. 386–7.
[5] Quoted in R. R. Davies, *Lordship and Society*, pp. 213–14.

Welsh lordship. In terms of patronage, likewise, the individual Welsh lordship was subsumed into the framework of the lord's overall needs. Offices were converted into sinecures and granted to deserving seignorial servants: thus Richard Eccleshall, a royal clerk, had accumulated the posts of *rhaglaw* (bailiff) in at least four north Wales commotes by 1340, while the king's surgeon was rewarded for his skill by being promoted to the office of *rhingyll* (beadle) of a commote in Anglesey. Close confidants might aspire to even richer rewards: thus Edward III discharged his debt, literally and metaphorically, to Walter Mauny in 1341 by granting him the office of sheriff of Merioneth for life and by bestowing all the rights and profits of the county on him. Ecclesiastical patronage in Wales was likewise harnessed to seignorial ends. No one exploited this power more blatantly or irresponsibly than the Black Prince: he presented his clerks to local churches such as Llan-faes (Anglesey); he promoted others to be canons, archdeacon, and precentor in the cathedral churches of Wales; he even managed to foist two of his closest confidants—John Gilbert, his confessor, and William Spridlington, one of his auditors—on the bishoprics of Bangor and St Asaph respectively. The revenues of Welsh lordships were similarly frequently earmarked to provide pensions for the lord's retainers. Much of the income of John of Gaunt's two major Welsh lordships of Monmouth and Cydweli, for example, was assigned in advance as annuities for some of his prominent retainers, such as Sir Richard Burley, the marshal of his army in Spain in 1386–7. The lordships of Wales had been fully subordinated to the needs and priorities of the English inheritances of which they were now a part; they were the colonial outposts of the ruling classes of medieval England.

For their lords the prime function of the lordships of Wales, as indeed of manors in England, was to provide them with resources in men, money, and power. For a military aristocracy, men were a vital source of power, and Wales provided men in abundance. English kings and lords had recruited Welshmen into their armies from at least the twelfth century; but it was in the years 1280–1350 that this recruitment reached its peak. During these years Welsh footmen, both archers and spearmen, frequently accounted for as much as half of the infantry in many English expeditionary armies to Scotland and France: 5,300 Welshmen were among the 7,800 infantry raised by Edward I for Flanders in 1297; in the next year 10,500 Welshmen were raised for the massive army which Edward I led to Scotland; Edward II likewise looked to Wales for more than half of the infantry forces for his Scottish expedition of 1322 and so did his son in 1334–5. The importance of Welsh troops gradually declined as the century progressed and the king came to rely on smaller, more compact and more mobile armies and placed greater emphasis on hobelars and mounted archers. Even so, military service remained an important bond between

English lords and their Welsh tenantry. Each lord regarded his own lordship as his own private pool of potential recruits; he dressed his own men in distinctive uniforms; he ensured that they fought under his own standard. Thus it was to his own men of Chirkland that the earl of Arundel regularly turned for his troops and it was from their midst that he was to recruit Owain Glyn Dŵr as one of his esquires for the Cadzand expedition of 1387; to Flintshire and south Wales the Black Prince sent an urgent request for extra troops as he sat before Calais in 1347; and to his Marcher estates Edmund Mortimer looked for recruits for his Breton expedition in 1375. The captaincy of contingents of Welsh troops was one of the few ways in which the leaders of native Welsh society—men such as Sir Gruffudd Llwyd (d. 1335) in the Principality or Llywelyn ap Madog (d. 1343) in Dyffryn Clwyd—could be recruited fully into the lord's service and could open careers of great military distinction for themselves—as did Sir Hywel 'y Fwyall'—of the Axe—(d. c.1380), who retired after notable service in France to take up the post of constable of Cricieth castle, or Sir Gregory Sais (d. 1390) from Flintshire, whose military service took him from Castile to Berwick and from Poitou to Pembroke. Nor were the lord's military demands on his lordship confined to the troops he recruited within it; they also impinged on it in the horses and supplies he commandeered, demands for financial support for the troops chosen to serve him, and heavy financial subsidies towards the cost of his expedition (such as the aid peremptorily demanded by the Black Prince from the men of Flintshire in 1346, or the subsidy of 200 marks levied by the earl of Surrey from his tenants of Bromfield and Yale in 1339). In one way or another, the men of Wales were deeply involved in the military enterprises of their lords.

The demands of the lord from his lordship in time of peace were no less exacting. 'There is a fair lordship there', remarked the council of the Black Prince gloatingly in its report on Bromfield and Yale in 1347, 'well worth two thousand marks a year'.[6] The 'fairness' of lordship was equated with its yield. One way in which that 'fairness' could be realized was by exploiting the demesne resources of the lordship. Arable demesne farming by English lords in Wales in the fourteenth century was largely confined to the river valleys and coastal plains of the south and east. There it could form a major item of seignorial revenue, as it did for example in the Clare lordships of Caerleon and Usk or in the Lancaster lordship of Monmouth. But most of Wales lay too far from obvious market outlets and too remote from the normal circuit of the lord's household for arable demesne farming to be continued there. Thus, none of the manors of the native princes of Gwynedd was retained as a working unit into the fourteenth century. Even in the south-east, demesne farming had been abandoned on virtually every

[6] *Register of Edward the Black Prince*, I, 96–7.

manor by the last quarter of the fourteenth century—at Brecon, for example, in 1373 and Newport by the 1380s. The lords of Wales were becoming rentier landlords as well as absentees.

The pastoral resources of Wales offered much better prospects for seignorial enterprise and profit-making. Earlier attempts had been made to explore these resources; but it was only with the advent of peace in the fourteenth century that the opportunities could be realized to the full. Vaccaries were established (as in the foothills of the lordship of Brecon) where large herds of cows could be reared and then sent to restock English manors or to cater for the needs of the lord's larder. In 1349, for example, twenty drovers drove over 400 head of cattle from Brecon to the Bohun household at Pleshy (Essex). But it was sheep farming, above all, which promised the richest returns in Wales. The English lords drew on all their entrepreneurial skills to take full advantage of the opportunity: they appointed professional stock-keepers; bred their flocks selectively; exchanged sheep between different manors to improve the quality of their flocks; took the pastures and flocks of Cistercian abbeys in Wales on lease; and marketed their wool through international agencies. By 1350 the earl of Arundel had flocks of over 5,000 sheep on his Shropshire and Marcher estates; by 1373 the Bohun flock on the Epynt mountains in Brecon exceeded 3,000; and several other Marcher lords—such as the Mortimers in the middle March, the earl of Warwick in Elfael, the Greys in Dyffryn Clwyd, and Guy Brian in Laugharne—likewise had large flocks.

Demesne farming, however, was expensive in effort and investment. A shorter route to seignorial profit lay through the exploitation of the tenantry. Seignorial policy in this respect naturally varied from one lordship to another and indeed from one lord to the next; but there is little doubt that English lordship in Wales in the fourteenth century was on the whole assertive and exploitative to a remarkable degree. Native customs were, it is true, respected; but every effort was made to ensure that obligations were scrupulously recorded and renders and dues promptly paid. It was for that reason that a remarkable series of cadastral surveys—notably the surveys of Bromfield and Yale (1315 and 1391), Dyffryn Clwyd (1324), Denbigh (1334), the northern Principality (1352), Chirkland (1391), and Oswestry (1393)—were drawn up during the course of the century; they are as eloquent of the determination of foreign lordship to exploit native society to the full as is Domesday Book for Norman England. Further evidence of that determination is not difficult to find. It is to be seen in the way that the land-market was carefully and profitably controlled: thus the lords of Bromfield and Yale and Dyffryn Clwyd alike decreed that all land-transactions under the Welsh device of *prid* required a seignorial licence, while in Flintshire in 1351 the Black Prince ordered the seizure of all Welsh land purchased in fee without his permission. Every opportunity was taken to declare Welsh lands escheat (i.e. forfeit to the lord) and to lease them on English terms for an annual rent, thereby bringing them more firmly under seignorial control.[7] The results could be quite spectacular: thus, in the lordship of Denbigh, 29,000 acres out of a total surveyed acreage of 68,000 acres in four commotes were classified as escheated land and in 1334 yielded some 53 per cent of the lordship's income of over £1,000. Native Welsh customs, such as *amobr* (virginity dues), and native offices, such as those of *ceisiad* (serjeant of the peace), were shamelessly exploited for maximum profit. English lordship in Wales also waxed powerful and profitable by extending its control over forest, waste, and pasture and by compelling tenants to take their corn to seignorial mills to be ground. These were areas which hitherto had been jealously guarded by community custom and by the rights of kin-groups; but they were now brought firmly under seignorial control. The sense of resentment within the native community at such seignorial aggression was intense: 'he has completely ejected us from our wood, pasture, mountain and mills', said the men of Dyffryn Clwyd of their lord, 'and this of his own will and without any manner of deserts'.[8] For the lord, however, the profits from such aggressive lordship more than compensated for the sense of grievance they occasioned. The seignorial mills in the Mortimer lordships of the middle March accounted for over a sixth of the lord's revenue, while in Brecon the income from the Great Forest more than doubled between 1340 and 1400, at a time when other sources of revenue remained stagnant.

But it was through the exercise of its judicial power that foreign lordship made its greatest profits in post-Conquest Wales. Here there was virtually no limit to the lord's authority. He did not share his jurisdictional power with the king, nor was he normally supervised by or answerable to him. In contemporary phraseology he had 'regal jurisdiction' and 'cognizance of all pleas personal, real and of the Crown'.[9] All writs within his lordship were issued in his name; offences were committed against his peace, not that of the king; he had power to issue legislation for his tenants and did so; the only fount of appeal against the decision of his courts or of his officials, in the March and the Principality alike, was his own council. This was seignorial jurisdiction as ample and untrammelled as it was known in medieval society. It formed the most regular, intrusive, and masterful way in which foreign lordship impinged on its Welsh subjects—coercing and chastising them; controlling them and their land, the major source of their wealth; and bringing judicial authority to bear on the local community.

Nor were the lords of Wales content with the regular sources of jurisdiction at their command. From the mid-fourteenth century, in

---

[7] See below, p. 432.
[8] *Cal. Anc. Pets.*, p. 168, n. 5359 (1324). Cf. below pp. 431–2.
[9] *Calendar of Charter Rolls 1341–1417*, pp. 289–90.

Principality and March alike, a new arm of judicial power was added, namely the session in eyre. The justices at these sessions were drawn from the lord's councillors and legal advisers; they were given the most ample authority in judicial and administrative matters, including the right of pardon and the power to review and revise judgements given in inferior courts; they were expected to yield handsome profits for the lord and rarely failed to do so. Thus at least four such sessions were held in the lordship of Denbigh 1359–70, while the 1373 sessions in Brecon yielded almost £2,000 to the lord. Judicial profits, ordinary and extraordinary, in fact formed one of the most distinctive and lucrative features of the revenues of Welsh lordships. More than twenty per cent of the income of Chirkland in the 1340s came from this source, while in the upland lordship of Maelienydd in the 1350s the figure rose to over sixty per cent. Two features in particular stand out with regard to this judicial income: proportionately far more of it was derived from the native communities of upland Wales than from the Anglicized lowland tenantry; secondly, it contributed a far more significant share of seignorial income in Wales than did judicial revenue on seignorial estates in England. Judicial power and judicial profits made lordship in Wales peculiarly attractive.

So also did the huge sums which the Marcher lords could exact as casual or extraordinary revenue. Until the sixteenth century Wales enjoyed the privilege of being exempt from English parliamentary taxation; but it paid heavily for that privilege in the subsidies which it was required to yield to its own lords, royal and Marcher. A whole galaxy of pretexts was manufactured in order to raise such subsidies. Massive communal fines were imposed for offences against the lord (such as appropriating land without his permission, evading tolls, or giving false judgements); 'gifts', 'aids', 'tallages', and 'mises' were levied under a host of specious excuses, such as saluting him on his first entry into his estates, helping him in his financial need, or contributing to his war expenses; large sums were collected in return for the grant or the confirmation of charters of liberties; and, increasingly and most regularly, huge communal fines were exacted in order to buy off the prospect of a visit of the lord's justices in eyre. The sums so collected were certainly impressive: in Chirkland in the 1340s they accounted for at least twenty per cent of the lord's revenue, in Cydweli and Brecon under Henry V for forty per cent. There can be little doubt that Wales was as heavily and regularly taxed by its lords as were the counties and boroughs of England by the king.

Lordship in Wales was hugely profitable to the English lords in the fourteenth century. The Black Prince's estates in the Principalty and Flintshire brought in an income in excess of £5,000 annually, while the families of Clare and, later in the century, Mortimer and Fitzalan had estates in Wales which yielded them more than £2,000 annually. These are indeed impressive figures, especially when it is recalled that several English comital families were well content with an income of £1,000 or so per annum. What is more, the English lords bent every effort to squeeze the maximum profit from their Welsh estates and to maintain and even augment their income from them in the face of the mounting economic crises of the fourteenth century. None was more determined or more grasping than the Black Prince. He and his officers set out purposefully 'to restore the peace and estate of the Prince's lands':[10] *quo warranto* inquiries were instituted; new surveys were commissioned; central officials were dispatched into the Principality to counter administrative slackness; justices in eyre were appointd to maximize judicial revenue; local officials were made directly accountable to the Prince's auditors rather than to the local chamberlain; heavy criminal fines and subsidies were imposed; and peremptory orders were issued for the more rapid collection of local revenues. The results of this tornado of reforms are not precisely known;[11] but the evidence of other Welsh lordships is eloquent as to what the answer might have been. The annual income of the earls of Arundel from Chirkland increased from £300 in the 1320s to over £500 in the 1370; the value of the Bohun complex of estates (Brecon, Hay, Huntington) rose by at least forty per cent in the same period; and there was a similar, if smaller, increase in the yield of the Lancaster lordships (Monmouth, Ogmore, and Cydweli). All these dramatic increases in seignorial revenue were achieved, it should be noticed, across the decades when Wales, like other countries, was ravaged by recurrent outbreaks of plague. The 'fairness' of lordship in Wales, to which the Black Prince's commissioners gloatingly referred in 1347, was being achieved by the systematic financial rape of the country. It required an escort of eleven archers to accompany the treasure-carts laden with £1,400 of the yield of the Mortimer estates in Wales as they trundled on their way to London in December 1387.

Lordship in Wales yielded profits for the English lords; it also yielded power. The lordships of Wales were counters on the chess-board of English politics in the later Middle Ages. As such, their history in 'political' terms is essentially part of the political story of medieval England. It was in the arena of national politics, and specifically of the king's court, that the distribution and redistribution of power in Wales was largely determined— whether by the award of a marriage (such as that of one of the Clare heiresses to Hugh Audley in 1317, who thereby became lord of Newport), the grant of the wardship of a minor and the custody of his estates (such as

---

[10] *Register of Edward the Black Prince*, I, 29.

[11] The valor compiled after the Prince's death, and based on an average of the revenues of the years 1372–5 suggests clearly, however, that the financial and administrative reforms led to a sharp increase in revenue. The northern lands of the Principality were expected to yield £3,041 annually, the southern lands £1,619 (compared with £2,258 and £1,059 in the early fourteenth century).

the grant of the custody of much of the huge Mortimer inheritance in Wales to a consortium headed by the earl of Arundel in 1384), or the award of key offices and sinecures in the Principality (such as the virtual life-grant of the post of justiciar of north Wales to Roger Mortimer of Chirk for much of Edward II's reign, thereby entrenching further the power of the Mortimers within the country). Royal favour and support were the most vital factors in shaping the fortunes of the English aristocracy in Wales. They could help to make or to restore a family: it was Edward III's favour which ensured that Richard Fitzalan, earl of Arundel, secured the rich lordship of Bromfield and Yale on the earl of Surrey's death in 1347, and it was that same favour which allowed Roger Mortimer, earl of March (d. 1360), to reconstitute the great empire which his grandfather had built in Wales a generation earlier. Equally, the withholding of royal favour could bring a family down and keep it there: the Mortimers of Chirk were never allowed, through royal indifference, to recover from the débâcle of 1322, while the Montagues, having waxed rich in one generation through Edward III's beneficence, declined sharply in the next, when that beneficence was withdrawn and they were required to surrender the lordship of Denbigh, worth over £1,000 per annum. In much the same fashion, territorial disputes in Wales quickly became entangled in the conflicts of national politics. The protracted and bitter quarrels over the succession to Powys and the title to Gower in the early fourteenth century, for example, were in essence merely local and domestic squabbles; but they were quickly sucked into the maelstrom of the bitter politics of Edward II's reign. The dispute over Gower in particular helped to crystallize the growing opposition to the greed and methods of the Despensers and gave their opponents both a pretext and a place to force a showdown in the form of a civil war in the Welsh March in May 1321.

The kings and barons of England, therefore, used Wales as one of the pitches on which they played their power-games; they lined up, or tried to line up, the communities of their Welsh lordships in support of their ambitions and manœuvres. Wales in this respect was no more than an adjunct of the political life of England. Yet there were several distinctive features to Wales's role in the political life of medieval England. Its very distance from the centre of English politics was one of these features. Disgruntled barons could retire here to lick their wounds to prepare revenge. Richard Marshal, earl of Pembroke, had done so in 1233–4; the disaffected barons in 1297 did the same, holding their assembly in Wyre forest on the edge of the March; the earl of Hereford and the Mortimers followed suit in 1321 as they laid their plans to overthrow the Despensers. Contemporaries readily recognized the attractiveness of Wales in this respect: 'it was there', as one chronicler remarked, 'that the barons had their safest refuge; it was difficult for the king to penetrate it without a strong force'.[12] Furthermore, the strongly militarist traditions of Wales and the acceptance of the practice of 'private' war there, as a means of settling differences, further encouraged the barons to retreat to Wales, as they did in 1233 and 1321, to confront their opponents, without necessarily incurring the charge of having defied the king and starting a civil war.[13] In this respect, Wales, and the March in particular, could act as an apron-stage for English political disputes.

Another distinctive feature of Wales in political terms was that it was a land of compact territorial blocks. Here the large self-contained lordship (not, as in much of England, the individual manor interspersed with the manors of other lords) was the unit of territorial, and thereby of political, power. Hence it was easy to assemble in Wales, in a very short time, a remarkably extensive and compact power base—through inheritance, marriage, force, and royal favour. The Braose and Marshal families and Hubert de Burgh had already shown how it could be done in the thirteenth century. They were not without their imitators in the fourteenth century. The first and one of the most successful was the younger Despenser. He only secured his initial foothold on Wales in 1317 as husband of one of the Clare co-heiresses; yet by the time of his downfall in 1326 he had assembled, through royal indulgence and his own utterly unscrupulous methods, a remarkable empire which stretched virtually unbroken from the Wye to the Teifi, from Castle Goodrich to Pembroke (see map 12). His Welsh estates, including those which he held in custody, must have brought him almost £5,000 in annual revenue; on their own they made him into one of the richest landowners of his day. Between them the king, the two Despensers and Edmund, earl of Arundel, held almost three-quarters of Wales under their sway in the years 1322–6. On Despenser's downfall in 1326, his empire was replaced by that put together with even more astonishing speed by Roger Mortimer of Wigmore (see map 13). Mortimer indeed publicly acknowledged that his territorial base in his years of supremacy (1327–30) lay in Wales, by adopting the novel title of earl of March on his elevation to comital status in 1328.[14] None used Wales to promote his political and territorial ambitions in the fourteenth century so ruthlessly and spectacularly as did Despenser or Mortimer; but even for less greedy men the compactness of power and the uninhibited quality of lordship in Wales were highly attractive. Richard Fitzalan, earl of Arundel (d. 1376), bent every effort to bring the four rich lordships of Clun and Oswestry (old Fitzalan lordships), Chirkland (a recent acquisition, first

[12] *Vita Edwardi Secundi. The Life of Edward the Second*, ed. N. Denholm-Young (1957), p. 117.
[13] 'In order to cover themselves that this was not done against the king', as the younger Despenser put it in 1321: *Cal. Anc. Corr.*, p. 259.
[14] See maps 12–13.

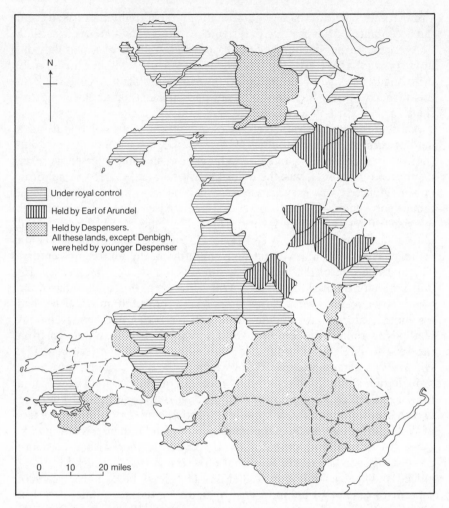

Under royal control

Held by Earl of Arundel

Held by Despensers.
All these lands, except Denbigh,
were held by younger Despenser

0   10   20 miles

MAP 12. The Political and Territorial Control of Wales, 1322–6

secured through political forfeiture in 1322 and restored to the family in
1332), and Bromfield and Yale (secured in 1347 on the death of the earl of
Surrey without an heir of his body) under his control. When to this array of
estates—yielding well over £2,000 in annual income—is added the
justiciarship of the northern Principality, which the earl initially acquired
in 1330 and which was converted into a life-grant for him in 1337, the
importance of Wales in Arundel's calculations can readily be appreciated.
For much the same reason, it was to Cheshire and Wales that Richard II
looked in the 1390s when he sought to redraw the map of territorial and

political power of his kingdom in his own interests. He added the county of
Flint and the Arundel lordships in north-east Wales to his palatinate of
Chester to form a new principality of Chester in September 1397. Between
them, the existing Principality of Wales and the new Principality of Chester
gave Richard a formidable territorial base, which was further enhanced by
the redistribution of other lordships in Wales to his close favourites,
notably Lescrope, Despenser, Exeter, and Aumale. It was little wonder
that rumours circulated that Richard II intended to rule his kingdom
henceforth from Wales and Ireland.

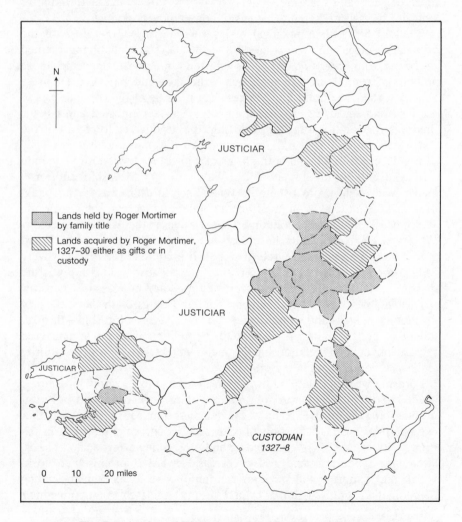

MAP 13. The Domination of Wales by Roger Mortimer of Wigmore, 1327–30

Wales, therefore, was one of the favourite hunting-grounds of the
empire-builders of medieval English politics. By the same token it was an
area in which the political upheavals of the period had the most dramatic
impact. Since it was a land of large lordships it was relatively easy to
change its political complexion by a few strokes. Thus as a result of the
downfall of Thomas of Lancaster and his allies in 1322, more than half of
the Marcher lordships of Wales (and far more than that in terms of wealth
and area) were confiscated and assigned to new lords. Much the same
bouleversement happened in 1326–7 and again in 1397. Wales registered
more dramatically than any other part of the dominions of the king of
England the seismographic changes of contemporary politics.

The lordships of late medieval Wales were convulsed, therefore, by the
political fortunes and misfortunes of their lords. Their inhabitants seemed
to be the innocent victims of seignorial ambitions, financing those
ambitions from their own inadequate incomes and paying even more
heavily if their lord fell on evil times. Yet the role of the communities of
the lordships of Wales *vis-à-vis* their lords was less innocent and passive
than this formulation suggests. Lordship, be it native or foreign, was the
framework of authority and power to which they were habituated. They
yearned for it: the tenants of the Mortimer lordships longed for 'a definite
lord'; those of Bromfield and Yale pleaded for 'good lordship' and for 'a
leader who might protect them'.[15] When such lordship was forthcoming,
they basked in the glow of its protection and in its success. Iolo Goch, the
Welsh poet, could hardly contain his superlatives in the two odes of eulogy
(W. *cywyddau mawl*) which he addressed to his local lords, Edward III and
Roger Mortimer, earl of March (d. 1398). It mattered little that they were
foreign lords. In such a society the hiatus or collapse of lordship was the
disaster. It left men feeling 'impoverished' (as the burgesses of Chepstow
put it), helpless against local strong men and thugs or the ambitions of
neighbouring lords and communities.[16] The collapse of lordship—through
failure of heirs, minority, widowhood, or political disaster—endangered
the delicate nexus of relationships, worship, and service on which authority
and social control ultimately relied.

Lordship was essential; but even in Wales it had to be 'good' lordship. It
needed to establish a measure of rapport with the local community—by not
overstepping the mark in terms of the demands it made, keeping a weather
eye open for local disaffection (as Edward II's commissioners did in the
Principality in 1315–16),[17] suspending and prosecuting extortionate officials,
attending to petitions and grievances (as Edward II promised to do in
1322), and flattering the sense of self-importance of local men—calling
them together for discussion or even, as in 1322 and 1327, summoning their

---

[15] *Cal. Anc. Corr.*, p. 131; *Cal. Anc. Pets.*, p. 296.
[16] *Cal. Anc. Corr.*, p. 72; *Cal. Anc. Pets.*, pp. 478–9.   [17] See above, p. 387.

leaders to parliament. Effective lordship and a contented community depended in particular on gaining the support and co-operation of the natural leaders of society. 'It is not easy', so some of the most experienced men of Pembroke had noted shrewdly, 'to control the Welsh except through one of their own race.'[18] That truism had to be learnt anew in each generation in every area of Wales. Medieval lords, it is true, paid a price for surrendering much of their authority into the hands of local *potentes*. Powerful family lineages frequently came to monopolize local offices (as did the lineage of Ithel Fychan in Tegeingl or the descendants of Iorwerth Ddu in Chirkland and Maelor Saesneg) and abuse them for their own ends. Yet, in the last resort, there was no alternative, for in the ordering of relationships between a distant lord and a local community, a due distribution of patronage to the leaders of native society was essential. It worked to the mutual advantage of both parties.

No career, perhaps, shows this more clearly than that of Sir Gruffudd Llwyd. He was of impeccable Welsh aristocratic stock, that of Ednyfed Fychan, Llywelyn ab Iorwerth's steward; but already by 1283 he had enlisted in Edward I's service as a yeoman. So began a career of unwavering, if occasionally very sorely tried, loyalty to the English Crown extending over more than fifty years. He reaped his reward in abundance: he was raised to the status of knight (a rare honour for a Welshman and prized all the more for that); secured valuable lands and profitable leases; held in turn the shrievalties of Caernarfon, Anglesey, and Merioneth; enjoyed the rich sinecure of the forestership of North Wales for ten years; and was employed almost without a break as the king's chief recruiting officer for troops in north Wales from 1297 to 1327. He had made himself indispensable to the Crown. But there was more to his career than offices and rewards. He was a vital bridge between the monarchy and the native community in north Wales. To contemporary Welshmen he was known as 'the man of the court' and it was a small token of the affection in which he was held at court that, when his son died *en route* to Scotland in 1322, the king contributed towards the expenses of his funeral at the Dominican church at Newcastle-on-Tyne. But Sir Gruffudd was also a man of the country: sensitive missions in Wales were entrusted to him and he acted as an important channel between royal lordship and Welsh community. The family of Einion Sais performed much the same function in the lordship of Brecon as Sir Gruffudd in north Wales. The service of the family to the Bohuns as lords of Brecon extended over more than a century. It stood and suffered with its lord—whether against the prince of Gwynedd in the 1260s, Edward I in 1297, or Edward II in 1327. The reward for such loyalty was an ample stock of patronage: a saddle for a horse, timber from seignorial forests for building houses, annuities, offices in abundance

[18] *Cal. Anc. Corr.*, p. 48.

(notably that of sheriff of Brecon which was virtually a family preserve), lucrative custodies, and leases. No one could be in doubt that there was a special bond between Einion Sais's family and the lords of Brecon. It worked to the mutual advantage of both parties.

The return on 'good lordship' was a contented community. 'They were all at one with their lord', as a royal commissioner reported jealously on relations between the men of Brecon and their lord in 1297.[19] But 'good lordship' could only be achieved through constant vigilance and, above all, sensitivity. If lordship became simply an instrument of extortion, if it trespassed heedlessly into areas—such as the control of escheats or access to pasture and woodland—which native society regarded as its own, if it rode roughshod over what were considered to be well-established customs, if it denied some of the fruits of patronage to local men, then the community could quickly be alienated from its lord.[20] Such alienation happened more than once in fourteenth-century Wales. The high-handed behaviour of the Grey lords of Dyffryn Clwyd drove their tenants in desperation to offer the king 600 marks in order to persuade him to keep the lordship in his own hands or transfer it to another lord. The two Mortimers—Roger of Wigmore (d. 1330) and his uncle and namesake of Chirk (d. 1326)—were held in similar bad odour by their Welsh tenants: the men of Cardiganshire complained bitterly of the 'excessive hardship' of their lordship;[21] the community of north and south Wales warned in 1322 that if the Mortimers were restored, they themselves would be forced to flee their lands; and when Roger Mortimer of Wigmore won his way back to favour in 1327, the men of the Principality were indeed driven to the edge of rebellion and their leaders, notably Gruffudd Llwyd and Rhys ap Gruffudd, conspired to overthrow him. The younger Despenser was likewise loathed, not surprisingly in view of the contemporary indictment of him as 'the greediest of men'. Even he was sensitive enough to realize that the attitude of his men of Glamorgan towards him was 'sullen and morose'.[22] The Black Prince was in danger of treading along the same path by his single-minded obsession with raising as much money as possible, at any cost, from his lands in Wales. Even the earl of Arundel, the Prince's justiciar in north Wales, was prompted to warn him that some of the Prince's commands 'seem to the Prince's good men in those parts to be very grievous and damaging to them'.[23]

The results of such alienation between lordship and community could be

---

[19] *Cal. Anc. Corr.*, p. 101.   [20] See below pp. 431–4.

[21] 'Propter nimiam duriciam dominii', Public Record Office, Chancery Miscellanea, C. 47/10/32 no. 21.

[22] 'Homo cupidissimus', quoted from the Lanercost Chronicle in J. Conway Davies, 'The Despenser War in Glamorgan', *Trans. Royal Historical Society*, 3rd ser., IX (1915), 21–64 at p. 27 n. 4; *Cartae et alia munimenta de Glamorgan*, ed. G. T. Clark, III, 102.

[23] *Cal. Anc. Corr.*, p. 244.

damaging. The community might at the very least become uncooperative; it might sit tightly on its hands when its lord was in dire trouble, as did the leaders of Glamorgan society, both English and Welsh, in the younger Despenser's hour of crisis in 1326. It could show its ill-will by being slow in paying its revenue or indeed by refusing to pay what it regarded as an unwarranted demand. In these circumstances there was a limit to what seignorial threat or distraint could achieve by way of retaliation. As the fourteenth century wore on, the community's resistance was manifested in an ever-lengthening list of arrears, or uncollected revenue, on the lord's annual accounts. The community could protect itself against further seignorial oppression by securing a charter of liberties which in effect circumscribed its lord's freedom of action in future. It might extort such a charter from its lord when he was in a corner (as did the men of Maelienydd in 1297 and those of Gower in 1306); alternatively, it might pay a large fine to secure such a concession (as did the community of Chirkland in 1324, 1334, and 1355, or that of Cydweli from Duke Henry of Lancaster in 1356).

Finally, the community might in despair resort to violence, if only as a warning that there was a threshold of tolerance which not even the most hard-nosed and insensitive of seignorial regimes dared cross. On St Valentine's Day 1345, Henry Shaldeford, recently appointed as the Black Prince's attorney in north Wales, was murdered on his way to Caernarfon. It was the climax of anti-English violence in north Wales in the 1340s, which had already included the murder of the sheriff of Merioneth, the seizure of his records, and a riotous assault on the town and castle of Rhuddlan. Tension was clearly running high; the Welsh, as a contemporary report remarked, were 'greatly agitated and in a highly volatile mood'. The tension sprang from deep suspicions of, and resentment at, recent high-handed administrative and fiscal reforms initiated by the Prince's councillors, such as the collection of debts and an inquiry into administrative irregularities; it also drew on an even more dangerous sense of alienation among many of the leaders of the native community in north Wales, lay and ecclesiastical. They felt that they were being excluded from the positions of trust and authority (including high ecclesiastical office) which should be theirs. The storm eventually blew over; but it sent a deep shudder down the spines of English settlers and administrators in Wales. 'The Welsh have never been so disposed', warned the terrified burgesses of Denbigh, '. . . to rise against their liege lord to conquer the land from him.' Even the Black Prince's steward foresaw that if redress were not forthcoming, 'it will be impossible for any Englishman or English official to dwell in these parts'. The ultimate price of a failure of 'good' and sensitive lordship in Wales might be a revolt of the native community against foreign lordship in general.[24]

[24] *Cal. Anc. Corr.*, pp. 239 ('molt merveilous et estrange'), 230, 233.

CHAPTER 16

PEACE, COEXISTENCE, AND CHANGE IN FOURTEENTH-CENTURY WALES

WALES in the fourteenth century enjoyed an unprecedented period of peace. With the exception of the rebellion of Llywelyn Bren in Glamorgan in 1316, there was no major revolt or war in the country between 1295 and 1400. To a society where raids and pillage had been for so long a normal, indeed essential, part of life and the struggle to contain and to counter the advance of Anglo-Norman lords and English kings a consuming preoccupation for over two centuries, peace was indeed a novel experience. But even the nervous English settlers in newly conquered north Wales began to believe that the days of military emergency were indeed at an end: already in 1316 in Dyffryn Clwyd the best armour was replaced by the best beast as the heriot payable by English military tenants. Now that peace had at last broken out, Wales suddenly seemed to be grossly overprovided with castles. Some key castles, such as Caernarfon or Pembroke, were kept in a state of military preparedness; but, even in those, anxious surveyors fought a losing battle against a seemingly inexorable process of neglect and dilapidation. Elsewhere, castles were left uncompleted as monuments to the over-ambitiousness and over-anxiety of an earlier age—as happened to the great Clare castle at Tregrug in Usk lordship—or crumbled into premature decay. Many of them survived as the administrative and judicial headquarters for their respective lordships; but the days of their military grandeur and usefulness were now over. At Llansteffan, for example, the main gatehouse, the military strong-point of the castle, was abandoned; a large storage barn was erected in the outer ward, and residence was probably restricted to the inner ward. Elsewhere, castles were indeed rebuilt but increasingly to meet the dictates of comfort rather than defence. Finely decorated chimneys, fireplaces, and glass windows might be installed (as at Grosmont (Monmouth) or Chirk), or an enterprising residential lord might embark on a major rebuilding with a clear emphasis on domestic comfort as well as military defence (as at Carew (Pembroke)), or might even desert the gloom of the castle for the spaciousness and elegance of an adjacent stately home (as happened at Tretower Court (Blaenllyfni)). The castle seemed to be entering on the last phase of its history in Wales.

With peace and security came prosperity and confidence. None benefited more than the tiny boroughs which had hitherto huddled nervously in the shadow of castles and behind hastily constructed ditches and ramparts. Their populations now grew rapidly, spilling beyond the safety of town-walls, whether in ancient boroughs, such as Kidwelly, or in recent foundations like Denbigh. The towns proclaimed their new-found confidence in a variety of ways: more ample charters of liberties (such as those of Swansea in 1306 and Cardiff in 1340) were now secured from their lords; borough seals were engraved; 'booth-halls', where tolls were paid and the official weights and measures kept, were built; guilds were formed and guild chapels, such as the corvisors' chapel in the Priory church at Brecon, were established; impressive gate-towers, of which the Monnow Gate at Monmouth remains the outstanding example, were erected; secure stone town-walls were constructed, as at Tenby and Chepstow; and civic churches, such as those of Brecon and Tenby, were redesigned and rebuilt. Many Welsh towns waxed prosperous in these peaceful conditions: the farm (i.e. the annual lease paid to the lord for the right of self-governance) of the borough of Brecon, for example, more than doubled between 1340 and 1399. Individual townsmen also prospered and extended the range and quantity of their trade. Some—such as John Owen of Kidwelly or Thomas Rede of Carmarthen (and Bristol)—became traders of international standing, exporting hides, leather, and especially wool, in large quantities, and importing wine, salt, and iron. More significantly, peace allowed the burgesses to extend their grip over local and regional marketing within Wales. No part of the country now lay outside the reach of a network of market towns. The tempo of economic life in Wales was accommodating itself increasingly to the calendar of urban activity, notably the weekly market and two or three annual fairs. Townsmen and peasants were coming to form a coherent economic community, whose interests were increasingly seen as mutual and complementary. It was a sign of the new-found confidence of the burgesses and the advantage of ready access to liquid capital which they enjoyed that they were now beginning to venture into the increasingly active market in Welsh land. The success of burgess families, such as the Colliers of Harlech, the Boldes of Conway, or the Forts of Llansteffan, in this respect, was yet another reminder that military conquest was soon followed by economic mastery.

Peace also allowed the large English communities which had settled in lowland Wales to face the future with much more confidence, to think of themselves as well-established settlers rather than as nervous frontiersmen. Many of them in the coastal lowlands and river valleys of south and east Wales—notably in Pembroke, Gower, the Vale of Glamorgan, Gwent, and Brecon—belonged to families which had been established there for generations; others, especially in north-east Wales, were recently arrived prospectors in search of land and fortunes in the wake of the Edwardian

Conquest. Unlike the English communities in Ireland, these alien settlers in Wales were in little danger of becoming isolated or of 'going native'. Their leaders—'gentlemen' (L. *gentiles homines*; Fr. *gentils*) as they were beginning to call themselves—often held lands in England, as well as in Wales, and moved easily in English county society. Furthermore, travel from lowland Wales into the west Midlands or across the Severn estuary to Somerset and Devon was relatively easy; it fostered a whole range of contacts—social, marital, cultural, ecclesiastical, and commercial—between lowland Wales and England. The social and economic configuration and customs of these Anglicized regions of Wales were now barely to be distinguished from those of southern England. Wales had become firmly and irreversibly a country of two peoples and two cultures. The relationship between them would henceforth be a leitmotiv of its history.

Now that peace had at last arrived, much of the effort and capital hitherto invested in military enterprises could be directed to more domestic ends. Several of the major monasteries felt sufficiently secure to embark on major rebuilding projects: the great abbey church at Tintern and the abbot's lodgings there were entirely rebuilt in the late thirteenth–early fourteenth centuries; so also was the church of Neath abbey; and at Brecon priory the claustral buildings were redesigned. Within native Wales the advent of peace and the need to repair war-damage prompted important building enterprises at the cathedral church of St Asaph and the monasteries of Strata Florida and Valle Crucis (where a contemporary inscription extols the work undertaken by Abbot Adam). But it is in the diocese of St Davids that the most striking evidence of this architectural renaissance is to be seen, notably in the great buildings associated with Bishop Henry Gower (1328–47) and his successors. Their building enterprise included work at the episcopal palace at Lamphey (Pembroke), in the hospital of St David, founded by Gower himself, at Swansea, and at the castle there; but their glories are undoubtedly the rebuilding undertaken at the cathedral at St Davids and the episcopal palace there. The richly decorated style and the distinctive arcaded parapets characteristic of this work bespeak affluence and confidence; they also proclaim a readiness to import the expertise of English craftsmen, while impressing upon it the hallmarks of the ecclesiastical patron himself. At the parish level, likewise, much ecclesiastical rebuilding and renovation was undertaken. It was in the fourteenth century that the movement began which was to give pre-Reformation Wales its impressive collection of roods, lofts, and screens.

Nor was it churchmen alone who delighted in the opportunities offered by peace. Laymen also began to build non-defensive, single-storeyed hall-houses, which were to remain such a distinctive feature of the vernacular architecture of Wales until the sixteenth century. Cefn y Fan (Caernarfon),

Plas Ucha (Merioneth) and Tŷ Draw, Llanarmon Mynydd Mawr (Chirk) are all examples which may well date from the fourteenth century. The house built by Rhys ap Roppert (d. 1377) at Rhydorddwy (Flintshire) does not survive; but the contemporary description of it as consisting of a hall, two chambers, a kitchen, and a small chamber indicates clearly that it was of the same kind. None of these houses was more spacious, none more replete with modern conveniences, than the one which Owain Glyn Dŵr built for himself at Sycharth (Chirk) in the later fourteenth century and which is memorably, if extravagantly, portrayed in the poem by Iolo Goch. In death, likewise, the squirearchy of Wales now displayed their status and wealth in the English fashion, commissioning sepulchral effigies and slabs, especially in north-east Wales.

The leaders of native Welsh society learnt to practise the arts of coexistence as well as to indulge in the pleasures of peace. Native Welshmen in the March had done so for generations; their colleagues in north and west Wales now followed suit. The framework of governance and justice, it is true, was firmly English and the highest posts in administration in Principality and March alike were normally reserved for Englishmen, especially from the border shires. Ordinances were issued periodically to bring the governance of Wales more into line with English practice: 'come est fait en Engleterre', 'as is done in England', was the recurring refrain of such ordinances.[1] It is through the documentation of this alien governance that fourteenth-century Wales has been, and indeed of necessity has to be, studied. Yet the impression conveyed by this official documentation of the nature and distribution of power in Wales is at best incomplete, at worst misleading. Beneath the façade of alien governance much of the reality of local power continued to reside in the hands of the native leaders of Welsh society, 'the great ones of the country' or 'the great men of north Wales', as they were referred to by contemporaries.[2]

Many of these native leaders were drawn from families which had once waxed rich and powerful in the service of the Welsh princes but which had now transferred their loyalty and service to the new English lords of Wales. Such a one was Sir Rhys ap Gruffudd (d. 1356), who was virtual governor of south-west Wales in the first half of the fourteenth century. Sir Rhys's genealogy was impeccably Welsh: like Sir Gruffudd Llwyd, whose career has been outlined earlier,[3] he was a direct descendant in the fourth generation of Ednyfed Fychan (d. 1246), steward of Llywelyn the Great and (in the apt phrase of the genealogists) 'the root of the nobility of

---

[1] *Calendar of Close Rolls 1339–41*, pp. 250–3. The phrase is used seven times in these ordinances issued for the governance of north Wales in 1339.

[2] *Cal. Anc. Pets.*, p. 398, no. 11883; *Cal. Anc. Corr.*, p. 233.

[3] See above, p. 409.

Wales' (W. *gwraidd bonedd Cymru*).[4] Sir Rhys's power, like that of his
fellow Welsh squires, was founded on territorial wealth as well as noble
pedigree. The estates of such squires were often widely dispersed and
thereby gave a more than local dimension to their power. Thus, the landed
fortunes of Gwilym ap Gruffudd ap Tudur (d. 1375), one of the leading
Welshmen of north Wales, were distributed from Anglesey in the west to
Flintshire in the east, those of Owain Glyn Dŵr from Cardigan in the west
to the borders of Shropshire in the east. In their own world and by its
standards these men were rich and powerful: they owned serfs and used
them to work their estates; they had the cash to buy and sell land in order
to consolidate their territorial power; they appointed their own estate-
officers and held their own courts. Their wealth is difficult to gauge; but it
is indicative that the earliest (and incomplete) rental of a Welsh
squire—that of Gwilym ap Gruffudd ap Gwilym of north Wales in
1413—lists rents totalling £112 annually.

The power of such men could not be ignored; nor was it. On the
contrary, English kings and lords made use of them as agents of their
authority and thereby entrenched their control over native society even
further. They were allowed to corner lucrative leases of land for their own
ends: Sir Rhys ap Gruffudd, for example, secured the lease of valuable
royal manors in southern Cardiganshire and Carmarthenshire in 1309 and
took over key royal estates in the Tywi valley in 1318. They accumulated
local offices and thereby gave a veneer of official respectiability to their
power: Sir Rhys was appointed deputy-justiciar of south Wales on more
than one occasion and secured constableships, foresterships, stewardships,
and custodies throughout the country. In much the same fashion they
hoarded the higher, if not very often the highest, ecclesiastical offices for
their kinsmen. Sir Rhys ap Gruffudd was no exception: the archdeaconry
of Anglesey was virtually a family preserve, held by his second cousin,
Ieuan ap Gruffudd Llwyd, and then by a third cousin, the powerful Master
Hywel ap Goronwy who master-minded the dangerous conspiracy of
1345.[5] These squires further enhanced their local standing with the king's
aid by securing commissions to raise and lead contingents of Welsh troops
in the king's army. In what was still a militarist society, there was no surer
or more lucrative way to confirm one's standing, authority, and reputation.
So it was that Sir Rhys ap Gruffudd led armies of Welsh troops on service
to Scotland and France for over thirty years. Such loyal service deserved its
reward, which in turn engendered further respect and authority in the
locality. Sir Rhys ap Gruffudd scaled the whole ladder of promotion in
royal service—from king's yeoman to esquire of the household, and so,
eventually, to the accolade of knighthood; among the tokens of royal and

    [4] Quoted in Glyn Roberts, *Aspects of Welsh History* (Cardiff, 1969), p. 245.
    [5] See above p. 411.

princely favour he enjoyed was the courser which the Black Prince gave him in Normandy in 1347. So were loyalty and service rewarded; and so was royal patronage distributed to confirm and enhance the standing of local Welshmen.

It is easier to trace the official careers and rewards of such men than it is to characterize the nature of their power within native society. Yet that power, in what was largely a self-governing society, does not admit of doubt. Its genial aspect was displayed in open-handedness and largess; so it was that the standing of one native squire was measured proudly in 'the sixteen tuns of wine he consumed yearly in his household'.[6] That standing was likewise manifested in conspicuous consumption and display in life and death—in fine clothes and food, wide parklands and large houses, heraldic shields and funerary effigies. Such men were the natural leaders of society, acting as its proctors in negotiations with Marcher lords and English officials, taking precedence in the swearing of fealty, assessing taxes, and collecting subsidies. They were addressed, in deeds and poetry alike, as 'squires', 'barons', and 'lords'. Each of them, great and small, had his *plaid*, a retinue of followers bound to him by ties of blood, tenancy, service, reward, and often, no doubt, threat. 'Providers of two hundred households' was the poet's genteel fashion of describing the authority they wielded.[7] That authority could be, and regularly was, abused: justice was perverted; public office was converted into a source of private wealth; aids and forced labour were ruthlessly exacted. Occasional campaigns against such abuses could do no more than punish wrongdoers at a profit without eradicating the source of oppression. Thus Sir Rhys ap Gruffudd was regularly mulcted for such oppression, but his service was too invaluable and his position too entrenched for the English government to remove, or to want to remove, him. Peace in Wales was bought, in good measure, by the effective surrender of much of the reality of power into the hands of these native squires.

The squires fulfilled another important function in native society; they were the patrons and upholders of Welsh literary culture. Many of them indeed were poets in their own right: Iolo Goch and Dafydd ap Gwilym, the two greatest Welsh poets of the fourteenth century, were of impeccably noble stock. Others were distinguished patrons and collectors of manuscripts. None excelled the remarkable Hopcyn ap Tomas ab Einion of Ynysdawy in Gower, truly the Maecenas of fourteenth-century Wales. He was the subject of at least five formal eulogies by different poets; he himself was respected and consulted as a 'master of brut' or native prophetic writing; he had collected one of the richest native literary libraries in private hands

---

[6] *Chronicon Adae de Usk*, ed. E. Maunde Thompson (1940), p. 70.
[7] *Cywyddau Iolo Goch ac Eraill*, ed. H. Lewis, T. Roberts, I. Williams (2nd edn. Cardiff, 1937), p. 15 ('cynheiliaid deucan aelwyd').

in medieval Wales, and it was he who probably commissioned *The Red Book of Hergest*, the largest and single most important source of medieval Welsh literary texts. Few squires were such ardent bibliophiles as Hopcyn; but others commissioned new copies of Welsh law-texts (as did Llywelyn ap Tudur of Meirionydd) or translations of devotional works (as did Gruffudd ap Llywelyn ap Phylip of Cantref Mawr). Official duties for the English government were in no way incompatible with such native literary tastes. Rhydderch ab Ieuan Llwyd of Glyn Aeron (Cardiganshire) served as deputy-justiciar of his county but also continued a well-established family tradition as leading patron of poets, devotee of native Welsh law, and collector of literary antiquities. The native squirearchy had come to terms with the obligations and opportunities of English rule without in any way surrendering, as so many of their successors in the sixteenth century were to do, their delight in and responsibility towards their native literary tradition.

The support of these squires of *uchelwyr*, as they were now often referred to, was crucial to the remarkable Welsh literary renaissance of the fourteenth century. Welsh literature appears to have undergone a severe crisis of both patronage and confidence immediately in the wake of the Edwardian Conquest. But during the fourteenth century that crisis was triumphantly resolved. It was then that the rules of Welsh poetic practice were laid down, albeit rather idiosyncratically, for the first known time in written form in the Grammar normally associated with Einion Offeiriad and probably composed in the 1320s. Einion's treatise revealed one way in which a conservative literary tradition might come to terms with changed circumstances—by admitting some of the themes and forms of popular vernacular poetry into the canon of official poetic practice. During the course of the century collections of most of the cardinal texts of Welsh medieval poetry and prose were assembled in composite volumes, of which the most famous are Llawysgrif Hendregadredd (probably composed in its original form at Strata Florida soon after 1300), Llyfr Gwyn Rhydderch (likewise belonging to the early fourteenth century), and Llyfr Coch Hergest (compiled towards the end of the century). It is little wonder that the period has been seen as 'the most important century in the recording of Wales's literature'.[8] The heritage of the past was being preserved and organized.

But the period was one of innovation as well as conservation. In prose, it is true, the great age of native tales had come to an end: to be replaced by a period rich in translations from French, Latin, and English and in the copying of religious, legal, and technical works. But in poetry radical innovations were introduced, in substance and form, which were to remain

---

[8] D. Huws, 'Llawysgrif Hendregadredd', *National Library of Wales Journal* 22 (1981), 1–22 at p. 13.

basic to Welsh poetry for centuries to come. Many of these innovations were quite possibly borrowed from a sub-literary tradition associated with popular poets (W. *y glêr*). In particular, the *cywydd* metre (couplets of seven-syllabled lines rhyming asymmetrically) gradually took the place of the stately, ponderous *awdl* (ode); at much the same time, that most distinctive feature of Welsh poetry, *cynghanedd* (a complex pattern of consonantal alliteration and internal rhyme) reached its maturity and came to be regarded as an indispensable part of the *cywydd*. These innovations of form allowed Welsh poetry to become more flexible in its expression, more innovative in its themes, and less archaic in its vocabulary. One of the earliest and most daring exponents of these novelties in poetry was also the greatest poet who has written in the Welsh language, Dafydd ap Gwilym (*fl.* 1320–80). The genius of Dafydd rests not only or even mainly in his confident mastery of the forms of his art but rather in his boundless gusto, his unrestrained delight in nature and woman, his fascination with the paradoxes of life, his unfailing good humour, and the engaging warmth and informality of his work. He stands head and shoulders above his contemporaries; but he shares with them a new-found serenity and a delight in the joys of domestic bliss, hospitality, and human company. Even in its poetry Wales seemed to be at peace and at peace with itself.

Wales in the fourteenth century may have been a country at peace; but it was also a country where the distinction between conqueror and conquered, settler and native, English and Welsh, was more clearly defined in formal and institutional terms than ever before or later. The distinction was not, of course, a novel one. For example, when Gerald of Wales came to Llandaff on his travels in March 1188 he noted how the English stood on one side, the Welsh on the other, to listen to his sermon. But it was during the thirteenth century, and especially the fourteenth, that the distinction became accepted as a basic feature of the governance of much of Wales. Henceforth, men could not afford not to know where they stood racially. That is why the burgesses of Llan-faes (Anglesey) felt so uncomfortable when they discovered that they had 'neither the status of Englishmen nor even that of Welshmen'.[9] Wales was now formally a land of two peoples; it was imperative to know to which one belonged.

The distinction between English and Welsh within Wales was expressed in a variety of ways. The two peoples were often treated separately for administrative purposes, granted separate charters of liberties and assessed separately for revenue-dues and subsidies. Such administrative separation was expressed most graphically in the division of lordships—from Clun in the east to Narberth in the west and from Denbigh in the north to Ogmore

---

[9] *Cal. Anc. Pets.*, p. 82, no. 2803A.

in the south—into Englishries and Welshries or, as in Gower, into an English and a Welsh county. Such a division was no doubt largely an administrative convenience; it was, nevertheless, one which was expressed in racial terms. Welsh and English were also treated separately at law: their affairs were often dealt with in separate courts; they might be tried by separate or at least by mixed juries; and even where they shared the same court they often chose—and were allowed to choose—different rules for initiating actions, verifying claims, procedure, and the acceptable forms of proof. The two peoples often paid different financial dues: Welshmen still contributed towards ancient communal renders, while their English neighbours paid rents assessed in proportion to the acreage of their holdings. Even the labour services owed from each group might be separtely itemized (as in Newport), and so might be the pannage dues in respect of their pigs (as in Hay). Above all, perhaps, the division of English and Welsh was most vividly expressed, in a landed society, in the sharp distinction between their customs regarding the inheritance and transmission of territorial wealth. English practice favoured primogeniture, descent through females in the absence of male heirs, dower rights for widows, and a considerable measure of freedom in the alienation of land. Welsh practice, on the contrary, may be said in general to favour partibility between male heirs (legitimate and otherwise), the exclusion of claims to land through or by females, and strict prohibition on the permanent alienation of inherited land.

The distinction between English and Welsh permeates the terminology and documentation of late medieval Wales. There was, of course, much that was artificial and administratively contrived about it; its significance and relevance also clearly varied greatly from place to place and period to period. Yet it was a distinction which was profoundly significant, especially in what it proclaimed about perceptions and attitudes in post-Conquest Wales. It was founded, at best, on an awareness of the profound differences in customs, law, and social organization between English and Welsh and of the need to respect those differences. Unfortunately, such respect could easily be the pretext for a self-serving administrative conservatism, as was manifested in the statute issued by the lord of Dyffryn Clwyd in 1361, prohibiting unlicensed purchases or leases of land by Englishmen from Welshmen and vice versa. The racial cleavage was also founded in some measure on an understandable distrust of the Welsh and fear for the security of English settlers in Wales. The government's nervousness about the reliability of the Welsh surfaces from time to time—in the authorization to the custodian of Glamorgan in 1316 to remove the Welsh from the plains and to instal Englishmen there for the greater safety of the land, the encouragement to Englishmen in north Wales in 1339 to secure the leases of Welsh land 'so that the peace will be assured and security improved by Englishmen so placed',[10] or the injunction in 1347 that no English living in Wales were to be chosen for the Welsh forces raised to serve in France.

Much the most nervous group in Wales were the residents of the newly established English boroughs there. They exploited the English–Welsh distinction to their maximum advantage, both politically and commercially: they spoke recurrently and hysterically about the 'malice', 'malevolence', and 'enmity' of the Welsh; they bemoaned their 'exiled status' as settlers in a foreign country; they insisted to the full on their exclusive commercial privileges as 'the English burgesses of the English boroughs of Wales'; and they conducted campaigns to oust Welshmen who had settled in their boroughs (as in Cricieth in 1337 or Beaumaris in 1345) and to prevent them from securing tenements in towns through marriage.[11] The racial distinction was likewise used from time to time for the fiscal advantage of lords; they retained Welsh customs, such as *amobr* (virginity due), or prohibitions on the alienation of land, simply as pretexts to fill their coffers, and deliberately tried to sustain the administrative, legal, and tenurial distinctions to their own advantage. It is little wonder in these circumstances that 'to hate like an Englishman' became a virtual Welsh proverb, or that a contemporary jury should observe of Welsh and English in Wales that 'as far as possible they maintain each other's cause'.[12] So long as this racial cleavage was sustained and insensitively exploited there was little prospect that the cessation of hostilities in Wales could be converted into genuine social concord.

Yet, behind the façade of an institutionalized racial distinction, Welshmen and Englishmen within Wales were reaching accommodation with each other, as indeed they had done for generations. The pace of assimilation obviously varied from one area to another. It was most rapid in those parts of the March where English settlers and native Welsh had lived cheek by jowl with each other for a long time: it was tardiest in recently settled districts of north and west Wales, where memories of recent conquest and the nervous arrogance of English settlers made for continuing tension. Even in the towns, the most secure and privileged bastions of Englishness, Welshmen soon established themselves in considerable members, in spite of Edward I's ordinance that 'no Welshman should stay or hold burgages' in them.[13] By 1330, at least a third of the burgesses of Ruthin and half or more of those of Aberystwyth or Beaumaris—all three of them Edwardian plantation boroughs—were

---

[10] *Calendar of Close Rolls 1339–41*, p. 251.

[11] *Register of Edward the Black Prince*, III, p. 125; *Cal. Anc. Corr.*, p. 231; Public Record Office, Chester 2/73, m. 3 v.; *Cal. Anc. Pets.*, p. 439, no. 13029.

[12] *Cywyddau Dafydd ap Gwilym a'i Gyfoeswyr*, ed. I. Williams and T. Roberts (2nd edn. Cardiff, 1935), p. 146; *Calendar of Inquisitions Miscellaneous 1307–49*, p. 16, no. 56.

[13] *Record of Caernarvon*, p. 132.

Welshmen; in Neath the charter of 1359 conceded, albeit reluctantly, that resident Welshmen could enjoy the privileges associated with burgage tenure. In the countryside, likewise, Welshmen were soon settling in areas which were administratively designated as Englishries—whether in Denbigh in north Wales, or in much older enclaves, such as English Coety and English Ogmore in Glamorgan or the English county of Gower—and English colonists, for their part, returned the compliment by buying land in the Welshries. This process of assimilation and accommodation was accelerated by intermarriage between natives and settlers, especially among the wealthier families. Some immigrant families, such as the Conways of Rhuddlan, might claim proudly that they only formed marriage-alliances with fellow-settlers; but in truth they were the exception not the rule. Old Anglo-Norman families—such as Le Soer and Berkerolles in Glamorgan or Harvard and Waldeboef in Brecon—and recently established settlers— such as Hanmer and Puleston in Maelor Saesneg, Holland and Thelwall in Denbigh, Le Marreys and Stalworthman in Dyffryn Clwyd—were quite content to choose their brides from among native Welsh dynasties.[14] The linguistically mongrel names which the offspring of such mixed marriages bore—names such as Tangwystl daughter of William of Pulford or Almaric ab Ithel ab Einion—are among the striking testimonies to the gradual assimilation of the two peoples.

The same process of assimilation was at work in other spheres of life. Law provides an obvious example. Though the wings of native Welsh law had been severely clipped in the Principality lands by the Statute of Rhuddlan of 1284, it continued to flourish. The most comprehensive collections of native law almost all belong to the fourteenth and fifteenth centuries. Some of them, admittedly, have an antiquarian air, but most of them were compiled to be studied by native lawmen and to be cited by them in formal court decisions and extracurial arbitrations. Indeed, native law was still evolving as new legal formulae, processes, and terminology were invented to cope with changing social conditions and with the legal issues which they raised. In very different parts of Wales—in the heartlands of north and west Wales, but equally in some of the older Marcher lordships of the east, such as Clun or Brecon—native law showed a remarkable resilience and adaptability and was still frequently used and quoted, especially in matters of contract, trespass, and land.

Yet the later Middle Ages also witnessed throughout Wales the gradual adoption of English law, in substance and in procedure. This victory of English law was assured not so much by royal statute or seignorial ordinance but by the ready availability of English writs, the regular application of English procedures and terminology in the local courts, the

---

[14] Cf. above, p. 102.

frequent visits of English judges and lawyers on sessions to Wales, and, above all, the imitation and borrowing of the legal procedures current among English settlers in Wales. Welshmen themselves frequently hastened the process, requesting, as did the men of Gower in the late thirteenth century, that the 'law of Hywel' be replaced by inquest and the 'law of twelve'. Even when the substance and terminology of Welsh law were preserved—as in pleas such as *sarhad* (trespass) and *amobr* (virginity due)—the procedure more often than not was now that of English law. English legal terms were increasingly borrowed into Welsh, and even genuinely Welsh actions—such as those relating to Welsh mortgage (W. *prid*)—were deeply influenced by the formulae and procedures of English common law. When the Act of Union of 1536 eventually formally imposed English law on the whole of Wales, it was but completing a process which had already been well under way for generations.

Nowhere did this process of legal assimilation have more far-reaching results than in the field of land law. In essence, native Welsh law and English custom stood poles apart on the vital issues of the tenure and transmission of land. Yet in the later Middle Ages in Wales, both English and Welsh showed a remarkable willingness to borrow each other's practices. Already in south-east and south-west a mongrel institution called a Welsh fee had appeared, namely land held by English feudal tenure but divisible among male heirs according to native practice. It was a survivor of this hybrid practice which George Owen recorded in sixteenth-century Pembrokeshire when he referred to land held by 'English law and Welsh division'. In north Wales English settlers soon familiarized themselves with the formulae of Welsh mortgage (W. *prid*); they applied them to buy land from Welshmen in the countryside and, supreme irony, they even employed them to convey burgages in English boroughs, such as Conway and Rhuddlan. Much more significant ultimately, however, was the adoption of English conveyancing methods and inheritance practices by the native Welsh. They began to transfer their lands by charter; confirmed their territorial arrangements by final concord; prosecuted their claims to land through the writ of novel disseisin (occasionally Welshed as *cwyn newydd difeddiant*); entailed their estates in order to avoid the Welsh custom of partibility; and flouted native law further by seeking permission for their daughters to inherit in the absence of direct male heirs of the body and by dowering their wives with a share of their land. In the forefront of this movement for the adoption of English land law and practices were the richer native families, who quickly recognized the advantages of unitary succession and freedom of alienation. Already by 1310 Gruffudd ap Tudur ap Madog had conveyed many of his extensive lands throughout north Wales to the exclusive control of his eldest son, thus laying the foundations of the future Penrhyn estate; and a few years later Owain Glyn Dŵr's grandfather likewise arranged for the conveyance of his property in tail (i.e. to a designated line of descendants). They were soon followed by other land speculators and estate builders, men who had often amassed their fortunes through the Welsh device of *prid*, but who then proceeded to convert their holdings into estates held by English tenure. The consequences of this shift towards English land tenure and practice were only beginning to become evident towards the end of the fourteenth century; but it eventually led to a fundamental change in the distribution and descent of landed wealth in Welsh society.

The same process of accommodation and assimilation is to be seen in other directions. It is evident in the adoption of English-style surnames by leading Welsh families: the sons of Gruffudd ap Gwenwynwyn of Powys adopted the surname Pole in preference to their tongue-twisting patronymic, while the native dynasty of Afan paraded its assimilation into Glamorgan county society by sporting the spurious Normanized surname, De Avene. But English settler families were likewise anxious to merge into their adopted Welsh habitat, as some of their names—such as Gruffudd ap David Holland of Denbigh or William Fychan ap Gwilym Sourdevall of Brecon—reveal. The common use of aliases, one Welsh and the other English, likewise bespeaks an anxiety to find an identity which was acceptable in both communities: William son of Walter Haunton of Caernarfon was known as William ap Wat to his Welsh friends, just as Iorwerth ap Morgan ab Iorwerth Foel of Chirkland called his son Morgan Yonge to please his Cheshire in-laws. Welsh families, such as that of Owain Glyn Dŵr, sent their sons to the inns of court in London to master English law and to learn English manners; but equally some of the major settler families and alien religious houses in Wales were beginning to return the compliment by acting as patrons to Welsh bards. Shrewd contemporaries recognized that the cultural divide between the English and Welsh, though still marked, was becoming less obvious. The Welsh, commented Ranulf Higden from Chester, were beginning to till gardens and fields, live in towns, ride around, wear stockings and shoes, and even sleep under sheets. 'So they semeth now in mynde', he concluded, 'More Englische men than Walsche kind'.[15]

In these circumstances the formal legal and administrative distinction between Welsh and English within Wales appeared increasingly anachronistic. Even the authorities recognized as much occasionally: in Dyffryn Clwyd in 1400 the Welsh sergeant was placed in charge of English and Welsh tenants alike. In that very year the revolt of Owain Glyn Dŵr brought this uncertain process of accommodation to an abrupt end, but only temporarily. The contrast between Wales and Ireland in this respect is striking and

[15] *Polychronicon Ranulfi Higden*, ed. C. Babington and J. R. Lumby (Rolls Series, 1865–86), I, 411.

instructive. In Ireland the formal racial distinctions between English settlers and native Irish were, if anything, being further entrenched in the fourteenth century as the English government and Anglo-Irish lords fought a losing battle against 'the wild Irish, our enemies'. Those distinctions were further reinforced by the Statutes of Kilkenny in 1366, at the very time when they appeared, at least from many directions, to be withering in Wales. For English government, lords, and settlers, Wales and Ireland appeared to present two contrasting examples of the colonial experience.

Such shifts in attitudes were doubtless accelerated by the profound economic changes of these years. In Wales, as in Europe generally, the fourteenth century was an era of unprecedented calamities. The forces of nature seemed to be conspiring against man. The weather may well have deteriorated: summers were shorter and wetter, winters longer and colder. Great storms battered the coasts; in Glamorgan, Cydweli, and western Anglesey a change in sea levels buried large tracts of coastal lowlands under shifting sand-dunes. The great famine of 1315–17 inaugurated the century of calamities: food was desperately short in many parts of the country and the bishop of Bangor was not alone in bemoaning 'the bad years' and the 'the murrain of his beasts'.[16] Then in mid-century the advent of plague delivered the *coup de grâce*. The Black Death reached the borders of Wales in the spring of 1349; before the year was out it had penetrated every part of the country. Statistics on mortality rates are few and localized; but they register vividly enough the devastating impact of the disease. In the rich manor Caldicot on the Severn estuary, thirty-six out of forty customary tenants fell victim to plague; at the other end of the country, at Degannwy (Caerns.), the demesne manor was totally emptied by the death or flight of its tenants: most reliable and most dramatic are the figures of tenant mortality from the lordship of Dyffryn Clwyd, for they reveal a fourteen-fold increase in the scale of mortality in 1349. Some of the highland and sparsely populated areas of the middle March may have escaped lightly; but the plague returned with devastating, if diminishing, results in 1361–2, 1369 (when south-east Wales was badly affected), and seven times thereafter before 1420.

The impact of The Great Mortality, *Y Farwolaeth Fawr* as it was known in Welsh, was immediate and profound. Seignorial income fell dramatically. The farmers of the lordships of Pembroke and Abergavenny were allowed remittances of £80 and £40, respectively, in their leases, because 'of the deadly pestilence which lately raged in these parts',[17] while in the Duchy of Lancaster lordship of Ogmore (Glamorgan), seignorial income in the 1360s was still thirty per cent below its pre-plague level. Seignorial accounts

[16] *Cal. Anc. Pets.*, p. 499, no. 15659.
[17] *Calendar of Fine Rolls 1347–56*, p. 240.

abound with references to vacant or abandoned land and sharply reduced income from mills, pasture, meadow, tolls, and fisheries. Labour problems became acute: villein services on lowland Anglicized manors contracted dramatically, nowhere more than in Caldicot, where the number of such works available to the lord plunged from over 2,000 in the 1340s to 114 by 1362; wages rose in spite of local ordinances and penalties; while attempts to curtail the movement of labour impress more as an expression of determination than by their success.

Initially, it is true, landlords in Wales, as in England, did enjoy a measure of success in their attempts to preserve the status quo. By the 1360s seignorial income had recovered to pre-plague levels in several Marcher lordships; indeed, in a few lordships, such as Chirkland, it even scaled new heights. But such success was short-lived; even in the short term it could only be achieved through an unacceptable level of seignorial pressure. As the population continued to fall and plague recurred, far-reaching changes in the pattern of seignorial authority and in the landscape of social and economic power in Wales began to reveal themselves. The first tell-tale signs appeared in the seignorial accounts. The officers of the Principality lands were compelled to institute a Great Roll of Debts in 1351; their example was soon imitated in Marcher lordships. The lengthening lists of arrears and deferred instalment-payments on these rolls were a sure sign of a mounting financial *malaise*. By the end of the century, seignorial income in very different parts of Wales—in Denbigh and Ogmore, Chirk and Glamorgan—had begun a downward slide which was to gather pace dramatically in the next century. Much the same was true of ecclesiastical estates: the value of episcopal temporalities fell sharply and many monasteries found themselves confronted simultaneously with the twin problems of acute financial difficulties and a sharp drop in recruitment. High labour costs and low and uncertain profit margins soon placed a large question mark against the worthwhileness of direct agricultural exploitation by lay and ecclesiastical landlords. By the end of the fourteenth century all the major English landlords had abandoned demesne farming on their Welsh estates. Initially their decision appeared to be no more than a sensible, and quite possibly temporary, response to changed economic circumstances. But it proved to be permanent, and contributed further to the erosion of the lord's effective power and interest in his lordship. He was now little more than an absentee, rent-collecting landlord; others would gradually begin to fill the vacuum of leadership and social power created by his growing estrangement from his lordship.

Equally dramatic changes were taking place on the face of the Welsh landscape. In some areas the population contraction was so severe that villages and hamlets were now no more than shadows of their former selves. Particularly was this true of lowland Glamorgan: so depopulated were a group of three hamlets near Barry (Cwmcidi, Uchelolau, and Merthyr Dyfan) that their parishes were amalgamated into one, while the tiny village of Radyr disappeared altogether to be incorporated into a deer park. Towns also suffered: leading boroughs, such as Cardiff and Tenby, declined markedly in size; others, such as Caerffili, Cricieth, and Harlech, stagnated; while a few anaemic ones, notably Cefnllys in Maelienydd and Bere in Merioneth, disappeared altogether. Much arable land lay abandoned for decades on end: in lowland Glamorgan half of the land of customary tenants and cottagers in Ogmore was still classified as being 'in decay' as late as 1428. Well might a contemporary Welsh poet pray that Gwynedd might be spared the plague lest its 'fruitful acres' be converted into 'bleak pasture and escheated land'.[18] His prayer went largely unanswered, for throughout Wales much of the land left vacant after the plagues could only be let, if at all, as pasture. Initially, such leases *ad herbagium* may have been regarded as a temporary expedient, but it soon became evident that they represented the beginnings of a major shift in land usage. In the changed economic circumstances of the time, pastoral husbandry flourished and the opportunity was seized, particularly in north-east Wales, to build fulling mills and promote the local cloth industry.

The tempo of economic and social change was accelerating in other directions also. Population mobility increased dramatically as men travelled in search of higher wages and cheaper and better lands. 'Aliens' (L. *extranei*) are frequently recorded as taking over vacant tenements, often on favourable terms. Many such 'aliens' were doubtless serfs anxious to shake off the taint and obligations of personal unfreedom and to begin a new life in a new lordship. For there can be little doubt that the later fourteenth century witnessed the beginnings of the dramatic collapse of serfdom in much of medieval Wales. The unfree population declined much more sharply than did the overall population—through flight as well as through disease. By 1381 the population of one of the major bond centres in Dyffryn Clwyd had fallen from 212 to 47 and in one vill in Denbigh from forty to five bond tenants by 1397. Much the same story was repeated throughout the Principality: thus early in Henry V's reign the bond vills of the commotes of Tal-y-bont and Ystumanner in Merionethshire were said to be 'completely depopulated'.[19] Seignorial administrators made desperate attempts to halt the process, using a mixture of threat, force, bribes, and cajolery. But in the end their efforts were to be in vain and might even

---

[18] 'Na wna, Iôr, wen Wynedd/Ddaear ffraeth yn dduoer ffridd/ . . . yn dir asêd': T. Roberts, 'Englynion Gwynedd gan Gruffudd ap Maredudd ap Dafydd', *Transactions of the Anglesey Antiquarian Society and Field Club*, 1982, 123–9 at p. 124.

[19] Quoted in J. B. Smith, 'Crown and Community in the Principality of North Wales in the Reign of Henry Tudor', *WHR*, 3 (1966–7), 145–71 at p. 153.

provoke a riot (as happened at Abergavenny in 1400 when the steward was kiled by a crowd of bondmen).

The beginnings of the process of surrender can be traced in the records of the period. Occasionally, as on the estates of the bishop of St Asaph in 1355, bondmen were formally and communally enfranchised; more commonly they secured remission of all or part of their bond dues on an individual basis, often in return for increased rents; most common of all, former bond tenements were leased to free tenants on non-bond terms. The estate-surveys of the time, conservative as they often are, betray a recognition of the changes that were afoot. They introduced a new category of 'freemen holding bond land' into their classifications, as they did in Chirkland in 1355 or in Whitecastle (Monmouth) in 1386. On occasion they went even further: in new surveys, compiled at Caldicot and Hay before the end of the century, the time-honoured distinction between free and unfree tenure was replaced by a new division between free tenants on the one hand and copyholders and tenants-at-will on the other. A new tenurial dispensation was gradually, and often very uncertainly, being shaped in Wales; the economic transformation of the later fourteenth century was the catalyst in the process.

That transformation also initiated a major redistribution of territorial wealth, and thereby ultimately of social power, within the country, especially in native Welsh society. The customary practices of that society, notably its prohibition on the alienation of hereditary land and the practice of partibility among male heirs, militated against the accumulation of estates and, above all, against the transmission of such estates in their integrity from one generation to the next. Some native Welsh families, it is true, had shown remarkable ingenuity and success in circumventing these obstacles—notably by using the Welsh device of *prid* to buy up individual strips (as Tudur ab Ithel Fychan had done to remarkably good effect in the township of Whitford (Flints) in the years 1316–66) and by paying for licences to hold their lands by English tenure and the rules of descent of English law. But, once again, it was the changed circumstances of the post-plague period which dramatically transformed the opportunities for such men.

Land was now abundant: in Dyffryn Clwyd alone, in 1360, £61 was realized from the lease of vacant lands. Whole tenements as well as individual strips were up for offer. Even conservative landlords had to bow to the pressure: in 1359 the Black Prince accepted a fine of £400 from the men of Tegeingl and Hopedale (Flints) for the right to buy and sell land freely. The tempo and scale of the land market quickened perceptibly. Certain groups were particularly well-placed to take advantage of the opportunity now presented to them. Wealthy burgesses with ready cash and an entrepreneurial approach were one such group: among their number were Richard Golding, a rich Beaumaris burgess, and Bartholomew Bolde of Conwy, whose territorial purchases laid the foundations of the fortunes of the Bulkeley family. Enterprising clerics formed another such group: the land-jobbing activities of the rector of Ceidio (Dyffryn Clwyd) can be traced for twenty years after 1365, culminating in a large fine in order to convert his newly gotten gains into a single holding held by English tenure. Thrusting squires also saw their opportunity: some made large outright purchases, as did Gruffudd ap Madog Gloddaith, who paid £40 down in 1396 for an estate in Anglesey; most of them proceeded in a more piecemeal fashion, as did Iorwerth Ddu ab Ednyfed Gam of Chirkland, who turned the misery of the times and the misfortunes of his kinsmen and neighbours into an opportunity to assemble a considerable estate for himself and thereby to make his contribution to the future wealth of the Mostyn family.

The scale and tempo of this story of territorial consolidation varied enormously from place to place—in part according to circumstances, notably the pattern of mortality and the tenurial structure of each district, and in part in proportion to the enterprise, ruthlessness, and liquid assets of the local squirearchy. What, however, hardly admits of doubt is that many parts of Wales, especially native Wales, witnessed a significant redistribution of rural wealth in the century or so after 1350. Multiple holdings and consolidated estates were being built out of the debris left by the plague mortality. This was a key period in the pre-history of many of the estate complexes of early modern Wales. It was also a key period in the polarization of rural wealth. In the township of Ogmore (Glamorgan) in the mid-fourteenth century, 133 acres of arable had been held by twenty-two tenants; by 1428 the number of tenants had been reduced to six and one of these, Thomas Aythan, had cornered twenty cottages and a hundred acres for himself. The future lay with Thomas Aythan and his like.

The generations after 1350 were a momentous period in the social and economic transformation of medieval Wales. The face of the country was being altered; territorial power was being radically redistributed; old classifications and categories were being undermined; established patterns of seignorial authority and control were being eroded; and the framework of inheritance and tenurial customs, which had prevailed in native Wales for generations, was being dismantled. Certain groups, families, and individuals doubtless benefited handsomely from this transformation. But the very rapidity and character of the transformation also begat acute social tensions. For some—Welshmen excluded from the privileges of English tenure and status or serfs denied access to the liberties of free men—the tension arose out of the growing discrepancy between their legal status, on the one hand, and their social position and ambitions, on the other. Such a disjunction has often been recognized as one of the most fertile seedbeds of revolt. For others, the tension arose out of a profound sense of disorientation, in particular of the collapse of the values, categories, and social landscape to which they had long been accustomed. It is perhaps no coincidence that the later fourteenth century seems to witness the appearance of a corpus of macabre poetry, unremitting in its condemnation of the vanity and futility of the world, delighting in emphasising the transitoriness of worldly wealth, scathing in its denunciation of the methods and newly won fortunes of the *nouveaux riches*, and bitter in its condemnation of the inversion of social values. This was indeed for many men a world out of sorts, a 'truly gloomy, dread world' (*byd dudrist, byd ergryd oergrai*) as the poets called it.[20] In a world which felt itself so turned upside down, tension might relieve itself through revolt.

[20] *Cywyddau Iolo Goch ac Eraill*, p. 125 (Gruffudd Llwyd); *Cywyddau Dafydd ap Gwilym a'i Gyfoeswyr*, p. 139 (Gruffudd Gryg).

CHAPTER 17

TENSION AND REVOLT, 1370–1415

WALES may have been at peace in the fourteenth century; but that did not mean, of course, that all sources of social tension and friction had been removed. Far from it. The rapidly expanding corpus of written evidence—notably the abundant individual and communal petitions, the charters of liberties granted to local communities, and, to a lesser degree, the native poetry—reveals clearly a wide range of festering grievances. Many of these grievances, it is true, are scarcely to be distinguished from the complaints common in all medieval communities. Financial *gravamina* figure with predictable regularity: errors in extents went uncorrected; increased rents were demanded arbitrarily; Welsh renders and dues—such as investiture fees (W. *gobrestyn*) and virginity fines (W. *amobr*)—were ruthlessly exploited; and, as in England, the practices of prise and purveyance (that is, the commandeering of goods for consumption by the lord and his men in return for promise of future payment) were regularly abused in Principality and March alike. The list of administrative grievances was likewise a series of variations on well-worn themes—the sale and leasing of offices to the highest bidder; the deliberate proliferation of offices and a proportionate increase in the number of hangers-on and their fees; and the blatant abuse of official power, especially in judicial matters. Complaints about the administration of justice figure equally prominently, all the more so since Welshmen found it difficult to adjust to the judicial regime and obligations imposed on them by their English governors. Suit of court, often exacted from tenants of very small holdings, and fines for failure to perform it were, in particular, a recurring source of complaint. Nor is this surprising when it is recalled that in Caernarfonshire alone in 1321–2 almost seven hundred people paid fines for non-suit of court, yielding almost £27. But perhaps the broadest-based social grievances, the ones which affected most members of each local community, were those which arose out of the lord's exploitation of his economic monopolies, notably forests, mills, and tolls. Throughout Wales and throughout the fourteenth century there were vigorous protests against the tightening seignorial grip over forests. Lords clamped down on their tenants' freedom to take timber for building and fuel, hunt in the forest, make assarts there, and send their animals, especially their pigs, to pasture in the woodland. They thereby converted the forest into one of the most resented, oppressive, and profitable emblems of seignorial authority. It was little wonder that one of the reflex reactions of the community to the death or downfall of its lord, as in Chirkland in 1330, was to destroy the fences around his woodland and to indulge in a great spree of hunting in his forest. Mills were another favourite target of communal resentment, for they were an equally potent symbol of seignorial monopoly and profiteering. Tolls were hated for much the same reason: they represented an attempt to control and regulate trade to the profit of the lord and of the alien boroughs in Wales. It is easy to understand the resentment when it is recalled that the men of Brecon were fined £500 in 1352 for evading the seignorial tolls and that the men of Denbigh were willing to raise £400 in 1356 in order to secure 'the right to buy and sell without paying toll', even for a limited period.[1]

Resentment against seignorial control of forests, mills, and tolls was, of course, by no means peculiar to Wales or to the fourteenth century. On the contrary, it was a sentiment common in peasant societies in many parts of Europe across the centuries. Yet in Wales such resentment had to it a potentially more dangerous edge, for it could be presented as the animus of a native conquered people against its foreign lords. For there is no doubt that control of forests, mills, and rural trade was interpreted, rightly or wrongly, as a recent English innovation and one which flew in the face of age-old Welsh customs. Much the same confrontation between native custom and alien practice emerged over the issue of the control of escheated land. The native community in Principality and March alike claimed that according to Welsh law escheated land—that is, land forfeited for a major offence, for failure to pay rent or dues, or, most commonly, through failure of male heirs—should revert to the kin-group or at least to the local community. How much this right was prized can be readily appreciated by reference to the huge communal fine of £1,000 which the men of the county of Carmarthen and its associated lordships were willing to pay to secure confirmation of the right in 1415. But equally the English lords quickly recognized that control of escheated land had huge potential for them: it could be a lucrative source of revenue and, even more important, it provided an ideal opportunity for them to place their relations with their Welsh tenants on a more secure basis and one more closely approximate to the nature of English landlordship. The issue was one which became particularly significant in the late fourteenth century, as the high level of mortality suddenly swelled the pool of escheated land. Thereby relationships between lord and community were embittered at the very time when other grievances were accumulating.

One of those grievances related to the status of Welsh law. This was an issue which evoked contradictory responses. On certain matters native

---

[1] *Register of Edward the Black Prince*, III, 486.

Welsh communities were certainly anxious to protect and defend their right to use native law. The first clause of the charter of liberties conceded by Duke Henry of Lancaster (d. 1361) to the Welshmen of Cydweli in 1356, for example, decreed that they should 'have record and judgement according to the law of Hywel Dda'.[2] Yet in other directions Welshmen were anxious to liberate themselves from the restrictive strait-jacket of native law. Particularly was this so in regard to the sale and alienation of land. Welsh law strictly prohibited any outright alienation of hereditary land; at best a short-term lease or vifgage (W. *prid*) was all that was allowed. Such a prohibition, devised to protect the interests of the kin-group, proved increasingly irksome. From at least the opening decade of the fourteenth century, the communities of north and west Wales recurrently petitioned for the right to sell or give their lands, according to the law and customs of England. It was a request which the king equally regularly declined to endorse, except as a temporary concession in 1316. 'The King does not feel advised to abrogate the ancient customs of Wales'[3] was the stock reply to such requests. Such deference to Welsh custom was in fact dictated by profiteering self-interest: through licences granted for *prid*-conveyances, the operation of the custom of escheat, and punitive communal fines for unlicensed alienation of land, the rigidity of Welsh law was turned into a lucrative source of seignorial revenue. Indeed, the English lords were willing to turn Welsh law to their advantage in more general terms: by the end of the fourteenth century they were hiring professional experts in native law (W. *dosbarthwyr*) to reverse judgements given according to Welsh law in Welsh courts and thereby to provide the pretext for imposing large fines on the local communities. So it is that one of the most striking paradoxes of late medieval Wales is the way in which the self-interested defence of Welsh law and custom by English Crown and Marcher lord became a major source of friction in their relationships with the native community.

But perhaps the single most immediate source of that friction, especially in north and west Wales, lay in the status and privileges of the 'plantation' boroughs. Welshmen may have settled in considerable numbers in some of these boroughs and the English burgesses had certainly begun to adjust to their Welsh environment;[4] but the opportunities for tension remained manifold throughout the fourteenth century. The towns continued to extend the orbit of their trading monopoly: that of Brecon, for example, embraced the whole of the lordship (even to the extent of suffocating the subsidiary burgh at Llywel), while the exclusive trading zone of Aberystwyth covered the whole district from the river Aeron to the river Dyfi. Nor did the townsmen let slip any opportunity to assert their commercial privileges:

[2] Public Record Office, Duchy of Lancaster Miscellaneous Books (DL 42), 16 fol. 43 v.
[3] *Cal. Anc. Pets.*, p. 99, no. 3179 (*c.*1322).   [4] See above, p. 413.

thus nine Welshmen were arrested at Clynnog in 1375, ten miles from Caernarfon, for brewing ale for sale 'contrary to regulation and to the prejudice of the liberty of the town'.[5] Whenever the boroughs thought that their monopolies were in danger of being undermined, they quickly ran for royal support and played the trump card of their precarious status as alien settlers in a foreign land. So it was that the burgesses of Beaumaris appealed successfully in 1366 for a confirmation of the discriminatory ordinances of Edward I; Conway, Cricieth, and Caernarfon secured a like confirmation six years later. The hopes of Welshmen that the barriers of racial and commercial exclusiveness would be eroded by the passage of time were recurrently shattered: occasional orders for the expulsion of Welshmen from boroughs were issued (as happened at Hope in 1351), and Welshmen might be embarrassed by peremptory inquiries as to how they—'mere Welshmen' (L. *meri Wallici*) and 'foreigners' (L. *forinseci*), as they were derogatorily called—had dared to assume the right to trade and to enjoy the privileges of burgesses. In such a fraught atmosphere, town–country hostility could not be expected to subside. It is little wonder that the Welshmen of Tegeingl (Flints.) conducted campaigns in the 1330s and again in the 1370s to secure the abrogation of the privileges of the towns of Rhuddlan and Flint; equally, it is no surprise that the English boroughs in north Wales should be the prime target for Owain Glyn Dŵr's followers in their initial foray in September 1400.

Such individual and communal grievances are characteristic, to a greater or lesser degree, of all societies in all periods. What rendered these grievances more explosive in fourteenth-century Wales was that they could readily contribute towards, and feed upon, a more generalized hostility towards England and the English, and more specifically towards English rule and settlers in Wales. Such hostility flowed as a silent undercurrent throughout the period, welling occasionally to the surface in a sudden but limited outburst of fury. It drew upon a bitter sense of disinheritance, both particular and general. At the particular level, native communities throughout Wales—in Anglesey and Dyffryn Clwyd, in Caernarfon and Glamorgan—continued to nurture a deep sense of wrong at past territorial expropriation and forcible, and often unjust, exchanges of land at the hands of Normans and English. Even more deep-seated psychologically, and ultimately more menacing, was the sense of a loss of glory and power as a people. Welshmen in the fourteenth century were haunted by bitter memories of conquest and treachery and by the disjunction between past greatness and current misery and failure. The perfidy of the English was the obvious and natural explanation for their predicament. Thus Sir Gruffudd Llwyd in a letter, which he wrote to the brother of King Robert I

<hr />

[5] *Caernarvon Court Rolls 1361–1402*, ed. G. P. Jones and H. Owen (Caernarvon, 1951), p. 113.

of Scotland in 1316, spoke of the way in which the Scots and Welsh alike had been expelled from their rightful inheritances by the English. More poignant was the note written at the end of a Welsh translation of Geoffrey of Monmouth's *History* commissioned by a leading Welsh squire in the later fourteenth century: in it the author bemoaned the woes of the descendants of the Britons, who 'to this day suffer pain and deprivation and exile in their native land'.[6]

This ideology of disinheritance drew on native Welsh traditions which had been accumulating for centuries. Age only served to confirm the authority of such myths.[7] To them was now added a clearer vision of the universal history of the Britons, or the Welsh, than had perhaps hitherto been achieved. This universal history, like that of so many of the peoples of Europe in the Middle Ages, began with an emphasis on the Trojan origins of the Britons. So it was that medieval Welsh authors busied themselves translating the most popular account of the Trojan wars, that attributed to Dares Phrygius, into the vernacular. Where Dares's narrative ended, Geoffrey of Monmouth's *History of the Kings of Britain* provided for the Welsh a ready-made and fully convincing, if not altogether flattering, account of their ancestors until the reign of Cadwaladr in the seventh century. The popularity of Geoffrey's account can be gauged by the fact that his *History* survives in Welsh translation in at least twelve copies in the fourteenth century, three of them being entirely new versions. From Cadwaladr's period onwards the Welsh had to rely on their own resources to provide a connected history of their country down to recent times. *Brut y Tywysogyon* or *The Chronicle of the Princes* represents their response to that challenge. It does not survive in its original Latin version or versions; but three independent Welsh translations of it are extant from the fourteenth century, tracing the history of Wales down to 1282 and, in one case, even further. The cryptic annalistic entries of the *Brut* stand in striking contrast to the flamboyant and well-polished narrative of Geoffrey's *History*; yet, together with the translation of Dares Phrygius, they were seen to provide a universal account of the history of the Britons (or the Welsh) from their Trojan origins to the débâcle of 1282. That they were indeed seen as providing such a coherent story is vouched for by the fact that in two manuscript traditions the three texts are associated with each other. Not for the first or last time in history, conquest and foreign rule had served to sharpen historical sensibilities. In the absence of political independence, the identity of the Welsh as a people was to be grounded in a vision of their past.

But the vision of the past was also a vision of the future. It was thereby a

[6] B. F. Roberts, 'Un o lawysgrifau Hopcyn ap Tomas o Ynys Dawy', *BBCS* 22 (1966–7), 223–8 at p. 227.
[7] See above pp. 78–80.

charter for action as much as a source of nostaglia. History, prophecy, and poetry were close bedfellows in medieval Wales; never more so than in the post-Conquest generations. The corpus of native vaticinatory poetry (W. *cywyddau brud*) increased apace from the fourteenth century. Richly garnished as it is with cryptic astrological, zoomorphic, and heraldic references, it is, and no doubt often was, impenetrably obscure and rarely precisely datable. Yet its recurring themes constitute a vital insight into the political aspirations of the native community. One such theme is the expectation of a messianic deliverer (W. *y mab darogan*). Best of all would it be if such a deliverer were drawn of the stock of the ancient princes; legitimacy would thereby confirm his pretensions. 'Is there' asked one of the poets 'a champion of the line of Llywelyn who will stand forth?'[8] Two such deliverers did put forward their claims in the fourteenth century and both, appropriately enough, were of impeccably princely stock: Owain Lawgoch (d. 1378) was the grandson of the brother of Llywelyn ap Gruffudd and thereby represented the direct line of Gwynedd, while Owain Glyn Dŵr combined in his veins the blood of the dynasties of Deheubarth and Powys. The ambition of these men and of the poet-prophets who supported them was not only to restore their native dynasties but also to reinstate, and indeed to create, a unitary Welsh kingdom. It was as 'prince of Wales', not of Gwynedd or Powys or Deheubarth, that both Owain Lawgoch and Owain Glyn Dŵr put forward their claims. The experience of conquest had enabled the Welsh to aspire to a notion of political unity which had consistently eluded them in practice in the days of native rule.

Mythology, prophecy, legitimist descent, messianic expectation, and national unity were, therefore, among the vital ingredients of the 'political' ideology of native Wales in the fourteenth century. It is easy to dismiss such ideology as bardic ranting, particularly in the light of the overwhelmingly administrative character of the official documentation of the period. Contemporaries, including shrewd English observers, thought otherwise. It was the author of the contemporary *Life of Edward II* who analysed the situation most clearly: 'The Welsh habit of revolt against the English is a long-standing madness . . . And this is the reason. The Welsh, formerly called the Britons, were once noble crowned over the whole realm of England; but they were expelled by the Saxons and lost both name and kingdom . . . But from the sayings of the prophet Merlin they still hope to recover England. Hence it is that they frequently rebel.'[9]

Given this recognition of the Welsh inclination for rebellion, it is small wonder that the English should be on their guard. Political quiescence, it is

[8] *Cywyddau Iolo Goch ac Eraill*, p. 109. ('Oes dewrfalch sy falch a saif/O Lywelyn â'i loywlaif?').
[9] *Vita Edwardi Secundi*, ed. N. Denholm-Young, p. 69.

true, might lull them into believing that the Welsh had at last been tamed. Their occasional bouts of restlessness could be attributed cavalierly to their well-known 'light-headedness' (L. *levitas cervicosa*); and they themselves could be dismissed as 'men of poor reputation' or 'bare-footed rascals' whose pranks deserved scant consideration.[10] The Welsh for their part had learnt to play the role of natives under colonial governance, that of an apparently submissive deference and somnolent acquiescence, provided their customs were respected. Yet a basic nervousness remained. It might focus on uncertainty about the ultimate loyalty of some of the most prominent leaders of Welsh society such as Sir Gruffudd Llwyd. His career between 1315 and 1330 demonstrated that the line between deep personal commitment to the English Crown, on the one hand, and plots nurtured by injured pride and fanned by an ideology of disinheritance and deliverance, on the other, was indeed a thin one. Nervousness might also be prompted by disturbing rumours of 'nightly gatherings of Welshmen called Dadelowes' and confirmed by an occasional violent incident, of which the most notable was the murder of Henry de Shaldeford in 1345.[11]

In such circumstances it was little wonder that the English government should take precautions 'in case the Welsh should rise suddenly'.[12] Throughout the fourteenth century this fear of internal unrest was regularly coupled with another anxiety—that Wales might be used by England's enemies as a point of entry for an attack on England itself. It was a spectre which was first raised by the Scots. A Scottish invasion of Wales launched from Ireland seemed a distinct possibility several times in the fraught years 1315–17, and the prospect of Scottish invasion was revived again in 1325–7, 1335, and 1339. By the latter date an even more menacing threat loomed on the horizon, that of a French invasion. That spectre was certainly raised in 1339, 1346, and 1359; it doubtless explains the periodic injunctions to the English burgesses in north Wales 'to keep their town at their own peril',[13] the occasional frenzied order for the repair of castles, and the dispatch of archers to reinforce the garrisons. The proverbial fecklessness of the Welsh and the ambition of the French and the Scots to exploit it for their own ends were reasons enough for the English government to be concerned, if not unduly worried, about Wales. 'Beware of Wales' might well be the government's watchword.

Tension within Wales grew palpably in the last thirty years of the fourteenth century. Hindsight, admittedly, may prompt the historian to

---

[10] *Proceedings and Ordinances of the Privy Council*, ed. Sir Harris Nicolas (1834–37), I, 134; *Eulogium Historiarum*, ed. F. S. Haydon (Rolls Series, 1858–63), III, 388.

[11] *Flintshire Ministers' Accounts 1301–28*, ed. A. Jones (Flintshire History Society Publications, III, 1913), pp.82–3; for the Shaldeford incident see above, p. 411.

[12] *Calendar of Close Rolls 1339–41*, p. 251.

[13] *Register of Edward the Black Prince*, III, 221.

interpret the period too readily as one of accumulating tensions which eventually exploded into revolt in 1400. Yet, there is little doubt that in Wales, as in England, economic and social dislocation, seignorial pressure, political *malaise*, and external threat made these years particularly fraught ones. Fears of external invasion mounted rapidly after the resumption of England's war with France in 1369, all the more so since England was now very much on the defensive. Garrisons were stationed at most of the Welsh castles in 1370; the measures were repeated in 1372 and 1377 (when the garrison at Pembroke was augmented to almost 150 men); regular reviews of the victuals and state of repair of the castles were ordered; the fear of a threat from the north was renewed by a Scottish raid on Beaumaris in 1381; and the general jitteriness was compounded by rumours and plots—such as the astounding story that a Castilian spy had been shown all the secrets of the castles of south Wales in the 1380s.

Such external threats were taken all the more seriously since they were accompanied by the very real prospect that a legitimist pretender might seek to establish himself in Wales in the person of Owain ap Thomas ap Rhodri or Owain Lawgoch ('Owain of the Red Hand'). His credentials were excellent. He was a great-nephew of Llywelyn ap Gruffudd; he was a soldier of vast experience, who had served in Spain, France, Alsace, and Switzerland; he had attracted into his circle a handful of Welsh exiles, many of whom—including the most colourful of them Ieuan Wyn, *Poursuivant d'Amour*—were of noble stock; he commanded the confidence of leading Frenchmen, such as Du Guesclin and the duke of Anjou, and the active support of Charles V; above all, his cause had begun to attract the sympathy and active financial support of some leading men in north Wales. The government of England had good cause to be alarmed; the prognostications of the poets seemed at last about to be realized. In May 1372, at Paris, Owain proclaimed his intention to recover Wales, which 'is and should be mine by right of succession, by kindred and by inheritance'.[14] He borrowed a huge sum of money from Charles V and set sail from Harfleur. The expedition was diverted to Guernsey and was eventually aborted when the king of France found himself in need of Owain's services elsewhere. Owain, however, did not abandon his ambition. When reports of a new expedition—this time with Castilian aid—were circulated in 1377, the English government was sufficiently concerned to dispatch a spy to assassinate Owain. The spy's mission was accomplished on a July morning in 1378 at the town of Mortagne sur Mer in Poitou. Therewith was finally extinguished the dynasty of Gwynedd; but Owain Lawgoch's career and exploits had served to confirm the political expectations of Welshmen. His mantle as the legitimist, messianic deliverer must pass to another.

[14] Quoted in E. Owen, 'Owain Lawgoch—Yeuain de Galles: Some Facts and Suggestions, *Trans. Cymm. Soc. 1899–1900*, 6–105 at p. 61.

Tension within Wales was exacerbated in these years by the insensitive greed of its English lords. They made every attempt to sustain their high level of income in spite of the sharp and continuing fall in the population since the 1350s. Rents and farms were beginning to falter by the 1370s; but shortfall in these directions was often made good by the vigorous exploitation of other sources of revenue. In Principality and Marcher lordships alike, court profits were ruthlessly exploited; heavy communal subsidies and fines were imposed (such as those in the Principality lands in 1384 and 1394–5, or the 'gift' of £1,333 granted to Henry of Bolingbroke on his first visit to Brecon in 1397); non-performance of antiquated customs was used as a pretext to impose punitive fines (as in Chirkland in 1389, where a fine of £500 was imposed on the community for failing to carry timber to Chirk castle). Some lords admittedly experienced difficulty in collecting the whole of the revenue they claimed; but on the whole it is the degree of success they enjoyed and the unremitting pressure which they applied which are striking. Thus, when the income from John of Gaunt's extensive estates in Wales fell into arrears in the late 1380s, a special commission was established to expedite the collection of revenue. The results were impressive: during the 1390s at least 92 per cent of the income due from the Lancaster estates found its way into the duke's coffers within two years. Adam of Usk calculated that Wales yielded £60,000 a year to the coffers of English kings and lords in the late fourteenth century. Wales was still held firmly in the vice of a ruthlessly exploitative lordship.

Under these conditions it is hardly to be wondered that the native community grew increasingly restless. One group within that community had its own reasons for resentment. Native churchmen saw their church increasingly exploited as a source of patronage, income, and preferment for an alien hierarchy. In the last quarter of the fourteenth century only one Welshman, John Trefor, bishop of St Asaph 1395–1410, was promoted to a Welsh see. Instead, Welsh bishoprics were used as rewards for deserving governmental servants, such as Adam Houghton, bishop of St Davids 1362–89, or for royal confidants, such as Alexander Bache, royal confessor and bishop of St Asaph 1390–4, or Tideman of Winchcombe, royal physician and bishop of Llandaff 1393–5. Such appointments were, of course, not new; but they now became almost universal, partly because Welsh bishoprics were pawns in the games of English factional politics and, above all, because after the schism of 1378 the papacy was in no position to provide a counterweight to royal influence in the choice of bishops.[15] Some of the men so chosen were men of considerable ability, but they often showed scant respect for the sensibilities of their Welsh flocks. Thomas Ringstead, bishop of Bangor 1357–66, made his views offensively clear.

[15] Thus a papal attempt to install a Welshman, Lewis Aber, as bishop of Bangor in 1398 was overridden.

His bequest of £100 to the cathedral was to be cancelled in the event of a Welshman being chosen as his successor, while another bequest of the same sum to help five poor scholars from the diocese to attend Oxford or Cambridge was specifically not open to any Welshman. Another menancing threat to the ecclesiastical careers of Welshmen in the period after 1350 was the sharp increase in the number of prebends and sinecure rectories reserved for royal clerks. The practice is particularly clear in the diocese of St Davids, both in the cathedral church itself and in the collegiate churches of Abergwili and Llanddewibrefi. 'Royal control', it has been justly observed, 'meant, by and large, excluding Welsh clerics from the highest ranks of ecclesiastical preferment'.[16]

Nor was this the only grievance. The later fourteenth century witnessed a revival of the practice of appropriating parochial revenues in order to bolster the tottering finances of English and Welsh monasteries, bishoprics, and cathedral chapters. An under-endowed church was thereby further impoverished and indigent vicars left to manage on inadequate stipends. Pluralism (i.e. the holding of more than one ecclesiastical benefice) haemorrhaged the pitiful resources of the Welsh church even further. The returns to the papal inquiry of 1366 into pluralism revealed that fifteen out of the twenty-two canons of Abergwili and ten out of twelve of those of Llanddewibrefi were pluralists; most of them were not even resident in the diocese. It is little wonder in these circumstances that Owain Glyn Dŵr's ecclesiastical programme should include demands for the annulment of all appropriations of Welsh churches by English monasteries and for the appointment of Welshmen only to Welsh benefices. The high level of clerical taxation formed another broad-based source of complaint. During Edward III's reign the clergy paid proportionately more taxation than did the laity; and the Welsh clergy, being under the jurisdiction of the province of Canterbury, was not exempt from such taxation. Resistance to clerical taxation grew particularly strident from the 1370s, as the clergy found itself ground between the upper and nether millstones of royal and papal demand. In north Wales the clergy proved increasingly 'contrary and rebellious', and in south Wales likewise the clerical tax-collectors reported despairingly that they met 'great rebelliousness' and even physical resistance.[17] The clerical cauldron seemed to be coming to the boil.

Disaffected churchmen were a potentially dangerous group in any medieval society. Drawn as they were from leading native families, they identified themselves readily with the grievances and aspirations of their lay kinsfolk. As men of education and wide horizons, they naturally occupied a premier role in articulating the grievances of the native

---

[16] Glanmor Williams, *The Welsh Church from Conquest to Reformation* (2nd edn. Cardiff, 1976), p. 139.
[17] Quoted in Glanmor Williams, *The Welsh Church*, p. 141.

community. Nor were they averse to taking part in local unrest. The Shaldeford incident in 1345 had been master-minded by Master Hywel ap Goronwy and among his fellow-conspirators were the deans of St Asaph and Llŷn, the archdeacon of Bangor, and the abbot of Aberconwy. Churchmen were prominent also as guardians of native Welsh literary tradition and political mythology; while the importance of monasteries as centres of political disaffection had long since been recognized. Already in 1330 it was claimed that unlawful assemblies were being held in the abbey of Strata Marcella (Powys) 'to excite contentions and hatred between the English and the Welsh'.[18] The revolt of Owain Glyn Dŵr was to confirm amply that monasteries and the houses of friars remained powerful centres of Welsh sympathies and aspirations.

Disillusion within Wales extended further than the ranks of churchmen. Relations between the burgesses of English towns in Wales and the Welshmen of the countryside were still fraught in the closing decades of the fourteenth century in places as far apart as Carmarthen and Hope (Flints.). Nor were relations always smooth in the countryside: the lord of Dyffryn Clwyd complained of the malice and audacity of Welshmen in trying to undermine his family's title to land granted to it at the Edwardian Conquest, while in Narberth in the 1390s the council of the earl of March felt that an ability to compose the differences between the Welsh and English of the lordship was an important qualification in the appointment of a steward. On a broader front, the last quarter of the century witnessed a resumption and intensification of the campaign of the English counties bordering on Wales against alleged raids by Welshmen, the jurisdictional abuses encouraged by Marcher liberties, and the frightening increase in the number of Welshmen who were settling in the English border counties. What was particularly disturbing about this campaign was the openly racialist tone of its attack on 'pure Welshmen' and the descendants of 'pure Welshmen' and its invocation of the ordinances of Edward I. Racial tension and hysteria were being deliberately raised.

That tension in its turn fed on individual incidents whose significance often escapes us but which could only have contributed further to straining relationships. In 1385 John Lawrence, deputy-justiciar of south Wales and burgess of Carmarthen, was killed on the road to Cardigan by a leading Welsh squire of northern Carmarthenshire; the Welsh poem prompted by the latter's forthcoming trial clearly suggests that it was regarded as a *cause célèbre*. In 1389 there were reports of great unrest among the Welsh after the death of a prominent Welshman in custody during a judicial visitation to Wales by the earl of Arundel. North-east Wales in particular was unusually volatile during these years: it was racked by a bitter family feud

[18] *Calendar of Close Rolls, 1330–33*, p. 150.

in 1391, and three years later a violent demonstration at the justice's sessions at Flint in 1394 threatened to get out of hand. It is difficult to gauge the significance of events such as these; but in all of them prominent leaders of the native community were involved. The route from local lawlessness to a more general revolt could be a short one.

A more generalized and obvious cause of concern lay in the remarkable vacuum of lordship that was created in Wales in the late 1390s. The quiescence of Wales politically and the contentment of the leaders of the native community depended very considerably on the availability of a focus of service, worship, patronage, and reward.[19] In this context, the events of the years 1397-9 had a devastating impact not only on the distribution of power but also on political stability in Wales. Three of the greatest Marcher lords forfeited their lordships, and in two cases their lives, in Richard II's *coup d'état* in July 1397: Thomas, duke of Gloucester (Caldicot and Huntington), Thomas Beauchamp, earl of Warwick (Elfael and, until 1396, Gower), and above all Richard Fitzalan, earl of Arundel (Bromfield and Yale, Chirkland, Oswestry, Clun). Two deaths from natural causes greatly compounded the impact of this territorial avalanche: those of Roger Mortimer, earl of March, much the most powerful Marcher lord in July 1398 (sixteen Marcher lordships including Denbigh in the north, a large assemblage of lordships in the middle March, and Usk and Caerleon in the south-east), and John of Gaunt in February 1399 (Monmouth, Cydweli). Finally Thomas Mowbray, duke of Norfolk (Gower and Chepstow), and Henry Bolingbroke, heir to Gaunt's estates and also lord of Brecon through his wife, were exiled for life in 1398-9. Richard II installed his own favourites—notably Lescrope, Despenser, Exeter, and Aumale—in the lordships so confiscated or brought into custody; but hardly were they installed than they, and Richard himself, were swept from power. Never, not even during the tumultuous reign of Edward II, had there been such an earthquake on the map of lordship in medieval Wales. The seismic impact of these changes extended much further than mere title to lordship; the ties of service and reward, often carefully cultivated within families over generations, had suddenly been severed.

Such a vacuum of leadership and loyalty was all the more dangerous in Wales since it allowed a festering sense of disenchantment with English rule to well to the surface once more. There are hints—by the nature of the evidence and of the issue they can be no more—that this was indeed happening in the closing decades of the fourteenth century. The disenchantment sprang in part from a sense of outrage at the legalized discrimination against Welshmen and at the insensitive trampling on their

---

[19] See above, pp. 408-10.

sense of former glory. 'Where once there were Britons', so declaimed one outraged poet, 'now the English hold sway. What a daily tragedy for Welshmen!'[20] More specifically, the disenchantment focused on a conviction that the leaders of Welsh society were not now regarded or rewarded as their status or their deserts merited. No Welshman was now knighted as in the days of Edward III; social values were inverted as low-born men were promoted and noblemen overlooked; the Welsh were 'reeling like drunken crows'. This was indeed a 'sorry world' (W. *byd dudrist*).[21] The poem in which these sentiments were expressed was addressed to Owain Glyn Dŵr; it is one of the few contemporary hints of the storm that was brewing.

That storm broke on 16 September 1400. On that day Owain Glyn Dŵr was proclaimed prince of Wales by some of his followers at Glyndyfrdwy (Merioneth) and forthwith set out on a raid on many of the leading English boroughs of north-east Wales. So began a revolt which engulfed much of Wales during the next few years and whose dying embers were not finally extinguished until well into the reign of Henry V. Initially, the outbreak seemed to be little more than an outburst of pique and frustration by a few disaffected and high-spirited Welsh noblemen—Owain Glyn Dŵr and his friends in the north-east and Owain's cousins, Rhys and Gwilym ap Tudur, in Anglesey. Henry IV led a short punitive expedition into north Wales in October, meeting little opposition. Had he and his advisers shown rather more imagination and magnanimity at this juncture in dealing with the complaints of the rebels and in extending a pardon to them, the short-lived revolt might have been finally extinguished. Instead, the government rubbed salt in the wounds of discontent by holding judicial sessions in north Wales and exacting large subsidies from the population; it even went some way to meet the demands of the Commons in the Hilary parliament of 1401 for penal legislation against the Welsh as a people. Welshmen were to be excluded from acquiring land in England or in English towns in Wales and from being enrolled as burgesses; 'entire Englishmen' were to be protected from conviction at the suit of Welshmen in Wales. The Welsh response was not slow in coming: Conway castle was seized dramatically on Good Friday 1401 by Gwilym and Rhys ap Tudur and held for a full two months, much to the embarrassment of the English authorities; Owain Glyn Dŵr himself emerged from hiding, carried his revolt into the uplands of mid-Wales, and by autumn 1401 had tightened his grip sufficiently on north-west Wales to threaten Harlech and Caernarfon castles. Attempts at negotiation with him bore no fruit. Instead, both sides dug in their heels: Henry IV led a second expedition into Wales in October 1401, hoping to

[20] *Cywyddau Iolo Goch ac Eraill*, p. 109 ('Lle bu'r Brython, Saeson sydd/A'r boen ar Gymry beunydd').
[21] *Cywyddau Iolo Goch ac Eraill*, p. 125 ('Cymry . . . Cenedl druain fel brain brwysg').

terrorize the country into submission by executing some of Owain's prominent supporters and by harrying the countryside. Owain for his part made it clear that his revolt now had national pretensions by soliciting help from the king of Scotland and the native Irish lords.

Owain's pretensions grew apace during 1402. He effected the capture of two leading English notables—his old enemy, Reginald Grey of Ruthin, in the spring and Edmund Mortimer, the uncle of the young earl of March, in midsummer. He used both as pawns for his own purposes, extorting a massive ransom of ten thousand marks for the release of Grey and forging a marriage-alliance with Edmund Mortimer when the royal government dragged its feet on the question of his release. Even more ominously Owain extended the sphere of his military activity to encompass east and south-east Wales: in June he inflicted a signal military defeat on a border military force near Pilleth (Pyllalai), to the east of Radnor, and before the summer was out his revolt had extended into Glamorgan and Gwent. Even boroughs such as Usk, Caerleon, Newport, and Cardiff were targets for his attacks. In August 1402 a third royal expedition was directed at Wales from three bases on the English border; but it achieved little more in terms of permanent success than its predecessors and was brought to an ignominious end by torrential rain. It was little wonder that the contemporary St Albans chronicler believed that Owain Glyn Dŵr dabbled in magic and used it to control the weather for his own purposes.

Owain's revolt had now lasted far longer than any other in the history of Wales since the Conquest. During the next three years it scaled even greater heights; indeed, it appeared for a while as if the grandiose schemes of its leader might not, after all, lie beyond the realm of the attainable. During the course of 1403 Owain extended his sway into south-west Wales, the one major area of the country where he had hitherto made little headway. Before the end of the year his forces were laying intermittent siege to castles from Brecon in the east to Aberystwyth in the west, Beaumaris in the north to Cardiff in the south, while the men of Herefordshire were driven in despair to conclude a truce with Owain. Well might they do so, for there was little hope of salvation from a hard-pressed king who led yet another short expedition into Wales, his fourth and last, in September 1403, providing short-term relief but in no way offering a long-term solution. But it was in two other directions that 1403 was a notable year for Owain. It witnessed the first serious attempt to link his revolt in Wales with domestic disaffection in England: the Percies and Glyn Dŵr joined forces against Henry IV, and though their alliance faltered badly when Hotspur, the earl of Northumberland's son, was defeated and killed at the battle of Shrewsbury (21 July 1403) it had at least opened the prospect of channelling discontent in England to bolster Owain's ambitions in Wales. In the same year, Owain received the first substantial practical help from the French. In October, forces from France and Brittany helped Henry Don in the siege of Kidwelly, while a month later a French fleet under Jean d'Espagne assaulted the town and castle of Caernarfon. These twin developments were of momentous significance: they propelled the Welsh revolt into the arena of English politics and international conflict. It was at that level alone that Owain Glyn Dŵr had any prospect of achieving some measure of real success and permanence for his ambitions.

The pinnacle of those ambitions was reached in 1404. Effective English control in most of Wales was now restricted to a few coastal and lowland areas, and to isolated castles and boroughs. During the course of the year two of Wales's premier castles, Harlech and Aberystwyth, were captured; Cardiff likewise was possibly taken and burnt; while lowland castles such as Abergavenny and Coety (Glamorgan) were closely besieged. With such successes to his credit Owain could assume the pretensions of a national prince instead of those of a guerrilla leader. So it was that he assembled at Machynlleth a parliament of his own or, as Adam of Usk had it, 'imitated or contrived' one.[22] An even more impressive testimony to his growing self-confidence was the embassy which he dispatched from Dolgellau (Merioneth) on 10 May to the French court, requesting an alliance and practical help in the form of supplies of arms and a French expeditionary force. The formal alliance was concluded in the most solemn fashion on 14 July 1404. The military aid was not immediately forthcoming; but Owain could rest content in the knowledge that his cause had now been formally woven into the fabric of the Anglo-French conflict. Owain's status was reinforced from another direction during the course of the year: in August 1404 Lewis ab Ieuan (alias Lewis Byford) was provided to the see of Bangor and promptly acknowleged Owain's supremacy in north-west Wales; and before the year was out John Trefor, the talented and experienced bishop of St Asaph since 1395, defected to the Welsh cause. Owain was rapidly assembling the credentials and status of an independent prince, both within and without Wales.

Compared with the achievements of 1404, the next year was one of very mixed fortunes for Owain. Some of the well-laid plans of the past, it is true, came to fruition. Domestic discord in England once more enhanced Owain's prospects and even tempted him to dream wild dreams. In February 1405 Lady Despenser was only just prevented from seeking exile in Wales with the two young Mortimer heirs, whose uncle was already an ally of Glyn Dŵr and who could claim a superior title to the English throne to that of Henry IV. It was around this Mortimer claim and the ambitions of the Percies that one of the most extraordinary incidents of the whole

----

[22] *Chronicon Adae de Usk*, p. 86.

revolt turned. During the course of the year Owain, the earl of Northumberland, and young Edmund Mortimer concluded a Tripartite Indenture whereby they agreed to divide England and Wales between them. The grossly inflated ambitions of the three parties indicated that they were losing touch with political reality. That truth was underscored when the rebellion of Northumberland's allies collapsed in late May. The French alliance proved of much greater value and posed a real threat to the English king. A substantial force—estimated (no doubt with much exaggeration) by contemporary French sources at over ten thousand men—landed in Milford Haven in early August, captured the town (though not the castle of) Haverford, marched on Carmarthen and captured it, and proceeded speedily westwards, camping eight miles short of Worcester by the end of the month. No French army had ever achieved a comparable advance into the king of England's realm hitherto; it was an ample vindication of the value of the French alliance. Yet the French expedition into Wales was not well attuned either to Glyn Dŵr's tactics or ultimately to his resources. Unless it could link successfully with insurrectionary forces in England, its chances of effecting a lasting change in Henry IV's fortunes, and thereby in Owain's prospects, were limited. It was on his own resources that Owain would ultimately have to rely. Those resources were already under strain. During the spring and summer he had suffered a series of military defeats, especially in south-east Wales. Among those captured were his son, Gruffudd, his secretary, and his close confidant and brother-in-law, John Hanmer. Support for him was beginning to crumble: chronicle and record evidence agree that much of Glamorgan had submitted to the king by the end of the year; even in north Wales fair-weather friends, such as Gwilym ap Gruffudd, were already concluding that Owain's days of glory were numbered. 'And then', remarked a native Welsh annalist of the year 1405, 'was the turning of the tide for Owain'.[23]

The tide turned much further, and irretrievably so, in 1406. Owain and his advisers admittedly showed the largeness of their vision and their appreciation of the continuing need to exploit international disagreements to further their cause, by switching the ecclesiastical allegiance of Wales to the Avignonese papacy and by propounding a radical ecclesiastical programme to liberate the Welsh church from the control of the English church and state. But a second French expeditionary force did not materialize; the prospect of any help from Scotland largely evaporated with the capture of the heir to the Scottish throne by English sailors; while the flight of the earl of Northumberland and Lord Bardolf to Wales only proved in what desperate straits they were. In spite of an occasional

---

[23] Quoted in J. E. Lloyd, *Owen Glendower* (Oxford, 1931), p. 154.

flamboyant gesture—such as the attack on Kidwelly castle launched in August by Henry Don—support for the revolt was visibly crumbling. By the end of the year the men of Gower, the Vale of Tywi, Ceredigion, and Anglesey had all made their submissions. Glyn Dŵr was firmly on the defensive.

Thereafter he never regained the initiative. The French alliance had effectively collapsed by autumn 1407; the earl of Northumberland and Lord Bardolf were killed at the battle of Bramham Moor in February 1408 and with them in effect disappeared any substantial opposition to Henry IV's rule in England. During 1408 the last two major strongholds under Owain's control—Harlech and Aberystwyth—were at last recaptured. It was a measure of the renewal of English confidence that royal nominees were chosen to replace Owain's supporters as bishops of Bangor and St Asaph and that by October 1409 it was even possible for the new bishop of Bangor, Benedict Nicholls, to be enthroned in his own cathedral. Glyn Dŵr's revolt was not crushed; it simply petered out. A hard core of followers stuck stubbornly by him; three of the most prominent of them—including his cousin, Rhys ap Tudur of Anglesey—were caught and executed in 1410. An occasional border foray, a local outburst of disorder, or the capture of a prominent English supporter (notably Dafydd Gam of Brecon in 1412) showed that the last embers of revolt had still not been finally extinguished; in the upland districts of north and west Wales English officers still dared not move about their business except under escort, and English garrisons still stood by nervously in Welsh castles. Glyn Dŵr himself, unlike so many earlier leaders of Welsh revolts, remained uncaptured. He disappears from the records during 1415. 'Very many', noted the Welsh annalist scrupulously, 'say that he died; the seers maintain that he did not.'[24] He had joined that pantheon of heroes from Welsh history and legend, such as Cadwaladr and Arthur, whose time had been but was also to be.

It is with the character of Owain Glyn Dŵr himself that any consideration of the great revolt of the years 1400–8 must begin. It was his proclamation as prince of Wales which inaugurated the revolt; the movement was consistently known to the English authorities as his revolt. Local leaders there appeared in plenty, but Owain's ultimate leadership was never challenged and on occasion it was imposed masterfully over his followers. By any standards he was a consummate leader of men, who showed great dignity and remarkable vision in the pursuit of his chosen course and who commanded intense loyalty from his closest companions. Yet, in many respects, his career before 1400 hardly hinted at the making of a great

[24] J. E. Lloyd, *Owen Glendower*, p. 154.

national leader. He belonged to a native family which had apparently
accommodated itself readily to English rule and which moved easily in the
mixed society of the March. His grandmother was a Lestrange and his own
wife a Hanmer, the daughter of a chief justice of the King's Bench. His
father had served the earl of Arundel as steward of Oswestry and had acted
as keeper of the lordship of Ellesmere. By native Welsh standards the
family was rich, and Owain was able to provide himself with a splendid new
moated house at the family seat at Sycharth (Chirkland) and to enjoy the
comforts of a fine new lodge in his other estate across the Berwyn
mountains at Glyndyfrdwy (Merioneth). His own youthful career bore the
hallmarks of the training of an English county squire: he had probably
served a period of legal training at the Inns of Court and had certainly
enjoyed an exciting military apprenticeship, serving in the garrison at
Berwick in 1384, campaigning with the king in Scotland in 1385, and taking
part, under the command of the earl of Arundel, in the notable naval
victory at Cadzand in March 1387. Owain indeed deserved the title of
'formidable squire' (*armiger formosus*).[25]

Yet there was another dimension to Owain's career which, like so much
of native Welsh life, is concealed from view in the record evidence. Owain
was the subject of at least six extant Welsh praise poems (W. *cywyddau
mawl*) addressed to him by poets before 1400. This degree of close and
cloying poetic attention may well, of course, be primarily a comment on his
own munificence and literary taste; but equally it may already reflect a
heightened level of attention and expectation on the part of the
professional bardic order. The responsibilities of a remarkably distinguished
descent weighed heavily on Glyn Dŵr's shoulders. Through his father, he
was the direct male descendant of the princely dynasty of northern Powys
and through his mother of the even more distinguished stock of Lord Rhys
of Deheubarth. Legitimist Welsh dynastic hopes thereby focused on him,
especially after the extinction of the direct Gwynedd line with the murder
of Owain Lawgoch in 1378. It was an awesome responsibility and one
which others would not allow him to overlook, even if he had been minded
to do so himself. Its importance may in fact have loomed ever larger in
Owain's mind as his own sense of disappointment and frustration—amply
hinted at in the poetry—grew in the 1390s. He was not knighted as
Welshmen of his birth, standing, and proven prowess had been earlier in
the century; he was denied local office; and the deaths of his would-be
patrons—Sir David Hanmer in 1387 and the earl of Arundel in 1397—
deprived him of those whose help might have secured his promotion and
thereby flattered his sense of self-importance. Owain Glyn Dŵr could now
speak as the leader of the *exclus*, the native Welsh squires who felt that
their importance and deserts were being overlooked.

[25] *Historia Vitae et Regni Ricardi Secundi*, ed. G. B. Stowe (Pennsylvania, 1977), p. 168.

More positively, Glyn Dŵr was clearly closely attuned to the ideology of prophecy, expectation, and deliverance which flows as a strong undercurrent through the history of native Wales in the post-Conquest period. His formal declarations are couched in the phraseology of that ideology; he deferred to its spokesmen recurrently. His own household soothsayer, Crach Ffinnant, had accompanied him to Berwick in 1384 and was at his side when the revolt was launched in September 1400. It was to Hopcyn ap Tomas ab Einion of Ynysdawy, noted Welsh bibliophile and patron and 'maister of brut', that he turned for a prophetic interpretation of the outcome of the revolt in 1403. His letter to Robert III of Scotland in 1400 referred recurrently to 'the prophecy' and spelt out for the king's information their common descent from Brutus, 'your most noble ancestor and mine'.[26] When the Tripartite Indenture was drawn up in 1405, the much-augmented Wales claimed by Owain, extending northwards from Worcester to the source of the Trent and thence to the source of the Mersey, had as one of its boundaries 'the ash trees of Meigion', a location redolent with associations with a seventh-century victory by Cadwallon and embroidered with further tales in the prophecies of Merlin. It is in the context of such prophecies and historical mythology that the character of Owain's revolt begins to become comprehensible.

It was from the outset a national revolt. Owain, it is true, may have been stung into action by local and personal insults, such as a boundary-dispute with his neighbour Reginald Grey of Ruthin or by deceitful conduct by Grey over the delivery of a military summons. There are also clear hints that Owain and his Anglesey cousins could have been bought off by limited concessions in 1400–1. Nevertheless, the initial act of the rebellion—the proclamation of Owain as prince of Wales, nothing less, on 16 September 1400—announced it to be, from its outset, national in its pretensions. Owain dwelt recurrently in his propaganda on the need 'to deliver the Welsh people from the captivity of our English enemies who have oppressed us and our ancestors for a long time past' and told the king of France how 'my nation (*nacio mea*) has . . . been trodden underfoot by the fury of the barbarous Saxons'.[27] His formal title in his diplomatic documents was 'Owen by the grace of God prince of Wales'; his great seal, which in artistry and design bears comparison with those of contemporary princes, displays the four lions rampant of Gwynedd, recalling his claim thereby to be the heir of the pretensions of Llywelyn ap Gruffudd, the first native prince of Wales, and indeed also of the previous legitimist pretender, Owain Lawgoch. As his confidence and hopes soared from 1403 onwards, so the lineaments of what may be termed a national policy began

---

[26] *Chronicon Adae de Usk*, p. 72.
[27] *Welsh Records in Paris*, ed. T. Matthews (Cardiff, 1910), pp. 113, 40. The preferred date for the former letter is 1403, not 1404.

to appear, at least in certain directions. Its most famous and precise expression is to be found in the letter, dated at Pennal (Merioneth) on 31 March 1406 'and in the sixth year of our principate', announcing his adherence to the Avignonese papacy in order to please his French ally. It is in effect a programme for establishing an independent Welsh church as the ecclesiastical counterpart of an independent Welsh principality. St Davids was to be elevated to the status of a metropolitan church and was to be given authority not only over the other three Welsh dioceses but also over five dioceses in western England. Only ecclesiastics versed in Welsh were to be provided to Welsh benefices, while appropriations of Welsh parishes to English monasteries and colleges were to be revoked forthwith. In the most innovative and forward-looking clause in the agreement, two universities were to be founded, one in north and the other in south Wales. Owain's revolt was to be given the status of a crusade and plenary remission was to be extended to all those who fell in the Welsh cause.

There is a breath-taking amplitude, even bravado, about this so-called Pennal programme. It bespeaks the breadth of vision of the much-travelled and widely experienced ecclesiastics in Owain's entourage, notably his chancellor Gruffudd Young and John Trefor of St Asaph. Whether Owain had developed comparable ideas for the secular governance of his principality is doubtful. Wales was governmentally fragmented; it had never developed, before or after the Conquest, the institutions of a common polity. Scottish parallels might have suggested themselves, given the frequent dispatch of messages and messengers thither, as a goal to which to aspire. Owain did indeed acquire some of the basic paraphernalia of princely power—a great and a privy seal, a chancellor, and a secretary; he made impressive efforts to cast his written instruments in the correct diplomatic form and to give the proper credentials to his ambassadors; his summons of four men from each commote of Wales to his second recorded parliament at Harlech in summer 1405 again indicates an awareness of the need to provide an institutional outlet for the broad degree of support he commanded. But Owain was too concerned with the problems of military survival to be able to attend—as far as we know—to the problems of providing a proper infrastructure of authority and finance for his ambitions. His principality was national in terms of its pretensions, ideology, and military scope, rather than in terms of practical governance and achievement.

Owain certainly came to command support for his movement on a scale, both geographical and social, such as had never hitherto been witnessed in Wales. Churchmen of all kinds were among his most enthusiastic supporters. It was perhaps not surprising that Franciscan friars should figure prominently as early followers, given their unequalled record of conspiracy against Henry IV. Nor is it surprising that native Cistercian houses, such as Strata Florida, Whitland, Aberconwy, and even Llantarnam (Caerleon) in the south-east, or native houses of Augustinian canons, such as Beddgelert (Caernarfon) and Bardsey (Caernarfon), should be solid in their support, for since the thirteenth century they had rarely faltered in their commitment to the native cause and to the succouring of its mythology and traditions. Equally crucial was the early support of higher Welsh secular clerics, such as the dean of St Asaph or the archdeacon of Anglesey. Their social standing and wide-ranging family connections gave them much the same importance in Glyn Dŵr's revolt as they had enjoyed in earlier native conspiracies. They were soon joined by even more powerful and experienced ecclesiastics—notably Gruffudd Young, Lewis ab Ieuan, and John Trefor. Their university training and experience of the papal court brought a new dimension to Glyn Dŵr's cause; they were largely responsible for the polished image which it presented to the outside world and for the wide international contacts which it quickly established. The revolt also quickly triggered the enthusiasm of Welsh students in Oxford and evoked a ready response among the poorly paid parochial clergy in rural Wales.

Even more crucial for Owain Glyn Dŵr than the support of ecclesiastics was that of his fellow squires, high and low, throughout Wales. They were the natural leaders of native society; they controlled a web of formal and informal authority over the local population. They were initially slow to respond to Glyn Dŵr's call, but by 1403–4 they were defecting to him in droves. A roll-call of their names would include a goodly proportion of the leaders of local society—men such as William Gwyn, steward of Llansteffan and sometime deputy-justice of south Wales; Rhys Ddu, a former sheriff of Cardiganshire and zealous official in Richard II's service but who now graduated to control of Aberystwyth castle for Glyn Dŵr before ending his life on the scaffold in London; Henry Don, the buccaneering bully-boy of Cydweli and Gaunt's steward there, who brought military experience in Gascony and Ireland to the aid of Glyn Dŵr's campaign in the south-west; or Hywel ap Tudur ab Ithel Fychan, the most powerful Welshman in Flintshire, who brought with him the support of a galaxy of relatives when he defected to Glyn Dŵr in 1403. And so the list could be lengthened. These men were well-versed in the practice of authority; they had almost to a man held local office. They were equally well-versed in the arts of war, having led contingents of Welsh troops in the service of king, prince, or Marcher lord. They formed a closely integrated group, bound to each other by a common ethos and even more firmly by bonds of kinship and marriage. Each of them had his group (W. *plaid*) of dependants, whose support was theirs at their bidding. They could now pursue their local ambitions, too often frustrated by an alien administration, under the cloak of a national revolt. They did so exultantly, no doubt with very varying degrees of commitment to the cause itself.

Beyond the ranks of the squirearchy, Owain came to command a remarkable measure of general support within Wales, so that, in these terms at least, there is no reason to doubt that his was a popular revolt. Migrant wage-labourers from England flocked to his cause; the bards and minstrels were quickly condemned in parliament as among his most fervid and effective propagandists; townsmen in long-established English towns, such as David Perrott of Tenby, were suspected of flirting with his cause; even lowland gentry with unmistakably non-Welsh names, such as Philip Skidmore of Troy (Monmouth) or John Fleming of Ogmore (Glamorgan), were seduced to join him. As to the native population of the countryside, native annalist and hysterical English correspondents were at one in observing how they defected *en masse*—'all the Welsh nation, except a few' is the recurrent phrase—to Glyn Dŵr's cause.[28]

Resistance to the revolt was naturally led by the English settlers in Wales—both the townsmen of the small boroughs and their cousins in the countryside, such as the Bedells of Hay, the Mortons of Kidwelly, or the Colliers of Harlech. Many of the settlers lost their goods and their livelihood as a result of the revolt; they must have genuinely believed the contemporary report that it was indeed Owain's intention 'to destroy the English language' in Wales.[29] In these circumstances it is little wonder that they gave their all to thwart his plans: they manned the walls of the local castles side by side with the professional soldiery; they imported supplies from Chester or Bristol to meet the needs of the besieged; they lent large sums of money to keep unpaid and impatient soldiers on duty; they rebuilt the town-walls, often at their own expense. Yet though the legislation and correspondence of the period suggest that the Welsh stood solidly by Glyn Dŵr and were, therefore, to be distrusted, this was in fact far from being so. Even in the heartland of Owain's area of support in north-west Wales, several leading Welshmen stood aside from or even actively opposed his cause, men such as Hwlcyn Llwyd and Ieuan ap Maredudd, both of them leading squires in Caernarfonshire who died resisting Owain's assault on the town and castle of Caernarfon in the winter of 1403–4. Elsewhere in Wales, especially in the south and east, native opposition to Owain was doubtless more widespread. Thus Maredudd ap Madog of Maelienydd refused to join Glyn Dŵr though 'his brethren and kinsmen became rebels';[30] while the premier Welsh family in Brecon (Llywelyn ap Hywel and his kinsmen, notably his son, the redoubtable Dafydd Gam) stood firm

---

[28] *Royal and Historical Letters of Henry IV*, ed. F. C. Hingeston (Rolls Series 1860–1965), I, 140, 142, 148.
[29] *Proceedings of the Privy Council*, II, 55, 60; *Eulogium Historiarium*, III, 393.
[30] *Calendar of Patent Rolls 1401–5*, p. 212.

in its loyalty to English lordship and paid a heavy price in losses, ransoms, and harassment. For many such men Glyn Dŵr's revolt presented the prospect of a disturbing reversal of the political and social order to which they and their ancestors had long since adjusted and from which they had profited. As a sixteenth-century antiquarian crisply observed of Dafydd Gam, 'he was a great stickler for the Duke of Lancaster' (as indeed his forebears had been for over a century and a half for the lords of Brecon); for him such a tradition of service determined his political loyalties clearly and definitively.[31] He was to die in the service of his lord on the field of Agincourt.

For many other Welshmen such certainties were a luxury they could not afford. They had to trim their sails to the prevailing wind, if they were to survive and to retain their lands. As one of them observed with disarming frankness, he was 'for the safety of his goods in the company of Owain Glyn Dŵr until he had put his goods into safe keeping'.[32] There were many like him, both as individuals and as communities. Thus the men of upland Brecon submitted to Henry IV in February 1404 but only on condition that the king defeated the rebels in Glamorgan; if he failed to do so, they would have no option but to renege on their submission. Like every other revolt, that of Glyn Dŵr developed its own momentum; as contemporaries fully recognized, that momentum could not be reversed until English lordship in Wales once more offered a credible and effective focus of protection.

Why then did the revolt last so long? The Welsh certainly made full use of their terrain and of their opportunities. Their leaders, after all, were men of considerable military experience. They frequently took the enemy off its guard, as at Conway in April 1401. They used their superior numbers and their mass levies to terrorize isolated castle garrisons into surrender, as at Llansteffan and Castellnewydd Emlyn in 1403. Although they won a few striking military victories—notably at Hyddgen (Powys) in 1401 and Bryn Glas (Usk) in 1402—they were more frequently than not badly worsted in open battle. Their preference was for the sudden ambush or raiding foray and, equally, for the swift flight, especially when confronted with a major expedition. In short, their tactics were those of the guerrilla. They conducted great devastating raids, those into south-east Wales and Herefordshire being particularly well recorded. Their aim in such raids was in part to terrorize, to capture distinguished prisoners who could then be ransomed for large sums of money, of which the Welsh were so desperately short (Reginald Grey's ransom brought them ten thousand marks, that of Dafydd Gam allegedly seven hundred marks), and to drive local communities to plead for local truces, for which a price again had to be paid. The men of Herefordshire and Shropshire concluded such truces in

[31] David Powel, *The History of Wales . . . augmented by W. Wynne* (1784), p. 320.
[32] *Calendar of Patent Rolls 1405–8*, p. 328.

1403–4, in spite of government disapproval, while in the autumn of 1405 the men of Pembroke raised £200 in silver among themselves to pay for a three-month truce with Owain. Welsh tactics had one other high priority—to secure desperately needed stocks of victuals, food, arms, horses, and other supplies. This is a recurrent theme of contemporary reports, just as much as it was a prominent feature of English policy to cut off access to English markets and provisions. Both parties recognized that in a guerrilla war, starvation is one of the few ways to effect a surrender.

The Welsh showed remarkable stamina; but it has to be recognized that the achievement and duration of their revolt probably owed most to the domestic preoccupations of Henry IV. Until 1408 Henry was never free from plots and rumours of plots against himself and his dynasty. The plotters, almost without exception, made use of the Welsh revolt to try to destabilize Henry's regime. The wild stories of large sums of money being sent from religious houses in England to Wales and of some leading English officials and commanders in Wales acting as double agents, to their own benefit, are possibly not without a small kernel of truth. At the very least they suggest the atmosphere of suspicion and treachery, of plot and revolt, within England which is an essential backcloth to Glyn Dŵr's success. It was to Glyn Dŵr's credit that, on the whole, he exploited this disaffection cleverly for his own ends. He was even more successful in harnessing his revolt to broader international conflicts, in both state and church. He was receiving help, official or otherwise, from the Scots by 1401 and from the French by at least 1403; he concluded a formal alliance with the French king in 1404 and arranged to transfer his loyalty to the Avignonese papacy in 1406. His appreciation of the need to exploit international tensions to promote the cause of his revolt is one of the most impressive features of Owain's policy.

The military shortcomings of the English and the problems they faced also contributed their fair share to the long-drawn-out character of the revolt. The English were undoubtedly vastly superior in military technology and supplies. In particular, they were able to make full use of sea power to supply besieged garrisons and to launch lightning raids, such as that led by Stephen Scrope, deputy-lieutenant of Ireland, against Anglesey in June 1405. They used cannon and gunpowder, both for defence (as at Pembroke and Tenby) and in order to reduce captured castles (as at Aberystwyth and Harlech). Individual commanders, notably from the border counties (such as Edward Charlton of Powys, Richard Grey of Codnor, or John Greyndour), showed considerable initiative and enjoyed a good measure of success. But the English military enterprise in Wales on the whole faced problems which were never properly overcome. The four royal campaigns into Wales 1400–3 were sorry affairs, inadequately prepared and totally lacking in the stamina which, as Edward I had so clearly shown, was a prerequisite of any sustained success in the country. Furthermore, Henry IV and his commanders in Wales were constantly hampered by a shortage of cash which severely inhibited their military plans. The nature of the Welsh terrain and the guerrilla-type character of the revolt—in this respect it posed a marked contrast to the opposition presented by Llywelyn ap Gruffudd—made a nonsense of any notions of a grand strategy. Much of the English campaigning was piecemeal and uncoordinated, concentrating on the problems of local survival or busying itself with the relief of a hard-pressed castle (such as Coety castle (Glamorgan) closely besieged twice in 1404–5). All these problems were greatly compounded by the fragmentation of authority in medieval Wales, where each lordship was virtually a self-contained unit, jealous of its military independence as of all other aspects of its autonomy. The revolt did at least compel the English government and Marcher lords to confront some of the issues posed by such fragmentation for the first time since the Edwardian Conquest. Civilian governance was replaced in several lordships by military rule; commanders were hired to serve by indentures of war with a specified number of troops for fixed periods, even in Marcher lordships. Most innovative of all, military lieutenancies were created which embraced whole regions and ignored lordship boundaries. As early as November 1401 the earl of Worcester was appointed royal lieutenant throughout south Wales; the practice reached its logical conclusion with the appointment of the Prince of Wales as military lieutenant for the whole of Wales in March 1403.

In the end, however, success was achieved through attrition rather than by counter-attack. The Welsh simply did not have the resources to sustain a national revolt. An amateur army of peasants and labourers could not ignore the seasonal demands of cultivation. The Welsh lacked sea power, other than that provided by French or Scottish allies or by the seizure of an occasional ship. They lacked siege-engines; they lacked the provisions to sustain a long siege. Their campaigns were generally short-lived and largely confined to summer forays. It is the long list of castles which they failed to take, in spite of being held often by small garrisons, rather than those which they captured which is noteworthy. Even in areas such as Cydweli, which they regularly attacked over a period of three years, they failed to dislodge the local administration completely and in the areas under their control there is no evidence that they were able to establish an effective alternative local administration. By 1406 their stamina was visibly faltering; the harsh winter of 1407–8 proved the final blow. Throughout Wales the English forces won the upper hand and the wheels of local government and revenue-collection began to turn again. The process of pacification was painfully slow under Henry IV, but immediately on Henry V's accession it was quickly concluded. The local communities of north Wales made their formal submissions and were pardoned. Magnanimity was the keynote: former rebels were restored to their property; succession according to Welsh law was guaranteed; community petitions received a favourable response; an inquiry was established into the misdemeanours of royal officials in north Wales; and even a gift of £200 was made to the men of Caernarfonshire and Merionethshire to help them restock their holdings. In July 1415 plans were afoot to receive Glyn Dŵr into the king's obedience, but death saved him from that humiliation. The government remained nervous about affairs in Wales, and not without good reason; but when Glyn Dŵr's surviving son, Maredudd, was offered a pardon in 1417 and at last accepted it in 1421, the revolt could be finally proclaimed dead and buried.

Such a protracted and wide-ranging revolt left its mark deeply on Welsh society and the Welsh consciousness. Immense devastation had been caused. 'It was Owen Glyndoores policie', so remarked the Tudor antiquary, Sir John Wynn, 'to bring all thinges to wast, that the Englishe should find not strength nor restinge place in the Countrey.'[33] Such indeed seems to have been the case—houses and crops were burnt, mills destroyed, ecclesiastical buildings (including the cathedral at Bangor and the canons' houses at St Asaph) laid waste, animals slaughtered or driven away. The English responded in kind: 'the King', remarked a contemporary letter, 'has proclaimed "havoc" of the whole of Wales'.[34] Towns such as Conway and Nefyn suffered a set-back from which they never fully recovered. Monastic revenues, already in disarray after the ravages of plague, spiralled downwards; while the small priory of St Mary's Cardiff was in effect extinguished by the revolt. Some of the rich lowland communities of south Wales were particularly severely affected: in the mesne-lordship of Ogmore (Glamorgan) more than half of the customary and cottager land still lay vacant in 1428; the two small villages of Sutton and Northdown remained mere shadows of their former selves; mills were not rebuilt and seignorial revenue remained depressed for over a generation. Elsewhere, notably in the upland Welshries, local communities proved more resilient and seignorial revenue recovered more quickly, but even here there was considerable social and economic dislocation as a result of the death of rebels and the flight of tenants, especially serfs. The pace of recovery was further slowed down by the huge communal fines that were imposed on rebel districts—a total of 1,400 marks (exclusive of individual fines) on Anglesey, 500 marks on Caernarfonshire, 300 marks on Merionethshire, 1,000 marks on Brecon, £500 each on Glamorgan and Abergavenny, and so forth.

The impact of the revolt on native Welsh society, and particularly on the

---

[33] Sir John Wynn, *History of the Gwydir Family*, ed. J. Ballinger (Cardiff, 1927), p. 53.
[34] *Anglo-Norman Letters and Petitions from All Souls MS. 182*, ed. M. D. Legge (Oxford, 1941), p. 374.

fortunes of its natural leaders, varied widely. Some families suffered greatly and were virtually obliterated: thus the sons of Tudur ap Goronwy, who had lorded it so powerfully in Anglesey and north-west Wales in the later fourteenth century, never recovered their power and influence; and, likewise, the family of William Gwyn ap Rhys Llwyd, former steward of Cydweli and later doughty defender of Aberystwyth castle for Glyn Dŵr, never regained his lands. But those who survived the revolt were generally allowed to redeem their lands, for a price: Henry Don secured his pardon in 1413 and was soon lording it again over native society in Cydweli, while Maredudd ab Owain, one of the leading Cardiganshire rebels, paraded his new-found loyalty by accompanying Henry V to Agincourt, as indeed did many other erstwhile rebels. Some of the craftier Welsh rebels turned a timely defection very much to their advantage, none more so that Gwilym ap Gruffudd, who, with a fine sense of timing, made his submission in 1405, secured the forfeited lands of Gwilym ap Tudur as well as those of other rebels in Anglesey, and completed the process of parading his loyalty to the English regime by taking an Englishwoman as his second wife and by largely disinheriting his son by his first, Welsh wife. For many of the Welsh squirearchy, therefore, the revolt of Owain Glyn Dŵr was a watershed both in their loyalties and in their fortunes. At a more general level, it greatly facilitated and accelerated those social and economic movements which were already afoot in Wales before the end of the fourteenth century—the movement from Welsh to English tenure and land law, the decline of bond status, the acceleration of the land market, the redistribution of rural wealth, and the accumulation of consolidated estates by yeomen and gentlemen, English and Welsh alike.[35] The social geography of early modern Wales was gradually coming into view, and Glyn Dŵr's revolt was undoubtedly an important catalyst in the process.

The revolt also served to focus attention on two cardinal issues, to which the English government would sooner or later have to attend. One was the institutional fragmentation of Wales and the anomalous character of its relationship to the kingdom of England. The Commons in parliament were loud in their criticism of the Marcher lords, notably of their failure to defend their castles and lordships adequately and to reside in them, echoing thereby contemporary complaints against 'absentees' in Ireland. They could not see why they should be required to vote subsidies in parliament to recover control of a country which lay outside the administrative, fiscal, and judicial ambit of ordinary English governance. They were also critical of the failure to apply the hard-line policies of 'the noble and wise' Edward I towards the Welsh[36] and questioned the propriety of such Marcher practices as redemption-fines for felonies and

---

[35] See above, pp. 427–30.   [36] *Rotuli Parliamentorum*, III, 476.

the custom of disclaimer (whereby a man arrested in one lordship for an offence could claim to be extradited to his native lordship) as being contrary to English common law. In short the revolt had highlighted, however briefly, the institutional, legal, and fiscal anomaly that was Wales. That anomaly could ultimately only be rectified by incorporating the country fully into the kingdom of England.

The revolt had also highlighted another issue—that of the status and legal position of Welshmen within Wales. The revolt put paid to any move towards dismantling the concepts and machinery of racial distinction in Wales. The Welsh had been shown in their true colours. They were not submissive and deferential natives. They were not even the merely troublesome and lightweight people of contemporary reputation. They were a perfidious people, on a par with 'the wild Irish, our enemies'. The reaction to their treachery vented itself in particular in parliament and manifested itself in the petitions, statutes, and ordinances issued against Welshmen as Welshmen, especially in 1401–2. No Welshman was henceforth to buy land in England or in English towns in Wales or to be accepted as a burgess; not even an English burgess who henceforth married a Welshwoman was to enjoy the privileges of burgess status. No Welshman was to hold any major office in Wales and the ban was extended to any Englishman married to a Welshwoman since the outbreak of the revolt. No Welshman was to carry arms in any town, market, church, assembly, or on a highway. No Welshman was to hold a castle, fortress, or defensible house, other than such as existed in the days of Edwrd I. The garrisons of castles and towns in Wales were to be composed of Englishmen, strangers to the district; they were not even to include men of mixed race. Finally, judicial discrimination was ensured in a statute that no Englishman was to be convicted in Wales by, or at the suit of, a Welshman.

This body of legislation was more comprehensive by far than any other issued hitherto on the legal disabilities of Welshmen. It was also more specifically racist in character, referring for example to 'an entire Welshman, born in Wales and having a mother and father born in Wales' and to 'men of the half-blood of the Welsh party'.[37] It was echoed in local directives, which may have been more truly effective in practice than general legislation. The steward of Cydweli was reminded in 1407 that no Welshman was to be allowed to hold office in the town or to carry arms within Wales; likewise at Brecon a year later it was decreed that no Welshman was to be a burgess, and in the confirmation of the town's charter in 1411 its liberties were henceforth specifically restricted to those 'whom we deem to be Englishmen and to such of their heirs as are English

---

[37] 2 Henry IV, c. 12; *Record of Caernarvon*, 240. The ordinances issued by Prince Henry's council in June 1401 even went so far as to forbid English men and women from marrying or consorting with Welsh women and men under pain of forfeiture.

both on their mother's and father's sides'.[38] Much of the legislation was no doubt occasioned by temporary hysteria; in practice much of it was quickly overlooked or ignored. Yet for decades it was to be invoked to embarrass Welshmen—to bar them from or to drive them out of office, to exclude them from enrolling as burgesses, to inhibit them from devising their lands by English law or from purchasing lands in England or in English boroughs in Wales, and to uphold the commercial privileges of those boroughs. Even successful and well-proven Welshmen had to secure licences and letters of denization in order to escape the terms of the legislation. That legislation entrenched and indeed sharpened the categorizations of a colonial society (much as the Statute of Kilkenny had done so in Ireland in 1366). It thereby formally ensconced some of the racial discrimination upon which the revolt of Glyn Dŵr had itself fed. It also provided the ingredients for a new mythology of deprivation and discrimination to add to an already centuries-old ideology of grievance, loss, and messianic deliverance. That mythology would only begin to wane when 'entire Welshmen' were placed on the same footing as 'entire Englishmen'. The revolt of Owain Glyn Dŵr, it may be argued, had postponed that process, at least statutorily, by a century. But it was also, as it proved, the last sustained native Welsh protest against the experience of conquest; the Welsh people would henceforth have to cultivate their identity as a people within the experience of conquest, not in protest against it.

[38] William Rees, 'The Charters of the Boroughs of Brecon and Llandovery', *BBCS* 2 (1923–5), 243–61 at p. 251. The charter granted to Welshpool in June 1406 was likewise restricted to those who were loyal to the king during the rebellion. It included several clauses directed against Welshmen, and decreed that henceforth cases in the borough court were only to be pleaded in French or English.

EPILOGUE

BY 1415 Wales had been conquered, finally and irreversibly. The story of that conquest dominated the history of the country for the 350 years covered by this volume. What was surprising was that conquest had taken so long. Already by 1093 the odds against the survival of Wales's political independence seemed hopeless. But the Welsh showed remarkable resourcefulness and resilience. For almost two centuries they survived and even, periodically, flourished. They took full advantage of their own terrain, climate, and hardiness; they exploited the lack of stamina and frequent diversions of the Anglo-Norman invaders; they capitalized on the domestic preoccupations and periodic impotence of the English monarchy. They did more: in the thirteenth century they deliberately cultivated an ideology of national unity and took the first tentative steps in laying the foundations of a native principality of Wales. Yet in truth, the chances of the survival of Wales, even of a truncated Wales, as an independent or quasi-independent political unit (or units) were virtually nil. Native Wales failed to develop the structures of authority, the traditions of loyalty and deference, the financial and territorial basis, the economic wealth, or the governmental framework to enable it to become a single polity. The attempts by the thirteenth-century princes of Gwynedd to make good these shortcomings were hurried, tentative, and ultimately unsuccessful. Even had they enjoyed more success, they could have done little more than delay Wales's ultimate political subjection. Once the English monarchy turned the full force of its attention and power onto native Wales, the days of its political independence would be numbered. The choice for its petty principalities lay between being reduced into dependent, client units or political extinction. The two devastating onslaughts of 1276–7 and 1282–3 showed how quickly and thoroughly the latter objective could be achieved.

Even the completion of the process of conquest did not bring political or governmental unity to Wales. Indeed, the country's natural particularism had been further entrenched by the piecemeal and protracted character of the Anglo-Norman conquest. The Statute of Rhuddlan might declare majestically in 1284 that 'the land of Wales' had been 'annexed and united . . . to the Crown of the realm as a member of the said body'. The truth was quite otherwise. The extinction of the native principality of Wales and of its dynasty in 1282–3 did not bring about either the unification of Wales within itself or its incorporation into the body of the English realm. Instead

Wales remained for the rest of the middle ages an ill-assorted jigsaw of private lordships and royal shires, lacking all unity in law and government. It was treated, in effect, as a collection of colonial annexes dependent on the Crown and higher aristocracy of England.

Its people were likewise treated anomalously. They were, ultimately, subjects of the king of England, yet they suffered, in the words of the Act of Union of 1536, from 'the distinction and diversity' drawn between them and the king's subjects in England. For all practical purposes they lay outside the legal, administrative, fiscal, and governmental framework of the English kingdom. Their native leaders were likewise excluded from most of the higher governmental offices within Wales and from participation in the political life of the kingdom of England, including its parliament. Within Wales itself, the sentiments of exclusion and inferiority were further nurtured by the legal privileges, commercial monopolies, and administrative liberties bestowed upon, and assiduously cultivated by, English settlers. Such 'distinction and diversity' were a sure recipe for a sense of alienation and deprivation. It was upon such discontent that the revolt of Owain Glyn Dŵr fed. His revolt was the massive protest of a conquered people against the experience and consequences of conquest.

The shadow of conquest lay heavily over the history of Wales in these centuries; but more important, ultimately, in the evolution of Welsh society was the settlement of peoples which came in the wake of that conquest. Between the late eleventh and early fourteenth century a major influx of alien colonists (in relation to the existing size of the population of Wales) settled in the country. This alien settlement was part of the movement of peoples in search of new lands common throughout much of Europe in these centuries. In Wales, as elsewhere, it was a movement undertaken under the aegis and within the framework of lordship; its aim was to underpin the process of military and political subjection. Its impact on the composition of the population of Wales was dramatic and permanent. In the southern coastal belt of the country and in the valleys of the south-east, the native population was displaced or reduced to a minority. From the twelfth century onwards the separate existence of these alien settlements was formally recognized in the creation of administrative districts called Welshries and Englishries and in the definition of the differences—legal, financial, tenurial, and commercial—between them. Such distinctions were employed to bolster privilege as well as to recognize diversity. Wales was now a country of two peoples, two cultures, two (or more) languages, and, in a measure, two social and economic formations. The two peoples were unequal in numbers, status, and authority: a small, settler minority enjoyed the power and privileges of a conquering élite over a conquered native population, deeply conscious of its past glory and present plight. Such a duality within the bounds of a small country created profound problems of loyalty and coexistence. On the degree to which those problems could be resolved, or at least reduced, would depend social peace and the assimilation of the two peoples. The revolt of Owain Glyn Dŵr showed that there was still a long way to go to achieve that goal.

In the three-and-a-half centuries which separated the death of Gruffudd ap Llywelyn (1063) from that of Owain Glyn Dŵr (c.1415) Wales had undergone a social and economic transformation that was arguably more profound and significant than the military and political conquest of these years. The dimensions of that transformation have often been underestimated by the artifical disjunction of political and social history and by fracturing the history of Wales along the lines of native power and alien settlement. If the history of the country is regarded as a whole, the nature of the transformation is more evident. A thinly populated and underdeveloped society, dominated by a class of warrior freemen or nobles, was gradually converted into a relatively well-settled country, served (especially in the south) by a network of small towns and market-centres. It was a country where the population and the area of cultivated land had grown rapidly, where the regular exploitation of a rural peasantry rather than the plunder of their animals and chattels was the mode of domination, where rural wealth circulated more freely than hitherto, and where money was becoming a unit of account and exchange. The pace of transformation naturally varied immensely from one part of Wales to another; indeed, in many respects the changes of these centuries served to deepen the regional differences within Wales. Yet by 1415 many of the major features of Welsh society and economy as they were to remain until the Industrial Revolution had already taken shape—the distribution of the population, the pattern of settlements, the forms and emphases of agriculture, the network of towns, the rhythm of markets, the lines of trade, and the distribution of wealth and power within society. Wales in 1415 bore closer resemblance to the Wales of George Owen of Henllys (1552–1613) or even Thomas Pennant (1726–98) than to the Wales of Gruffudd ap Llywelyn (d. 1063). In the process, Wales's ties with Ireland and with the western sea-ways of Britain declined markedly; Wales's orientation lay now firmly, if not exclusively, eastwards, towards England. Wales's military conquest therefore, was accompanied by a gradual process of social and economic assimilation which was laying the foundations for closer integration with England. Once that happened, the path back to native political independence would be closed.

Ecclesiastically, likewise, Wales by 1415 had become firmly part of the province of Canterbury and of the western church in general. Anomalies there still were in its religious practices and in some of its ecclesiastical institutions; but those anomalies were now little more than antiquarian curiosities or acceptable regional traits. From the level of the parish to that of the cathedral, in worship and religiosity, in the calendar of its saints, and in the forms of its monastic life, Wales's common heritage with the rest of western Christendom was now much more striking than were the differences. Owain Glyn Dŵr's so-called 'Pennal policy' of 1406 represented the last attempt for centuries to treat the church in Wales as a single, united national church. Ecclesiastical annexation was part of the price of political subjection. When the status of Wales as a 'separate nation' (L. *natio particularis*) was raised at the Council of Constance in 1417, the English spokesman asserted robustly that 'the whole of Wales was peacefully obedient in spiritual matters to the archbishop of Canterbury as its primate and in temporal matters to his most serene majesty the king'. This assertion of the effective incorporation of Wales ecclesiastically and politically into England was accompanied by the claim that England was to be equated with Britain (*'inclyta natio Anglicana alias Brytannica'*).[1] So had the English appropriated the mythology of an unitary empire of Britain, which had for so long been a source of memories, inspiration, and hope for the Welsh.

Wales in these centuries had also drawn closer culturally to England and to Europe. Its architecture and sculpture were largely derivative, often no more than late and mediocre reflections of those of England. Yet it preserved its pride in its linguistic unity and separateness, and it had in no way surrendered its own literary identity. Its literature had not yet lost the patronage or the confidence which were essential for it to thrive. It absorbed some of the current popular works, in religious and lay literature, from Latin and French; but it made them its own. It also collected and preserved its own treasures, literary and legal, particularly in the fourteenth century. Above all, within two generations or so of the Edwardian Conquest its poetry showed triumphantly how it could respond, in substance and form, to the challenge of a new world. The remarkable poetic renaissance, which spanned the generations from Dafydd ap Gwilym (*fl.* 1320–80) to Dafydd ab Edmwnd (*fl.* 1430–90), was the best possible answer to the question of whether military and political conquest would lead to cultural surrender.

Much the same could be said of the Welsh people's awareness of themselves as a single people. The Edwardian Conquest of 1277–83 had shattered any prospect of establishing a native, unitary Welsh polity; the eventual collapse of Glyn Dŵr's rebellion confirmed that there was no hope of resurrecting that polity, even in the most favourable of political circumstances. Wales had been reduced to a 'land' (*terra Wallie*), an annex of the kingdom of England. Yet the Welsh were, arguably, more sensible of their unity as a people in the fourteenth century that at any earlier stage

---

[1] A. O. H. Jarman, 'Wales and the Council of Constance', *BBCS* 14 (1950–2), 220–2.

in their history. Conquest and the experiences that came in its wake had been powerful catalysts in creating and sustaining that sensibility. So also had been the nurturing of a mythology of common descent, disinheritance, and expectation. The revolt of Owain Glyn Dŵr, whatever else it may have been and whatever other grievances and aspirations it drew upon, was ultimately founded on a vision of national unity and national deliverance. The failure of that revolt meant that the prospect of unitary native rule and political independence had gone for good. If the Welsh were to survive as a people, they would henceforth have to cultivate and sustain their identity, as in the past, by other means. In that sense, the collapse of Glyn Dŵr's revolt closed the era of conquest; it thereby inaugurated the prelude to the making of modern Wales.

THE DESCENT OF THE MAJOR ANGLO-NORMAN LORDSHIPS IN WALES 1086–1400

The following list lays no claims to comprehensiveness or finality. Its purpose is to help the reader to identify quickly the major changes in the descent of some of the main Anglo-Norman lordships in Wales in the period 1086–1400. Three major caveats need to be borne in mind using the list: (i) there are many uncertainties in our knowledge of the descent and control of several lordships in the period before 1200; (ii) Anglo-Norman control of many lordships was precarious well into the thirteenth century and was sometimes little more than nominal; (iii) no account is taken of minorities, custodies, and dower- or jointure-rights in lordships or of short periods of confiscations. A fully documented check-list of the descent and control of castles and lordships is an urgent desideratum of Welsh medieval scholarship.

Abbreviations used in this appendix:

    f.   = forfeiture

    m. -   = descent through marriage, either of daughter, grand-daughter, or sister of previous lord;

    o.s.p.   death without heir of the body

    o.s.p.m. death without surviving male heir of body

Where a valuation is quoted at the end of the entry, this represents an estimate of the yield of the lordship in the fourteenth century. (For sources see R. R. Davies, *Lordship and Society in the March of Wales 1284–1400*, pp. 196–8).

ABERGAVENNY (UPPER GWENT, GWENT UWCHCOED)

–temp Henry I:	Hamelin de Ballon
c.1119–41/2:	Brian fitz Count
1141/2–1165:	Miles of Gloucester, earl of Hereford, and his sons o.s.p.; m. -
1165–1230:	Braose o.s.p.m.; m. -
c.1240–73:	Cantilupe o.s.p.; m. -
1273–1389:	Hastings o.s.p.
1389–	Beauchamp (cadet branch)
Valuation:	£505–£667.

BLAENLLYFNI

–1165:	*see* BRECON; m. -
c.1190–1310:	Fitzherbert/Fitzpeter

1310–22:	Mortimer of Chirk, f.
1322–6:	Despenser jun., f.
1327–30:	Mortimer (of Wigmore), f.
1330–54:	Talbot
1354–	Mortimer

BRECON

c.1093–c.1125:	Bernard of Neufmarché o.s.p.m.; m. -
c.1125–65:	Miles of Gloucester, earl of Hereford, and his sons o.s.p.; m. -
c. 1165–1208; 1213–30:	Braose o.s.p.m.; m. -
1241–1373:	Bohun (except 1322–6), o.s.p.m.; m. -
1380–8:	Henry Bolingbroke, earl of Derby and later duke of Hereford
1399–	part of Duchy of Lancaster
Valuation:	£1,543

BROMFIELD AND YALE (MAELOR GYMRAEG A IÂL)

1282–1318; 1322–47:	Warenne o.s.p.; m. -
1318–22:	Thomas of Lancaster, f.
1347–97; 1399–	Fitzalan
Valuation:	£830–£967.

BUILTH (BUELLT)

c.1100–1208; 1213–30:	Braose o.s.p.m.
1230–42; 1256–77:	largely under control of native dynasty of Gwynedd
1242–56; 1277–	Crown or king's eldest son (as prince of Wales after 1301). Normally leased by the Crown to one of the Marcher families: Giffard, Bohun, and, especially, Mortimer
Valuation:	£200

CAERLEON AND USK (LOWER GWENT, GWENT ISCOED)

c.1086:	Thurstin fitz Rou
c.1090–c.1119:	Wynebald de Ballon and sons o.s.p.m.
c. 1119–38:	Walter fitz Richard of Clare o.s.p.;
? 1138–76:	Gilbert fitz Gilbert of Clare, earl of Pembroke (d. 1148/9), and his son Richard Strongbow o.s.p.m.; m. -
1189–1245:	Marshal o.s.p.m.; m. -
1245–1314:	Clare o.s.p.; m. -
1317–22:	Amory, f.;
1322–6:	Despenser jun., f.;
1327–60:	Elizabeth de Burgh, sister of last Clare and widow of Amory; o.s.p.m.; m. -
1360–8:	Lionel, duke of Clarence o.s.p.m.; m. -
1368–	Mortimer
Valuation:	£967

CANTREF BYCHAN (LLANYMDDYFRI)

c.1110–36; 1158–62:	Richard fitz Pons and his descendants known as Clifford,
1136–58; 1162–1282:	under control of native dynasty of Deheubarth
1283–99:	Giffard; m. -
1299–1391	Audley o.s.p.m.; m. -
1391–	Tuchet

CAUS

pre-1086–1322	Corbet o.s.p.m.; m. -
1347-	Stafford
Valuation:	£264

CEMAIS

c.1115–1326	Fitzmartin o.s.p.; m. -
1326–92	Audley o.s.p.; m. -
1392	Tuchet
Valuation:	£112

CERI AND CEDEWAIN

1279–	Mortimer (except for short periods of forfeiture)

CEREDIGION

1110–37	Gilbert fitz Richard of Clare and his son;
1137–1277/82	mainly under control of native dynasty of Deheubarth
1277/82–	Crown

CHEPSTOW (STRIGOIL)

c.1067–75	William fitz Osbern, earl of Hereford and his son Roger, f.
c.1080–96	William count of Eu, f.
c.1119–1245	as for CAERLEON and USK; m. -
1245–1306	Bigod o.s.p.;
1310–99	Thomas of Brotherton, (son of Edward I) earl of Norfolk, and his daughter Margaret, countess and later duchess of Norfolk, o.s.p.m.; m. -
1399–	Mowbray

CHIRKLAND

1282–1322	Roger Mortimer of Chirk, f.
1322–6	Fitzalan, f.
1327–30	Roger Mortimer of Wigmore, f.
1332–	Fitzalan (forfeited 1397–9)
Valuation	£500

CILGERRAN

See PEMBROKE

CLUN

pre-1086–*c.*1150	Say o.s.p.m.; m. -
*c.*1150/1202–	Fitzalan (except for brief periods of forfeiture)
Valuation:	£251–£398

CYDWELI (Kidwelly)

*c.*1106– ?*c.*1130:	Roger, bishop of Salisbury,
?*c.*1130–1216:	Londres o.s.p.m.; m. -
1245–83:	Chaworth o.s.p.m.; m. -
1296–1361	Henry (d. 1345) younger son of Edmund, earl of Lancaster (d. 1296), and his son Henry, duke of Lancaster (d. 1361) o.s.p.m.; m. -
1361–99	John of Gaunt, duke of Lancaster
1399–	part of Duchy of Lancaster
Valuation:	£520

DENBIGH

1282–1311	Lacy o.s.p.m.; m. -
1311–22	Thomas, earl of Lancaster, f.
1322–6	Hugh Despenser sen., f.
1327–30	Roger Mortimer of Wigmore, f.
1332–54	Montague
1355–	Mortimer (of Wigmore)
Valuation	£1,000 +

DYFFRYN CLWYD

1282	Grey, in senior line until 1323; in junior line (the Greys of Ruthin) thereafter
Valuation	£492–£545

ELFAEL

?*c.*1100–1208; 1213–30	Braose o.s.p.m.; m. -
1233–1309	Tony o.s.p.m.; m. -
1309–15; 1337–	Beauchamp
Valuation	£194

EWYAS LACY

pre-1086–1095	Lacy, f.;
1095–*c.*1121	junior line of Lacy o.s.p.m.; m. -
*c.*1121–37	Payn Fitz John o.s.p.m.; m. -
1137–55	Roger son of Miles of Gloucester o.s.p.;
*c.*1155–1241	Lacy o.s.p.m.;
1241–1314	(a) Geneville o.s.p.m.; m. -
1314–	Mortimer
1241–1316	(b) Verdon o.s.p.m.; m. -
1316–69	Burghersh o.s.p.m.; m. -
1369–	Despenser

GLAMORGAN (Morgannwg)

c.1090–1107	Robert fitz Hamo o.s.p.m.; m. -
c.1121–83	Robert earl of Gloucester (d. 1147) and his son William (d. 1183); o.s.p.m.; m. -
1189–1216	John, count of Mortain, later king of England
1217–1314	Clare o.s.p.; m. -
1317–26, 1337–	Despenser
Valuation	£1,276

GOWER (Gŵyr)

c.1107–84	Beaumont o.s.p.
1203–8; 1213–1322	Braose m. -
1322–6	Hugh Despenser jnr. f.
1331–54	Mowbray
1354–97	Beauchamp
1397–	Mowbray
Valuation	£386

HAVERFORD

–1245	*see* PEMBROKE; m. -
1245–89	Bohun and Mortimer
1289–1308	Crown
1308–24	Valence
1324–	Crown or Prince of Wales
Valuation	£161

ISCENNEN

1282–1322	Giffard, f.
1322–6	Despenser, jun., f.
1327–37	Crown
1337–40	Wylington
1340–61	Lancaster o.s.p.m.; m. -
1361–99	John of Gaunt, duke of Lancaster
1399–	part of Duchy of Lancaster
Valuation	£158

KIDWELLY

See CYDWELI

LAUGHARNE

See TALACHARN

LLANSTEFFAN

temp. Henry I–c.1190	Marmion o.s.p.m.; m. -
c.1190–1338	Camville o.s.p.m.;
1338–77, 1391–	Penres

MAELIENYDD, GWRTHEYRNION, CWMWD DEUDDWR

c. 1100–1277	Held spasmodically by Mortimer
1277–1322, 1327–	Mortimer
Valuation	£334

MOLDSDALE AND HAWARDEN

twelfth century–1329	Montalt o.s.p.;
1329–37	Crown
1337–	Montague

MONMOUTH AND THREECASTLES

pre 1086–1256	William fitz Baderon and his descendants who assumed the surname 'de Monmouth'
1256–67	Lord Edward, son of Henry III
1267–1361	Edmund of Lancaster, son of Henry III, and his descendants in the cadet line o.s.p.m.; m. -
1361–99	John of Gaunt, duke of Lancaster
1399–	part of Duchy of Lancaster
Valuation	£527

MONTGOMERY

*c.*1070–1102	Montgomery, earls of Shrewsbury, f.;
*c.*1110 ?–1207	Bollers o.s.p.;
1214–	Crown or eldest son of King. Frequently leased to family of Mortimer

NEWPORT (Gwynllŵg)

–1314	*See* GLAMORGAN, m. -
1317–18	Audley
1318–26	Despenser jnr. f.
1327–47	Audley o.s.p.m.; m. -
1347–	Stafford
Valuation	£537

OSWESTRY

*c.*1080– *temp.* Henry I	Rainald of Bailleul and son
temp. Henry I–	Fitzalan (forfeitures 1327–30, 1397–99)
Valuation	£376

PEMBROKE

1093–1102	Arnulf of Montgomery f.
1102–38	Crown
1138–76	Gilbert fitz Gilbert of Clare and descendants o.s.p.; m. -
1189–1245	Marshal o.s.p.m.; m. -
1247–1324	Valence o.s.p.; m. -
1339–89	Hastings o.s.p.;

| 1389– | Crown |
| *Valuation* | £320 |

RADNOR

*c.*1095–1230	Braose o.s.p.;
1230–	Mortimer
Valuation	(with Gwrtheyrnion) £314

TALACHARN (Laugharne)

| ? twelfth century–1390 | Brian |
| 1390– | Scrope |

USK

See CAERLEON

BIBLIOGRAPHY

PRIMARY SOURCES

A. 1063–1282
  1. General
  2. Narrative Sources
    2.1 Narrative Sources written in Wales
    2.2 Narrative Sources written in England
    2.3 Other narrative and literary sources
  3. Record Sources
    3.1 Welsh secular record sources
    3.2 English government records and collections
    3.3 Miscellaneous baronial record sources
    3.4 Record Sources: ecclesiastical
    3.5 Other Record Sources
  4. Texts of Medieval Welsh Law
  5. Literary Sources
  6. Antiquarian Works and Genealogies
  7. Commentaries on Sources

B. 1282–1415
  1. Narrative Sources
  2. Official Sources
    2.1 General
    2.2 Surveys and Extents
    2.3 Financial Records
    2.4 Judicial Records
    2.5 Other miscellaneous record sources
    2.6 Ecclesiastical Records
  3. Literary Sources

SECONDARY SOURCES

A. BIBLIOGRAPHIES

B. WORKS OF REFERENCE
  1. General
  2. Atlases, Dictionaries and Gazetteers
  3. General Periodicals
  4. Local Periodicals

C. GENERAL WORKS

1. Relating to Wales as a whole
2. Works on local history

D. GENERAL AND POLITICAL HISTORY

1. Native Wales to 1272
2. The Anglo-Norman Settlement of Wales (to 1272)
3. Royal Policy in Wales 1066–1272
4. Edwardian Conquest and Settlement and Native Response 1272–1317
5. Wales in the Fourteenth Century
6. The Revolt of Owain Glyn Dŵr

E. ECONOMY AND SOCIETY

1. General
2. Agriculture and Rural Life
3. Settlement Patterns and Land Tenure
4. Economic Developments in the Later Middle Ages
5. Towns, Trade and Industry
6. Social Bonds and Perceptions
7. Native Welsh Law

F. CHURCH AND RELIGION

1. General
2. The Secular Church
3. The Monastic Orders
4. Religious Devotion

G. LITERATURE AND CULTURE

1. Latin and French Literature in Wales
2. Native Welsh Literature
3. Place- and Personal-Names
4. Architecture, Sculpture and Artefacts

This bibliography lays no claim to being comprehensive. Its aim is to provide the reader with a guide to the main printed primary and secondary sources upon which this volume has been based. It should also thereby serve to indicate to the reader the most obvious bibliographical routes to follow should he wish to pursue a topic discussed in the volume. Works cited refer almost exclusively to Wales itself. This is inevitable for reasons of space; but the reader should be aware that some of the most fruitful approaches to, and questions about, medieval Welsh society arise from comparisons and contrasts with other medieval societies. Indeed, one of the aims of the present volume, as indeed of the series to which it belongs, has been to bring the history of Wales out of isolation to which it has too often been consigned and to which its own practitioners seem sometimes to have been anxious to consign it.

All works published in London, unless otherwise stated.

PRIMARY SOURCES

A. 1063–1282

1. *General*

A Calendar of the Public Records relating to Pembrokeshire, ed. H. Owen. 3 vols. (Cymmrodorion Record Series, 1914–18)
A Catalogue of the Manuscripts relating to Wales in the British Museum, ed. E. Owen. 4 vols. (Cymmrodorion Record Series, 1900–22)
A Source-Book of Welsh History, ed. Mary A. Salmon (1927)

2. *Narrative sources*

2.1 *Narrative sources written in Wales*

Annales Cambrie, ed. J. Williams ab Ithel (Rolls Series, 1860)
'Annales de Margam, 1066–1232', *Annales Monastici*, i, ed. H. R. Luard (Rolls Series, 1864)
Brenhinedd y Saeson or The Kings of the Saxons, ed. and trans. T. Jones (Cardiff, 1971)
Brut y Tywysogyon. Peniarth Ms. 20 version, ed. T. Jones (Cardiff, 1941)
Brut y Tywysogyon or The Chronicle of the Princes. Peniarth Ms. 20 version, ed. and trans. T. Jones (Cardiff, 1952)
Brut y Tywysogyon or The Chronicle of the Princes. Red Book of Hergest Version, ed. and trans. T. Jones (Cardiff, 1955)
'Cronica de Wallia and other documents from Exeter Library MS. 3514', ed. T. Jones, *BBCS* 12 (1946–8), 27–44
Historia Gruffud vab Kenan, ed. D. Simon Evans (Cardiff, 1971)
History of Gruffydd ap Cynan (1054–1137), ed. and trans. A. Jones (Manchester, 1910)

2.2 *Narrative sources written in England*

Most chronicles written in England during this period contain some reference to events in Wales; but only those which contribute substantially to the construction of a narrative of events in Wales are listed here.

Anglo-Saxon Chronicle, ed. D. Whitelock *et al.* (1965); or ed. G. N. Garmonsway (2nd edn. 1973)
Annales Cestrienses, ed. and trans. R. C. Christie (Lancashire and Cheshire Record Society, 1887)
Annales Monastici, ed. H. R. Luard. 5 vols. (Rolls Series, 1864–9), esp. the annals of Dunstable, Tewkesbury, Waverley, Winchester, and Worcester.
Chronicles of the Reigns of Stephen, Henry II and Richard I, ed. R. Howlett. 4 vols. (Rolls Series, 1884–9)
Chronicles of the Reigns of Edward I and Edward II, ed. W. Stubbs. 2 vols. (Rolls Series, 1882–3)

Chronicon ex chronicis, ed. B. Thorpe. 2 vols. (English Historical Society 1848–9)

Dickinson, J. C. and Ricketts, P. T., 'The Anglo-Norman Chronicle of Wigmore Abbey', *Trans. Woolhope Field Club* 39 (1969), 413–46

Flores Historiarum, ed. H. R. Luard. 3 vols. (Rolls Series, 1890)

Gervase of Canterbury, *Historical Works*, ed. W. Stubbs. 2 vols. (Rolls Series, 1879–80)

Gesta Regis Henrici Secundi, ed. W. Stubbs. 2 vols. (Rolls Series, 1867)

Gesta Stephani, ed. and trans. K. R. Potter and R. H. C. Davis (2nd edn. Oxford, 1976)

Henry of Huntingdon, *Historia Anglorum*, ed. T. Arnold (Rolls Series, 1879)

Matthew Paris, *Chronica Majora*, ed. H. R. Luard. 7 vols. (Rolls Series, 1872–83)

Orderic Vitalis, *Historia Ecclesiastica*, ed. and trans. M. Chibnall. 6 vols. (Oxford, 1969–80)

Ralph of Coggeshall, *Chronicon Anglicanum*, ed. J. Stevenson (Rolls Series, 1875)

Ralph of Diceto, *Opera Historica*, ed. W. Stubbs. 2 vols. (Rolls Series, 1876)

Roger of Howden, *Chronica*, ed. W. Stubbs. 4 vols. (Rolls Series, 1867–71)

Roger of Wendover, *Chronica*, ed. H. O. Coxe. 4 vols. (English Historical Society, 1841–4)

'Walter of Coventry', *Historical Collections*, ed. W. Stubbs. 2 vols. (Rolls Series, 1872–3)

2.3 Other narrative and literary sources

Gerald of Wales, *Opera*, ed. J. S. Brewer, J. F. Dimock, and G. F. Warner. 8 vols. (Rolls Series, 1861–91). The Itinerary through Wales and The Description of Wales are published in vol. vi. There are various English translations, of which the most recent is by Lewis Thorpe (Harmondsworth, 1978)

— *Speculum Duorum*, ed. M. Richter *et al.* (Cardiff, 1974)

— *The Autobiography of Giraldus Cambrensis*, ed. and trans. H. E. Butler (1937)

— 'De Invectionibus', ed. W. S. Davies, *Y Cymmrodor*, 30 (1920)

John of Salisbury, *Letters*, ed. W. J. Millor, H. E. Butler, C. N. L. Brooke. 2 vols. (1955–78)

Rhigyfarch, *Life of St. David*, ed. J. W. James (Cardiff, 1967). For an English translation see A. W. Wade-Evans in *Y Cymmrodor*, 24 (1913), 1–73

Vitae Sanctorum Britanniae et Genealogiae, ed. A. W. Wade-Evans (Cardiff, 1944)

Walter Map, *De Nugis Curialium*, ed. and trans. M. R. James, J. E. Lloyd, and E. S. Hartland (Cymmrodorion Record Series, 1923); new edn. by C. N. L. Brooke and R. A. B. Mynors (Oxford, 1983)

3. Record Sources

3.1 Welsh secular record sources

Davies, J. Conway, 'A Grant by David ap Gruffydd', *NLWJ* 3 (1943–4), 29–32

— 'A Grant by Llywelyn ap Gruffydd', *NLWJ* 3 (1943–4), 158–62

Gresham, C. A. 'The Aberconwy Charter', *Arch. Camb.* 94 (1939), 123–62; also *BBCS* 30 (1982–3), 311–47

Jones, E. D., Davies, N. G., Roberts, R. F., 'Five Strata Marcella Charters', *NLWJ* 5 (1947–8), 50–4

Williams-Jones, K., 'Llywelyn's Charter to Cymer Abbey in 1209', *Jour. Merioneth Hist. Soc.* 3 (1957) 45–78

'Wynnstay Mss.: Charters of Trefeglwys', *Arch. Camb.*, 3rd ser., 6 (1860), 330–3

See also below 3.2 and 3.4

3.2 *English royal government records and collections*

Abbreviatio Placitorum (Record Commn., 1811)

Book of Fees 1198–1223, 3 vols. (1921–31)

Calendar of Ancient Correspondence concerning Wales, ed. J. G. Edwards (Cardiff, 1935)

Calendar of Chancery Warrants 1244–1326 (1927)

Calendar of Close Rolls 1272–1422 (1900–32)

Calendar of Fine Rolls 1272–1471 (1911–49)

Calendar of Inquisitions Miscellaneous 1216–1422 (1916–68)

Calendar of Inquisitions Post Mortem 1216–1392 (1898–1974)

Calendar of Liberate Rolls 1226–1272 (1916–64)

Calendar of Patent Rolls 1232–1422 (1906–11)

Calendar of Various Chancery Rolls: Supplementary Close Rolls, Welsh Rolls, Scutage Rolls 1277–1326 (1912)

Calendar of Charter Rolls 1266–1516 (1903–27)

Catalogue of Ancient Deeds. 6 vols. (1899–1915)

Close Rolls 1227–1272 (1902–38)

Curia Regis Rolls 1199–1242 (1922–79)

Diplomatic Documents 1101–1272, ed. P. Chaplais (1964)

Documents of the Baronial Movement of Reform and Rebellion, ed. R. F. Treharne and I. J. Sanders (Oxford, 1973)

Domesday Book, 4 vols. (Record Commn., 1783–1816)

Foedera, Conventiones, Litterae, etc. ed. T. Rymer (revised edn. 4 vols. in 7 parts. Record Commn., 1816–69)

Issues of the Exchequer, Henry III–Henry VI, ed. F. Devon (Record Commn., 1847)

Littere Wallie, preserved in Liber A in the Public Record Office, ed. J. G. Edwards (Cardiff, 1935)

Patent Rolls 1216–32 (1901–3)

Pipe Rolls 31 Henry I, ed. J. Hunter (1833, rep. 1929)

Pipe Rolls 2, 3, 4 Henry II, ed. J. Hunter (1844)

Pipe Rolls 5 Henry II– (Pipe Roll Society 1884–)

Red Book of the Exchequer, ed. H. Hall. 3 vols. (Rolls Series, 1896)

Regesta Regum Anglo-Normannorum 1066–1154, 4 vols. (Oxford, 1913–69)

Rotuli Chartarum 1199–1216, ed. T. D. Hardy (Record Commn., 1837)

Rotuli Curiae Regis 1194–9, ed. F. Palgrave (Record Commn., 1835)

Rotuli de Oblatis et Finibus . . . regis Johannis, ed. T. D. Hardy (Record Commn., 1835)

Rotuli Litterarum Clausarum 1204–27, ed. T. D. Hardy (Record Commn., 1833–44)

Rotuli Litterarum Patentium 1201–16, ed. T. D. Hardy (Record Commn., 1835)

Rotuli Parliamentorum, 7 vols. (Record Commn., 1783–1832)
Royal and other Historical Letters illustrative of the Reign of Henry III, 2 vols. (Rolls Series, 1862–6)
Treaty Rolls 1234–1325, I–II, ed. P. Chaplais (1955–72)
The Welsh Assize Roll 1277–84, ed. J. Conway Davies (Cardiff, 1940)

3.3 *Miscellaneous baronial record sources*

'Accounts of the ministers for the lordships of Abergavenny and Three Castles 1256–7', ed. A. J. Roderick and W. Rees, *South Wales and Monmouth Record Society* 2 (1950), 67–125; 3 (1954), 21–47; 4 (1957), 5–29,
Cartae et alia Munimenta quae ad Dominium de Glamorgancia pertinent, ed. G. T. Clark, 6 vols. (2nd edn. Cardiff, 1910)
'Charters of the Earldom of Hereford, 1095–1201', ed. D. G. Walker, *Camden Miscellany* 2 (1964), 1–75
Earldom of Gloucester Charters. The Charters and Scribes of the Earls and Countesses of Gloucester to A.D. 1217, ed. R. B. Patterson (Oxford, 1973)

3.4 *Record Sources: ecclesiastical (including monastic)*

Calendar of entries in the Papal Registers relating to Great Britain and Ireland: Papal Letters, 5 vols. (1893–1904), *Petitions to the Pope* (1896)
'Cartularium prioratus S. Johannis evangelistae de Brecon', ed. R. W. Banks, *Arch. Camb.*, 4th ser., 13 (1882), 275–308; 14 (1883), 18–49, 137–68, 221–36, 274–311
Cartularium S. Johannis Baptistae de Carmarthen, ed. T. Philips (Cheltenham, 1865)
Cartulary of Haughmond Abbey, ed. Una Rees (Cardiff, 1985)
Cartulary of Shrewsbury Abbey, ed. Una Rees. 2 vols. (Aberystwyth, 1975)
Charles, B. G. 'An Early Charter of the Abbey of Cwmhir', *Trans. Radnorshire Soc.*, 40 (1970), 68–73
Councils and Ecclesiastical Documents relating to Great Britain and Ireland, ed. A. W. Haddan and W. Stubbs. 3 vols. (Oxford, 1869–78)
Councils and Synods 1205–1313, ed. F. M. Powicke and C. R. Cheney (Oxford, 1964)
Davies, J. Conway, 'Ewenni priory: some recently-found records', *NLWJ* 3 (1943–4), 107–37
— 'Records of the Abbey of Ystrad Marchell', *Montgomeryshire Colls.* 51 (1949–50), 3–21, 164–87
Davies, Wendy E., *The Llandaff Charters* (Aberystwyth, 1979)
Descriptive Catalogue of the Penrice and Margam Abbey Manuscripts, ed. W. de Gray Birch. 6 vols. (1893–1905)
Episcopal Acts and cognate documents relating to Welsh Dioceses 1066–1272, ed. J. Conway Davies. 2 vols. (Historical Society of the Church in Wales, Cardiff, 1948–53)
Historia et Cartularium Monasterii S. Petri, Gloucestriae, ed. W. H. Hart. 3 vols. (Rolls Series, 1863–7)
Jones, E. D., Davies, N. G., Roberts, R. F., 'Five Strata Marcella Charters', *NLWJ* 5 (1947–8), 50–4

Jones, O. E., 'Llyfr Coch Asaph. A Textual and Historical Study' (MA thesis, Univ. of Wales, 1968)

Letters of Pope Innocent III (1198–1216) concerning England and Wales. A Calendar with an Appendix of Texts. Ed. C. R. and M. G. Cheney (Oxford, 1967)

Liber Landavensis. The Text of the Book of Llan Dav, ed. J. Gwenogvryn Evans and J. Rhys (Oxford, 1893; reissued Aberystwyth, 1979)

Monasticon Anglicanum, ed. W. Dugdale. Rev. edn. by J. Cayley *et al.* 6 vols. in 8 parts (1817–30)

Morgan, R., 'An Early Charter of Llanllugan Nunnery', *Montgomeryshire Colls.* 73 (1983), 116–19

'Register of Aberconway', ed. H. Ellis, *Camden Miscellany* I (1847), 1–23

Registrum epistolarum fratris Johannis Peckham, ed. C. T. Martin. 3 vols. (Rolls Series, 1882–5)

Tibbot, G. 'An Abbey Cwmhir Relic Abroad', *Trans. Radnorshire Soc.* 6 (1935), 64–7

Valuation of Norwich, ed. W. E. Lunt (Oxford, 1926)

Worcester Cartulary, ed. R. R. Darlington (Pipe Roll Society, 1968)

3.5 *Other Record Sources*

Ancient Charters Royal and Private prior to A.D. 1200, ed. J. H. Round (Pipe Roll Society, 1888)

British Borough Charters, 1042–1660, ed. A. Ballard, J. Tait, and M. Weinbaum. 3 vols. (Cambridge, 1913–43)

Calendar of Documents preserved in France 918–1206, ed. J. H. Round (1899)

4. *Texts of Medieval Welsh Law*

Ancient Laws and Institutes of Wales, ed. and trans. Aneirin Owen (Record Commn., 1841)

Cyfreithiau Hywel Dda o Lawysgrif Coleg yr Iesu, Rhydychen, LVII, ed. M. Richards (Cardiff, 1957)

Damweiniau Colan, ed. D. Jenkins (Aberystwyth, 1973)

Facsimile of the Chirk Codex of the Welsh Laws, ed. J. Gwenogvryn Evans (Llanbedrog, 1908)

The Latin Texts of the Welsh Laws, ed. H. D. Emanuel (Cardiff, 1967)

The Laws of Howel Dda, ed. T. Lewis (1912)

The Laws of Hywel Dda, ed. and trans. Melville Richards (Liverpool, 1954)

Llyfr Blegywryd, ed. S. J. Williams and J. E. Powell (3nd edn. Cardiff, 1961)

Llyfr Colan, ed. D. Jenkins (Cardiff, 1963)

Llyfr Iorwerth, ed. A. R. Wiliam (Cardiff, 1960)

Welsh Medieval Law, ed. A. W. Wade-Evans (Oxford, 1909)

5. *Literary Sources*

The list in this section, as in the section on secondary works on literature, is highly selective. Comprehensive lists of texts and commentaries will be found in *Llyfryddiaeth Llenyddiaeth Gymraeg*, ed. T. Parry and M. Morgan (Cardiff, 1976) with supplement in *BBCS* 30 (1982–3), 55–121

Breudwyt Ronabwy, ed. M. Richards (Cardiff, 1948)

Brut Dingestow, ed. H. Lewis (Cardiff, 1942)

Brut y Brenhinedd. Llanstephan Ms. 1 Version, ed. B. F. Roberts (Dublin, 1971)

Clancy, J. P., *Medieval Welsh Lyrics* (1965)

— *The Earliest Welsh Poetry* (1970)

Fouke le Fitzwaryn, ed. E. J. Hathaway and others (Anglo-Norman Text Society, 1971)

Geoffrey of Monmouth, *The Historia Regum Britanniae*, ed. A. Griscom (New York, 1929)

— *History of the Kings of Britain*, ed. and trans. Lewis Thorpe (Harmondsworth, 1966)

— *Life of Merlin*, ed. B. Clarke (Cardiff, 1973)

Gruffydd, R. G., 'A Poem in Praise of Cuhelyn Fardd from the Black Book of Carmarthen', *Studia Celtica* 10–11 (1975–6), 198–209.

Hen Gerddi Crefyddol, ed. H. Lewis (Cardiff, 1931)

Llawysgrif Hendregadredd, ed. J. Morris-Jones and T. H. Parry-Williams (Cardiff, 1933)

Llyfr Du Caerfyrddin, ed. A. O. H. Jarman (Cardiff, 1982)

Llyfr Gwyn Rhydderch: Y Chwedlau a'r Rhamantau, ed. R. M. Jones (Cardiff, 1973)

The Myvyrian Archaiology of Wales, ed. O. Jones, E. Williams, and W. Owen (2nd edn. Denbigh, 1870)

The Oxford Book of Welsh Verse, ed. T. Parry (Oxford, 1962)

The Oxford Book of Welsh Verse in English, ed. G. Jones (Oxford, 1977)

Pedeir Keinc y Mabinogi, ed. I. Williams (2nd edn. Cardiff, 1951) Among the many English translations of the medieval Welsh prose tales the most accessible is *The Mabinogion*, ed. Gwyn and Thomas Jones (1949). The most recent version in modern Welsh (with a valuable introduction by B. F. Roberts) is by Dafydd and Rhiannon Ifans (Llandysul, 1980)

Poetry in the Red Book of Hergest, ed. J. Gwenogvryn Evans (Llanbedrog, 1911)

Roberts, B. F., 'Dwy Awdl Hywel Foel ap Griffri', *Bardos*, ed. R. Geraint Gruffydd (Cardiff, 1982), 60–75

The Text of the Mabinogion and other Welsh Tales from the Red Book of Hergest, ed. J. Rhŷs and J. Gwenogvryn Evans (Oxford, 1887)

Trioedd Ynys Prydein. The Welsh Triads, ed. Rachel Bromwich (2nd edn. Cardiff, 1978)

6. *Antiquarian Works and Genealogies*

Bartrum, P. C., 'Notes on the Welsh Genealogical Manuscripts', *Trans. Cymm. Soc.* 1968, 1, 63–98; 1976, 102–8.

— *Early Welsh Genealogical Tracts* (Cardiff, 1966)

— *Welsh Genealogies A.D. 300–1400*, 8 vols. (Cardiff, 1974)

— *Welsh Genealogies A.D. 1400–1500*, 18 vols. (Aberystwyth, 1983)

Dwnn, Lewys, *Heraldic Visitations of Wales*, ed. S. R. Meyrick. 2 vols. (Llandovery, 1846)

Leland, J., *The Itinerary in Wales in or about the years 1536–9*, ed. L. Toulmin Smith (1906)

Lewis Rice, 'A Breviat of Glamorgan 1596–1600', ed. W. Rees, *South Wales and Monmouth Record Society* 3 (1954), 92–150

Merrick, Rice, *A Booke of Glamorganshire Antiquities*, ed. J. A. Corbett (1887); also ed. B. L. James (Barry, 1983)

Owen, George, *The Description of Pembrokeshire*, ed. H. Owen. 4 vols. (Cymmrodorion Record Society, 1902–36)

Pennant, Thomas, *Tours in Wales 1770–73*, ed. J. Rhŷs. 3 vols. (Caernarfon, 1883)

Powel, David, *The Historie of Cambria* (1884), ed. W. Wynne (1784)

Wynn, John, *History of the Gwydir Family*, ed. J. Ballinger (Cardiff, 1927)

7. Commentaries on Sources

Borst, K. G. 'A Reconsideration of the *Vita Sancti Cadoci*', *Celtic Folklore and Christianity*, ed. P. K. Ford (Santa Barbara, 1983), 1–15

Brooke, C. N. L., 'The Archbishops of St. David's, Llandaff and Caerleon-on-Usk', *Studies in the Early British Church*, ed. N. K. Chadwick *et al.* (Cambridge, 1958), 201–42

— 'St. Peter of Gloucester and St. Cadoc of Llancarfan', *Celt and Saxon. Studies in the Early British Border*, ed. N. K. Chadwick (Cambridge, 1963), 260–76

Davies, Wendy E., 'Saint Mary's Worcester and the *Liber Landavensis*', *Journal of the Society of Archivists* 4 (1970–3), 459–85

— '*Liber Landavensis*. Its Construction and Credibility', *EHR* 88 (1973), 335–51

Elton, G. R., *The Sources of History. England 1200–1640* (1969)

Emanuel, H. D., 'An Analysis of the Composition of the *Vita Cadoci*', *NLWJ* 7 (1951–2), 217–27

Evans, D. L., 'Llyfr Coch Asaph', *NLWJ* 4 (1945–6), 177–83

Greenway, W., 'The Annals of Margam', *Trans. Port Talbot Hist. Soc.* 1 (1963–7), 19–31

Harris, S. M., 'The Kalendar of the *Vitae Sanctorum Wallensium*', *Journal Hist. Soc. Church in Wales* 3 (1953), 3–53

Hughes, Kathleen, 'The Welsh Latin Chronicles: *Annales Cambrie* and Related Texts', *Proc. British Academy*, 59 (1973), 233–58 (for an important review see D. M. Dumville in *Studia Celtica* 12–13 (1977–8), 461–7).

Jack, R. I., *The Sources of History. Medieval Wales* (1972)

Jones, E. D., 'The Book of Llandaff', *NLWJ* 4 (1945–6), 122–57

Jones, T., 'Historical Writing in Medieval Welsh', *Scottish Studies* 12 (1968), 15–27

Kirby, D. P., 'A Note on Rhigyfarch's Life of St David', *WHR* 4 (1968–9), 292–9

Lewis, C. W., 'The *Liber Landavensis* and the Diocese of Llandaff', *Morgannwg* 4 (1960), 50–65

Lloyd, J. E., 'The Text of Mss. B. and C. of *Annales Cambrie* for the period 1035–93 in parallel columns', *Trans. Cymm. Soc.* 1899–1900, 165–79

— 'The Welsh Chronicles', *Proc. British Academy* 14 (1928), 369–91

B. 1282–1415

Sources which cover the pre-1282 as well as the post-1282 period are normally referred to in Section A above.

1. *Narrative Sources*

See also Section A.2 above.

Adam of Usk, *Chronicon*, ed. and trans. E. Maunde Thompson (2nd. edn. 1904)
Bartholomew de Cotton, *Historia Anglicana*, ed. H. R. Luard (Rolls Series, 1859)
Chronicle of Bury St. Edmunds 1212–1301, ed. Antonia Gransden (1964)
Eulogium Historiarum, ed. F. S. Haydon. 3 vols. (Rolls Series, 1858–63)
Historia Vitae et Regni Ricardi Secundi, ed. G. B. Stow, jun. (Pennsylvania, 1977)
Nicholas Trevet, *Annales*, ed. T. Hog (English Historical Society, 1845)
Pierre de Langtoft, *Chronicle*, ed. T. Wright. 2 vols. (Rolls Series, 1846–8)
Ranulph Higden, *Polychronicon*, ed. C. Babington and J. R. Lumby. 9 vols. (Rolls Series, 1865–86)
Thomas Walsingham, *Historia Anglicana*, ed. H. T. Riley. 2 vols. (Rolls Series, 1863–4)
— *Annales Ricardi Secundi et Henrici Quarti*, ed. H. T. Riley (Rolls Series, 1866)
Vita Edwardi Secundi, ed. N. Denholm-Young (Oxford, 1957)
Walter of Guisborough, *Chronicle*, ed. H. Rothwell (Camden Society, 1957)
'Wigmore Chronicle', *Monasticon Anglicanum*, ed. W. Dugdale (2nd edn. 1817–30), VI, i, 348–55
'A Wigmore Chronicle', ed. J. Taylor, *Proc. Leeds Philosophical and Literary Society* 11 (1964–6), 84–6

2. *Official Sources, Records, Letters, etc.*

2.1 *General*

See also Section A.3 above.

Anglo-Norman Letters and Petitions from All Souls Ms. 182, ed. M. D. Legge (Anglo-Norman Text Society, 1941)
Antient Kalendars and Inventories of the Treasury of His Majesty's Exchequer, ed. F. Palgrave (Record Commn., 1836)
Book of Prests of the King's Wardrobe for 1294–5, presented to J. Goronwy Edwards, ed. E. B. Fryde (Oxford, 1962)
Calendar of Ancient Petitions relating to Wales, ed. W. Rees (Cardiff, 1975)
Documents Illustrative of English History in the Thirteenth and Fourteenth Centuries, ed. H. Cole (Recod Commn., 1844)
Feudal Aids, 6 vols. (1899–1920)
Issues of the Exchequer, Henry III–Henry VI, ed. F. Devon (Record Commn., 1837)
John of Gaunt's Register 1372–6, ed. S. Armitage-Smith. 2 vols. (Camden Society, 1911), *1379–83*, ed. E. C. Lodge and R. Somerville. 2 vols. (Camden Society, 1937)
Letters of Edward, Prince of Wales 1304–5, ed. H. Johnstone (Roxburghe Club, 1931)
List of Welsh Entries in the Memoranda Rolls 1282–1343, ed. N. M. Fryde (Cardiff, 1974)

'Original Documents' published as a supplement to *Archaeologia Cambrensis* 1877, 1879

Original Letters illustrative of English History, 2nd ser., ed. H. Ellis. 4 vols. (1827)

Placita de Quo Warranto (Record Commn., 1818)

Proceedings and Ordinances of the Privy Council, ed. N. H. Nicolas. 7 vols. (Record Commn., 1834–7)

'Recognizance Rolls of the Palatinate of Chester', *Annual Report of the Deputy Keeper of the Public Records* 2 (1875), Appendix

Register of Edward the Black Prince, 4 vols. (1930–3)

Royal and Historical Letters during the Reign of Henry IV, ed. F. C. Hingeston. 2 vols. (Rolls Series, 1860, 1965)

Statutes of the Realm (Record Commn., 1810–28)

Statutes of Wales, ed. I. Bowen (1908)

Welsh Records in Paris, ed. T. Matthews (Carmarthen, 1910)

2.2 *Surveys and Extents*

The Black Book of St. David's 1326, ed. J. W. Willis-Bund (Cymmrodorion Record Series, 1902)

The Extent of Chirkland (1391–3), ed. G. P. Jones (Liverpool, 1933)

'Extent of Merionethshire *temp*. Edward I', *Arch. Camb.*, 3rd ser., 13 (1867), 184–92

The First Extent of Bromfield and Yale A.D. 1315, ed. T. P. Ellis (Cymmrodorion Record Series, 1924)

Lordship of Oswestry, 1393–1607, ed. W. J. Slack (Shrewsbury, 1951)

The Record of Caernarvon, ed. H. Ellis (Record Commn., 1838). The Anglesey section of the survey of 1352 is published in translation by A. D. Carr in *Trans. Anglesey Antiquarian Society* 1971–2, 150–272

'Records of Denbighshire. The Lordship of Dyffryn Clwyd in 1324', ed. R. I. Jack, *Trans. Denbs. Hist. Soc.* 17 (1968), 7–53

'Survey of Anglesey' in F. Seebohm, *The Tribal System in Wales* (2nd edn. 1904), Appendix, 3–25

A Survey of the Duchy of Lancaster Lordships in Wales 1609–13, ed. W. Rees (Cardiff, 1953)

Survey of the Honour of Denbigh 1334, ed. P. Vinogradoff and F. Morgan (1914)

2.3 *Financial Records*

Cole, E. J., 'Account of the Keeper of Radnor Castle, 9–10 Edward III', *Trans. Radnorshire Soc.* 33 (1963), 36–43

— 'Maelienydd, 30–31 Edward II', *Trans. Radnorshire Soc.* 34 (1964), 31–9

Flintshire Ministers' Accounts 1301–28, ed. A. Jones (Flints. Hist. Soc., 1913)

Flintshire Ministers' Accounts 1328–53, ed. D. L. Evans (Flints. Hist. Soc., 1929)

Griffiths, J., 'Documents relating to the rebellion of Madoc 1294–5', *BBCS* 8 (1935–7), 147–59

— 'Two Early Ministers' Accounts for North Wales', *BBCS* 9 (1937–9), 50–70

— 'Early Accounts relating to North Wales *temp*. Edward I', *BBCS* 14 (1951–2), 235–42, 302–13; 15 (1954), 126–56; 16 (1955), 109–34

Jones, F., 'The Subsidy of 1292', *BBCS* 13 (1948–50), 210–30

Lewis, E. A., 'Account Roll of the Chamberlain of the Principality of North Wales
    1304–5', *BBCS* 1 (1921–3), 256–75
— 'Account Roll of the Chamberlain of West Wales 1301–3', *BBCS* 2 (1923–5),
    49–86
The Marcher Lordships of South Wales 1415–1536. Select Documents, ed. T. B.
    Pugh (Cardiff, 1963)
The Merioneth Lay Subsidy Roll 1292–3, ed. K. Williams-Jones (Cardiff, 1976)
Ministers Accounts for West Wales 1277–1306, I, ed. M. Rhys (Cymmrodorion
    Record Series, 1936)
Morgan, R., 'A Powys Lay Subsidy Roll, 1293', *Montgomeryshire Colls.* 71 (1983),
    91–112
Pierce, T. Jones, 'A Lleyn Lay Subsidy Account', *BBCS* 5 (1929–31), 52–71
— 'Lleyn Ministers' Accounts 1350–1', *BBCS* 6 (1931–3), 255–75
Rees, W., 'Accounts of the Ministers for the lands of the Crown in West Wales,
    1352–3', *BBCS* 10 (1939–41), 60–83, 137–56, 256–71
Waters, W. H., 'Account of the sheriff of Caernarvon, 1303–4', *BBCS* 7 (1933–5),
    143–53

2.4 *Judicial Records*

Abbreviatio Placitorum, ed. G. Rose and W. Illingworth (Record Commn., 1841)
Caernarvon Court Rolls 1361–1402, ed. G. P. Jones and H. Owen (Caernarfon,
    1951)
*The Court Rolls of the Lordship of Ruthin or Dyffryn Clwyd of the Reign of Edward
    I*, ed. R. A. Roberts (Cymmrodorion Record Series, 1893)
Flint Pleas 1283–5, ed. J. G. Edwards (Flints. Hist. Soc., 1921)
Jones, G. P., 'Anglesey Court Rolls, 1346', *Trans. Anglesey Antiq. Soc.* 1930,
    33–49; 1932, 42–9; 1933, 44–9
Jones, W. G., 'The Court Rolls of the Borough of Cricieth', *BBCS* 2 (1923–5),
    149–60
Lewis, E. A., 'Proceedings in the Small Hundred Court of Ardudwy, 1325–6',
    BBCS 4 (1928), 153–60
Select Cases in the Court of the King's Bench, ed. G. O. Sayles. 7 vols. (Selden
    Society, 1936–71)
Waters, W. H., 'A North Wales Coroner's Account', *BBCS* 4 (1927–9), 348–50
— 'Documents relating to the Sheriff's Turn in North Wales', *BBCS* 6 (1931–3),
    354–60
— 'Documents relating to the office of escheator for North Wales for the year
    1309–10', *BBCS* 6 (1931–3), 360–8

2.5 *Other Miscellaneous Record Sources (including borough records)*

Baronia de Kemeys. Documents and accounts relating to the lordship of Cemais, ed.
    T. D. Lloyd (Cambrian Archaeological Association, 1861)
Cardiff Records, ed. J. H. Matthews. 6 vols. (Cardiff, 1898–1911)
Charters granted to the Chief Borough of Swansea, ed. G. Grant Francis (1867)
Crecy and Calais (1346–7) From the Public Records, ed. G. Wrottesley (William
    Salt Archaeological Collection, 1897)
Daniel-Thyssen, J. R., *Royal charters and historical documents relating to the town*

and county of Carmarthen, 1201–1590, ed. A. C. Evans (Carmarthen, 1876)

Davies, J. Conway, 'Some Owen Glyndwr Documents', *NLWJ* 3 (1943), 48–50

Griffiths, R. A., 'The Cartulary and Muniments of the Fort Family of Llanstephan', *BBCS* 24 (1970–2), 311–84

Pierce, T. J. and Griffiths, J., 'Documents relating to the early history of the borough of Caernarvon', *BBCS* 9 (1937–9), 236–47

Rees, W., 'The Charters of the boroughs of Brecon and Llandovery', *BBCS* 2 (1923–5), 243–61

Waters, W. H., 'Documents relating to the early history of Conway', *Trans. Caerns. Hist. Soc.* 8 (1947), 5–9

2.6 *Ecclesiastical Records*
See also above Section 3.4

Canivez, J. M., *Statuta capitulorum generalium ordinis Cisterciensis*, 8 vols. (Paris, 1933–41)

Emanuel, H. D., 'A Fragment of the register of Stephen Patrington, bishop of St. David's, *Journal Hist. Soc. Church in Wales* 2 (1950), 31–45

— 'Early St. David's Records' *NLWJ* 8 (1953–4), 258–63

The Episcopal Registers of the diocese of St. David's 1397–1518, ed. R. F. Isaacson. 3 vols. (Cymmrodorion Record Series, 1917–20)

Jones, F., 'Medieval Records relating to the diocese of St. David's', *Journal Hist. Soc. Church in Wales* 14 (1964), 9–24

Pryce, A. I., 'The Register of Benedict, bishop of Bangor 1408–17', *Arch. Camb.* 77 (1922), 80–108

Taxatio Ecclesiastica Angliae et Walliae auctoritate Papae Nicholai IV circa A.D. 1291 (Record Commn., 1802).

3. *Literary Sources*
See also Section A. 5. above.

Y Bibyl Ynghymraec, ed. T. Jones (Cardiff, 1940)

Buched Dewi, ed. D. S. Evans (Cardiff, 1959)

Cywyddau Dafydd ap Gwilym a'i Gyfoeswyr, ed. I. Williams and T. Roberts (Cardiff, 1935)

Cywyddau Iolo Goch ac Eraill, ed. H. Lewis, T. Roberts, and I. Williams (1st edn. Cardiff, 1925; 2nd edn. Cardiff 1937)

Dafydd ap Gwilym. Fifty Poems, trans. H. I. and D. Bell (Y Cymmrodor, 1942)

Dafydd ap Gwilym, A Selection of Poems, ed. R. Bromwich (Llandysul, 1982)

Gramadegau'r Penceirddiaid, ed. G. J. Williams and E. J. Jones (Cardiff, 1934)

Gwaith Dafydd ap Gwilym, ed. T. Parry (1st edn. Cardiff, 1952; 2nd edn. Cardiff, 1963)

Gwassanaeth Meir, ed. B. F. Roberts (Cardiff, 1961)

Llyfr Ancr. The Elucidarium and Other Tracts in Welsh from Llyvyr Agkyr Llandewivrevi, A.D. 1346, ed. J. Morris-Jones and J. Rhŷs (Oxford, 1894)

Roberts, T., 'Englynion Gwynedd gan Gruffudd ap Maredudd ap Dafydd', *Trans. Anglesey Antiq. Soc.* 1982, 123–7

Williams, I., 'Awdl i Rys ap Gruffydd gan Einion Offeiriad', *Y Cymmrodor* 26 (1916), 115–46

Ystorya de Carolo Magno, ed. S. J. Williams (2nd edn. Cardiff, 1968

SECONDARY SOURCES

A. BIBLIOGRAPHIES

Dr. P. H. Jones of the College of Librarianship Wales, Aberystwyth is actively preparing a new edition of *The Bibliography of the History of Wales* for the Board of Celtic Studies. I have greatly benefited from his kind permission to consult the fiches of the work prepared to date.

Annual Bibliography of British and Irish History, ed. G. R. Elton (1975–)

Annual Bulletin of Historical Literature (Historical Association, 1915–)

Bibliography of English History to 1485, ed. E. B. Graves (Oxford, 1975)

Bibliography of the History of Wales (2nd edn. Cardiff, 1962). Supplements in *BBCS* 20, 22–3, 25

Bibliotheca Celtica. A Register of publications relating to Wales and the Celtic peoples and languages (Aberystwyth 1909–38, 1954–)

Martin, G. H. and McIntyre, S., *A Bibliography of British and Irish Municipal History*, 1 (Leicester, 1972)

Llyfryddiaeth Llenyddiaeth Cymraeg, ed. T. Parry and M. Morgan (Cardiff, 1976). Supplement in *BBCS* 30 (1982–3), 55–121

Rees, W., 'Bibliography of the Municipal History of Wales and the Border Counties', *BBCS* 2–3 (1925–6), 321–82

Welsh History Review. The December issue of each volume includes a useful check-list of articles relating to the history of Wales recently published. A comprehensive list of 'Theses on Welsh History presented before 1970' appeared in vol. 5 (1970–1), 261–304 with supplements in vols. 7, 9, 11.

Writings on British History (1901–33, 1934–66)

B. WORKS OF REFERENCE

1. *General*

Davis, G. R. C., *Medieval Cartularies of Great Britain* (1955)

Dictionary of National Biography (1885–1900)

Dictionary of Welsh Biography down to 1940 (1959). The Welsh-language supplement for 1941–50 (1970) also contains important addenda to the original volume.

Emden, A. B., *A Biographical Register of the University of Oxford to 1500*, 3 vols. (Oxford, 1955–9)

— *A Biographical Register of the University of Cambridge to 1500* (Cambridge, 1963)

G. E. C(okayne), *The Complete Peerage of England, Scotland, Ireland, Great Britain and the United Kingdom*, 12 vols. (1910–50)

Giuseppi, M. S., *Guide to the Manuscripts preserved in the Public Record Office*, 2 vols. (2nd edn. 1960)

Handbook of British Chronology, ed. F. M. Powicke and E. B. Fryde (2nd edn. 1961)

Handbook of Dates for Students of English History, ed. C. R. Cheney (1945)

Ker, N. R., *Medieval Libraries of Great Britain* (2nd edn. 1964)

Mullins, E. L. C., *Texts and Calendars. An Analytical Guide to Serial Publications*, 2 vols. (1958–83)

Sanders, I. J., *English Baronies. A Study of their Origin and Descent 1086–1327* (Oxford, 1960)

2. Atlases, Dictionaries and Gazetteers

A Gazetteer of Welsh Place-names. Rhestr o Enwau Lleoedd, ed. Elwyn Davies (2nd edn., Cardiff, 1958)

Geiriadur Prifysgol Cymru. In progress. 34 fascicules issued to date (Cardiff, 1950–)

Lloyd-Jones, J., *Geirfa Barddoniaeth Gynnar Gymraeg*, 8 parts issued (Cardiff, 1931–63)

Richards, G. Melville, *Welsh Administrative and Territorial Units* (Cardiff, 1969)

Rees, William, *South Wales and the Border in the Fourteenth Century*. Four Sheets. (Ordnance Survey, 1932)

— *An Historical Atlas of Wales from Early to Modern Times* (2nd edn., 1959)

3. General Periodicals

Archaeologia Cambrensis, 1846–

Board of Celtic Studies, Bulletin, 1921–

Y Cymmrodor, 1877–1949

Historical Society of the Church in Wales, Journal, 1949

Honourable Society of Cymmrodorion, Transactions, 1893–

Llên Cymru, 1950–

National Library of Wales, Journal, 1939–

Welsh History Review, 1960–

Ysgrifau Beirniadol, 1965–

4. Local Periodicals

Anglesey Antiquarian Society and Field Club, Transactions, 1913–

Brycheiniog, 1955–

Caernarvonshire Historical Society, Transactions, 1939–

Cardiganshire Antiquarian Society, Transactions, 1909–39

Carmarthenshire Antiquarian Society and Field Club, Transactions, 1905–

Ceredigion, 1950–

Denbighshire Historical Society, Transactions, 1952–

Flintshire Historical Society, Journal, 1911–25, 1952–

The Glamorgan Historian, 1963–

Merioneth Historical and Record Society, Journal, 1950

Montgomeryshire Collections. Transactions of the Powysland Club, 1868–

Morgannwg. Transactions of the Glamorgan Local History Society, 1957–

The Pembrokeshire Historian, 1959–

Radnorshire Society, Transactions, 1931–

Shropshire Archaeological Society, Transactions, 1878–
South Wales and Monmouth Record Society, 1932–50
West Wales Historical Records, 1910–29
Woolhope Naturalists' Field Club, Transactions, 1851–

C. GENERAL WORKS

1. *Relating to Wales as a whole*

Bowen, E. G. (ed.), *Wales. A Physical, Historical and Regional Geography* (1957)
Chadwick, N. K. (ed.), *Studies in Early British History* (Cambridge, 1954)
— *Celt and Saxon. Studies in the Early British Border* (Cambridge, 1963)
Davies, Elwyn (ed.), *Celtic Studies in Wales. A Survey prepared for the Second International Congress of Celtic Studies* (Cardiff, 1963)
Davies, Wendy E., *Wales in the Early Middle Ages* (Leicester, 1982)
Lloyd, J. E., *A History of Wales from the Earliest Times to the Edwardian Conquest* (3rd edn.1939)
Millward, R. and Robinson, A., *The Welsh Border* (1978)
Pierce, T. Jones, *Medieval Welsh Society*, ed. J. B. Smith (Cardiff, 1972)
Richards, Robert, *Cymru'r Oesau Canol* (Wrexham, 1933)
Roderick, A. J. (ed.), *Wales Through the Ages*, 2 vols. (Llanybie, 1959–60)
Roberts, Glyn, *Aspects of Welsh History* (Cardiff, 1969)
Sylvester, Dorothy, *The Rural Landscape of the Welsh Borderland. A Study in Historical Geography* (1969)
Thomas, D. (ed.), *Wales: A New Study* (Newton Abbot, 1977)
Williams, Glanmor, *Religion, Language and Nationality in Wales* (Cardiff, 1979)

2. *Works on local history*

The line between 'national' and 'local' history is often very indistinct in Wales. Much material of more than 'local' significance is therefore to be found in local histories and journals. Some of these are itemized in the appropriate sections below, but general attention is drawn to the following:

An Atlas of Anglesey, ed. G. M. Richards (Llangefni, 1971)
Atlas Brycheiniog (Llandysul, 1960)
Atlas of Caernarvonshire, ed. T. M. Bassett *et al.* (Caernarfon, 1977)
Atlas Hanesyddol Ceredigion, ed. W. J. Lewis (Aberystwyth, 1955)
Atlas Meirionydd, ed. Geraint Bowen (Bala, 1975)
Bradney, J. A., *A History of Monmouthshire*, 4 vols. (1903–33)
Carr, A. D., *Medieval Anglesey* (Anglesey Antiquarian Society, 1982)
Clark, G. T., *The Earls, Earldom and Castle of Pembroke* (Tenby, 1880)
Davies, J. Conway, 'Lordships and Manors in the County of Montgomery', *Montgomeryshire Colls.* 49 (1946), 74–150
Dodd, A. H., *A History of Caernarvonshire 1284–1900* (Denbigh, 1968)
Eyton, R. W., *Antiquities of Shropshire*, 12 vols. (1854–60)
Fenton, R., *A Historical Tour Through Pembrokeshire* (1881)
Glamorgan County History, vol. iii, ed. T. B. Pugh (Cardiff, 1971)
History of Flintshire, vol. i, ed. C. R. Williams (Denbigh, 1961)

Jones, Theophilus, *History of the County of Brecknock*, 4 vols. (new edns. 1909–30)

Lloyd, J. E., *The Story of Ceredigion (400–1277)* (Cardiff, 1937)

— (ed.), *A History of Carmarthenshire*, 2 vols. (Cardiff, 1935–9)

Lloyd, J. Y. W., *The History of the Princes of Powys Fadog*, 6 vols. (1881–7)

Morgan, R., 'The Territorial Divisions of Medieval Montgomeryshire', *Montgomeryshire Colls.* 69 (1981), 9–44; 70 (1982), 11–32

Payne, F., *Crwydro Sir Faesyfed*, 2 vols. (Llandybie, 1966–8)

Pratt, D., 'Fourteenth-Century Bromfield and Yale: A Gazetteer of Lay and Ecclesiastical Territorial Units', *Trans. Denbs. Hist. Soc.* 27 (1978), 89–149

Victoria County History of England,

Cheshire, vols. ii–iii (1979–80)

Herefordshire, vol. i (1908)

Shropshire, vols. i–iii, viii (1908–79)

D. GENERAL AND POLITICAL HISTORY

1. *Native Wales to 1272*

Barrow, G. W. S., 'Pre-Feudal Scotland: Shire and Thanes', *The Kingdom of the Scots* (1973), 7–68

Bartrum, P. C., 'Plant yr Arglwydd Rhys', *NLWJ* 14 (1965–6), 97–104

Binchy, D. A., *Celtic and Anglo-Saxon Kingship* (Oxford, 1969)

Carr, A. D., *Llywelyn ap Gruffydd* (Cardiff, 1982)

Charles, B. G., *Old Norse Relations with Wales* (Cardiff, 1934)

Charles-Edwards, T. M., 'The Heir Apparent in Irish and Welsh Law', *Celtica* 9 (1971), 180–90

Davies, R. R., 'Law and National Identity in Thirteenth-Century Wales', *Welsh Society and Nationhood. Essays to Glanmor Williams*, ed. R. R. Davies and others (Cardiff, 1984), 51–69

— 'Llywelyn ap Gruffydd, Prince of Wales', *Jour. Merioneth Hist. Soc.* 9 (1981–3), 264–77

Davies, Wendy E., 'Land and power in early medieval Wales', *Past and Present* 81 (1978), 3–23

— *Early Medieval Wales* (Leicester, 1982)

Dumville, D. M., 'Kingship, Genealogies and Regnal Lists', *Early Medieval Kingship*, ed., P. H. Sawyer and I. N. Wood (Leeds, 1977), 72–105

Jenkins, Dafydd, 'Kings, Lords and Princes. The Nomenclature of Authority in Thirteenth-Century Wales', *BBCS* 26 (1974–6), 451–62

Jones, G. R. J., 'The Defences of Gwynedd in the Thirteenth Century', *Trans. Caerns. Hist. Soc.* 30 (1969), 29–43

King, D. J. Cathcart, 'Two Castles in Northern Powys: Dinas Brân and Caergwrle', *Arch. Camb.* 123 (1974), 113–39

Lloyd, J. E., 'Llywelyn ap Gruffydd and the Lordship of Glamorgan' *Arch. Camb.*, 6th ser., 13 (1913), 56–64

Loyn, H. R., *The Vikings in Wales* (1976)

Moore, D. (ed.), *The Irish Sea Province in Archaeology and History* (Cardiff, 1976)

Ó Corráin, D., 'Nationality and Kingship in Pre-Norman Ireland', *Nationality and the Pursuit of National Independence. Historical Studies*, 12 ed., T. W. Moody, (Belfast, 1978), 1–35

Palmer, A. N., 'The Welsh Settlements east of Offa's Dyke during the eleventh century', *Y Cymmrodor* 10 (1890), 29–45

Pierce, T. Jones, *Medieval Welsh Society* (Cardiff, 1972), esp. chaps. I and XIV

Richter, M. 'David ap Llywelyn, the First Prince of Wales', *WHR* 5 (1970–1), 205–19

— 'The Political and Institutional Background to National Consciousness in Medieval Wales', *Nationality and the Pursuit of National Independence. Historical Studies*, 12 ed., T. W. Moody (Belfast, 1978), 37–55

Roderick, A. J., 'Marriage and Politics in Wales, 1066–1282', *WHR* 4 (1968–9), 3–20

Smith, J. B., 'The "Cronica de Wallia" and the Dynasty of Dinefwr. A Textual and Historical Study', *BBCS* 20 (1962–4), 261–82

— 'Owain Gwynedd', *Trans. Caerns. Hist. Soc.* 32 (1971), 8–17

— 'Castell Gwyddgrug', *BBCS* 26 (1974–6), 74–77

— 'The Treaty of Lambeth, 1217', *EHR* 94 (1979), 562–79

— 'Dower in Thirteenth-Century Wales. A Grant of the Commote of Anhuniog, 1273', *BBCS* 30 (1982–3), 348–55

— 'Llywelyn ap Gruffydd and the March of Wales', *Brycheiniog* 20 (1982–3), 9–22

— 'Llywelyn ap Gruffydd, Prince of Wales and Lord of Snowdon', *Trans. Caerns. Hist. Soc.* 45 (1984), 7–36

Smith, Llinos B., 'Llywelyn ap Gruffydd and the Welsh Historical Consciousness', *WHR* 12 (1984–5), 1–28

— 'The Gravamina of the Community of Gwynedd against Llywelyn ap Gruffydd', *BBCS* 31 (1984), 158–76

Stephenson, D., 'Llywelyn ap Gruffydd and the Struggle for the Principality of Wales 1258–82', *Trans. Cymm. Soc.* 1983, 39–61

— *The Governance of Gwynedd* (Cardiff, 1984)

— 'The Politics of Powys Wenwynwyn in the Thirteenth Century', *Cambridge Medieval Celtic Studies* 7 (1984), 39–61.

Stewart-Brown, R., *The Serjeants of the Peace in Medieval England and Wales* (Manchester, 1936)

Treharne, R. F., 'The Franco-Welsh Treaty of Alliance in 1212', *BBCS* 18 (1958–60), 60–75

Walker, D. G., 'A Note on Gruffydd ap Llywelyn', *WHR* 1 (1960–3), 83–98

Williams, G. A., 'The Succession to Gwynedd 1238–47', *BBCS* 20 (1962–4), 393–413

2. The Anglo-Norman Settlement of Wales and the Making of the March (to 1272)

Alcock, L., *Dinas Powys* (Cardiff, 1963)

Altschul, M., *A Baronial Family in Medieval England. The Clares 1217–1314* (Baltimore, 1965)

Barker, P. A. and Higham, R., *Hen Domen Montgomery. A Timber Castle on the English-Welsh Border*, I (1982)

Barraclough, G., *The Earldom and the County Palatine of Chester* (Oxford, 1953)

Barrow, G. W. S., 'The Pattern of lordship and feudal settlement in Cumbria', *Journal of Medieval History* I (1975), 117–38

Boon, G. C., 'Two Medieval Coin-Hoards from Cardiff, 1980', *Morgannwg* 24 (1980), 92–5

Cam, H. M., 'The Medieval English Franchise', *Speculum* 32 (1957), 427–44

Crouch, D. A., 'Oddities in the Early History of the Lordship of Gower, 1107–1166', *BBCS* 31 (1984), 133–42

Darby, H. C., *The Domesday Geography of Northern England* (Cambridge, 1962)

— *The Domesday Geography of Midland England* (2nd edn. Cambridge, 1971)

Davies, R. R., 'The Law of the March', *WHR* 5 (1970–1), 1–30

— 'Kings, Lords and Liberties in the March of Wales, 1066–1272', *Trans. Royal Historical Society*, 5th ser., 29 (1979), 41–61

Dolley, R. H. M., 'The 1962 Llantrithyd Treasure Trove and some thoughts on the first Norman coinage of Wales', *British Numismatic Journal* 31 (1962), 74–9; 33 (1964), 169–71

Douglas, D. C., *The Norman Achievement* (1969)

Edwards, J. G., 'The Normans and the Welsh March', *Proc. British Academy* 42 (1956), 155–77

Eyton, R. W., *Antiquities of Shropshire*, 12 vols. (1954–60)

Flanagan, M.-T., 'Strongbow, Henry II and Anglo-Norman Intervention in Ireland', *War and Government in the Middle Ages. Essays in Honour of J. O. Prestwich*, ed. J. B. Gillingham and J. C. Holt (Woodbridge, 1984), 62–78

Glamorgan County History III. The Middle Ages, ed. T. B. Pugh (Cardiff, 1971)

Griffiths, R. A., 'The Norman Conquest and the Twelve Knights of Glamorgan', *Glamorgan Historian* 3 (1966), 153–69

Gwynne, T. A., 'Domesday Society in Herefordshire', *Trans. Woolhope Field Club* 41 (1973), 22–33

King, D. J. Cathcart, 'Pembroke Castle', *Arch. Camb.* 127 (1978), 75–121

King, D. J. Cathcart and Spurgeon, C. J., 'The Mottes in the Vale of Montgomery', *Arch. Camb.* 114 (1964–5), 69–87

Le Patourel, J., *The Norman Empire* (Oxford, 1976)

Lewis, F. R., 'A History of the Lordship of Gower from the missing cartulary of Neath Abbey', *BBCS* 9 (1939–9), 149–54

Lloyd, J. E., 'Wales and the Coming of the Normans', *Trans. Cymm. Soc.* 1899–1900, 122–79

— 'Carmarthen in Early Norman Times', *Arch. Camb.*, 6th ser., 7 (1907), 281–92

Mason, J. F. A., 'Roger de Montgomery and his sons 1067–1102', *Trans. Royal Historical Society*, 5th ser., 13 (1963), 1–28

Meisel, J., *Barons of the Welsh Frontier. The Corbet, Pantulf and Fitzwarin Families 1066–1272* (Lincoln, Nebr., 1980)

Morgan, R., 'Trewern in Gorddwr', *Montgomeryshire Colls.* 64 (1976), 121–32

Nelson, L. H., *The Normans in South Wales 1070–1171* (Austin, Tex., 1966)

Otway-Ruthven, A. J., 'The Constitutional Position of the Great Lordships of South Wales', *Trans. Royal Historical Society*, 5th ser., 8 (1958), 1–20

Rees, W., 'The Medieval Lordship of Brecon', *Trans. Cymm. Soc.* 1915–16, 165–244.

— 'The Lordship of Cardiff', *Trans. Cardiff Naturalists' Society*, 63 (1932), 18–35

Rodd, Lord Rennell of, *Valley on the March. A History of a Group of Manors on the Herefordshire March of Wales* (1958)

Round, J. H., 'The Family of Ballon and the Conquest of South Wales', *Studies in Peerage and Family History* (1901), 181–215

— 'Domesday Herefordshire', *Victoria County History, Herefordshire*, ed. W. Page (1908), 263–307

Rowlands, I. W., 'The Making of the March. Aspects of the Norman Settlement of Dyfed', *Proceedings of the Battle Conference*, 3, ed. R. A. Brown (Woodbridge, 1981), 142–57

— 'William de Braose and the Lordship of Brecon', *BBCS* 30 (1982–3), 123–33

Smith, J. B., 'The Lordship of Glamorgan', *Morgannwg* 9 (1965), 9–38.

— 'The Middle March in the Thirteenth Century', *BBCS* 24 (1970–2), 77–93

Spurgeon, C. J., 'Gwyddgrug Castle and the Gorddwr Dispute in the Thirteenth Century', *Montgomeryshire Colls.* 57 (1961), 125–36

Stenton, F. M., *The First Century of English Feudalism* (2nd edn. Oxford, 1961)

Tait, J., 'Flintshire in Domesday Book', *Flints. Hist. Soc.* 11 (1925), 1–37

Taylor, A. J., 'Usk Castle and the Pipe Roll of 1185', *Arch. Camb.* 99 (1947), 249–56

Tout, T. F., 'Wales and the March during the Barons' War 1258–67', *Collected Papers*, II (Manchester, 1933), 47–100

Walker, D. G., 'Miles of Gloucester, Earl of Hereford', *Trans. Bristol and Gloucs. Arch. Soc.* 77 (1958–9), 66–84

— 'The "Honours" of the Earls of Hereford in the Twelfth Century', *Trans. Bristol and Gloucs, Arch. Soc.* 79 (1960–1), 174–211

— 'William Fitz Osbern and the Norman Settlement in Herefordshire', *Trans. Woolhope Field Club* 39 (1967–9), 402–12

— *The Norman Conquerors* (Swansea, 1977)

— 'The Norman Settlement in Wales', *Proceedings of the Battle Conference*, 1, ed. R. A. Brown (Woodbridge, 1978), 131–43

— 'The Lordship of Builth', *Brycheiniog* 20 (1982–3), 23–33

Wightman, W. E., 'The Palatine Earldom of William fitz Osbern in Gloucestershire and Herefordshire', *EHR* 77 (1962), 6–17

— *The Lacy Family in England and Normandy* (Oxford, 1966)

3. *Royal Policy in Wales, 1066–1272*

Barlow, F., *Edward the Confessor* (1970)

Brown, R. Allen, 'A List of Castles 1154–1216', *EHR* 74 (1959), 249–81

Carpenter, D., 'King, Magnates and Society. The Personal Rule of King Henry III, 1234–58', *Speculum* 60 (1985), 39–70

Davies, R. R., 'Henry I and Wales', *Studies in Medieval History presented to R. H. C. Davis*, ed. H. Mayr-Harting and R. I. Moore (1985), 132–47

Edwards, J. G., 'The Early History of the Counties of Carmarthen and Cardigan', *EHR* 31 (1916), 90–8

— 'Henry II and the Fight at Coleshill. Some Further Reflections', *WHR* 3 (1966–7), 251–65

Holt, J. C., *Magna Carta* (Cambridge, 1965)

King, D. J. Cathcart, 'Henry II and the Fight at Coleshill', *WHR* 2 (1964–5), 367–75

Le Patourel, J., 'The Plantagenet Dominions', *History* 50 (1965), 289–308

Lewis, C. W., 'The Treaty of Woodstock. Its Background and Significance', *WHR* 2 (1964–5), 37–65

Painter, S., *The Reign of King John* (Baltimore, 1949)

Poole, A. Lane, *From Domesday Book to Magna Carta* (2nd edn. Oxford, 1955)

Powicke, F. M., *Henry III and the Lord Edward*, 2 vols. (Oxford, 1947)

— *The Thirteenth Century* (2nd edn. Oxford, 1962)

Prestwich, J. O., 'The Military Household of the Norman Kings', *EHR* 96 (1981) 1–35

Roderick, A. J., 'The Four Cantrefs. A Study in Administration', *BBCS* 10 (1939–41), 246–56

— 'The feudal relations between the English Crown and the Welsh Princes', *History* 37 (1952), 201–12

Smith, J. B., 'Magna Carta and the Charters of the Welsh Princes', *EHR* 99 (1984), 344–62

Stenton, F. M., *Anglo-Saxon England* (3rd edn. Oxford, 1971)

Studd, J. R., 'The Lord Edward's Lordship of Chester 1254–72', *Trans. Hist. Soc. Lancs. and Cheshire* 128 (1979), 1–25

Walker, R. F., 'Hubert de Burgh and Wales 1218–32', *EHR* 87 (1972), 465–94

Warren, W. L., *King John* (1961)

— *Henry II* (1973)

4. *Edwardian Conquest and Settlement and Native Response, 1272–1317*

See also section 3 above.

Bullock-Davies, Constance, 'Minstrels at the Court of Edward I', *Trans. Cymm. Soc.* 1972–3, 104–23

— *Menstrellorum Multitudo. Minstrels at a Royal Feast* (Cardiff, 1978)

Carr, A. D., 'The Last Days of Gwynedd', *Trans. Caerns. Hist. Soc.* 43 (1982), 7–22

Chrimes, S. B., *King Edward I's Policy in Wales* (Cardiff, 1969)

Colvin, H. M. and others, *The History of the King's Works. The Middle Ages*, 2 vols. (1963)

Davies, J. Conway, 'Felony in Edwardian Wales', *Trans. Cymm. Soc.* 1916–17, 145–96

Douie, Decima L., *Archbishop Pecham* (Oxford, 1952)

Edwards, J. G., 'Sir Gruffydd Llwyd', *EHR* 30 (1915), 589–601

— 'The Battle of Maes Madog and the Welsh War of 1294–5', *EHR* 39 (1924), 1–12

— 'The Site of the Battle of "Meismadoc"', *EHR* 46 (1931), 262–5

— 'The Treason of Thomas Turberville, 1295', *Studies in Medieval History presented to F. M. Powicke*, ed. R. W. Hunt *et al.* (Oxford, 1948), 296–309

— 'Edward I's Castle-Building in Wales', *Proc. of the British Academy* 32 (1950), 15–81

— 'Madog ap Llywelyn, the Welsh leader in 1294–5' BBCS 13 (1948–50), 207–10
— 'The Building of Flint', Flint. Hist. Soc. Publ. 12 (1951), 1–20
— The Principality of Wales 1267–1961. A Study in Constitutional History (Caernarfon, 1969)
Fryde, N. M., 'A Royal Enquiry into Abuses. Queen Eleanor's Ministers in North-East Wales 1291–2', WHR 5 (1970–1), 366–76
Griffiths, J., 'The Revolt of Madog ap Llywelyn, 1294–5', Trans. Caerns. Hist. Soc. 16 (1955), 12–24
Griffiths, R. A., 'The Revolt of Llywelyn Bren', Glamorgan Historian 2 (1965), 186–96
— 'The Revolt of Rhys ap Maredudd, 1287–8', WHR 3 (1966–7), 121–43
Hays, R. W., 'The Welsh Monasteries and the Edwardian Conquest', Studies in Medieval Cistercian History, ed. J. F. O'Callaghan (Shannon, 1971), 110–37
Johnstone, H., Edward of Caernarvon 1284–1307 (Manchester, 1946)
Jones, F., 'Welsh Bonds for Keeping the Peace, 1283 and 1295', BBCS 13 (1948–50), 142–4
— 'The Subsidy of 1292' BBCS 13 (1948–50), 210–30
Kaeuper, R. W., 'The Role of Italian Financiers in the Edwardian Conquest of Wales', WHR 6 (1972–3), 387–403
Lloyd, J. E., 'Edward I's Commission of Enquiry of 1280–1. An Examination of its Origin and Purpose', Y Cymmrodor 25 (1915), 1–20
— 'The Death of Llywelyn ap Gruffydd', BBCS 5 (1929–31), 349–53
Loomis, R. S., 'Edward I, Arthurian Enthusiast', Speculum 28 (1953), 114–27
Maud, R., 'David, the Last Prince of Wales', Trans. Cymm. Soc. 1968, 1, 43–62
Morris, J. E., The Welsh Wars of Edward I. A Contribution to Medieval Military History (Oxford, 1901)
Pierce, T. Jones, 'Einion ab Ynyr (Anian II), Bishop of St. Asaph', Flints. Hist. Soc. 17 (1957), 1–14
Prestwich, M. C., War, Politics and Finance under Edward I (1972)
— 'A New Account of the Welsh Campaign of 1294–5', WHR 6 (1972–3), 89–94
Roberts, G., 'Biographical Notes', BBCS 17 (1956–8), 41–9
— Aspects of Welsh History (Cardiff, 1969)
Simpson, W. D., 'Harlech Castle and Edwardian Castle Plan', Arch. Camb. 95 (1940), 153–69
Smith, J. B., 'The Origins of the Revolt of Rhys ap Maredudd', BBCS 21 (1964–6), 151–63
— 'Offra Principis Wallie Domino Regi', BBCS 21 (1964–6), 362–7.
— 'Welsh Dominicans and the Crisis of 1277', BBCS 22 (1966–8), 353–7
Smith, Llinos B., 'The Statute of Wales, 1284', WHR 10 (1980–1), 127–54
— 'The Death of Llywelyn ap Gruffydd. The Narratives Reconsidered', WHR (1982–3), 200–14
Stephenson, D., The Last Prince of Wales (Buckingham, 1983)
Taylor, A. J., 'Master James of St George' EHR 65 (1950), 433–57
— 'The Death of Llywelyn ap Gruffydd', BBCS 15 (1952–4), 107–9
— 'Castle Building in Wales in the Thirteenth Century. The Prelude to Construction', Studies in Building History, ed. E. M. Jope (1961), 104–33
— The History of the King's Works in Wales 1277–1330 (originally pub. in The

History of the King's Works, ed. H. M. Colvin, I (1963); repub. as a separate volume 1973)
— 'Who was "John Pennardd, leader of the men of Gwynedd"?', *EHR* 91 (1976), 79–97
— 'A Fragment of a Dona Account of 1284', *BBCS* 27 (1976–8), 253–62
— 'Castle Building in Thirteenth Century Wales and Savoy', *Proc. British Academy* 63 (1977), 104–33
Tennant, W. C., 'Croes Naid', *NLWJ* 7 (1951–2), 102–15
Walker, R. F., 'The Hagnaby Chronicle and the Battle of Maes Moydog', *WHR* 8 (1976–7), 125–30
Waters, W. H., 'A First Draft of the Statute of Rhuddlan', *BBCS* 4 (1927–9), 344–8
— *The Edwardian Settlement of Wales in its administrative and legal aspects* (Cardiff, 1935)
— 'The Making of Caernarvonshire', *Trans. Caerns. Hist. Soc.* 4 (1942–3), 1–18

5. *Wales in the Fourteenth Century*

See also section 4 above

Carr, A. D., 'Welshmen and the Hundred Years' War', *WHR* 4 (1968–9), 21–46
— 'An Aristocracy in Decline. The Native Welsh Lords after the Edwardian Conquest', *WHR* 5 (1970–1), 103–29
— 'Rhys ap Roppert', *Trans. Denbs. Hist. Soc.* 25 (1976), 155–70
— 'A Welsh Knight in the Hundred Years' War: Sir Gregory Sais', *Trans. Cymm. Soc.* 1977, 40–53
Chotzen, T. M., 'Yvain de Galles in Alsace-Lorraine', *BBCS* 4 (1927–9), 231–40
Davies, J. Conway, 'The Despenser War in Glamorgan', *Trans. Royal Historical Society*, 3rd ser., 9 (1915), 21–64
— *The Baronial Opposition to Edward II. It Character and Policy* (Cambridge, 1918)
Davies, R. R., 'Baronial Accounts, Incomes and Arrears in the Later Middle Ages', *Economic History Review*, 2nd ser., 21 (1968), 211–29
— 'Richard II and the Principality of Chester, 1397–9', *The Reign of Richard II. Essays in Honour of May McKisack*, ed. F. R. H. Du Boulay and C. M. Barron (1971), 256–79
— 'Colonial Wales', *Past and Present* 65 (1974), 3–23
— 'Race Relations in Post-Conquest Wales', *Trans. Cymm. Soc.* 1974–5, 32–56
— *Lordship and Society in the March of Wales 1282–1400* (Oxford, 1978)
Evans, D. L., 'Some Notes on the History of the Principality of Wales in the time of the Black Prince', *Trans. Cymm. Soc.* 1925–6, 25–110
— 'Walter de Mauny, Sheriff of Merioneth 1332–72', *Jour Merioneth Hist. Soc.* 4 (1961–4), 194–203
Fryde, N. M., 'Welsh Troops in the Scottish Campaign of 1322', *BBCS* 26 (1974–5), 82–9
— *The Tyranny and Fall of Edward II, 1321–6* (Cambridge, 1979)
Griffiths R. A., *The Principality of Wales in the Later Middle Ages. The Structure and Personnel of Government. I. South Wales 1277–1536* (Cardiff, 1972)

— 'Wales and the Marches', *Fifteenth-Century England 1399–1509*, ed. S. B. Chrimes and others (Manchester, 1972), 145–65

Hewitt, H. J., *The Organization of War under Edward III* (Manchester, 1966)

— *The Black Prince's Expedition of 1355–7* (Manchester, 1958)

Holmes, G. A., 'A Protest against the Despensers', *Speculum* 30 (1955), 207–12

— *The Estates of the Higher Nobility in Fourteenth-Century England* (Cambridge, 1957)

Jack, R. I., 'Welsh and English in the Medieval Lordship of Ruthin', *Trans. Denbs. Hist. Soc.* 18 (1969), 23–49

Jenkins, Dafydd, 'Law and Government in Wales before the Act of Union', *Welsh Studies in Public Law*, ed. J. A. Andrews and D. Jenkins (Cardiff, 1970), 7–29

Lewis, N. B., 'The English Forces in Flanders, August–November 1297', *Studies in Medieval History to F. M. Powicke*, ed. R. W. Hunt *et al.* (Oxford, 1948), 310–18

McFarlane K. B., *Lancastrian Kings and Lollard Knights* (Oxford, 1972)

— *The Nobility of Later Medieval England* (Oxford, 1973)

McKisack, M., *The Fourteenth Century 1307–99* (Oxford, 1959)

Maddicott, J. R., *Thomas of Lancaster 1307–22* (1970)

Morgan, P. J., 'Cheshire and the Defence of the Principality of Aquitaine', *Trans. Hist. Soc. Lancs. and Cheshire* 128 (1979), 139–60

Morgan, R., 'The Barony of Powys 1275–1360', *WHR* 10 (1980–1), 1–42

Owen, D. H., 'The Englishry of Denbigh. An English Colony in Medieval Wales', *Trans. Cymm. Soc.* 1974–5, 57–76

Owen, E., 'Owen Lawgoch: Yvain de Galles', *Trans. Cymm. Soc.* 1899–1900, 6–18

Parry, B. R., 'A Note on Sir Gruffydd Llwyd', *BBCS* 19 (1960–2), 316–18

Phillips, J. R. S., *Aymer de Valence, Earl of Pembroke 1307–24. Baronial Politics in the Reign of Edward II* (Oxford, 1972)

Pratt, D., 'Bromfield and Yale in English Politics 1387–99', *Trans. Denbs. Hist. Soc.* 30 (1981), 109–47

Prince, A. E., 'The Strength of English Armies in the reign of Edward III', *EHR* 46 (1931), 353–71

Pugh, T. B., *The Marcher Lordships of South Wales 1415–1536* (Cardiff, 1963)

Reeves, A. C., *Newport Lordship 1317–1536* (Ann Arbor, Mich., 1979)

— *The Marcher Lords* (Llandybie, 1983)

Sherborne, J. W., 'Richard II's return to Wales', *WHR* 7 (1974–5), 389–402

Smith, J. B., 'Cydfodau o'r Bymthegfed Ganrif', *BBCS* 21 (1964–6), 309–24; 25 (1972–4), 128–34

— 'The Regulation of the Frontier of Meirionydd in the Fifteenth Century', *Jour. Merioneth Hist. Soc.* 5 (1965–6), 105–11

— 'Crown and Community in the Principality of North Wales in the Reign of Henry Tudor', *WHR* 3 (1966–7), 145–71

— 'Gruffydd Llwyd and the Celtic Alliance', *BBCS* 26 (1974–6), 463–78

— 'Edward II and the Allegiance of Wales', *WHR* 8 (1976–7), 139–71

— 'Marcher Regality. Quo Warranto Proceedings relating to Cantrefselyf in the Lordship of Brecon, 1349', *BBCS* 28 (1978–80), 267–88

— 'The Legal Position of Wales in the Middle Ages', *Law-Making and Law-Makers in British History*, ed. A. Harding (1980), 21–53

Smith, Llinos B., 'The Arundel Charters of the lordship of Chirk in the fourteenth century', *BBCS* 23 (1968–70), 153–66

— 'Seignorial Income in the Fourteenth Century: The Arundels in Chirk', *BBCS* 28 (1978–80), 443–57

Somerville, R., *A History of the Duchy of Lancaster* I (1953)

Strayer, J. R. and Rudisill, G., jun., 'Taxation and Community in Wales and Ireland 1272–1327', *Speculum* 29 (1954), 410–16

Tout, T. F., *The Place of Edward II in English History* (2nd edn. 1936)

Tuck, J. A., *Richard II and the English Nobility* (1973)

Usher, G. A., 'The Black Prince's Quo Warranto Inquiry (1348)', *WHR* 7 (1974–5), 1–12

Williams, Glanmor, 'Prophecy, Poetry and Politics in Medieval and Tudor Wales', *Religion, Language and Nationality in Wales* (Cardiff, 1979), 71–86

6. *The Revolt of Owain Glyn Dŵr*

Allmand, C. T., 'A Bishop of Bangor during the Glyn Dŵr Revolt', *Journ. Hist. Soc. Church in Wales* 18 (1968), 47–56

Bradley, A. G., *Owen Glyndwr and the last struggle for Welsh Independence* (1901)

Davies, R. R., 'Owain Glyn Dŵr and the Welsh Squirearchy', *Trans. Cymm. Soc.* 1968, ii, 150–69

Gabriel, J. R., 'Wales and the Avignon Papacy', *Arch. Camb.*, 7th ser., 3 (1923), 70–86

Goodman, A. E., 'Owain Glyndŵr before 1400', *WHR* 5 (1970–1), 67–70

Griffiths, R. A., 'Some Partisans of Owain Glyn Dŵr at Oxford', *BBCS* 20 (1962–4), 282–92

— 'Some Secret Supporters of Owain Glyn Dŵr?', *Bulletin of the Institute of Historical Research* 37 (1964), 77–100

— 'Gentlemen and Rebels in Later Medieval Cardiganshire', *Ceredigion* 5 (1964–7), 143–67

— 'The Glyn Dŵr Rebellion in North Wales through the eyes of an Englishman', *BBCS* 22 (1966–8), 151–68

Jack, R. I., 'New Light on the early days of Owain Glyn Dŵr', *BBCS* 21 (1964–6), 163–6

— 'Owain Glyn Dŵr and the Lordship of Ruthin', *WHR* 2 (1964–5), 303–22

Jacob, E. F., *The Fifteenth Century 1399–1485*(Oxford, 1961)

Jarman, A. O. H., 'Wales and the Council of Constance', *BBCS* 14 (1950–2), 220–2

Kirby, J. L., *Henry IV of England* (1970)

Lloyd, J. E., *Owen Glendower* (Oxford, 1931)

Messham, J. E., 'The County of Flint and the Rebellion of Owen Glyndwr in the Records of the Earldom of Chester', *Flints. Hist. Soc. Publications* 23 (1967–8), 1–34

Morris, W. H., 'Cydweli and the Glyn Dŵr Revolt', *Carms. Antiquary* 3 (1959–61), 4–16

Phillips, J. R. S., 'When did Owain Glyn Dŵr die?', *BBCS* 24 (1970–2), 59–77

Roberts, Enid P., 'Tŷ Pren Glân mewn top Bryn Glas', *Trans. Denbs. Hist. Soc.* 22 (1973), 12–47

Roberts, Glyn, 'The Anglesey Submissions of 1406', *BBCS* 15 (1952–4), 39–61

Smith, J. B., 'The Last Phase of the Glyn Dŵr Rebellion', *BBCS* 22 (1966–8),
    250–60
Williams, Glanmor, *Owen Glendower* (1966)
Williams-Jones, K., 'The Taking of Conwy Castle, 1401', *Trans. Caerns. Hist.
    Soc.* 30 (1978), 7–43
Wylie, J. H., *History of England under Henry IV*, 4 vols. (1884–98)
— *The Reign of Henry V*, 3 vols. (1914–29)

E. ECONOMY AND SOCIETY

1. *General*

Bowen, E. G. (ed.) *Wales. A Physical, Historical and Regional Geography* (1957)
Davies, R. R., *Lordship and Society in the March of Wales 1282–1400* (Oxford,
    1978)
Dodgshon, R. A. and Butlin, R. A., (eds.), *An Historical Geography of England
    and Wales* (1978)
Griffiths, R. A., 'Medieval Severnside', *Welsh Society and Nationhood. Essays to
    Glanmor Williams*, ed. R. R. Davies *et al.* (Cardiff, 1984), 70–89
Hallam, H. E., *Rural England 1066–1348* (1981)
Jones, G. R. J., 'Post-Roman Wales', *The Agrarian History of England and Wales*,
    I, ii, ed. H.P. R. Finberg (Cambridge, 1972), 281–382
Linnard, W., *Trees in the Law of Hywel* (Aberystwyth, 1979)
Millward, R. and Robinson A., *The Welsh Borders* (1978)
North, F. J., 'The Map of Wales', *Arch. Camb.* 90 (1935), 1–69
Pierce, T. Jones, *Medieval Welsh Society*, ed. J. B. Smith (Cardiff, 1972)
Rees, W., *South Wales and the March 1284–1415. A Social and Agrarian Study*
    (Oxford, 1924)
Sylvester, D., *The Rural Landscape of the Welsh Borderland. A Study in Historical
    Geography* (1969)
Thomas, D., (ed.), *Wales. A New Study* (Newton Abbot, 1977)
Vinogradoff, P., *English Society in the Eleventh Century* (Oxford, 1908)

2. *Agriculture and Rural Life*

Baker, A. R. H. and Butlin, R. A., *Studies of Field Systems in the British Isles*
    (Cambridge, 1973)
Davies, Margaret, 'Rhosili Open Field and Related South Wales Field Patterns',
    Agricultural Hist. Rev. 4 (1950), 80–96
Dodgshon, R. A., *The Origin of British Field Systems. An Interpretation* (1980)
Emery, F. V., 'West Glamorgan Farming, *circa* 1580–620', *NLWJ* 9 (1955–6),
    392–400; 10 (1956–7), 17–32
— 'The Farming Regions of Wales', *Agrarian History of England and Wales*, IV,
    ed. J. Thirsk (Cambridge, 1967), 113–60
Finberg, H. P. R., 'An Early Reference to the Welsh Cattle Trade', *Agricultural
    Hist. Rev.* 2 (1954), 12–14
Gray, H. L., *English Field Systems* (Cambridge, Mass., 1913)
Hooke, D., 'Llanaber. A Study in landscape development', *Jour. Merioneth Hist.
    Soc.* 7 (1973–6), 221–30

Howells, B. E., 'Pembrokeshire Farming, *circa* 1580–1620', *NLWJ* 9 (1955–6), 239–50, 313–33, 413–39
— 'The Distribution of Customary Acres in South Wales', *NLWJ* 15 (1967–8), 226–33
— 'Open Fields and Farmsteads of Pembrokeshire', *Pembrokeshire Historian* 3 (1971), 7–27
Kelley, R. S., 'The Excavation of a Medieval Farmstead at Cefn Graeanog, Clynnog, Gwynedd', *BBCS* 29 (1980–2), 859–908
Payne, F. G., 'Cwysau o Foliant Cyson', *Y Llenor* 26 (1947), 3–24
— *Yr Aradr Gymreig* (Cardiff, 1954)
— 'The Welsh Plough-Team to 1600', *Studies in Folk Life . . . to I. C. Peate*, ed. D. Jenkins (1969) 235–51
Pierce, T. Jones, 'A Note on Ancient Welsh Measurements of Land', *Arch. Camb.* 97 (1943), 195–204; see also *Arch. Camb.* 101, ii (1950–1), 118–22
Thomas, Colin, 'Thirteenth-Century Farm Economies in North Wales', *Agricultural Hist. Rev.* 16 (1968), 1–14
— 'Peasant agriculture in medieval Gwynedd: an interpretation of the documentary evidence', *Folk Life* 13 (1975), 24–37

3. *Settlement Patterns and Land Tenure*

Barnes, F. A., 'Land tenure, landscape and population in Cemlyn, Anglesey', *Trans. Anglesey Antiq. Soc.* 1982, 15–91
Barrow, G. W. S., 'The Pattern of Lordship and Feudal Settlement in Cumbria', *Journ. Medieval History* 1 (1975), 117–38
Davies, Wendy E., 'Land and Power in Early Medieval Wales', *Past and Present* 81 (1978), 3–23
— *An Early Welsh Microcosm. Studies in the Llandaff Charters* (1978)
Gresham, C. A. 'The Interpretation of Settlement Patterns in North-West Wales', *Culture and Environment. Essays in Honour of Sir Cyril Fox*, ed. I. Ll. Foster and L. Alcock (1963), 263–79
— 'Tre Ferthyr and the Development of Cricieth', *Trans. Caerns. Hist. Soc.* 27 (1966), 5–37
— *Eifionydd. A Study in Landownership from the Medieval Period to the Present Day* (Cardiff, 1975)
Jones, G. R. J., 'The Distribution of Medieval Settlement in Anglesey', *Trans. Anglesey Antiq. Soc.* 1955, 27–96
— 'The Tribal System in Wales: a Reassessment in the light of Settlement Studies', *WHR* 1 (1960–3), 111–33
— 'The Pattern of Settlement on the Welsh Border', *Agricultural Hist. Rev.* 8 (1960), 66–81
— 'The Distribution of Bond Settlements in North-West Wales', *WHR* 2 (1964–5), 19–37
— 'The Llanynys Quilletts: A Measure of Landscape Transformation in North Wales', *Trans. Denbs. Hist. Soc.* 13 (1964), 133–58
— 'Rural Settlement in Anglesey', *Geography as Human Ecology*, ed. S. R. Eyre and G. R. J. Jones (1968), 199–230

— 'Early Territorial Organization in Gwynedd and Elmet', *Northern History* 10 (1975), 3–27

—— 'Multiple Estates and Early Settlements', *English Medieval Settlement*, ed. P. H. Sawyer (1979), 9–34

Owen, D. H., 'Tenurial and Economic Developments in North Wales in the Twelfth and Thirteenth Centuries', *WHR* 6 (1972–3), 117–42

— '*Treth* and *Ardreth*. Some Aspects of Commutation in North Wales in the Thirteenth Century', *BBCS* (1972–4), 446–53

Palmer, A. N. and Owen E., *History of Ancient Tenures of Land in North Wales and the Marches* (2nd ed. Wrexham, 1910)

Pierce, T. Jones, 'Aber Gwyn Gregin', *Trans. Caerns. Hist. Soc.* 23 (1962), 37–43

Smith, Llinos B., 'The gage and the land market in late medieval Wales', *Economic Hist. Rev.*, 2nd ser., 29 (1976), 537–50

— '*Tir Prid*. Deeds of gage of land in late medieval Wales', *BBCS* 27 (1977), 263–77

Thomas, Colin, 'Social Organisation and Rural Settlement in medieval North Wales', *Jour. Merioneth Hist. Soc.* 6 (1973), 121–31

— 'Field-Name Evidence in the Reconstruction of Medieval Settlement Nuclei in North Wales', *NLWJ* 21 (1979–80), 340–56

— 'Place-Name Studies and Agrarian Colonization in North Wales', *WHR* 10 (1980–1), 155–71

4. *Economic Developments in the Later Middle Ages*

Butler, L. A. S., 'The Study of Deserted Medieval Settlements in Wales (to 1968)', *Deserted Medieval Villages*, ed. M. W. Beresford and J. G. Hurst (1971), 249–76

Carr, A. D., 'The Barons of Edeyrnion 1282–1485', *Jour. Merioneth Hist. Soc.* 4 (1961), 187–93, 289–301

— 'Medieval Gloddaith', *Trans. Caerns. Hist. Soc.* 38 (1977), 7–32

— 'The Making of the Mostyns. The Genesis of a Landed Family', *Trans. Cymm. Soc.* 31 (1982), 5–27

Gresham, C. A., 'The Bolde Rental', *Trans. Caerns. Hist. Soc.* 26 (1965), 31–49

Griffiths, R. A., 'The Rise of the Stradlings of St. Donats', *Morgannwg* 7 (1963), 15–47

Lewis, E. A., 'The Decay of Tribalism in North Wales', *Trans. Cymm. Soc.* 1902–3, 1–75

Rees, W., 'The Black Death in Wales', *Trans. Royal Historical Society*, 4th ser., 3 (1920), 115–35

Webster, P. V. and Caple, R., 'Radyr Deserted Medieval Settlement, 1975–8', *BBCS* 29 (1980–2), 190–200

5. *Towns, Trade, and Industry*

Beresford, M. W., *New Towns of the Middle Ages* (1967)

Bromberg, E. I., 'Wales and the Medieval Slave-Trade', Speculum 17 (1942), 263–9

Carter, H., *The Towns of Wales. A Study in Historical Geography* (2nd edn. Cardiff, 1966)

Dolley, M. and Knight, J. K., 'Some Single Finds of Tenth- and Eleventh-Century English Coins from Wales', *Arch. Camb.* 119 (1970), 75–82

Griffiths, R. A. (ed.), *Boroughs of Medieval Wales* (Cardiff, 1978)

Hewitt, H. J., *Medieval Cheshire. An Economic and Social History of Cheshire in the Reigns of the Three Edwards* (Manchester, 1929)

Jack, R. I., 'The Cloth Industry in Medieval Ruthin', *Trans. Denbs. Hist. Soc.* 12 (1963), 10–25

— 'The Cloth Industry in Medieval Wales', *WHR* 10 (1980–1), 443–60

— 'Fulling Mills in Wales before 1547', *Arch. Camb.* 130 (1981), 70–130

Jones, I. G. (ed.), *Aberystwyth 1277–1977* (Llandysul, 1977)

Lewis, E. A., 'The Development of Industry and Commerce in Wales during the Middle Ages', *Trans. Royal Historical Society* 2nd ser., 17 (1903), 121–75

— *The Medieval Boroughs of Snowdonia* (1912)

— 'A Contribution to the Commercial History of Medieval Wales', *Y Cymmrodor* 24 (1913), 86–188

Lobel, M. D. (ed.), *Historical Towns. Maps and Plans of Towns and Cities in the British Isles*, 1 (1969)

Morgan, R., 'The Foundation of the Borough of Welshpool', *Montgomeryshire Colls.* 65 (1977), 7–24

Owen, D. H., 'The Two Foundation Charters of the Borough of Denbigh', *BBCS* 28 (1978–80), 253–66

Pierce, T. Jones, 'The Old Borough of Nefyn', *Trans. Caerns. Hist. Soc.* 18 (1957), 36–53

Pratt, D., 'The Lead-Mining Community at Minera in the Fourteenth Century', *Trans. Denbs. Hist. Soc.* 11 (1962), 28–36

— 'The Medieval Borough of Holt', *Trans. Denbs. Hist. Soc.* 14 (1965), 9–74

Rees, W., *Cardiff. A History of the City* (2nd edn. Cardiff, 1969)

— *Industry Before the Industrial Revolution*, 2 vols. (Cardiff, 1968)

Reynolds, S., *An Introduction to the History of English Medieval Towns* (Oxford, 1977)

Sanders I. J., 'The boroughs of Aberystwyth and Cardigan in the early fourteenth century', *BBCS* 15 (1952–4), 282–93

Soulsby, I. N., *The Towns of Medieval Wales. A Study in their History, Archaeology and Early Topography* (Chichester, 1983).

6. *Social Bonds and Perceptions*

See also section 7.

Charles-Edwards, T. M., 'Some Celtic Kinship Terms', *BBCS* 24 (1970–2), 105–22

— 'Kinship, Status and the Origins of the Hide' *Past and Present* 56 (1972), 3–33

— 'Honour and Status in some Irish and Welsh Prose Tales', *Eriù* 29 (1978), 123–41

Davies, R. R., 'The Survival of the Blood Feud in Medieval Wales', *History* 54 (1969), 338–57

— 'Buchedd a Moes y Cymry', *WHR* 12 (1984–5), 155–79.

Ellis, T. P., *Welsh Tribal Law and Custom in the Middle Ages*, 2 vols. (Oxford, 1926)

Fox, R., *Kinship and Marriage* (Harmondsworth, 1967)

Jones, F., 'An Approach to Welsh Genealogy', *Trans. Cymm. Soc.* 1948, 303–466

Jones, W. R., 'England against the Celtic Fringe', *Journal of World History* 13 (1971), 155–71

— 'The Image of the Barbarian in Medieval Europe', *Comparative Studies in Society and History* 13 (1971), 376–407

Maitland, F. W., 'The Laws of Wales. The Kindred and the Bloodfeud', *Collected Papers* I, ed. H. A. L. Fisher (Cambridge, 1911), 202–29

Pierce, T. Jones, 'The Laws of Wales. The Kindred and the Bloodfeud', *Medieval Welsh Society* (1972), 289–307

Seebohm, F., *The Tribal System in Wales* (2nd edn. 1904)

7. Native Welsh Law

Aberystwyth Studies, 10. The Hywel Dda Millenary Volume (Aberystwyth, 1928)

Charles-Edwards, T. M., 'The Heir Apparent in Irish and Welsh Law', *Celtica* 9 (1971), 180–90

Davies, R. R., 'The Twilight of Welsh Law, 1284–1506', *History* 51 (1966), 143–64

— 'Law and National Identity in Thirteenth-Century Wales', *Welsh Society and Nationhood. Essays to Glanmor Williams*, ed. R. R. Davies *et al.* (Cardiff, 1984), 51–69

Edwards, J. G., *Hywel Dda and the Welsh Lawbooks* (Bangor, 1929)

— 'The Historical Study of the Welsh Lawbooks', *Trans. Royal Hist. Society*, 5th ser., 12 (1961), 141–55

— 'The Royal Household and the Welsh Lawbooks', *Trans. Royal Hist. Society*, 5th ser., 13 (1962), 163–76

Ellis, T. P., *Welsh Tribal Law and Custom in the Middle Ages*, 2 vols. (Oxford, 1926)

Emanuel, H. D., 'Llyfr Blegywryd a Llawysgrif Rawlinson 821', *BBCS* 19 (1960), 23–8

— 'Studies in the Welsh Laws', *Celtic Studies in Wales*, ed. Elwyn Davies (Cardiff, 1963), 71–100

Huws, D., 'Leges Howelda at Canterbury', *NLWJ* 19 (1975–6), 340–4; 20 (1977–8), 95

— *The Medieval Codex with reference to the Welsh Law Books* (Aberystwyth, 1980)

Jenkins, Dafydd, 'Llawysgrif Goll Llanforda o Gyfreithiau Hywel Dda', *BBCS* 15 (1951), 89–104

— 'Iorwerth ap Madog', *NLWJ* 8 (1958), 164–70

— 'A Lawyer looks at Welsh Land Law', *Trans. Cymm. Soc.* 1967, ii, 220–48

— *Cyfraith Hywel* (Llandysul, 1970)

— (ed.) *Celtic Law Papers introductory to Welsh Medieval Law and Governance (Studies presented to the International Commission for the History of Representative and Parliamentary Institutions*, 42, (Brussels, 1973)

— 'The Significance of the Law of Hywel', *Trans. Cymm. Soc.* 1977, 54–76

— 'The Medieval Welsh Idea of Law', *Tijdschrift voor Rechtgeschiedenis* 49 (1981), 323–48

— *Agricultural Co-operation in Welsh Medieval Law* (St Fagan, 1982)

Jenkins, Dafydd and Owen, Morfydd, E. (eds.), *The Welsh Law of Women* (Cardiff, 1980)
— 'Welsh Law in Carmarthenshire', *Carmarthenshire Antiquary* 18 (1982), 17–27
— 'The Welsh Marginalia in the Lichfield Gospels', *Cambridge Medieval Celtic Studies* 5 (1983), 37–66; 7 (1984), 91–120
Lewis, T., *A Glossary of Medieval Welsh Law* (Manchester, 1913)
Owen, Morfydd, *see* Jenkins, D.,
— 'Y Cyfreithiau', *Y Traddodiad Rhyddiaith yn yr Oesau Canol*, ed. G. Bowen (Llandysul, 1974), 196–244
Patterson, Nerys W., 'Honour and Shame in Medieval Welsh Society. A Study of the Role of Burlesque in the Welsh Laws', *Studia Celtica* 16–17 (1981–2), 73–103
Pierce, T. Jones, 'The Law of Wales. The Last Phase', *Medieval Welsh Society* (Cardiff, 1972), chap. xv
Reynolds, Susan, 'Law and Communities in Western Christendom, *c.*900–1140', *American Journal of Legal History* 25 (1981), 205–24
Stephenson, D., *Thirteenth Century Welsh Law Courts* (Aberystwyth, 1980)
Walters, D. B., *The Comparative Legal Method. Marriage, Divorce and the Spouses' Property Rights in Early Medieval European Law and Cyfraith Hywel* (Aberystwyth, 1982)
Welsh History Review. Special Number: The Welsh Laws (1963)

F. CHURCH AND RELIGION

1. *General*

Brett, M., *The English Church under Henry I* (1975)
Chadwick, N. K. (ed.), *Studies in the Early British Church* (Cambridge, 1958)
Cheney, C. R., *From Becket to Langton* (Manchester, 1956)
Davies, J. Conway, *Episcopal Acts relating to Welsh Dioceses 1066–1272* 2 vols. (Hist. Soc. of the Church in Wales, 1946–8)
Hughes, K., 'The Celtic Church: Is This a Valid Concept?', *Cambridge Medieval Studies* 1 (1981), 1–20
Le Neve, J., *Fasti Ecclesiae Anglicanae 1300–41, XI. The Welsh Dioceses*, ed. B. Jones (1965)
Pantin, W. A., *The English Church in the Fourteenth Century*
Southern, R. W., *Western Society and the Church in the Middle Ages* (Harmondsworth, 1970)
Walker, D. G. (ed.), *A History of the Church in Wales* (Penarth, 1976)
Williams, Glanmor, *The Welsh Church from Conquest to Reformation* (2nd edn. Cardiff, 1976)

2. *The Secular Church*

Brooke, C. N. L., 'The Church and the Welsh Border in the Tenth and Eleventh Centuries', *Flints, Hist. Soc. Pub.* 21 (1964), 32–45
— and Morey, A., *Gilbert Foliot and his Letters* (Cambridge, 1965)
Charles-Edwards, T. M., 'The Seven Bishop-Houses of Dyfed', *BBCS* 24 (1971), 247–62
Cule, J. H., 'Some Early Hospitals in Wales and the Border', *NLWJ* 20 (1977–8), 97–130

Davies, Wendy E., 'The Consecration of the Bishops of Llandaff in the Tenth and Eleventh Centuries', *BBCS* 26 (1974–6), 53–73

— 'Braint Teilo', *BBCS* (1974–6), 123–37

Davies, W. S., 'Materials for the Life of Bishop Bernard of St. David's', *Arch. Camb.*, 6th ser., 19 (1919), 299–322

Emanuel, H. D., 'Beneventana Civitas', *Journ. Hist. Soc. Church in Wales* 3 (1953), 54–63

Greenway, W., 'Archdeacons of Carmarthen in the Fourteenth Century', *Carmarthenshire Antiquary* 3 (1959–61), 63–71

— 'Archbishop Pecham, Thomas Bek and St David's', *Journ. Ecclesiastical Hist.* 11 (1960), 152–63

—'The Election of David Martin, Bishop of St. David's 1293–6, *Journ. Hist. Soc. Church in Wales* 10 (1960), 9–16

— 'The Election of John of Monmouth, Bishop of Llandaff 1287–97', *Morgannwg* 5 (1961), 3–22

— 'The Papacy and the Diocese of St. David's 1305–1417', *Church Quarterly Review* 161 (1960), 36–48; 162 (1961), 33–49

Hays, R. W., 'Welsh Students at Oxford and Cambridge Universities in the Middle Ages', *WHR* 4 (1968–9), 325–61

Howell, M., 'Regalian Right in Wales and the March. The Relation of Theory to Practice', *WHR* 7 (1974–5), 269–88

Jones, E. J., 'Bishop John Trevor (II) of St. Asaph', *Journ. Hist. Soc. of Church in Wales* 23 (1968), 36–46

Jones, W. B. and Freeman, E. A., *The History and Antiquities of St David's* (1886)

Lewis, F. R., 'The Rectors of Llanbadarn Fawr', *Arch. Camb.* 92 (1941–2), 233–46

Lloyd, J. E., 'Bishop Sulien and his family', *NLWJ* 2 (1941–2), 1–6

Palmer, A. N., 'The Portionary Chruches of Medieval North Wales', *Arch. Camb.*, 5th ser., 3 (1886), 175–210

Pryce, H., 'Ecclesiastical Sanctuary in Thirteenth-Century Welsh Law', *Journ. of Legal History* 5 (1984), 1–13

Richter, M., 'Professions of Obedience and the Metropolitical Claims of St. David's', *NLWJ* 15 (1967–8), 197–214

— 'Canterbury's Primacy in Wales and the First Stage of Bishop Bernard's Opposition', *Journ. Ecclesiastical History*, 22 (1971), 177–89

Roberts, E. P., 'Llys Ieuan, Esgob Llanelwy', *Trans. Denbs. Hist. Soc.* 23 (1974), 70–103

Thomas, D. R., *History of the Diocese of St. Asaph*, 3 vols. (Oswestry, 1908–13)

Thompson, A. Hamilton, 'The Welsh Medieval Dioceses', *Journ. Hist. Soc. Church in Wales* 1 (1947), 91–112

Usher, G. A., 'Welsh Students at Oxford in the Middle Ages', *BBCS* 16 (1955), 193–8

Victory, Sian, *The Celtic Church in Wales* (1977)

Walker, D. G., 'The Medieval Bishops of Llandaff', *Morgannwg* 6 (1962), 5–32

Williams, Glanmor, 'Henry de Gower (? 1278–1347), Bishop and Builder', *Arch. Camb.* 130 (1981), 1–19

Williams-Jones, K., 'Thomas Becket and Wales', *WHR* 5 (1970–1), 35–65

3. *The Monastic Orders*

Birch, W. de Gray, *A History of Margam Abbey* (1897)
— *A History of Neath Abbey* (1902)
Cowley, F. G., *The Monastic Order in South Wales, 1066–1349* (Cardiff, 1977)
Donkin, R. A., *The Cistercians. Studies in the Geography of Medieval England and Wales* (Toronto, 1978)
Donnelly, J. S., 'Changes in the Grange Economy of English and Welsh Cistercian Abbeys', *Traditio* 10 (1954), 399–458
Easterling, R. C., 'The Friars in Wales', *Arch. Camb.*, 6th ser., 14 (1914), 323–56
— 'Anian of Nanneu', *Flints. Hist. Soc. Journ.* 5 (1914–18), 589–601
Gresham, C. A., 'The Aberconwy Charter', *Arch. Camb.* 94 (1939), 123–62; also *BBCS* (1982–3), 311–47
— 'The Cymer Abbey Charter', *BBCS* 31 (1984), 142–57
Hays, R. W., *The History of the Abbey of Aberconwy 1186–1537* (Cardiff, 1963)
Johns, C. N., 'The Celtic Monasteries of North Wales', *Trans. Caerns. Hist. Soc.* 21 (1960), 14–43
Knowles, D., *The Monastic Order in England* (Cambridge, 1940)
— *The Religious Orders in England*, 3 vols. (Cambridge, 1948–59)
— , Brooke, C. N. L., and London, V., *The Heads of Religious Houses. England and Wales 940–1216* (Cambridge, 1972)
— and Hadcock, R. N., *Medieval Religious Houses. England and Wales* (2nd edn. 1971)
— and St. Joseph, J. K. S., *Monastic Sites from the Air* (Cambridge, 1953)
Lewis, F. R., 'The Racial Sympathies of the Welsh Cistercians', *Trans. Cymm. Soc.* 1938, 103–18
Little, A. G., *Studies in English Franciscan History* (1917)
O'Sullivan, J. F., *Cistercian Settlements in Wales and Monmouthshire, 1140–1540* (New York, 1947)
Pierce, T. Jones, 'Bardsey. A Study in Monastic Origins', *Medieval Welsh Society* (Cardiff, 1972), 391–409
— 'Strata Florida Abbey', *Ceredigion* 1 (1950–1), 18–33
Radford, C. A. Ralegh, 'The Cistercian Abbey of Cwmhir, Radnorshire', *Arch. Camb.* 131 (1982), 58–70
Rees W., *A History of the Order of St. John of Jerusalem in Wales and on the Welsh Border* (Cardiff, 1947)
— 'The Friars at Cardiff and Newport', *South Wales and Monmouth Rec. Soc.* 4 (1958), 51–6
Ward, J. C., 'Fashions in Monastic Endowment. The Foundations of the Clare Family 1066–1314', *Journ. Ecclesiastical History* 32 (1981), 427–51
Williams, D. H., 'The Cistercians in Wales. Some Aspects of their Economy', *Arch. Camb.*, 114 (1965), 2–47
— *The Welsh Cistercians. Aspects of their Economic History* (Pontypool, 1969)
— 'Fasti Cistercienses Cambrenses', *BBCS* 24 (1970–2), 181–229
Wiliams, S. W., *The Cistercian Abbey of Strata Florida* (1889)
Williams-Jones, K., 'Llywelyn's Charter to Cymer Abbey in 1209', *Jour. Merioneth Hist. Soc.* 3 (1957), 45–78

4. *Religious Devotion*

Foster, I. Ll. 'The Book of the Anchorite', *Proc. British Academy* 36 (1950), 197–226

James, J. W., 'The Welsh Version of Rhigyfarch's "Life of St. David"', *NLWJ* 9 (1955–6), 1–21

Jones, T., 'Pre-Reformation Welsh Versions of the Scriptures', *NLWJ* 4 (1946), 97–114

Lewis, H., 'Englynion i'r Offeren', *BBCS* 5 (1929–31), 14–18; 'Credo Athanasius', *BBCS* 5 (1929–31), 193–203

McKenna, C. A., 'Molawd Seciwlar a Barddoniaeth Grefyddol Beirdd y Tywysogion', *Ysgrifau Beirniadol*, 12 ed. J. E. Caerwyn Williams (Denbigh, 1982), 24–39

Williams, Ifor, 'An Old Welsh Verse', *NLWJ* 2 (1941–2), 69–75

Williams, J. E. Caerwyn, 'Medieval Welsh Religious Prose', *Proc. Second International Congress of Celtic Studies* 1963 (Cardiff, 1966), 65–97

— 'Rhyddiaith Grefyddol Gymraeg Canol', *Y Traddodiad Rhyddiaith yn yr Oesau Canol*, ed. G. Bowen (Llandysul, 1974), 312–408

G. LITERATURE AND CULTURE

1. *Latin and French Literature in Wales*

Bartlett, R., *Gerald of Wales 1146–1223* (Oxford, 1982)

— 'Rewriting Saints' Lives: The Case of Gerald of Wales', *Speculum* 58 (1983), 598–613

Bromwich, R., 'Concepts of Arthur', *Studia Celtica*, 10–11 (1975–6) 163–81

Bullock-Davies, C., *Professional Interpreters and the Matter of Britain* (Cardiff, 1966)

— ' "Exspectare Arturum": Arthur and the Messianic Hope', *BBCS* 29 (1980–2), 432–40

Chadwick, N. K., 'Intellectual Life in West Wales in the last days of the Celtic Church', *Studies in the Early British Church*, ed. N. K. Chadwick (Cambridge, 1958), 121–82

Chambers, E. K., *Arthur of Britain* (reprinted with a valuable supplementary bibliography by B. F. Roberts, Cambridge, 1964)

Davies, J. Conway, 'Giraldus Cambrensis', *Arch. Camb.* 99 (1946–7), 85–108, 256–80

— 'The *Kambriae Mappa* of Giraldus Cambrensis', *Journ. Hist. Soc. Church in Wales* 2 (1950), 46–60

Davies, Wendy E., 'The Latin Charter Tradition in Western Britain, Brittany and Ireland in the early medieval period', *Ireland in Medieval Europe*, ed. D. Whitlock *et al.* (Cambridge, 1982), 258–80

Huws, D., 'A Welsh Manuscript of Bede's *De Natura Rerum*', *BBCS* 27 (1976–8), 491–504

Jones, T., 'The Early Evolution of the Legend of Arthur', *Nottingham Medieval Studies* 5 (1964), 3–21

Lapidge, M., 'The Welsh Latin Poetry of Sulien's Family', *Studia Celtica* 8–9 (1973–4), 68–106

Legge, M. D., *Anglo-Norman Literature and its Background* (Oxford, 1963)

Loomis, R. S., *Wales and the Arthurian Legend* (Cardiff, 1956)

— (ed.) *Arthurian Literature in the Middle Ages. A Collaborative History* (Oxford, 1959)

Peden, A., 'Science and Philosophy in Wales at the time of the Norman Conquest: A Macrobius Manuscript from Llanbadarn', *Cambridge Medieval Celtic Studies* 2 (1981), 21–45

Powicke, F. M., 'Gerald of Wales', *Christian Life in the Middle Ages and Other Essays* (Oxford, 1935), 107–29

Richter, M., 'The Life of St. David by Giraldus Cambrensis', *WHR* 4 (1968–9), 391–7

— 'Gerald of Wales. A Reassessment on the 750th Anniversary of his death', *Traditio* 29 (1973), 379–90

— *Giraldus Cambrensis. The Growth of the Welsh Nation* (2nd edn. Aberystwyth, 1976)

Roberts, B. F., *Gerald of Wales* (Cardiff, 1982)

— 'Sylwadau ar Sieffre o Fynwy a'r *Historia Regum Britanniae*', *Llên Cymru* 12 (1973), 127–45

Walker, D. G., 'Gerald of Wales, Archdeacon of Brecon', *Links with the Past. Swansea and Brecon Historical Essays*, ed. O. W. Jones and D. G. Walker (Llandybie, 1974)

— 'Gerald of Wales. A review of Recent Work', *Journ. Hist. Soc. Church in Wales* 24 (1974), 13–26

— 'Cultural Survival in an Age of Conquest', *Welsh Society and Nationhood. Essays to Glanmor Williams*, ed. R. R. Davies *et al.* (Cardiff, 1984), 35–50

2. Native Welsh Literature

Bowen, D. J., 'Agweddau ar ganu'r Bedwaredd Ganrif ar Ddeg a'r Bymthegfed', *Llên Cymru* 9 (1966–7), 46–73

— 'Y Cywyddwyr a'r Noddwyr Cynnar', *Ysgrifau Beirniadol* 11, ed. J. E. Caerwyn Williams (Denbigh, 1979), 63–109

Bowen, G. (ed.), *Y Traddodiad Rhyddiaith yn yr Oesau Canol* (Llandysul, 1974)

Bromwich, R., 'The Character of the Early Welsh Tradition', *Studies in Early British History*, ed. N. K. Chadwick (Cambridge, 1958), 83–136

— 'Tradition and Innovation in the Poetry of Dafydd ap Gwilym', *Trans. Cymm. Soc.* 1964, i, 9–40

— *Dafydd ap Gwilym* (Cardiff, 1974)

— 'Gwaith Einion Offeiriad a Barddoniaeth Dafydd ap Gwilym', *Ysgrifau Beirniadol*, 10, ed. J. E. Caerwyn Williams (Denbigh, 1977), 157–81

Charles-Edwards, G., 'The Scribes of the Red Book of Hergest', *NLWJ* 21 (1979–80), 246–56

Charles-Edwards, T. M., 'The Date of the Four Branches of the Mabinogi', *Trans. Cymm. Soc.* 1970, 263–98

Evans, D. S., *Llafar a Llyfr yn yr Hen Gyfnod* (Cardiff, 1982)

Griffiths, M. E., *Early Vaticination in Welsh* (Cardiff, 1937)

Gruffydd, R. G. 'The Early Court Poetry of South-West Wales', *Studia Celtica* 14–15 (1979), 95–105

Hamp, E. P., 'On Dating and Archaism in the Pedeir Keinc', *Trans. Cymm. Soc.* 1972–3, 95–103

Huws, D., 'Llawysgrif Hendregadredd', *NLWJ* 22 (1981), 1–26

Jarman, A. O. H. and Hughes, G. R. (eds.), *A Guide to Welsh Literature*, vols. 1–2 (Swansea, 1976–9)

Jones, R. M., 'Y Rhamantau Cymraeg a'u cysylltiadau â'r Rhamantau Ffrangeg', *Llên Cymru* 4 (1956–7), 208–27

Jones, T., 'Historical Writing in Medieval Welsh', *Scottish Studies* 12 (1968), 15–27

Jones, T. Gwynn, 'Catraeth and Hirlas Owain. A Study with critical texts, translations and notes', *Y Cymmrodor* 32 (1922), 1–57

Lewis, H., 'Rhai Cywyddau Brud', *BBCS* 1 (1921–3), 240–55, 296–309

Lewis, S., *Braslun o Hanes Llenyddiaeth Gymraeg hyd at 1535* (Cardiff, 1932)

— *Gramadegau'r Penceirddiaid* (Cardiff, 1967)

Lloyd, D. M., 'Meddwl Cymru yn yr Oesoedd Canol', *Efrydiau Athronyddol* 13(1950), 3–19

— *Rhai Agweddau ar Ddysg y Gogynfeirdd* (Cardiff, 1977)

Lloyd-Jones, J., 'The Court Poets of the Welsh Princes', *Proc. British Academy* 34 (1948), 167–97

Llwyd, Alan (ed.) *Llywelyn y Beirdd* (Gwynedd, 1982)

MacCana, P., *The Mabinogi* (Cardiff, 1977)

Matonis, A. T. E., 'Traditions of Panegyric in Welsh Poetry. The Heroic and the Chivalric', *Speculum* 53 (1978), 667–88

McKenna, C. A., 'The Theme of Sovereignty in *Pwyll*', *BBCS* 29 (1980–2), 35–52

Parry, T., *Hanes Llenyddiaeth Gymraeg hyd 1900* (3rd edn. Cardiff, 1953) English translation by H. I. Bell, *A History of Welsh Literature* (Oxford, 1955)

— 'The Welsh Metrical Treatise attributed to Einion Offeiriad', *Proc. British Academy* 47 (1961), 177–95

Reiss, E. A., 'The Welsh Versions of Geoffrey of Monmouth's *Historia*', *WHR* 4 (1968–9), 97–127

Roberts, B. F., 'Un o lawysgrifau Hopcyn ap Tomos o Ynys Dawy', *BBCS* 22 (1966–8), 223–8

— 'The Red Book of Hergest Version of Brut y Brenhinedd', *Studia Celtica* 12–13 (1977–8), 147–86

Roberts, E. P., 'Uchelwyr y Beirdd', *Trans. Denbs. Hist. Soc.* 24 (1975), 38–73

Roberts, T., 'Englynion Marwnad i Llywelyn ap Gruffydd', *BBCS* 26 (1974–6) 101–2

Rowlands, E. I., 'Nodiadau ar y Traddodiad Moliant a'r Cywydd', *Llên Cymru* 7 (1963), 217–45

— 'Iolo Goch', *Celtic Studies. Essays in Memory of Angus Matheson*, ed. J. Carney and D. Greene (1968), 124–46

Rowlands, J. (ed.), *Dafydd ap Gwilym a Chanu Serch yr Oesoedd Canol* (Cardiff, 1975)

Sims-Williams, P., 'The Evidence for Vernacular Irish Literary Influence on Early Medieval Welsh Literature', *Ireland in Early Medieval Europe*, ed. D. Whitelock *et al.* (Cambridge, 1982), 235–57

Smith, J. B., 'Einion Offeiriad', *BBCS* 20 (1962–4), 339–47

Surridge, M., 'Romance Linguistic Influence on Middle Welsh', *Studia Celtica* 1 (1966), 63–93
Williams, J. E. Caerwyn 'Beirdd y Tywysogion. Arolwg', *Llên Cymru* 11 (1970–1), 3–95
— *Canu Crefyddol y Gogynfeirdd* (Swansea, 1977)
— *The Poets of the Welsh Princes* (Cardiff, 1978)

3. *Place- and Personal Names*

Charles, B. G., *Non-Celtic Place-names in Wales* (1938)
— 'The Welsh, their Language and Placenames in Archenfield and Oswestry', *Angles and Britons. O'Donnell Lectures* (Cardiff, 1963), 85–110
— 'English Place-names in Laugharne', *Carmarthenshire Studies . . . Presented to Francis Jones*, ed. T. Barnes and N. Yates (Carmarthen, 1974), 122–35
Davies, Ellis, *Flintshire Place-Names* (Cardiff, 1959)
Lloyd, J. E., 'Welsh Place-names. A Study of some Common Name Elements', *Y Cymmrodor* 11 (1980), 15–61
Lloyd-Jones, J., *Enwau Lleoedd Sir Gaernarfon* (Cardiff, 1928)
Morgan, P. and T. J., *Welsh Personal Names* (Cardiff, 1985)
Pierce, G. O., 'Enwau Lleoedd Anghyfiaith yng Nghymru', *BBCS* 18 (1958–60), 252–65
— *The Place-names of Dinas Powys Hundred* (Cardiff, 1968)
Richards, G. M., 'Hafod and Hafoty in Welsh Place-names', *Montgomeryshire Colls.* 56 (1959–61), 13–20
— 'Cynaeafdy and Hendre in Welsh Place-names', *Montgomeryshire Colls.* 56 (1959–61), 177–87
— 'The Significance of Is and Uwch in Welsh Commote and Cantref Names', *WHR* 2 (1964–5), 9–18
— 'Gwŷr, Gwragedd a Gwehelyth', *Trans. Cymm. Soc.* 1965, i, 27–45
— 'The Distribution of Some Welsh Place-names', *Lochlann* 3 (1965), 404–14;4 (1969), 179–225
— 'Ecclesiastical and Secular in medieval Welsh Settlement', *Studia Celtica* 3 (1968), 9–18
— 'The Population of the Welsh Border', *Trans. Cymm. Soc.* 1970, i, 77–100
Thomas, R. J., *Enwau Afonydd a Nentydd Cymru* (Cardiff, 1938)
Williams, I., *Enwau Lleoedd* (Liverpool, 1945)

4. *Architecture, Sculpture and Artefacts*

Avent, Richard, *Cestyll Tywysogion Gwynedd. Castles of the Princes of Gwynedd* (Cardiff, 1983)
Brown, R. Allen, *English Castles* (3rd edn. 1976)
— 'Royal Castle-Building in England 1154–1216', *EHR* 70 (1955), 353–98
Butler, L. A. S., 'Medieval Floor-Tiles at Neath Abbey', *Arch. Camb.* 122 (1973), 154–8
Cadw. Welsh Historic Monuments. The individual guides to abbeys, castles, and other sites in public care, published successively by The Ministry of Works,

Department of the Environment, The Welsh Office, and Cadw are of primary
importance.

Gresham, C. A., *Medieval Stone Carving in North Wales. Sepulchral Slabs and
Effigies of the Thirteenth and Fourteenth Centuries* (Cardiff, 1968)

Haslam, R., *The Buildings of Wales: Powys* (Harmondsworth/Cardiff, 1979)

Hilling, J. B., *The Historic Architecture of Wales. An Introduction* (Cardiff, 1976)

Hogg, A. H. A., 'A Fourteenth-Century House-Site at Cefn y Fan', *Trans. Caerns.
Hist. Soc.* 15 (1954), 1–8

— and King, D. J. Cathcart, 'Early Castles in Wales and the Marches', *Arch.
Camb.* 112 (1963), 77–124

— 'Masonry Castles in Wales and the Marches', *Arch. Camb.* 116 (1967), 71–132;
119 (1970), 119–24

King, D. J. Cathcart, 'The field archaeology of mottes in England and Wales',
Chateau Gaillard. Etudes de Castellologie Médiévale 5 (1972), 101–12

— *Castellarium Anglicanum. An Index and Bibliography of the Castles in England,
Wales and the Islands*, 2 vols. (1983)

— and Alcock, L., 'Ringworks of England and Wales', *Chateau Gaillard* 3 (1969),
90–128

Laing, Lloyd, *The Archaeology of Late Celtic Britain and Ireland c.400–1200 A.D.*
(1978)

Lewis, J. M. *Welsh Medieval Paving Tiles* (Cardiff, 1976)

— *Medieval Pottery and Metalware in Wales* (Cardiff, 1978)

Lewis, Mostyn, *Stained Glass in North Wales up to 1850* (Altrincham, 1970)

Nash-Williams, V. E., *Early Christian Monuments of Wales* (Cardiff, 1950)

Peate, I. C., *The Welsh House. A Study in Folk Culture* (rev. edn. Liverpool, 1944)

Radford, C. A. Ralegh, 'The Native Ecclesiastical Architecture of Wales c.1100–
1282. The Study of a Regional Style', *Culture and Environment. Essays in
Honour of Sir Cyril Fox*, ed. I. Ll. Foster and L. Alcock (1963), 355–72

Royal Commission on Ancient Monuments in Wales and Monmouthsire. Inventories
of the Ancient Monuments. Particular attention is drawn to the following
volumes: *Anglesey* (1937); *Caernarvonshire* 3 vols. (1956–64); *Glamorgan* (in
progress 1976–)

Siddons, M., 'Welsh Seals in Paris', *BBCS* 29 (1980–2), 531–44

Smith, P., *Houses of the Welsh Countryside. A Study in Historical Geography*
(1975)

— and Hague, D. B., 'Tŷ Draw. A Fourteenth-Century Cruck Hall', *Arch. Camb.*
107 (1958), 109–20

Taylor, A. J., *see above* Section D. 4

Thomas, W. G., 'Medieval Church Building in Wales', *The Irish Sea Province in
Archaeology and History*, ed. D. Moore (Cambrian Archaeological Association,
1970), 93–8.

Williams, D. H., *Welsh History Through Seals* (Cardiff, 1982)

INDEX

D. and M. in brackets after an entry refer to the numbered diagram or map respectively in the text on which the person or place entered appears. Many of the titles of a subject index are entered under 'Wales' or 'Welsh' and their sub-headings.

Aber, Lewis 439 n.
Aberafan (Glamorgan M.3) 500, 167
Aberconwy (Arllechwedd M.8) abbey of 197, 201, 251, 261, 266, 343, 355, 359, 373, 451; abbot of 343, 441; hall of 355; Treaty of (1277) 335–7, 345
Abercorram, later Laugharne 37
Aberdaron (Llŷn M.8) 76; church of 188, 196; *clas* of 133
Aberdyfi (Meirionydd) 11; partition of (1216) 277–8, 243
Aberffro (Anglesey M.8) 9, 149–50, 154, 256; church of 105; as principal seat of Gwynedd 217, 253
Abergavenny (M.3) 143, 165, 167, 272, 306, 312, 316, 378, 428; castle of 445; Henry of, bishop of Llandaff (1193–1218) 193; mint at 162; priory of 181
Abergavenny, lordship of (M.10) 35, 41, 84, 171, 277, 339, 425, 466; English and Welsh in 100–1, 159–60, 275, 291; honour of 47, 94
Abergele (Rhos) 125
Abergwili (Carms.) collegiate church of 376, 440
Abergwyngregyn (Arllechwedd M.8) 119, 254, 355
Aberlleiniog (Anglesey M.3), castle of 31, 90–1
Abermenai (Anglesey) 11
Aberystwyth (Ceredigion M.9) 39, 88, 91, 227; borough of 348, 372, 421, 433; burgesses of 385; castle at 226, 241, 295, 333, 338–9, 348, 383, 444–7, 451, 454, 457
Abingdon, abbey of 169
Abingdon, Richard, chamberlain of north Wales (1284–6) 366
Adam, bishop of St Asaph (1175–81) 193
Afan (Glamorgan M.3, M.5) 91; land reclamation in 153; local Welsh ruler of 96, 222, 282–3, 424
Alexanderstone (Brecon) 90
Amlwch (Anglesey) 148
Anglesey, Môn (M.2) 9–11, 31, 34–5, 51, 87,

140, 143, 334, 349, 351–2, 425, 434, 447; agricultural wealth of 238; archdeaconry of 416, 451; community of nobles of 68, 117; commutation of renders in 163; county of 365; mills in 155; position after 1277: 336, 342; settlement in 147–8, 129–30; sheriff of 380, 383, 386, 409
Anhuniog (Ceredigion), commote of 337 n.
Anian, bishop of Bangor (1267–1305) 318, 326, 342–3, 373, 395
Anian II, bishop of St Asaph (1268–93) 194, 202, 374–5; his quarrel with Llywelyn ap Gruffudd 192, 325–6
Anian Sais, bishop of Bangor (1309–28) 375
Annales Cambrie 317
Anselm, archbishop of Canterbury (1093–1109) 179, 189
Arberth *see* Narberth
Archenfield, Ergyng (M.1) 6, 26, 41, 174, 183; customs of 65, 124, 131; food renders in 64; free Welshmen of 118
Ardudwy, *cantref* of (M.2) 8, 21, 117, 130; commutation in 163
Arfon *cantref* of (M.2) 20; commutation of renders in 163; *see also* Caernarfon
Arllechwedd *cantref* of (M.2) 21; dean of 343
Armes Prydain 80
Arthur 79, 106, 122, 355; tales in Welsh about 105, 106
Arundel, earls of *see* Fitzalan
Arwystli, *cantref* of (M.7) 13, 30, 43, 50, 57, 62, 68, 140, 231, 238, 261; annexation of 49, 229–31; dispute over (1278–82) 344–7; dynasty of 44, 59, 72, 75, 217, 231; ecclesiastical status of 183; men of 129
Athée, Gerard d' 296
Athelstan, king of England (925–39) 3
Atiscross, hundred of (M.1) 4, 31
Audley, family of 235; Hugh 403; James 28
Aythan, Thomas 429

Bache, Alexander, bishop of St Asaph (1390–4) 439
Bailleul, Reynold of 30